W9-BLS-630

FOG 795

KNOW YOUR MERCHANDISE

KNOW YOUR

GREGG DIVISION   McGRAW-HILL BOOK COMPANY
NEW YORK   CHICAGO   DALLAS   SAN FRANCISCO   TORONTO   LONDON   SYDNEY

ISABEL B. WINGATE, Ph.D.

Professor of Retail Management
Institute of Retail Management
New York University

KAREN R. GILLESPIE, Ed.D.

Professor of Retail Management
Institute of Retail Management
New York University

BETTY G. ADDISON, M.S.

Instructor of Retailing
Laboratory Institute of Merchandising
Formerly Teacher of Merchandising in
New York City High Schools

Merchandise

DESIGN BY BARBARA DU PREE KNOWLES ♦ DRAWINGS BY MARTA CONE

KNOW YOUR MERCHANDISE, *Third Edition*

Copyright © 1964, by McGraw-Hill, Inc. All Rights Reserved. Copyright 1953, 1951, 1944, by McGraw-Hill, Inc. All Rights Reserved. Printed in the United States of America. This book, or parts thereof, may not be reproduced in any form without permission of the publishers. Library of Congress Catalog Card Number 62-12488.

6 7 8 9 LK-64 2 1 0 9 8 7

70990

Preface

Know Your Merchandise, Third Edition, is a thorough revision of the most widely used textbook on merchandise information. The book is designed for two groups of students: (1) those preparing for careers in retailing and distribution and (2) those seeking guidance and information for intelligent personal buymanship. The latter group includes regular and adult students pursuing homemaking and similar curricula.

In an economy where changes in technology, improvement of existing products, and introduction of completely new products are taking place almost daily, a merchandise text must consider the latest developments. As an example, after fifty years of research, DuPont introduced a new poromeric, or porous polymer plastic, for the manufacture of shoes to be marketed under the trade name of *Corfam*. DuPont has also developed a new resilient nylon "Fiber H," which will be widely used in women's and girls' hosiery. Both these new developments are mentioned in the revised text.

In addition to a complete up-dating of the previous edition and the expansion of certain units, as well as the introduction of new topics, this third edition has many new photographs and drawings, some of which show step-by-step manufacturing processes.

Labels, advertisements, consumer magazines, radio, and television offer a great deal of product information. But this information must be interpreted—the salesman and the consumer must know what the product really does for the buyer. This book explains in simple language the composition of various products and, more importantly, how these products can be used most effectively by the consumer.

PLAN OF THE BOOK

The book has two main divisions: Part I, Textiles, and Part II, Nontextiles. During the preparation of this edition, the authors were fully aware that many teachers would not wish to follow the sequence of organization of the text. In view of this possibility, the authors provided the book with a highly flexible organization. Thus a teacher may prefer to teach these main parts in reverse order.

Part I, Textiles

The book opens with an introductory chapter entitled "Know Your Merchandise" that discusses the importance of merchandise information to the salesperson and to the consumer, giving the reader the various concepts about buying information. An important feature of the book is presented in this introductory chapter, namely, instruction to the salesperson on how to construct selling sentences. By these sentences, facts are changed from just merchandise information (what the product is) into impressive statements giving advantages of the merchandise (what the product does for the customer).

Following the introductory chapter, the succeeding chapters of Part I present a thorough and interesting discussion of textile information—from the natural fibers of cotton, silk, and wool to the man-made fibers of acrylics through vinyons, their structure, manufacture, and ultimate uses. A chapter on color, line, and design has been added to help the students know and appreciate harmonious combinations in both apparel and homefurnishings.

Part II, Nontextiles

Part II is a thorough presentation of the nontextile merchandise usually found in a well-stocked departmentized store. The plastics chapter now includes the recently developed plastics such as the epoxies, ethylenes, and urethanes. The chapter on rubber has also been expanded to include recent improvements in rubber technology, as well as new units on paint and allied products, and automotive products. Part II also has a new unit on umbrellas in addition to other updating, as well as the recent Federal Trade Commission Guides for Shoe Advertising and Labeling and the Trade Practice Rules for the Household Furniture Industry.

Additional Merchandise Terms

In addition to the merchandising terminology used throughout the book, a section entitled "Additional Merchandise Terms" appears at the end of each chapter. These additional terms with their definitions are related to the chapter and will help the reader expand his technical vocabulary and his understanding of merchandise.

Student Activities

Each unit concludes with two kinds of activities:

Do You Know Your Merchandise? These are stimulating thought-provoking questions based on the unit, which will test the student's understanding of the material presented.

Interesting Things to Do. These projects challenge the student, relate his experiences to the unit material, and thus make the instruction more meaningful.

SUPPLEMENTARY MATERIAL

The Teacher's Manual and Key contains: (1) teaching suggestions based on the authors' vast experience in teaching merchandise-information classes, (2) a bibliography of related books and periodicals, (3) sources of audio-visual materials, (4) sample selling sentences, and (5) complete solutions to all "Do You Know Your Merchandise?" questions.

ACKNOWLEDGMENTS

A great many people assisted the authors in the preparation of this major revision. Included in this group are those teachers who responded to questionnaires and indicated their desire to see the addition of certain topics that were not covered in earlier editions. In addition, many teachers made valuable suggestions regarding course content, instructional level, organization, and emphasis.

ISABEL B. WINGATE   KAREN R. GILLESPIE   BETTY G. ADDISON

Contents

TEXTILES PART ONE

NONTEXTILES
PART TWO

PART ONE: TEXTILES

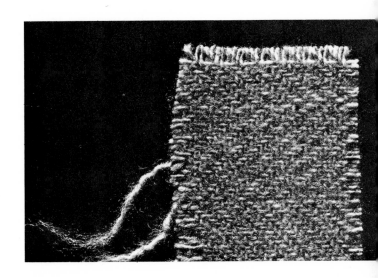

Know Your Merchandise

CHAPTER 1

UNIT 1 USE OF MERCHANDISE FACTS

If you could step back into history about one hundred years and enter a typical American home, you would realize the tremendous changes that have taken place since then in the material well-being of the American consumer. Clothes made from natural fibers were often hand woven as well as hand-made; home furnishings, too, were often made by the homeowner or some local craftsman. Gardens supplied much of the produce consumed, and farming was a common occupation of a large portion of the population. Services were few since most people took care of their own work and helped neighbors when necessary. Modern conveniences, made possible by electric power and gas lines, were unknown. Drudgery was the lot of the average housewife whose hard work was matched by that of the man in the family toiling in the fields to provide necessary food and shelter for his family.

Just about one hundred years later, we find the marvels of the industrial era and the atomic age available for most of the populace. Daily, research workers are creating new products or improving those already devised. There is nothing static about the progress and the merchandise available today. Tomorrow something new and better may be ready to amaze, to amuse, or to satisfy some consumer need or want.

This rapid development and change means that retailers must be alert to carry the new products and to know the benefits to be derived from their use. Consumers, likewise, should know what to look for in making buying decisions about the products they select for their use.

THE ROLE OF MANUFACTURERS, RETAILERS, AND CONSUMERS

People living in the United States enjoy one of the highest living standards in the world. Throughout the country, many families own their own homes, have TV and radio sets, automobiles, washing machines, and other electrical and gas appliances, complete wardrobes of fashionable clothes and accessories for various occasions, and have the money for needed food, medical requirements, education, and recreation. In addition, the citizens of this great country plan for future purchases, save money for that "rainy day," plan for retirement, plan for college education for their children, and for other special needs and wants. All this is possible because we produce goods and services at a rate unparalleled elsewhere in the world; because we distribute these goods efficiently; and, because as consumers, we eagerly accept the products that the manufacturers have designed and created and that retailers and other distributors have made available. We also use the services that are increasingly important in our complex system of living, offered by such persons as doctors, lawyers, teachers, clergymen, repairmen, clerks, technicians, writers, artists, and entertainers. Advertisements tell us about these available products and services; shelves in stores are stocked with products; and consumers, paid for their labors in providing these goods and services, in turn have the money to purchase them, thus completing the cycle that makes our economy such a success.

DISTRIBUTORS AND CONSUMERS MUST KNOW THEIR MERCHANDISE

This book is concerned primarily with two groups of people, the consumers —which includes everyone, since all must eat, wear clothing, and live in some type of shelter—and the distributors who make these items available to the consumers. According to United States government statistics, one out of every eight persons gainfully employed is employed in distributing goods; therefore, a large percentage of the persons in this country act in some way to sell products. The more efficiently they sell them, the more costs are cut; the more other goods and services are purchased, the more the entire economy is stimulated. This book aims to develop knowledge in young people, so that they can select merchandise wisely and know enough about it to help to sell it so that both consumers and distributors are benefited.

SOURCES OF BUYING INFORMATION

Among the most important sources are the manufacturers and dealers who supply the merchandise from which the customer must choose. Through advertising and labels, manufacturers and distributors provide the facts about their products; through display and sampling, they present the products themselves; and through personal salesmanship, they help the customer to relate these facts about the products to her personal and special needs.

For example, a customer needed a new handbag for daytime use. She visited the handbag department in her favorite department store. The salesperson showed her an attractive genuine leather handbag. He emphasized the durability of the genuine leather; the style rightness of this leather; the features in the construction of the bag; the leather lining and the useful fittings. After the salesperson had finished, the customer remarked, "Is genuine leather really better than handbags made from *bonded* leather I've read about?"

The salesperson reached for a bonded leather handbag. "When the handbag is new, the bonded leather, which is made from real leather fibers held together with a plastic gluelike substance, looks almost as rich in appearance as the genuine leather. The price, of course, is somewhat higher for the real leather product. However, as the bag is used, the surface color and texture of the bonded leather wear down leaving a less attractive-looking bag. The genuine leather handbag merely mellows with age and becomes richer and glossier as it is used."

When the salesperson discovered that price was not the most important factor to the customer, he stressed again the attractiveness of the genuine leather, its suppleness, and its durability which justified several dollars difference in price. The customer purchased the handbag of genuine leather and thanked the salesperson for his assistance. Undoubtedly the satisfied customer will return to this salesperson who had shown such a complete knowledge of the merchandise.

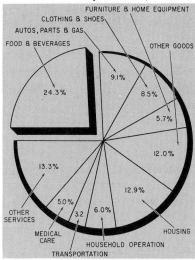

Consumers Expenditures, 1960*

* Survey of Current Business, adapted from Table 6, Aug. 1961 and Table 15, July, 1961

The salesman who knows his merchandise and can talk about it intelligently is making a career for himself and profits for the store. He is developing a clientele of satisfied customers who will come back to him.

SELLING POINTS

Selling points are the facts a salesperson stresses in the belief that they will help the customer decide that the merchandise in question will satisfy her need or that of her family. If the customer accepts the fact as contributing to the satisfaction of her need, this fact becomes a buying point to her.

Selling points may be analyzed as follows:

Suitability

Suppose you are selling novelty jewelry on an aisle table of a large department store. A young woman, apparently an office worker, fingers each article in turn on your table. Then, somewhat bewildered she looks at you and says, "I want something to brighten up this black suit." You show her a simulated stone novelty pin and pin it on her suit. You give her a mirror, so that she can see the effect for herself. The customer buys the pin. You, the salesperson, merely demonstrated the merchandise in use. What were the selling points? The color and sparkling beauty of the simulated stones which brightened the black suit were the selling points. In other words, the pin satisfied the customer's needs because it was suited for a particular purpose. This selling point is called *suitability*.

Durability

To the woman who wants to conserve wool fabrics for several seasons, the salesman can appeal with the selling point called *durability*. A durable cloth is one which will give long wear.

Versatility

Merchandise that has many uses is versatile. For example, there is a table that can be used (1) as a bedside table; (2) as a table for a person in bed with the top swung over the bed to support books or food; (3) as a table to sit around. The outstanding selling point of such a table is its *versatility*.

Style and Fashion

Some people confuse the words *style* and *fashion*. Those who are expert enough to sell merchandise want to use these words correctly. A *style* in merchandise is the distinctive shape or form of a product. For example, a leg-of-mutton sleeve is a style of sleeve, but it is not in fashion at the present time. A *fashion* is a style that has popular acceptance. The "continental" is a style of young men's suit that was in fashion during 1959–61. The Model T Ford is a style of automobile that has been out of fashion since the 1920's. The square-toe shoe is a style of toe that became fashionable in 1961. Customers sometimes refer to an item as being "in style" when they mean "in fashion." The salesperson needs to know what styles are in fashion as this is an important selling point to stress during his sales talk.

Attractiveness

An enthusiastic buyer of notions returned from a buying trip. He called together his salespeople to show them his purchases, among which was a gross of printed percale aprons. Now to most salespeople an apron is a useful article but not one to become enthusiastic about. But these aprons were different. They were in small floral prints, cut in youthful styles with fagoting around the ruffled edge and a large apple appliquéd to a roomy pocket. These aprons were attractive to the salespeople, who would consequently use attractiveness as a selling point, because the article had sufficient intrinsic beauty to appeal to the customer.

Comfort

A customer selected a pair of shoes from a display on a counter of a basement shoe department. She asked the salesman to help her try them on. The salesman told her they were too short for her, but she insisted on buying them. He told her she would not be comfortable in them if she did much walking. Still she insisted she wanted them. So the salesman sold them to her, but marked them "T.S." (too short) to protect the store against a possible return because of customer dissatisfaction. Comfort is a very important selling point in selling shoes, as well as outer garments, and many items of furniture. Comfort is a selling point for an article which will improve the personal well-being of the purchaser.

Pride of Ownership or Possession

Many of our greatest art collections have been assembled for reasons of sentiment—a desire to have the finest paintings—to own the best collection of books on a particular subject. A human want is satisfied by possession of rare or unique objects. Pride of ownership is the selling point to use for a customer who has this feeling. The same selling point can be used for the customer who wants to "keep up" with his friends. A girl usually feels that if her friend has a new dress for the prom, she must have one, too. She must not run a chance of being a wallflower.

Price

To the young man or woman who has a weekly allowance, as well as to many other thrifty shoppers, the price of an article plays an important part in buying decisions. The salesman often has to justify what seems to the customer to be a high price for an article. He does this by showing certain features about the article which make it worth the price asked.

In times of national crises, price becomes more important than ever to the customer who gets a fixed salary, because at such times prices rise, but income remains the same. The customer must buy wisely and be sure she gets her money's worth. Price, then, is a selling point that appeals to the person with a limited amount of money to spend for a certain article.

Safety and Health

Newly developed products, tested only for their intended uses, sometimes reach consumers. Thus toy-airplane glues that were dangerous when inhaled, hair sprays that ignited in the presence of a flame, fabrics that were highly inflammable, and pencil-slim heels that caught in escalator gratings have been among the hazardous products sold in recent years. Even foods have occasionally been found to contain harmful residue from chemical sprays used to protect them, as in the case of cranberries a few years ago. Protection is provided in some cases by government rulings and laws. Conscientious manufacturers, producers, and retailers also give exhaustive tests to products to assure their safety in use and to provide warnings against possible misuse. Customers like to be sure that the products they purchase are safe and not harmful to health.

Care Required

One of the most frequent questions a salesperson has to answer when he is selling is about the care required to keep an article in usable condition. Typical questions are: "How can I keep this silver bowl from tarnishing? Can I store my fur coat here for the summer? Can I have this blouse dry-cleaned? How do I wash a nylon sweater? Can I wear this blouse, when I take it from the automatic dryer, without ironing?"

If the salesperson can answer these questions accurately and thus make the care of the merchandise seem easy, then his answer becomes a selling point. What customer is not impressed by the fact that the article she is buying is going to be easy to care for?

PUTTING MERCHANDISE KNOWLEDGE TO USE

As you read the discussions about the various items of merchandise, two factors were stressed: knowledge of what merchandise *is* and interpretation of that knowledge to tell what the merchandise *does* for the user. This combination of *is* and *does* information is the essence of good selling information. Elmer Wheeler, noted for his sales ability, called such interpretations *selling sentences.*

Building Selling Sentences

Impressive sales talks, informative signs, effective advertising, dynamic display messages may all use selling sentences to get important messages to the customer. Selling sentences may be created from the ingredients of any product, added—where suitable—to the selling points that have been listed in the foregoing paragraphs. To show how this formula might work, the following illustration is provided.

The merchandise is a child's pair of shoes. The manufacturer has listed the following "is" features of the shoe. They are blucher oxfords made from boarded cowhide leather with a vinyl plastic tip, bend leather oak-tanned soles, Goodyear Welt construction; and they are available in black and brown colors.

The customer for these shoes, however, does not understand these terms. He is seeking "does" information such as: how comfortable are the shoes for a chubby child's foot, how sturdy and long wearing are they, how healthful are they for feet, how popular is the style, and how appropriate are the shoes for school use?

The salesman has the problem of making meaningful statements about these shoes to the customer. The following chart illustrates how the salesman can translate these technical terms into customer's language and make impressive selling sentences.

> > SELLING SENTENCE CHART ‹ ‹

IS Information		DOES Information
Technical terms	Translation of technical terms	Salesman's translation of technical terms into selling sentences that tell the customer what he wants to know.
Blucher oxford	Shoe that laces. Lace stays across instep are loose. This oxford has a one-piece tongue.	Because this shoe has loose lace stays, it allows plenty of room for a chubby child's foot. This shoe will never bind the foot but will allow it to be comfortable yet well supported. The one-piece construction of the tongue permits no seams to rub across the instep portion of the foot. The blucher oxford is a popular style for school.
Boarded cowhide	Leather from the cow, which has been creased in various directions, to give a bumpy-textured surface.	Cowhide is a fine, sturdy, long-wearing leather that has been made soft and supple to give the upper part of the foot all the flexibility needed. This interesting bumpy texture known as "boarding" will prevent minor scratches and scars from showing as the child wears these shoes. This helps the shoes to stay new looking longer.
Vinyl tip	The front of the toe section has a reinforcement of leather-appearing vinyl plastic.	Vinyl, one of the toughest plastics known, has been made to look like leather and attached to the tip over the toes of this shoe. Even though the child drags his toes along the sidewalk and kicks various objects, he will not be able to scuff this tough, long-wearing tip. The vinyl protects the foot and keeps the shoe looking attractive.
Oak-tanned, bend leather sole	The center back of the animal's hide is known as the "bend" This has been preserved with a vegetable tanning agent, oak bark.	The strongest, longest wearing leather from the animal comes from his center back section and is known as the "bend." This bend leather makes these soles the finest made. The tannage that imparts the most porosity for foot health and yet prevents slippage of the leather when sidewalks are wet has been used for the soles of these shoes. This quality leather provides added safety and health features for the wearer.
Goodyear Welt construction	The insole (section inside the shoe against which the foot rests) and the narrow strip of leather known as the welt have been stitched with a hidden seam. The outsole	No sturdily built shoe is finer for comfort than this Goodyear Welt constructed oxford. No stitches nor seams nor tacks are inside the shoe to press against the foot in any way. All inside stitching is hidden between the layers of soles used on the shoes. This assures complete foot comfort

IS Information		DOES Information
Technical terms	Translation of technical terms	Salesman's translation of technical terms into selling sentences that tell the customer what he wants to know.
	has then been stitched to the welt around the outside edge of the shoe.	for the wearer. The outsole, however, is visibly stitched on the outside in a manner that makes it easily resoleable. This sturdy shoe is constructed to hold its shape, support the foot, and yet to be easily repaired if necessary.
Colors	Brown and black.	These are traditional colors for shoes that permit them to be worn with a variety of clothing colors. Two pairs of these shoes, one in black and one in brown, will permit a child to have the right color shoe for all the school clothes in his wardrobe.

Throughout the book you will be asked to write selling sentences based on the facts you have learned about merchandise. Use this chart as a guide in preparing your selling sentences.

KINDS OF MERCHANDISE—TEXTILE, NONTEXTILE, AND COMBINED

Textiles are products made of cotton, linen, silk, wool, rayon, or other natural or man-made raw materials, which have been woven, knitted, felted, or braided into cloth. All other products such as those made from metals, plastics, rubber, paper, china, glass, wood, leather, and fur are known as *nontextiles*. Some stores carry exclusively one or the other type of merchandise. For example, a drapery and curtain shop may have only textile products while a jewelry store may carry just nontextile items made from metals and stones. Some stores carry ties, shirts, and underwear, and men's jewelry, belts, wallets, and other small leather goods.

Not all merchandise can be classified as strictly textile or nontextile. Some items contain both. A lamp, for example, may have a china base and a silk shade. A pair of shoes may have leather uppers, rubber soles, fabric lining, and fabric laces. A fabric may be made from cotton, or linen, or some other fiber, yet have a plastic finish. Likewise, a plastic may have a fabric backing. A handbag may be made from leather or plastic but lined in fabric. Furniture may be made primarily from wood, braced with metal, but upholstered with fabric covers. Thus, while there are some clear differentiations in merchandise, some products combine both textiles and nontextiles.

Foods, of course, are not textiles and are generally classified separately. They include grocery products, meats, produce, baked goods, frozen foods, and dairy products. Some courses in home economics are devoted wholly to foods.

Left: Yard goods.
Center: Clothing.
Right: Home furnishings.

Articles of Textile Merchandise.

Articles of Nontextile Merchandise.

Top and center row: Articles of plastic, leather, glass, and ceramics. **Bottom row:** Articles of wood, metal, and plastic.

PUTTING THIS MERCHANDISE KNOWLEDGE TO USE ❯❯❯❯❯❯❯❯❯❯

❯ DO YOU KNOW YOUR MERCHANDISE?

1. Explain the importance of distribution in our economy.
2. What are the major classes of goods and services that are included in the consumer expenditures?
3. (*a*) What is meant by "Selling Sentences"? (*b*) What information does the customer seek from the salesperson?
4. What sources of information does the consumer tap as she hunts for the right merchandise?
5. In what respects is the retailer the purchasing agent for the consumer?
6. (*a*) How can the salesperson help the customer find the best merchandise to round out her home assortment? (*b*) What are the main selling points he can use?
7. What are the major items of merchandise included in the terms: (*a*) textiles, (*b*) nontextiles, (*c*) foods?

❯ INTERESTING THINGS TO DO

1. Make a rough survey of all merchandise in your home. (*a*) What items need replenishing almost at once? (*b*) What items should be bought within the week? within a month? (*c*) Are there some major purchases, much needed, that are having to be deferred even longer because of lack of purchasing power? (*d*) Do you feel that your present household assortment is pretty well balanced? (*e*) Would you suggest any changes in your family's buying habits that would result in a better assortment of goods than you now have without increasing the total family spending for merchandise?
2. Go into a large retail store, preferably a large department store, and count the number of departments selling textile merchandise and the number of departments selling nontextile merchandise. (*a*) What can you conclude as to the relative importance of the two types of merchandise sold in retail stores? (*b*) What merchandise is made both of textiles and nontextiles?
3. The next time you purchase something in a retail store, observe what selling points the salesperson gives you about the merchandise. Write up the sale as it took place. (*a*) Was the salesperson well informed about the merchandise he sold you? (*b*) If not, why not? (*c*) Would you return to this salesperson for further purchases?

ADDITIONAL MERCHANDISE TERMS ❯❯❯❯❯❯❯❯❯❯❯❯❯❯❯❯❯❯❯❯

Buying points are facts about a product that the customer considers important in satisfying his needs.

Customer is any individual or firm to whom a seller sells and with whom he maintains or hopes to maintain a continuing relationship.

Felted cloth is a fabric made by steaming, pounding, and pressing masses of raw material together to form a cloth.

Knitted cloth is a fabric made by looping a single continuous thread around needles. As each consecutive loop is made, it is transferred to the other needle.

Merchandise is any finished goods ready for consumer purchase.

Retail salesperson sells merchandise to the ultimate consumer.

Woven cloth is a fabric made by the interlacing of two sets of threads (yarns) at right angles.

How Cloth Is Made— Fibers Used

CHAPTER

2

UNIT 2 WHAT IS CLOTH?

Have you ever tried to darn a hole in a sock? Have you ever watched a hole in a cloth be rewoven? If you have had either of these experiences, then you will know that in each instance a new cloth or *fabric* is made to fill in the hole.

If a sock is to be repaired, the darning thread selected is usually of the same color as the sock proper; and it is cotton if the sock is cotton; wool, if the hose is wool; nylon, if the sock is nylon. But why? The darner of the hole wants to have the new cloth to look and feel like the rest of the sock. In other words, color and texture should match.

Texture is the way the cloth looks and feels. In reweaving a hole in a fabric, it is extremely important to match exactly the color, the size of the thread, and the texture.

Cloth and *fabric* mean the same thing—an article that is constructed, fabricated, or put together. A house is made or constructed of brick and mortar, or wood, for example.

A *cloth* is made from raw materials, such as cotton, linen, silk, wool, nylon, or rayon. Such a cloth would be a *textile fabric*, which can be made by the following processes: weaving, knitting, felting, braiding, bonding, or laminating.[1] Some examples of textile fabrics made by these methods include: weaving—broadcloth shirting, bed sheeting, flannel suiting, velvet; knitting—sweaters, jersey, fabric gloves; felting—felt hats; braiding—braided rugs; bonding—durable disposable napkins; laminating—flannel-backed denim dungarees. Each of these methods will be discussed in the following section called

[1] See Methods of Making Cloth, Chapter 4.

"Kinds of Textile Cloths." *Nontextiles* include all articles that are made by methods other than those described for making textiles. Examples of nontextiles are foods, jewelry, cosmetics, stationery, leather goods, furs, silverware, household utensils, rubber goods, china, glassware, and furniture. All of these items are discussed in Part II.

Textiles are fabrics, or the fibers from which the fabrics are made. The word textiles comes from the Latin *textilis* meaning "to weave." While the original meaning of textiles pertained to woven fabrics only, the present definition includes additional methods of construction, such as: knitting, felting, crocheting, knotting, braiding, bonding, and laminating. Textile merchandise comprises any and all types of textile fabrics, other merchandise being called *nontextile merchandise*.

KINDS OF TEXTILE CLOTHS

Woven Cloth. Most of us remember from kindergarten days the paper mats we made of different colored strips of paper. We had a piece of paper cut with slits through which we ran strips of paper, over and under, across and back. This passing of a strip over and under another strip of paper is the same kind of operation as that used in weaving a cloth.

Knitted Cloth. Most of us either know how to knit, or have seen someone knitting. To knit, a strand of yarn is looped and interlaced around needles.

Different Cloth Constructions for Typical Uses.

Upper left: Lace. **Lower left:** Knitted fabric. **Center:** Woven fabric. **Upper right:** Felted fabric. **Lower right:** Braided fabric rug.

《 Laminated cloth

Braided cloth 》

As each new loop is made, it is slipped from one needle to the other. This looping of the yarn forms a fabric of rows or ridges.

Felted Cloth. Textile merchandise can also be made by taking masses of raw wool or cotton (cleaned, of course) and, with steam and pounding, pressing them into a cloth—a felt for a hat, as an example. (See page 14.)

Braided Cloth. To braid, three strands of yarn or narrow-cut fabric are used. By intertwining these strands, a narrow band like braided hair is made. The braid can be laid in the shape of the article desired and then sewed in place. (See above.)

Bonded Cloth. To visualize the method of constructing bonded fabrics, which are often called "nonwoven goods," one should think of a thin layer of absorbent cotton that can be sprayed with a plastic to make it hold (be bonded) together. This is but one of several methods used in bonding. The bonding process differs from felting in that in the latter process steam and pressure cause the wool or the fur to hold together. (See page 14.)

Laminated Cloth. Almost everyone is familiar with plywood—layers of wood held together by laminating. Two or more textile cloths can be stuck together with plastic to make them reversible and to add warmth. When one mends clothing by ironing a plasticized tape patch onto a fabric, one is doing a laminating process. (See above.)

Knotted Cloth. A fabric called *fish net* is made by tying knots into the cotton yarn to form a four-cornered mesh like the Gloucester fishing nets. While the fabric is done by machine, the fishing nets may be done by hand. Tatting is a kind of narrow knotted lace used for edging handkerchiefs. It is done by hand by tying a series of knots in the form of a small design. (See page 79.)

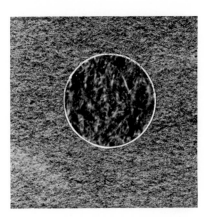

◀ Bonded cloth

Felted cloth ▶

Crocheted Cloth or Lace.   A single strand of cotton or linen is used. With a crochet hook, a loop is made; then a second loop is pulled through the first loop, a third through the second, and so on, until a chain is formed from this single strand. By looping back into this chain, various designs can be formed. (See page 79.)

PUTTING THIS MERCHANDISE KNOWLEDGE TO USE ❯ ❯ ❯ ❯ ❯ ❯ ❯ ❯ ❯ ❯

❯ DO YOU KNOW YOUR MERCHANDISE?

Copy the following questions and replace the question mark with the name of the cloth construction.
1. Nonwoven goods, such as disposable napkins, are generally made by a ? process.
2. Cotton broadcloth shirtings are made by ?.
3. Jersey is made by ?.
4. Bed sheeting is made by ?.
5. Tatting is a lace done by ?.
6. Men's everyday winter hats for business wear are usually made by ?.

❯ INTERESTING THINGS TO DO

1. Examine items in your wardrobe, i.e., your suits, your socks or stockings, dungarees, sweaters. Try to determine the method by which each cloth is made.
2. Examine items in your home to determine whether they are textile or nontextile.
3. For those items you believe to be textile fabrics, try to determine the method by which each cloth is made.

UNIT 3 FIBERS USED FOR CLOTH— THE NATURAL FIBERS

The label shown below is a tag that is attached to an article of clothing. It tells the customer six important facts about the textile merchandise:

1. It is made of all cotton (shown on reverse side of label).
2. The brand name is Cone.
3. It is guaranteed by *Good Housekeeping*.
4. American craftsmen make it here.
5. The garment will not shrink more than 1%— so little that one need not think about it.
6. Instructions for caring for the article of clothing are also given on the reverse side.

A Cone Fabric with RETENTO finish

SANFORIZED

Residual shrinkage not over 1%

LITTLE OR NO IRONING REQUIRED

CARE INSTRUCTIONS

This fabric is WASHABLE by AUTOMATIC WASHING MACHINE, by hand or may be sent to your laundry. Deep shades or reds should be washed separately for first few launderings to remove excessive dye.
  • Retains Color and hand after repeated washings
  • Dries quickly
  • Use any all-fabric or oxygen type powdered bleach

©CONE MILLS INC.
New York 18, N. Y.   A CONE FABRIC

Tag printed in U.S.A.   C-300-5

The first fact, "all cotton," and the manufacturer's name are required by law to be on the label. This law is called "The Textile Fiber Products Identification Act." It was signed by former President Eisenhower and became effective March 3, 1960. This law requires manufacturers to label their fabrics, indicating the kinds of raw material that went into them.

The raw materials from which textile cloths are made are called "fibers"; therefore, the content of this cloth is known as "fiber content." A *textile fiber* is the smallest unit in a textile cloth.

The law mentioned above was enacted to protect the consumer from any possible misrepresentation of cloth contents. The knowledge of what a cloth is made of can be of great help to a customer in selecting the appropriate fabric for a particular use. Facts about the merchandise can also help the consumer to judge its durability and to care for the article properly. For

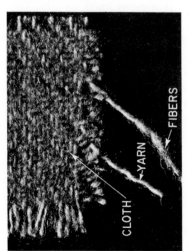

CLOTH — YARN — FIBERS

example, if the customer knows that a fabric is all cotton, she can usually expect it to be washable, and to be comparatively economical to buy and own, inasmuch as the United States grows a large supply of cotton, and modern processes control shrinkage and make cotton colorfast. Cotton cloths are therefore good for sportswear and children's clothing.

A cloth may be made of one kind of fiber, such as cotton, or it may be made of a mixture of two or more kinds of fibers. Fibers are of different kinds, lengths, shapes, fineness; they are combined in different ways by manufacturing processes to form cloths.

To discover a fiber in a piece of cloth, unravel a thread, called a *yarn*, from the cloth, untwist the yarn and notice all the tiny hairlike filaments. Each hairlike filament is a fiber.

USES OF TEXTILE FIBERS

Suppose we think of some of the garments we wear to see what fibers are used:

1. Dresses can be made of cotton, linen, silk, wool, rayon, acetate, nylon, acrylic, polyester fibers, or mixtures of these. There are many more fibers—some quite new.

2. Underwear can be made of the same fibers.

3. Hats are made of wool, cotton, fur, felt, straw, metal threads, linen, cotton, silk, and man-made fiber mixtures. Man-made fibers are discussed in Unit 3.

4. Gloves are made of cotton, wool, silk, rayon, polyester, nylon (or combinations of these). When made of these fibers, gloves are called *fabric gloves* and are textile fabrics. When they are made of leather, gloves are non-textiles.

5. Hosiery is commonly made of cotton, wool, silk, rayon, acrylic, polyester, and nylon.

6. Men's suits are generally made of wool, silk, rayon, acetate, cotton, linen, mohair, polyester, or mixtures of two or more of these fibers.

7. Men's neckties are made of silk, rayon, nylon, cotton, wool, polyester, or mixtures.

If we think of fabrics we use in home furnishing, we have:

1. Rugs made of wool, the most commonly used fiber; of silk, as in some valuable orientals; of cotton, as in tufted and rag rugs; of linen, as a backing for valuable antique hooked rugs; of jute, as backing for Axminster rugs; of rayon, frequently used in chenille bath rugs, and in broadlooms. Orlon acrylic, nylon, and other man-made fibers are now also being used for rugs. These fibers are durable. Stains can be removed from them easily.

2. Draperies and upholstery of cotton, linen, silk, rayon, acetate, mohair, and nylon are common. Curtains come in cotton, rayon, nylon, glass fiber, and polyester. In fact many new fibers are now being used in this field.

3. Sheets and pillow slips are made of cotton and sometimes of linen, nylon, or even silk.

4. Face towels and guest towels are made of cotton, linen, or mixtures of the two. Turkish towels are generally cotton, with the exception of the back scratcher or friction towel, which is preferably linen. Face cloths are cotton. Dish towels, glass towels, and dishcloths are usually cotton, linen, ramie, or mixtures of these fibers. However, rayon may be used as decoration, or in a mixture with cotton or linen.

Sources of Textile Fibers. Silkworm is the producer of silk fibers. Cotton boll yields cotton fibers. Sheep's body covering gives wool fibers. Mohair fibers are hair from the Angora Goat. Flax fibers come from inside the stalks of the bundle of flax stalks. The test tube represents synthetic fibers like rayon, nylon, acetate, Dacron polyester, Orlon acrylic, and Dynel modacrylic.

KINDS OF NATURAL FIBERS

There are two major classes of textile fibers: (1) natural fibers (fibers grown in nature); (2) man-made fibers (manufactured or so-called synthetic fibers).

From the listing of items of merchandise and their usual fiber content on page 16, it will be noticed that cotton, linen, silk, and wool have many uses. These fibers may therefore be considered as major textile fibers because of their extensive use in the manufacture of textile fabrics. Furthermore, they may be classed as *natural fibers* because they grow in nature and are not man-made. These fibers can be classified into (1) animal; (2) vegetable; (3) mineral.

Animal fibers	Vegetable fibers	Mineral fibers
Silk	Cotton	Asbestos
Wool	Linen	Metal threads (gold,
Hair	Hemp	silver, tinsel yarn)
	Jute	
	Ramie	
	Kapok	
	Paper	
	Straw	
	Grass	

Animal Fibers

Silk, the Luxurious Fiber. Silk fibers are the longest natural fibers. They are animal fibers and are the product of the silkworm. Silkworms feed on either mulberry leaves or on the scrub oak (vegetables). A chemical change takes place in the silkworm—a conversion from a vegetable to an animal product. The color of cultivated silk from silkworms feeding on the mulberry leaves is yellow to gray. Wild silkworms that feed on scrub oak produce silk which is usually deep yellow to brown.

The wild silk is coarse, uneven, and is frequently used in its natural color,

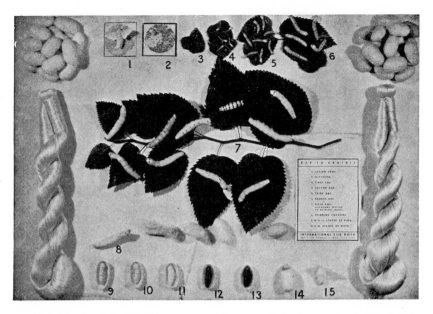

Metamorphosis of the Silk Worm. *(Courtesy of the International Silk Guild)*

1. Laying eggs.
2. Hatching.
3. First age.
4. Second age.
5. Third age.
6. Fourth age.
7. Fifth age (Silkworm feeding on mulberry leaves.)
8. Spinning cocoons.
9,10,11,12. Stages of the chrysalis.
13,14,15. Stages of moth.

Placing full-grown silkworms in cocoon spinning rack with compartments. *(Courtesy of the Japanese Silk Assoc., Inc.)*

Moths emerging from cocoons.

because it does not take dye as well as cultivated silk. Pongee and shantung are made from wild silk. When silkworms are cultivated, the eggs are placed in an incubator, under controlled conditions of temperature and moisture, where they soon hatch into worms about the size of a hair ⅛ of an inch long. For the next 30 days these worms are fed a diet of mulberry leaves. During this period, complete control must be exercised over all external conditions, such as cleanliness, temperature, smell, and noises.

The food consumed by the worm is changed within its body into the substance that is later excreted as silk filaments. When the worm has grown to about 3 or 3½ inches, it stops eating and is ready to spin its cocoon. It then raises its head and attaches a few threads to the twigs that are prepared for this purpose and begins to excrete a fluid from two glands, one on each side of its head. When these fluids reach the air, they unite to form a single thread or filament which is composed of the silk itself, or *fibroin*, and a protective gummy covering, called *sericin*. After the cocoon is completed, the worm inside shrinks into a hard, brown, nutlike chrysalis. If the worm is allowed to live, it will emerge within 8 to 15 days as a moth, mate, lay about 350 eggs, and die, thus starting the life cycle anew. The entire life of the silkworm is about two months.

Some silk fibers are as long as 1,350 to 4,000 feet. These fibers are unwound (reeled) directly from the cocoons which are composed of one long silk filament. But to obtain these long fibers, the larvae inside the cocoon must be killed. Because of the length and strength of these long *reeled silk* fibers, fabrics made from them are durable. But not all silk fibers are of this length.

If the moth emerges, the cocoon is broken and also the long silk filament. The resultant short fibers are straightened, drawn out, and then spun into yarn. This yarn is called *spun silk*. Any tangled ends of fiber which cannot be reeled from the cocoon and the fibers from defective cocoons are also used for spun silk. Spun silk yarns can be used in silk broadcloth, plush, and velvet, as well as in upholstery fabrics, hosiery, underwear, sweaters, and scarfs.

Because spun silk is made of short fibers, it is not very smooth and has a cottony feel. It does not have the luster, the strength, nor the elasticity of reeled silk. Spun silk is less expensive than reeled silk.

Silk noil is waste silk produced during the manufacture of spun silk. According to the Trade Practice Rules for the Silk Industry, fabrics made from silk noil (or silk waste) must be so labeled. One of the most important uses of silk noil is in powder bags for military purposes. It can also be used in dress fabrics. Such cloths are cottony to the touch; are very dull in luster; and are quite rough in texture. See page 48 for noil-silk yarn.

Japan, Italy, and China produce raw silk. The United States imports its silk from the first two countries. Brazil also produces silk. Several times during the history of the United States, attempts were made to cultivate and produce silkworms. The failure of these undertakings, from a commercial standpoint, is due, not to the type of climate, but to the great amount of hand labor involved.

Wool and Hair, the Warm Fibers. The wool fiber serves as a protective covering for the sheep. It is shorn from a live sheep or is pulled from a dead one. Wool fiber is animal. It is yellowish to brown and sometimes black in color. Wool is an animal fiber because it is composed chiefly of a protein substance called *keratin*. Hair fibers may be considered along with wools because, like wool fibers, hairs are the growth on the skins of animals. Wool comes from different varieties of sheep, while hair fibers come from various kinds of rabbits, camels, goats, cats, horses, and cows. Countries producing the best wool for clothing are Australia, England, New Zealand, Scotland, South Africa, United States, and Uruguay. Coarse wools used for carpets come from Argentina, China, Siberia, and Turkey. Much of our carpet wool now comes from Argentina.

Everyone has heard of the excellence of merino wool. In this connection, the average customer often thinks of Australia synonymously with merino wool. Indeed the best grade of merino wool comes from Australia. Because of favorable climatic conditions and the excellent care given the sheep, the finest fiber wool is produced in Australia. However, much of the wool raised in the United States, especially in Ohio, West Virginia, and Pennsylvania, can compare favorably in quality to Australian wool.

Generally speaking, merino wool is shorter in fiber than English wools from Lincolnshire and Leicestershire, which average the longest fibers.

It is difficult to generalize about grades of wool. The grade of wool depends not only on the country from which it comes, but also on the breed of sheep and the part of the body from which the wool is taken. Wool from the head, belly, and breech is poorer grade than wool from the shoulders and sides of the sheep.

Formerly, wool was removed from the sheep's body by a skillful shearer who clipped the wool by hand. Now the clipping is done by machine. In the Northern Hemisphere, domestic and territory sheep are clipped in the spring; in the Southern Hemisphere, in our fall.

Fleece wool is wool shorn from a living sheep. Wool can also be removed from dead sheep which have been slaughtered or have succumbed to disease. Skins of dead animals are treated with lime paste and sweated; the fibers are then pulled from the skin. Wool so obtained is called *pulled wool*. It is not considered as good grade as fleece wool, but it can be used in felts, flannels, and bed blankets.

Mohair, alpaca, and *cashmere* are goats' hair. Mohair is from the Angora goat raised extensively in Cape Colony and Turkey and also in Arizona, California, New Mexico, Oregon, and Texas. Alpaca comes from a kind of goat found in the mountains of Peru; while cashmere is a very soft hair from the cashmere goat of China, India, Iran, Iraq, Mongolia, and Tibet. Cashmere fleece is the finest when the animal lives at high altitudes. Cashmere fibers from China, Mongolia, and Tibet are usually finer than those from India, Iran, and Iraq.

The *llama* and *vicuña* fibers are obtained from goatlike animals found in

South America. Although these fibers are soft and attractive, only a comparatively small amount of them is used for textile purposes. Vicuña is very rare and is not domesticated.

Camel's hair is obtained from Africa, Asia, China, and Russia. Horsehair is imported for the most part from South America.

Hair fibers are generally more wiry and stiffer than wool fibers. Hair does not felt as well as wool. Wool fibers range from 1 to 8 inches in length, while hair fibers range from 4 to 12 inches.

Vegetable Fibers

Cotton, the Economical Fiber.   This fiber is most used in consumers' goods. It is grown in Asiatic Russia, Bengal, Brazil, China, Egypt, Hawaii, India, Japan, Mexico, Peru, Thailand, the continental United States, and the West Indies. The United States grows a large portion of the world's supply.

Cotton fibers come from a plant, somewhat like a hollyhock, which ranges in height from 2 to 20 feet, depending on the variety. Cotton is a white or yellow-white vegetable fiber contained in the cotton boll. (See illustration, page 22.) Cotton fiber is chiefly composed of cellulose—a solid, inert substance that is a part of plants.

Before the cotton fiber has ripened, the fiber is tubelike, and the central canal or tube is filled with a substance called *lumen*. When the cotton fiber ripens, the lumen goes down to the stalk of the plant; and the fiber flattens and twists like a ribbon. This twist can be seen under a microscope. When cotton is mercerized, that is, treated with a chemical to give luster and strength to the fiber, the microscopic twist disappears and the fiber becomes cylindrical. With this chemical treatment, the fiber also absorbs dye better. Cotton cloths usually mercerized are sateen, broadcloth, and batiste. Cotton fibers range from ¾ of an inch to nearly 2 inches in length.

VARIETIES OF COTTON.   There are several varieties of cotton, depending in a large measure on the climatic conditions under which they are grown. The cotton with the longest and finest staple (fiber) is used for the finest, sheerest cotton goods, such as organdy and batiste. The short-fibered cottons are used for the coarser cotton materials, such as unbleached muslin.

Cottons grown in the United States may be classified according to length of fiber, beginning with the longest:

1. Sea island (supply negligible because of the ravages of an insect, the boll weevil.) Fibers, 1⅜ inch-1⅞ inch.
2. Pima. Fibers 1⅜ inch-1¾ inch.
3. Peeler. Fibers 1⅛ inch-1¼ inch.
4. Upland. Fibers ¾ inch-1½ inch.

Foreign-grown cotton fibers, also listed according to length, are Egyptian, Indian, and Peruvian. Cotton is also grown in Bengal, China, and Thailand. Fibers are yellowish brown in color and are seldom exported.

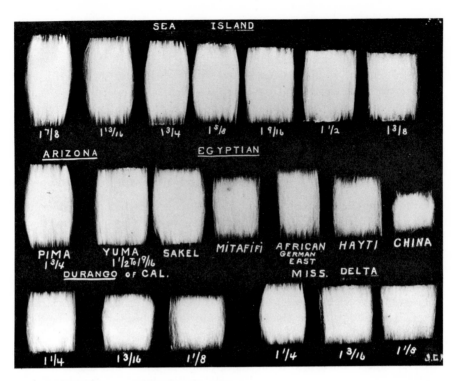

Varieties of Cotton and Their Fiber Lengths.

Cotton Bolls. *(Courtesy American Viscose Corp.)*

HOW COTTON IS GROWN AND HARVESTED.   There are three main steps:

1. *Planting and Picking.*   The cotton seeds are planted in the spring. The boll pods of the cotton shrub mature and are picked in the latter part of July or early August. Much cotton picking is still done by hand, but the recent invention of the mechanical picker has increased production on farms that are large enough to afford the high cost of such machinery.

2. *Ginning.*   After the cotton bolls are picked, they are sent to the cotton gin where the seeds are separated from the fiber.

3. *Baling.*   After the cotton fibers are removed from the boll, they are placed in bales of 500 pounds each and are sent to the mills. Here the cotton is removed from the bales and put through several machines that clean it. In the next chapter, the making of various kinds of cotton yarn will be discussed.

BY-PRODUCTS OF THE COTTON INDUSTRY.   The seeds that are removed are pressed out to make soaps and also cottonseed oil for salad dressing. The hull that is left after the oil is removed is used in making cattle food, fuel, and fertilizer. The very short fibers that remain on the seed are called *cotton linters* and are used in the manufacture of rayon, paper, absorbent cotton, mattresses, gun cotton, photographic films, and cotton wadding.

Flax or Linen, the Hygienic Fiber.   The fibers obtained from inside the woody stalk of the flax plant are called *flax*; after woven into cloth, it is called *linen*. Like cotton, flax is composed chiefly of cellulose and is therefore a vegetable fiber.

Flax is a slender, erect annual plant which has blue blossoms. It is cultivated for two purposes: (1) for seed, and (2) for fiber. In this country in the states of Minnesota, Michigan, and the Dakotas we raise flax principally for seed, rather than for fiber. This is largely because of the expense and care involved in the cultivation and preparation of flax for spinning. Also flax raised for seed does not produce good fibers, and vice versa.

The Argentine produces the most flaxseed in South America; and India, Canada, Lithuania, French Morocco, and Latvia also produce flaxseed.

Flax is grown for fiber in the U.S.S.R., Poland, Lithuania, Latvia, Ireland, Belgium, France, Egypt, northern Italy, Holland, and Germany.

Linen has been in consumer use for centuries. The cultivation, preparation, and manufacturing of linen cloth is a very old textile industry. Egyptian mummies have been found wrapped in linen cloth. Ireland was cultivating flax two and a quarter centuries ago. European farmers taught the Irishmen the secrets of the manufacturing of linen.

CULTIVATION AND PREPARATION OF FIBERS FOR YARN MAKING.   Flax is planted in soil in a temperate climate where there is copious rainfall, for dry weather of too long duration will stunt and ripen the fiber prematurely. Careful weeding of the flax field is important during the early stages of its growth. When harvesting time arrives, the stalks are pulled by hand and assembled in bundles. The reason for pulling the stalks up by hand is that great care must be taken not to break the length of the fiber, which is inside the wooded stalk.

◄ **Irish Flax in Bundles.** *(Courtesy William Ewart & Sons, Ltd., Belfast)*

Fibers are prepared for yarn making by two processes: (1) retting and (2) scutching.

Retting. Flax fiber is removed from the stalk by a process called *retting*—actually rotting. One method of retting is to place the bundles of flax in a rectangular hole in the ground filled with fresh water. A stone is placed on top of the bundles to keep them completely submerged until the stalk separates easily from the fiber. This is called the *lint-hole* method and is common in Ireland. In Russia, the stalks are spread out on a field and the dew rets (rots) the stalks. In Belgium, flax in bundles is anchored in the River Lys where the flow of the current rets the stalks. The stalks are then spread out in rows to dry. A quicker method is to boil the flax in a dilute sulfuric acid solution followed by careful washing. While this method is quick, it is more costly and there is a tendency to weaken the fibers.

Scutching. This process breaks the woody part of the stalk and separates the flax fiber from the stalk. The stalks are run through rollers that break them. Then the rolled stalks of flax are held over a metal plate while dull-edged revolving blades remove the woody stalk from the flax fiber. The scutched flax is then sorted and graded.

Linen fibers are longer than cotton fibers. They range from 18 to 20 inches. Linen fibers are also coarser than cotton. Linen launders easily because hot water and soap do not harm the fiber. In fact, the fibers are stronger wet than dry. Linen can, therefore, be called a "hygienic fiber."

Minor Vegetable Fibers.   While cotton, linen, silk, and wool rank first among natural fibers from the standpoint of extent of use in consumers' goods, there are other natural textile fibers that have their places in textile fabrics. Following is a description of these minor fibers.

Hemp is a fiber grown in Central America, Mexico, Philippine Islands, the continental United States (Kentucky), the West Indies, and Yucatan. Manila hemp is a white fiber and is stronger than the other varieties. Hence it is used mainly in making ropes. The United States imports much hemp from the Philippines. India also raises hemp, but the Indian variety is not so strong as either the American or Manila hemp. Nevertheless, it is used in canvas and in cables. France, Italy, Japan, and Poland also raise hemp. Hemp is stronger than linen, cotton, or jute. It is dark brown in color and cannot be bleached without considerable loss of strength.

Jute fiber comes from a plant that grows about 12 feet high and is chiefly produced in India. The physical structure of jute is similar to flax; both fibers are obtained by stripping the branches and leaves from the stalk and then retting (like flax) the stalks to loosen the outer bark from the fibers inside. After this process, the fibers are dried and cleaned.

Jute fibers are shorter and weaker than flax. While linen becomes stronger when it is wet, jute becomes much weaker. Jute is likewise weakened by chemical bleaches and therefore cannot be bleached white. It is used for bags, sacks, cordage, burlap, and bindings in carpets and rugs.

Sisal is a larger, stiffer, harder fiber than jute or hemp. The United States imports most of it from Haiti, Java, and Kenya. The fibers are dried, bleached, and sold in bales. Since sisal is too coarse for making into fine yarn, it is used for cordage and coarse sacking. It also appears in women's straw hats.

Ramie, or *rhea*, the substitute for linen, is a textile fiber that can be used for the same purposes as linen.

A customer was examining the raveled edges of a doilie of a luncheon set. She liked the salmon-colored background and the white woven-in design. The cloth had a silky sheen too. The customer remarked to the salesperson, "I don't think this doilie is linen. The luster seems too high for linen." The salesperson replied, "This is a ramie cloth." "What's that? Is it any good?" queried the customer. "Yes, it is extremely durable. It washes better than many linens—more like cotton. Ramie is stronger than linen; will resist mildew and will absorb more moisture than will linen."

Chinese grass cloth is ramie. This fiber is also made into twine, ropes, nets, and sewing thread. It can be mixed with wool or with silk in woven goods. But its best use is as a substitute for linen, although it does not make up into so sheer or so fine a cloth as does linen. Inexpensive dish towels and bedding can be made of ramie.

Ramie comes from China and Egypt, and experiments in growing ramie have been made in Florida, eastern Georgia, and some parts of the Gulf States.

Paper is primarily cellulose and is derived from wood, bamboo, jute, straw, and cotton, linen and hemp rags. In sheet form, paper is a nontextile, but when cut into strips and twisted into yarn, it becomes a textile. Fiber rugs are made of paper. Paper usually becomes weak when wet.

One type of prairie *grass* used in rugs comes from Minnesota and Wisconsin. *Rush* is usually made from reeds that grow in sluggish waters of Europe and the Far East. Rush is used for rugs and chair seats.

Straw fibers come from the stems, stalks, leaves, and barks of plants growing in Ceylon, Italy, and Panama. These fibers are commonly used in hats. (See Chapter 12.)

Kapok is a lustrous vegetable fiber that comes from a plant or tree grown in Africa, Brazil, Central America, Java, South Asia, and the West Indies. It is used as a stuffing for pillows and life preservers.

Mineral Fibers

Asbestos, the Fire-Resistant Fiber. We all know for what uses asbestos is important—anything that is to resist fire. Asbestos is obtained from rocks, primarily in Quebec, Canada. While it is not resilient enough to be spun into yarn and woven into cloth, it can be mixed with a sufficient amount of cotton to be used in a fabric such as a theater curtain. Most of us are familiar with its use in mats to place over the flame of the stove to prevent food burning. Asbestos is mixed with man-made fibers in use as ironing-board covers.

Metal Threads. Tinsel yarns made of gold and silver were used from the earliest times to achieve luxury in clothing and in decoration. Now these tinsel yarns have been almost entirely replaced by man-made metallic yarns that are less expensive and nontarnishable. (See page 57.)

PUTTING THIS MERCHANDISE KNOWLEDGE TO USE ❯ ❯ ❯ ❯ ❯ ❯ ❯ ❯ ❯ ❯

❯ DO YOU KNOW YOUR MERCHANDISE?

1. Which fibers usually make the warmest fabrics: (*a*) silk and wool or (*b*) cotton and linen? Why?
2. What is ramie? Explain its uses.
3. Why is cotton considered an economical textile from the consumer's point of view?
4. Define a textile fiber. Name eight natural textile fibers.
5. (*a*) Distinguish among mohair, alpaca, cashmere, llama, and vicuña. (*b*) How do hair fibers differ from wool?
6. (*a*) What is kapok? (*b*) Where does it grow? (*c*) What are its uses?
7. (*a*) Give the essential differences between hemp and jute. (*b*) For what purposes is each used?

❯ INTERESTING THINGS TO DO

1. Collect labels from garments which you have purchased recently. Underline the fiber content. Classify the natural fibers into animal, vegetable, mineral.
2. Clip advertisements from newspapers in which the fiber content of an article is given. Underline and classify the natural fibers.
3. Trace a map of the world. On the map indicate the sources of the natural fibers.

UNIT 4 FIBERS USED FOR CLOTH— THE MAN-MADE FIBERS

KINDS OF MAN-MADE FIBERS

When a shortage of natural fibers threatened, scientists tried to find new man-made fibers to replace the natural fibers. In 1878, the silkworm disease threatened the European silk industry. It was then that Count Chardonnet experimented with nitrocellulose dissolved in alcohol and ether—a process that, many years later, came to be known as "the nitrocellulose process of making rayon."

Nowadays the urge to discover new fibers seems to come from the desire to create something new for the consumer. One object of advertising has been to create a feeling of obsolescence on the part of the consumer—to make her think that the article she is using is out of date. She must have the new fur-like fabric, the new triacetate jersey dress for traveling.

Synthetic fibers are manufactured or man-made fibers. They have come on the market so rapidly that it is almost impossible to keep up with their brand names.

But all brands of man-made fibers can be classified into family groupings. Each family has a name like the names Smith, Jones, or Brown.

These family names are called *generic names*, and members of each family have certain similar characteristics. Consequently, if one learns the family, or generic, names and their attributes, then, with the use of a table such as the one on page 37, one can attempt to judge the appropriateness of a cloth for a given use and can estimate how the fabric will perform in use.

Under the Textile Fiber Products Identification Act, all fibers must be declared in percentage by weight. For example, a man's suit would be labeled 50 per cent Dacron polyester, 50 per cent cotton. Under this law, the Federal Trade Commission (F.T.C.) has defined 16 generic names of textile fibers, to which it can add more. The difficulty with the definitions is that each name is defined in technical chemical terms. This language must be simplified for the consumer.

Following is the alphabetic list of the 16 generic names:

1. Acetate
2. Acrylic
3. Azlon
4. Glass
5. Metallic
6. Modacrylic
7. Nylon
8. Nytril
9. Olefin
10. Polyester
11. Rayon
12. Rubber
13. Saran
14. Spandex
15. Vinal
16. Vinyon

CANBERRA CLOTH
BY
LANGROCK-PRINCETON
50% DACRON - 50% COTTON
WASH - RINSE - DRIP DRY
NEVER WRING OR SPIN DRY
TOUCH UP WITH WARM IRON

HOW SYNTHETIC FIBERS ARE MANUFACTURED

It is possible that observation of the silkworm as it makes its cocoon may have served as a basis for creating man-made fibers. The silkworm ejects (extrudes) through its glands a liquid substance that becomes a solid filament of fiber when it comes in contact with cool air.

The chemist conceived the idea of extruding a man-made liquid through fine holes in a thimblelike device called a *spinneret*. The substance could then be hardened into a filament (fiber) of an indefinite length. A *filament*, then, is a synonym for fiber. The term is applied to long man-made fibers. *Continuous filament* is a synthetic fiber of indefinite length.

In general, this is the basic method used for making all synthetic fibers. However, the chemical solutions and methods of hardening the fiber vary. But man has studied the molecular structure of natural fibers so that he may know how to arrange molecules as nature does. Then he extrudes his laboratory-mixed liquid substance in a manner similar to the method used by the silkworm.

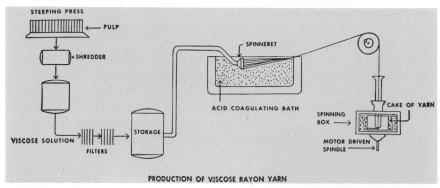

PRODUCTION OF VISCOSE RAYON YARN

The Viscose Process.

Upper left: Cotton bolls. **Lower left:** Wood. **Center:** Spinneret. **Right:** Cake of yarn.

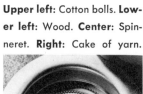

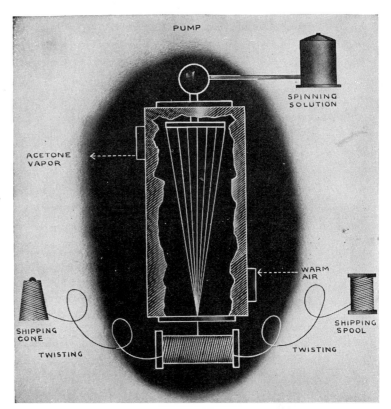

PUMP

SPINNING
SOLUTION

ACETONE
VAPOR

WARM
AIR

SHIPPING
CONE

SHIPPING
SPOOL

TWISTING

TWISTING

The Acetate Process.
*(Courtesy Tennessee
Eastman Corp.)*

Rayon, the Absorbent Fiber

Rayon and acetate are the oldest man-made fibers, rayon, the most used. The generic term *rayon* was coined by the National Retail Dry Goods Association (now N.R.M.A.) in 1924. It is the generic name of man-made vegetable fibers produced in the following manner.

The chief chemical constituent of the rayon fiber is cellulose, the same substance found in cotton, linen, and the other natural fibers. Cellulose is obtained from wood pulp or cotton linters (fuzzy waste fibers that stick to the cotton seeds).

To make rayon, wood pulp or cotton linters containing the necessary cellulose are treated with certain chemicals to form a thick solution. This solution is forced through holes in the spinneret to form threads and then is hardened. These threads or fibers are rayon—vegetable fibers made of pure cellulose. If a dull rather than a shiny fiber is desired, microscopic solids can be put in the solution before it is hardened into fiber.

How the Processes of Making Rayon Derive Their Names. Rayon is made by two different processes. The names for the two types of rayon are sometimes difficult to remember. Perhaps a study of the derivation of the names of the processes will help to fix the names in your mind.

1. Cuprammonium process, developed in France in 1890, derives its name from the copper (cupra) oxide and ammonia used to convert the pure cellulose into solution to be forced through the spinneret.

2. Viscose process, discovered by two English chemists in 1892, derives its name from the consistency of the solution which is forced through the spinneret. This liquid is called viscous solution, because it is thick and has the viscosity of honey or of molasses. From viscous is derived the term *viscose*.

By law, the generic name *rayon* must appear in close conjunction with the brand name. In Chapter 4, the important characteristics of rayon cloths will be discussed.

Viscose and cuprammonium rayon fibers are practically pure cellulose; that means that these two processes begin with cellulose and, going through chemical treatment, are changed back again into cellulose. The rayon fiber is vegetable like cotton and linen.

Acetate, the Beautiful Fiber

Acetate is the generic name of man-made fibers made by chemically treating pure cellulose waste cotton which is converted into a solution, which in turn produces a combination fiber composed of cellulose and acetic acid (acetyl). The final acetate fiber is both vegetable *and* chemical. Acetate, therefore, has some of the properties of cotton and some of the acetate plastic.

The acetate process, patented by two English chemists in 1894, derives its name from the acetic anhydride and glacial acetic acid and acetone—the chemicals used in making this fiber. In 1924, the Celanese Corporation of America developed the acetate process in the United States.

Acetate is *not* rayon, because the fibers differ from rayon chemically, react differently in use, and require different care by the consumer. For example, a pressing iron that is too hot will melt acetate fibers. An unsightly glaze appears permanently on the surface of the fabric. To make a colorfast fabric, the dyestuff is put into the solution before it is forced through the spinneret. In this fashion, color is locked permanently into the fiber.

Azlon, "the Soft Blender"

Azlon is the official generic name of man-made fibers derived from *protein*. Azlon received impetus in use during World War II. These fibers resemble wool in many respects. The protein for these fibers is obtained from casein in milk, soy beans, fish, and corn. There are no azlon fibers produced currently in the United States, but a number are being manufactured in Europe. These fibers are used in blends with wool for suits, coats, and knitted outerwear. When the fibers are used in this country, *Azlon* will be found on the labels.

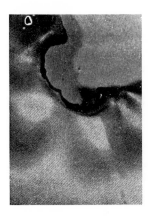

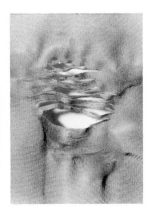

Burning Test of Rayon and Acetate. Left: Acetate (hard brownish residue left). **Center:** Rayon (paperish brown ash). **Right:** Effect of acetone on acetate and rayon.

Rubber, the Elastic Fiber

Because rayon, acetate, azlon, and some rubber fibers are obtained from natural sources, they are being described before those which are of a plastic type "made in test tubes."

The natural base for rubber is latex, a fluid tapped from the bark of the rubber tree. The liquid latex, which has been preserved in ammonia, is then formed into threads by being forced through tiny holes. After that, the threads are hardened and finally vulcanized. Synthetic rubber is also used as a raw material for this class of fibers. Rubber, therefore, is a generic name of fibers made from natural or synthetic rubber. See Part II, Chapter 17.

Rubber threads, called yarns, are wrapped with either natural or synthetic fibered yarns and then woven or knitted into cloth.

Such yarns are used in shirring in dresses and in bathing suits. They are also woven into foundation garments, underwear, tops of hosiery, swimming trunks, surgical stockings, and the elastic insteps of women's pumps.

Glass, the Nonflammable Fiber

Students of chemistry have probably used filters made of spun glass. But the 1930's saw the development of glass fibers for textile fabrics—particularly for draperies for homes and theater lobbies.

To make glass fibers, glass marbles are melted in an electric furnace. The molten glass is drawn down through a bushing which has microscopic holes at one end. Each hole makes a fiber or filament, which is then hardened. Fibers are spun into yarn and woven into fireproof fabrics, such as draperies, curtains, and wallpaper. *Glass* is the generic name for these fibers.

Metallic, the Luxury Look

While the use of gold and silver threads dates back to Biblical days, their use today is limited primarily to royal and ecclesiastical garments and religious decorations. Real gold and silver threads are heavy and harsh and will tarnish.

Consequently, the man-made metallics have taken their place because they are soft, lightweight, do not tarnish and are relatively inexpensive. They are made like a sandwich. A layer of aluminum foil is "sandwiched in" between two layers of clear plastic (a man-made substance that can be shaped and molded by heat). Color can be added to the plastic before the "sandwich" is made. Sometimes the inside layer is colored and shows through the clear plastic outer layers. *Metallic* is the generic name of these man-made fibers.

Nylon, the Strong Fiber

Nylon was the first man-made textile fiber which had been built up from all-chemical material. Rayon and acetate were made from wood pulp or cotton linters (cellulosic, natural raw materials).

Nylon was discovered by research chemists of the Du Pont Company. Although the public knew about its discovery October 30, 1938, it was about a year later before retailers in Wilmington, Delaware, had a limited supply of nylon hosiery for sale. It was not until the spring of 1940 that retailers in all parts of the country received limited quantities of nylon hosiery. From its successful early beginning in the hosiery field, it has spread in use to nearly every article of wearing apparel and to home-furnishing items such as carpets, draperies, and upholsteries.

Nylon is the generic name of plastic fibers (polyamide plastic) made from coal, air, and water. From coal, coal tar is derived; oxygen and nitrogen are two elements obtained from air; hydrogen is derived from the water. Coal tar, oxygen, nitrogen, and hydrogen are basic materials from which compounds are made. These compounds are carried through a complex series of chemical reactions to form a material which can be forced through tiny holes in a spinneret to form continuous filaments like rayon. Nylon can be made permanently dull in luster by putting microscopic solids into the solution before it is forced through the spinneret.

Because of nylon's great strength, it is used wherever durability is important. Other attributes of nylon will be discussed in Chapter 4.

There are various kinds of nylon with somewhat different chemistry and produced for specific uses by various companies both here and abroad. Nylon, however, is the generic, or family, name of all fibers, of the polyamide plastic type.

Acrylic, the Warm, Lightweight Fiber

Another man-made class of fibers made from a type of plastic called "acrylic resin" is commonly known under the brand names of Orlon (the trademark of E. I. du Pont de Nemours & Co.) and Acrilan the trademark of Chemstrand Corporation). Acrylic resin is a compound derived from elements found in coal, air, water, petroleum, and limestone. Acrylic, therefore, is the generic name of fibers made of "acrylic resin."

Acrylics are not quite so strong as nylon but are soft, lightweight, bulky without being heavy.

Consumers first saw Orlon on the retailers' shelves as sheer curtaining in the fall and winter of 1949–1950. Since then it has become very popular for sweaters, coats, and dresses. It has now entered the carpet field.

Likewise, Acrilan has been well received by consumers for use particularly in blankets and rugs. For other trade names of acrylic fibers see chart on page 37.

In Chapter 4, the attributes of acrylics will be discussed more fully.

Modacrylic, the Fleecy, Furlike Fiber

The word *modacrylic* is a short form of "modified acrylic." The generic term means that the ingredients in the acrylic resin are not 100 per cent acrylic plastic but are combined with other chemicals. Modacrylic, therefore, is the generic name of man-made fibers with a modified acrylic base. The resultant fibers will not burn, are soft, can be permanently shaped by heat and pressure, and make up into furlike fabrics for coatings, collars of snow suits, mittens, and hoods of parkas. Familiar trade names of these fibers are Dynel and Verel.

Polyester, the Resilient Fiber

Polyester is the generic name of fibers made from basic chemicals coming from coal, air, water, and petroleum. The polyester is another type of plastic resin exemplified in Dacron, Kodel, Vycron, and Terylene (Canada). It is characterized in fabrics by crease resistance and shape retention. It is frequently blended with cotton for men's dress shirts, women's dresses, and men's suits. These fibers are also used for curtains. For further discussion of their characteristics, see Chapter 4.

Saran, the Tough Fiber

Most people immediately think of Saran Wrap which is a nontextile because it is in sheet form and is not made into cloth by any method described earlier in this chapter.

The same polyvinyl plastic resin as is used for Saran Wrap can be extruded through a spinneret and hardened into fibers for textile weaving. Saran is the generic name of man-made fibers of the polyvinyl type.

Saran is very resistant to hard wear and is best suited for automobile seat covers, railroad upholstery, women's belts, handbags, doll's hair, and chair seats. It can be used for strings of tennis racquets, leaders for fish lines, and suspenders.

The brand name Velon (accent on the last syllable) is familiar to consumers for use in curtains, upholstery, and tapes for venetian blinds. It is also made of a polyvinyl resin.

Vinyon, the Industrial Fiber

Vinyon is the generic name for fibers made of a chemical substance called *vinylchloride*. The American Viscose Company makes a product called *Vinyon H. H.*

These fibers make good filter cloths, fender cloths, rope, fishing lures, paint rollers, and insect screening. See page 37 for characteristics and fiber trade names.

Olefin, the Lightweight Fiber

Man-made fibers in this class are newcomers to the field. One type of olefin is produced from ethylene to form a polyethylene resin fiber. Because of the fiber's low heat resistance and waxy "hand," it has proved suitable for ropes, filter cloths, and webbing.

Another member of the class of olefin fibers is made from propylene gas and was developed as a textile fiber in Italy in 1957. Because of its low cost of production, and because it can be made with a soft touch, it blends well with wool fibers; it can be used in suitings, knitted goods, stuffing for pillows, automobile upholstery, outdoor furniture, and carpets.

U.S. trademarks for olefin fibers include Prolene, Reevon, Royalene, and Wynene.

Vinal, the Fiber with a Potential

Originally developed by the Japanese, *vinal* is the generic name for polyvinyl alcohol fibers. At present this class of fibers is not being manufactured in this country.

Nytril, Soft Fibers

Still another type of vinyl plastic, but differing in its complex chemical substance from the previous classification, is *Nytril* derived from ammonia and natural gas.

Due to their cashmerelike softness, nytril fibers are suitable for deep furlike luxury coatings, sweaters, hand knitting yarns, and in blends with wool, cotton, and other fibers for coat and suit fabrics.

Spandex, the Expandable Fiber

This type of man-made fiber is composed mainly of a chemical plastic substance called polyurethane. Its generic name is *spandex*. (See Chapter 4 for a full description.) There is no rubber present in this fiber. For textile purposes it is extruded through a spinneret as are other plastics.

Recently the fibers have won popularity in the foundation-garment field. They not only expand to fit the body firmly, but also contract and keep their shape indefinitely. Spandex is also used in the tops of men's socks to hold them up so garters are not needed.

PUTTING THIS MERCHANDISE KNOWLEDGE TO USE ❯ ❯ ❯ ❯ ❯ ❯ ❯ ❯ ❯ ❯

❯ DO YOU KNOW YOUR MERCHANDISE?

1. Give uses of the following man-made fibers in textile fabrics: (*a*) nylon; (*b*) saran; (*c*) polyester; (*d*) acrylic; (*e*) glass; (*f*) rayon; (*g*) acetate.
2. (*a*) What is rayon? (*b*) How does rayon differ from acetate? (*c*) What can you tell a laundress about ironing fabrics of acetate?
3. (*a*) Why are some man-made fibers dull in luster? (*b*) How is delustering accomplished?
4. (*a*) Define plastic. (*b*) Give a list of generic names of fibers which are plastic.
5. (*a*) What man-made fibers have both natural and chemical bases? (*b*) How are man-made metallics constructed?
6. (*a*) Why is spandex particularly well suited for use in foundation garments? (*b*) Why is nylon particularly suited for use in carpets?

❯ INTERESTING THINGS TO DO

1. Over a three-week period, clip advertisements from papers in which fiber content of an article is given. Underline the fibers described; classify the fibers by generic names.
2. Make a chart of the results of the above project to show the (*a*) article in which the fibers appear; (*b*) the brand name of the fibers.
3. Determine the fibers, by generic and brand names, that appear most frequently in the ads; and the kind of textile fabrics in which each fiber is most used.

UNIT 5 HOW TO REMEMBER GENERIC NAMES OF FIBERS AND THEIR CHARACTERISTICS

CONFUSION OVER TOO MANY FIBER GENERIC NAMES AND BRANDS

Having read the descriptions and important characteristics of the three families of natural fibers and sixteen families of synthetic fibers, you may be confused as to how to remember the differences between them.

You can easily remember that there are but three families, or classes, of natural fibers that grow in nature:

1. Animal (wool, hair, silk)
2. Vegetable (cotton, linen, etc.)
3. Mineral (asbestos and tinsel)

The man-made fibers are somewhat more difficult to classify. Probably the easiest way to remember them is to think of the fibers that are based on:

Natural Substances	Chemically Derived Substances	Natural *and* Chemically Derived Substances
Rayon (cellulose)	Nylon (polyamide)	Rubber (natural and/or synthetic base)
Acetate (cellulose)	Acrylic (resin)	Glass (mineral and chemical base)
Azlon (protein)	Modacrylic (modified acrylic)	Metallic (mineral and chemical [metal and plastic])
	Polyester (resin)	
	Saran (polyvinyl)	
	Vinyon (vinyl chloride)	
	Olefin (polyethylene and polypropylene)	
	Vinal (polyvinyl alcohol)	
	Nytril (vinylidene dinitrile)	
	Spandex (polyurethane)	

Identification of Generic Names of Fibers in Labels and Advertising

Fortunately, there is no problem of identification of these fibers by the consumer. The Textile Fiber Products Identification Act requires that each fiber be labeled in order to protect the consumer from misrepresentation as well as manufacturers from their competitors.

It is now illegal to label a cloth "Made from 'Flufftex'—the Miracle Fiber." The T.F.P.I.A. requires:

1. The generic names of fibers contained in a fabric in order of prominence.

2. Percentage of each fiber present, by weight, except those under 5 per cent.

3. Name or symbol of the product manufacturer.

4. If imported, the name of the country where the product was processed or manufactured.

Wool products have been labeled by law since the Wool Products Labeling Act of 1939. The object of the T.F.P.I.A. is to identify in labels and in advertising the fibers used in wearing apparel and in household textiles. But the definitions of the generic names of fibers are difficult to understand because they are given in terms of chemical structure rather than in terms of performance in use. From consumer surveys, it is evident that consumers want information on labels concerning performance and care.[1]

More than a knowledge of the kind of fiber used in a fabric is necessary in order to estimate a fabric's suitability for a given use. The kind of fibers, the

---

[1] Isabel B. Wingate, "The Informative Label as a Consumer Guide"—a thesis submitted in partial requirement of the degree of Ph.D. in the Graduate School of Education, Yeshiva University, June 1961.

type of yarn used, the cloth construction, the types of finishes—all determine the color, "hand" (touch or feeling), weight, wearing quality, draping quality, attractiveness, and style of a fabric.

What Facts Should the Consumer Know?

The *grade* of a fabric is determined by (1) the kind and quality of fibers used; (2) the grade of yarn; (3) the construction; and (4) the finish. If all factors but one are good grade, the final grade cannot be good.

The consumer, therefore, needs a general knowledge about the characteristics of each of the various fibers; the different kinds of yarns and their uses; the kinds and qualities of cloth constructions; and the kinds, uses, and permanency of various types of fabric finishes such as water repellency, shrinkage control, fire retardant, and permanent starchless. (See Chapter 5.)

Generic Names of Synthetic Fibers	Characteristics	Fiber Trade Names
Acetate	Silky feeling, draping quality, stability. Triacetate—less sensitive to heat than acetate, wrinkle resistant.	Chromspun, Celaperm, Estron, Acele, Arnel (triacetate)
Acrylic	Warmth without weight, bulky, stability	Acrilan, Orlon, Creslan, Zefran, Courtelle
Azlon	Soft, blends well with other fibers	No longer made in U. S.
Glass	Nonflammable, wrinkle resistant, drip-dry	Fiberglas
Metallic	Luxurious, nontarnishable, lightweight	Lurex, Lamé, Reymet, Metlon
Modacrylic	Fleecy, furlike, quick drying	Dynel, Verel
Nylon	Very strong, abrasion resistant, elasticity	Du Pont Nylon, Caprolan, Chemstrand Nylon, Enka Nylon, I.R.C. Nylon
Nytril	Very soft, press retention, good launderability	Not in production
Olefin	Lightweight, abrasion resistant, easily cleaned	Reevon, Avisun, Wynene
Polyester	Resiliency, wrinkle resistant, pleat retention	Dacron, Kodel, Vycron, Terylene (Canada), Fortrel
Rayon	Absorbency, versatility, easily dyed, creping property	Coloray, Cupioni, Bemberg, Avron, Avicron, Enka Rayon, Colorspun, Fortisan, Spunlo, Cordura (strong) Topel, Zantrel, Corval
Rubber	Elasticity (stretch and recovery)	Lastex, Lacton, Laton, Contro
Saran	Tough, wear resistant, flexible, water resistant	Saran, Velon
Spandex	Expandability and elasticity, abrasion resistant	Vyrene, Lycra
Vinal	Heat and chemical resistant, strong	Vinylon
Vinyon	Low melting point, unaffected by sunlight and water	Vinyon, Bristrand

In addition to this general knowledge, the consumer should know how to estimate the probable performance of blends of various fibers in different percentages, the use of regular and novelty yarn, and the types of cloth construction and finishes employed, since all these factors are likely to affect the finished fabric in its numerous uses. Such knowledge will help her select a fabric more intelligently and will help her care for it more efficiently. The informative label, if read carefully, and if referred to while the article is in use, should prove a most helpful guide.

The chart on page 37 gives the generic names of the fibers and describes in a few words their chief characteristics. If these words are memorized in connection with the generic name, a guide to the fiber's main characteristics will be fixed in mind. While each brand of fiber classified under a generic name is slightly different from other brands, just as members of the same family have different characteristics, they are in general very much alike because they stem from similar chemical combinations.

PUTTING THIS MERCHANDISE KNOWLEDGE TO USE ❯❯❯❯❯❯❯❯❯❯❯

❯ DO YOU KNOW YOUR MERCHANDISE?

1. (a) By what law is the labeling of wool products governed? (b) How long has this law been in effect?
2. What are the chief objectives of the T.F.P.I.A.?
3. What information in addition to fiber content do consumers want on labels to help them select and care for textiles properly?
4. What is the objection to the definitions of generic names in the T.F.P.I.A.?
5. What facts in addition to fiber content are needed for a consumer to estimate a fabric's suitability for a given use?
6. (a) If a fabric has good quality fibers, good grade of yarns, a firmly woven construction, a color that is not sunfast, how would you grade the fabric? (b) Why?

❯ INTERESTING THINGS TO DO

1. Visit a department store, the girls going to a ready-to-wear department; the boys, to a sports-jacket department. Look through a rack of dresses or jackets observing labels on each. Keep note of three points: (a) fiber content, (b) performance, what the article will do in use—resist shrinkage, be sunfast, etc., (c) instructions for care.
2. On the basis of your observations, (a) Do you find all labels complying with the law? (b) How many labels listed features of performance? (c) How many labels listed instructions for care?
3. (a) In this study, how many labels were attached to a single dress or jacket? (b) Whose labels were they? The fiber manufacturer's, the weaving mill's, the converter's (finisher), the garment manufacturer's? (c) What conclusions can you draw from this study of garment labels?

ADDITIONAL MERCHANDISE TERMS ❯❯❯❯❯❯❯❯❯❯❯❯❯❯❯❯❯❯❯❯❯

Bushing is a detachable metal lining used as an insulating part.
Vulcanize means to treat rubber latex chemically in order to improve its strength, hardness, and elasticity.

How Cloth Is Made— Yarns

CHAPTER
3

UNIT 6 WHY ARE YARNS IMPORTANT?

QUALITY OF YARN

A *textile* fabric is a cloth the basic unit of which is composed of textile fibers. If the quality, or grade, of these fibers is good, there is a possibility that the fabric may be strong. The strength of fabrics depends, however, on many factors—the qualities of the fibers, the quality of the yarns (strands of twisted fibers), the method of construction (weaving, knitting, or felting), and the type of finish used. Each of these factors may be likened to a link in a chain. The chain can be considered textile fabric with each link an integral part. For example, the fibers unprocessed are not fabric. Yarns (the second link) as such are not fabric. The fabric has to be put together (constructed) by weaving, knitting, felting or other methods (third link). Fabrics cannot be sold as they come from the loom or a knitting machine, because such fabrics are not ready for their intended use. Some fabrics may need to be colored to make them suitable for use; others may require bleaching or stiffening. These processes performed after the fabric is constructed are called *finishes*.

A chain is no stronger than its weakest link. Consequently, if fibers, construction, and finishes are strong, but the yarn, weak, the fabric will not have the maximum strength. Each link must be equally strong to make a strong cloth which we say is durable or long wearing.

The Fabric Chain. If one of these links is weak, the entire fabric suffers in durability.

FIBERS   YARN   CONSTRUCTION   FINISH

Chapter 2 considered the kinds and characteristics of fibers used in a textile fabric, their classification and labeling, facts needed to judge the quality of any fabric. The second step to judge a fabric is to know the type of yarn used, because the quality of yarn also affects the cloth.

A *yarn* is a strand made of fibers twisted together. Probably the easiest way to see how this is done is actually to make a yarn. Anyone can make a cotton yarn from a bit of absorbent cotton. First pull out the fibers into a very thin, filmy sheet; then narrow this sheet until it is ribbonlike; then alternately pull and twist the ribbonlike sheet until a yarn is formed. If these steps have not been carefully followed, the yarn may break or be uneven.

Your handmade yarn is probably fairly bumpy. In colonial times, all yarns were made by hand. Now all this is done by machinery. In manufacturing cotton yarn, great care is taken to make the filmy sheet of even thickness and of the same width, so that the yarn made from it will be smooth and even. The cloth made from an even yarn will then be smooth.

How Twist of Yarn Affects the Fabric

If you have just tried to make a cotton yarn, you found that the tighter you twisted the yarn, the stronger the yarn became. If you twist a yarn too tightly, however, it will break. So too, a fabric made of tightly twisted, evenly spun yarn will tend to be stronger than one made of loosely twisted and irregularly spun yarn. A salesperson should know that fabrics with loosely spun novelty yarns, although they have style value, may not be so durable as fabrics made of more evenly and tightly twisted yarn.

A yarn that is twisted so tightly that it begins to knot is called a *crepe yarn*. Crepe yarns used in hosiery dull the luster of the fabric and decrease the tendency to snag. In dress fabrics, such as flat crepe, the crepe yarn is woven crosswise of the cloth to give the fabric its crinkled surface.

How Ply Yarns Affect the Fabric

The cotton yarn you have made is called a *single*, because it is composed of one strand of fibers twisted together. Notice the amount of strength you need to break it in half. Then twist the two broken pieces of yarn together. This combined yarn is called a *two-ply yarn*. Now break this yarn. Notice that at least twice as much strength is needed to break the two-ply yarn as is needed to break the single. As a rule, a ply yarn is stronger than a single yarn of the same diameter.

A cotton broadcloth shirting of good quality is made of two-ply yarns both ways (north-south and east-west) of the fabric. Such broadcloth shirtings are sold as *2 × 2 broadcloths* ("2 × 2" refers to the two-ply yarn both ways). A poor quality cotton broadcloth shirting is made with single yarns both ways. The single yarn is not so strong as the ply yarn, so the strength of the yarn in a broadcloth materially affects the durability of the finished shirting.

The appearance and texture of a fabric may be affected by the combination of two kinds of fibers in the ply yarn. For example, a single cotton yarn and a single wool yarn may be twisted together to form a two-ply yarn. The texture of a fabric may also be affected by a variation in the twist of the single yarns used for the ply yarns. One or more tightly twisted single yarns and one or more loosely twisted single yarns may all be spun together into a ply yarn. The resultant ply yarn is bumpy and often has a knotty texture. Bouclé yarn is made in this manner.

How Size of Yarn Affects the Fabric

Size or Number of Sewing Thread. If a salesperson were to recommend a sewing thread to be used on slip covers and drapery fabrics, she might suggest a number 40; for use on gingham or percale, she would suggest a number 60. As a seamstress knows, the higher the number, the finer the cotton sewing thread. Cotton thread is made of carded and combed yarn twisted together to give added strength. Cotton thread used for sewing, embroidery, and darning is made of several long-fibered cotton yarns twisted together. A three-cord thread is made by twisting three yarns together; six-cord is made by twisting six yarns together. This cord should be even enough in diameter to go through a needle, smooth enough to resist friction of sewing, strong enough to hold seams firmly, and elastic enough to resist puckering and breaking.

Size or Count of Yarn. Yarns used to make cloth or to make thread are given numbers to indicate their fineness or coarseness. But the numbering to denote size of cotton yarn is called the *count of yarn.* The count of cotton yarn is determined by the number of yards of yarn that can be spun from one pound of cotton fiber. If 840 yards are spun from one pound of cotton, that yarn is called *Number 1;* if 1,680 yards are produced from one pound, the count is 2. An "s" after the number indicates single yarn, as differentiated from ply yarn. Hence, a number 10s cotton yarn would be a single yarn which is 10 times as fine as number 1s. In cotton, the finer the yarn, the higher the count. Illustration:

Cotton Fibers	Amount of Yarn Spun	Count
1 lb.	840 yards	#1
1 lb.	1,680 yards	#2
1 lb.	8,400 yards	#10

The term *count of yarn* is used also for wool, for spun yarns of silk, rayon, acetate, and other synthetics, even though the method of figuring is not the same for all. This means that in each of these yarns the higher the count, the finer the yarn. In linen also, the same principle of numbering holds true, but instead of *count,* the word *lea* (pronounced lē) is used.

In numbering the size of reeled silk, filament rayon, acetate, nylon, and other synthetic yarns, the term *denier* (pronounced den'yer) is used instead of *count*. To determine denier, 450 meters of yarn are weighed on a scale. If this amount of yarn weighs exactly 5 centigrams, the yarn is number 1 denier. If 450 meters of yarn weigh 10 centigrams, the denier is number 2. A number 2 denier yarn would be coarser than number 1 denier. The higher the number, the coarser the yarn. The reverse is true for cotton, linen, and man-made spun yarns.

Denier is important to the salesperson selling nylon hosiery, because nylon is sold by denier. The marks 15s and 30s on stockings mean 15 denier and 30 denier. The 15s stockings are made of finer yarns than the 30s.

The size of the yarn used in a fabric may vary in strength and in appearance. Some fabrics are made of yarns that are all about the same size; for example, batiste and organdy. Other fabrics may have larger crosswise yarns and finer vertical yarns. Broadcloth is an example of a fabric made of larger crosswise yarns.

Different-sized yarns may be combined to form cords either in the warp or in the filling, or in both. Dimity is an example of a fabric with cords warpwise.

How the Color of the Yarn Affects the Fabric

Yarn Dyeing.   When a salesperson picks up a checked gingham, she knows she has a selling point for that fabric because it is *yarn dyed*. This means that the colored yarns that form the check were dyed *before* the cloth was woven. Hence the dye could easily penetrate to the center of the yarn and color it thoroughly. If the cloth is dyed *after* the fabric is woven, the cloth is said to be *piece dyed*. A yarn-dyed fabric, whether in solid color, figured, checked, or plaid, is generally "talked up" on the basis of the depth and richness of color and the likelihood of the colors being permanent.

Warp Printing.   Sometimes the lengthwise (warp) yarns in a fabric are printed with a design *before* the fabric is woven. This method of coloring is called *warp printing*. Then when the crosswise yarns are woven in, they create a hazy outline of the pattern. Fabrics made in this way are called *warp-printed fabrics*. Some typical uses of warp prints are taffetas for dinner and formal wear and floral warp prints for draperies.

Space Dyeing.   It is possible to dye the filling yarns in spaced patterns as well as the warps, so that designs emerge when the cloth is woven. The effect is similar to warp printing, except that if yarns are raveled from the fabric, you can see that both warps *and* fillings have different colors on them.

PUTTING THIS MERCHANDISE KNOWLEDGE TO USE ❯❯❯❯❯❯❯❯❯❯

❯ DO YOU KNOW YOUR MERCHANDISE?

1. (*a*) What is a yarn? (*b*) What are the steps in making cotton yarn?
2. How does the twist of yarn affect the fabric?
3. (*a*) What is a ply yarn? (*b*) How do ply yarns affect the fabric?
4. (*a*) Explain the meaning of 2x2 broadcloth shirting. (*b*) Why would a 2x2 broadcloth be of better grade than 2x1?
5. (*a*) Define count of yarn. (*b*) To what kinds of yarn does count apply?
6. (*a*) How does the size of yarn affect the fabric? (*b*) Explain how the color of the yarn affects the fabric.

❯ INTERESTING THINGS TO DO

1. Obtain some absorbent cotton and make (*a*) a tightly twisted single yarn; (*b*) a two-ply yarn; (*c*) a novelty yarn.
2. Copy any newspaper advertisements containing terms used in this unit. Underline the terms and explain the meaning of each.
3. Obtain samples of the following: (*a*) printed dress percale, (*b*) cotton organdy, (*c*) cotton voile, (*d*) wool flannel, (*e*) rayon satin or rayon crepe, and (*f*) silk or rayon flat crepe. Mount each fabric in a scrapbook. Stick it with Scotch tape at the top edge only. Opposite each fabric write: (1) Single or ply yarn (identify horizontal and crosswise yarn), (2) Tight or loose twist (determine this by the ease with which you can untwist the yarn), (3) Texture (dull, shiny, fuzzy, smooth, etc.), (4) Size of yarn (coarse, medium coarse, fine—judged by comparing diameters of each yarn).

UNIT 7 KINDS OF YARN

COTTON (Carded and Combed Yarns)

When the yarn manufacturer produces a filmy sheet of fibers by disentangling and straightening the fibers, he is doing the first step in yarn making, called *carding*. Narrowing this sheet by pulling it out is called *drawing*. Twisting this ribbonlike sheet of fibers into a yarn is called *spinning*. Yarns made by this method are called *carded yarns*. This type of yarn may be somewhat uneven. Fabrics made from carded yarns include unbleached muslin used for ironing-board covers and dusting cloths, muslin sheeting, dress percale, denim for slacks, and broadcloth.

In fact, all cotton yarns must be carded; but only when the yarn is to be

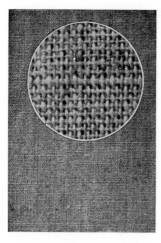

◀ Carded broadcloth

Combed broadcloth ▶

fine, smooth, and very even is it put through an additional process called *combing*. This process eliminates short fibers from the filmy sheet and lays the fibers more nearly parallel. About 8–10 per cent of cotton yarns are combed—the majority are carded only. Fine cotton muslins like batiste, lawn, and voile are usually made of combed yarns.

Sometimes yarn is purposely made irregular in order to produce a bumpy surface. This type of yarn is called *slub yarn*. Fabrics in which slub yarn is used are shantung, slub broadcloth, and slub poplin.

WOOL (Carded and Combed Yarns)

Wool yarns are also carded, combed, or both, depending on the texture (roughness or smoothness) of the fabric. For example, when the salesperson sells a tweed suiting, he is selling a wool cloth made of carded yarn. When he sells a wool gabardine, he is selling a wool cloth made of carded and combed yarn.

How to Recognize Carded and Combed Yarns in Cotton or Wool Fabrics

Appearance of the Texture of the Fabric. Fabrics made of combed yarns are usually smoother, flatter, and less fuzzy on the surface than fabrics made of carded yarns.

Examination of the Yarn. If the salesperson can unravel a yarn from a fabric, he can determine whether the yarn is combed or merely carded. The fibers in a combed yarn will be parallel and of equal length, while fibers in a carded yarn will be of unequal length and will branch out from the center of the yarn.

Why should a well-informed salesperson want to know about carded and combed yarns?

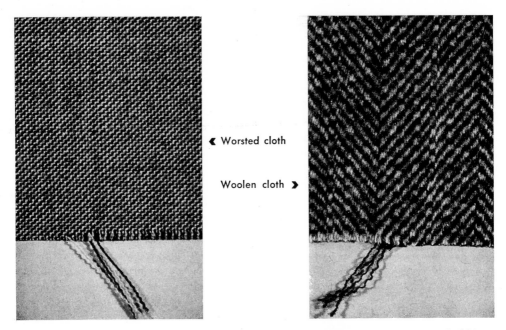

◀ Worsted cloth

Woolen cloth ▶

Selling Points of Cotton and Wool Fabrics Made of Combed Yarn and Carded Yarn

Wool fabrics made of combed yarn are likewise attractive, because they generally have a smooth surface which shows the pattern of the weave. Carded wool yarns may be used to produce a rough texture or a fuzzy one. Fabrics made of carded wool yarns include tweed, shetland, and broadcloth. These fabrics are called *woolens*. Fabrics made of combed wool yarns are called *worsteds*. Examples of worsteds are tropical, sharkskin, and gabardine.

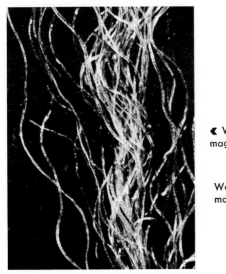

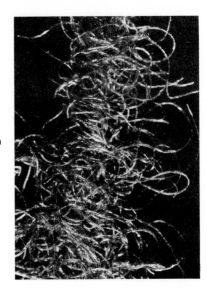

◀ Worsted yarn magnified.

Woolen yarn magnified. ▶

Fabrics of carded cotton yarn are more uneven in texture, thicker and thinner in places, as can be seen when they are held against the light. This unevenness in texture often makes a fabric less attractive. For example, a carded muslin sheet is less attractive than a combed percale sheet. Carded muslin feels heavier and rougher than combed percale.

The price of fabrics made of combed yarns is usually higher than that of fabrics made of carded yarns. In order to justify the price, the salesperson can point out the more attractive appearance of combed-yarn fabrics. This selling point, attractiveness, is the result of the additional process through which all combed yarns must pass.

In the preceding paragraphs carding and combing have been described as the ways of manufacturing cotton and wool yarns. But the terms *carded* and *combed yarns* do not apply to linen, silk, or to the man-made fibers.

LINEN (Poorly Hackled or Well-hackled Yarn)

Grading and Dressing.   After the flax fiber is separated from its woody stalk, it is sorted and graded and subjected to a finishing process called *dressing*.

Hackling.   When the flax has been dressed, the fibers are put through a series of combs made of pointed steel pins set in wooden bars. This operation separates the short, tangled fibers from the long fibers. The short fibers are called *tow* and are used in crashes and in heavy, coarse materials such as dress linen and kitchen toweling. The long fibers called *line* are adaptable to such cloths as handkerchief linen and fine table damasks where evenness and fineness of yarn are essential. *Line yarns* are made by laying the fibers parallel and end to end in the form of a ribbon on a moving belt. The ribbon can be made narrower and drawn out until it is the desired width for its intended use. A tow linen yarn may be compared to a carded cotton yarn, while a line linen yarn resembles a combed cotton yarn.

  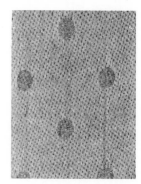

Left: Linen crash made of tow yarns. **Center:** Handkerchief linen made of line yarns. **Right:** Linen damask with beetle finish.

Spinning. Spinning consists of twisting the ribbons of fibers together. Some yarns require more twist than others. But, as the linen fibers are much longer and stronger than cotton fibers, not as much twisting is required to hold them together in the yarn.

The quality of the yarn used in a cloth is very important, as the best grade of yarns makes the most attractive and also the most durable cloth. For example, an ordinary crash dish towel is made of tow linen, whereas the best grade of dress crash is a combination of *line and tow* linen. Poor grades of crash are made with yarns of good strength, but are not so smooth and even as better grades.

SILK (Reeled and Spun Yarn)

Two types of silk are produced: reeled silk from the long fibers and spun silk from the short, uneven fibers.

Reeled Silk

It was pointed out in Chapter 2 that only certain cocoons were selected for breeding purposes and that the moths are allowed to emerge. All other cocoons are put through a stifling process in order to kill the chrysalis inside.

The smooth, lustrous silk made of long fibers is called *reeled silk*, because the long fibers are simply unwound, or reeled, from the unbroken cocoon and then twisted very slightly to make yarn. Fibers for this yarn range in length from 1,350 to 4,000 feet. On account of the length and strength of reeled-silk fibers, fabrics made from them are usually very durable.

Yarns made of reeled silk have no twist if used in a satin, or a tight twist if used in a crepe. The tighter the twist of the yarn, the duller the luster. Satins, therefore, with no twist are more lustrous and smoother than crepes which have tight twists. The number of strands twisted together in each yarn will affect the durability; as a rule, the greater the number of threads (strands) twisted together, the stronger the yarn. This is particularly true in silk hosiery.

Spun Silk

This yarn is made from the short fibers of unequal length that have been grouped together and then spun. As the short fibers tend to stick out from the center of the yarn, *spun-silk* yarns have a low luster and may have a fuzzy surface.

Since the sources of spun silk are broken cocoons, tangled ends of fiber, and defective cocoons, spun-silk yarns do not have the elasticity or strength of reeled silk. Spun silk is less expensive than reeled silk and is frequently used in the crosswise direction of a cloth, especially in tightly twisted crepe yarns.

Left: Crepe satin with creped yarn in the filling and reeled silk yarns in the warp. **Center:** Jacquard made of reeled silk. **Right:** A dress fabric made of noil silk.

How to Recognize Fabrics Made of Reeled or Spun Silk

If the fabric is silk, is it made of spun or reeled silk? Spun-silk fabrics, because they are made of short fibers, are less lustrous, fuzzier, softer, and have less strength than reeled silk. To distinguish between the two, a yarn may be unraveled. If the yarn is found to be made of long fibers lying parallel, the fabric is made of reeled silk. If the fibers are short, uneven in length, and tightly spun, the yarn is spun silk.

There is no need to learn to identify noil silk because according to the F.T.C. ruling on silk, noil silk must be identified on the label. *Noil silk* is waste from the making of spun-silk yarn (waste of the waste). Fabrics of noil silk are often incorrectly called *raw silk* by consumers. Raw silk is composed of silk fibers before they are made into yarn.

MAN-MADE YARNS (Filament and Spun)

In general, most of the man-made yarns, with the exception of rubber and metallic, fall into two kinds: filament and spun yarns. There are, of course, other types of bulky, texturized, or novelty yarns, which will be discussed later in the chapter.

Yarns made of natural fibers, such as cotton, wool, and reeled silk, are composed of fibers of definite length. For example, worsted yarns are made of fibers from 2 inches to 8 inches in length. Woolen yarns are made of fibers under 2 inches in length. A polished cotton fabric may have fibers averaging $1\frac{3}{5}$ inches. On the other hand, reeled-silk fibers are not short but can be 4,000 feet long. But waste silk is made of shorter fiber.

Manufactured (man-made) fibers can be made continuous as long as the viscous solution continues to be forced evenly through the spinneret. Yarns made from long, continuous filaments are called *filament yarns*. Filament rayon yarn was the first type yarn made in the United States. Textile companies that make synthetic fibers usually make yarn as well. But few fiber and yarn manufacturers also make cloth.

To make a short-fibered man-made yarn, the fibers are processed as described up to the time the filaments leave the spinneret. At this point, the filaments are chopped to different lengths, which can be varied as desired. If a yarn is to be spun like cotton, fibers are cut 1 to 2 inches long. If a yarn is to be spun like silk or wool, it is cut in 2- to 7-inch lengths. These cut lengths are known as rayon *staple fiber*. These fibers are made by different processes and in bright and dull luster. They can be spun into yarn to resemble cotton, wool, silk, or linen. Yarns spun from staple fibers are called *spun yarn*. A new process has been developed that crimps, or kinks, the fiber to make it appear like wool. Yarns made from crimped fibers produce a wool-like textured fabric. Crimped staple fibers blend with wool, cotton, and other synthetics.

How Rayon and Acetate Yarns Are Made

To gain an accurate picture of yarn making, it is necessary to go back to the step in making rayon and acetate where the solution is ready to be forced through the spinneret.

In the viscose process, as the filaments are drawn away from the spinneret, they are hardened by acid before they have a chance to run or stick together. Each hole in the spinneret makes a filament and all filaments from one spinneret make a yarn.

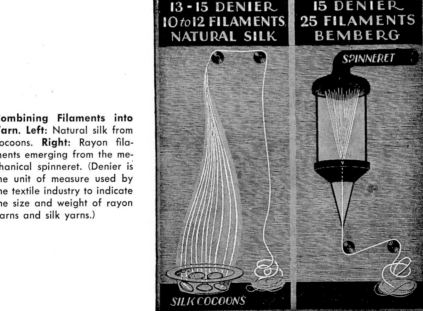

Combining Filaments into Yarn. Left: Natural silk from cocoons. **Right:** Rayon filaments emerging from the mechanical spinneret. (Denier is the unit of measure used by the textile industry to indicate the size and weight of rayon yarns and silk yarns.)

13 - 15 DENIER
10 to 12 FILAMENTS
NATURAL SILK

15 DENIER
25 FILAMENTS
BEMBERG

SPINNERET

SILK COCOONS

In the viscose process the hardened filaments are carried to a revolving spindle that puts in the desired twist while winding the filaments on another spool. The yarns are then wound onto cones or into skeins. This is called *spool spinning*. Another method is called *box spinning*. In this method, the hardened fiber is guided over a reel, down a glass funnel, and into a so-called spinning box or revolving cylinder. The funnel moves up and down slowly in the center of the spinning box. The rim of the cylindrical spinning box revolves faster than the speed at which the parallel filaments enter the box; therefore, the filaments as they enter the box are twisted together. Then by the revolutions of the box, centrifugal force throws the twisted filaments to the side wall of the cylinder. When the spinning box is full of yarn, the cylinder of yarn is removed.

The American Bemberg Corporation, which makes a second type of rayon cuprammonium, has patented a stretch-spinning process which increases the normal elasticity of the yarn. To explain: The solution is forced through the spinneret, which has holes larger in diameter than the final fiber is to be. As the fibers come from the hardening bath, they are pulled or stretched and then spun or twisted into yarns. Since fibers can be drawn out to a very fine diameter, Bemberg can make very fine yarns. Many fibers can be twisted tightly together, an operation which decreases the luster of the yarn. Such yarns make up into Bemberg sheer rayon crepes.

Spinning acetate yarns is a simple operation. The solution is forced through the spinneret from which the filaments go to a hollow tube down which they pass to a spindle. Air in the tube causes the acetone in the solution to evaporate, which hardens the filaments. Threads so hardened are wound on a bobbin. Acetate yarns do not have to be made into skeins but can be wound into the form for use by the weaver or the knitter.

Kinds of Rayon and Acetate Yarns

Filament Yarns.   These are made from long, continuous filaments (fibers) and require only a slack twist of from 3 to 6 turns to the inch to hold in the ends of the fibers. If the crepe yarn is needed, 45 turns or more are necessary.

Spun Yarns.   These are made from staple rayons or acetates (short fibers from 1½ to 6 inches long). Since the fibers are short, more twist is advisable than for filament yarn. Spun yarns, therefore, are given 15 to 25 turns to the inch. These yarns can be spun by the cotton method, by the worsted method (wool), or by the silk method. When rayon or acetate is spun by the cotton method, the spun yarns take on the appearance and feeling of cotton; when spun by the worsted method, the appearance and feeling of a worsted.

Characteristics of spun rayon and acetate yarns:
1. Spun yarns make a more fluffy fabric than filament rayons.
2. They have a subdued luster more like natural fiber.
3. They resist wrinkling.

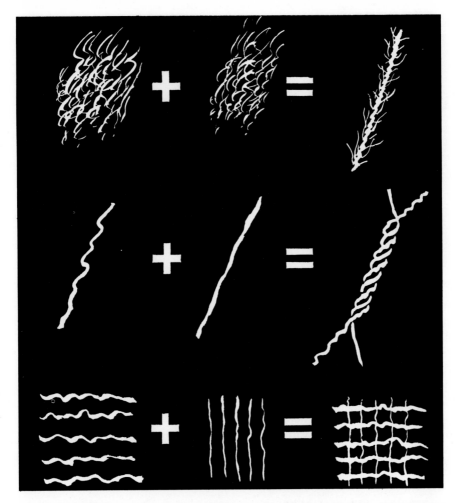

How a Combination Rayon Yarn Is Made and Is Woven into Cloth. Top: Blending acetate staple fiber with viscose rayon staple or natural fibers before spinning into yarn. **Center:** Twisting acetate continuous-filament or spun yarn with viscose rayon or natural-fiber yarn to produce plied yarn. **Bottom:** Weaving acetate continuous-filament or staple yarn with yarn of viscose rayon or of natural fibers. *(Courtesy Tennessee Eastman Corp.)*

4. Garments and curtains made of spun yarn hang in graceful folds (drape well).

5. Garments made of spun yarn may appear to have a warm texture but they lack excessive warmth and are cooler in summer than natural fibers.

6. Spun yarns made of fibers of different lengths and spun in varied twists produce fabrics of interesting textures.

7. Spun yarns offer great blending possibilities because staple yarns are made in a great variety of thicknesses, lusters, and lengths. Spun rayon or acetate will combine with silk, wool, cotton, and other man-made fibers.

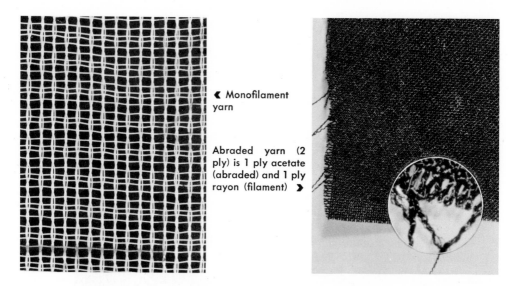

◀ Monofilament yarn

Abraded yarn (2 ply) is 1 ply acetate (abraded) and 1 ply rayon (filament) ❯

Abraded Yarns   The word *abraded* comes from *abrade*, meaning to rub off or to wear away by friction. To make an abraded yarn, filament yarn is run over a roughened surface. This process breaks or snags an outer layer of filaments. These abraded yarns are then twisted with nonabraded yarns in ply form.

The purpose of making abraded yarn is to produce wool-like textures requiring a fuzzy surface. Such fabrics are warmer and softer than filament yarn.

Combination Yarns.   Sometimes a ply yarn is made by combining two different types of single yarns. For example, a single rayon yarn might be twisted with a single acetate yarn which would be called a *combination yarn.* Rayon yarn can be combined with natural fibered or man-made fibered yarns.

Properties of Rayon and Acetate Yarns

Strength of Yarns.   As in yarns made of natural fibers, the strength of the yarn depends to a great extent on the fibers composing the yarn. The quality of rayon and acetate yarns varies just as the quality of yarns made of cotton, silk, linen, or wool. High-strength rayon yarns are made of filament rayon fibers that are specially treated, primarily stretched, before hardening. It is also possible to make strong yarns if new rayon fibers, especially engineered for strength, are used.

Elasticity or Resiliency of Yarn.   Rayon is more elastic than linen and may be as elastic as the average cotton. Rayon is not so elastic as silk. The patented stretch-spinning process of the American Bemberg Corporation increases the normal elasticity of their yarn and makes it very suitable for knitted goods. However, the elasticity of most fabrics depends more on their construction (weave or knit) and finish than upon the yarn itself. The exceptions would be yarns made of spandex fibers, elastic (rubber) yarns, and stretch yarns sold under trademarks like Helanca by Du Pont and Agilon by Deering Milliken & Co. These stretch yarns are made of long continuous nylon filaments that are made soft, fluffy, and stretchy by patented processes. These yarns are found in adults' and children's hosiery and underwear.

Fineness of Yarn. Fineness of yarn depends on (1) the diameters of the fibers composing the yarn, and (2) the number of fibers in the yarn. As the tensile strength of rayon fiber was raised, it became possible to spin finer filaments. It was found that if more of these fine filaments were used in a given weight yarn, the yarn would be softer and more pliable.

Effect of Physical Properties of Rayon and Acetate Yarns on the Final Fabrics

Luster. The process of making rayon and acetate yarns outlined above would result in bright lustrous yarn. But some fabrics are more attractive when dull.

A certain amount of dullness can be created by twisting the yarn tightly— the tighter the twist, the duller the yarn. The luster can be regulated by adding a dulling agent, such as a kind of mineral oil, to the spinning solution that forms tiny bubbles on the surface of the fiber so that light cannot be reflected. Another method of making dull yarns is to put microscopically fine material into the spinning solution that becomes a part of the fiber itself when it hardens. Yarns made by this method are called *pigment yarns*. Fabrics made of these yarns are called pigment fabrics, a term confined mostly to the trade.

Rayon can be made in three different lusters: bright, semidull, and dull or chalky. Acetate is made in two lusters: bright and dull. The luster of rayon and acetate is permanent because the dulling agent is a part of the fiber.

Color. The viscous solution of which rayon is made is brown or honey colored, and the rayon yarns (with the exception of acetates) are washed and bleached in skein form. Most rayon yarns will remain white and do not tend to yellow with age, laundering, or exposure to light. White rayons have this advantage over white silks and wools. Fibers can be colored by injecting dye into the spinning solution. The resultant yarn is called *solution dyed* or *spun dyed*. Familiar trade names of solution-dyed acetates are Chromspun and Celaperm. In rayon, there is Jetspun and Coloray. Rayons can be dyed easily with the same dyestuffs used for cottons and linens. Acetates, however, have to be dyed with special dyestuffs.

How Nylon and Other Plastic Yarns Are Made

It has been stated that the most common types of nylon and other plastic yarns are made in filament and spun types. To make the latter kind of yarns, the long continuous fibers must be chopped up into short lengths similar to the way rayon staple fiber is made. The length of the fiber will depend on the type of texture desired in the final cloth. If the texture of the fabric were to resemble cotton, the staple fiber would be about 1½ inches long; if to resemble worsted, about 5 inches long.

Since nylon and many of the plastic yarns are so very strong, one fiber can be used as a yarn. Because the filament can be made of indefinite length, there will be no definite end to the fiber as there would be if a natural fiber like cotton, silk, or wool were used. Yarns made of one single fiber are called *monofilament yarns*. The more common types of yarns are composed of many fibers and therefore are called *multifilament yarns* (*multi* means many). Monofilament nylon yarns are used in hosiery, women's blouses, nightgowns, and sheer curtains.

The sizes of filament yarns are figured on a denier basis. Hosiery, for example, is labeled as 15 denier. A 20-denier yarn would be coarser than 15 denier. Spun yarns are figured on a count basis like cotton. The newer synthetic yarns can be delustered and yarn or solution dyed.

SUMMARY OF YARN CHARACTERISTICS

Following is a chart that will help you remember how various yarns are made and their characteristics.

Fibers	Method of Manufacturing into Yarn	Name and Characteristics of Yarn Made
Cotton	Carding or carding *and* combing	Carded cotton yarn: uneven, irregular, often bumpy. Combed cotton yarn: even, regular diameter.
Linen	Poorly hackled or well hackled	Tow yarn: very uneven, irregular diameter. Line yarn: regular, even.
Silk	Long fibers reeled from cocoon, short waste fibers spun	Reeled-silk yarn: smooth, even, regular. Spun-silk yarn: fuzzy dull.
Wool	Carded or carded *and* combed	Woolen yarn: fuzzy, uneven, may be bumpy. Worsted yarn: even, regular.
Rayon	Long fibers grouped together, short fibers spun	Filament rayon yarn: smooth, even, regular. Spun rayon yarn: fuzzy, dull, may be irregular.
Acetate	(same as rayon)	(same as rayon)
Metallic	Carded cotton wrapped with metallic foil, called *core yarn*. Other fibers may be used as core. Plastic "sandwich" type	Metallic core yarn. Metallic with plastic yarn.
Rubber	Vulcanized natural rubber thread wrapped with any type of tex-	Rubber core yarn: texture of fibers that wrap it.

Fibers	Method of Manufacturing into Yarn	Name and Characteristics of Yarn Made
	tile fibers. Synthetic rubber may be used instead of natural rubber.	
Nylon and other synthetics	Long fibers grouped together, short fibers spun	Filament yarns: smooth, even, regular. Spun yarn: fuzzy, dull.

PUTTING THIS MERCHANDISE KNOWLEDGE TO USE ❯ ❯ ❯ ❯ ❯ ❯ ❯ ❯ ❯ ❯

❯ DO YOU KNOW YOUR MERCHANDISE?

1. (*a*) What is the difference between a muslin sheet and a percale sheet as far as yarn is concerned? (*b*) How can a salesperson determine whether a fabric is made of carded or combed yarns?
2. Why should a salesperson know whether a fabric is made of carded or combed yarns?
3. (*a*) What is the importance of knowing the sizes of cotton thread? (*b*) Why is denier important in nylon hosiery?
4. (*a*) In what types of yarn are most synthetics made? (*b*) What is the difference in texture between a fabric made of a filament synthetic yarn and a spun synthetic yarn?
5. Explain how handkerchief linen differs from dish toweling.
6. (*a*) How can you distinguish reeled-silk yarn from spun-silk yarn? (*b*) Name a fabric commonly made of reeled silk. (*c*) Name a fabric that may have spun-silk yarn in it.

❯ INTERESTING THINGS TO DO

1. Obtain samples of rayon fabrics, preferably rayon challis and rayon taffeta. Rayon flannel and rayon satin will do just as well. Note the appearance of each fabric—the smoothness or fuzziness of the surface. Feel the comparative warmth of each sample. Which is spun rayon? Check your answer by unraveling the yarn to determine the length of the fibers and the evenness and smoothness of the yarn. Paste both samples with a write-up of your findings in a scrapbook.
2. Make the same experiment with silk flat crepe and rayon flat crepe. Identify the type of yarn both ways in each sample. Describe the texture of each cloth. Write up your findings in a scrapbook.
3. In the same fashion, compare a cotton crash (Indian Head) and a dress linen. Write your findings.

UNIT 8 NOVELTY YARNS AND BLENDS OF FIBERS

NOVELTY YARNS

In order to obtain a variety of pleasing effects in the texture of a cloth, novelty yarns are used, inasmuch as conventional types of yarn, like carded and combed, filament or spun, would not suffice.

Some examples of novelty yarns include:

1. Bouclé. This is made in ply yarn composed of single yarns of different sizes and amounts of twist, which is woven or knitted into a fabric. (See illustration.)

2. Crimp. This is made of synthetic fibers that have been crimped or permanently waved to look like wool.

3. Thick and Thin Yarn. It is possible to make man-made fibers of varied diameters (widths) by forcing the solution through the spinneret at different speeds. By making yarn of fibers of varying diameters, yarn with thick-and-thin places in it is produced.

4. Slub and Nub Yarns. If you know a fabric called "shantung," you know that the crosswise yarns in it are very bumpy. These yarns are what give the characteristic texture to the fabric. One method of making slub yarn is to drop tufts or small masses of fibers into the filmy sheet of fibers in a hit-or-miss fashion. When all fibers are twisted into yarn, the strand is bumpy in those spots where masses of fibers were dropped. These enlarged places on a yarn are called "nubs" if rounded, and "slubs" if soft and elongated. (See illustration.)

5. Plastic-coated Yarns. To protect either natural or synthetic yarns from friction (abrasion) and to keep metal (tinsel) yarns from tarnishing, yarns can be dipped in plastic to coat them. Such yarns will not absorb water, and therefore are suitable for rainwear.

6. Metallic Yarns. These yarns have been described in the previous chapter under "natural mineral fibers" (tinsel threads) and under "man-made fibers" (metallic) and also in the table on page 54.

YARNS MADE OF BLENDS

The word *blend* has come into common use by the salesperson and consumer. What is a blend then? A yarn that contains two or more different kinds of fibers is a *blended yarn*.

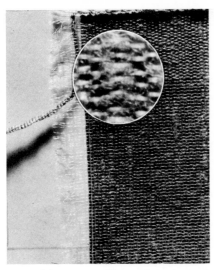

Thick slub yarn in filling of a piece of shantung.

Bouclé fabric with metallic foil yarn at top and bottom, and thick spun yarn at upper right.

How is blending done? It may be compared to blending butter and sugar to make a cake. The ingredients, be they food or fibers, are mixed (blended) together first. In textiles, one can blend almost any fibers together to make a yarn; for example, Dacron polyester and cotton, silk and cotton, nylon and wool, Dacron polyester and acetate.

Fabric made of filament yarns in warp and filling. Multifilament yarns at left side and crepe yarn showing at bottom.

Fabric made of noil silk in warp and filling.

Advantages and Disadvantages

The future possibilities of these blends seem limitless. Advantages of blending are to give a fabric the desirable characteristics of all fibers present in the blend. Blending might increase the uses of a fabric; give a different feeling, appearance, and style value; lower the fabric's cost. Technicians, however, must experiment to learn what percentages of each fiber are best in a blend, in order to achieve fabric performance in use that will meet consumer demand. For example, a 65 per cent Dacron polyester and 35 per cent cotton blend has been found to be good for a man's cotton broadcloth dress shirt. Why? Because Dacron polyester gives added strength to the yarn, sheds water and hence dries quickly, is resilient and therefore resists wrinkling; cotton absorbs moisture of perspiration to keep the wearer comfortable, washes easily, is a relatively inexpensive fiber, and blended with Dacron polyester irons more easily than all cotton.

It must be remembered that all fibers have certain advantages and certain disadvantages in specific uses. Blending fibers, therefore, in appropriate percentages aims to bring to the yarn and cloth the advantages of each fiber. For example, nylon added to wool gives strength and resistance to abrasion and shrinkage in laundering to the wool. Wool in the blend gives warmth, absorptive quality, and resilience (wrinkle resistance) to the yarn.

It is the work of the textile technologist to select the fiber or yarn in appropriate proportion to be used in a given cloth for a particular use. The new synthetic fibers and yarns are doing much to give wrinkle resistance, ease-in-care properties, and durability to the blended yarn in which they are used. But the synthetic fibers have their drawbacks just as natural fibers do. For example, many plastic yarns "pill" (form little balls of fiber on the surface of the fabric); they often give the wearer the discomfort of having a garment stick to the body due to static electricity; they may have problems of dyeing yet to be solved. But textile laboratories are rapidly finding solutions to all these problems.

PUTTING THIS MERCHANDISE KNOWLEDGE TO USE ❯❯❯❯❯❯❯❯❯❯

❯ DO YOU KNOW YOUR MERCHANDISE?

1. Explain how fibers in a yarn are blended.
2. What are the purposes of blended yarns?
3. Give the advantages of a 55 per cent Dacron polyester and 45 per cent wool blended yarn for a man's suit.
4. (a) Explain the difference between a nub and a slub yarn. (b) Name a fabric that has slub yarns in it.
5. (a) Describe two methods of making metallic yarn. (b) Which of these methods has been discovered more recently?
6. (a) What type of texture would result from the use of thick-and-thin yarn? from crimped fibered yarns? (b) Why are some yarns coated with plastic?

1. Copy any newspaper advertisements containing terms used in this chapter. Underline the terms and explain the meaning of each.
2. (*a*) For girls: Go to the knitting-yarn department of any dry-goods or department store. Make a list of the various kinds of yarn from labels on the balls or skeins. At home, underline the terms that you have learned in connection with the study of yarn.

   (*b*) For men: Go to a men's shirt department in a department store. Make a list of the various terms appearing on the labels. At home, underline those terms that you have learned in connection with the study of yarn.
3. Obtain samples of as many all-cotton, all-linen, all-silk, all-wool, and all-rayon or all-synthetic fabrics as you can. Mount them in the scrapbook used for Units 1 and 2. Label the yarns in each direction of the cloth as follows: (*a*) single or ply yarn, (*b*) tight or loose twist, (*c*) texture, (*d*) size of yarn (coarse, medium, fine).

ADDITIONAL MERCHANDISE TERMS ❯❯❯❯❯❯❯❯❯❯❯❯❯❯❯❯❯❯❯❯❯❯

Dope-dyed yarn is composed of a strand of man-made fibers that have the dyes hardened into the viscous solution. Synonymous with "solution dyed."

Denier is a unit expressing the fineness of silk, rayon, or nylon yarns in terms of weights in grams per 9,000 meters of length; thus 100-denier yarn is finer than 150-denier yarn.

How Cloth Is Made— Weaving, Knitting, Felting, and Lace Construction

CHAPTER 4

UNIT 9 THE BASIC WEAVES

When a hole is worn in a sock, it should be darned properly so that the sock will give more wear and be comfortable. If the hole is darned correctly, a new cloth is made.

In good darning the north-south yarns are put in parallel to each other first, then the east-west yarns are interlaced parallel to each other in order to insure a flat, comfortable surface. The darning of this hole is the construction of new cloth similar to weaving a new fabric.

CONSTRUCTION OF A WOVEN FABRIC

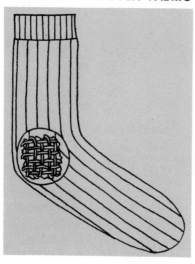

Woven fabrics are made with two sets of yarns, a lengthwise set called *warps* and a crosswise set called *fillings*. Warp yarns run parallel to the woven finished edges or *selvages*. The filling yarns interlace the warp yarns at right angles and fill in the spaces between them. The warp yarns are generally stronger and closer together than the filling yarns because they are subjected to greater strain.

The greater number of warps a cloth has to the square inch, the more closely woven it is. To see the closeness of the weave, hold the cloth to the light, or use a magnifying glass called a *pick glass* or

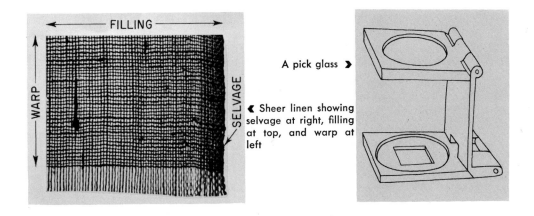

FILLING

WARP

SELVAGE

A pick glass ❯

❮ Sheer linen showing selvage at right, filling at top, and warp at left

linen tester to count the number of warps and filling yarns in a square inch. To make counting easier, unravel about ¼ inch from two adjacent edges of a cloth. If the fabric is black, place it on a white surface, or vice versa. Then look down through the pick glass and count the yarns seen through the opening in the lower part of the pick glass. The number of yarns in warp and in filling to the square inch is called the *count of cloth*. For example, if a cloth has 72 yarns to the inch in one direction and 68 yarns to the inch in the other, the count of the cloth is 72 x 68—meaning 72 warp yarns and 68 filling yarns in the square inch. The warp is usually expressed first; the higher the count number, the closer the yarns and the firmer the cloth. Closely woven or high-count fabrics are usually stronger, keep their shape better, shrink less, and have less slippage at the seams than loosely woven fabrics of the same weight and texture. For example, a cotton organdy has a much higher count than a cheesecloth. In plain-weave cotton muslins, particularly sheeting, the count of cloth is a very important factor in determining the grade of the fabric. For example, a sheet with a minimum of 180 to 199 yarns (warp and filling added together) is a percale sheet of "B" grade; a minimum of 200 or over is "A" grade; a minimum count of 112 to 127 is poor-grade muslin sheeting; 128 to 139 minimum is "C" grade muslin; 140 to 179 minimum is "A" grade muslin.

PREPARATION FOR WEAVING

From primitive times to the present day, with its high-spun precision methods of production, weaving has been fundamentally the same. Primitive man first used reeds and grasses, which he interlaced or wove into mats and baskets. Later, man discovered how to suspend warp yarns from a horizontal branch of a tree. The filling yarn was passed over and under the warp yarns by means of a sharpened stick. The next development was the making of a box frame similar to a cigar box, across which warp yarns were stretched. From this box frame developed the hand loom of colonial times. (A *loom*

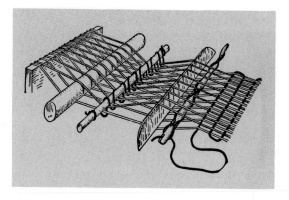

Primitive Weaving Apparatus.

A sword separates alternate warp yarns to form the shed. The needle carrying the filling yarn is being passed through the shed. *(Courtesy Ciba Review.)*

is the name given to the frame or machine on which a cloth is woven.) This hand loom had an advantage over the earlier methods of weaving in that the filling did not have to be passed over and under the individual warp yarns. Certain warp yarns could be separated from others by raising them all at once so that the filling could be passed through the separated warps. Today the power loom performs the weaving operations speedily and automatically.

Warping

Before a cloth can be woven, the warp yarns are strung into the frame of the loom. This method resembles the stringing of warps into the early box frame loom. See the illustration on page 63.

The harness is the upright frame (C) that holds flattened wires called *heddles.* Each heddle has an eye, like a darning needle, through which a warp yarn is threaded. Each harness controls a series of heddles (D) which are raised or lowered to allow the filling yarns to pass through the separated warps. In the simplest weave—the plain weave—there are only two harnesses—one harness to control warps 1, 3, 5, 7, etc., and a second harness to hold and control warps 2, 4, 6, 8, etc.

STEPS IN THE WEAVING OPERATION

Shedding. The warps are separated according to the desired weave, so that the filling yarns can be sent through easily. This separating process is called *shedding,* because the raising of the heddles holding the warp yarns makes a shed through which the filling yarn can pass.

Picking. The filling yarn is then sent through the shed by means of the shuttle (a boatlike wooden or metal bobbin). This operation is called *picking.* Hence the name for *pick glass* used to "pick out" the count of cloth.

Battening or Beating-up.   The filling yarn is then pushed or beaten with the reed against the preceding filling to make the fabric firm. This is called *battening*.

These processes are continued until the cloth is the desired length.

Letting Off and Taking Up.   Finally, the warp is released from the warp beam, and the woven fabric is wound or taken up on the cloth beam.

The appearance and the strength of fabrics can be varied according to the type of weave used. Certain ways of interlacing the yarns produce designs in the fabric (called *structural designs*) which differ from designs placed on the cloth after it is woven (called *surface designs;* for example, prints). A structural design is woven into the cloth and cannot be pulled out.

Fabrics, therefore, which are made of identical fibers that are spun into the same type of yarn, can differ in appearance and texture because of the structural designs in which they are woven.

BASIC WEAVES

There are three basic weaves, namely the plain, twill, and satin; each of these, in turn, has several variations.

Plain Weave

A large portion of all woven fabrics is made in this simple weave that resembles darning. By holding such a woven fabric up to the light, or examining it under a magnifying glass, one can see that it consists of an even

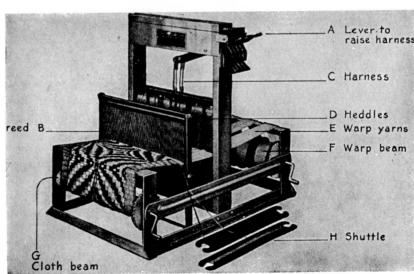

Hand Loom.

(Courtesy Structo Manufacturing Company)

A Lever-to raise harness

C Harness

D Heddles

E Warp yarns

F Warp beam

reed B

H Shuttle

G
Cloth beam

interlacing of every other warp and filling yarn. The structural design of this weave is checkerboard. See page 65. This construction is an inexpensive one to weave, since it requires only a simple two-harness loom. If a plain-weave fabric is closely woven, it can be firm and strong. All kinds of fibers can be used in the weave. Furthermore, plain-weave fabrics can be easily cleaned or laundered because of their flat surfaces. Gingham, voile, cheesecloth, batiste, nainsook, lawn, organdy, cambric, sheeting, crepe, percale, chambray, crash, chintz, cretonne, and shantung are representative cotton fabrics made in the plain weave. Typical linen fabrics in plain weave are dress linen, handkerchief linen, art linen, cambric, crash, theatrical gauze. Common wool fabrics in plain weave are crepe, tropical worsted, challis, and homespun. Silk fabrics in plain weave include taffeta, shantung, pongee, chiffon, flat crepe, georgette, broadcloth. A few rayon fabrics in plain weave are taffeta, crepe, chiffon, georgette, and ninon.

Because the pattern of a plain-weave fabric is not very interesting, the use of crepe yarns to make a crinkly surface will give an added selling point of attractiveness. Slub yarns crosswise of a cloth will produce bumpy surfaces, such as shantung and crash. Yarn-dyed stripes, checks, plaids, and warp prints also give an attractive appearance to cloths in plain weave.

The weaver can further enhance the appearance or change the texture of a fabric in plain weave by varying the structural design. The same two-harness loom can be used. There are two common structural variations of the plain weave (1) rib; (2) basket. See page 65.

Rib Variation of the Plain Weave.   A ribbed, corded, or crossbar effect may be made by using heavier yarns in either the warp or filling or in both. Striped dimity and crossbar nainsook for men's summer underwear are made in this way. The use of ribs or cords produces the *rib variation* of the plain weave. Fine and heavy warps can be alternated at regular intervals. Broadcloth, poplin, rep, faille, and grosgrain have ribs made by using filling yarns that are heavier than the warp. If the rib yarns are very much heavier than the other yarns, the rib yarns might rub against the finer yarns and cut them. This often occurs in the case of dimity. Sometimes a heavy rib yarn is covered by fine yarns, as in faille or bengaline; in such cases there must be a sufficient number of fine yarns to cover the rib yarn. (A cloth becomes unattractive if the ribs show where the finer covering yarns are worn away.) The separation or shifting of fillings or of warps results from a poor balance (proportion) of warp to fillings.

Basket Variation of the Plain Weave.   Instead of weaving a fabric by passing one filling yarn over and under every other warp yarn, one, two, three, four, or more filling yarns may be passed at the same time over and under one, two, three, four, or more warp yarns. This variation gives a structural design in a splint basket effect. Though this variation may be more attractive than the plain weave (over one and under one), a basket construction can-

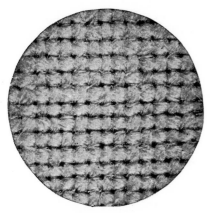

Plain weave.

Rib variation of plain weave.
(Courtesy American Viscose Corp.)

Basket variation of plain weave.
(Courtesy American Viscose Corp.)

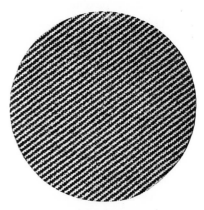

Twill weave.
(Courtesy Tennessee Eastman Corp.)

Magnified satin weave.

Pile weave.

not be woven as closely. Thus, as in all loosely woven fabrics, basket weave stretches easily, may shrink when washed, and the yarns in it tend to slip out of place. A fabric in this weave, called monk's cloth, is generally used for bedspreads and draperies rather than for clothing, because the loosely woven yarns may catch and pull out. But a very common fabric in this weave used for clothing is men's Oxford shirting.

Twill Weave

The checkerboard design produced by the plain weave is not particularly interesting. If all fabrics were made of this weave, the structural design would become monotonous. Designers of textile fabrics therefore use other patterns. Gabardine, used for slacks and men's and women's suits, is an example of the second major weave called *twill*. Instead of being made by a regular interlacing of every other yarn, as is the plain weave, the twill weave is formed by passing a filling yarn over and under one to three warp yarns, lapping backward one warp yarn in each successive line.

The structural design looks like stairs, and the surface of the fabric shows diagonal ridges called "wales." Because this method of weaving allows for a very close and firm construction, twill weave can be the firmest, most compact weave made. Hence, fabrics in twill weave are very durable and can be dust resistant, which makes them desirable as slip covers. Pillow tickings are made in twill weave, because down or feather stuffing cannot work through a closely constructed cloth. Because of this closeness of yarns, however, dirt collects between the ridges; and a twill-weave fabric is, therefore, not so easy to keep clean as a fabric woven in the plain weave. Cotton fabrics in the twill weave besides gabardine are chino cloth, denim, and jean. Common wool fabrics in the twill weave are serge, gabardine, flannel, worsted cheviot, covert cloth, flannel, and tweed for men's suits. Silk fabrics in the twill weave include foulard, silk serge, and surah. Rayon or acetate fabrics in the twill weave include gabardine, flannel, foulard, serge, whipcord, and surah.

Variations of the Twill Weave.

The herringbone pattern is a structural design like the backbone of a herring. Ridges run diagonally from upper left to lower right of a cloth and then reverse in the opposite direction. This is one method of varying the twill-weave pattern. Tweeds for women's and men's coats are frequently made in herringbone variation of the twill. Many blends of different fibers are used in twill fabrics.

Satin Weave

Many people think of satin as the name of a shiny, smooth material. Satin is also the name of a weave that produces a smooth lustrous surface because of the way in which the yarns are interlaced. The luster is increased if the long fibers of silk, rayon, acetate, nylon, or mercerized cotton are used in its construction. The word *satin,* then, denotes the third major weave. The expression *silk satin* or *rayon satin* or *crepe satin* is the name of the specific fabric made in satin weave.

In the plain and in the twill weaves, the yarns are interlaced at frequent intervals so that there is no smooth surface to reflect the light and enhance the luster. In the satin weave, the yarns are interlaced at less frequent intervals, thus allowing some smooth unbroken yarns to remain on the surface and reflect the light. The yarns that lie loose on the surface of the fabric over several other yarns are called *floats.*

By examining carefully the shiny side of a satin fabric you can see the floats on the surface. As the warps float in a satin weave, the sheen or luster runs in the direction of the float (warpwise). The longer the float, the higher the luster of the fabric. In judging the durability of satins, the length of the float must be considered. Although long floats make a more lustrous fabric, they are more likely to snag and to show wear than satins made with short floats. Reeled silks, filament rayons, acetates, and nylons are particularly adapted to the satin weave, because long fibers give luster and do not pull out with friction to make a fuzzy surface. Mercerized cotton, however, may be used to form floats, too; but cotton must necessarily have shorter floats than silk, rayon, or nylon, because cotton fiber is shorter. A short fiber in a long float is likely to become fuzzy in use.

Sateen is a cotton material commonly used for linings. It has a short four-float. If you smooth a sateen in the direction of the shine, you will find the fabric is shiny crosswise—just the opposite direction from a rayon or a silk satin. The floats are made by floated fillings rather than by floated warps. Hence, sateen is a four-float fillingwise, and is called a *sateen weave* instead of a *satin weave.*

Whenever a warp floats, the weave is *satin;* whenever the filling floats, the weave is *sateen.* Cotton-backed rayon satins or silk satins are made with the warp of rayon or silk and the filling of cotton. The warps float and hence show more on the right side than the filling, which appears mostly on the back in a satin weave. The warp-float creped-back satin is made with filling yarns of crepe texture. These creped fillings show on the back of the fabric, whereas the surface is formed by the rayon or silk warp floats. A selling point for a cloth with a silk or rayon satin face and creped back is that both sides of the fabric can be used. Skirt, waist, and sleeves of a dress may be made with the crepe side out and the trimmings, namely, the collar, cuffs and belt, can be made with the satin side out.

Selling Points of Basic Weaves

The selling points of the basic weaves may be summarized briefly:

Plain weave—comparatively inexpensive; easy to clean
Twill weave—interesting design; firm, strong
Satin weave—attractive luster; smooth surface

❯ DO YOU KNOW YOUR MERCHANDISE?

1. Why should a salesperson know the different weaves used in fabrics he sells?
2. What are the selling points of a closely woven fabric?
3. How would you point out to the customer the durability of the following materials: (*a*) percale sheeting, (*b*) rayon satin coat lining (4 float), (*c*) men's worsted gabardine slacks?
4. Define herringbone, selvage, pick glass, loom, shedding, weaving.
5. Name the weave of the following fabrics: silk foulard, dress linen, wool serge, Oxford shirting, cotton broadcloth, cotton batiste.
6. (*a*) Why is a satin weave an attractive weave? (*b*) What limitations do satin weaves have?

❯ INTERESTING THINGS TO DO

1. Analyze ten fabrics used in your own wardrobe. For each fabric give the name, weave, and selling points.
2. Make a loom and weave a sample of each basic weave studied in this chapter. A small loom may be made by using a piece of cardboard 2 inches by 3 inches. Thread the warp either around straight pins placed at each end, or through slits cut at each end. Another method of making a simple loom is to use a cardboard or wooden box, approximately 6 inches by 4 inches. Make slits or stick pins in the box at the two opposite short ends of the box. Use string, heavy thread, or knitting yarn as warps.
3. Go to a department store and visit the domestics department where bed sheets are sold. Copy the labels appearing on percale and on muslin sheets.
   When you get home, underline the count or type, if given, and any other terms with which you are familiar. Define each term on the labels.

UNIT 10 FANCY WEAVES

There are three kinds of fancy weaves; namely, pile, leno, and figured weaves.

PILE WEAVE

The pile weave has three variations; namely the uncut pile as in terry cloth; the cut pile, as in velvet and velveteen; and the double cloth, as in reversible coating.

Why do most people like to dry themselves with a Turkish towel after a bath? Why do they not use a huck face towel. Huck face towels are smoother and so do not absorb as much water or feel as invigorating as the Turkish towels, which are rough and absorbent. If you examine a Turkish towel carefully, you will see that the weave looks different from those already discussed. It is made of loops that are held together by a background of plain or twill weave. The loops are known as *pile*, and so we say the cloth is made in *pile weave*. Pile-weave fabrics are made with loops on one or both sides of the cloth.

In the pile weave, two sets of warp yarns are used. One set is held tight in the loom and forms the background or groundwork of the fabric. The tension on the other set can be released so that when each filling is battened, the filling yarns then push the slack warp yarns into loops, first on one side and then on the other. Turkish towels and terry-cloth bathrobes are made in this way. These are made of *uncut* pile.

Silk Velvet or Velvet Rugs

Velvet is also made in pile weave, but the pile of silk velvet is *cut*. As in Turkish toweling, one set of warp is held tight in the loom to form the groundwork of the fabric; but in velvet the other set of warp is looped over wires inserted in the loom. When a section of cloth is woven, the wires are raised, cutting with their sharp edges the yarns looped over them. Silk velvet and velvet rugs are made in this way.

Velveteen and Corduroy

You know how cotton sateen is made by floating filling yarns over four or five warp yarns. To make corduroy and velveteen, extra filling yarns form floats that are cut after weaving; and the short cut ends of filling yarn are brushed up to form pile on the surface of the cloth. If the back of the velveteen is twill weave, it is better grade because it will be more durable than a plain-weave back.

Transparent Velvet (All Rayon or Silk Back and Rayon Face)

By weaving two layers of cloth together by means of extra sets of filling yarns that pass back and forth between the two cloths thus joining them together, a double cloth is made. A sharp blade moves between the layers of fabric and cuts the joining threads, thereby leaving two distinct fabrics, each with a pile on one side. Transparent velvet is made in this way.

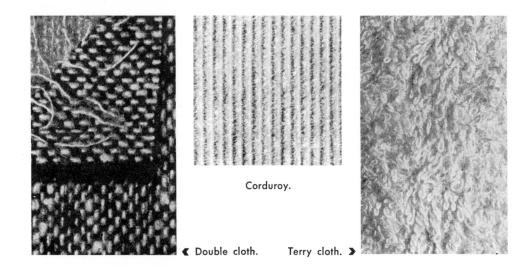

Corduroy.

◀ Double cloth.　　Terry cloth. ▶

Double-Cloth Reversible Coating

Sometimes the two cloths are not cut apart. This is the way reversible coat fabrics, motor robes, some blankets, and double-faced ribbons are woven. (See illustration of double cloth.)

How to Judge Durability of Pile Fabrics

Not only the quality of the yarn used for the pile, but also the background weave is important in judging the durability of pile fabrics. In order to hold the pile so that it cannot be pulled out easily, two or more rows of filling should be used between two rows of pile. In addition to this, the background weave should be closely woven for greater durability. A twill-back cloth makes a stronger bath towel or velveteen than a plain-weave back.

In selling a bath towel, the salesperson should emphasize the importance of a thick pile, for the thicker the pile, the more absorbent the towel. On the other hand, he should point out that very long pile loops, while attractive and absorbent, often mat in laundering and are less desirable than shorter loops, because shorter loops do not pull out so easily.

How to Care for Pile Fabrics

To restore the appearance of a velvet or a velveteen fabric that has become matted, steaming, which raises the pile, is effective. The fabric should be held or hung near the steam of a shower bath, but must not be allowed to get wet. Another method of steaming a fabric at home is to place a damp cloth over a hot iron which is standing on end; or use a steam iron omitting damp cloth;

then, keeping the pile side away from the cloth, pass the back of the velvet slowly over the damp cloth.

See Chapter 13, page 245, for a discussion of the care of Turkish towels.

See Chapter 13, page 245, for a discussion of the care of Turkish towels.

LENO WEAVE

When a salesperson is selling marquisette for a window curtain, he should point out the importance of the weave. Marquisette is a lacelike construction called *leno weave* because it is made on a special leno loom that twists pairs of warp yarns like a figure eight. A filling is passed through a loop made by the twisting warps. See page 72. The selling points of this kind of weave are that it provides, as in marquisette, a lacelike appearance; it is porous enough to allow the penetration of air and light; and yet it does not allow the filling to slip appreciably because it holds each filling in position by the twists of warp above and below it.

Inexpensive dishcloths and mosquito netting may be made similarly.

FIGURED WEAVES

Figured weaves may be divided into Jacquard designs and into embroidered effects. The latter are broken down into lappet, clipped spot, and Schiffli.

Jacquard Design

Large, intricate woven-in designs are made on a special loom called the Jacquard, named after its inventor, Joseph Marie Jacquard. Such designs are repeated at intervals through the entire cloth, as in damask, brocade, or tapestry. A Jacquard weave, therefore, is a figured weave made by combining two or more basic weaves; it may be a combination of satin and sateen as in damask.

The Jacquard loom is more elaborate than the harness loom. The structural design is punched into pasteboard cards similar to punched business-machine cards. Just as the holes in the pianola roll govern the notes to be played, so the holes in the Jacquard cards govern the warp yarns to be raised. To produce the intricate designs, each warp yarn is separately controlled, so that each warp can be raised according to the pattern desired. Because of the elaborate machinery necessary and the skill required in making the Jacquard designs, fabrics in this weave are more expensive than those done on ordinary looms. For a picture of a fabric made in Jacquard weave, see page 135.

Small, far less intricate patterns than a Jacquard are made with a special attachment to the harness loom. This method is not so elaborate as the Jacquard and therefore is not so expensive to make. The loom used is called *dobby*. The name of the weave, therefore, is "dobby." *Dobby-weave fabrics* have small, often geometrical woven-in designs.

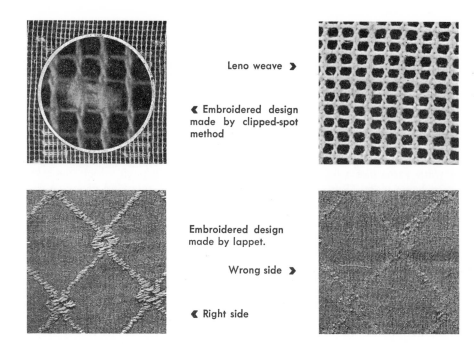

Leno weave ❯

❮ Embroidered design made by clipped-spot method

Embroidered design made by lappet.

Wrong side ❯

❮ Right side

Birds-eye, used for diapers, huck toweling, waffle cloths, and white-on-white men's shirtings are made in this way.

Embroidered Effects and Machine Embroidery

Lappet.   Patterns are sometimes embroidered onto the fabric while the cloth is being woven. This is done by special needles, called *lappets,* threaded with embroidery yarn, which are set at right angles to the frame of the loom. With these needles, simple designs such as dots, squares, stars, floral sprays are embroidered over the regular filling yarns. In lappet designs, the embroidery yarn is floated on the right side of the fabric to form the design. The pattern runs in a zig-zag line and is made of one continuous yarn. Embroidered voile, organdy, and batiste can be made in this way. However, because the design requires more yarn than the following methods, this embroidered effect is not common. The background of these cloths is usually in the plain weave.

Clipped Spot.   By using extra filling yarns, an embroidered patterned effect called *clipped spot* may also be made. These extra filling yarns are larger in size than the regular fillings and may be in different colors. The embroidery filling yarns are carried by extra shuttles that weave this yarn into the cloth at desired intervals. The yarn is cut off after each filling in the design, leaving cut, fuzzy ends on one side of the fabric.

Schiffli (machine embroidery). A machine called a "Schiffli" makes it possible to do more intricate designs than lappet or clipped spot. This machine can embroider in any direction—it can even make eyelets, whereas the lappet can only make zig-zag lines in one direction and the clipped spot makes patterns only crosswise. Many embroidered organdies, eyelet batistes, and piqués are embroidered by Schiffli.

PUTTING THIS MERCHANDISE KNOWLEDGE TO USE ❯❯❯❯❯❯❯❯❯❯

❯ DO YOU KNOW YOUR MERCHANDISE?

1. Examine each of the following articles of apparel and home furnishings. List them on a separate piece of paper, and write opposite each the name of the weave used for the fabric: (*a*) window curtain, (*b*) man's everyday shirt, (*c*) handkerchief, (*d*) dish towel, (*e*) bath towel, (*f*) huck towel, (*g*) formal dinner cloth, (*h*) man's tweed topcoat, (*i*) dishcloth, (*j*) girl's sport jacket.
2. If you were selling ready-to-wear, how would you know in what weave a gabardine jacket is made? a rayon crepe blouse?
3. Explain why a damask tablecloth is usually more expensive than a printed crash fabric.
4. How would you point out the durability of the following fabrics: (*a*) silk velvet, (*b*) Turkish toweling with Jacquard border, (*c*) marquisette?
5. Name the weave in which each of the following fabrics is made: (*a*) reversible coating, (*b*) terry-cloth robing, (*c*) diaper cloth, (*d*) Schiffli-embroidered batiste, (*e*) velveteen.
6. Give the selling points of a wool blanket made of double cloth.

❯ INTERESTING THINGS TO DO

1. Visit the yard-goods department of a store and from observation make a list of at least ten fabrics sold there. Give the name of each fabric; the name of the weave together with any variation; and the uses of the fabric. Mount fabrics in your scrapbook with "the write-up" of each.
2. Select one item of textile merchandise in which you are interested. Clip the advertisements for this item in newspapers over a period of one month. How many of the ads give the construction of the fabric? What facts can you deduce from your study?
3. Visit a large yard-goods department of a store. Make a list of all fabrics that are Schiffli embroidered. What facts can you deduce as to the popularity of Schiffli this season? On what fabrics is Schiffli most used?

UNIT 11 KNITTING, FELTING, AND LACE CONSTRUCTION

Mrs. Hollins went shopping for "T" shirts for her husband. She was served by a very well-informed salesperson who pointed out the selling points.

"You see, madam, since these shirts are knitted, they are very comfortable because they give with the movements of the body. If these undershirts were made of some woven material they would appear bulky under a dress shirt. Knitted shirts conform to the body contours, and they absorb perspiration readily. They're also very easy to take care of, for they can be laundered in a mechanical washer and do not require ironing."

HOW KNITTED FABRICS ARE MADE

Fabric knitting is done primarily by two methods: by weft knitting and by warp knitting.

Weft Knitting

Those who have done hand knitting know that one knitting needle holds one row of loops. The free needle is used to interloop the yarn with each successive loop. As this looping is done, the new loop formed is transferred from one needle to the other. The knitting process continues until the fabric is the desired size. Knitting, therefore, is the method of making cloth by the use of needles, one or more yarns forming a series of connecting loops that support each other like a chain. This method of knitting is called *weft* knitting, because rows of loops are formed crosswise of the fabric.

Plain Knitting. A beginner generally learns to do plain knitting. This is a knitting stitch identified by crosswise ridges on both sides of the fabric. These ridges are called *courses*. Scarves, dishcloths, carriage covers, and face cloths can be made in plain knitting and can be done either by hand or by machine.

Stockinette Knitting. Cotton and wool jersey are made in what the hand knitter calls stockinette—the kind of knitting used in the legs of stockings.

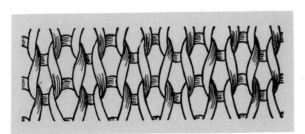

Knitted cloth showing rows of connecting loops.

The stockinette knitting stitch stretches to fit the body and comes back to shape better than plain knitting, so it is commonly used for hosiery, sweaters, and "T" shirts. Stockinette is identified by vertical ridges (*wales*) on the right side and horizontal ridges (*courses*) on the wrong side.

Rib Knitting. The top of a stocking is generally made in what is called *rib knitting*. This type of knitting has ribs and is more elastic than plain or even stockinette because it comes back to shape better after it has been stretched, and thus fits the body snugly. Cuffs of sweaters and snow suits, and children's heavy stockings are often made of rib knitting. Men's socks sold as 6 x 3 rib have a rib 6 loops of stitches wide and 3 loops between the ribs. *Rib knitting* is a knitting stitch done with vertical ribs (or wales) on both right and wrong sides of a fabric.

Figured Knitting. While it is possible to knit fancy patterns by hand, most of them are done by machine. Patterned golf socks and fancy vari-colored patterned sweaters are usually knitted by machine. For figured knitting, a special attachment regulates each needle to be used. Argyle socks may be knitted by hand.

Warp Knitting

Mesh Knits. One of the chief customer objections to knitted hosiery is the fact that loops often break and then runs form. There are runproof stockings, mesh underwear, and mesh hosiery that are made by a method called *warp knitting*—a process that makes a closer, flatter, less elastic fabric than stockinette or rib. While these mesh fabrics do not run, they may form holes. Warp-knitted fabrics have loops that interlock with one another in more than one direction of a fabric—not just crosswise as plain stockinette and rib knitting do.

Mesh fabrics frequently used for underwear and hosiery are made by this method. The crossings of the yarn are characterized by diagonal lines, making a diamond-shaped mesh (holes). This warp-knitting method may also be used for outerwear.

Tricot. Tricot (from the French verb *tricoter* meaning "to knit") is the name of a warp-knitted construction—a stitch less porous than mesh. One type of tricot construction is identified in women's underwear and gloves by a warpwise stripe (possibly a satin stripe) which, though run-resistant, may run downward if given too much strain. Fabrics of this type include sueded knitted cloths. Triacetate jersey dress fabrics, as distinct from wool or cotton jersey, are made in tricot rather than in stockinette. Arnel triacetate is commonly made in this construction. These jerseys do not wrinkle and so are excellent for traveling.

GAUGE OF KNITTED FABRICS

A woven cloth that has a high count is more closely constructed than a woven fabric with a low count. Similarly, a knitted cloth with a high gauge number is more closely knitted than a cloth with a low gauge number. *Gauge* is the term used to express the closeness of the knit.

The salesperson selling women's hosiery should know that a 51-gauge stocking is more closely knitted than one of 45 gauge. The gauge number is determined by the number of needles or stitches to the inch and a half; as a rule, the higher the gauge number, the stronger the fabric.

HOW ARE KNITTED FABRICS SHAPED?

One of the chief selling points of knitted fabrics is that they conform to the shape of the body. This is because the knitted loop construction is quite elastic. But elasticity of the knitting is not enough to make a knitted garment fit. Garments must be shaped.

Woven fabrics are made flat and then are cut and sewed to make the desired shape. Most knitted fabrics, however, would soon ravel if they were cut. If they are shaped in the knitting process, they fit much better. Shaping is done in one of the following ways.

Full-fashioned

The best method of making knitted garments to fit the shape of the body is called *full-fashioned*. The fabric is knitted in a flat piece, and stitches are added or decreased to widen or narrow the fabric to the shape required. The two edges are then sewed together on a machine. Full-fashioned knitted goods can be identified by the fashion-marks near the seam that are made when the stitches have been decreased. In hand knitting, two stitches are knitted as one to decrease the width. Hosiery and sweaters can be full-fashioned. Full-fashioned goods are usually more expensive than any other type, but fit best and keep their shape even after washing.

Semifashioned

Semifashioned fabric is only partly fashioned. It is not knitted flat, but on a circular machine that produces a tubelike fabric. Some shape is given by tightening the tension of the knitting needles at certain points, so that some stitches are closer together

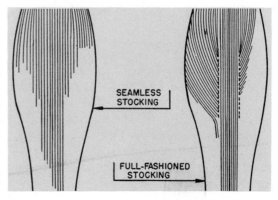

SEAMLESS STOCKING

FULL-FASHIONED STOCKING

than others. No real seam is necessary in this type of hosiery. The majority of men's socks are made in this manner, and many men prefer this type of sock because there is no seam under the ball of the foot as there is in full-fashioned socks. Women's seamless hosiery is of this type.

Tubular

Tubular knit fabrics are made in the form of a cylinder on circular machines, without any change of tension of the needles. Tubular knitted hosiery can be shaped, after the knitting is completed, by placing the stockings on forms and shrinking or stretching them to shape. When such stockings are worn and washed, however, they lose their shape and become baggy, for they revert to their tubular appearance.

SELLING POINTS OF KNITTED GARMENTS

Knitted garments, such as sweaters, hosiery, undergarments, and infants' wear, are comfortable because they give with body movements. They are elastic and do not wrinkle easily. They are porous, lightweight, absorbent, easy to launder, and do not require ironing. Knitted garments are generally considered warmer than woven ones of the same weight, fiber, and yarn, because the loops made in the knitting process form air pockets that keep the heat near the body.

When you wear a knitted wool sweater, the cold air must pass through the air pockets in the pores of the fabric before the outside air can reach the body. By the time the outside air does reach the body, the air is somewhat warmer.

OBJECTIONS TO KNITTED GARMENTS

As most people who have ever had a run in their stockings know, knitted garments have certain disadvantages. If one loop in the fabric is broken, it is very difficult to control the rip or run that soon occurs. Another objection is that knitted garments may fit the figure too closely, and so in a short time may stretch out of shape at elbows, knees, and other places where pressure is placed.

What advice should be given to customers about the care of knitted garments?

HOW TO CARE FOR KNITTED GARMENTS

Many objections to knitted garments may be overcome through a knowledge of their proper care. Although most knitted garments do not require ironing since they come back into shape when worn, some articles are softened and smoothed by ironing, as for example, cotton jersey polo shirts and some cotton knitted dresses. Rayon, silk, wool, or nylon knitted fabrics must be washed just as any woven fabric made of these fibers. Read the label to see whether the article is machine or hand washable. Follow instructions implicitly. Woolen garments, such as sweaters and hosiery, should be washed by hand, squeezing suds through the fabric. Sweaters and hosiery should be stretched back to shape, dried flat, called "blocking," or put on sweater or sock frames to dry. If no frame is available, the best way to bring sweaters back to shape is to draw an outline of the sweater on a piece of paper before washing. After the sweater has been washed, roll it in a Turkish towel to absorb moisture; then stretch it to the shape of the pattern and allow it to dry flat. Another way to restore the shape of a sweater is to note its length, width, and sleeve measurements before washing. After rolling it in the towel, place it on a flat surface and "work it" by gentle pushing with the hands to the required measurements.

If a run forms, it should be mended immediately. Pins should never be used as a substitute for mending, for they cause the loops to snag and runs to form.

LACEMAKING

Lace is a fabric made by looping, twisting, or knotting thread in different ways. Knotting was described in Chapter 2 as a method of making cloth. The method of looping and twisting as described in mesh and tricot fabrics is used to form nets of lace called *bobbinet* and *tulle*. Crocheting was also mentioned in Chapter 2 as a method of making cloth. Hence, lacemaking involves three methods of making cloth which you have already studied: knitting, knotting, and crocheting.

Real lace is made by hand. The delicacy and beauty of handwork are not to be compared with machine-made lace; however, lace machines have brought most laces within the buying power of the average woman. In fact, many machine laces are sold on the counters of our variety stores.

Kinds of Real Laces

One legend tells that the early Roman men of wealth, when their togas became frayed, had the edges mended by having them sewed or edged each time with a buttonhole stitching. When repair work of this kind was done several times, a new fabric was created along the edge. This new fabric closely resembled what later became known as lace.

Needle-point Lace. Even if we do not believe this legend in its entirety, we know from history that the first handmade needle lace originated in Venice, Italy, in the early sixteenth century. This kind of lace is called *needle point* because it is made with the point of a needle. The design is first

❯ ❯ Laces ❮ ❮

From Top to Bottom. Left-hand column: Handmade laces: Torchon, Cluny, Irish crochet, Tatting, Filet.

Right-hand column: Machine-made laces: French Val, Filet, Binche, Point d'Esprit net, Chantilly, Venetian, Fine Alençon, Princess (bobbin).

drawn on a piece of parchment which is stitched to a strong backing of linen. Next, the lines of the design are loosely stitched with linen thread. The pattern is then filled in with buttonhole stitches, which is slow work. When the filling-in is completed, the outlining threads which hold the lace to the parchment pattern are cut, and the lace is ready for use.

Needle-point Laces

Some of the common needle-point laces are:

Alençon—a lace used particularly in trimming slips and underwear. It is often écru color and is made in floral patterns outlined by a heavy thread.

Rose Point (de Venise)—a rather heavy, wide lace in a rose pattern. It is an exquisite and expensive lace.

Raised Point (de Venise)—also a rather heavy lace with a raised floral pattern. Parts of the design are joined together with bars that resemble thorns on rose bushes. This lace is also very beautiful and expensive. Machine-made lace in this and in rose pattern is called *Venetian lace*. The word *point* signifies handmade lace. Venetian lace makes attractive blouses.

Bobbin Lace

Bobbin lace, when made by hand, is often called *pillow lace* because the pattern is first drawn on a pillow that is as wide as the lace is to be. Small pins or pegs are stuck into the pillow along the design. Small bobbins twisted with thread are looped around the pins that mark the design. When the lace is finished the pillow is removed.

Laces have two parts; a design, and a ground (background). In many needle-point laces, the design covers more area than the ground. In bobbin laces, many fabrics have a twisted net ground called bobbinet. The designs are somewhat clothy, like woven fabrics. When there is no design on the net, it is sold as *bobbinet*.

Some typical bobbin laces are:

Binche (pronounced "Bansh")—a coarse net ground similar to the design found in a cane-seated chair, ornamented by a design of flat sprigs. These sprigs are cut from fine linen cloth and sewed to this net ground. The sewing of fabric to a net ground is called *appliquéing*.

Chantilly—a filmy French lace made of silk. In machine-made construction, the same patterns are made of rayon. Machine-made Chantilly is termed *Chantilly-type* lace. The real Chantilly usually comes in black or white. Branchlike designs with bobbinet ground are identifying features. All-over-pattern Chantilly lace is used for formal dresses and bridal veils.

Cluny—a moderately heavy lace with open, geometrical designs. A shell pattern forming a scalloped edge is typical. It is used for trimming luncheon sets and dresses.

Duchesse—often considered the "Queen of Bobbin Laces." The lace is composed primarily of a clothy design, parts of which are connected by heavy joining threads. It is made in wide widths. Collars and trimmings are often made of duchesse. The owner of a piece of real duchesse lace would never cut it, but would find some other method of making it smaller—probably by turning under the unused part of it.

Torchon—a fairly coarse bobbin lace. It is often called "beggar's lace" because it is inexpensive (especially in machine types), and is used extensively for edgings on children's and women's dresses and underwear. It is serviceable and washes nicely. A shell pattern is typical of torchon.

Val—the short name for *Valenciennes*—a lace of French origin. It is identified by the bobbinet ground and the floral or sprig design. Frequently there are also small round dots in the ground. As this lace is light and filmy in texture, it is used as trimming for blouses, dresses, and infants' clothing. It is one of the most extensively used laces and is quite inexpensive in machine-made types.

Real lace can also be made by crocheting; by darning a design into a mesh ground with needle and thread; by knotting thread by means of a shuttle as in tatting. The most common crocheted lace is called *Irish crochet.* A familiar lace that can be made by darning is called *filet,* used for tablecloths, luncheon sets, and doilies.

Machine-made Laces

Nearly all common patterns found in real laces can be made with some simplification in machine-made types. There are also some novelty machine-made laces that are combinations of two or more designs found in real lace.

When the pattern in a machine lace is similar to that of real lace, the real-lace name holds. However, in needle-point laces made by machine, the word *point* is omitted. The word *type* is sometimes used with the name of the lace to signify that it is machine made, as in *Cluny-type* lace.

The first simple frame for making a loop net was invented about 1764, but the bobbinet machine was not invented until 1809. It was patented by John Heathcote but was modified later by several other inventors, notably John Levers. The Levers machine is very important in the lace industry.

Comparison of Real and Machine-made Laces

We make machine laces in this country, chiefly of cotton, rayon, and nylon, which are plentiful and can be produced at popular prices. The most successful lacemaking machines have been imported from abroad, primarily from Switzerland.

While machine-made laces come in different patterns and widths, ranging from the wide all-over lace cut from a bolt to the narrow edging used on babies' dresses, the machine-made lace does not rival the real lace in delicacy or beauty. For real laces, linen and silk are popular fibers because of their strength and beauty. The use of these strong fibers has been the reason that many ancient museum pieces of lace are still in splendid condition.

If there is any doubt in the salesperson's mind as to whether a lace is real or machine made, he can clear it up by considering the price, for real lace is more expensive than machine-made lace.

FELT FABRICS

The felt hat, the soft warm bedroom slippers, the college pennant, and the felt table pad are neither woven nor knitted. If one were to make a hole in one of these articles, or pull it apart, he would not find any yarn. *Felt fabrics* are made directly from the fibers that have been closely compressed and interlocked by heat, moisture, and pressure. No yarn making, weaving, or knitting is necessary. Wool fibers, because of their scaly surfaces, are best adapted to felting. When the wool fibers are subjected to heat, moisture, and pressure, the scales cause the fibers to interlock into a tight, compact mass called *felt*. Other fibers—such as fur, hair, or cotton—may be mixed with the wool during the felting process. Some other uses for felt are for blackboard erasers, corn plasters, phonograph pads, washers, and weather stripping.

Other methods of making cloth such as braiding, bonding, laminating were discussed in Chapter 2.

PUTTING THIS MERCHANDISE KNOWLEDGE TO USE ❯❯❯❯❯❯❯❯❯❯❯

❯ DO YOU KNOW YOUR MERCHANDISE?

1. Why do runs frequently form in knitted goods?
2. List the selling points and customers' objections to knitted fabrics.
3. Explain the difference between weaving and knitting.
4. Explain fully how you would recommend to a customer the laundering of a (a) wool sweater, (b) woolen socks, (c) nylon hosiery.
5. How would you tell a real lace from a machine-made lace?
6. What are the chief differences between needle-point and bobbin laces? Give examples of each type.
7. For what purposes are laces used?

❯ INTERESTING THINGS TO DO

1. Obtain a woman's stocking and a man's sock (these need not be new). Determine by which method of shaping each was made. List the selling points for each type.
2. Knit a fabric containing each of the following stitches: (a) plain,

(b) rib (knit 2 purl 2), (c) stockinette (knit one row, purl the next). Put each fabric, clearly identified, in your scrapbook.
3. Obtain samples of four types of machine-made laces. Identify the patterns as to type. Give possible uses of each lace. Put these laces in your scrapbook.

ADDITIONAL MERCHANDISE TERMS ≫ ≫ ≫ ≫ ≫ ≫ ≫ ≫ ≫ ≫ ≫ ≫ ≫ ≫ ≫ ≫ ≫ ≫ ≫

Circular-knit fabrics are made in the form of a tube and shaped by shrinking or stretching on forms. Synonym is "tubular."

Construction denotes the way the cloth is made. Cloth can be constructed from fibers or yarn in different ways.

Eyelets are small decorative holes, usually round, made in fabric to be worked around with buttonhole stitch.

Jacquard-knitted patterns are novelty fabrics having fancy designs knitted directly into the cloth.

Plain-weave fabrics have structural designs resembling a checkerboard.

Point is a word signifying handmade lace of needle-point variety.

Shuttle is a boatlike wooden or metal bobbin used to send the filling yarn through the warps.

Terry cloth is a fabric made in pile weave. Uncut loops of pile are to be found on both sides of the cloth.

CHAPTER 5

Facts About Finishes

UNIT 12 HOW CLOTH IS FINISHED

Customer to the salesperson: "I have here a copy of your advertisement for men's all-cotton broadcloth shirts. Here is the ad.

BROADCLOTH SHIRTS

Fine white broadcloth in regular or spread collar, single convertible cuffs. Wash & wear—no ironing required. Sizes 14-17.

3⁹⁵

MEN'S STORE

"What does 'wash and wear' really mean? Can a man really wear this shirt without ironing?"

Fortunately for the customer, the salesperson knew the correct answers to these questions. He explained that the shirt is treated with a plastic resin to make it shed water and therefore dry faster than untreated cotton. However, the resin-finish treatment to make a "wash and wear" fabric should not be confused with a fiber blend of 65 per cent Dacron polyester and 35 per cent cotton which also makes a "wash and wear" fabric. The latter is not a finish, but a blend of fibers. He also explained that while some men might wear such a cotton shirt without ironing while traveling, most shirts of this type are improved by at least a "touch up" on the collar, cuffs, and front closing. Should the customer want to do a complete ironing, this treated shirt is easier to iron than one not treated.

When the salesperson told the customer about a resin-treated broadcloth, he was talking about a very important finishing process—one that has recently given the homemaker ease in caring for apparel. A *finishing process* is a treatment given a cloth after it is woven or knitted.

WHY MUST FABRICS BE FINISHED?

Ask yourself this question: Is a piece of unbleached muslin attractive?

Probably your answer is "No." Is a sheer crisp pink organdy attractive? Most of you who know the fabric will answer "Yes."

The attractiveness of the organdy is due to its color and to its crisp appearance. Both the color and the crispness were processes given the fabric after weaving.

From this it is apparent that one very important purpose of a finishing process is to enhance the attractiveness of a fabric.

Fabrics that are identical in fibers, yarns, and weave can differ greatly according to the finish used. Compare two pieces of cotton lawn: both fabrics are similar in appearance when they come from the loom. In the finishing, one sample is bleached snow white, printed in a gay paisley design, and starched. The other sample is dyed a solid navy blue. It is soft and lifeless because it is not starched.

On the other hand, a finishing process may be used to give weight to an otherwise flimsy fabric of loose weave. For example, a sheet of low count may be so filled with starch that it feels firm before washing; but after washing such a sheet feels flimsy and light.

Just as there are entire industries devoted to the spinning, to the weaving, and to the knitting of fabrics, so there is an industry devoted to the changing of unfinished goods into finished materials. This industry is called the *converting industry,* for it changes, or converts, gray goods when they come from the loom or knitting machine into the finished salable cloth. The industry devoted to the coloring of fabrics, however, is not considered a part of the converting industry.

HOW FINISHING PROCESSES CREATE SELLING POINTS FOR THE CLOTH

Unfinished fabric are drab Cinderellas, uninteresting and unattractive, which can be changed into the most beautiful materials by the use of various finishes. Finishing processes may affect fabrics as follows:

1. Finishing processes are used to give attractiveness and beauty to the cloth, by whitening it, by adding luster, smoothness, crinkled effect, crispness.

2. They may change the texture of the fabric, by adding weight to make it heavier, giving it more elasticity, adding softness, or warmth.

3. They may affect the appearance of the cloth, hiding its defects and making it appear more desirable than it is, by adding sizing to make the fabric appear more closely woven, or raising a fuzz to cover defects in spinning or weaving.

4. They may make the fabric better suited for a specific use. For example, a water-repellent finish makes a fabric better suited for rainwear than one not so finished. A fabric with a wrinkle-resistant finish looks fresh longer. It is therefore better suited for traveling.

5. They may protect the wearer from bodily injury by fire.

6. They may make fabrics more sanitary by being resistant to odors of perspiration, by overcoming susceptibility to mildew and moth damage.

7. They may make fabrics easier to care for.

8. They may make fabrics retain their size, fit, and shape by controlling shrinkage and the possibility of stretching.

TYPICAL FINISHES

The type of finishing process applied is determined by the use for which the fabric is intended, as well as by the fiber of which the fabric is made.

Many finishing processes can be used for all fabrics, but some processes can be applied only to fabrics made of certain fibers. Finishes that can be used for most fibers are given in the order listed above as follows.

Finishes That Give Attractiveness to a Fabric

Bleaching. *Bleaching* is the process of removing the coloring matter from the fibers and thereby making them white in color. When the homemaker hangs her wash in the sun to dry, she wants to make her white clothes whiter, and so uses the natural and safest method of bleaching, namely, the ultra-violet rays of the sun.

Natural bleaching, or *"grassing,"* was the original bleaching method used. In this method, the fabrics were spread on the grass and exposed to the sun and dew. This method is still used in certain countries, and it has the advantage of not injuring the fabric; but it requires too much time, space, and tie-up of capital. A much more rapid method, one which is used commercially today, is the use of chemicals. Although chemicals can produce pure white materials more rapidly than the natural method, they may weaken the fibers. All fabrics that are to be solid white or white with a print are bleached. Likewise, light-colored fabrics are usually bleached before they are dyed.

Vegetable fibers, except jute, are generally bleached commercially with chloride of lime. Wool, silk, and jute are bleached with sulphur. Hydrogen peroxide can be used for all fibers, but is very expensive. White cotton or linen fabrics may be bleached at home by dipping them in chlorine solutions (sodium hypochloride). Bluing is not a bleach because it does not remove color. It merely aids in making white clothes a blue-white.

Chemical Printing. Crepe effects can be obtained after the cloth has been woven. The method of making crepe fabrics by varying the twist and tension in the yarn has already been discussed. To make crepe during the finishing process, certain parts of the fabric are printed with an alkali paste, such as caustic soda. When the fabric is washed, the parts printed with the alkali will shrink, whereas the unprinted parts will not. The unprinted parts will crinkle or crepe. Seersucker and crinkled bedspreads are often made by this method. The crepe is considered permanent.

Designs on pile-weave fabrics may be obtained after the pile fabric is woven, either by pressing, cutting, or by the use of certain chemicals that

❯ ❯ Typical Finishes ❮ ❮

Left: Chemical printing for creped stripes on seersucker. **Right:** Moiréing on taffeta.

eat out the pile and leave the groundwork intact. So-called brocaded velvets are a result of chemical printing to remove pile where desired.

Embossing. Most of the finishing processes discussed so far change the character of the fabric by using certain chemicals. Those methods that follow produce their effects on the fabrics by using some mechanical means.

Embossing is a process of pressing a design into a fabric by passing it through heavy rollers having a raised pattern.

Some inexpensive cloths are given a temporary crinkled effect by being passed between hot rollers filled with indentations. This manner of producing crepe is an embossing process. It is not permanent, and a fabric so treated will lose its crinkled appearance after laundering, whereas the method described under *chemical printing* produces crepe effects which will launder satisfactorily. The salesperson should make it clear to his customers that garments made of the embossed type of crepe are inexpensive, but that the crinkled surfaces do not last. However, there is now a method called *heat-setting* by which plastic is applied to the fabric as the cloth is embossed. The pressure and heat of the embossing rollers cause the embossed effect to be heat-set permanently. This finish is commonly applied to cotton. When the plastic-type synthetics are used, heat and pressure will fuse the fibers slightly so that the embossed design will last.

Moiréing. Rayon or silk may be given a watered appearance by passing the cloth, woven with heavy fillingwise ribs, between heavy rollers that have irregular lines raised on them. This is another method of embossing. The pressing down of parts of the surface brings out their luster and thus produces the moiré, or watermarking. Again, acetate, nylon, and other plastic synthetics would be permanently moiréd by fusion of the fibers by heavy heated rollers. Rayon, silk, and cotton would require setting of the design to make it permanent.

Calendering. Before most fabrics can be sold, they must be pressed or calendered. The exception to this are wool fabrics, which are sponged and pressed in a manner similar to that used by a tailor when pressing a suit. *Calendering* is the process of passing the fabric between smooth hot rollers. Those cloths that have a flat, smooth surface have been calendered more than once to give a satiny look.

Finishes Affecting the Stiffness, Softness, Weight, and Elasticity of a Fabric

Sizing and Weighting. *Sizing* may be defined as a finishing process commonly applied to cotton to give weight, crispness, or stiffness, or to hide defects of a fabric. Unfortunately, most of the dressing used is soluble, so that the fabrics that have been so treated will not be so attractive after being laundered as fabrics without such dressing. Various starches, glues, and gums are used to give body, stiffness, and weight. Oils and fats are used to give softness; waxes, paraffin, shellac, and plastic are used to give glazed effects. Plastic-resin glazes are permanent; they can be laundered and will not rub off. Cotton organdy and glazed chintz are examples of fabrics which may be so treated. Everglaze and Vita Glaze are two brand names of permanent glazes. Fabrics that are loosely woven can be sized to imitate a more tightly woven cloth. The salesperson should know whether the fabric has a permanent stiffness in these cases.

Generally, linens are not sized but may have a little starch put into the fabric in finishing to give that leathery stiffness of new linen fabrics.

Silk can be *weighted* in the finishing process by adding metallic salts that give a heavy feeling and stiffness to the fabric. Weighting may come out in part or entirely in washing and dry cleaning. Then the fabric feels limp. Heavily weighted silks will deteriorate in sunlight. For these reasons the Federal Trade Commission specifies that weighted silk must be labeled in per cents of metallics present in the cloth. Water-soluble finishes may be added to silk, rayon, and other synthetics to increase their weight and to give a more closely woven appearance. When the fabric is washed, the finish may come out giving the water a cloudy appearance. For this reason, F.T.C. has a ruling also on this type of finish. If the finishing material amounts to over 15 per cent in black and 10 per cent in other colors, then the percentage of finishing materials must appear on the label.

Wool can be given added weight by the addition of moisture and a chemical. This is not a permanent finish. A loose weave in wool may be covered up by steaming the very short waste fibers into the back of the fabric. This is called *flocking* and will not last permanently, for the short fibers soon come out with friction. Small rolls of wool in the pockets of wool overcoats are usually indications of flocking.

SIMPLE TESTS TO DETECT SIZING OR WEIGHTING IN FABRICS. To detect sizing in cotton, rub a corner of the fabric to see whether a powdery substance comes off, revealing a loose weave. Holding the fabric up to the light may also reveal whether it is loosely woven.

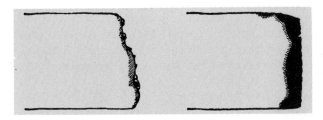

Burning Test for Silk.

Left: Pure silk fabric—gummy beads remaining along burned edge. **Right:** Weighted silk fabric — charred edge resembling a metal screen.

Another way to test for sizing is to tear the fabric and notice whether dust flies and whether the dust particles cling to the edges of the fibers.

To identify weighting in silk, the burning test is a very simple method. Cut off a small piece from the seam of the fabric to be tested. If the fabric burns with a crisp ash and has the odor of burning feathers or hair, it is pure silk. If the fabric does not ignite, but merely chars, it is weighted silk. Weighted-silk fabrics also can be recognized because they waterspot easily. Weighted silk is not very common. It can sometimes be found in an imported taffeta, men's silk ties, and lamp shades.

To identify flocking in wool garments, brush the back of the cloth with a stiff brush. If short fibers have been used to cover up a loose weave, they will come out with friction.

Elasticity—Crease-resistant Finishes. Many fabrics made of linen, cotton, or rayon crease very readily and must be pressed frequently in order to be restored to their fresh appearance. There are several crease-resistant finishes now used on such fabrics that add elasticity and cause them to resist creasing and to lose their wrinkles after hanging. The crease-resistant solution (usually made of a chemical resin base) is applied either to the fabric during the dyeing process or to the face of the fabric after it has been dyed and dried. Fabrics so treated will crease less and will lose their creases after wear or packing if they are simply hung up.

Left: Untreated cotton cloth.

Right: Cotton fabric treated for crease resistance. *(Courtesy United Piece Dye Works)*

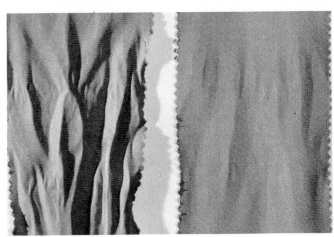

Crush-resistant velvets will soon return to their original appearance after wear. If the pile of such velvet becomes spotted by water, it will become smooth again after drying. Velvets so treated can be dry-cleaned repeatedly without losing their crush-resistant properties. This finish makes velvet a much less fragile material.

Tebilized and *Vitalized* are some brand names of crease-resistant finishes. In no case is a fabric 100 per cent noncrushable or creaseproof; therefore, the merchant should not advertise fabrics as noncrushable. Crease-resistant treatment of fabrics minimizes slippage at the seams and sagging. It also improves laundering properties.

Finishes That Protect the Wearer from the Weather

Warmth. Either a mechanical process or a chemical process may be used to give warmth to a fabric.

NAPPING. *Napping* raises the loose ends of the short fibers to produce a fuzz or nap. Cotton can be napped to resemble wool, as in cotton flannel. Many woolen fabrics are napped to give them their characteristic rough finish; spun rayon can be napped to resemble wool. Revolving cylinders covered with fine wire teeth are generally used to draw up the nap. Teazles (little burrlike plants) are sometimes used on the better grade woolens to raise a nap. Napping increases the warmth of a fabric.

MILIUM TREATMENT. Results of research have indicated that cold does not actually penetrate a fabric but leaks through the cloth in proportion to the fiber's heat-reflecting scales. As synthetic fibers do not have these scales, a substitute for their heat-reflecting properties has been developed in a finishing process called *Milium* developed by Deering Milliken & Company, Inc. The fabric is treated with an aluminum derivative that causes external heat rays to bounce off the surface of the cloth and the internal heat rays to rebound to the body, thus keeping the wearer of the treated fabric warm. Hence Milium may result in the use of lighter and less bulky clothing and bed coverings during the winter months.

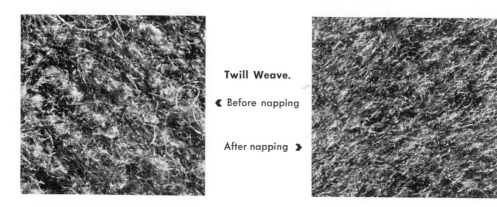

Twill Weave.

❮ Before napping

After napping ❯

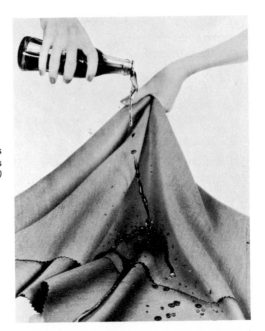

Fabric has been treated to resist spots and stains. Note how the liquid runs off. *(Courtesy United Piece Dye Works)*

Waterproofing and Water-repellent Finishes. There are several patented processes that close the pores of the fabric, thus making the cloth rainproof and moistureproof. Raincoats, umbrellas, and galoshes are some of the articles often treated in this manner. It is important to find out the degree of water repellency the article possesses, for some fabrics will withstand a brief 15-minute shower; others, several hours of rain; still others, all-day rain without wetting through. Usually the label indicates whether the water-repellent fabric can be laundered or dry-cleaned. Instructions on the label should be followed to insure long service.

Water-repellent finishes must not be confused with waterproof finishes. In the water-repellent type, the pores of the fabric are open for circulation of air; in the *waterproof* type, the pores of the fabric are closed to air.

Wax emulsions, insoluble metallic soaps, or compounds of nitrogenous bases are used to make fabrics water repellent. As these chemicals combine with the fiber, the cloth feels softer and less oily; and the finish does not tend to wash out. Other finishes merely coat the yarn and are not fast to laundering or cleaning; fabrics so finished must be refinished after being cleaned. Some laundries and dry cleaners can replace such a water-repellent finish.

To waterproof a fabric, a rubber coating can be applied to the right side of a cloth. Most men can remember having had one of these raincoats, possibly with hat to match, and how warm and uncomfortable they were in them. Nowadays, we have plastic-coated fabrics of nylon, cotton, rayon, etc., that are lighter and softer in weight, do not become stiff with age, and can be wiped off with a damp cloth. The plastic may be applied on one side of the cloth only, as in raincoats, some kinds of baby pants, bibs, and imitation leather goods. Or the cloth may be dipped in plastic for use in shower-bath curtains, play-pen pads, and mattress covers.

Fabrics treated with water-repellent finishes give better service because they:

1. Shed water, rain, and snow
2. Stay clean longer
3. Resist spots and stains. (Spots can generally be sponged off and grease stains removed with cleaning fluid.)
4. Resist perspiration

Familiar brand names of water-repellent finishes include Aridex, Cravenette, Neva-Wet, Rainfoe, Impregnole.

Fabric Finish to Protect the Body from Injury

Flame-retardant or Fire-resistant Finish. In the days of the coal or the wood stove, the heated flatiron was a real fire hazard when it was placed flat on an ironing board without a metal stand. But the automatic heat-controlled iron helped to eliminate the hot-iron hazard. Nevertheless, fire insurance companies tell us that our homes are full of real fire hazards, many of which can be easily eliminated. One method of checking these hazards is by purchasing fire-resistant draperies, curtains, ironing-board covers, children's sleeping garments, and so on. Or, if a housewife already has these articles, not fireproofed, in use, she can fireproof them at home by dipping the cloth into a solution of 30 per cent boric acid and 70 per cent borax. Another method of fireproofing is to spray the cloth with such a solution. Then the treated fabric should be ironed with a warm, not a hot, iron. This home treatment is not permanent and the treatment has to be repeated after each laundering.

When the converter applies a *fire-resistant* finish, he may use chemicals (namely carbonates and aluminum salts) that melt and cover the fabric with nonflammable film and give off a noncombustible vapor. A fabric so treated is fire resistant. Water-repellent fabrics that cannot be immersed in solution can be sprayed on the surface. Although animal fibers will burn, they do not catch on fire so quickly, nor burn so readily, as vegetable fibers. The cellulose of which vegetable fibers are primarily composed is particularly inflammable. Typical brand names of fire-resistant finishes include Banflame, Flamefoil, Fire Chief, and Pyroset.

The purpose of this finish is to protect the wearer or user of this fabric from bodily injury by fire. Some types of flame-resistant finishes also make a cloth mildew resistant.

Finishes to Protect the Cloth from Deterioration

Perspiration-resistant Finish. The objectionable odor of perspiration can be overcome by either the application of antiperspirants to the skin or by the treatment of the fabric with chemicals (germicides, fungicides) that are odorless, do not stain the fabric, do not affect the dye or any other finishes applied to the fabric. Fabrics so treated are sterile and can be used as shoe linings to protect the wearer against athlete's foot. This finish is semipermanent, and has been found to wash as many as 40 times. Puritized, Sanitized, Telosobent, and Vita-Fresh are brand names of such odor-resistant finishes.

Mildew-resistant Finish. Mildew is a parasitic growth that primarily attacks the vegetable (cellulosic) fibers, but may attack wool if left damp for a long period. To resist this attack, fabrics can be treated with metallic compounds (chromium, mercury, lead, zinc, salts, copper) or with creosote, rubber, or coal-tar products. Cotton, linen, wool, and filament rayon may be made mildew resistant.

Moth-repellent Finish. When the homemaker stores her winter clothes during the summer months, she usually sprays each garment thoroughly with a moth-repellent solution. Frequently, she puts mothballs or crystals into the garment closet. While this method is effective, the fabric finisher can make a fabric permanently moth repellent by adding colorless chemicals similar to dyestuffs to the dye bath. However, this method is more expensive than to spray the finished fabric with colorless, odorless, moth-proofing chemical.

Vegetable fibers and those with plastic bases are not palatable to moths, and therefore need no protection. Boconize and Erustomoth are brand names of moth-repellent finishes.

Ease-in-Care Finishes

One of the greatest boons to the homemaker is the finish that eases her ironing job each week. Advertisements and labels have referred to them as "drip-dry," "wash-and-wear," "easy," or "minimum care."

As has been explained, these finishes are of a plastic-resin nature that are, for example, applied to a cotton. This treatment causes the fabric to dry more rapidly and to iron more easily—if and when ironing will improve the appearance of the fabric. Recently, a nonresin finish has been applied to shirtings. This is done by changing the molecular structure of the cotton to give the fiber more resilience. Belfast is a finish of this type, trademark of Deering Milliken & Co.

When these finishes first appeared, the homemaker took the advertising literally. She washed everything that had a drip-dry, wash-and-wear label in her automatic washer. She let them go all through the final wringing cycle. Of course, they were full of wrinkles and had to be ironed. Finally, she learned to take out drip-dry items before the wringing took place and to use the washing-machine setting called "modern fabrics" or "fine fabrics" for all the drip-dries.

Two labels giving valuable information to the consumer on performance and care of the fabric. *(Courtesy Cluett, Peabody & Co. and Dan River Mills, Inc.)*

While not all minimum-care fabrics are made by finishing treatments, the fiber blends 65 per cent Dacron polyester and 35 per cent cotton also make care of fabrics easier for the consumer.

Judging from the author's experience, it was found that wash-and-wear shirts trap soil—particularly around the collar and cuffs. This is due to the presence of resin treatment (finish) or the resin fibers themselves. It is, therefore, necessary to rub some soap on the soiled spots before putting them into the washer. At any rate, it is advisable to send a resin-treated cotton shirt to the commercial laundry occasionally, to restore its appearance. Again, from the author's experience, it cannot be said that minimum-care fabrics never have to be ironed. It has beeen found that a touch-up of collars, cuffs, dress or shirt closings, and hems greatly improves the general appearance of the garment.

Finishes to Control Shape and Size of Fabrics

Tentering. When the salesperson sells a customer a sheer cotton marquisette curtain, he should recommend that the curtain be dried on a stretcher to insure its drying evenly. After a fabric has been finished or dyed, it is made even in width by a process called *tentering*.

To tenter a cloth, the fabric is gripped tightly along both selvages and is pulled along a frame in the presence of steam. After the tentering process, the fabric is dried and calendered. If the cloth is stretched too much, as is sometimes done by unreliable manufacturers, it will return to its original size after laundering. This is often the cause of excessive shrinkage of fabrics.

Tentering is a *must* for all fabrics.

Control of Shrinkage by Finishing. Fabrics that are labeled *preshrunk* are very deceiving. This does not mean, as most people are led to believe, that they have been treated so that they will not shrink any more. According to the Federal Trade Commission ruling of June, 1938, the term *preshrunk* on a label or in an advertisement must be followed by "will not shrink more than (amount) %." This *residual shrinkage* is the maximum amount of shrinkage a consumer may expect after she has laundered it or had it laundered. A salesperson should know how to interpret *residual shrinkage*. For example, a 4 per cent residual shrinkage on a .45-inch dress actually means that the dress will shrink almost 2 inches! This amount is excessive and should be recognized as such by both the salesperson and the customer. Fabrics bearing the trademark "Sanforized" will not shrink more than 1 per cent. This trademark is applied to cotton or linen woven fabrics and products made therefrom which, before tailoring or manufacture, have been mechanically treated under the control and periodic testing of the trademark proprietor so as to substantially eliminate subsequent shrinkage. "Sanforized-Plus" is a trademark signifying a regularly checked standard of wash-and-wear performance. Fabrics so labeled have met rigid test requirements for shrinkage, smoothness after washing, crease recovery, tensile strength, and tear strength as prescribed by the trademark owner.

In wool fabrics, shrinkage can be accomplished by the finisher so that only a certain amount of shrinkage remains. One method is to treat wool with a synthetic resin. Not only does a fabric so treated resist shrinkage, but the finisher claims that stains apparently are more easily removed from wool so treated, and that the cloth can be dry-cleaned or laundered more easily. A tag or label affixed to the merchandise should bear the trademark of the shrinkage-resistant process. Familiar trademarks for wool fabrics that are shrinkage-controlled are Resloom and Lanaset.

Finishes Commonly Applied to Fabrics Made of the Various Fibers

A knowledge of the finishing processes used on fabrics made of a given fiber is important in order to understand the effect they have on the appearance and wearing qualities of these fabrics.

If the salesperson is familiar with typical finishes usually applied to cloth made entirely of one fiber, then he is better able to judge the type of finishes applied to blended fabrics and to estimate the cloth's performance in use.

In blended fabrics, the finishes applied are governed by the texture, appearance, and use of the cloth. If a fabric is an Orlon acrylic and wool blend, then the fabric would be processed as a wool. If it were a Dacron polyester and cotton blend, it would be finished as a cotton.

What Are Permanent Finishes?

A fabric whose finish will retain its specific properties such as smoothness, wrinkle resistance, shrink resistance during the fabric's normal or reasonable period of wear and laundering or cleaning is considered to have a *permanent finish*.

The finisher selects the finishing treatments that are required for a fabric to perform adequately in a given use. For example, a summer sports dress

Cotton	Linen	Silk	Wool	Synthetic Fibers	
Brushing & shearing	Bleaching*	Bleaching*	WOOLENS	RAYON AND ACETATE	NYLON
Gassing & singeing	Beetling*	Water-soluble finish	Bleaching	Water-soluble finish	Heat-set*
Bleaching*	Shrinkage control*	Spot-resistant	Fulling or milling	Shrinkage control*	Plastic-resin stiffness*
Mercerizing*	Starchless*	Weighting	Preshrinkage	Moiréing*	Embossing*
Control of shrinkage	Fire-resistant	Water-repellent	Flocking	acetate-permanent	Nonslip*
Air-condi-tioning	Water-repellent	Tentering	Napping	Embossed-permanent if heat-set	Tentered
Starchless*	Wash & wear	Calendering	Tentering	Heat-set	Calendered when needed
Glazing*	Wrinkle-resistant		Steaming	Starchless*	POLYESTERS
Wrinkle-resistant	Perspiration-resistant		Sponging	Crease- or wrinkle-resistant*	Wrinkle-resistant*
Creping	Tentering		Pressing	Water-repellent*	Shape retention*
Fire-resistant	Calendering		Water-proofing	Perspiration-resistant	Heat-set*
Mildew-resistant			Water-repellent	Fire-resistant	Tentered
Water-repellent			Moth-repellent*	Napped	Calendered
Wash & wear			WORSTEDS	Tentered	ACRYLIC & MODACRYLIC
Perspiration-resistant			Fulling	Calendered	Crease-resistant*
Napping			Preshrinkage		Permanent pleating
Tentering			Napping		Water-repellent*
Calendering			Brushing		Heat-set*
			Sponging		GLASS FIBERS
			Pressing		Crimp setting*
			Water-repellent		Wrinkle-resistant*
			Moth-repellent*		

must be both colorfast to light and to washing, preferably in a mechanical washer. Hence the finish should be fast to the particular hazard it will encounter in use. For instance, if a cotton glazed chintz is used in a woman's peasant skirt, the wearer will expect to wash it and will expect it to look like new after ironing. If she cannot do so without the fabric losing its glazing, then the finish would not be considered permanent because the glazing did not remain during the fabric's normal period of wear and laundering.

The above chart gives the finishes that can generally be applied to the different fibers, remembering that a choice is made of processes in line with the intended uses of the fabric. Finishes that usually can be considered permanent are marked (*).

The use for which a cloth is intended determines the type of finish needed. Also the degree of permanency of a finish to be expected by a customer depends on the kind of finish applied and the care which is given the cloth while it is in use. Salespeople should advise their customers on the care required to insure satisfaction with a fabric's service. This information may often be obtained by reading the label attached to the fabric. A salesperson can also tell his customer to keep the label so she may refer to it when the article needs cleaning.

PUTTING THIS MERCHANDISE KNOWLEDGE TO USE

❯ DO YOU KNOW YOUR MERCHANDISE?

1. Explain four purposes of finishing processes, giving examples for each.
2. (*a*) What is the safest method of bleaching? (*b*) Why is this method not used much commercially? (*c*) How may cotton sheets be bleached at home?
3. Give the selling points for: (*a*) crush-resistant velvet, (*b*) Sanforized cotton broadcloth, (*c*) water-repellent ski cloth, (*d*) cotton flannel for sleeping pajamas, (*e*) organdy with permanent finish.
4. What is the difference between the terms *waterproof* and *water-repellent?*
5. Define: tentering, calendering, napping, flocking, brocaded velvet, embossing, weighting, grassing, preshrinkage, chemical printing.
6. How are fabrics made mildew resistant? flame resistant? perspiration resistant?

❯ INTERESTING THINGS TO DO

1. Rub a white handkerchief briskly against a piece of colored costume cambric approximately 4″ x 4″. Notice whether color is transferred to the handkerchief. If this is the case, then the cloth is heavily sized.
2. Hold the fabric against the light. Then tear the cloth quickly. Notice whether particles fly as it is torn. If so, the cloth is sized.
3. Mount part of the torn sample on a piece of paper. Then wash the other part in warm water and a neutral soap. Rub the cloth on a washboard. Dry and iron the sample. Compare the washed fabric with the unwashed cloth. Notice any difference in the weight, crispness, and color.

UNIT 13 COLORING OF CLOTH: DYEING AND PRINTING

Overheard at the fashion fabric counter:

Customer: Will the color run if I wash this fabric?

Salesperson: No, we can guarantee that it will wash satisfactorily. It has been tested by the government standard test. Here is the label.

Customer: Will it fade if I wear it in bright sunlight?

Salesperson: No. It has been tested for sunfastness too. It was found to be fast for sportswear. (Salesperson shows the customer the label that gives the rating on sunfastness.)

These are only two of the many varied questions that a salesperson may be called upon to answer regarding colored fabrics in his stock.

All the questions of this type can readily be boiled down to one: "Is the fabric colorfast?"

WHAT IS COLORFASTNESS?

If a fabric after being washed, during its normal life, shows no change of color, that fabric is colorfast to washing. If a fabric can be placed in bright sunlight for a certain number of hours without change of color, that fabric is colorfast to sunlight. If drops of water fall on a fabric and, after it is dry, leave no rings, then the cloth is considered fast to water-spotting. There are other elements such as perspiration, friction, and pressing to which many cloths are fast.

Colorfastness, therefore, means that a cloth will not change color when it is subjected to a certain element or elements for a given time.

No fabric is absolutely colorfast to all elements. If a cloth is fast to the elements required for its intended use, then that fabric will give satisfaction. For example, an evening dress should be fast to perspiration but it does not have to be fast to sunlight. A man's blue wool-flannel slacks should be fast to sunlight, to friction, to frequent pressing, and to dry cleaning, since wool flannel tends to shrink if laundered. Consequently, this fabric does not have to be fast to washing but must be fast to dry cleaning.

POINTS TO NOTICE ON A LABEL

No matter how beautiful a colored fabric may be, it will soon lose its value if it is not colorfast for its intended use. Too many times salespeople have heard complaints from customers who have been disappointed because colors faded, or ran, or rubbed off. Even a label marked *fast color* may be misleading. One salesperson sold some drapery fabric marked *fast color.* When the customer washed the draperies, they ran (or bled) in the water. She attempted to put salt in the water to prevent the colors from bleeding any further, but to no avail. The customer therefore came back to the store with her complaint.

These draperies, marked *fast color,* were fast only to sunlight. That is, they had not faded when exposed for a normal length of time to the sunlight. The colors were not fast to washing, however; therefore, the label should rightfully have read: "Fast to sunlight. Dry-clean this fabric. Do not wash."

In selling merchandise labeled *colorfast,* the salesperson should understand the meaning of the word. The word *colorfast,* unless it is qualified, means little, for it may refer to any one or more of the following: fast to washing, fast to sunlight, fast to perspiration, fast to crocking (rubbing off of the color), fast to spotting, fast to pressing, fast to dry cleaning. An ever-increasing amount of textile yardage is being made colorfast for its intended uses. Consequently, if consumers use the fabric as intended and care for it as designated on the label, they should have satisfaction from the merchandise.

Salespeople should be careful not to tell their customers that a fabric is washable when the label distinctly gives instructions to dry-clean the article. The final answer to whether a fabric is colorfast is to read the label.

UNITED STATES GOVERNMENT TESTS FOR COLORFASTNESS

The National Bureau of Standards of the U. S. Department of Commerce has set up standard tests, designated as CS 59–44 tests, to determine a fabric's fastness to sunlight, fastness to perspiration, fastness to laundering, fastness to cleaning, fastness to crocking, and fastness to dry and wet pressing. If, after subjecting a cloth to one of these tests, a fabric shows no appreciable change of color, then the retailer is safe in telling his customers that a fabric is colorfast to the element for which the cloth has been tested.

The L22 standards and those set by reliable manufacturers protect the consumer by giving her a quality of fabric suited to its intended use. Seals of approval, quality recommendations of testing bureaus, serve as consumer guides to selection of textile fabrics.

Salespeople should understand the meaning of the word *colorfast* on a label. Labels should be carefully read to understand the degree of colorfastness to be expected, and customers should be advised intelligently about the care of the fabrics they purchase.

As a rule, a fabric that is labeled *vat dyed* may be considered to possess a high degree of colorfastness and may be washed under most conditions, either in cold or in boiling water. Vat dyes used on cotton are fast to light, to perspiration, to rubbing. They will not run in washing and will not stain other materials washed with them.

For example, to determine whether a color will rub off with friction, a machine called a Crock-Meter is used. This machine has an automatic "finger" to which is fastened a white cloth. This finger passes the white cloth over the colored test sample twenty times in about ten seconds. If the white sample is not discolored, then the tested fabric is said to be "colorfast to crocking."

Suppose a manufacturer or a retailer wished to test the colorfastness of a fabric to washing. He would use the United States government standard washing test. He would use a Launder-Ometer, standard testing device, or a washing machine. Three very rigid tests must be made to determine whether the fabric must be laundered carefully at home or may be sent to a laundry.

The tests for colorfastness to perspiration, cleaning, and pressing are also standardized.

VOLUNTARY STANDARDS OF QUALITY

Textile manufacturers set up standards of quality for products they make. By so doing, the manufacturer assures his product a uniformly controlled quality.

The L22 standard is a voluntary one worked out by textile-mill men through their affiliation with various organizations, such as the American Standards Association, the American Association of Textile Chemists and Colorists, Textile Distributors Institute, American Society of Testing Materials, apparel manufacturers, and the National Retail Merchants Association who acted as sponsor. These groups, working together over several years, developed standards or minimum requirements based on features of an item of apparel that consumers considered essential in a given use. Such essentials include strength of a fabric, shrinkage, colorfastness to light, to laundering, and dry cleaning, yarn slipping or shifting, ability of fabric to keep its original touch and appearance, strength of seams and features of the garment other than the fabric. Those textile manufacturers who subscribe to the L22 stand-

 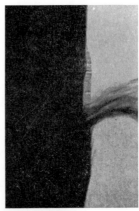 

Methods of Coloring Textile Fabrics.

Top left: Printed fabric (each yarn is black and white). **Center:** Piece-dyed fabric. **Right:** Yarn-dyed fabric (each yarn is black or white). **At left:** Cross-dyed rayon suiting with black yarns of viscose rayon and white yarns of acetate.

ards may print a tag with the L22 designation telling the customer the type of performance guaranteed for this article. This standard covers some seventy-five different items of apparel and home furnishings.

Seals of approval or certificates of having passed standard laboratory tests are worthy consumer guides to the quality of fabrics. *Good Housekeeping Magazine* stamps seals of recommendation on its satisfactory lab-tested articles. The American Institute of Laundering certifies its tested fabrics similarly; the Consumer Bureau of *Parents' Magazine,* private and public testing companies like Better Fabrics Testing Bureau and U. S. Testing Company print their seals of quality for use in advertising and labeling.

Consumers Union and Consumers' Research, nonprofit organizations, test merchandise of all kinds and rate in their monthly publications the items tested. The publication of Consumers Union is *Consumer Reports;* that of Consumers' Research is *Consumers' Bulletin.*

Information on performance of textiles can be reliable if based on standards of quality kept by government agencies and reliable mills and garment manufacturers. It therefore is important that the salesperson read all labels carefully so that he can interpret them to his customer.

HOW FABRICS ARE COLORED

The various dyeing and printing processes are discussed in the following sections.

Dyeing

By the addition of different colors and of different patterns, fabrics can be varied tremendously in appearance. Many more designs can be produced on the surface of fabrics, after they have been constructed, than can be made by structural patterns during the construction of the cloth.

Dyeing may be done in the fiber stage (*stock-dyeing*); in the yarn stage (*yarn-dyeing*); or after a cloth is woven (*piece-dyeing*). The dyes can best penetrate the fibers in stock-dyeing. Whenever a yarn is composed of a number of colors, the fibers of various colors are mixed together in a vat before the yarn is spun. This method of stock-dyeing can produce fast colors, and it is frequently used in wool fabrics. Next come fabrics dyed in the yarn before weaving. In general, yarn-dyeing produces faster colors than piece-dyeing, in which the woven fabric is immersed in a dye bath to produce a solid color, or printed fabric, because the dyes can more easily penetrate the yarn than the cloth itself. The method of dyeing, whether stock, yarn, or piece, is only one factor that determines the colorfastness of the dye. Other points to be considered are the chemical content of the dyestuff itself and the affinity (attraction) of the dye for the particular fibers.

Cross-dyeing is another way of piece-dyeing fabrics that are made of a mixture of animal and vegetable fibers. Since animal and vegetable fibers are dyed with different types of dyes, a dye may be used that will affect only one type of fiber, leaving the other one white, as, for example, a very fine white cotton stripe in wool suiting. If, however, the cotton-and-wool suiting is to be dyed one solid color, a *mordant* must be used. A mordant is a chemical that has an affinity (a liking) for both the dyestuff and the fabric. Color can be mixed with synthetic resins and applied directly to a cloth. No preliminary treatment is necessary. This method is called *pigment dyeing or printing,* a technique developed since 1937. See left and right illustrations, page 104.

Because the variety, quantity, and uses of natural dyes are limited, and because they are expensive, they have been replaced largely by chemical dyes. The principal sources of commercial dyes used today in factories and in the home are coal-tar derivatives, by-products of the coke industry.

The selection of the proper dyestuff for a fabric to insure adequate performance in its intended use is not an easy task. The new synthetics have given the chemist complex problems; and with the advent of blends, the problem has become even more complicated.

Printing

The gay South American or Mexican designs on cotton or rayon cloths are not woven into the cloths, but are printed onto the fabrics after they are woven. Whereas in *piece-dyeing* the fabric is immersed in the dye bath, in *printing* the dyestuff is placed on the surface of the cloth, either as a design or as a solid color. The dye naturally need not penetrate as deeply in the printing. Printing can be done either by hand or by machine. Most printing today is done by machine, although there are still some beautiful designs put on by hand, often found in hand-blocked tablecloths.

Hand printing is usually more expensive, for it requires much time and hand labor. Although machine-printed fabrics also require a great amount of skill in the preparation of the design, the comparative speed in the printing process, plus the greater quantity of cloth that can be produced from the same design, lessens the expense.

Hand-printing Methods. *Hand-block* printing is done by wooden or metal blocks on each of which is cut a portion of the design to be printed. There is a separate block for each color. Each portion of the design is then stamped carefully to complete the various colors of the pattern. Since this is done by hand, there cannot be so much precision as in machine printing. Patterns in hand-block work may not be identical in spacing, and one color may run into another. Hand-blocked linen tablecloths and real India prints are examples of this type of printing.

Batik printing is quite the opposite of block printing. Instead of placing the colors directly onto the fabric, parts of the fabric are brushed with wax to resist the dye, and then the whole is dipped in the dye solution. Those parts that are not covered with wax will take the dye. This process may be

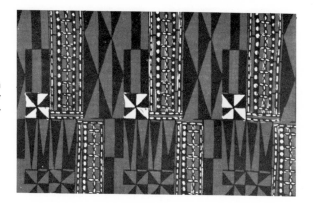

Hand Printing by Stencil on a Cotton Kimono. *(Courtesy American Craftsmen's Council)*

repeated several times so that several colors can be produced. After the dyeing is completed, the wax is removed either by dipping the fabric into a solvent like benzine, or by covering it with blotters and pressing it with a hot iron so that the melted wax is absorbed by the blotter.

Stencil printing is also a method of hand printing by which certain portions of the fabric are made to resist the dye. A stencil of paper or of metal cut in the desired design is placed over the fabric. The dye "takes" only in the cut-out spaces.

Tie-dyeing is a type of hand printing in which the designs are not very clearly outlined. It is done by tying pieces of string around parts of the cloth where the dye is to be resisted. The fabric is then dipped in the dye, and the pattern is formed generally like sunbursts. The tying and dyeing can be repeated several times with different colors, thereby producing varied effects.

Painting designs by hand is most frequently done on silk. The outline of the design is first made on the fabric with wax, and colors are then filled in with a paintbrush. Fabrics so treated are usually quite expensive because of the handwork and artistry that are required.

Airbrushing is another method of hand printing. Delicate shaded effects can be produced by using an airbrush that blows colors onto the surface of the fabric in varying amounts.

Machine-printing Methods. *Direct printing* is used on the majority of the many-colored printed fabrics on the market today. As its name implies, the colors are printed directly onto the fabric, much the same as in the hand-blocked method. Instead of individual wooden blocks that print the different parts of the design, a succession of copper rollers are used. Each roller is engraved with a part of the design, and there is a separate roller for each color. The cloth then passes between a succession of rollers until the design is complete. When they are dry, the printed fabrics are passed over hot rollers and steamed to set the colors. The design may sometimes be printed so that the pattern coincides on both sides of the fabric to imitate a woven

Methods of Machine Printing Textile Fabrics. Left: Cloth printed by direct method *(Aridye Corp.).* **Center:** Screen-printed cloth *(Roto-Matic Screen Printer, Ltd.).* **Right:** Discharge printed cloth *(Aridye Corp.).*

design that is yarn dyed. This is called *duplex* printing. The fabric is printed first on one side and then on the other, so that the outlines on each side are identical, thus giving a reversible fabric. Some examples of printed fabrics are cretonne, printed dress linen, printed percale, printed rayon and silk crepes, and printed wool challis.

Photographic printing produces some delicately shaded effects of rich coloring by reproducing a design on the cloth by a similar method to that used for newspaper photograph reproduction.

Screen printing is a method of printing cloth in which the fabric is placed under a silk screen treated to keep the dye from passing through at certain points. A "squeegee" held by a handle is pulled over the screen to spread the dye.

Printing by the Silk-screen Process. *(Courtesy the Scalamandre Museum of Textiles)*

Resist printing, like the batik or the stencil hand-printing methods, uses certain resist substances to cover those parts of the design that are not to take the dye. The design is first printed with a chemical paste that covers those places that are to resist the dye. The entire cloth is dyed, and then the paste is removed. This procedure may be repeated so that more than one color can be used. Batik, stencil, and tie-dyeing are hand methods of resist printing. Yarn-dyed fabrics in prints or checks may be imitated in the resist method by treating certain yarns chemically to resist the dye. When the piece is dipped in the dye, those yarns that have been treated will resist the dye.

Discharge printing is frequently used on fabrics that ordinarily have only two colors, such as dotted materials, or a white design with a colored background. The discharge method is just the reverse of resist. The whole cloth is first dyed one complete color, then run through a roller printed with a chemical paste that removes the color from certain portions of the fabric. The white portion from which the color has been discharged may be either the design or the background; however, the chemical used sometimes weakens the white portions. White-dotted fabrics, for example, may wear out first in the white dots, because the chemical used has weakened the fabric in those dots. In a discharge print, the colored parts of the fabric are the same color on both sides of the fabric, whereas in a cloth printed by direct printing, the colored section on the wrong side is often lighter than that on the right side.

How to Identify Piece-dyed and Printed Fabrics

To tell how a cloth is dyed, first look at the fabric. Is it all one color or are there designs in it? If the fabric is all one color, it is probably either piece dyed or yarn dyed. As it takes less dye and as it is less expensive to dye a cloth *after* weaving, the piece-dyeing method is very popular. If you unravel a solid colored linen crash or Indian Head (cotton crash), and find that the dye has not penetrated to the center of the yarn, the fabric is piece dyed.

When a cloth has a design, it is either woven-in or printed after weaving. Woven-in designs are yarn dyed. To determine whether a design is printed, unravel a yarn in the part of the cloth where the design occurs. If a yarn is of different colors, then the design is printed. If the yarn is all one color, it may be considered yarn dyed. Furthermore, if a cloth is lighter in color on the wrong side than it is on the right side, the design may be considered a "printed" one.

PUTTING THIS MERCHANDISE KNOWLEDGE TO USE ❭❭❭❭❭❭❭❭❭❭❭

❭ DO YOU KNOW YOUR MERCHANDISE?

1. To what elements should the color of a bathing suit be fast? a bed blanket? a ski suit?
2. What may the word *colorfast* mean?

3. (*a*) What is the difference between printing and dyeing? (*b*) What is meant by a piece-dyed fabric?
4. How can a salesperson determine whether a plaid fabric has been yarn dyed or printed?
5. (*a*) What is the difference between direct printing, resist printing, and discharge printing? (*b*) Give an example for each method.
6. Where do dyers obtain most of the commercial dyes they now use?

❯ INTERESTING THINGS TO DO

Make the following tests for colorfastness. When the tests are completed, mount in your scrapbook the original piece of fabric plus the tested sample. Record the results of each test opposite each fabric.

1. For colorfastness to washing: launder the colored fabric and then compare it with an original piece that has not been laundered. Note whether any change of color has occurred. Another method is to sew the colored fabric onto a white cloth, and then wash to see if the colors "bleed" or run. If only the water, and not the white fabric, is discolored, the color can be considered fast to washing.
2. For colorfastness to sunlight: place the experimental piece in the sunlight for at least two weeks. Then compare it with the original piece of cloth.
3. For colorfastness to crocking: rub a white cloth briskly over the dark fabric to be tested, and notice whether the color rubs off onto the white fabric. Wet and wring the white cloth. Rub it against the colored fabric. Notice any rubbing off of color.
4. For colorfastness to spotting: drop some water on the colored fabric, allow it to dry, and see whether spots remain.

ADDITIONAL MERCHANDISE TERMS ❯❯❯❯❯❯❯❯❯❯❯❯❯❯❯❯❯❯❯❯❯❯

Beetling is a finishing process done by flattening the yarns in order to make a smooth, firm, leathery-feeling cloth.

Brushing and shearing is a finishing process used to give cotton a smooth surface. The loose ends of cotton fibers are first raised and then cut off.

Creped fabrics have a crinkled surface produced either by printing the fabric with an alkali which causes the treated parts to shrink and the untreated parts thereby to crinkle; or by embossing.

Duplex printing is a method of direct printing in which the design is printed similarly on both sides of the fabric, thus imitating a yarn-dyed pattern.

Gassing or singeing is a finishing process that is used to remove all short ends of fuzz on the surface of a fabric by passing the cloth over a gas flame. This produces a smooth finish.

Mercerizing is a finishing process of immersing cotton yarns or cloth under tension in a bath of caustic soda. This produces a strong, lustrous, pliable cotton that is more susceptible to dye stuff than unmercerized cotton.

Milling is a process of tumbling the fabric in soap and water to shrink the fabric. It is used extensively on woolens but only slightly on worsteds to soften the cloth. Synonymous with fulling.

Shrinkage control is a finishing process for preshrinking a fabric to assure the consumer that the cloth will shrink no more than 1 per cent when laundered.

Starchless finish is one that makes a cloth permanently stiff and crisp by use of a plastic resin. No starch is used.

Wash-and-wear is a type of fabric that requires minimum care to keep its attractive appearance.

Care and Selling Points of Fabrics

CHAPTER
6

CARE OF TEXTILE CLOTHS MADE OF NATURAL FIBERS

Shall I wash it? Shall I dry-clean it? These are very common questions in a customer's mind either when she buys an item of textile merchandise or when it becomes soiled and she wants to clean it properly.

If she has these questions in mind when she buys the article, then the salesperson should answer the question. If the salesperson is familiar with the properties of textile fibers, yarns, construction, finishes, and coloring of cloth, he can apply this information. In any event, the salesperson should read the label attached to the article, because the law now requires an identification of the fibers, the manufacturer, and the country of origin if the item is imported. In addition, many manufacturers are supplying instructions for care and often some information on expected performance of the article in use.

One of the best methods of closing a sale is for the salesperson to be able to tell the customer how to care for that particular article. For instance, if he is selling wash-and-wear shirts, he can say, "Wash-and-wear Dacron polyester-and-cotton blends require little or no ironing when hand-washed or when slow-spin rinsed by machine (no wringing) and dried on a hanger."

The N.R.M.A. is promoting the use of Sure Care Symbols which are to be attached to the article. Stores keenly interested in the use of these symbols are promoting them to aid the consumer in the care of her purchase.

The informed salesperson knows that Dacron polyester sheds wrinkles, because it is quite resilient, and also sheds water, so that Dacron polyester blended with cotton has the properties cotton needs to insure minimum care. He also knows that a polyester blended with cotton makes any "touch up" or all-over ironing easier.

Let us see first what facts can be learned about care of fabrics made

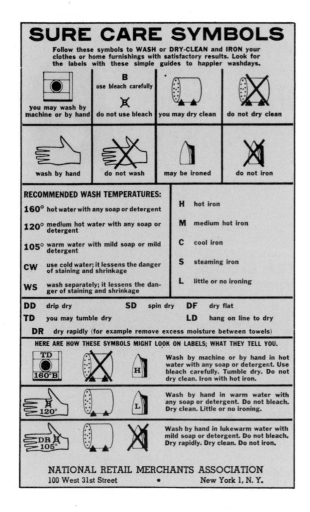

SURE CARE SYMBOLS

Follow these symbols to WASH or DRY-CLEAN and IRON your
clothes or home furnishings with satisfactory results. Look for
the labels with these simple guides to happier washdays.

	B use bleach carefully do not use bleach	you may dry clean	do not dry clean
you may wash by machine or by hand			
wash by hand	do not wash	may be ironed	do not iron

RECOMMENDED WASH TEMPERATURES:

160°	hot water with any soap or detergent	**H**	hot iron
120°	medium hot water with any soap or detergent	**M**	medium hot iron
105°	warm water with mild soap or mild detergent	**C**	cool iron
CW	use cold water; it lessens the danger of staining and shrinkage	**S**	steaming iron
WS	wash separately; it lessens the danger of staining and shrinkage	**L**	little or no ironing

DD	drip dry	**SD** spin dry	**DF** dry flat
TD	you may tumble dry		**LD** hang on line to dry
DR	dry rapidly (for example remove excess moisture between towels)		

HERE ARE HOW THESE SYMBOLS MIGHT LOOK ON LABELS; WHAT THEY TELL YOU.

TD **160°B**		**H**	Wash by machine or by hand in hot water with any soap or detergent. Use bleach carefully. Tumble dry. Do not dry clean. Iron with hot iron.
H **120°**		**L**	Wash by hand in warm water with any soap or detergent. Do not bleach. Dry clean. Little or no ironing.
DR H **105°**			Wash by hand in lukewarm water with mild soap or detergent. Do not bleach. Dry rapidly. Dry clean. Do not iron.

NATIONAL RETAIL MERCHANTS ASSOCIATION
100 West 31st Street   •   New York 1, N. Y.

entirely of one fiber. Then if we know how to care for these cloths, we can better determine how to care for blended fabrics.

CARE OF COTTON FABRICS

Proper care of fabrics will prolong their length of service; will help to keep their original appearance and texture during their use. Practically all cottons are washable because cottons are 25 per cent stronger wet than dry. Most of them are machine washable. *Washable* means that a fabric can be laundered. The method may not be given on the label.

How to Launder Cottons

Now that washing machines have been designed so that the temperature of the wash and rinse waters can be controlled, as well as the speed and time of washing action and spinning, all the laundress has to do is to sort the clothes and select the appropriate washing cycle by pushing a button or dial. Many of the new machines have special cycles for washing wash-and-wear fabrics. Some machines cool the warm wash water before rinsing and spinning, in order to avoid setting of wrinkles. In some cases, the last spin or all spins are omitted for this reason.

Mechanical Washing. All cotton fabrics, unless they have a wash-and-wear finish (synthetic resin) can go through the normal washing cycle. To all white clothes, bleach may be added according to instructions given with the washing machine. Bleach should not be used on a resin-finished cotton unless the label says so. It is inadvisable to wash white and colored clothes at the same time for two reasons: (1) any fabric that is not colorfast may run into other fabrics (nylon picks up color very quickly); (2) since warm, not hot, water should be used for washing colored fabrics, the white fabrics may not come out so white as if washed in hot water with a bleach.

All-cotton fabrics can be washed by either of three methods: (1) mechanical washer at home; (2) automatic laundry outside the home; (3) commercial laundry. Very fine sheer cottons are best washed at home. Often the label will tell what methods are suitable for the fabric. The automatic dryer can also be used for fabrics that are machine washable. Colored fabrics should be dried separately for the first few times to prevent crocking (rubbing off of dye). Sheer fabrics should be dried at low heat; knit goods, at medium heat to prevent shrinkage; all others, at high heat.

Hand Laundry. For sheer cottons and those with doubtful colorfastness, washing by hand is the safest method. To determine whether or not a fabric is hand washable, wash an inconspicuous part of the fabric in a garment first (under a collar, cuff, or arm). Let it dry before you decide to wash the entire garment. If there is a change of texture and/or fading of color, it should be sent to a dry cleaner.

If you do all your laundering by hand, light and dark colors should be washed separately. It is advisable to soak white and light clothes for 10 to 15 minutes in cool water to remove surface dirt. Colored clothes should not be soaked.

If the colored fabrics are labeled *colorfast,* they may be fast to one or more factors, such as sunlight, perspiration, washing, or crocking. Vat-dyed fabrics are usually colorfast to washing and sunlight. Colored clothes that are not guaranteed fast colors should be washed in lukewarm mild suds and hung so that the colored sections do not touch the white or light-colored parts.

To whiten discolored cottons, bleaching powders may be used, because cottons are not affected by alkalines. Bluing is used to give a blue-white appearance.

Pressing Cotton Fabrics

Medium- and heavy-weight cottons may be pressed with a hot iron. Sheer cottons must be pressed with a warm iron. For a fresh appearance, cottons should be ironed when they are fairly damp. Automatic ironers may be used on all but sheer delicate cottons.

Removal of Stains

Stains should be removed before the actual washing, as they may become "set" or fixed by laundering.

Paint, varnish, or grease may be removed with turpentine or benzine.

Bloodstains may be removed by soaking in cool water, and then washing

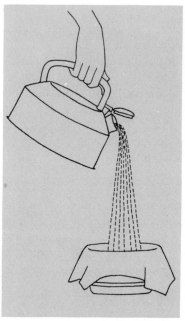

with soap and a little borax in warm water. Fresh bloodstains are much easier to remove than those that have become set.

Beverage or fruit stains can usually be removed by placing the stained part over a bowl and pouring boiling water through it from a height.

Ink. Ink eradicators are often effective, as is a treatment in which a bleach is alternated with oxalic or hydrochloric acid. These methods can be used only on white cottons, for they will bleach colored fabrics. Another method is to soak the fabrics in sour or in cultured milk such as yoghurt. After the spot disappears the fabric should be thoroughly rinsed.

Scorch. To remove scorched spots from cotton, if the fiber itself is not damaged, the fabric should be placed in the sunlight until the scorched place is bleached.

Grass stains may be removed by soaking in milk or in naphtha soap and warm water.

Iodine or mercurochrome, when fresh, may be washed out with soap and water. Old stains may be removed by soaking in alcohol.

Perspiration stains may be removed by washing in soap and water. Stains that cannot be removed in this way may be taken out by using some bleach, such as a mild solution of peroxide and ammonia.

Iron Rust. Salt and lemon juice are simple applications that often prove effective. Another method is that of holding the spot over a steaming teakettle and applying with a medicine dropper hydrochloric (muriatic) acid diluted with an equal amount of water. The application should always be followed by a rinse in clear water.

Mildew. Cottons that are not sized do not mildew easily. It is the starches, flour, gums, or chemicals used in certain processes, plus dampness, that create the mildew. Fresh mildew spots can be removed with strong soap and water, followed by sun bleaching. A solution of one teaspoon of sodium hydrosulphite in a glass of water is a very effective bleach. It must be used quickly and rinsed well to prevent destruction of color and weakening of fabric. For colored fabrics, a paste made of powdered chalk, plus exposure to sunlight, is an effective treatment.

CARE OF LINENS

Linens are easy to launder but not quite so easy as cottons. Linen fibers are weakened more quickly by alkalis than are cotton fibers. Bleaches containing chlorine or hypochlorites, if they are used cold and diluted, do not harm linen; but concentrated solutions will destroy the fiber. Borax, ammonia, phosphate of soda, laundry soap, and hot water are harmless to linen. With these points in mind, linen can be washed at home by machine or hand methods. Heavier fabrics—such as dish towels, table linens, and sheets—may be sent to a commercial laundry.

Linens, especially damask, should never be heavily starched, because the heavy iron necessary for pressing such a cloth may break the fiber. The sun is the best and the safest bleaching agent, and white linens dried in the sun will keep their whiteness.

Linens, after being washed and dried, should be sprinkled and ironed damp on the right side and then on the wrong side. To produce luster, the iron should be moved crosswise of the cloth from selvage to selvage. Face towels, like table linens, should be creased as few times as possible. All creases should be measured evenly.

Linens can be stored safely in cedar closets or chests that are not too warm. Starch should be removed from the fabric before it is stored, since starch plus dampness causes mildew. All linens should be kept away from radiators, stoves, or steampipes, because heat makes linen fibers brittle.

Since linen is a vegetable fiber like cotton, the same general rules for spot removal can be applied to linen.

CARE OF SILK

All silk cloths are classified as fine fabrics, because special care has to be given them to cleanse them properly. "Fine fabrics," however, does not mean that they are not durable. If given the proper care, they will wear longer than some fabrics that may appear stronger.

A general rule for silk is to clean it as soon as it becomes soiled. This is why silk hosiery should be washed after each wearing. Perspiration, being primarily acid, is apt to weaken silk if it is allowed to remain in the fabric. Another general rule for silk is to dry-clean it unless the label specifically says it may be washed. Then instructions on the label should be followed carefully. Dry cleaning is a method of removing soil from fabrics by means of a solvent.

Usually silks are best washed by hand. Neutral soap flakes, containing no free alkali (no laundry soap), should be used. A lukewarm soap solution should be made and squeezed through the fabric; the lukewarm rinse water should be squeezed, not wrung, from the fabric several times; the article should be rolled in a towel to absorb moisture; it should be dried slightly and ironed on the wrong side while damp. If the silk has dried completely, a damp pressing cloth should be placed over it to iron through. Dry heat will weaken the fibers in silk fabrics, which should therefore not be hung near radiators or placed in hot dryers. To remove wrinkles from silk garments, ironing through a damp pressing cloth is suggested.

Removal of Stains

Spots should be removed from silk as soon as possible. Stains may be removed as follows:

Grease stains may be removed with dry-cleaning fluid or with special chalklike ingredients that tend to absorb the grease.

Water Spots. If the fabric is weighted silk, the spot can be rubbed with tissue paper, with another part of the fabric, or with a nickel coin. The object is to equalize the weighting. If the fabric is pure silk, hold it in steam and iron damp.

Ink. Sometimes an ink stain will come out if washed in soap and water before the stain has had time to dry. If the stain does not come out or has dried, the fabric should be soaked overnight in milk, or better, in a cultured milk (yoghurt) obtained from the grocery or delicatessen. Rinse out the milk after soaking. Roll in towel and dry.

Fruit Stains. Acid-type stains can be removed by a treatment with ammonia and alcohol mixed in equal proportions. If the dye is fast, these alkalis should not injure silk if they are not left too long on the fabric before rinsing.

Coffee and Chocolate. Soft water should be poured from a height through the stain. Then the cloth should be washed in lukewarm water and soap. Cold water should remove cocoa stains.

Perspiration. One part of diluted hydrochloric acid to 75 or 100 parts of water should remove stains of perspiration.

Milk or Cream. Cold water or cold water and soap are used for these stains.

Rust. Oxalic acid, citric acid, or tartaric acid may prove useful to take out rust. After the treatment, the acid must be rinsed from the fabric.

CARE OF WOOL FABRICS

The frequent brushing of wool fabrics keeps them clean longer; any dirt on a wool fabric will mix with the oil that wool absorbs from the skin, resulting in a greasy spot. Furthermore, wools should be aired out-of-doors to remove body odors and to prevent attack by moths. Wool does not show soil readily; but once it becomes dirty, it is more difficult to clean than cotton or linen. Hence any spots or stains should be removed as soon as they are discovered. Often it is possible to remove grease spots by rubbing them up and down with warm soapy water. If the rest of the fabric is very soiled, the cleaned spot may show up in contrast to the rest of the fabric. Should a grease spot not come out with soap and water or should a ring occur, the article should be sent to a dry cleaner.

Hand-washable woolens should be treated as "fine fabrics." See the units on the care of silk, rayon, and acetates. While some labels on blankets and wool garments say that they are machine washable if cold water and the fine- or delicate-fabric setting is used, many homemakers prefer to wash small

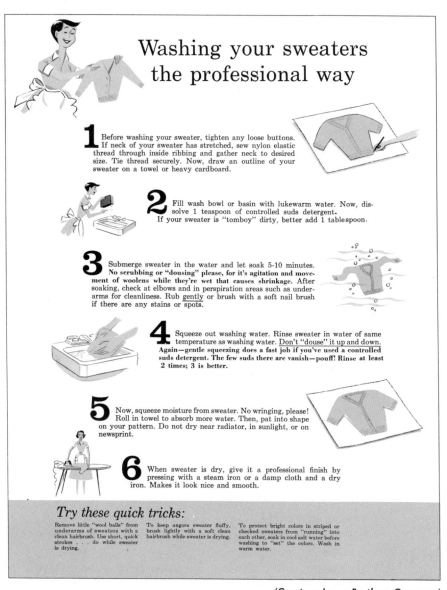

Washing your sweaters the professional way

1 Before washing your sweater, tighten any loose buttons. If neck of your sweater has stretched, sew nylon elastic thread through inside ribbing and gather neck to desired size. Tie thread securely. Now, draw an outline of your sweater on a towel or heavy cardboard.

2 Fill wash bowl or basin with lukewarm water. Now, dissolve 1 teaspoon of controlled suds detergent. If your sweater is "tomboy" dirty, better add 1 tablespoon.

3 Submerge sweater in the water and let soak 5-10 minutes. No scrubbing or "dousing" please, for it's agitation and movement of woolens while they're wet that causes shrinkage. After soaking, check at elbows and in perspiration areas such as underarms for cleanliness. Rub gently or brush with a soft nail brush if there are any stains or spots.

4 Squeeze out washing water. Rinse sweater in water of same temperature as washing water. Don't "douse" it up and down. Again—gentle squeezing does a fast job if you've used a controlled suds detergent. The few suds there are vanish—pouff! Rinse at least 2 times; 3 is better.

5 Now, squeeze moisture from sweater. No wringing, please! Roll in towel to absorb more water. Then, pat into shape on your pattern. Do not dry near radiator, in sunlight, or on newsprint.

6 When sweater is dry, give it a professional finish by pressing with a steam iron or a damp cloth and a dry iron. Makes it look nice and smooth.

Try these quick tricks:

Remove little "wool balls" from underarms of sweaters with a clean hairbrush. Use short, quick strokes . . . do while sweater is drying.

To keep angora sweater fluffy, brush lightly with a soft clean hairbrush while sweater is drying.

To protect bright colors in striped or checked sweaters from "running" into each other, soak in cool salt water before washing to "set" the colors. Wash in warm water.

(Courtesy Lever Brothers Company)

articles, like wool sweaters and hosiery, by hand. These articles are best dried on frames to insure proper size. The blend of nylon or Dacron polyester with wool improves washability, because the man-made fiber helps keep wool from shrinkage and adds strength to the fabric. Some woolens are *labeled shrink-resistant* or *shrinkage controlled* because they have had special treatment. In this case, some woolens can be automatically washed at 120 degrees (high warm) temperature, if they have fast colors.

Woolens should not be completely dried but pressed while damp through a damp cloth (wool setting). Steam ironing is suggested. Woolens should not be bleached or starched. Spots can be removed as follows:

Removal of Stains

Shine can be removed temporarily by (*a*) steaming, (*b*) sponging with a solution of ammonia in water, (*c*) felting the fabric and then raising a nap. The last process may decrease the size of the garment.

Scorched spots may be removed by sponging with lukewarm soapy water. When the fiber is really burned to the core, the cloth will probably have to be dyed a darker color.

Ink stains. See Care of Silk.

Unless the label indicates that a wool fabric has been made moth resistant, it should be cleaned and stored when not in use. A fabric may be sprayed with moth repellent. Paradichlorobenzine crystals or moth balls may be placed in the closet or chest where woolens are stored.

PUTTING THIS MERCHANDISE KNOWLEDGE TO USE ❯❯❯❯❯❯❯❯❯❯

❯ DO YOU KNOW YOUR MERCHANDISE?

1. Explain how you would launder a: (*a*) mercerized cotton broadcloth blouse, (*b*) silk-crepe scarf, (*c*) pair of all-wool socks.
2. (*a*) How would you remove a grease stain from silk? (*b*) from wool?
3. Why is it suggested that starch be removed from linen and cotton fabrics before they are stored for any length of time?
4. (*a*) Define "fine fabric." (*b*) Name a "fine fabric." (*c*) Explain how you would launder it.
5. Why is it important to sort soiled clothes before they are put in a washing machine?
6. If you spilled ink on wool-flannel slacks, how would you remove it?

❯ INTERESTING THINGS TO DO

1. (*a*) Collect, during the term, labels that are attached to apparel or household textiles. (*b*) How many of these labels give instructions for care? (*c*) How do instructions for care of fabrics differ from those you have studied?
2. (*a*) Clip 50 advertisements of wearing apparel and household textiles from newspapers featuring minimum care, drip-dry, wash-and-wear. (*b*) List all items in two columns; apparel, household textiles. (*c*) Which articles emphasize ease in care most in the advertisements?
3. If you do your own ironing, keep track, over a period of one month, of the articles that were sold to you as "minimum care" items. Which articles really needed some "touch up" or all-over ironing? If you do not do your own ironing, consult your mother or some woman who is familiar with this problem.

CARE OF FABRICS MADE OF SYNTHETIC FIBERS

CARE OF RAYONS

Like silk, rayons should be regarded as "fine fabrics." They have to be cleaned or laundered in a special way.

A fabric that can be boiled or bleached with commercial bleaches without any deteriorating effect would not be considered a fine fabric. A muslin sheet, which can be treated in this manner, is not a fine fabric. Rayon or silk sheer dresses are fine fabrics. Most wool garments have to be cleansed in a special way peculiar to wool. Such wool fabrics would be considered "fine."

Some stores have made it a practice to include cleaning instructions in a package containing rayon. Now the informative label, which many manufacturers are affixing to their merchandise, includes care of the article.

Instructions for Laundering

1. If a fabric is marked *washable,* the owner should not wait until the fabric becomes too soiled to launder it. It should be remembered that most rayons lose more strength when wet than when dry, and hence it is necessary to cleanse them gently. If there is no indication on the label as to what method to use in washing, then the owner should interpret the label to mean "hand washable." If an automatic washer is specified, the machine should be set for the washing of modern fabrics, fine fabrics, delicate fabrics, or the like. Most sturdy rayon fabrics, such as rayon twills and sharkskins, are machine washable, but one should be sure the garment seams are well bound. White and colored fabrics, fast to washing, can be laundered at 160 degrees Fahrenheit. Rayons of a sturdy type may be dried in an automatic dryer at low heat.

2. Examine the fabric for any spots, small tears or holes. Mend all tears or holes first. Mark the soiled spots with white thread, so they may be specially treated before or during washing.

3. If there is some doubt whether the dye is fast, wash an inconspicuous part of the fabric first. After the cloth is dried, compare the washed with the unwashed portion. If there is no appreciable difference between the washed and unwashed portions, then the entire article may be washed. If there is fading or streaking, the article should be dry-cleaned.

4. Garments made of rayon fabrics that are likely to stretch or shrink should be measured carefully before hand washing.

5. Make suds in a bowl with lukewarm water (about 90 degrees) and neutral soap flakes (no free alkali).

6. For hand washing, the hands should make a cupping motion to force the soap solution through the fabric. Very soiled spots should be given more

of this treatment than the rest of the fabric. In case one soapy water does not suffice to clean the fabric, use as many as are needed—do not increase the temperature of successive waters. Bleaching is needed only very occasionally. If the cloth has a resin-type finish, the fabric should not be bleached unless the label so states. Rayon may be starched if a crisp feeling is desired.

7. For rinsing, use clear water of 100 degrees Fahrenheit.

8. Do not wring the fabric. Roll it in a Turkish towel and knead out the moisture into the towel. Unroll the towel at once. Lay the garment or article flat and gently pull it to shape. Throw woven rayons over a line or a chair. Knitted underwear, sweaters, and knitted dresses should be dried flat on a table or board, because if knitted garments are hung, they may stretch and dry longer and narrower than the original measurements. Clothespins and clothes hangers should be avoided when fabric is wet, as these often leave permanent distortions in the fabric. Then, too, the weight of the fabric may start a runner.

9. Rayons, if dried out-of-doors, should be hung in a cool shaded spot. Some rayons may be weakened by ultraviolet rays of the sun. Rayons should not be dried near a radiator or a hot stove.

10. Rayon sheer and loosely constructed dress fabrics and underwear may be ironed with the iron set to "rayon" which is warm, not hot; they should be ironed on the wrong side when the garments are slightly damp. If the garment is bone dry, a damp pressing cloth of ordinary muslin sheeting should be placed over the fabric. By placing a wool cloth between the pressing cloth and the fabric, a hotter iron may be used to remove deep wrinkles. A steam iron protects the fabric, and no dampening is needed to press dry fabrics.

Sturdy rayons can be ironed like cotton because rayon and cotton are cellulosic.

Fabrics which must be dry-cleaned should be sent to a reliable cleaner. It is not recommended that dry cleaning be done at home.

A deodorant may weaken a rayon fabric. Let the deodorant dry thoroughly before putting on a dress or blouse.

CARE OF ACETATE FABRICS

It should be remembered that acetate is a combination of vegetable and chemical properties; therefore, the care of acetate will differ somewhat from that of rayon, which is an all-vegetable fiber.

Like rayons, acetates are "fine fabrics" and must be cared for as such. And, like rayon, acetate loses some of its strength when wet; but some sturdy, well-constructed acetate fabrics may be machine washable provided the wash load is light and the washing time is short. *Wash load* refers to the number of garments or pounds that can be put in an automatic washer at one time. Avoid wrinkles by taking fabrics out before the spin-drying cycle. Colored fabrics can generally be washed safely at 100 degrees Fahrenheit, while some heavy, sturdy white fabrics will stand 160 degrees but more safely 120 degrees (high warm). White fabrics should be washed separately from colored ones. Usually an automatic dryer is not recommended; but, if used, low heat is required.

If the label indicates that the fabric is hand washable, the article must be washed by hand and the instructions for rayon will apply. While the fabric is still dripping wet (do not wring), hang it on a hanger and let it drip over a tub or bowl. If pressing of an acetate fabric is needed, do so as lightly as possible on the wrong side while the cloth is slightly damp. Since acetate is a plastic, it must be ironed at heat as low as possible or else the fibers will fuse or glaze. Once this happens, there is no remedy for it.

Acetate and rayon blends, if labeled *machine washable,* should be put in a light wash load and a short washing time. (See temperatures for water in the preceding paragraphs.) Articles should be removed before the spinning cycle to avoid wrinkles and hung to *drip dry.* This is a method of drying a fabric without wringing or squeezing it. Men's slacks may be put on stretchers. If some pressing is needed, use a low heat setting.

CARE OF NYLON

Test the washability by washing some inconspicuous part of the article first (say the hem). If that part washes satisfactorily, then the entire item may be washed similarly. If the article is a mixture of nylon and some other fiber, then the fabric should be laundered as if it were made entirely of the other fiber. Soft water, a synthetic detergent, or a soap-and-water softener in warm water is advisable. Nylon fabrics may be washed by machine or by hand depending on their sturdiness. In any case, any instructions on the label should be followed. Bleaches such as are used on cotton are suitable, but instructions on the bottle should be followed. White articles should be washed separately from colored clothes because nylon picks up dye easily.

Some fabrics are heat set and may need no ironing, because nylons drip dry. If an automatic dryer is used, it should be set to low heat. Spin drying will cause wrinkles. Curtains, for instance, can be washed and rehung with neither ironing nor stretching. A moderate iron (set for rayon) is satisfactory for nylon. If the iron is tried first on a seam, then the correct temperature can be determined.

Any cleaning fluid satisfactory for other fibers can be used on nylon. Again, a small inconspicuous spot may be tested first, or the article can be sent to a reliable cleaner.

Nylons stored in a dark, cool place (like a bureau drawer) do not deteriorate.

CARE OF ACRYLICS

In almost every case, acrylic fibers are washable; however, if acrylics are blended with other fibers, the other fiber should be considered. In any case, the washing instructions on the label should be kept and followed. Acrylic fabrics drip dry and require little or no ironing. If the fabric is ironed, it should be set to "rayon." For brand names of acrylic fibers, see Chapter 2.

With most of the man-made fibers, a detergent rather than a soap helps to overcome static electricity. A *detergent* is an agent or solvent used for cleansing a fabric. Detergent is applied to washing products called "synthetic detergents" as opposed to soap. Brand names include: Tide, Vel, Dreft, All, and many others. *Soap* is a cleansing agent produced by the action of caustic soda and a fat.

CARE OF THE MODACRYLICS

The same rules for laundering nylon and acrylics should be followed for modacrylics. However, since this class of generic fibers is not so resistant to heat as the acrylics, it is preferable to use a hand electric iron with a cotton pressing cloth between the fabric and the iron. A steam iron is not recommended. The iron temperature should be set to "rayon."

CARE OF THE POLYESTERS

The rules for caring for nylon should be followed. Polyesters blended with cotton dry faster, resist wrinkling, and are easier to iron.

CARE OF VINYL-TYPE FIBERED FABRICS—SARAN, VELON

Since fabrics made of these fabrics do not absorb moisture, upholsterings made of them can be wiped clean with a damp cloth or stubborn stains can be removed by brushing with soapy water. Usually, the color is a part of the fiber, so there is no danger of the color rubbing off. Like all plastics, cloths made of these fibers drip dry. When vinyl fibers are blended with fibers of other kinds, the instructions for care should be followed implicitly.

MAN-MADE METALLIC FIBERS AND THEIR CARE

A plastic commonly used to make this fiber is of a polyester variety; therefore, fabrics made of these yarns should be cared for like the polyesters.

The fabrics made with some natural metallic core yarns should be cared for according to the way the other fibers and yarns in the cloth would be cared for.

CARE OF GLASS-FIBERED CLOTHS

Cloths made of glass fibers can be wiped clean with a damp soapy cloth or by dunking them in a tub of soap and water and then hanging them without wringing to drip dry. Curtains made of glass fibers can be hung at the windows immediately after washing to drip dry. Fabrics made of these fibers do not soil easily, because glass does not absorb moisture or collect dirt. While draperies of glass fibers can be dry-cleaned, some cleaners object to doing them because fibers sometimes loosen, come off, and may clog the machines eventually.

PUTTING THIS MERCHANDISE KNOWLEDGE TO USE ❯ ❯ ❯ ❯ ❯ ❯ ❯ ❯ ❯ ❯

❯ DO YOU KNOW YOUR MERCHANDISE?

1. How would you clean an automobile seat cover made of Saran?
2. Describe the procedure for washing a 100 per cent spun Orlon acrylic sweater.
3. Give instructions for laundering a woman's white nylon slip.
4. Give instructions for laundering a baby's all Dacron polyester bonnet.
5. What precautions should be taken in ironing an all acetate sharkskin blouse?
6. Explain how you would launder an acetate-and-nylon blend used in men's slacks.

❯ INTERESTING THINGS TO DO

1. From a scrap bag select some fabrics that you think are made of synthetic fibers.
   Unravel a few yarns from each sample. Drop these yarns in acetone, a small bottle of which you can obtain from a drugstore. Watch the result for about 5 minutes. Acetate will dissolve. Describe in your scrapbook the effect acetone had on acetates and on the other materials.
2. Use the same samples as for the previous experiment. Set the electric iron to the temperature used on cotton fabrics. When the iron is at the maximum heat, iron each fabric in turn. Note the effect of heat on acetate.
3. In the textile or chemistry laboratory, take yarns or small pieces of fabric containing as many of the synthetic fibers as possible. (*a*) *Alkali Test.* Boil for 5 minutes in a 10 per cent solution of sodium hydroxide. Rinse out the solution and put the residue on blotting paper. Which fibers were dissolved? Which fibers will be weakened or destroyed by alkaline soaps and bleaches? Write up the results in your scrapbook. (*b*) *Acid Test.* Place a similar set of fabrics or yarns in concentrated sulfuric acid for 5 or 10 minutes. Take care not to touch the solution with your hands, but use glass rods to stir and tongs to remove residue to a blotting paper. Which fibers were dissolved? What effect would acid perspiration or antiperspirants containing mild acid have on rayon fabrics?

UNIT 16 SELLING POINTS OF TEXTILE FABRICS

The customer has become increasingly well informed about the merchandise she is buying. Research surveys show that a customer will "shop" many stores, learn many facts about color and design, texture, wearing quality, prices of carpets before she finally makes a purchase.

Furthermore, consumers as a group have made our government realize that they want to know what they are buying. The result has been The Wool Products Labeling Act and Rules of Trade Practice for various segments of the textile industry; that is, hosiery, shrinkage control, silk finishes, etc. Also the F. T. C. is responsible for the generic fiber classifications under the Textile Fiber Products Identification Act.

If the customer knows what she wants, the salesperson should certainly know what he has to sell. The selling points of an article that a salesperson presents should be the same points the intelligent customer considers when she buys that article. For example, Miss Lane wants to buy a pair of Bermuda shorts to wear during a weekend visit to the country. She knows her hostess has a badminton court and plays the game frequently. Should the weather be slightly cool, Bermuda shorts would be more comfortable than short shorts. The salesperson finds her size in black corduroy and conducts her to a fitting room.

The buying point that Miss Lane had in mind was *suitability* for a particular use, namely, for playing badminton during a weekend in the fall. The chief selling point for the salesperson to stress was the *suitability* of the dark-colored fabric for active sport during a cool fall weekend in the country. It is apparent that *buying points* are the features of an article that a customer considers in buying, while *selling points* are the features of an article that a salesperson stresses in selling. In reality, *selling points* are *buying points*.

SELLING POINTS OF COTTON FABRICS

Let us find out what a salesperson of all-cotton fabrics can tell about them; in other words, their *selling points*.

The salesperson should tell his customer that cotton fabrics are:

1. *Economical* because cotton is one of the most plentiful fibers.

2. *Versatile* because cotton can be used for many purposes—as a sturdy fabric for stratosphere balloons and the sails of boats and as the sheerest organdie or batiste for women's or infants' wear.

3. *Easy to care for* because cottons are usually machine washable at home, colorfast when vat dyed, preshrunk when Sanforized. Many garments and household textiles can be sent to a commercial laundry. The synthetic resin finishes on cottons will give them quick drip-drying features and little or no ironing.

4. *Styled attractively* for apparel and accessories, as well as for household textiles. Some textures are shiny (polished) like silk; some are napped to resemble wool; while others are bumpy to give the handmade look.

5. *Comfortable* because cotton is absorbent. For knitted underwear and men's shirts, cotton is appropriate because it absorbs perspiration. Cotton is a vegetable fiber; and in summer, cotton fabrics, particularly in sheer weight, are cool. On the other hand, napped cottons are relatively warm.

6. *Durable,* when cotton is spun into strong yarns and woven into close, well-balanced cloths (warp and filling counts nearly equal).

SELLING POINTS OF LINEN FABRICS

1,500 WOMEN'S 100% LINEN HANDKERCHIEFS
in Colorful Gay Floral Prints (colorfast).
Regularly 65¢ each. Now 2 for $1.
Handkerchiefs—Street Floor.

Mrs. Dorn clipped this advertisement from her morning paper and resolved to go to the store immediately before all the linen prints were sold.

Why was Mrs. Dorn so anxious to buy some of these handkerchiefs? She was price conscious and therefore knew that this price was very low for an all-linen handkerchief. She also knew that linen is stronger than cotton and that linen yarn will not lint as cotton does. It launders easily too.

The salesperson should tell the customer that linen fabrics are:

1. *Versatile.* Linens, like cottons, can be used for many purposes—for apparel, for the table, for home furnishings. A linen towel (if in a good quality) is particularly suitable for drying dishes because it does not lint.

2. *Scarce.* Since the United States grows only a small amount of linen for fiber (mainly in Oregon), we have to depend on importation for our supply.

3. *Cool,* because linen is a vegetable fiber. Linen fabrics in sheer weights are very comfortable in summer. In this case, comfort would also be a selling point because linen fabrics will improve the personal well-being of the wearer.

4. *Easy to care for and hygienic,* because hot water and soap do not harm the linen fibers; like cotton, they are stronger when wet than when dry. Most linens are machine washable. Linen does not soil as quickly as cotton because the fibers are smoother, harder, and longer. Linens can be finished to drip dry. They can also be made wrinkle resistant.

5. *Durable* because linen fiber is longer and stronger than cotton fiber of the same size.

SELLING POINTS OF SILK FABRICS

It was stated that silk fabrics are "fine fabrics" because they require special care. The salesperson can tell the customer also that silk fabrics are:

1. *Attractive* because they can be made in sheer and dainty textures. Silk is the finest of the natural fibers—so fine that it weighs very little when

Two labels showing fiber content of fabric.

packed for traveling. Silk takes a deep, rich dye, so that the colors of silk fabrics are varied and beautiful. Satins and velvets have a luxurious sheen.

2. *Easy to drape* in graceful folds. This quality of silk is due to the fact that silk is very elastic. This same quality of elasticity accounts for the fact that the wrinkles tend to hang out overnight.

3. *Warm* in proportion to their weight, because silk is an animal fiber and therefore keeps the heat near the body.

4. *Durable* because the silk fiber is the strongest natural fiber in commercial use. The durability of silk is shown by the fact that many silk gowns of generations past, which are now exhibited in museums, are in a perfect state of preservation.

SELLING POINTS OF WOOL FABRICS

Before a salesperson shows a customer a coat, suit, or dress, he should determine the use for which the garment is intended. Woolen cloths have characteristics that are quite different from worsted cloths, and consequently the salesperson should find out how the customer expects to use these fabrics. For example,

Woolen cloth is generally:
1. *Soft* because woolens have
    a. short, elastic wool fibers
    b. slack-twisted, carded yarn
    c. fuzzy or hairy surface

Worsted cloth is generally:
1. *Firm* because worsteds have:
    a. longer fibers
    b. tighter twist yarn
    c. harder surface

Woolen cloth is generally:

2. *Comfortable* because of
   a. the thermostatic (warmth quality of wool fibers)
   b. elasticity of the fabric
   c. ease in tailoring

3. *Attractive* because of
   a. soft, cushionlike texture
   b. deep, rich colors
   c. good draping quality

Worsted cloth is generally:

2. *Durable* because of
   a. tightly twisted combed yarn
   b. close weave
   c. clear surface (with the exception of sparse nap on a worsted flannel)

3. Easy to keep pressed because of
   a. tightly twisted yarn
   b. close weave
   c. hard surface

In general, woolen fabrics are less expensive than worsteds and can be more easily adulterated (mixed with poorer grades of raw materials) than worsteds.

SELLING POINTS OF RAYON AND ACETATES

Because of the difference in chemical composition of the fibers, acetates have properties different from the rayons. These physical properties affect the fiber in use. Following are the general selling points of both rayons and acetates:

1. The lustrous or the dull rayon is *fast to laundering* and should not change luster in use.

2. Rayons *take dye well;* that is, they have good color and are reasonably fast to light and laundering if the fabric is well finished.

3. White fabrics tend to *remain white* after laundering or exposure to light. They are not apt to yellow with age.

4. Rayons and acetates *resist light better than silk*—an important factor in draperies. Acetate is more resistant to light than rayon.

5. Although some rayon and acetate yarns are weaker when wet, their *original strength returns after they dry.* Newer types of rayon have greater tensile strength when wet. Under humid conditions, some rayon yarns become tender, but return to their original condition after the humidity has left.

6. Fabrics *do not mold or mildew,* and are not affected by salt water (important factor in use at seashore for garments and draperies).

7. Acetate does not absorb readily; it therefore *does not soil easily* or retain perspiration odor. Rayon absorbs perspiration readily and therefore keeps the skin dry.

8. The fibers *may be processed* (cut) *to resemble natural fibers.*

9. Because the *fibers lack elasticity,* garments may bulge or possibly break at points of strain. A crease-resistant finish will do much to overcome this drawback. For example, a resilience is given to pile that makes it resist crushing and enables it to come back to its original condition when pressure is removed and when it is exposed to the air.

When the manufacturer places an informative label on a fabric, he usually stresses any special finishes that have been applied to the fabric. These special finishes—such as sunfast, vat dye, crease-resistant, water-repellent, permanent moiré—all add selling points for the fabric. In case the garment costs slightly more because of the special finishes applied, then the label shows the salesperson how to justify the additional cost.

Information about finishes on a label tells the salesperson what the customer can expect of the fabric in use. The customer therefore should carefully consider what she expects of the garment or home furnishing in use and let this be a guiding factor in selection.

10. Acetate is affected by heat more than rayon; therefore, acetates *should be ironed with a warm,* but not a hot *iron.* Acetates may be injured by dry-cleaning fluids containing acetone or chloroform. It is quite important that a dry cleaner know that a fabric contains acetate.

11. *Acetate* fabrics are *warmer than rayons* because acetates are poorer conductors of heat.

SELLING POINTS OF NYLON FABRICS

The salespeople who have sold nylon fabrics will know that:

1. Nylon *is elastic,* an important factor in knitted goods. Fabrics whose fibers possess elasticity do not wrinkle as much as inelastic materials, for example, hosiery.

2. Nylon *filaments, when dry, are stronger than any other fibers* (twice as strong and only half as heavy as the same size of aluminum wire). Because of nylon's strength, one filament can be used as a yarn; therefore, nylon hosiery can be very sheer yet reasonably strong. Hence garments made of nylon will be durable.

3. Nylon *does not mildew* and is not attacked by moths.

4. Nylon can be dyed with the same dyestuffs as used for acetates. It *can be dyed* in various colors—*in the yarn or in the piece.*

5. Nylon *dries quickly,* because it is smooth and retains little moisture. This is important for articles like hosiery, girdles, underwear, blouses, bathing suits, and boat sails.

6. Nylon is *wear and tear resistant.* For uses in hosiery, reinforcements, and blanket bindings, this is an important selling point.

7. Nylon *can be heat-set.* This means that the article will keep its shape, and pleats stay in permanently.

SELLING POINTS OF FABRICS MADE OF ACRYLIC FIBERS

Most women consumers and some men are familiar with the cashmerelike feeling of the Orlon acrylic sweater. The salesperson, therefore, can tell his customers that acrylic fibers are:

1. *Soft* when made of staple fibers in spun yarns.

2. *Warm,* especially when "high bulk" yarns containing many small air pockets are used. In pile fabrics, acrylics resemble fur.

3. *Bulky* but not heavy because acrylic spun yarn is fluffy (a loftiness) and contains small air pockets for warmth but little weight.

4. *Comfortable.* The fact that acrylics are warm and lightweight makes fabrics made of them desirable for winter apparel and blankets.

5. *Varied textures* are possible. Smooth, shiny fabrics are produced by using filament yarns; soft downy textures are made with spun yarns.

6. *Good resistance to sunlight, soot, smoke, fumes* and thus are well adapted to use in curtains, carpets, and sportswear.

7. *Easy to care for* because they resist wrinkling, shrinking, sagging, stretching or wilting. They need little or no ironing.

8. *Good colorfastness.* Dyed in a wide color range; they can be solution dyed.

SELLING POINTS OF FABRICS MADE OF MODACRYLIC FIBERS

The salesperson should know that these fibers are not completely acrylonitrile (ack-ril-o-nye-tril)—a chemical compound derived from coal, air, water, petroleum, and limestone. Properties of modacrylics will therefore be somewhat different from the acrylics.

The salesperson may tell his customer that generally the modacrylics are:

1. *Warm* and *soft* to the touch.

2. *Nonallergic,* so that they make excellent soft stuffings for pillows and comforters.

3. *Resilient.* This property keeps the fibers from matting.

4. *Nonabsorptive.* For this reason a pile fabric does not weaken or flatten. If rain or snow hits a pile fabric, it dries rapidly. Fabrics, therefore, are particularly suited for coat collars, mittens, hoods of parkas. Blended with other fibers, modacrylics are used in furlike coat fabrics for women. The price is far less than for fur.

5. *Resistant to ultra violet light, to fire, inorganic acids, bacteria,* and *abrasion.* Some of these modacrylics have better heat resistance than others, but none of them are outstanding in this property. *Abrasion* means the act of rubbing or wearing away.

SELLING POINTS OF FABRICS MADE OF POLYESTERS

Most salespeople know that Dacron polyester fibers have been used successfully for men's ties. Since these accessories have to be tied many times, they must be wrinkle resistant. Consequently, the salesperson can tell his customer that polyesters are:

1. Very *wrinkle resistant* and springy both wet and dry.

2. *Resistant to dirt, stains,* and *moisture* because these fibers are non-absorptive.

3. *Smooth* and *crisp looking* even in humid weather.

4. *Easy to care for.* They drip dry and require little or no ironing. Pleats

and creases in trousers can be "heat set" to last through many wearings and washings.

5. *Resistant to sun,* to *abrasion,* to *moths.*

6. *Nonallergic.* Suitable for pillow stuffing.

7. *Lightweight and strong,* therefore durable.

Since vinyon, azlon, olefin are not yet used extensively in soft lines, their selling points need not be learned by salespeople until there is more extensive use in these lines.

SELLING POINTS OF FABRICS MADE OF VINYL PLASTIC FIBERS

Salespeople should tell their customers that fabrics of these fibers are:

1. *Tough* and *strong.* This is why tennis racquet strings, outdoor furniture, and automobile seat covers are made of this class of fibers. A monofilament yarn can be used for curtains.

2. *Quick drying* and easy to clean (wipe off).

3. *Resistant to mildew, moths, abrasion, soil, grease,* and *chemicals.*

SELLING POINTS OF SPANDEX FIBERS

1. *Resilient, form-fitting* properties. This is why spandex has become so popular in foundation garments and tops of men's socks.

SELLING POINTS OF CLOTHS MADE OF METALLIC FIBERS

These fibers have:

1. A *luxurious appearance* whether they be made of real gold, silver foil, or aluminum.

2. *Resistance* to *sunlight, abrasion, chemicals,* etc., insofar as the plastic components of their man-made fibers are resistant to these elements. Core yarns are resistant to dyestuffs since the foils used to wrap the yarn are resistant.

3. *Durable* because synthetics and metal laminated are strong. Core yarns are essentially ply yarns, they therefore are strong.

SELLING POINTS OF FABRICS MADE OF GLASS FIBERS

Salespeople should be familiar with the selling points of glass fibers as used in draperies and curtains, for they appear most frequently in this area. They should tell their customer that glass fibers are:

1. *Fireproof* and therefore are well-suited for draperies and curtains in the home or in theater lobbies and hotels.

2. *Nonabsorptive,* therefore dry rapidly.

3. *Strong* but have limited stretch, although this feature has been improved.

4. *Resistant to microorganisms* or *insects,* and *sunlight.* They can be made wrinkle resistant. They can be "heat set" and can be treated to resist abrasion.

5. *Water repellent* because the fibers are nonabsorptive.

SELLING POINTS OF CLOTHS MADE OF RUBBER YARNS

These fabrics are made of yarns either of natural or of synthetic rubber. In any case, the coagulated rubber thread is used as a core of a yarn with rayon, cotton, or other fibers wrapped around it.

Fabrics with rubber yarns have:

1. *Elastic* and *enduring form-fitting properties;* therefore are well-suited for bathing suits, garters, suspenders, surgical bandages, and tops of hosiery.

2. Properties of the fibers wrapped around them.

SELLING POINTS OF BLENDS (Fabrics Made of Blended Yarns)

It would be impossible to discuss the selling points of all possible blends. Furthermore, not all possible blends have been discovered nor their uses studied. Accordingly, let us consider some of the most common blends.

55 per cent Dacron polyester and 45 per cent wool in men's suiting. The fabric has a wool-like feel and appearance. Dacron polyester gives durability and ease of care. Researchers have found that 50 per cent or more of Dacron polyester is needed in the blend to bring out its best qualities, namely, wrinkle-resistance, crease and shape retention, and nonabsorptive quality.

65 per cent Dacron polyester and 35 per cent cotton in a man's shirt or woman's blouse. The fabric has the absorbency of cotton, together with the minimum-care features of Dacron polyester.

If acrylic fibers are blended with other man-made or natural fibers, the acrylics contribute ease of care, shape retention, and strength. (Acrylics may also contribute bulkiness without being heavy and warm.) Other fibers can bring to the fabric absorbency or cross-dyed textures and effects.

PUTTING THIS MERCHANDISE KNOWLEDGE TO USE ❯ ❯ ❯ ❯ ❯ ❯ ❯ ❯ ❯ ❯

❯ DO YOU KNOW YOUR MERCHANDISE?

1. Give the selling points of the following rayon fabrics: (*a*) crease-resistant transparent velvet, (*b*) sanitized rayon shoe lining, (*c*) printed rayon shantung dress, (*d*) rayon curtains.
2. Why would a customer prefer all-linen dish towels to all-cottons?
3. Give reasons why silk can be considered a luxury fabric.
4. Give the selling points of the following fabrics for use in wool slacks: (*a*) wool flannel (woolen), (*b*) worsted flannel (worsted).
5. Why are mothproofing treatments valueless on nylon, acrylic, polyester, and other synthetic fibers?
6. Why are Orlon acrylic sweaters warm and comfortable?
7. Why are beach-chair seats frequently made of Saran fibers?

1. In the classroom, feel and carefully examine at least five fabrics whose fiber content you know. Write the selling points of each fabric. If possible, place each fabric in your scrapbook and opposite each cloth, write its selling points.
2. (*a*) Read the labels on the bed pillows that you have in your home. (*b*) List the fibers used for stuffing. (*c*) What are the selling points of each kind of fiber?
3. (*a*) Clip newspaper advertisements for wool clothing. (*b*) List the selling points given in each advertisement.

ADDITIONAL MERCHANDISE TERMS ❯❯❯❯❯❯❯❯❯❯❯❯❯❯❯❯❯❯❯❯❯❯

Bluing is a liquid, bead, or flake-type tint which makes fabrics appear whiter.

Fused means that textile fibers have been melted with heat. Slight fusion will make pleats in dresses and trousers permanent.

Nonallergic means that a substance contained in an article (a stuffing, a dye, or a finish) does not cause a person to have an unpleasant reaction.

Touch-up refers to pressing certain portions of a fabric with an electric or steam iron in order to give a smoother appearance.

Washing cycle is the time the automatic washer takes to cleanse a load of clothes (normally 30 minutes).

Water softener is a chemical compound added to the rinse water and/or the soap to prevent the formation of soap film that may make a fabric appear gray.

Color, Line, and Design In Clothing and Home Furnishings

CHAPTER

7

UNIT 17 CHOICE OF COLOR FOR CLOTHING

If you are short in stature, how many times have you wished you could be taller? If you are very tall for your age, how many times have you envied the person who is of average height? You may have wished you were smaller in the hips or broader in the shoulders. Maybe you would like to be both broader and taller, or possibly shorter and narrower.

Your secret desires can be fulfilled at least partially by selecting a garment with features that do for you what you want.

COLOR FASHIONS

Most of our fabrics are either solid color or patterned. By *patterned* we mean that either (1) the design is woven or knitted into the cloth by the use of different colored yarns in the form of checks, plaids, stripes, geometrical (dobby), or Jacquard designs; or (2) the designs are printed on the cloth by rollers, photography, screen, stencil, wood block, and others. A *design* is an arrangement of forms and/or colors intended for use or ornament in or on various materials.

The solid or mottled colors are usually raw stock (fiber dyed) or piece dyed. Solid colors may be more in fashion during one season than they are in another. Often a plain-color season follows one or two popular-print seasons. It seems that women become tired of prints sooner than they do of plain colors.

HOW TO ANALYZE A COLOR

For purposes of this discussion, *color* is a sensation which, for most people, affects them pleasantly or otherwise. These effects of color are psychological and personal. As a salesperson, you should not try to have a customer buy a color that she dislikes, even though it may be stylish. A customer will be more satisfied with colors that appeal to her.

Color is any one of the hues of the rainbow or spectrum or any tint produced by the blending of those hues. A *hue* is an attribute of color by which colors may be described as red, yellow, green, or blue; or as intermediate between these, as red-yellow or yellow-green. The intensity of a color is called *chroma,* the degree of departure from white.

CLASSIFICATION OF COLORS

Colors can be classified as *chromatic* and *achromatic.* Chromatic colors are, for example, reds, greens, purples, browns, and pinks. Achromatic colors are black, white, and their intermediates—various shades of gray. If a chromatic color and white are combined, we have a *tint.* A chromatic color combined with black will make a dark color called a *shade.* When black and white are combined, we have a grayish color, depending on the amount of each present. Tints and shades constitute the *value* of a color. Hence the three measurements of color are hue, chroma, and value. All three measurements are important in color identification. Colors can be further classified as *primary, secondary,* and *tertiary. Primary colors* are those from which all other colors may be derived or obtained by mixture. The primary colors are red, yellow, blue, as mixed in pigments for printing. The mixing of red and yellow produces the secondary chromatic color, orange; similarly, yellow mixed with blue produces green; and blue mixed with red produces purple. Mixing of secondary colors produces tertiary colors; for example, purple mixed with green gives a grayed aqua. The best way to learn about these combinations is to practice mixing paint. The chromatic colors, based on their positions in the spectrum, may be laid out in a color wheel as on page 131.

Color Harmony

To determine what colors go together, take a fabric color and analyze it somewhat as follows:

Powder blue, as to chromatic color, belongs to the blue-green family; as to white, considerable white has been used both to whiten the blue and to dull it; as to black, very little is used, the purpose being to gray it a little.

Color harmony is a combination of those colors that have something in common. They may have the same amount of lightness and darkness; they may belong to the same color family, or they may contrast.

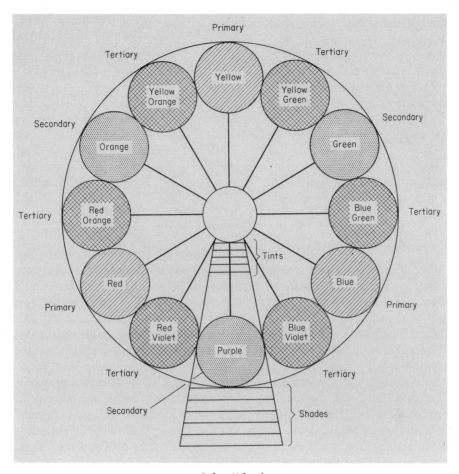

> > Color Wheel < <

Blended Harmony.   Colors blend when they belong to the same color family but are in different shades of a particular color. For example, two blues would be in blended harmony if both are in the same position in the color wheel or spectrum but one is darker than the other. Likewise, a pure blue will harmonize with a blue-green or blue-purple.

Contrasted Harmony.   When two colors contrast sharply they may make a pleasing effect. For example, two reds of the same color but widely separated in tone (one dark red and the other pink) would be a contrasted color scheme. To use together complementary colors is another way to create contrasted harmony. Complementary *colors* are opposites on the color wheel, shown above. When complementary colors are mixed together, they produce gray. Green complements red; purple complements yellow; and orange complements blue. Similarly, red-orange complements blue-green. It has been found by experiment that a degree of deviation from a complementary color produces an especially pleasing effect. Thus, instead of using a pure green in combination with red, it is probably better to use a blue-green or a yellow-green. And instead of a yellow-orange with a blue-purple, use a yellow or an orange. Such complementary combinations of colors in displays have great attention value but must be used sparingly in clothing. It is often best for the complementary color to be simply an accent, such as a flower on the lapel.

Some color combinations tend to clash and should generally be avoided. They neither harmonize nor contrast. Commonly accepted examples are yellow-orange and green; or yellow-orange and red. Note how these clashing colors are related to one another on the color wheel.

PLANNING PLEASING COLOR COMBINATIONS

In addition to making sure that colors to be used together have something in common, select one color to dominate the color scheme. For instance, a blue coat of pure color would look well with a light-blue hat, matching gloves, and a pale yellow-orange scarf.

If the dominant color is dulled and toned down, the secondary color can be more intense. Here there would be a good balance because of the intensity of the secondary color (say the deep-blue hat) used in a smaller area which would balance the less intense color of the larger area, such as a gray-blue coat. The third area, perhaps a light-blue scarf, would blend with one of the main colors. If a fourth color is to be introduced in this color scheme, it should be an accent color. It can be vivid, but it should be in the smallest area. In this case, the wearer of this costume decides on some orange-red earrings. A good rule to follow is to combine no more than three colors and an accent in a costume. *Costume* is a term used to refer to all garments and accessories worn at one time.

Suitability of Colors

We have seen that we have light colors and dark colors. In the Middle Atlantic States, we think of light colors particularly for summer and dark colors for winter. Black is really the warmest color we can wear, because it stops the rays of the sun and throws none of them back. On the other hand, white is the coolest color, because it throws back the sun's rays; however, dark-colored cottons are becoming increasingly important for the city dweller. In general, light colors—such as white, lilac, pink, powder blue—tend to make the figure appear larger. Black, navy blue, dark brown, and gray are basic colors suitable to all ages. If a person has gray hair, she should not wear brown or beige unless the eyes are strikingly brown; whereas gray is usually becoming. Yellows and tans may make an older person seem sallow.

With gray hair, solid colors in dusty pastels often look well. With white hair, black and white or clear hues are appropriate.

The selection of an appropriate color or colors in a costume is pretty much of a personal matter. Determine first what colors look best on you. Be honest with yourself. You should remove all makeup from the face and wash it thoroughly with soap and water. Sit down at a window facing north. This light will show the real color of the skin and eyes. If your skin has a sallow appearance, you should avoid wearing chartreuse (yellow-green) or olive. If your skin has pinkish tones, then wearing pink will enhance your coloring. If you have a dark, ruddy, brunette coloring of the skin, then red, brown, violet, and green are usually flattering, but gray should be avoided. Blondes appear to advantage in blues, greens, and dark shades of red. Tans and yellows should be avoided. The redhead looks well in blues and greens.

Your height and weight are also important factors to consider in choosing colors for yourself. A short, slim person usually looks best in one color, preferably a light one to enhance his or her size. The short, stout figure looks best in dark, solid colors; while the tall person can wear bright colors becomingly. The normal figure can wear almost any color but should avoid all extremes.

SILHOUETTE OR LINE OF A GARMENT

A *silhouette* is the outline of a garment. You may think of the silhouette of a woman's dress or man's coat in terms of a triangle. Sometimes Dame Fashion decrees that the triangle rest on its base to emphasize the full, bell-shaped skirt or the coat fitted at the waist and flared at the bottom. In this case, the eye is attracted to the line of the skirt. Consequently, the width of shoulders and bust is minimized. Then again, the triangle may be inverted so that the top is emphasized by broadening the shoulders. Enlarging the size of the sleeves will also give a broadening effect. If the eye is attracted to the shoulders, then the size of the waist and hips is minimized.

Another principle of line concerns the use of vertical and horizontal lines. To make a tall person seem shorter, he or she should emphasize the horizontal, not the vertical line. A woman can wear horizontal stripes or inserts of lace in a gown to bring down her height. A short person, on the other hand, emphasizes the vertical line to appear taller. A short, slender woman may wear narrow vertical stripes to give her height. A short, stocky man will appear taller and slimmer in a slightly longer jacket and narrower trousers than those worn by the normal figure. In selecting a collar, line is very important. A round collar will make the face of a person with a round face seem rounder; whereas a long, pointed collar will make a long face seem even longer.

The choice of silhouette is pretty much a personal one. But if the consumer knows her figure faults and the lines that will detract from them, a selection of the proper garment will give satisfaction in its use.

Top:
Broad shoulders emphasized by narrow skirt and minimized by flare skirt.

Bottom:
Same chubby figures showing advantages of vertical stripes over horizontal stripes to give a more slender and taller effect.

Woven-in designs are called *structural designs.* They are an integral part of the fabric. Such designs like intricate Jacquard patterns are found in brocades and damasks and are generally more expensive than printed designs. The reason for this is the expense and operation of the Jacquard loom. The designer of Jacquards not only has to be artistic but also has to know the principles of textile engineering in order to execute a design adaptable to the Jacquard loom. Less expensive are the small, less intricate, often geometrical designs woven on the dobby loom.

Plaids, stripes, and checks are also woven-in figures. The size of these designs, like those in Jacquard, should be an important factor in fabric selection by the consumer.

There are two general types of printed designs: (1) *space patterns,* (2) *cover,* or all-over, *designs.* The first type shows considerable areas of background because the designs are spaced. In the second type, the design covers the entire cloth, so that it is difficult to tell where one design begins and another ends.

In selecting designs for the various figure types, it may be said that, in general, large designs make a large person look larger and vice versa. Large plaids and wide stripes, especially horizontal stripes, would have this effect. A short person of normal girth can appear to advantage in fabrics with small patterns. The average, normal figure can select almost any type of design if it is not extreme. If older persons want to wear patterns, they would do well to choose small, dark, inconspicuous ones.

A word in general about prints: they need a relief of a solid color; that is, a solid-colored hat and accessories. Two printed patterns should not be combined.

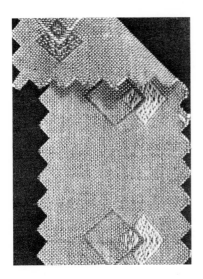

◀ Dobby weave, turnover showing right side

Jacquard weave, turnover showing right side ❯

Textures in Rayon Fabrics. Left: Rayon tweed, a wool-like texture *(American Viscose Co.).* **Center:** Rayon crashlike texture resembling linen *(Tennessee Eastman Corp.).* **Right:** Rayon shantung, a silklike texture; slub yarns are in filling *(Tennessee Eastman Corp.).*

CHOICE OF TEXTURE OF THE FABRIC

As we have discovered, fabrics have rough, smooth, bumpy, knotted, and hairy textures. In some years, the rough textures like tweeds are stylish because they give a hand-crafted appearance. This style may be followed by a less rough or crepey texture and then by a smooth texture. But, no matter what Dame Fashion decrees, the average woman who knows what texture most becomes her can generally find a becoming modification of the current style.

In general, it may be said that the tall man or woman of average build can wear rough-textured fabrics like tweeds, homespun, and hopsacking. The short person appears best in smooth-textured fabrics like gabardine, serge, and worsted cheviot. Likewise, the stout person looks best in dull, smooth-textured fabrics. Fortunately for the average figure, he or she can wear any textured fabric and look well.

PUTTING THIS MERCHANDISE KNOWLEDGE TO USE

❯ DO YOU KNOW YOUR MERCHANDISE?

1. (*a*) What colors should blondes avoid? (*b*) What colors should blondes wear?
2. (*a*) What colors are flattering to brunettes? (*b*) What colors should brunettes avoid?
3. (*a*) What lines in a garment tend to reduce height? (*b*) increase height? (*c*) add width? (*d*) reduce width? (*e*) add height and width at the same time?
4. (*a*) What textures, lines, colors, and patterns should a stout woman wear? (*b*) a stout man?
5. (*a*) What textures, lines, colors, and designs should a short, stocky woman wear? (*b*) a short, stocky man?
6. (*a*) What textures, lines, colors, and designs should a tall, slender woman wear? (*b*) a tall slender man?

1. The teacher should divide the class into committees of not more than five students in each.
(*a*) Borrow from the textile department *large* pieces of fabric of different textures, colors, and designs. Test the effects of the features of different fabrics on each student and record the result in your scrapbook. (*b*) Make a statement of colors, textures, and patterns most becoming to each student. Make a second list of colors, textures, and patterns to avoid.
2. (*a*) Demonstrate with a yardstick held against each student in turn the effect of vertical, horizontal, and diagonal lines. (*b*) What lines are most becoming to the builds of various students? (*c*) List for each student the lines he should and those he should not wear.
3. (*a*) Attend a fashion show for customers held in a department store. (*b*) Select three costumes that are most becoming to the models wearing them. (*c*) Describe each model as to figure type, skin, and hair coloring. (*d*) Describe the colors, silhouette, design, and texture of the fabric each model wore.

UNIT 18 CHOICE OF COLOR FOR HOME DECORATION

The purchase of a rug or carpet for an important room like a living room requires considerable thought. A *rug* is a floor covering made of thick, heavy fabric, woven in definite sizes and designs. A *carpet* is a floor covering sold by the square yard. A survey shows that it takes a customer 1½ years to come to a decision.[1] During that time she "shops" various stores to determine styles, color, textures, fibers, prices. Customer surveys also show that color in rugs is the consumer's primary consideration. When a salesman approaches the customer, he therefore asks, "Are you mainly interested in patterned goods or do you want plain colors?" At present, the emphasis in selling and advertising has shifted from the price of rugs to a stressing of color and texture. The principles of color harmony are equally applicable to home decoration as they are to costume.

While the rug may be considered the "heart of the room," other areas also use textile fabrics in decoration: the draperies, curtains, upholstery, and pillows.

[1] Talk by Mr. Eugene Connet, American Carpet Institute, to a group of graduate students, New York University School of Retailing, April, 1961.

GUIDING FACTORS IN COLOR SELECTION

In home decoration, there are six room areas that have to be considered. The first step or principle is to visualize where the colors have to be used and the comparative size of the areas:

1. Walls
2. Ceiling
3. Floor
4. Upholstery
5. Draperies
6. Accents

The second step is to select one color to dominate the color scheme. But this color should not overpower the scheme but be balanced by visualizing the colors to be used and the comparative size of the areas for each. For example, if walls and ceilings are neutral gray, the color scheme involves mainly (1) floor covering, (2) upholstery and (3) draperies. The floor covering, which is the third largest area, can be a strong color such as red, brown, or blue, with upholstery and draperies in less intense, toned-down colors. If the dominant color is dull or toned down, then the secondary color can be more intense. Here balance would be achieved by using a toned-down color in a large area and a more intense, secondary color in a smaller area. The third color used in the third largest area should tend to blend with one of the main colors. The fourth color should be an accent color and should be used on the smallest area (possibly a pillow for a couch). Being used in a small amount, the color can be vivid. As in apparel, three colors and an accent are usually considered the maximum number of colors to be used.

Style Trends

There are style trends in the use of color. The *monochromatic scheme* (use of shades of one color) was very popular in the middle 1950's. In fact, one color was used in varied shades and textures in a room and even for an entire house. Then, again, there may be a trend to use a *multicolor scheme*. For instance, if walls and ceiling are a light, neutral shade, with a room-sized Kerman Oriental rug on the floor showing a border of oak parquet flooring, a color in the rug, say blue, may be used for the draperies in solid color; neutral gray, for the upholstery of the couch and overstuffed chair; and an accent of red, for a pillow on the couch. In this scheme, the rug is the part of the room to which one's attention is drawn, and rightly so because of its artistic design, luxurious appearance, and warmth.

Other factors besides the choice of harmonious colors are involved in the selection of colors for home decoration. These factors are: (1) the size of the room, (2) the exposure of the room, (3) the use of the room, and (4) the influence of style and pattern.

The Size of the Room

Colors have different effects in rooms where they are used. For instance, red, orange, yellow are called *advancing colors*. They have warmth and give a large room cheerfulness; but when used in a small room, the room seems smaller. Blue, green, and violet are retreating or cool colors. They are best used in small rooms to create an illusion of greater size. To make a low-ceilinged room seem higher, it should be painted in cool-colored tints or in white and vice versa. Wall-to-wall carpets in cool, solid colors make a room seem larger than do rugs in bold designs.

The Exposure of the Room

Rooms facing north, or those with little light from outside, give an impression of warmth if lemon yellow, or the yellow family are used. Conversely, if a room is light with sun pouring in most of the day, the use of cool colors—greens, blues, violets—makes the room seem cooler.

Use of the Room

Foyers, hallways, hotel lobbies, and rooms opening on streets or areas of heavy traffic present floor-covering problems. In general, the rug salesman would be wise to advise his customer to choose dark colors in strong hues, because these colors show dirt less.

If a room is used constantly, such as a living room, bedroom, or nursery, it is best decorated in restful colors. If a room is lived in but a few hours or minutes of the day, it can be decorated in more vivid colors. Examples of the less-used rooms are dining rooms and guest rooms, which can be done in the advancing color yellow.

Influence of Style and Design

The interior decorator is professionally familiar with the styles in architecture, furniture, rugs, and upholstery of the various decorative periods. With his background, he is in an enviable position to know what fabrics, colors, and textures to suggest for decor of these periods.

Relatively few customers can afford the services of a professional decorator when they wish to decorate their homes. They must rely on the salesman's advice and their own knowledge. Hence a brief summary of the various decorative periods, both traditional and contemporary, will be helpful. The traditional periods will be broadly classified, and only the most salient points will be mentioned in relation to each.

PUTTING THIS MERCHANDISE KNOWLEDGE TO USE

❯ DO YOU KNOW YOUR MERCHANDISE?

    1. (*a*) What are the types of color harmony? (*b*) Give an example of each in home decoration.

2. What factors besides the choice of harmonious colors are involved in selection of colors for home decoration?
3. Define (*a*) advancing colors, (*b*) retreating colors. (*c*) Give an example when each should be used.
4. For a room whose windows open on a dark air shaft, what colors would you suggest for its decoration?
5. (*a*) What color and texture rug would you suggest for the foyer of a city apartment? (*b*) for a child's nursery in a suburban home?
6. (*a*) What colors and textures would you recommend for floor covering and draperies for a hotel lobby? (*b*) for a sunny living room in a suburban, contemporary-style home?

❯ INTERESTING THINGS TO DO

1. (*a*) Visit model homes or decorated suites in the home-furnishing department of a store. (*b*) Make a list of furniture items in the set. (*c*) List colors of all fabrics used and where used. (*d*) Comment on the effectiveness of this color scheme.
2. (*a*) Find examples of bad taste in home decoration in your own home, in advertisements, in model homes, etc. (*b*) Indicate what articles are in poor taste and why. (*c*) How would you remedy the situation?
3. (*a*) Draw or cut out from an advertisement a room drawn in black and white. (*b*) Put in with crayon the colors that you feel would make a harmonious color scheme.

UNIT 19 PERIOD STYLES IN INTERIOR DECORATION

THE ENGLISH PERIODS

Five periods stand out as influences on later interior designs.

Jacobean Period—1603–1685 (Charles I, Charles II, and James I of England)

This was an age of heavy, square, oak and walnut furniture. These were masculine eras. Appropriate floor coverings are Oriental or plain-colored carpets in bold colors. Brocade, ribbon fabrics, elaborate needle point, tapestry, leather are suitable for upholstery. Chenille, brocade, velvet, and velour are appropriate for both draperies and upholsteries. The two kings, Charles I and II, supported a luxurious court life, so that decorative fabrics continued to be rich and elegant.

This king and queen enjoyed home life and were not concerned with ceremonial court life. For this reason, rooms became more livable and furniture smaller and more comfortable. At this time, the English were trading with the Far East; consequently, Chinese and Oriental rugs became popular. Since domesticity was the keynote of this reign, the less formal fabrics such as chintz, cretonne, polished cotton, and needle point are appropriate in this decor.

Queen Anne—1665–1714

This monarch was a sister of Mary, a pious and devout woman who spent much time in making beautiful hangings and furniture covers. Trade with China grew, a factor that increased the use of Chinese, Persian, and Indian floor coverings. Furniture was light and graceful. Decorative fabrics included brocade, Chinese embroidery, needle point, chintz, and India prints.

Georgian Period—1660–1820

This is often called the "Age of Mahogany." The wood was shipped to England originally as a possible source of quinine for curing fevers; an overshipment of this hardwood led to the making of it into furniture. With good success, a fashion for mahogany was begun. The period of George I, II, and III is one of luxury and elegance accented by a strong French influence. During the Georgian Period, famous English cabinetmakers were at work: Thomas Chippendale (1718–1779), The Adam Brothers (1760–1792), George Hepplewhite (1765–1795), and Thomas Sheraton (1751–1806).

Chippendale. Chippendale was probably the most famous of all English cabinetmakers. His designs were well proportioned, graceful, sturdy but not heavy. He is noted for his exquisitely carved ornamentation. Probably he is best known for his chairs with ball-and-claw feet. His clients liked the Chinese influence, so that many of his furniture pieces were designed to please his clients. Rugs with Chinese designs on blue grounds, as well as luxurious wall-to-wall broadloom carpeting are suitable. Upholstery and drapery fabrics include brocade, damask, needle point, tapestry, velour, satin, velvet.

The Adam Brothers. The Adam Brothers were architects. They became interested in excavations at Pompeii which explains why they featured classic designs. These were formal and balanced with a bit of the feminine influence. Being architects, they excelled in pieces such as bookcases, sideboards, and cabinets. Typical decorative designs are urns, wreaths, husks, and honeysuckle. Not only did the Adams design furniture but also carpets, upholsteries, tapestries, and silverware. Their designs were also repeated on walls and ceilings. Orientals or Chinese rugs would, therefore, be inappropriate for this period. The Adams favored cool, delicate, pastel shades. Appropriate fabrics include brocade, lightweight satin-striped silks, and moirés.

Hepplewhite. Hepplewhite is noted particularly for his chairs and his secretaries. His designs were influenced by the classic revival and were characterized by femininity and charm. The backs of the chairs were in the shape of a shield, a hoop, or a heart. They were often ornamented with three feathers taken from the coat of arms of the Prince of Wales. Fabrics for upholstery and draperies were damask, satin in stripes, figured moiré, with trimmings of ribbons and tassels. Plain carpeting in light colors or with small patterns and fine textures as well as French or Oriental designs can be used.

Sheraton. Sheraton was a man of many trades. First he was a genius as a designer and cabinetmaker, an author, a self-taught scholar, a bookseller, drawing teacher, and preacher. Sheraton's designs were more classical and conservative than those by Hepplewhite. While his designs were simple and charming, they were always firm and stable in construction. Ornamentation included rosettes, urns, wreaths, and garlands. Plain or classic-patterned broadloom carpeting in subdued tones is appropriate.

English Regency—1811–1820

This was the age of Beau Brummel, a friend of George IV, who was the fashion plate of those days. It was he who made George IV fashion conscious. He became tired of the formal classic styles of the previous Georgian Period and wanted something new. In the early days of the Regency, furniture was classic but later showed the Empire influence from France. Furniture was made of mahogany or painted black or gilt. Chairs had broad backs and rolled over at the top; legs curved in. Patterns in floor coverings used roses, ribbons, and festoons. Plain color or classic designs embossed and sculptured were used in floor coverings. Strong, rich colors were to be found in drapery and upholstery fabrics. Satin, taffeta, moiré, and vertical stripes were used as decorative fabrics.

Victorian Period—1837–1901

It was Albert, Queen Victoria's consort, who took the initiative in the decorative arts. The Queen, being of a sentimental nature, would permit nothing to be discarded.

During this period, one could choose his own style. It was also a time when machine-made furniture was coming into vogue—a factor that probably contributed to a decline in home decoration. William Morris, best known for his invention of the Morris chair, tried unsuccessfully to stem the tide of commercially made furniture.

The gewgaws, fussiness, the dust-catching bric-a-bac, elaborate floral patterns in wallpaper and carpets, the horsehair-covered sofa are symbols of

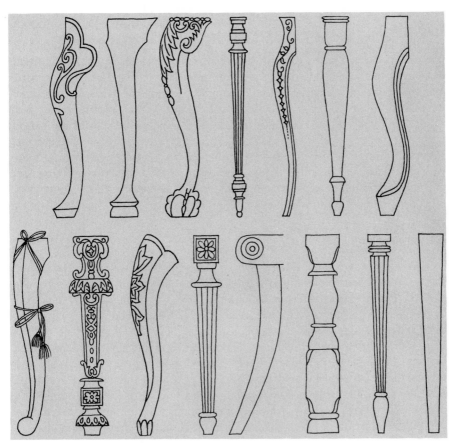

Chair Legs from Various Periods. Top row: Queen Anne, Georgian, Chippendale, Adam, Hepplewhite, Sheraton, and Regency. **Bottom row:** Victorian, Louis XIV, Louis XV, Louis XVI, Empire, Early American (Pilgrim), Federal, and Contemporary.

this era. Brussels carpeting, often with beige background with large red roses, was typical of parlor floor coverings. The modern, machine-made hooked type of figured carpet, rag rugs, or plaid carpeting are appropriate in the Victorian decor. Brocade and damask, draperies with ball fringes and tassels, horsehair upholstery, friezé, plush, velvet, and velour are suitable fabrics.

THE FRENCH PERIODS

French interiors were greatly influenced, as in England, by the tastes of reigning kings, as well as by political events.

Louis XIV—1638–1715

He was known as the "Sun King" because he loved brilliance. He was also called the "Grand Monarch" because he was known for his cultivation of the arts. During his reign, the silk fabric weaving at Lyons flourished; and its fine quality brocades and damasks won international fame. Louis XIV himself was a vain person; in interior decoration, he preferred the masculine, ornate, massive styles in straight lines with complete symmetry. His great personal interest in decoration laid a foundation for later French decoration. It was Louis XIV who built the beautiful Palace of Versailles. Designs of the period were palm leaves, shells, fruits, scrolls, garlands, birds, feathers, and ribbons. Colors in fabrics were rich and strong; there were solid-colored carpets, some with designs of the period; Chinese, Aubusson, a kind of handmade tapestry, and some Oriental designs in floor coverings. In decorative fabrics, damasks, brocades, satins, tapestry, velvet were important.

Louis XV—1715–1774

This king was influenced by two of his favorites, Mmes. DuBarry and Pompadour. Their femininity is reflected in the design and furnishings of the period. The massive furniture of Louis XIV was replaced by delicately designed pieces with curved lines, elaborately ornamented with love knots, cupids, scrolls, darts, and flowers. Pastoral scenes were popular, as well as inlay work and bronze mountings. Woods were mahogany, oak, rosewood, and walnut. Some of the furniture was painted in gold or in colors. Walls and fabrics for decoration favored pastel colors. The chaise longue covered with brocade, satin, or damask was popular. Other fabrics included needle point, prints, taffeta, toile de Jouy, friezé, and cretonne. Appropriate floor coverings would be Aubusson in pastel shades, Oriental rugs, and plain broadlooms.

Louis XVI—1774–1793

This period represents a return to the simplicity of the classic influence. We have seen how at this same time the Adam Brothers in England were also influenced by the symmetry and reserved classic style. The designs of the period were inspired by the beautiful Marie Antoinette, wife of Louis XVI. Flowers, garden tools, cupids' bows, shepherds' crooks, bows or ribbons were typical of the period. These designs were smaller, and ornamentation was more reserved, daintier, and lighter than in the previous period. Floor coverings and fabrics similar to those of Louis XV were appropriate. Striped fabrics became very popular.

Directoire—1794–1804

This is the period in French history that repudiates all the grandeur and extravagance of the former monarchies. The slogan of the French Revolution had been Liberty, Equality, and Fraternity. This idea was reflected in interior decoration. While the classical influence remained, emblems of the French

Revolution—such as wreaths, triumphal arches, arrows, clasped hands—were popular as well as the classical designs of swans, lyres, and stars. Ebony, mahogany, and satinwood in natural wood finishes were used. Colors were quite strong. Floor coverings were designed with patterns of the period; plain carpeting was suitable but not Oriental or Chinese. Satin, particularly in stripes was important. Fabrics similar to those in the Louis XIV period may be used.

Empire Period—1804–1815

This was the Napoleonic Era. All furniture and decorations reflected the glory of Napoleon's conquests. Furniture became heavy and massive, made of ebony, mahogany, or satinwood. Designs were perfectly symmetrical, imperialistic in classical effect. Napoleon's own invention, the "bee" emblem, is found everywhere. The bee is a symbol of Corsica, Napoleon's birthplace. Likewise, military symbols, Napoleon's initial "N," Roman laurel wreaths, and acanthus leaves, and Egyptian patterns (like the obelisk and sphinx) are typical designs of the period. Decorative fabrics included damask, brocades, taffeta, moiré, and satin. Plain carpeting or Empire designs in strong colors can be used.

French Provincial

This period is not dated because it represents the type of decor that the average Frenchman used in his home in small towns and villages where life contrasted sharply with the glamour of the French Court. Peasants toiled for the necessities of life. Their furniture was simple and sturdy, made of beech, maple, walnut, and fruit woods. Rugs were hand hooked or made of rags. Fabrics for decoration were homespun, crash, cretonne. Designs were frequently small but rather gay with wild-flower patterns and plaids.

AMERICAN PERIOD STYLES

At first American interiors continued the styles of the European countries from which the early settlers had come. Later on these styles were modified, so that gradually an American style evolved.

Early American (New England)—1620–1720

Early American furniture in New England was quite primitive compared with the Southern Colonial of the same period. The pilgrims in New England were determined pioneers, toiling hard for the bare necessities. They built their own homes and furnishings. Furniture was simple, crude, rustic, and sturdy; pine, ash, cherry, maple, and oak were used. The women wove their own cloth and made hooked and rag braided rugs. Appropriate decorative fabrics are chintz, crash, homespun, monk's cloth, and organdy.

Colonial—1607–1776

In the South, the settlers were mostly wealthy cavaliers who came to America to seek adventure. They became owners of great plantations and lived a life of luxury due largely to the warm climate and to slave labor. Very little furniture was made in the South in the early years. The finest pieces of Georgian furniture were imported from England. The earliest southern homes were Jacobean, but later they became Georgian in style. Designs and fabrics reflected the life of the South. Appropriate floor coverings are solid-color rugs, or those with multicolor floral, leaf and scroll, or floral and scroll designs. Since most of the fabrics were imported from England, brocades, damask, velvet, satin, velour, and needle point were used.

The early colonists, who lived in the country, were conservative people who continued to follow the Jacobean decor until early in the nineteenth century. They developed designs and useful types of furniture not found among city dwellers. For example, the Windsor chair is an American Provincial product. Colors were primary hues and patterns were traditional.

Pennsylvania-Dutch styles were simple, but they ornamented their furniture more than the New England country people. They used elaborate painted designs of tulips, pomegranates, dates, and unicorns.

While the early New England Pilgrims had a hard life with a few conveniences and comforts in home decoration, evidence of improved living conditions was reflected in their home decorations as soon as families began to prosper. Houses and interior decoration became essentially Georgian but were influenced by the austerity of the earlier colonial style. In fact, furniture took on the appearance of the current styles in England. Trade with the Far East brought Chinese, Indian, and Persian carpets to the colonial home. The eighteenth century floral designs harmonize well with Georgian furniture. Hooked rugs in floral designs, embossed, or in plain colors, are suitable in carpets.

Federal Period—1776–1810

This was an era when American cabinetmakers became skilled in modifying the designs of the Adams, Hepplewhite, and Sheraton. Furnishings became distinctly American. The outstanding furniture designer was Duncan Phyfe (1795–1847). He is sometimes called the American Sheraton. Santo Domingan mahogany and walnut were his favorite woods, which he turned into slender fluted legs and lyre-back chairs. Many of his pieces have been reproduced and are very popular in fine furniture today. The most popular motif of this period was the eagle, which was used to adorn sofas, bull's eye mirrors, clocks, chairs, desks, glassware, and porcelain. The Clipper Ship, representing trade with the Far East, became a familiar symbol. Imported floor coverings from China, India, and Persia, together with Adam designed carpeting and hooked rugs, were used. Fabrics of the Georgian period were used.

The period 1810–1850 is sometimes called "American Empire." It is really Federal with a French influence. Our cabinetmakers attempted to interpret the classical revival abroad. In so doing, furniture became heavier, more solid, with far less ornamentation than the French Empire. Cornucopias, eagle heads (often gilded), were typical designs of the period. There were gondola, sleigh, and four-poster beds, rectangular mirrors with heavy carved frames. Popular, too, were the Chinese and French scenic wallpapers. Draperies were made of damask, brocade, taffeta, or satin and were voluminous. Carpets could be plain, two-tone designs, or solid in strong colors.

Modern Style—1928–1948

It is difficult to fix the dates for this period, for some features of this era of simplicity are evident as early as 1911. All unnecessary details were eliminated; curves were replaced by straight lines; furniture followed architectural forms. Very little ornamentation was used. Furniture was functional, simple, and useful. Geometric designs and mechanical symbols prevailed. Fabrics for decoration included casement cloth, armure, tapestry, rough linen textures, chenille, and corded fabrics. Broadloom carpeting in soft solid colors or modern designs was used.

Contemporary—1948–

We are now living in this period. The design expresses the kind of world in which we live: efficient, comfortable, casual. Emphasis in furniture is on form, not details; many of our furniture pieces are designed to serve a dual purpose. It is an age of plastic, unbreakable sheet glass, glass brick, aluminum, and steel. One school of contemporary design attempts to interpret historical styles in terms of present-day living, while another school emphasizes functionalism and oversimplification. Fortunately, the family heirlooms can be combined with a contemporary decor. Fabrics for decoration emphasize texture and geometric design. They play a good part in covering large areas such as a floor from wall to wall and a picture window from ceiling to floor. Carpets may be solid color, two tone, carved or sculptured designs, textured or high-low pile.[1] Popular fabrics are antique satin, gauze, handwoven effects, and textured cloths.

If a salesman of floor coverings or decorative fabrics knows the essential features of the various period styles, he will be able to recommend appropriate fabrics, colors, and designs. The modern customer is more conscious of color, line, and design in her home furnishings than her mother was. She reads about appropriate decor in home magazines; she sees advertisements

---

[1] See Chapter 15 for description of these types.

on television, she hears about it on radio and by going to lectures; by discussing problems of decoration with her friends. Since we are a more mobile population than we were in the last generation, we are frequently decorating or "redoing" our homes.

PUTTING THIS MERCHANDISE KNOWLEDGE TO USE ❯ ❯ ❯ ❯ ❯ ❯ ❯ ❯ ❯ ❯

❯ DO YOU KNOW YOUR MERCHANDISE?

1. What fabric would you suggest for a chaise longue in Louis XVI style?
2. (*a*) For what designs is Duncan Phyfe known? (*b*) What fabric or fabrics would be appropriate for upholstering a Duncan Phyfe lyre-back chair?
3. (*a*) What are the essential differences between modern and contemporary styles? (*b*) What fabric or fabrics would be suitable for the curtaining of a picture window in a contemporary living room?
4. (*a*) What are the essential differences between Chippendale and Hepplewhite styles in furniture? (*b*) How do Louis XIV and Louis XV styles differ? (*c*) Explain the differences between Louis XVI and Directoire styles in home decoration. (*d*) between Directoire and Empire styles.
5. (*a*) Characterize French Provincial and American Provincial styles. (*b*) What fabrics would you suggest for a maple French Provincial armchair?
6. Why is it important for a salesman of carpets or draperies to know the features of decorative periods?

❯ INTERESTING THINGS TO DO

1. (*a*) A living room 22 feet x 12 feet is to be furnished. You are to choose the style of furniture you wish. Make a floor plan of the room. Fit in the furniture to scale. (*b*) Completely "furnish" this living room with rugs, draperies, curtains, and upholsteries. (*c*) Obtain fabrics or pictures of fabrics that you would use for each article of furnishing.
2. Visit model rooms in furniture or department stores. List all the articles you find made of textile fabrics in these rooms.
3. In your visit to model rooms, (*a*) state the style of the decoration of any one room; (*b*) classify the fabrics in the above-mentioned room in a table similar to the one given below.

Name of Fabric	Use	Colors	Texture

ADDITIONAL MERCHANDISE TERMS ❯ ❯ ❯ ❯ ❯ ❯ ❯ ❯ ❯ ❯ ❯ ❯ ❯ ❯ ❯ ❯ ❯ ❯ ❯

Broadloom is a carpet woven in a wide width.

Colonial Period is the style in home decoration from 1620–1720 in New England and from 1607–1776 in the South.

Color wheel is a circular form designed to show the proportion of primary colors in any tint or shade of color.

Decor is a shortened form of *decoration*.

Home decoration. See Interior Decoration.

Interior decoration is the co-ordinating of floor coverings, fabrics, and style of furniture to create a harmonious ensemble.

Interior decorator is a person who is familiar with principles and practices of interior decoration.

Neutral gray is an indefinite color with a grayish tint.

Period styles in interior decoration are the outstanding modes used in furniture and home furnishings in a particular historical period.

Provincial is the style in home decoration of people who lived in villages or in the country as opposed to that of urban dwellers.

Strong color is an intense or vivid color.

Infants' and Children's Wear

UNIT 20 INFANTS' WEAR

THINGS TO LOOK FOR IN INFANTS' WEAR

Young mothers like to see their babies in pretty, dainty clothes; but young mothers are also very conscious of the work involved keeping these clothes pretty and dainty. For that reason they look for garments that launder easily, that require little or no ironing, and that are fast colors. Modern production processes have created the drip-dries in cottons and cotton blends and in synthetics that give the mother the dainty clothes she wants for her baby without the work formerly connected with them.

WHO ARE THE PURCHASERS OF INFANTS' WEAR?

The obvious answer is mothers, of course. But in department and specialty stores, there is an increasing number of purchasers who are grandmothers. Stores like this clientele because they usually spend more on each item than a mother could normally afford. They also buy the "big ticket items" like snow suits, blankets, quilts, carriage covers, corduroy sets of overalls often called "crawlers," hat-and-jacket sets, and novelty items.

Another type of customer is the woman who buys gifts for new babies of relatives and friends. This woman will often select an article that is not too practical, like a dress or a little two-piece diaper set. Since most babies wear a kimono or nightgown for the first few months, "dressing up" only on very special occasions, the young mother will probably receive so many of the articles mentioned that her child will never have an opportunity to wear them out before he or she grows out of them. It would be more acceptable to the mother to receive a gift of a pair of corduroy overalls or a sweater of a one-year size which can be worn after the layette is outgrown.

WHAT IS A LAYETTE?

A *layette* is a combination of articles that a baby will need as soon as he is born. It is primarily textile with the possible exception of diaper pins, nursing bottles, scales, sterilizers, and the like.

Textile articles may include as few as 45 pieces to as many as 95 pieces. A layette may cost as little as $25 for the bare necessities up to $75 and more for more elaborate ones. One large department store in New York gives a free bassinette to the purchaser of a layette costing $50 or more. With each successive baby, the layette replacements may be fewer, because most babies outgrow their first clothes before they wear them out.

Following are articles included in a layette:

SHIRTS—tie or snap fasteners

DIAPERS (Use of a diaper service practically eliminates this item; however, it is advisable to have one or two dozen on hand in case of a nondelivery.)

GOWNS—nightgown

KIMONOS—loose-fitting garments with raglan sleeves. Open down the front, inspired by the Japanese kimono

QUILTED PADS—made of two layers of fabric with cotton, polyester, or wool between them. Two layers are stitched together with fine (quilting) stitches.

RUBBER AND STOCKINETTE SHEETS—a fitted rectangular-shaped knitted article for the crib. Keeps mattress dry.

TERRY TOWELS

WASHCLOTHS—a small square of knitted cotton cloth for washing the baby

RECEIVING BLANKETS—a very small square fabric, usually made of flannelette, used to wrap the baby in for the first few weeks of its life

CRIB SHEETS (fitted or flat)

BLANKETS (acrylic or wool, and light cotton for summer, optional)

QUILT FOR CRIB—a covering for the baby when in the carriage or crib, optional

Additional articles, not included in the layette which a baby needs as soon as he is taken out in the carriage or eats solid food, include:

SACQUES—sweaterlike garments usually tied at the neck—open down the front

BONNETS

CARRIAGE SETS—includes pillow and fancy case and a carriage cover

SWEATERS—for the child 3 months to 1 year

BOOTEES—knitted or crocheted covering for the feet and part of leg

SLIPPER SOCKS—knitted sock with plastic or soft leather foot

SLIPS to wear under dresses

TIGHTS—knitted fabrics which cover body snugly from waist to toe

BIBS

DRESSES

WASH SUITS

BABY PANTS—silk with water-repellent finish or all plastic, needed when he comes home from the hospital.

STYLES IN INFANTS' WEAR

A new style of garment that took the customer's eye and money during 1960 and 1961 was the stretch suit, a one- or two-piece garment covering the body closely but comfortably from neck to toe. It was made of all-nylon knitted or stretch yarn, or cotton or nylon terry. For summer, the feet and legs were not covered. Common colors included blue, pink, yellow, and white. The selling feature of the garment was that one size, because of the stretch yarns, would fit a newborn infant and would last until the child was as old as six months. It could be washed at home in an automatic washer and required no ironing. The first nylon stretch suits were not wholly satisfactory because yarns would break and form holes about a half inch from the front closing of the garment. The 100 per cent nylon pilled (formed little balls of fibers on the surface of the clothes).

Other than this new one- or two-piece suit, not very many articles have been especially styled for the new baby that differ radically from the traditional. The diaper suit or dress for baby boys or girls consists of a shirt or blouse and a pair of fabric panties coated inside with plastic. Baby girls' panties have become very feminine with rows of lace ruffles. The baby girl of two or three months can wear tights (leotard) with a smock-type blouse that hangs loosely from the shoulders and extends down to the hips. Or she can wear tailored overalls, those with frilly ruffles, and a blouse or "T" shirt to match. "T" or polo shirts are knitted with short or long sleeves, round neck, and can be made of nylon stretch yarns. The corduroy set of overall, blouse, fleece-lined jacket and bonnet or cap is intended for boy and girl babies of four months to a year or more. This outfit is particularly suitable for fall and spring. In winter, the baby in the carriage usually wears a one-piece snowsuit or pram suit with detachable hood, feet, and mittens. It is usually made of smooth nylon fabric or other synthetic fiber with a quilted lining. These fabrics are generally spot and water repellent.

FABRICS USED IN INFANTS' WEAR

Batiste, dimity, lawn, and blends with synthetics are sheer fabrics, normally appropriate for summer wear; but infant girls can wear sheer dresses all year round because a wool or acrylic sweater or sacque can be worn over the dress for warmth.

In warm apartments and well-heated homes, the flannelette (cotton flannel) or knitted sleeping garment is sufficiently warm. Outer garments for winter are a wool bunting (a fleecy bag with hood) or a snow or pram suit.

Natural Fibers: Cotton

How to Identify Names of Fabrics Used in Infants' Wear. Some of the most commonly used fabrics for infants are the cotton muslins. These fabrics

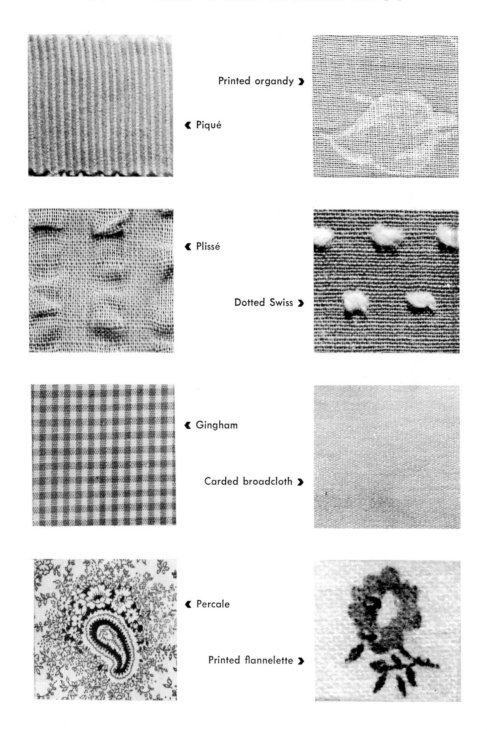

Printed organdy >

< Piqué

< Plissé

Dotted Swiss >

< Gingham

Carded broadcloth >

< Percale

Printed flannelette >

are always plain-weave cottons but some are very sheer like batiste, lawn, and organdy and some are heavy like a baby's crib sheet.

If we look at the list of fabrics and their uses on pages 156–157, we can remember them better if we learn them by their characteristic textures.

Cotton muslins, batiste, lawn, dotted swiss, organdy, gingham, percale are smooth-surface textures. However, batiste and percale are soft to the touch and usually lawn, dotted swiss, and organdy are fairly stiff or crisp. A good grade of batiste is the sheerest (thinnest), silkiest, and softest of the muslins. It is silky because it is well mercerized (see Chapter 5 for explanation of mercerization). If you should count the yarns to the inch in the fabric, there would be over 100 in warp and in filling in best grade (112 x 108). Lawn, named for a French town, Laon, is not mercerized. This is one way lawn differs from batiste. It can be stiffened (starched or permanent starchless) by finishing to make it appear fresh looking. In best grades, lawn has a lower count than batiste, say 100 x 96.

The finish of *percale* is dull and the cloth is a lot heavier than batiste or lawn. It is usually printed when used for clothing.

Gingham is about as heavy as percale. It is not printed but yarn dyed in the form of checks or plaids. This is a very popular fabric for infants' diaper sets, first overalls, dresses, shirts, and blouses. Its popularity carries over to toddlers (young children learning to walk), kindergarteners, and school children.

Organdy is always sheer and has a stiff crisp finish. Most of the organdy now sold is permanent starchless finish. It appears the same after washing and ironing as it did when new. Its count in good grades (88 x 76) is somewhat lower than good-grade batiste or lawn. The better grades are made of well-combed yarn while poorer grades are carded only.

Dotted swiss is identified by its woven-in dots done by the clipped-spot method. The fabric itself is either an organdy (good grade) or low-count lawn (poor grade). So here there is really no new fabric to identify. The woven dotted design changes its name to dotted swiss.

Dimity is a corded striped or checked sheer cotton fabric. The cords are made by weaving two, three, or more warp and/or filling yarns as one.

Cotton broadcloth is not a muslin although it is plain weave. It is slightly heavier than percale and has heavier, uneven, crosswise filling yarns. You can see them easily if you look at a white broadcloth shirt or a woman's broadcloth dress or blouse. These larger filling yarns take up more space than the warps. The count of cloth is, therefore, unbalanced (144 x 76 good grade or 100 x 56 poor grade).

Cotton crepe is a fabric in plain weave, but its texture is crinkled. We have found in Chapter 4 that crepes can be embossed and heat set to make them permanent. These fabrics are usually sold as cotton plissé crepe. Some of these crepes are made by printing with caustic soda. They may be printed or solid color. This type of fabric is often used for summer pajamas and kimonos. Seersucker is also a crepe. There are two types, one which is chemically printed and the other which is woven in by tightening certain warp yarns in weaving. The latter type is permanent and is called *woven seersucker*. The tight yarns are the plain stripes which alternate with the crinkled stripe. These stripes are yarn dyed. Seersucker is used for summer overalls, sun suits, dresses, and diaper sets.

Flat crepe is also a crinkled texture but the crinkle is put in by using crepe yarns, twisted to the point where they knot, in the filling (crosswise); the warp uses loosely twisted yarns. Flat crepes can also be made of silk, rayon, acetate, or other synthetics alone or in blends.

Bird's-eye is a smooth, soft cotton fabric frequently used for diapers. Its woven-in design represents a conventionalized bird's eye (diamond shape). The weave is dobby.

Corduroy and *piqué* have wales, or ridges, up and down the fabric. Corduroy is a pile weave done by the filling-float method. Piqué is a twill weave which has a backing or padding to make the wale stand out. Wales are of different widths: the narrowest is called *pin-wale* corduroy or piqué; the next widest wale is called *narrow wale* and the widest is called *wide wale*. The pin and narrow wales are most used for infants' wear.

Flannelette is a cotton fabric in plain weave with a napped texture either on one side or both sides. It is often printed. The napped finish makes the fabric soft, absorbent, and warm. Nap wears off in time, however.

Terry cloth is cotton in pile weave with uncut loops. (For construction, see Chapter 4.) It is frequently printed for use as a bathrobe or stretch suit. In heavier weights, it is used for a baby's towel and face cloth.

Lace is made of cotton or nylon and is used for trimming dresses, bonnets, and carriage sets. (For lace construction, see Chapters 2 and 4.)

Importance of Cotton in Infants' Wear. There are many good reasons why cotton is used so extensively.

EASE OF CARE. Seventeen of the 21 fabrics listed on pages 156–157 are usually cotton or a blend with a synthetic. Cotton is used most in infants' wear primarily because it is easy to launder. If it has a wash-and-wear (resin) finish, ironing is eliminated or certainly minimized.

SOFTNESS. Baby has a tender skin; therefore, soft fabrics of cotton are gentle and comfortable.

ABSORBENCY. The fact that cotton takes up bodily moisture and allows it to evaporate makes cotton comfortable.

WASHABILITY. Cotton fabrics can be laundered at home in an automatic washer. Most colors are now made fast for this type of laundering. For the most part, cottons can be dried in an automatic dryer as well. Instructions on the label usually specify the heat setting.

FRESHNESS. After cleansing, there is a hygienic freshness in the appearance of cotton fabrics.

PRICE. The fact that cotton is plentiful in this country brings cottons to a price level suited to every budget.

Natural Fibers: Silk and Wool

Silk is a luxury fiber and is not used extensively in infants' wear. Gift items of silk sacques, bonnets, and carriage sets are carried in many department and specialty stores.

Wool is a warm fiber; therefore, articles like blankets, sacques, sweaters, caps, and mittens are often made of wool. However, some stores carry no babies' wool sweaters. Mothers prefer the ease in care of Orlon acrylic. Since all-wool articles should be laundered by hand, there is a good explanation for the popularity of the acrylic fibers.

Linen is rarely found in a baby's wardrobe, unless it might be a handkerchief linen dress.

FABRICS MADE OF BLENDS AND OF SYNTHETICS

When cotton is used in a blend with Dacron polyester, nylon, or any other synthetic, it acquires the wash-and-wear, or minimum-care, feature as it.does when all-cotton is resin finished. Some mothers prefer a blend, because they think the fabric looks silkier and is softer.

Rayon, acetate, nylon, Dacron polyester are frequently used for carriage covers, bonnets, and dressy sacques. Again, their silky appearance is a selling point. Nylon lace is often used as trimming for dresses and bonnets. Nylon stretch yarn is found in stretch socks and in the stretch suit.

Orlon acrylic fibers are very popular in sweaters, caps, and bootees, sold as sets or as single items. Mothers like Orlon acrylic because it is easily laundered in the automatic washer and dryer. It requires no ironing, and it does not shrink. In fact, in knitted garments, it is more apt to stretch than to shrink. Acrylic fibers are very popular in crib blankets. They are soft, lightweight, yet warm enough for winter in a well-heated apartment or house located in the Middle Atlantic States. The chief selling point is that they can be laundered at home in an automatic washer-dryer without fear of shrinkage. Nylon blanket binding is attractive and more durable than acetate or rayon. Mothers should be cautioned about buying 100 per cent rayon blankets unless they are treated for fire resistance. Rayon is a cellulose fiber and, when napped, the air pockets between the fibers make the fabric highly flammable should a cigarette ash be dropped on it. Wool is slow to burn, and acrylics fuse but the fire does not flare up and spread as rapidly as cotton.

The following fabrics are suitable for the accompanying uses.

Fabric	Uses
Batiste	for dresses and slips
Bird's-eye	for diapers
Broadcloth	for wash suits, sunsuits, blouses and shirts
Corduroy	for overalls, hats and jackets
Crepe (cotton)	for summer pajamas, kimonos

Fabric	Uses
Dacron polyester	for bonnets
Dimity	for dresses, bonnets
Dotted swiss	for dresses
Flannelette	for sleeping garments, kimonos, receiving blankets and diapers
Flat crepe	for christening dresses, bonnets, sacques, summer coats, carriage sets
Gauze	for diapers
Gingham	for diaper sets, dresses, suits, shirts and blouses
Knitted cotton	for nightgowns, shirts, diapers, training pants
Lace	for edging dresses, pillows and carriage covers
Lawn	for dresses, bonnets
Nylon knit	for knitted stretch suits. Woven for bonnets.
Organdy	for bonnets, dresses
Percale	for suits, dresses, shirts, blouses
Piqué	for sunsuits, sacques, bonnets
Taffeta	for bonnets and carriage covers
Terry cloth	for beach robes, sunsuits and space suits

PUTTING THIS MERCHANDISE KNOWLEDGE TO USE ❯❯❯❯❯❯❯❯❯❯

❯ DO YOU KNOW YOUR MERCHANDISE?

1. How can you distinguish: (*a*) gingham from percale, (*b*) batiste from lawn, (*c*) cotton plissé crepe from flat crepe, (*d*) woven seersucker from plissé crepe, (*e*) corduroy from piqué, (*f*) corduroy from flannelette, (*g*) piqué from dimity, (*h*) lawn from organdy, (*i*) dotted swiss from organdy, (*j*) gingham from broadcloth?
2. What fabric would you recommend for a baby girl's diaper set?
3. Of what fabrics are crib sheets made?
4. (*a*) What fabrics are suitable for an 18-month-old boy's overalls? (*b*) What fabric is used for a pram set or snowsuit for a 9-month-old baby?
5. Mention three textile articles that would be appropriate for baby gifts.
6. (*a*) For what purposes is taffeta used in infants' wear? (*b*) Name as many cotton muslins as you can for garments in infants' wear.
7. (*a*) Define a "layette." (*b*) List 10 articles usually found in a layette.
8. (*a*) Of what fibers are crib blankets made? (b) Why are acrylic fibers used so often in blankets?
9. What fabric would you recommend for a baby's bonnet? Why?
10. What fabric would you recommend for a 3-month-old baby boy's stretch suit?

❯ INTERESTING THINGS TO DO

1. (*a*) Visit a store that has an infants' department. (*b*) See if there is any new style in infants' wear that has recently become popular. (*c*) Write up the selling points of this garment in your scrapbook.
2. (*a*) What fabrics do you prefer for a baby's kimono? Why? (*b*) Do you prefer wool or Orlon acrylic fiber for a baby's sweater? Why? (*c*) Do you prefer all-cotton or all-wool or a mixture for a tiny baby's winter undershirt? Why? (*d*) Do you prefer fitted or flat

crib sheets? (*e*) Do you prefer acrylic or wool fibers in babies' blankets?

3. Look through a mail-order catalogue that lists infants' wear. (*a*) Make a list of all layette items made of blends containing synthetic fibers, (*b*) of all layette items made of 100 per cent natural fibers.

4. (*a*) Clip from newspapers ads about articles of infants' wear and paste them in your scrapbook. (*b*) Write the selling points of each item.

UNIT 21 CHILDREN'S WEAR

When does an infant become a child? Some will say after his first birthday; some, after he is 18 months or 2 years old.

The infants' department in a store is not too helpful in answering this question, because some items, like waterproof panties large enough to fit a 2-year-old, are carried in the infants' department. Training pants also large enough to fit a 2½- or even a 3-year-old can be found in the infants' department. Yet sweaters to fit an 18-month-old or older and overalls for over a year old can be purchased in the children's department.

STYLES IN CHILDREN'S WEAR

When a child begins to walk, he becomes a toddler and is graduated from the infants' to the children's department. Toddlers' sizes run from 1–4 inclusive. A No. 1, No. 2 and No. 3 toddler will usually fit a child from one year to about 18 or 20 months, while a No. 4 will generally fit a 2-year-old. Regular sizes 2–6x fit the preschool child. Larger sizes will be found in the older children's department, called girls' or boys' departments, where sizes run from 7–14.

The Girl Toddlers

This particular age group from 1–2½ is rightly called *toddler* because at first children are unsteady on their feet.

So many mothers say, "Oh, I wish I had a girl instead of a boy. You can buy such cute things for girls." This is true, but toddler boys can look more mannish and can vary their apparel considerably more now than they could a generation ago.

Clockwise: Parka and slacks; daytime jumper dress; tennis dress; smock and panty; sunsuit.

In general, toddlers' sizes for girls can be classified as "dress-up" or party, everyday or play clothes, and swimwear.

Dress-up and Everyday. For dress-up, the girl can wear a short dress of organdy, dotted swiss, lace, batiste, taffeta, velveteen, or corduroy jumper with crepe blouse. Frequently, bloomerlike panties match the dress. Some panties have rows of lace ruffles. These may be called "rhumba panties." For everyday, there is the smock and pantie set of the same fabric. The smock is short and full, with a round low-necked collar to which the main fabric is shirred quite full.

Also for everyday wear, there is the two-piece tennis dress. This garment opens all the way down the front from neck to hem, is full skirted as a grown-up's tennis dress would be to allow freedom of movement in the sport. Some dresses have panties of matching fabric. This dress usually comes in 3 or 4 toddler and 2–6 or 6x sizes.

As a substitution for the tennis dress, there is an outfit called *skorts* in three pieces: a blouse, panties, and short skirt to go over the panties. The skirt may be accordion pleated.

Play Clothes. For active play, there are two-piece sets including a blouse and shorts. Each item can be purchased separately. There are two-piece pedal-pusher sets consisting of a blouse or knitted skirt and trousers that are tight fitted and come to the calf of the leg. Sometimes the pants are slit at the bottom and have been given the name of *toreador pants.*

Slacks, long trousers, or overalls with straps for toddlers are usually worn with a shirt of woven or knitted construction. For little girls, the overalls may be edged with ruffles.

For summer or resort wear, toddlers and little girls often wear one-piece sunsuits with straps.

At the seashore, the one- or two-piece girls' swimsuits are popular. The two-piece consists of a separate top and shorts or briefs. A terry-cloth robe may be worn over the swimsuit before and after a swim. Some robes have hoods.

Cabana sets consisting of shorts and shirt or blouse in bright-colored prints are popular for summer at the beach or in the country.

For outerwear, there are legging, coat-and-hat sets for spring, fall and winter; snow suits come in one- or two-piece styles. The car coat, which has been popular for adults, is also styled for the small child.

The Boy Toddlers

While there are not quite so many different styles for boys, there is always the opportunity to buy a pair of shorts and then to find a shirt to go with them. "Mix 'em and match 'em" as the store advertisement says. This combination of short and "T" shirt, sometimes called a *polo shirt,* can be found in summer or in winter weights, short or long sleeves. There are also matched shirts and shorts or shirts and overalls or slacks in different weights for year-round wear. Then there is the ever popular slack-and-jacket set in corduroy similar but more tailored than the girls' version. The Eton suit in grey or blue flannel consists of a collarless jacket and shorts. The plaid vest in cotton or rayon is styled like Dad's. It looks well with an Eton suit, white shirt, and bow tie.

Play and Outerwear. For hard play, the small version of the man's dungarees in blue denim plus a jacket of the same material is practical.

For beachwear, trunks or a bikini-type swimsuit are worn. Over it for protection against cold or sun, a terry-cloth beach robe, "T" shirt, sport shirt, or polo shirt can be worn. Cabana sets of shorts and shirts in brilliant colors are popular for all ages.

For outerwear, the water-repellent jacket with front zipper, similar to Dad's, is a *must* in a boy's wardrobe. Corduroy sets have been mentioned for fall and spring. The legging set, consisting of leggings, coat and hat to match, is traditional for "dress-up" attire; while the one- or two-piece snowsuit is an essential item for winter. The navy flannel Eton coat trimmed with naval insignia on the sleeve and cap to match is a staple style for spring and fall. Car coats, styled like father's, worn with overalls or snow pants are suitable for late fall, early spring, and mild winter days in the northern states.

Underwear

Underwear for young toddlers consists of a knitted "T" shirt and training pants (heavy knitted briefs). The older girl, wearing sizes 2–6x, can wear nylon or cotton knitted panties or tights like her mother. She can also wear a petticoat or a slip.

For little girls' underwear, cotton fabrics are very important because in knitted goods, particularly, cotton absorbs perspiration better than do rayon or nylon. Cotton knitted goods expand and contract with the movements of the body. Likewise, cotton underwear can be laundered either at home in an automatic washer or in the commercial laundry. White cotton fabrics used for children's wear can be bleached.

Sleepwear

One-piece or two-piece pajamas may be worn by toddlers. For cold weather, the garment may have feet. The knitted type for small children is called a *sleeper.* Small children, who do not keep covered at night, may wear over the sleeper a one-piece garment called a *blanket.* This is cut like a sleeper, has a front zipper, and is often made of acrylic fleece.

FABRICS USED IN CHILDREN'S WEAR

Following is a list of garments commonly worn by boys and girls from the toddler stage until school age. Opposite each article is a list of fabrics in which the garment is made:

Garments	Fabrics
Bathrobes	Quilted cotton, rayons or terry cloth
Beach robes	Terry cloth
Blouses or shirts	Broadcloth, gingham, percale, knitted cotton
Cabana sets	Printed broadcloth, percale, knitted top and woven twill shorts
Car coats	Fleece
Coat-and-legging sets	Tweed, flannel, wool fleece
Eton coat-and-jacket sets	Serge, flannel
Everyday dresses	Percale, broadcloth, polished cotton, seersucker
Jackets	Poplin, corduroy, bark cloth
Longies	Gabardine, bark cloth, corduroy, crash
Overalls and crawlers	Corduroy, denim, seersucker
Panties	Plastic-coated gingham, percale, broadcloth
Party dresses	Velveteen, corduroy, dotted swiss, organdy, taffeta, eyelet batiste, flat crepe
Pedal pushers	Polished satin, cords, crash, gabardine
Shorts	India madras plaids, batik prints, checks, twills, crash, cords, corduroy, polished cotton
Skorts	Polished cotton, broadcloth, percale
Sleepwear	Knitted cotton, flannelette, plissé crepe, batiste
Slips and petticoats	Nainsook (when well calendered, called "polished cotton"), flat crepe, tricot knit
Smock and pantie sets	Percale, gingham, embroidered lawn
Snowsuits	Cotton twill, poplin, nylon (smooth plain weave or ribbed)
Sunsuits	Plissé crepe, piqué, percale
Swimsuits and trunks	Stretch nylon, cotton knit, printed broadcloth, wool knit
Tennis dresses (two-piece)	Broadcloth, polished cotton, percale
"T" or polo shirts	Flat-knit cotton with all cotton or cotton and nylon neckband, or stretch nylon
Training pants	Cotton rib knit

You will be familiar with some of the fabrics from your study of infants' wear, but the majority are new.

In this group are several new cotton muslins in plain weave that have not yet been discussed. They include:

Nainsook, which is a fine, soft cotton muslin fabric, about as heavy as a very lightweight sheeting. It is not so fine or sheer as batiste or lawn. Recently, nainsook has been polished by calendering well on the right side. When so done, it is sold as "polished cotton." The name "nainsook" is an old name, which has been replaced by the name given.

Madras is a fine cotton fabric with a woven pattern in stripe, plaid, cord, or check. The name comes from Madras, India, where the fabric was first made. Over there, some of the dyes were not fast and "bled" (ran into each other). This feature has been emphasized as a fashion point and is often advertised as genuine Indian madras, guaranteed to bleed. Some homemakers object to this feature because, when laundered with white or light-colored clothes, bleeding madras will stain other garments. Madras of this type should be washed alone.

Batik prints are made by a form of resist printing that originated in Java. Parts of the fabric that are to resist (not take) the dye are covered with wax. In hand-done batik, a streaked or cracked effect is present where the dye has gone through the cracks in the wax. This effect can be imitated in machine printing.

Checks are small patterns, usually white combined with colors, woven in or printed on a fabric. Examples of checked designs are glen plaid, gingham, houndstooth, shepherd, gun club (large check over a smaller one found often in tweeds).

Crash is a coarse fabric having a rough texture obtained by weaving thick uneven carded yarns. It is woven of cotton, linen, or spun rayon; made in various weights for dresses, draperies, and tablecloths.

Bark cloth is a heavy cotton in a texture like tree bark. The coarse, thick yarns are in the warp. This fabric may be embossed and heat set.

Taffeta is a smooth-texture plain-weave fairly stiff fabric. It has a silky sheen. Originally it was made of silk but now may be rayon, nylon, or other synthetics.

Poplin is a plain-weave fabric made of cotton, wool, or rayon with a ribbed texture, heavier than broadcloth and with larger fillingwise ribs.

Cords are fabrics with ribbed stripes spaced at regular intervals. Cords run warpwise; made in nylon, cotton, rayon, and polyester.

Twills are a group of fabrics in twill weave. *Twill* may refer to denim, serge, jean, or gabardine.

Serge is a fabric in twill weave, made of wool, cotton, silk, or rayon yarns with the diagonal wale showing on both sides of the fabric.

Gabardine is a tightly woven twill fabric in cotton, rayon, silk, wool, or blends. It is distinguished by the fact that the diagonal wales appear raised on the right side only. The wrong side is flat.

Tweed is a rough-textured woolen fabric with a handcrafted effect. It is usually yarn dyed. It was originally made by country people in their homes along the River Tweed in Scotland. Tweeds in men's and boys' wear are twill weave but women's and girls' wear may be plain or basket weave as well.

Denim is a firm twill-weave cotton fabric. It derives its name from de Nîmes, a town in France. It comes in varied weights; the lighter ones for play clothes and draperies; the heavier weights for overalls, dungarees, and work clothes.

Flannel is an all-wool or a wool-and-synthetic blended fabric with a soft napped surface. It is usually twill weave for men's and boys' wear but may be plain weave for women's and girls' wear.

Fleece is the name of a wool, nylon, or an acrylic fabric that has a deep fleece-like napped surface.

Velveteen is a cotton fabric with a short, close pile made by the filling-float method. Velveteens with twill backs are more durable than those with plain-weave backs.

Quilted cotton is a fabric made of two thicknesses of cotton (percale or nainsook) with wool, cotton, or down batting in between for warmth. Running (quilting) stitches in patterns hold all layers together. Silk, nylon, rayon, acetate, or other synthetics may be quilted.

Selling Points of Fabrics for Children's Wear

In children's as in infants' wear, mothers are looking for fabrics that require minimum care to keep their original appearance.

Ease of Care. Again, the wash-and-wear feature is a very important selling point. This feature is accomplished by use of a 100 per cent plastic-type fiber; by a blend of rayon or cotton with a plastic-type synthetic; by a resin finish on a cotton. A 100 per cent cotton with this finish or a 65 per cent polyester and 35 per cent cotton will have this desirable feature. Since children's clothes need thorough laundering to get them really clean, a firmly constructed fast-colored fabric is required.

Durability. Mothers want a fabric that will withstand hard wear of active children who climb, slide, stretch, run, jump, and grab one another's clothes. All-cotton or cotton blended with nylon or polyester fibers will usually have this quality, particularly in twill weave. Not only must the fabric stand all these stresses and strains, but seams must be wide and stitching must be firm. Seams should be pinked (saw-tooth type edge cut by special pinking shears to prevent fabric from raveling) for firm fabrics and overcast (the sewing of the edges of a seam with long wrapping stitches to keep fabric from raveling) for pliable ones. The hems should have seam binding. The customer who buys children's wear should try to visualize the article after it has been washed and worn, for, say, six months. If the fabric and garment construction are first class, the article should look well after six months of wear.

Style. Mothers want their children dressed fashionably. Top-flight designers are creating high-fashion cottons and blends for everyday and party clothes.

Price. Purchasers of children's wear want style, durability, and minimum care at a reasonable price (within their budgets).

In this chapter, styles and fabrics used in infants' and children's wear have been discussed. The names and identifying features of fabrics commonly used for various items of apparel for these age groups have been presented. But no amount of reading about them can take the place of going to a store and seeing and feeling them. To really learn the names of fabrics, the experience of selling them in a store is an excellent way. Buying for one's family or for gifts is another good method of learning how fabrics are used.

PUTTING THIS MERCHANDISE KNOWLEDGE TO USE 》》》》》》》》》》

> DO YOU KNOW YOUR MERCHANDISE?

1. Of what materials are little girls' sunsuits made?
2. How can you distinguish: (*a*) broadcloth from percale, (*b*) cotton cord from cotton gabardine, (*c*) terry cloth from velveteen, (*d*) denim from serge, (*e*) madras from poplin?
3. What fabric or fabrics would you recommend for a little girl's party dress?
4. (*a*) Of what fabrics are beach robes made? (*b*) bathrobes?
5. Why is nylon tricot popular for girls' slips and petticoats?
6. (*a*) What is meant by bleeding madras? (*b*) Why do some people dislike bleeding madras?

> INTERESTING THINGS TO DO

1. (*a*) Arrange with one of your classmates to put on a demonstration sale in your class. (*b*) Use any article of infants' or children's wear that you can borrow from your relatives or friends. (*c*) In planning your sale, one of you will act as customer and the other as salesperson. (*d*) Follow the steps in the sale that you have learned in a class in salesmanship. Be sure the salesperson gives the selling points of the article he shows the customer.
2. Find out from "shopping" children's wear in stores or from reading ads whether any new styles in children's wear have appeared in the last six months. Describe these styles in your scrapbook.
3. (*a*) When you go to a store to "shop" children's wear, compare workmanship in two similar articles, such as overalls, (*b*) notice the evenness and width of seams, firmness of the stitches, and finishing of seams, (*c*) evenness of hems, stitching, and seam binding, (*d*) sewing on of buttons and buttonholes.

ADDITIONAL MERCHANDISE TERMS 》》》》》》》》》》》》》》》》》》》》》

Crawlers are overalls usually made with reinforced knees to protect the creeping infant.

Gathering is the drawing together of a fabric by sewing it with small running stitches.

Ruffles are shirred or gathered pieces of fabric used as trimming.

Women's Underwear, Hosiery, Foundation Garments

CHAPTER 9

UNIT 22 UNDERWEAR

THE IMPORTANCE OF THE VARIOUS FIBERS IN UNDERWEAR

One of the most interesting departments in which to sell is women's or girls' underwear. The merchandise is dainty and attractive and easy to care for. These are the chief selling points of women's underwear. On the other hand, comfort and durability are important selling points for men's and boys' underwear.

Nylon underwear for women has increased in importance because it is lustrous, soft, lightweight, attractive in pastel shades, but primarily because nylon is easily washed in the bathroom lavatory. It dries very rapidly and needs no ironing. Rayon and acetate are particularly important in foundation garments, bras, and panties. Spandex is an important fiber in this classification also.

A few generations ago, most women's undergarments were made of cotton. Starched cotton petticoats and muslin drawers with lace or embroidered ruffles were the style. But under tight-fitting sheathlike garments, cotton is not as appropriate as nylon or rayon because it does not cling to the body as well. Cotton underwear in white and pastel shades is inexpensive and is suitable for all ages.

The durability of cotton fabrics for underwear and sleeping garments depends not only on the workmanship used on the garment but also on the quality of the fiber, yarns, weave, and finish in the fabric proper and in the trimming as well. Blended with nylon or polyester fibers, minimum-care nightgowns, slips, shorts, and pajamas are important.

Silk lingerie is comfortable and not bulky. Silk knitted underwear has the "akin to skin" feeling, which makes it mold to the body. Since silk absorbs moisture readily, it is a healthy fiber to wear next to the body. Silk can be mixed with wool, cotton, rayon, or other fibers.

For summer athletic underwear, linen is cool; but it is more expensive than cotton or rayon, and it may feel clammy when saturated with perspiration. Handkerchief linen and linen cambric may be used. Linen cambric is heavier than handkerchief linen but lighter than crash. It is also used for blouses and sports dresses. Cambric may also be cotton.

Knitted underwear can be made of either woolen or worsted yarns. Woolen yarn makes a soft, fleecy, napped surface; worsted yarn makes a fine, smooth surface. Wool can also be mixed with cotton. Sometimes these mixtures are fleece lined. A backed cloth is made by knitting with three yarns at once: one yarn will make the right side; one will make the back; and one joins the two sides together. The back of the cloth is napped as a finishing process. This construction is very warm and is worn primarily for winter sports and by outdoor workers in cold climates. If a knitted cloth of one thickness is desired, wool and cotton can be blended in the fiber stage, then spun into yarn, and knitted into cloth. Infants' shirts, women's snuggies (tight-fitting knitted panties), and long underwear for skiing can be made in this way.

STYLES IN WOMEN'S AND GIRLS' UNDERWEAR

Styles in underwear are subject to the dictates of fashion as much as any item of wearing apparel. Consequently, when skirts are short and narrow, the undergarments must be made accordingly. The following basic information, however, remains unchanged.

Slips and Petticoats

A *slip* is a one-piece garment held up by shoulder straps, fitted at the waist with a form-fitting skirt a little shorter than the dress. Strapless slips are used for evening wear. Slips are made in white, black, navy, beige, red, pink, and other fashionable colors. Some slips are tailored with little or no trimming, while others are trimmed with Alençon-type lace, net, or embroidery.

Sizes of slips are according to bust measurement: 32, 34, 36, 38, 40, 42 inches, with extra sizes running up to 52. Women who wear half-size dresses may buy slips in the same half sizes.

Many women prefer to wear slips, particularly under dresses. Young women and girls often wear petticoats, sometimes called *half slips,* under suit skirts and opaque blouses.

A *petticoat* is an underskirt, gathered at the waist, and slightly shorter than the dress. It may be tailored with possibly an edging of lace at the bottom or it may be full and circular, gathered to an elastic band at the waist. The petticoat may be stiffened to be worn under a full skirt to give a bouffant effect. Sometimes a stiffened petticoat is "built in," or sewed, to the outer skirt.

Colors range from white and pastel shades (some are printed) to navy and black. The sizes of petticoats are according to waist measurements: 26–32 and 34–40 inches.

Gowns and Pajamas

Like slips, nightgowns and pajamas are made in tailored styles and with lace or ruffled trimming.

Gowns. Gowns are cut on the straight (with the warp) or on the bias (diagonally). Bias cut usually is fuller and flares attractively. Some styles have straps over the shoulder, and others are made with cap or puff sleeves. The short-length or waltz-length nightgown has become quite popular, particularly for summer.

Another style called "baby doll" is a two-piece set of loose blouse and short, full panties to match. In 1960 and 1961, the Hawaiian inspired Muu Muu won popularity. This was a very full garment hung from a round band fitted low around the neck. A shortened version of the Muu Muu was made with matching panties or shorts and was sold as a set. The Muu Muu found favor for sleepwear, for lounging, and for maternity wear. These items come in sizes small, medium and large.

Another style, which gained in popularity, was the "granny" nightgown made with a square-yoke neck, frequently pleated or edged with lace. This style calls for long, full sleeves shirred to a band edged with a ruffle at the wrist. The gown being long and full resembled the kind grandma used to wear. This style is warm for winter wear. A shortened version of this gown is a shirt length that buttons all the way down the front. Nursing mothers may prefer this style.

Dainty, feminine gowns are attractive when trimmed with lace—Alençon, val, binche, net. Embroidery and appliquéd lace or cloth designs are used as trimmings.

Pajamas. Pajamas are worn by both sexes. Women's pajamas, in strictly tailored styles, have a blouse or coatlike top and pants. In more feminine styles, fabrics are thinner and collars, cuffs, and yokes may be edged with lace. From time to time a new style is shown. It might have a high, tight-fitting (choker) collar or the Chinese coolie collar with "frogs" for the front closing. *Frogs* are narrow tapes arranged in fancy designs to outline and ornament a buttonhole.

For summer, both girls' and women's pajamas come in short lengths.

SIZES. Sizes in women's gowns and pajamas are determined by bust measure; that is, 32, 34, 36, 38, 40, 42 bust and larger. These sizes may also be designated small (32–34), medium (36–38), large (40–42).

Top row:
Waltz-
length
gown;
slip;
half-slip.

Center:
Ski
pajamas.

Bottom:
Tailored
pajamas;
baby-doll
pajamas.

Panties and Briefs

Panties for women come in several styles:

1. Brief—a very short close-fitting panty with elastic or bands at the bottom of the legs.

2. Panty—a garment with legs cut longer than a brief and with a band or elastic at the bottom.

3. Step-ins—a garment cut fuller than a panty. It hangs loose with no elastic at the bottom.

Panties and briefs come in the following sizes:

	Size	Hip Measure
Regular	4	32
	5	34
	6	36
	7	38
Large	8,9	40–42
Extra Large	10–12	44–52

Briefs and panties with elastic at the legs are regularly stocked in sizes 5–8, while band panties and step-ins come in sizes 5–8 and 9–10.

Colors are usually white, black, or pink. Some stores carry other pastel shades.

Tights. Tights made of stretch yarn are sold in either the underwear or the hosiery department. They come in several colors as well as black. Sizes are usually small, medium, or large. A familiar name is *leotard*.

Garments for Lounging

In their bedrooms, women often wear negligees (peignoirs). These are usually sheer, long garments with long, full sleeves, generally worn over a nightgown of similar fabric. For lounging at home, women often wear high-styled pajamas of elegant fabrics, a housecoat, or a robe.

Following is a list of garments of underwear. Opposite each item is a list of fabrics in which the garment is made.

FABRICS FOR WOMEN'S UNDERWEAR

Garments	Fabrics
Negligees	Chiffon, lingerie crepe, satin, velvet, all-over lace, flat crepe
Nightgowns	
(a) Granny	(a) Rayon challis, flannelette, batiste, tricot
(b) Regular	(b) Printed muslin, polished cotton, nylon tricot, flat crepe, challis, flannelette, pongee

Garments	Fabrics
Pajamas (lounging) and Housecoats	Polished cotton, sateen, satin, quilting, corduroy, flannel, pongee
Panties and briefs	Mesh knit, jersey knit
Petticoats	Taffeta, tricot knit, printed muslin, lawn or nainsook, stiffened net, nonwoven fabric
Slips	Batiste, tricot knit, flat crepe, satin

While some of the fabrics are familiar to you because they have been studied in the previous chapter, the majority of them are new. We shall discuss only the new ones.

Tricot is a warp-knitted fabric. *Tricot* comes from the French infinitive "tricoter" meaning to knit. It keeps its shape better than a weft-knitted fabric. Nylon can be heat set so it will not sag.

Satin is a shiny fabric made in satin weave. It can be made of silk, rayon, acetate, nylon, or other synthetics. Sometimes it has a crepe back. Then it is called "crepe satin."

Printed muslin is the term used in advertising and in selling. Actually, the fabric can be lawn or nainsook—more likely the latter than the former because it looks like a thin cotton sheeting.

Net is the short form for bobbinet. It is a hexagonal (6 sided) mesh of cotton, rayon, or nylon. The better qualities are fine meshes, having many holes to the inch.

Challis or challie is a very soft, lightweight fabric, which is often printed in small delicate floral designs. It was originally made of 100 per cent wool but is now made of spun rayon or nylon for nightgowns.

Pongee is a tan-colored silk or rayon fabric originally made of Chinese wild silk. It is also made in cotton. It has slub yarns that make it a somewhat rough texture.

Sateen is a cotton fabric in sateen weave. It is usually mercerized and well calendered.

Velvet is made in pile weave with a short, soft, thick-pile surface. The pile can be rayon, silk, or nylon, with a silk, cotton or rayon back. When the fabric is all cotton, it is called velveteen.

All-over lace is a fabric up to 36 inches in width, which is cut from a bolt like yard goods. The pattern is repeated "all over" the entire cloth.

Cotton knit is a weft-knitted fabric in stockinette or rib stitch.

Balbriggan is a lightweight knitted cotton fabric with a napped back. It is often in a tan shade. It gets its name from Balbriggan, Ireland, where it was first knitted.

Mesh knit is a fabric knitted in an open netlike structure.

Jersey knit is a fabric knitted in stockinette stitch—a kind of weft knitting. It is made in rayon, cotton, acetate, wool, silk, and synthetics. The warp knits are also called "jersey." A distinction should be made between them; the latter is called *tricot*.

SELLING POINTS OF WOMEN'S AND GIRLS' UNDERWEAR

Comfort. In selling underwear, remember that women want a soft, light-weight undergarment that will conform to body lines and will not show any bulkiness through the outer garment. It should be easy to slip on; should fit smoothly, not ride up; should not restrain bodily movements; should not cling to the outer garment; should not irritate the skin. If a stiffened petticoat is desired to make the outer garment stand out, it should do just that and not cling to the outer garment.

Ease of Care. Most of our underwear is made of synthetic fibers that dry quickly and need no ironing. Cottons are easily washed in an automatic washer, and the knitted type needs no ironing. Cotton batistes often have polyesters blended with them to make them drip dry quickly and iron easily (if they need any touch up).

Dainty and Attractive Appearance. Underwear is no longer all white. It is made in dainty pastels, prints, and edged with lace and often attractively embroidered. Some of the laces are quite filmy yet strong. There is an increasing amount of nylon lace being used.

Good Wearing Quality. When you buy or sell a garment, look to see if the parts of the garment are cut straight and are matched properly at the seams. Seams should be even, narrow, smooth (not puckery) with no pulled or trailing threads. Hems should be even. The quality of trimming (lace, embroidery, bindings) should be as good quality as the fabric itself. Trimming should be evenly and carefully sewed to the garment. If there are buttons on the garment, be sure they are sewed on securely and buttonholes are bound to cover all cut edges. No loose threads should be hanging from any part of the garment.

PUTTING THIS MERCHANDISE KNOWLEDGE TO USE ❯ ❯ ❯ ❯ ❯ ❯ ❯ ❯ ❯ ❯

❯ DO YOU KNOW YOUR MERCHANDISE?

1. For women's underwear, what inherent characteristics in the fabric itself make a garment easy to care for?
2. (*a*) Explain bias cut. (*b*) What are the advantages of a bias cut in a slip or in a nightgown?
3. (*a*) List the fabrics used for women's slips, (*b*) for petticoats, (*c*) for sleeping pajamas, (*d*) for lounging pajamas.
4. How can you distinguish (*a*) satin from sateen, (*b*) velvet from velveteen, (*c*) velveteen from corduroy, (*d*) rayon challis from flannelette, (*e*) polished cotton from sateen?
5. Give the selling points of a nylon-tricot petticoat with nylon lace.
6. (*a*) What is the difference between mesh knit and jersey knit? (*b*) For what articles is each type used?

1. (a) Cut out from your Sunday newspaper all advertisements for women's and girls' underwear. (b) List the fabrics in which they are made. (c) Mount each ad in your scrapbook and write the selling points of each garment.

2. *For girls:* go through your drawer of underwear: (a) Make a list of all garments with full description of the style and fabrics used in each. (b) From your experience in wearing these garments, which fabric do you like to wear best? why? (c) Which fabrics are easy to care for? why? (d) Which fabrics are not easy to care for? why?

3. *For boys:* ask your mother, sister, or female relative the following questions and write up the answers in your scrapbook: (a) What style nightgown do you prefer for summer? why? (b) for winter? why? (c) Which nightgowns are easiest to launder? (d) Do you iron your nightgowns? If yes, why?

UNIT 23   WOMEN'S AND GIRLS' HOSIERY

When we say "I must wash my nylons," we usually mean our nylon hosiery because that is what most business and professional women and homemakers consider a vital part of their wardrobes. The business woman or city dweller may wash a pair nightly.

TYPES OF HOSIERY

Then what other kinds of hosiery are there? Women and girls wear socks for sport, to high school, and at many campus colleges. Others wear long black or colored tights, which look like long stockings.

Some women are allergic to nylon and find they can buy silk hosiery in certain stores. Cotton, Orlon acrylic fiber, Dacron polyester fiber, nylon and blends of these are used for sportswear and for girls' socks. The synthetic fibers used for socks are staple fiber, and the yarns are spun.

Stretch Hosiery

What a boon stretch hosiery is to mothers with small children! One size in stretch hosiery will fit several age groups. Mother doesn't have to sort hosiery by owner. She can put all stockings in one drawer. Mothers and teen-age daughters may wear the same size in stretch nylons.

Stretch hosiery is made of stretch nylon yarn. Some familiar brand names are Helanca, Fluflon, and Agilon. There is no rubber in these yarns. Stretch yarn is made by a patented process from filament fibers that are miles long. These fibers are fluffed up to give them permanent elasticity.

Styles in stretch hosiery include these weights: (1) sheer, (2) medium, and (3) business sheer (service). They can be found with seams or seamless in plain knit or mesh. Some are run resistant. This means in full-fashioned hosiery that the stitch is locked both ways, so that, should a thread break, it cannot run. Colors in stretch nylons for women may be found in the same standard colors of regular nylons: neutral beige, brownish beige, grayish beige, a smoky gray sometimes called "charcoal."

Support Hosiery. Support stockings are advertised for relieving those who suffer from foot and leg fatigue as a result of long hours of standing. They are made of stretch yarn. These stockings are slightly heavier than the regular nylons and those currently on the market have seams. One well-known national brand *Supp-Hose* sells for $4.95 a pair. Experience has shown that they wear much longer than regular nylon hosiery. Consumers' Union questions whether these stockings prevent or relieve fatigue from standing. Elastic surgical stockings, they claim, are more effective for sufferers from varicose veins but are much heavier. Lycra spandex is also being used.

Over-the-Knee Hosiery. For women who prefer not to wear garters, there is the popular "over-the-knee" style with stretch top. *Spandex,* a generic name for fibers derived from a plastic substance called "polyurethane," is already being used in tops of men's hosiery and in foundation garments. Brand names are *Lycra* and *Vyrene.* A wholesale mail-order house gives the following instructions for ordering women's stretch hosiery:

Order size A if you wear:	Order size B if you wear:	Order size C if you wear:
8 Short or Slender	9 Long or Ample	10 Long or Ample
8 Medium	9½ Medium	10½ Medium
8½ Short or Slender	9½ Long or Ample	10½ Long or Ample
8½ Long	10 Short or Slender	11 Short or Slender
9 Short or Slender	10 Medium	11 Medium
9 Medium	10½ Short or Slender	11 Long or Ample
9½ Short or Slender		11½ Short, Medium, Slender

Courtesy National Wholesale Co., Inc., Lexington, North Carolina

STYLES IN REGULAR NYLON HOSIERY

Some stores advertise nylon hosiery as supersheer, sheer, and medium sheer. Styles include:

1. Plain knit, with or without seams, in short, medium, long lengths, and in supersheer, sheer, and medium sheer.

2. Mesh, with or without seams, in three lengths and three weights. Seamless styles are often called "bareleg."

3. Seamless sandal—foot with no heel or toe reinforcements. It is a style usually in supersheer weight to give the "bareleg" effect.

4. Knee-length seamless mesh to be worn without garters.

"Can't run" or "run-resist" features can be found in many of the above styles. Standard colors mentioned for stretch nylons are found in the styles above plus white, black, and fashion shades like green, red, blue.

Reinforcements are usually found at toe and heel. This is done by knitting in extra yarns to make the fabric heavier at points of most wear. A reinforcement high above the heel is called *splicing*. Sometimes the sole of a nylon stocking is reinforced with cotton for long wear.

Sizes of Hosiery

Sizes are determined by the length of the foot in inches, that is, 9, 9½, 10, 10½, 11. A size 9½ stocking should fit an average foot 9½ inches long. As to length: some women ask for the longest pair in the box. In some instances, the length of hosiery has been found to vary in the same box; but manufacturers who use quality control of their product are careful to finish each pair according to a predetermined standard. The average standard length of a woman's stocking is 30 inches from the heel to the top of the garter welt (reinforcement at the top of the stocking where garters are fastened). Now manufacturers are aware that some women desire longer hosiery either because their legs are long or because the length of their foundation garment necessitates a longer stocking. Manufacturers, therefore, will make a stocking that is longer than standard and one that is shorter than standard.

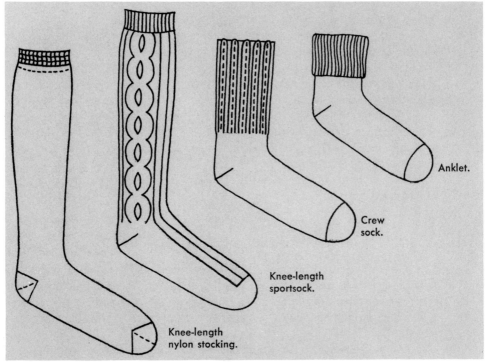

Anklet.

Crew sock.

Knee-length sportsock.

Knee-length nylon stocking.

HOW IMPORTANT ARE DENIER AND GAUGE?

Which is finer: 30-denier or 15-denier hosiery? The 15-denier is finer. *Denier* is the weight of the yarn, designated by number; the higher the denier number, the coarser, heavier, and stronger the yarn. A stocking of 30 denier would be twice as heavy and twice as strong as one of 15. It stands to reason then that, since we are demanding sheerer and sheerer hosiery, the yarns used are less and less strong; therefore, they do not give the length of service they once did.

What is gauge? *Gauge* is the number of knitted stitches (loops) to 1½ inches; the higher the gauge number, the closer the knitting. Sheer fabrics made with fine denier yarns can be strengthened by using a higher gauge number. It is easy to find a supersheer hose in 60 gauge, 15 denier fabric; 30 denier is often made in a 51 gauge for a medium-sheer stocking.

We have seen, then, that weight and size of yarn (denier) are related to gauge (closeness of the knit from the standpoint of attractive sheer appearance and relative wearing quality). In general we can say that a medium sheer should give longer wear than a supersheer.

WHAT ABOUT IRREGULAR HOSIERY?

Some stores feature irregular hosiery at lower prices than first quality. Many customers will want to know what's wrong with them.

Irregulars are really second quality or grade. It is probable that only an expert grader could tell why irregulars would not actually pass for first quality. In some instances, the irregularity may be a tiny blemish in the fabric or a slight variation from the standard in length. Most large hosiery manufacturers have quality controls backed by standards or strict specifications for first quality. If an inspector finds that a pair of hose does not meet these specifications implicitly, the article is graded "irregular." A customer may, therefore, derive just as much service from an irregular as from first quality and at a lower price.

Stockings with runs, mended places, defects in the fabric, knitting or finish are marked "seconds" and "thirds" according to the degree of defect.

HOW TO CARE FOR NYLON HOSIERY

All nylon hosiery, particularly the very sheer weight, should be handled with care. Rough hands, nails, or rings can snag the yarns. Some salespeople tell their customers to put on soft cotton gloves when they put on or take off nylon hosiery. If keys, coins, or rings are dropped on stockings, a run may develop.

Nylon hosiery should be washed in warm water in a mild soap solution. A strong soap or detergent can weaken the fabric. If new nylons are rinsed in lukewarm water before wearing, they tend to fit better. Nylons should never be dried near hot steampipes or near a stove. Fumes of strong chemicals may injure them.

Girls' and women's socks extend knee high, just above the ankles (anklets), or up to the calf of the leg. Socks come in plain, rib, or fancy stitches and in stretch styles. Regular and stretch-sock sizes are similar to sizes for stockings of similar type. The bulky rib-knitted all-cotton, all-wool, Orlon acrylic, or nylon in blends have been popular for wear with slacks or shorts. Socks are most common in all white, or white with colored border at the top. Some students wear socks with borders in their school colors; some even have the initials of their school woven into the top of the sock.

Knee-length socks in solid colors are important for wear with Bermuda or Jamaica shorts. Anklets are worn by small girls and by women, as fashion decrees.

SELLING POINTS OF HOSIERY

Appearance.   One of the most important reasons why women prefer sheer hosiery is because it looks trim and dressy and because the supersheers give a completely "bareleg" appearance. Fashionable color is also a factor in good appearance.

Suitability.   The salesperson should ask the customer if she wants a dressy-looking nylon stocking for evening or parties or if she wants one for business or everyday wear. If the former type is wanted, then the salesperson may show a supersheer; if the latter, a medium sheer.

If socks are needed, the salesperson should find out the kind of use to which they will be put: college wear with shorts or slacks; sportswear such as skiing, skating, golfing; or children's everyday wear. Based on this knowledge, he can select appropriate styles from his stock.

Fit.   Full-fashioned hosiery usually fits the leg more snugly than circular-knit hosiery (bareleg). Even though sport hose may be a bulky knit, it should fit the leg snugly. Sport socks, especially wool, are now treated in finishing so that they will not shrink out of size. Nylon or other synthetics blended with wool or cotton also help to prevent shrinkage. To insure exact fit, many women may prefer to dry wool socks on forms.

Durability (long wear).   The importance of proper denier and gauge for an intended use is one determinant of the length of wear a customer can expect from hosiery. The type of care she gives her hosiery is also a determinant of the amount of service she will get. Reinforcements on the sole, heel,

CHAPTER 9 · WOMEN'S UNDERWEAR, HOSIERY, FOUNDATION GARMENTS   **177** and toe help to lengthen the life of a pair of stockings. A run stop just below the garter welt and run-resist type of knitting should increase durability. A high-gauge fabric is closer knitted and stronger than a loosely constructed one. Coarser denier yarns are stronger than finer denier, and therefore denier is a factor in durability.

Style. Features of style may include a particular fashionable color, a fancy stitch in knitting, length of the sock or stocking, sheerness, and even the use of a new fiber.

Comfort. A stocking is considered comfortable if it does not bind the leg to restrict its movements; if it stays in place when worn; if it does not pinch the toes because it feels too short; if it has no uncomfortable seam over the ball of the foot; if it is warm in cold weather and cool in warm weather. If in selling, you can emphasize some of these features of comfort, you will be telling the customer about some of the points she looks for in buying.

Price. In general, all-cotton hosiery is the least expensive. Cotton blends and mixtures are next. In socks, wool is usually the most expensive, with blends of wool with synthetics next. Women's nylon hosiery sells from under $1 to about $2.50 a pair. High style features will add to price. Silk hosiery is usually more expensive than nylon. Price alone is not a measure by which you can judge how long a stocking will wear.

PUTTING THIS MERCHANDISE KNOWLEDGE TO USE ❯ ❯ ❯ ❯ ❯ ❯ ❯ ❯ ❯ ❯

❯ DO YOU KNOW YOUR MERCHANDISE?

1. Explain the following labels: (*a*) hosiery made of 30 denier 51 gauge, (*b*) hosiery made of 15 denier 60 gauge.
2. (*a*) What are the selling points of irregular hosiery? (*b*) List and explain the grades of hosiery.
3. Give complete instructions for washing nylon hosiery.
4. (*a*) How is stretch hosiery made? (*b*) For what purposes other than hosiery is stretch yarn used?
5. (*a*) Explain what is meant by "splicing," (*b*) by "run-resist," (*c*) by "bareleg" hosiery.
6. (*a*) What styles of women's hosiery are used for sport? (*b*) How can one try to prevent runs in regular nylon hosiery?

❯ INTERESTING THINGS TO DO

1. Find out how long a pair of stockings or socks will wear. For this experiment, use a new pair of nylon or all-lisle (cotton) hosiery. Boys may use a pair of their own socks. Wear the same pair of stockings every day, washing them every night in lukewarm water with neutral soap flakes. Dry them slowly away from radiators or steampipes. If the hosiery does not dry overnight, then another pair of hosiery may be worn on alternate days, and their wearing quality compared with the other pair.

Keep a record to show any changes in appearance of the hosiery and also any signs of wear.

2. (*a*) Make a list of the styles of women's and girls' sport socks. (*b*) Go to a store to see how many styles are actually carried and what fibers they are made of. (*c*) Which styles are most popular for school wear? (*d*) for active sports?

3. (*a*) Go to a mail-order office or the mail-order desk in a store operated by Sears, Roebuck or Montgomery Ward. From the catalogue see if the women's nylon hosiery is arranged by: (1) size, (2) price, (3) gauge and denier, (4) color, (5) mesh or plain knit, (6) length, (7) seams or seamless. (*b*) Make a list in the order in which the above items appear in the catalogue.

UNIT 24 FOUNDATION GARMENTS

Foundation garments support and control the figure in a manner that makes the lines of an outer garment fit and look better. While women are critical of the way a dress or suit may fit, few women realize that a properly fitting foundation garment improves the lines and fit of the outer garment. Like hosiery, foundation garments are becoming lighter in weight; and they have less boning. Most of them can be washed either in the automatic washer at home or by hand.

KINDS OF FOUNDATION GARMENTS

Some garments are intended to give only slight support; others give some support; while still others give a good deal of support and control. Generally speaking, the boned types give more support and control the figure more than the unboned stretch type.

Types of foundation garments include:

1. Stretch Panty or Panty Girdle. This is a pull-on type of girdle usually with no zipper closing. This garment has a crotch to form panties, which often can be detached for laundering. It has no bones and is knitted of all-stretch yarn or is made of plain-knitted fabric with merely elastic waist and leg bands. It may have only elastic or stretch panels. This garment is best suited to the slender or average figure and is especially suitable to wear under slacks and shorts. Sizes are small, medium, large, and extra large, running

24–32 inches waist size. In summer, the mature woman may find it comfortable under casual-style clothes. A longer version of this stretch style is called "pedal tights," intended especially for wear under pedal pushers. Inexpensive garments may be made of acetate 65 per cent, cotton 24 per cent, and rubber 11 per cent. More expensive versions may use nylon or spandex. These garments generally have detachable garters. A short-short version of the stretch panty is the sport brief intended for wear under Jamaica and Bermuda shorts.

2. Girdles. A girdle is also a pull-on step-in garment. It often has a few bones to keep the abdomen flat and to control the hips. Most girdles close with a zipper at the left of the center front. Garters are attached or are detachable. Sizes run from 27–40 inches waist measure.

3. All-in-Ones. As the name implies, this garment is a combination of bra and girdle, extending to below the buttocks. It is sized according to bust measure; that is, from 34 to 42 regular and 44 to 52 extra large, with bra cups A (small), B, and C. On the whole, this type of garment is worn by the more mature figure. All-in-ones are lightly boned with elastic hip panels; they may be cut low at the back; some are strapless for evening wear. They close at the left side with a zipper.

The bra section is sometimes semidetached in the front to give more freedom of movement.

One version of the all-in-one is somewhat shorter and is used primarily to cinch the waist and back.

4. Corsets. A corset is a heavily boned garment for the extra large figure. Fabrics used are heavier than those for the types previously mentioned. Special corsets for maternity wear and specially designed surgical corsets require professional fitting.

5. Bras. A bra, which is short for "brassiere," is made with or without straps. A bra may cover only the bust, or may extend to the waistline. The latter are called *long-line bras*. Sizes run from 32–44 (A, B, and C cups).

6. Garter Belts. Garter belts are functional items intended to hold up the stockings. They do not give support. Sizes usually run from 24–32 inches waist measure.

Fabrics Used

The closings, edgings, and padding of foundation garments use plush or flannelette, because of their softness.

It will be noted that labels on foundation garments are quite specific as to their fiber content under the T.F.P.I.A. Some typical examples were given

Garment	Fabric
All-in-ones	Cotton and/or nylon lace body, webbing (acetate, rubber, nylon, Dacron polyester); body 50 per cent nylon, 25 per cent rayon, 25 per cent rubber (cups 70 per cent acetate, 30 per cent nylon)
Bras	Schiffli-embroidered cotton broadcloth or nainsook; lace over satin; cotton broadcloth, sateen, nylon taffeta
Corsets	Coutil, heavy muslin, cotton-backed satin, Jacquard (elastic Jacquard), nylon taffeta, lace trimming
Garter belts	Cotton, nylon net, Schiffli-embroidered cotton or nylon; elastic webbing
Girdles	Broadcloth; mesh in cotton or nylon; satin, sateen, taffeta, coutil; all with elastic webbing
Stretch panties	All nylon stretch yarn in knitted jersey construction, cotton knit, elastic knits (acetate 65 per cent, cotton 24 per cent, rubber 11 per cent); kinds and meshes of spandex fibers and yarns

in the above listing of fabrics. On a label on a long-line bra, the fibers were identified as follows:

Cups
$\begin{cases} 60\% \text{ nylon} \\ 31\% \text{ acetate} \\ 9\% \text{ rubber} \end{cases}$
Rigid panel: 100% nylon
Elastic panels
$\begin{cases} 55\% \text{ rubber} \\ 27\% \text{ acetate} \\ 18\% \text{ polyester} \end{cases}$

You will know most of the fabrics used for foundation garments; four new ones are:

Webbing is a strong, closely woven fabric made in narrow widths for use as panels and insets in foundation garments. Elastic webbing is woven with rubber threads as part of the warp. Webbing may be made of stretch yarns, nylon, or spandex.

Coutil is very closely constructed cotton, cotton-and-rayon, cotton-and-nylon fabric with a firm herringbone twill weave. It is a very strong fabric.

Jacquard is a fabric with intricate woven-in designs, made on the Jacquard loom.

Schiffli is a kind of machine embroidery.

SELLING POINTS OF FOUNDATION GARMENTS

Improvement of Appearance. The garment should firm and smooth the figure, so that the dress or outer garment fits and looks better. The young average or slim figure needs no real support, so that a lightweight garment with little or no boning is satisfactory. The more mature figure, and especially the full figure, is improved by a properly fitting foundation garment. Ill-proportioned figures and those requiring special types of control should have the advice of a corsetiere before purchasing a foundation garment.

Comfort. Some women are so dependent on a foundation garment for support that they cannot go without it. In this case, comfort means support without restraint of bodily movements. The athletic type may want to move freely and yet to have a slight support. The matron may want to be cool in summer yet have some support from a foundation garment. The young college girl may just "feel better" with a stretch panty under her shorts.

Ease in Care. Women want a foundation garment that is washable, and if possible machine washable. They want it to dry quickly. Our synthetics and drip-dry finishes are the answer to this desire.

Attractiveness. Women want a foundation garment that is attractive in color with a femininity about it.

Price. The price should be reasonable, so that the average woman may own several garments without upsetting the budget.

PUTTING THIS MERCHANDISE KNOWLEDGE TO USE ❯ ❯ ❯ ❯ ❯ ❯ ❯ ❯ ❯ ❯

❯ DO YOU KNOW YOUR MERCHANDISE?

1. Distinguish among the following fabrics: (*a*) coutil from Schiffli-embroidered broadcloth, (*b*) nylon net from nylon lace, (*c*) cotton-backed acetate satin from sateen, (*d*) mesh from webbing, (*e*) stretch knits from elastic knits.
2. List the selling points of foundation garments.
3. What style in socks would you recommend for a woman to wear with Jamaica shorts for summer?
4. What are the advantages of spandex in women's foundation garments?
5. Why is stretch nylon yarn used so frequently in girdles?
6. (*a*) Explain the meaning of the underlined terms in the following label on a girdle.

> Body: 50% nylon, 25% rayon, 25% rubber. Webbing: acetate, rubber, nylon, Dacron polyester.

(*b*) What is your estimate of the wearing quality of such a garment? Why? (*c*) Will it be easy to care for? Why?

❯ INTERESTING THINGS TO DO

1. Ask your mother, sister, or female relatives the following questions: (*a*) What styles of foundation garments do you wear? (*b*) For what occasions is each style worn? (*c*) How do you cleanse these garments? (*d*) Are these garments comfortable? (*e*) About how much do you have to pay for each of these styles? (*f*) In what type of store do you buy these garments? (*g*) What features of a foundation garment are most important to you? (*h*) Did you have the services of a professional fitter? If so, what did she tell you about the garment? If not, who helped you in your selection? What did she tell you about the garment?
2. Write up the answers to these questions in your scrapbook.

ADDITIONAL MERCHANDISE TERMS ❯❯❯❯❯❯❯❯❯❯❯❯❯❯❯❯❯❯❯❯❯❯❯

Appliqué is a design of lace or of cloth which is sewed (appliquéd) to another fabric.

Fiber "H" is Du Pont's new kind of nylon, which is especially resilient; hence, the fiber is particularly comfortable in stockings.

Lounging pajamas are a garment of elegant fabric, with trousers designed for wear informally at home.

Undergarments. See underwear.

Underwear are articles of apparel worn under the dress, blouse and skirt, or shirt and trousers.

CHAPTER
10

Dresses and Sportswear

UNIT 25 DAYTIME DRESSES

SELECTION

"Chic," "elegante," "jolie" were adjectives used by the French press when Jacqueline Kennedy, the late President's wife, went to Paris about four months after her husband was inaugurated President of the United States.

Mrs. Kennedy has done a great deal to give the women's fashion industry new impetus, because the styles that she wears are chic, simple in line, and elegant in fabric. Her choice of clothing shows she likes fashion. She has an appreciation of what is in good taste; she has a look of individuality and flare. A *chic appearance,* then, means individual becomingness of the garment; a feeling for high-fashion design, color, and quality of workmanship. A person who makes a chic appearance is usually one who expresses her taste through the dress she wears. The upper social and high-income group is the one that can afford the best in clothing, which often comes at a high price. These garments are individually made in the establishments of exclusive fashion designers, not by mass production. The mechanized dress industry provides women in the middle- and lower-income groups with garments that reflect majority tastes. Women in these groups who have a knowledge of fashion, color, line, design, and fabrics will be able to select ready-to-wear garments which also will express their sense of style and their individual tastes. Ready-to-wear garments are articles of apparel which are made in a factory, as opposed to those made by dressmakers and custom tailors.

Determining Factors

Many types of costumes are worn for the different types of activities that women engage in during the day. The style of garment may differ with the climate; the kind of home one lives in (apartment or suburban home); the time of day; the kind of occupation.

For instance, the young suburban or urban homemaker may wear slacks and shirt, or shorts and blouse or skirt to do her housework. She may even take her children to the park or to the supermarket in this attire. In the afternoon, she may change to a one- or two-piece dress.

The older woman may wear a housedress or housecoat in the morning to change to a one- or two-piece street dress when she goes out.

The business and professional woman or volunteer worker will usually select a rather tailored dress in dark conservative colors for work in the city. In small towns or villages, women office workers may be less conservative in style. In large retail stores located in cities, women salespeople are often required to wear black or navy in conservative styles.

FABRICS USED IN DAYTIME DRESSES

Cotton or cotton and a polyester or a triacetate are popular for spring and summer in the northern and middle states, while in the south these fibers are worn the year around. Cotton is always important for houseworkers and nurses. On a warm July day, no fabric is more comfortable than cotton.

Left: Housecoat for a young woman.

Center: Robe for an older woman.

Right: Classic shirtwaist dress for business or shopping.

The textures of cotton may vary according to style. In some seasons, smooth, shiny cottons are the vogue; in other seasons, bumpy, slubby, or nubby surfaces are in style; in another season there may be a trend toward tweedlike or hand-woven textures. However, some fabrics are always in demand year in and year out regardless of season. Below are listed some of these so-called staple fabrics in cotton which are used for daytime dresses:

Plain Weave (no variation)			
Batiste	Crepes	Gingham	Percale
Bouclé (may be knitted)	Dotted swiss (plain	Indian Head	Ratiné
Chambray	ground with clip	Lawn	Seersucker
Chintz	spot dots)	Nainsook	Voile
Crash	Flannelette	Organdy	

Plain Weave (rib variation)		Plain Weave (basket variation)		Sateen Weave
Bedford cord	Dimity	Sailcloth	Oxford	Sateen
Broadcloth (slight	Poplin			
irregular rib)	Tissue gingham			

Twill Weave		Pile Weave		
Denim	Khaki twill	Corduroy	Terry cloth	Velveteen
Foulard	Piqué (padded twill)			
Gabardine				
Jean				

We often speak of linenlike textures. These fabrics are not necessarily all linen. They may be silk with a surface appearance like linen, or they may be a cotton or a blend with synthetics. As mentioned in Chapter 2, linen is mostly imported for clothing and is therefore not used as extensively as cotton or the synthetic blends for dresses. Linen is fairly expensive for use in moderate-price dresses. It is used for domestics, accessories, and play clothes. Handkerchief linen or linen crash (dress linen) are the most common dress fabrics.

DAYTIME AND SPECTATOR-SPORTS WEAR

For more tailored dresses for daytime and spectator-sports wear (a dress worn to watch a football game, a tennis match, or golf tournament) there are:

Bouclé—a bumpy-textured fabric, made of ply yarns in different tensions. It may be plain weave or knitted.

Broadcloth—a dull-textured, lightweight silk, in solid colors or stripes.

Tussah—a fabric woven from uncultivated (wild) silk worms of Asia. It has sparse, irregular ridges on the surface of the fabric. Tussah toile is also woven of wild silk to give a linenlike, homespun appearance.

Honan—a Chinese silk, similar to shantung, but the slub yarns are in both warp and filling.

Pongee—see page 171.

Shirting—a spun silk with a soft but firm feel.

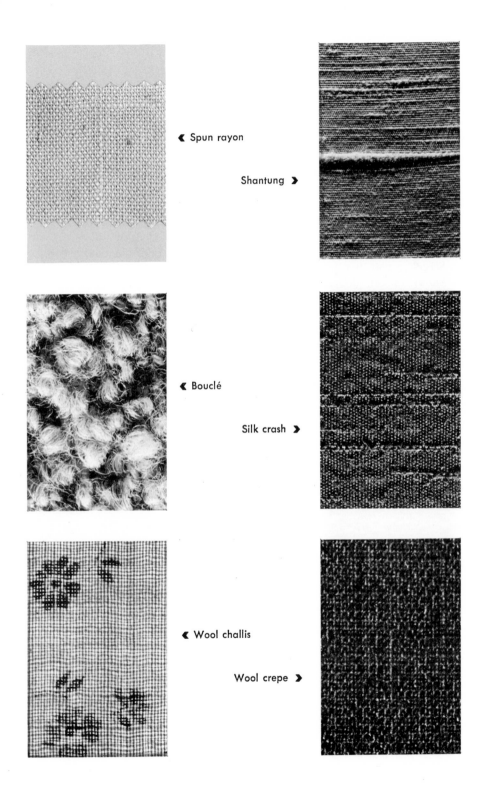

« Spun rayon

Shantung **›**

« Bouclé

Silk crash **›**

« Wool challis

Wool crepe **›**

Dress-up Occasions

For "dressier" occasions, there are the following fabrics:

Alpaca—a slightly shiny silk, woven to resemble the alpaca hair fiber. It is fine textured, with a slightly wiry feeling.

Crepe de chine—a slightly lustrous, medium-weight crepe with a soft, crinkly texture.

Faille—a soft, glossy, finely ribbed fabric.

Flat crepe—a firm, medium-weight crepe with very little crinkle (hence called "flat" crepe).

Gabardine—see page 163.

Grosgrain—a very heavy fabric with crosswise ribs or cords.

Ottoman—a heavy, glossy fabric with large widely spaced ribs.

Peau de soie—a soft, medium-weight fabric with faint diagonal wales.

Serge—a soft, fine fabric in twill weave; see page 163.

Surah—a soft, glossy fabric in twill weave with flat-topped wale or diagonal ridge.

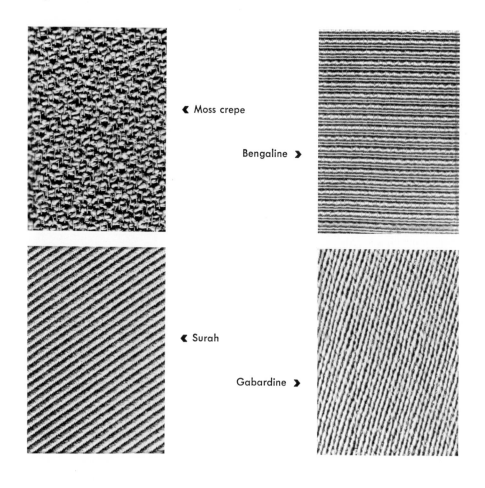

❮ Moss crepe

Bengaline ❯

❮ Surah

Gabardine ❯

In wools, there are lightweight and medium-weight dress fabrics in both woolen and worsted. Some are nubby and rough, while others are soft, and still others are firm and smooth surfaced. Some of the wool dress fabrics include:

Challis—a very sheer fabric in plain weave, usually printed with small floral designs; also made in rayon.

Flannel—see page 163.

Crepe—either a woolen or worsted fabric with a slightly crinkled surface.

Serge—see page 163.

Gabardine—see page 163.

Tweed—used for dresses in the lighter weights of the fabric. See also page 163.

Viyella flannel—a trade name for a cotton-and-wool flannel for the tailored type of dress. It is used also for shorts, sports dresses, and blouses.

Synthetics

As we have said, the synthetic fibers can be blended with one another or with natural fibers for dresses. Where used alone, they are made in textures resembling silk, cotton, linen, or wool.

Some of the more common fabrics made of synthetics are:

Alpaca crepe—a fabric in rayon and acetate in wool texture.

Bengaline—a heavy ribbed fabric similar to faille but with larger ribs running fillingwise; often made with rayon warp and cotton filling cord; also can be silk or wool warp with cotton or wool filling.

Challis—see Wool challis.

Crash—see page 163.

Faille crepe—see *Silk faille crepe*. Also made in rayon, acetate, or other synthetics and blends.

Flat crepe—see *Silk flat crepe*. Also made in rayon, acetate, or other synthetics and blends.

Foulard—a lightweight, soft, fine twill-weave fabric made of rayon, acetate, polyester, or other synthetic fibers. Can be made also in cotton or silk.

French crepe—often called *lingerie crepe*. A plain-weave acetate, rayon, or other synthetic fabric made by pressing the cloth over a fleece blanket. It is used for summer daytime dresses and blouses.

Jersey—see page 171.

Pebble or moss crepe—usually made of abraded yarns (rayon and acetate) in warp and filling. The plain weave is varied by skips of warp over two fillings and two fillings over two warps to give a pebbly appearance.

Poplin—see page 163.

Romaine crepe—a semisheer fabric of abraded yarns in warp and filling. It usually is made of rayon and acetate. It can also be made of wool. It is generally worn for street and "dressy" dresses. Also made in wool or silk.

Seersucker—a fabric with alternated plain and crinkled stripes. It may be acetate and rayon or other synthetics. It is also made of cotton, and silk. Seersucker is used in summer dresses.

Surah—see Silk surah. Also made in rayon, acetate, or other synthetics.

Taffeta—see page 163.

PUTTING THIS MERCHANDISE KNOWLEDGE TO USE ❯❯❯❯❯❯❯❯❯❯

❯ DO YOU KNOW YOUR MERCHANDISE?

1. Give the constructions of the following cotton dress fabrics: (*a*) bouclé, (*b*) flannelette, (*c*) batiste, (*d*) dimity, (*e*) corduroy.
2. (*a*) What is meant by a chic appearance? (*b*) Can one learn to dress in a chic manner?
3. How can you distinguish: (*a*) honan from shantung, (*b*) broadcloth from poplin, (*c*) flat crepe from faille crepe, (*d*) ottoman from bengaline, (*e*) wool challis from wool flannel?
4. What fabrics are best suited for house dresses?
5. What fabrics are best suited for street dresses?
6. What fabrics would you recommend for a salesperson to wear in a department store? Why?

❯ INTERESTING THINGS TO DO

1. (*a*) Go to a department store in your town to check on dress regulations for salespeople. (*b*) Observe the color, texture, fabric worn by a salesperson in the dress department. (*c*) Write down the names of the fabrics, colors, textures in your scrapbook.
2. (*a*) Ask your mother, female relative, or friend who is a homemaker which fabrics she prefers to wear mornings for housekeeping. Why? (*b*) List them in your scrapbook.
3. (*a*) Ask a business woman what fabrics she prefers to wear to business in the winter? (*b*) for summer? Why?

UNIT 26 AFTERNOON AND EVENING DRESSES

For occasions in the late afternoon and evening—such as cocktail parties, formal teas, concerts, dinners, theater, night clubs and dances—a woman wears a dressier garment, often in a more luxurious fabric, than she wears for street or business. Those fabrics that have sheen, are crisp, sheer, or have pile textures look attractive in later afternoon and evening styles. Silk and the synthetics fill these requirements in appearance.

Antique taffeta—a fabric woven to resemble those elegant fabrics of the eighteenth century. It is often made with spun slub filling yarns on the back and reeled silk or filament synthetic warp yarns on the face of the fabric. This fabric is also used for draperies.

Barathea—a heavy silk with a woven-in dobby pattern that resembles the bricks of a house. It is also used in men's neckties.

Brocaded taffeta—a fabric with a Jacquard pattern. There is a definite right and wrong side, and the fabric often has metallic yarns or gold- and silver-dyed yarns that look rich and luxurious. This fabric is also used in men's smoking jackets and robes. Brocade is indeed a luxury fabric and is best suited for formal afternoon and evening wear.

Moiré and moiré taffeta are characterized by designs that look like watermarks in the cloth.

Tissue shantung—a lightweight shantung. These crisp fabrics are very well suited to the bouffant styles (those that stick out in full-skirted cocktail and evening modes).

GLOSSY FABRICS

One of the most-used glossy textured fabrics is satin or crepe satin (satin with a crepe back). Satin brocade is a luxurious fabric in Jacquard weave but softer than brocaded taffeta. The design is slightly raised.

SHEER FABRICS

Fabrics that give a diaphanous appearance are particularly suited for summer afternoon and evening dresses. In fact, chiffon, the airy, sheer soft crepe, seems to float when worn on a dance floor. Yet it has been just as popular for dressy afternoon and cocktail wear as for formal evening.

Silk organdy, often called *silk organza* or *mousseline de soie,* a crisp sheer fabric very similar to cotton organdy. It is a youthful-looking fabric and makes beautiful teen-age formal dresses. This fabric may be made of synthetics as well as of silk.

Marquisette—a leno-weave fabric, often associated with cotton curtains made in silk or synthetics. It is used in the same type of dresses as chiffon.

Net or tulle—a very soft, fine transparent silk, synthetic, or cotton mesh, an excellent fabric for graduation, party, and formal dresses for the teen-ager. It is usually stiffened for these purposes. Tulle is a finer mesh (more holes to the inch) than net (bobbinet). A net even finer than tulle is called *silk illusion,* used chiefly for bridal veils.

Point d'esprit—a silk net with a woven, raised dot; also used for face veils.

Georgette—a silk or synthetic fibered fabric with a more crepy texture than chiffon. It often feels cottony to the touch.

All-over lace—a fabric cut from the bolt, is admirably suited for cocktail and evening dresses. It is usually made of silk, nylon, or cotton in chantilly, Alençon, or shadow patterns.

VELVETS

Velvet textures (pile weave) are one of the most luxurious of all textures. When made of all-silk, the fabric is soft, with a dense pile. It may be a solid color or a print.

Chiffon velvet—a finely woven all-silk fabric just described. It is expensive.

Brocaded velvet or burnt-out velvet is woven of two different fibers. The pile is usually rayon, and the back is often silk. Rayon is a vegetable fiber, and silk is an animal fiber. In the finishing process, the fabric is printed with acid paste that burns out the rayon pile and leaves the silk back. It is usually the background of the pattern that has the pile burned. This burning-out method is cheaper than a Jacquard weave would be.

Embossed velvet—a velvet whose pattern is made by embossing (pressing) it into the fabric. This method is relatively inexpensive and is not permanent—particularly in dry cleaning.

Transparent velvet—a fabric in pile weave. The back is either silk or rayon, and the pile is rayon. It is thinner and woven more loosely than Lyons velvet.

Lyons velvet—a heavy velvet originally woven in Lyons, France. It is heavier and stiffer than chiffon or transparent velvets. Originally made with silk pile and cotton back. If made of synthetic fibered pile, it is called *Lyons-type* velvet.

We have neglected to mention cotton and linen fabrics for afternoon and evening dresses. The sheer, crisp-finished cottons—such as lace, organdy, lawn, dotted swiss, voile—can be used appropriately, particularly for the teenager and for women's summer wear. Even gingham, generally worn for daytime and play clothes, is suitable in the evening if it is appropriately styled. Cotton piqué (a padded twill with vertical wales) is attractive in a dress with a tight-fitting bodice and full-gathered or flared skirt.

POINTS A SALESPERSON CAN EMPHASIZE IN THE CONSTRUCTION OF A DRESS

Since most dresses worn by the average woman are made in factories by mass production, the quality of the construction of the garment is obviously different from that of a custom-made dress. Some dress manufacturers, in order to sell a garment at a low price, will use inferior construction or workmanship. In order to determine how well made a dress is, here are some of the points to look for:

1. Be sure the vertical lines of the dress design run parallel with the warp—unless the skirt or blouse is cut on the bias (on the diagonal). In the sleeve, the warp should run straight from the shoulder seam to the back of

the wrist bone. The filling yarns in the sleeves and blouse should run similarly (crosswise). Both shoulder lines should be smooth. Armholes fit better if they are not cut too low.

2. Look to see how wide the seams are: (a) side seam should be 1 inch wide; (b) waist seam should be ½ inch wide; (c) hem should be 2½ inches wide.

3. Look at the workmanship to see if the seams are: (a) stitched with strong colorfast thread darker than the fabric; (b) pinked on firm fabrics; (c) overcast for pliable fabrics; (d) seam binding used for hem.

4. Look to see if: (a) placket closing of garment is one continuous, lengthwise seam; (b) front facings are turned over the hem. Bias facings are cut on the true bias; (c) the underfold of the pleat is deep, and pleats are pressed straight; (d) all fitted darts are straight and smooth; (e) pocket is reinforced by tape stitching at points of strain.

SIZES IN WOMEN'S AND GIRLS' DRESSES

In Chapter 8, we discussed children's clothing (girls') through size 14. This included a department often called the "Pre-teen" or "Sub-Teen." The next department, as far as sizes run, is the Junior Dresses. These sizes are adapted to a somewhat shorter, more girlish figure with a small waist and bust. Sizes here run 9, 11, 13, 15, 17.

Misses' sizes, which comprise the majority of garments sold to the normal, mature figure, are 10, 12, 14, 16, 18, 20. There is a tendency for stores to carry smaller sizes in this range; that is, 8 and even 6. But the average store usually has a good assortment of misses' sizes from 12–16 and usually 18.

Half sizes were designed to fit the woman 5'5" or under with relatively full hips. They are also shorter waisted and the arms are shorter and fuller than misses' sizes. Sizes run 12½, 14½ 16½, 18½–26½.

A tall, mature woman with full hips, arms, and bust would wear a woman's size 32–52.

Some dress manufacturers specialize in stout sizes to fit the woman with a large bust, large waist, and wide hips. Stout sizes run from 34½ to 52½.

PUTTING THIS MERCHANDISE KNOWLEDGE TO USE ❯ ❯ ❯ ❯ ❯ ❯ ❯ ❯ ❯ ❯

❯ DO YOU KNOW YOUR MERCHANDISE?
1. What fabrics would you recommend for cocktail dresses?
2. How can you distinguish: (a) antique taffeta from brocaded taffeta? (b) net from tulle? (c) georgette from chiffon? (d) marquisette from net? (e) brocaded velvet from chiffon velvet?
3. (a) For what figure type are half sizes designed? (b) women's sizes? (c) misses' sizes? (d) junior sizes?
4. What points should the salesperson stress in the contruction of a dress?

5. (*a*) Distinguish between Lyons velvet and Lyons-type velvet. (*b*) Lyons velvet and transparent velvet.
6. (*a*) By what other names is silk organdy called? (*b*) For what occasions is a silk organdy dress appropriate?

> INTERESTING THINGS TO DO

1. The girls should take a street dress from their wardrobe and examine it for all points of good garment construction. The boys can ask their mothers or sisters for a street dress for this purpose. (*a*) In what respects, if any, did the dress which you examined fall short of having good construction? (*b*) Record this information in your scrapbook.
2. Look through one rack of dresses in a store or in a wardrobe at home. (*a*) Write in one column the occasion for which each dress is suited. In the opposite column write the name of the fabric. (*b*) Record this information in your scrapbook.
3. (*a*) Watch for an announcement in the newspaper of a fashion show in a store in your nearest city or town. (*b*) Attend the showing. (*c*) Take notes on: occasion for which each dress would be worn; the fashion details of the dresses shown; the name of the fabric, color and texture in which it is made. (*d*) Report your visit to your class.

UNIT 27 BLOUSES AND SKIRTS

The salesperson who sells blouses and/or skirts has a good opportunity to make good sales because many women buy blouses in quantity for themselves and for gifts. One well-known company alone, Judy Bond, reported that in a recent year they had manufactured some 6 million blouses.

IMPORTANT POINTS IN A BLOUSE

If you are selling either blouses or skirts, don't let your customer leave without trying on the garment. Knowledge of size is not enough. A blouse should be chosen to fit the individual figure. When the customer has the blouse on, then you should look to see if:

1. Collar sets smoothly
2. Fullness at the bust is sufficient with no pull wrinkles below the bust
3. Upper armhole is smooth with seam of upper armhole parallel to the center front or center back
4. Blouse is smooth across the shoulders
5. Sleeves hang straight
6. Side seams hang straight

FABRICS USED

One of the most satisfactory fabrics is polyester (Dacron or Kodel) 65 per cent and cotton 35 per cent; however, this fabric might be too thin to wear with Bermuda shorts or too loose over a skirt. A fabric of this blend is usually durable and requires minimum care. Other satisfactory blends are 55 per cent or more polyester with rayon; 50 per cent or more polyester with acrylic; 80 per cent or more acrylic with cotton; or 55 per cent or more acrylic with wool. An all-cotton fabric with a special minimum-care finish is usually quite satisfactory as a blouse fabric; also a linen-crash or handkerchief-linen fabric if treated for crease resistance makes a very attractive, durable blouse.

For traveling or for general wear, a tricot Arnel triacetate is a good blouse fabric because it does not wrinkle and drips dry without ironing.

SELLING POINTS OF A GOOD BLOUSE

1. A blouse with a minimum of fussy frilling. If it has pleats, they should

Left:
Frilly blouse.

Right:
Tailored blouse.

be heat-set; and if there are ruffles, they also should be permanently heat-set. This type of blouse will appeal to the business woman and the young mother who has very little time to fuss with washing and ironing.

2. A fabric with a smooth surface will look fresher longer than one with a rough surface.

3. Seams, pockets, and collars should be smooth and not puckered when new. Seams should be wide enough not to pull out, and raw edges should not show.

4. Buttonhole stitches should be carefully finished so they will not pull out in wear or in laundering. Buttonholes cut crosswise stay buttoned better than those cut lengthwise.

5. Buttons should be smooth and all of the same thickness.

SKIRTS

In this section, separate skirts will be discussed, not those that are a part of a suit or a two-piece dress. Separate skirts are made in sizes according to waist measurement—from 24–46 inches.

Some skirts are cut on the straight of the material (with the warp), so that the side seams follow the grain of the goods, thus leaving a center seam that is slightly on the bias. In a bias-cut skirt, an allowance is usually made for sagging. Circle skirts are cut round like a circle. Other points in the garment construction follow those given under "Dresses."

Skirt fabrics are usually heavier than blouse fabrics. You are already familiar with all these fabrics. They may be knitted bouclé, cotton broadcloth, corduroy, crash, denim, tweed, faille, flannel, gabardine, mesh, Jersey knits, piqué, poplin, seersucker, serge, taffeta, terry cloth, tricot, velveteen, viyella flannel, and wool crepe.

PLAY CLOTHES OR SPORTSWEAR

So-called play clothes are not always used just for an active sport but, because they are designed for comfort, are often worn to the supermarket, to the park with the children, to do the household chores, to take the small children to school, and many other purposes. These apparel items may come under a larger classification of "Sportswear." Shorts or slacks and knitted shirts can be worn for playing badminton, boating, tennis, golf, hiking, bowling, and many of the activities mentioned below.

Some of the most popular articles originally designed for specific active sports are the ski suit for skiing; the walking shorts and shirt for hiking; the clam diggers (pants below the knees) designed for digging clams; the pedal pushers (three-quarter-length pants) designed for cycling; the polo shirt for playing polo; Bermuda shorts for resort wear in Bermuda and Jamaica shorts for Jamaica; the car coat for automobile riding. Additional uses for these articles now are, for instance, the ski suits worn everyday in the winter by

Clockwise:
Sweater and
slacks; striped
blouse and capri
pants; pullover
sweater and
pleated skirt;
ski suit with
stretch pants.

small children; polo shirts worn by women, girls, men, and boys for almost any type of casual attire; clam diggers used by women for gardening, shopping, housekeeping, as well as some of the active sports.

Bathing suits are designed in one- or two-piece garments, with or without straps. Some garments have very short, full skirts attached. They are made of cotton or wool knits, gingham, seersucker, elasticized faille and satin, and broadcloth. Skating outfits may consist of knitted tights with bodice and short skirt made of velveteen, corduroy, jersey, and elasticized satin.

Co-ordinates are two or more articles—such as shirt and slacks, skorts (short skirt), sweater, jacket, shorts, and culottes—which in color and fabric texture "go together." Items may be sold separately, so that a customer can buy as many articles as she wishes. Skirts, sweaters, and blouses of various styles are also sold as co-ordinates.

FABRICS USED

The type of fabric used in summer sportswear is not so heavy or warm as that worn in winter in the northern states. Fabrics for summer include denim, bleeding madras, hopsacking, crash, terry, cotton gabardine, chino, polished cotton for dungarees, slacks, shorts, culottes, clam diggers, pedal pushers. Shirts may be made of mesh, jersey knit, woven fabrics such as gingham, broadcloth, percale, terry cloth, seersucker, batiste, and chambray.

Fabrics for winter sportswear include wool flannel, viyella flannel, corduroy, wool gabardine for slacks; wool flannel, flannelette, corduroy, wool jerseys for sport shirts.

Our discussion in this chapter has centered primarily around the fabrics that are best suited for daytime and evening dresses and for sportswear. You have probably noticed that the same fabrics recur in various uses. You will also observe that in a given season some fabrics are more popular than others and may then become less important in another season.

FASHION FABRICS AND STAPLE FABRICS

You will probably notice fabrics with names unfamiliar to you. These names may be brand names or fashion names. However, if you know the staple names (a *staple* fabric is a cloth that must be kept in stock at all times to satisfy customer demand) and identifying features of the fabrics in this chapter, then it will be easier to recognize the fashion names. For instance, you now know how to recognize cotton gingham. If you should see it in a lighter weight and with a metallic yarn woven into it, the fashion name of the fabric might be "metallic tissue gingham." "Tissue" usually means lightweight. If you were to see a chambray, which, as a staple fabric, has colored yarns in the warp and white in the filling, with two different colored yarns in warp *and* filling, the fashion name might be "iridescent chambray." Suppose a silk shantung were made in twill weave instead of plain weave, then you could call it by a fashion name of "twilled shantung." With a knowledge of staple fabrics, you can often figure out where a fabric designer got his idea for a fashion fabric. Your buyer will often "glamorize" a fashion fabric by giving it a new name to appeal to the customer. If a fashion fabric is appropriate for its intended use; if customers find it satisfactory; and if they demand it over a long period of time by buying dresses and sportswear made of it, then that fashion fabric may become a staple fabric.

PUTTING THIS MERCHANDISE KNOWLEDGE TO USE ❭ ❭ ❭ ❭ ❭ ❭ ❭ ❭ ❭ ❭

❭ DO YOU KNOW YOUR MERCHANDISE?

1. If you are selling a good-quality silk-foulard blouse to be worn with a navy wool-faille spring suit, what selling points would you stress?
2. What are the names of some summer fabrics found in separate skirts for daytime wear?
3. Describe the following styles: (*a*) Bermuda shorts, (*b*) Jamaica shorts, (*c*) pedal pushers, (*d*) skorts, (*e*) culottes.
4. Describe the costume and fabric that you would recommend for playing tennis.
5. Give the selling points of a nylon elasticized swimsuit.
6. Why is a knowledge of staple fabric names helpful to a salesperson of dresses or sportswear?

❭ INTERESTING THINGS TO DO

1. (*a*) Visit a department store that carries patterns. Look at a brand, for example McCall, Vogue, or Simplicity. Find their patterns for women's sportswear. (*b*) List in one column the styles of garment patterns sold for sportswear. (*c*) In the opposite column, list the fabrics recommended by the pattern book for each style.
2. (*a*) You and a classmate put on, in class, a demonstration sale of an item of sportswear. (*b*) Ask your teacher if she will please discuss the sale with the class, after you have finished the demonstration.
3. (*a*) Cut out an ad of an article of sportswear from a newspaper or magazine. (*b*) Mount the ad in your scrapbook and write opposite it or under it all the selling points given for the article.

ADDITIONAL MERCHANDISE TERMS ❭ ❭ ❭ ❭ ❭ ❭ ❭ ❭ ❭ ❭ ❭ ❭ ❭ ❭ ❭ ❭ ❭ ❭ ❭

Bodice is the waist of a dress.

Casual style is an informal comfortable mode of dress, often worn at home, in the suburbs, or in the country.

Couturiere is a female fashion designer. Couturier is a male fashion designer.

Darts are tapered tucks sewed into a garment to shape it to the figure.

Flared skirt is a skirt fitted at the waist and hips and cut full at the bottom in a bell-shaped silhouette.

Full-gathered skirt is a skirt shirred onto a waistband to make it full all around.

Garment construction is the way a garment is cut and put together.

Hem is the edge of fabric at the bottom of a garment folded under and sewed.

Placket closing is the opening at the side of a skirt or dress for convenience in putting it on.

Pleats are creased folds stitched in a garment, usually a skirt. Pleats may be pressed to be knifelike or unpressed.

CHAPTER
11

Women's and Girls'
Outerwear

UNIT 28 COATS AND JACKETS

Mrs. Foster read an advertisement for car coats in her morning paper. The headline for this ad said "134 Years of Bargains—Lowest Prices in History." Mrs. Foster had read bargain ads for so many years that she would have been skeptical had she not known that this particular store had been in business for 134 years. She wanted a car coat to drive to the supermarket and to take the children to the park. So she clipped the ad and went to the store to look at the coats. She had trouble finding a salesperson who could tell her whether or not they were water-repellent. They were not. After all, the ad did not say they were, and what can one expect for $2.99? The lining was a cotton flannel, not so warm as a quilted or a wool lining. Again, what can one expect at this low price? Mrs. Foster tried on several models and liked one in green, in size 12. She had read in a fashion magazine that green was a popular fall color. Size 12 fitted her nicely. The shoulders were smooth and were just the right width, and the garment seemed roomy. The fabric in the body and sleeves of the coat was cut with the grain of the fabric, and the bottom of the coat seemed to hang evenly. The buttons were not sewed on firmly, but, in view of the low price, Mrs. Foster was willing to resew them. She was also willing to reinforce the sewing on the patch pocket to make it stronger. For the trimming on the collar, Mrs. Foster preferred the corduroy to a knitted fabric because it seemed to fit better and to look more like a fall coat than the knit. She examined the cotton poplin and noticed that it was closely woven.

Mrs. Foster is an example of a customer who knows how to make an intelligent selection. She not only knew the points to look for in garment construction and in fit, but she also considered the color and quality of the fabric. She did not expect perfection in all essentials at the price she had to pay. But at the price, the garment was a good value.

A car coat.

ESSENTIALS OF A WELL-MADE COAT

The *car coat* is a special type of short coat, which is a very popular item for casual wear for women, girls, and children.

For girls' wear, it is particularly important that coats of any style be roomy with large armholes and curved underarms to allow the arms to be raised above the head without pulling out the seams. Fullness of cut is also important for active women. Any outer garment should have adequately wide, even, pliable seams to keep them from pulling out. There should be reinforcements at points of strain. All buttons should be firmly sewed on, and buttonholes or loops should be made evenly and durably. Belts should be run through slides or stitched firmly at the sides of the garment, so there will be no slipping or loss of the belt. A coat collar should set up and fit snugly around the neck. If there are lapels, they should be the same width on each side and should roll back smoothly against the chest.

Linings for coats and jackets must be cut to fit the outer garment smoothly. All seam stitching of linings should be firm and even so the fabric will not pucker. In first-class tailoring, linings are closely hand stitched. Seams at armholes should not strain when the garment is put on. A loose stitching of the lining at the bottom of a coat, when attached to the outer garment, makes for good workmanship and also prevents the lining from showing below the outer garment.

FABRICS FOR COATINGS—NATURAL FIBERS

A spring coat in the northern states is usually a lighter weight and a lighter color than a fall coat. A winter coat is much heavier. Since World War II, however, there is a trend to lighter weight outer clothing supplemented by sweaters or warm dresses under it. It was found that servicemen were warmer with lightweight layers of clothing than with one very heavy outer garment.

Cashmere, Alpaca, Vicuna

One of the most popular coating materials in weights for spring, fall, and winter is the cashmere fleece. It is soft, lightweight, and warm. *Cashmere* is a goat fiber that comes from Outer Mongolia, Tibet, China, India, Iran and Iraq. Fibers from the first three countries are finer than from the last three. *Alpaca,* also a goat fiber, is used for lining sport jackets and also for the outer fabric of coats. *Vicuna,* from a South American goat of that name, is also used for coats, but it is rare and very expensive. Frequently wool is blended with cashmere and camel's hair. Many uninformed customers think that 100 per cent hair fiber is more desirable than a blend with wool. Actually, 35 per cent or 40 per cent wool blended with cashmere will improve the wearing quality. Also, there are various qualities of cashmere for sale. If you have studied furs, you will know that they have guard hairs to protect the down fur underneath. To avoid the expense of removing guard hairs, processors leave them in. They are long, coarse, and wiry, so that the coating feels harsh. One can tell if they are present by pulling fibers out at a seam. If some fibers are long and wiry, these are guard hairs and do not represent good quality cashmere.

Wool

Wool is always popular in all weights for coats. Its chief selling points in this use are:

Attractive Appearance. Wool can be dyed in rich, soft, muted colors or in intensely high shades. A thick nap of a woolen or an intricate woven design of a worsted appeal to the customer. Wool also drapes and fits well.

Feeling or Touch. A woolen usually has a soft, warm, springy feeling. Woolens are warmer, spongier, more pliable, and less firm than worsteds.

Ease in Care. Wool fabrics are slow to pick up soil because of the fibers' resilience. Because of the resilience, wrinkles tend to hang out. Wool absorbs moisture slowly; therefore, soil, which is carried in the moisture, can be sponged off the fabric before it dries. However, when soil finally becomes embedded in the fabric, it is very difficult to remove. Wool coats should be dry-cleaned.

Comfort and Protection. Wool has microscopic scales along the fiber, so that it naturally sheds water when the fabric is slanted. Because wool absorbs moisture slowly, it can hold much of it before it feels damp. This is the reason why the wearer of a wool garment is protected from sudden chill. In Chapter 2, we mentioned the fact that the wool nap traps the still air close to the fibers, so that these traps prevent the warm air from escaping from the body. Hence the wearer of wool is warm in cold weather. Some wool fabrics for spring are woven so loosely that the air passes through the open weave to ventilate the skin.

Microscopic view of wool fiber showing scales.

Suitability for Use. Wool fabrics are suitable for any climate because they can be made into lightweight porous coats for mild weather and napped, closer woven fabrics for cold weather. A zip-in fur or wool lining can be added to make a coat suitable for both mild and cool weather. When a polyester, acrylic, or nylon is added to wool, the abrasion resistance and strength of the fabric are improved.

Cotton

Cotton is admirably suited to the windbreaker type of water-repellent jacket and raincoat. A very close firm weave makes a poplin or twill excellent for this purpose. Cotton corduroy and cotton and rayon tackle twill, treated for water repellency, are also used in raincoats.

FURLIKE FABRICS—SYNTHETICS

In the past few years furlike fabrics, often incorrectly called "fake furs," have become extremely popular. They are made in styles similar to real fur coats and are sold at a fraction of the cost of real fur. Some fur fabrics are so well styled and the pile so well dyed that it is difficult for a customer to tell the difference at a quick glance. These fabrics are pile weave with woven or knitted backs. They may imitate seal, beaver, broadtail, mink, but in any advertising the F.T.C. ruling specifies that the name of the fur imitated be mentioned and the word "Imitation" added: "Imitation Beaver," "Imitation Broadtail," and so on. The ruling also specifies that the retailer call them "furlike fabrics" so that the customer will not confuse them with real furs. Various combinations of synthetic fibers are used, for example, Verel and Dynel modacrylic fibers, acrylics, and rayon.

Some familiar brand names are: Cloud 9, Borgana, O'llegro, Bakella, and Glenara. These fabrics are also used, in addition to full-length coats, for short dress jackets and coat collars.

NAMES OF FABRICS USED FOR COATS AND JACKETS

Raincoats are made of fabrics with plastic coatings or resin finishes that repel water. Nylon fabric is a popular raincoating because it is lightweight and dries quickly. Plastic film is a nontextile. Textile raincoats are more comfortable than the rubber or plastic-coated ones because they let the skin "breathe."

Wool or blends with synthetics include fleece, broadcloth, doeskin, flannel, hopsacking, tweed, cheviot, homespun, poplin, covert, some wool crepes, serge, bouclé.

Furlike fabrics include "Imitation Broadtail," "Imitation Beaver," "Imitation Mink."

Synthetics and/or silks include faille, ottoman, satin, velvet, taffeta, brocade for evening wear.

Cotton and synthetic blends are poplin, twills, piqué, bark cloth, denim, crash. Cottons are most often used in sports jackets and raincoats.

Fabrics New to You

Cheviot—a woolen or a worsted in twill weave. It is usually similar in appearance to a tweed, but it is a little lighter weight and somewhat smoother.

Covert—a sturdy cotton or wool fabric used originally for riding breeches (to ride to covert). It was originally made with two-ply yarns—one white and one colored to give a salt-and-pepper appearance. It may be made in solid color with a nap.

Doeskin—a fabric of wool, cotton, or synthetic fibers made with a nap resembling doeskin leather.

Homespun—a fairly coarse woolen coating in plain weave. The warp is white and the fillings are generally raw stock (fiber) dyed.

Hopsacking—a cotton, wool or synthetic blended fabric in loose, plain, or basket weave resembling a sacking used for holding hops. Used for sports jackets and casual style coats.

See Units 21, 22, 25, and 26 for a description of all other fabrics for feminine apparel. It is possible to have synthetic yarns blended or mixed in any of these.

PUTTING THIS MERCHANDISE KNOWLEDGE TO USE ❯❯❯❯❯❯❯❯❯❯

❯ DO YOU KNOW YOUR MERCHANDISE?

1. What are the selling points of wool for women's coatings?
2. (*a*) Define a furlike fabric. (*b*) What is the F.T.C. ruling on advertising of these fabrics? (*c*) Why have furlike fabrics become popular for winter coatings?
3. Give the selling points of a coat made of 70 per cent cashmere and 30 per cent wool.
4. How can you distinguish: (*a*) a good quality from a poor quality of cashmere? (*b*) a real fur from a furlike fabric? (*c*) a plastic-coated

fabric from a plastic film? (*d*) hopsacking from tweed? (*e*) fleece from doeskin?

5. What are the selling points of a good-quality car coat?
6. Why is a nylon fabric raincoat practical?

❯ INTERESTING THINGS TO DO

1. Collect all information you can find on furlike fabric winter coats: (*a*) *Suggestions:* (1) Look through mail-order catalogues. (2) Find out from shopping in department stores the names of the brands of furlike fabric coatings. (3) Clip ads in newspapers and magazines. (*b*) When you have collected all this information, prepare your findings in the form of a talk to give your class.
2. Borrow two raincoats from your family and prepare a sales demonstration for the class.
3. Compare prices, quality, colors, styles of women's cashmere coats in three different types of stores: (*a*) a high-style specialty store, (*b*) a semipromotional store, (*c*) a highly promotional store or discount house. Write up your findings in your scrapbook.

UNIT 29 SUITS AND SWEATERS

SUITS

While suit fashions change, certain classic styles are good for many seasons. These jacket styles are tailored very much like men's suit jackets and should fit the figure just as perfectly, if they are to be considered well made. They usually have a straight skirt with a kick pleat in the back or front; or a slit in the back or front; or slits on both sides to give room for walking.

Then there are more dressy suits. For example, fashion might decree accordion pleats and full backs with pleats and raglan sleeves. High-fashion suits may last only one season, only to be replaced by another fashion. This type of suit has been called a "dressmaker suit" because it looks as if a dressmaker had made it, rather than a man's tailor.

What then is the difference between a suit and a suit-type dress? A *suit* has a fully lined jacket, whereas a *suit-type dress* is generally unlined. Lately, fashion has called for a one-piece dress with a short sleeve or no sleeve to be worn under a waist-length fitted jacket with three-quarter or full-length sleeves. This is a very practical garment, because the dress with jacket can be worn for street or business and the jacket can be removed for dinner and evening.

Fabrics Used in Suits

There are suits for spring, summer, fall, and winter.

Summer suits, including suit-type dresses, may be made of seersucker, cotton or linen crash, cotton gabardine, or blended with synthetics, or 100 per cent synthetic fibers, polished cotton, cords (cotton or synthetic blends), cotton shantung. These cotton fabrics are cool and comfortable. Women like the minimum-care fabrics that can be laundered in automatic washers. They come in a variety of patterns and are comparatively inexpensive.

Spring and fall suits are generally made of wool covert, worsted poplin, some wool crepes, jersey, serge, flannel, mohair, fancy knits, cashmere, bouclé, wool shantung, sharkskin, gabardine. A heavier fabric is usually used for fall suits.

Winter suits come in wool tweed, heavy knits, wool broadcloth, fleece (wool or cashmere), homespun, hopsacking, cavalry twill, flannel.

Fabrics New to You. You will probably find only one or two of the suiting fabrics with which you are unfamiliar.

Cords—fabrics with vertical ridges (cords) which are often yarn dyed. Made in cotton, polyester blends, triacetate and cotton, acrylic blends, wool.

Wool broadcloth—a very soft twill-weave woolen with a thick nap that is pressed in one direction.

Hopsacking—See page 204 for description.

Cavalry twill—a firmly woven hard-finished worsted with a steep double twill. Used also for riding breeches, slacks, coats.

Sharkskin—a worsted fabric originally made in white, blue, navy, brown, black—now woven in plaids, stripes, and patterns.

In addition, there are fashion fabrics that cannot be described here because they vary widely in appearance and may be in fashion only one or two seasons.

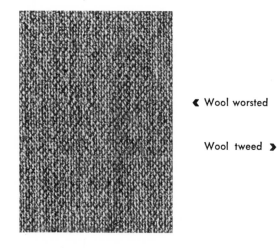

◀ Wool worsted

Wool tweed ▶

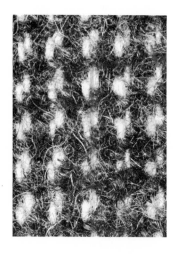

Linings. Coats, suits, and jackets must have linings that are easy to slip on, durable, and attractive. The cotton fabric that best meets these requirements is *sateen,* which is smooth because of its weave, durable and attractive because of its short floats and mercerized finish. Cotton may be mixed with rayon in such fabrics as *brocades* for coat linings and *twills. Flannelette* (cotton) is frequently used for lining of sports coats and jackets. *Silk* linings or blends and mixtures with synthetics make attractive linings. *Satin crepe* (crepe back and satin face) is silk, acetate, rayon, and synthetics. It is suitable for lining women's coats. Brocades and satin stripes are frequently used for the linings of furlike fabric coats. Zip-in linings are often made of real fur or wool flannel.

SWEATERS

The two classic styles in sweaters that every store must carry are the *cardigan* and the *pull-on.* A cardigan buttons down the front like a jacket; a pull-on is pulled on over the head. It usually has no buttons but may have two or three small ones at the closing of one shoulder seam. The sleeves may be short or long. These styles remain popular year after year. Then there are unique sweater styles which come in when Dame Fashion decrees.

A simple style in a woman's suit dress with a loose, straight jacket.

Sometimes there is a fashion demand for Tyrolean, Scandinavian, or Scottish sweaters. See the illustrations of a cardigan and of a pullover sweater on page 197.

The term *fashioned sweaters* does not refer to the way the sweater is styled but rather to a special kind of construction of the seams. We have described full-fashioned hosiery that must have seams because the stocking is shaped by knitting stitches together to make it narrower to fit the leg. The same thing is done in sweaters by turning the lines of knitting so that they run parallel to the seams. The result is a neater seam when fabrics are sewed together parallel to the lines of knitting. Fashioned sweaters keep their shape and appearance better than nonfashioned ones; however, if you look closely, you will see that not all sweaters are fashioned at every seam.

Fibers and Yarns Used in Sweaters

Natural and synthetic fibers, as well as blends, are used in sweaters.

Orlon Acrylic. One of the most popular lightweight sweaters worn by the majority of women is one made from Orlon acrylic fiber. Women like Orlon acrylic sweaters because they feel soft—almost like cashmere when new. These sweaters are machine washable and feel somewhat thicker than other synthetics. They are also colorfast. Frequently Orlon acrylic yarn is made bulky by Du Pont's patented process. One objection to Orlon acrylic is that it may pill, but these balls of fibers are all on the surface and can be literally shaved off with an electric razor.

Wool and Wool Blends. Almost every woman knows that an all-wool sweater tends to shrink; and once it has felted from shrinkage, there is no way of restoring its original softness. Therefore, most women wash wool sweaters by hand and block them to restore them to their original measurements.

A very warm sweater is one made of Shetland wool. Many of these are twice as thick as most wool or synthetic sweaters and hence considerably warmer. Lamb's wool is also a very warm fabric.

Wool, like nylon, will pill. Unfortunately, the pills cannot be removed by shearing. They can be pulled off, but in time the fabric loses wool and a thin spot or hole may result.

Cashmere is a very desirable fiber for sweaters. It is exceptionally warm, lighter in weight and softer than wool. Because of its high price, relatively few women can afford the luxury of a cashmere sweater.

Textured Nylons. Textured nylons are made of those knitted yarns that have been made bulky or napped. Sweaters made of textured nylon are sold under the familiar brand names of Ban-Lon, Tycora, and Renel. Consumer Union has tested sweaters made of these three brands of textured yarn and found they did not pill at all. Their test of a textured Dacron polyester was a close-knit, relatively smooth fabric. In a C.U. test this sweater tended to snag on slightly rough surfaces.

Selling Points of Sweaters

If you are selling women's sweaters, you can point out:

1. Evenness of the knitting
2. Fashioning (look for fashion marks along the seams)
3. Neatness and finishing of the seams
4. Quality of the buttons and how they are sewed on
5. Sewing of the buttonholes
6. Special features such as style, textured yarn, ease in care, warmth, softness.

❯ DO YOU KNOW YOUR MERCHANDISE?

1. (*a*) What is the difference between a suit and a suit-type dress? (*b*) Of what fabrics can each be made?

2. (*a*) What is meant by pilling? (*b*) What fabrics are apt to pill? Why?

3. (*a*) Name two classic styles in sweaters. (*b*) Why are they called classic styles?

4. (*a*) Of what fabrics are coat and suit linings made? (*b*) Why is sateen a good lining material?

5. How can you distinguish: (*a*) worsted sharkskin from serge? (*b*) cords from poplin? (*c*) wool broadcloth from flannel? (*d*) cavalry twill from tweed? (*e*) homespun from tweed?

6. (*a*) Of what fabrics can winter suits be made? (*b*) spring suits? (*c*) fall suits?

❯ INTERESTING THINGS TO DO

1. Make a survey of styles in women's sweaters. (*a*) Suggestion: Read fashion magazines such as *Vogue* and *Harper's Bazaar*. Study ads in magazines and newspapers. Shop high-fashion stores. (*b*) Write up your findings in your scrapbook.

2. Go over articles of outer apparel in your wardrobe. Feel in pockets of coats for balls of fibers (pills). Look on surfaces of sweaters, scarfs, suits, etc. Record your findings in your scrapbook.

3. Ask your mother, sister, or female relative the following questions and write up your findings in your scrapbook: (*a*) What kind of sweater do you like to wear best? Why? (*b*) Of what fibers is it made? (*c*) Is it full-fashioned? (*d*) What color is it? (*e*) Is it easy to wash or clean? (*f*) Do you have any objections to it? (*g*) Does it have a brand name?

UNIT 30 MILLINERY AND OTHER ACCESSORIES FOR WOMEN AND GIRLS

MILLINERY FOR WOMEN OF ALL AGES

Hat styles change from season to season as fashion dictates new materials and shapes. The hat manufacturers are always anxious to capture the woman's eye with appealing new silhouettes, colors, and sizes of hats. In recent years, the trend toward hatlessness of women and girls has made manufacturers redouble their efforts to create styles so attractive that every young girl and every woman may be enticed to buy one or more hats. Most outfits for street wear look more attractive when worn with an appropriate hat.

Why do women wear hats? Sometimes the weather necessitates the wearing of a hat. Hats protect the head from cold and shade the eyes from the summer sun. Sometimes the occasion demands a head covering. The person may be attending church, applying for a job, or attending a business or professional meeting. Such occasions frequently require the wearing of a hat. Some women like to accent their outfits with an attractive hat. Hats may add height to short women, may hide minor facial blemishes on others, may protect the hairdo, or hide straggly hair. Many women wear a hat because it is flattering and they feel more attractive in a hat.

HISTORY OF HAT STYLES

Records of millinery being worn both for decorative appearance as well as warmth and protection may be traced back through history some thousands of years. Through the ages, the materials used, the manufacturers' skills, hair styles, and men's headdress styles have influenced women's millinery fashions.

During the early periods, most headdresses were made from natural materials such as cotton, linen, silk, or wool. They were fairly simple in form— mostly draped kerchiefs and small caps. Embroidered decorations and flower trims were added later. By 1500 B.C., felt was used for caps.

Women continued through the centuries to wear kerchiefs or "wimples" with or without crowns. By the thirteenth century chinbands of white linen were being worn. These were fastened to forehead bands or to low crowns.

The Christian religion greatly influenced women in concealing their hair. This, naturally, affected hat styles during the medieval period. Many of the styles of headdress worn by religious orders today were developed at that period of history.

Cauls (ornamental caps resembling shower caps) and *turbans* that concealed the hair were worn during the fifteenth century. During the mid-sixteenth century, the *beret* came into style, and later a small brim was added to it. Toward the end of the century, the beret crown had grown very tall. By the seventeenth century, the *postilion,* a high-crowned, narrow-brimmed hat ornamented with ostrich plumes, became popular.

The period of the French Revolution brought many millinery style changes. As a result of Marie Antoinette's interest in rural settings and activities, straw hats with small crowns and wide brims with simple ribbon trim were in vogue. Straw then became the new, fashionable material for all the court ladies to wear.

From time to time, women have adapted men's hat styles for their own. Thus we have *derbies, slouch hats, sailors,* and *fedoras* that were originally worn by men.

Today there is no end of versatility in women's hats. They may be soft or stiff, made from woven or knitted fabric, fur or wool felt, or natural or synthetic straw. They may be large or small, shape retaining or crushable. They may be worn for daytime, evening, or casual occasions. They may be extremely simple or extravagantly ornate.

Although virtually any material may be used for millinery, the basic ones include felts, straws, and fabrics. Trimmings include feathers, ribbons, veiling, lace, artificial flowers and fruits, and metal and stone clips or pins.

Felt and Velour

Wool and fur fibers, because of their scaly structure, will interlock when steamed and pounded together to form a felted fabric that is neither woven nor knitted. *Wool felts,* which are somewhat harsh to the touch, are used in inexpensive millinery; while *fur felts,* which are softer and more luxurious, are used in better hats. Rabbit fur is used for the majority of fur felts. More costly, silkier felts are made from beaver fur. When these fur felts have a long, silky nap they are known as *velour.* A synthetic felt made of Dacron polyester fiber was developed by Du Pont in 1954. It is made of staple fiber by a method of heat-setting at 300–400 degrees. This heat treatment accomplishes what pounding and steam does for wool since it locks the fibers together.

Felt or velour is shaped initially over huge, perforated cones about 3 feet high. These fibers are then compressed repeatedly by steam and pressure until they have been matted to the right size to make a hat and brim.

Wool felt is heavily sized and therefore may waterspot easily. Fur felts rarely have much sizing and therefore are not affected when caught in the rain. Steaming and brushing a felt will usually restore all but the poorest quality to its original texture and appearance.

Straw

Both natural and synthetic straws are used for millinery. Natural straws are made from palm leaves, stems, rice shoots, and grasses. Bleaching makes the straw white or cream colored. Some hats, such as the *panama, leghorn, baku,* are woven by native workers into rough form. The finer these straws are, the more difficult they are to weave, and the more costly they will be when finished. *Toyo,* made from Japanese rice paper, imitates the panama and is made in a similar manner. The woven straw is then blocked to give it the final shape. *Blocking* is done by placing the straw on a wooden form in the shape of the finished hat. This block is then steamed to shape the straw. After drying, the shaped or blocked straw is removed.

Less costly straws are woven or plaited in narrow strips or braids which are then sewed together into the desired shape. These hats may also be formed over a block. Braid straws include Milan and Swiss braids. Stiffening is added to natural straws by use of a gelatinous glue.

Synthetic straws are made from cellophane, rayon, Dynel, and nylon. These may be made in various widths and in an unlimited color range. Synthetic straws range in price from inexpensive to fairly expensive.

Velvet and Other Fabrics

Cotton, rayon, and nylon velvet fabrics are also used for hats. Velvet is usually popular for between-season wear in August and September. Other fabrics also may be made into hats. Either soft, drapable hats or stiffened hats may be made from velvets and other fabrics. Buckram frames give the form to the shaped hats made from fabrics.

Fur Hats

Winter fashions often include fur hats. These may be made from any type of fur and in any style. Prices of fur hats range from inexpensive to very costly depending on the type of fur used and whether the fur is cut from whole animal skins or pieced from leftover sections of fur garments. Pieced furs must be so labeled according to the Fur Products Labeling Act discussed in the chapter on furs.

Trimmings

In addition to the body materials used to make hats, other materials are used for trimmings. Veilings, feathers, ribbons, and jewelry ornaments are the popular trimmings used.

Veilings. Veilings are made from fine to coarse nets, which are stiffened with glues and starches. These veilings may be steamed to shape but may become limp if they are soaked by rain. Veilings may trim a hat, may form the material of the hat, or may be used with flowers or bows to make *whimsies,* tiny umbrella-shaped coverings for the hair.

Feathers. Feathers from various types of birds with their delicate to dramatic colorings have long been used as a decorative accent on some types of millinery. In some seasons, hats entirely covered with feathers are in fashion. Poor-quality hats have the feather ornamentation glued on; while in better quality hats they will be sewed together.

Ribbons. Ribbons of different materials are used in a variety of ways to decorate ladies' hats.

MANUFACTURE OF MILLINERY

While certain materials and factors of workmanship affect the price of millinery, this product is more difficult to judge in determining value than other items of wearing apparel. There are many reasons for this. Millinery fashions change faster than any other item of clothing. Stores may change their entire stock of millinery every few weeks. Thus, designers are kept busy

> > Eight Basic Hat Styles < <

Turban

Sailor >

< Pillbox

Toque >

< Cartwheel

Hatlet >

< Beret

Cloche >

creating new styles. When a designer creates millinery for a custom house where the hats are handmade and only a few are constructed from any one design, the resulting hats are costly to produce. When, however, they are made from similar materials but in mass production for sale all over the country, the costs may be substantially curtailed. Sometimes a hat when first designed is expensive, but a few weeks later it may have been copied and appear at a fraction of its original cost.

In addition to materials and design, the actual workmanship affects the price of the hats. All parts and trim on better millinery are sewed into position. Less expensive millinery may have trimmings glued on. Inexpensive hats may use machine stitching for sewed parts while more costly hats may be completely hand sewed.

Linings in expensive hats may be made from luxurious fabrics or costly laces, while inexpensive hats may have no lining or merely a thin rayon one.

HAT STYLES

While certain styles of hats may or may not be fashionable in a given season, there are recurring hat styles that millinery salespeople should know.

Beret—a soft-crowned hat with a headband. Usually the crown of the hat may be pulled in different directions. The hat is made from any material.

Breton—a stiff hat with rolled brim. This is a youthful style featured for young girls usually; however, when the breton is in fashion, it is worn by women of all ages.

Bonnet—a hat with or without a protective brim which is shaped like a baby's bonnet or like a sunbonnet. It may have a ribbon that ties under the chin. This style is usually worn by young girls. It may be made from any material.

Calot—a small skull cap made from fabric or felt.

Cartwheel—a firm, large-brimmed hat named for the wheel which the shape and size of the brim resemble.

Cloche (pronounced "closh" from the French meaning "bell")—this bell-shaped hat usually has a small brim and is made from any material.

Derby—this hat has a stiff, rounded crown and a small rolled brim. It is commonly made from felt.

Halo—a beret-type hat with the crown pulled up high in the front to give a "halo" effect to the wearer.

Pillbox—a small, round-shaped, stiff hat that sits on the top of the head. It may be placed on the front, center, or back of the head. Any material may be shaped into a pillbox.

Sailor—an adaptation of the nineteenth-century hat worn by sailors. It has a small to large, stiff, straight brim and a low crown. It is made in all materials and is worn by women of all ages when it is in fashion.

Sou-western—adapted from the fisherman's hat, this brimmed hat with a deep sweep in the back has made a few limited appearances on the fashion scene. It may be made from any material that has sufficient body for this style.

Toque—a tall, brimless hat made from felt, straw, fur, or soft materials over a frame.

Turban—a brimless hat made from fabric draped gracefully around the head.

HAT SIZES

For infants, head coverings such as caps, hoods, and bonnets come in sizes according to age. They range usually from sizes for newborn babies to those 6 months of age; from 6 months to 1 year; and from 12 months to 24 months.

Young girls' hats are usually adjustable to fit all those in the age ranges of 3 to 6x. Girls age 6 to 12 years wear hat sizes ranging from 19½ inches to 21½ inches. Teen-agers' hats usually range from 21 to 22 inches in size. Women's hats are available in sizes 21¾ to 23½ inches with size 22–22½ as the most usual. Many styles of hats such as pillboxes, calots, and knitted caps fit all head sizes.

To measure the head, a tape measure should be placed around the head just over the eyebrows. A hat should never fit too snugly as it can cause a headache.

ARTIFICIAL FLOWERS

While many artificial flowers are made of nontextiles such as paper, wax, and glass, very often flowers on dresses and coats may be made of the same material as the garment. Transparent velvet, rayon taffeta, rayon satin, rayon lace, or rayon sheers can be used.

NECKWEAR AND SCARFS

Neckwear includes such items as collars, cuffs, and stoles. Collars, cuffs, and scarfs are made of dress fabrics that are familiar to you, such as velveteen, taffeta, organdy, handkerchief linen, crash, lace, satin, and polished cotton. Stoles can be made of knitted or woven wool, velvet, furlike fabrics, metallic cloth, brocade, satin, or crepe. The last three named may be silk.

HANDKERCHIEFS

Handkerchiefs for evening wear may be made of rayon or nylon lace, silk, or rayon chiffon.

For daytime use, particularly for display in a pocket, an embroidered handkerchief of linen or a fine cotton batiste or lawn is appropriate. Lace trimming is not uncommon. Handkerchiefs are also featured in stores as gift items for special occasions. For example, for St. Valentine's Day, handkerchiefs may be printed with hearts; for Christmas, with holly.

Selling Points of Handkerchiefs

When you sell handkerchiefs, you should mention:
1. Attractive appearance. Mention any new style feature.
2. Wearing quality or durability (including grade of fabric, workmanship, hand-rolled hem, grade of lace, trimming, embroidery, printed or woven design)
3. Purpose or occasion for its use
4. Price

HANDBAGS

Most handbags are made of nontextiles—leather or a plastic to simulate leather. Textile fabric handbags are very popular for summer and for evening wear.

The beach bag of sail cloth, crash, or duck with plastic lining is excellent for carrying wet bathing suits. Diaper bags of cotton, nylon, or synthetic leather also feature plastic linings.

Knitting bags are often made of tapestry, cretonne, crash, knitted goods or string.

Summer handbags are of linen or cotton crash, woven straw, homespun, bouclé, or fabrics to match hat, gloves or dress. For evening wear, handbags are made of moiré, faille, taffeta, tapestry, satin, metallic cloth or crepe.

PUTTING THIS MERCHANDISE KNOWLEDGE TO USE ❭❭❭❭❭❭❭❭❭❭

❭ DO YOU KNOW YOUR MERCHANDISE?

1. How important are hats for women for various occasions?
2. What are some of the factors that affect the style of women's hats?
3. How did the Christian religion affect hat styles?
4. How did straw become a fashionable material for hats?
5. Explain the difference between *wool* felt and *fur* felt. Which is better?
6. What is the difference between *felt* and *velour?*
7. How are straw hats shaped?
8. What factors affect the prices of fur hats?
9. Explain how the price of a hat is affected by the way it is manufactured.
10. (*a*) List popular styles of hats that have no brims. (*b*) List popular styles of hats with brims.
11. (*a*) For what occasions are fabric shoes suitable? (*b*) Name the fabrics used in women's shoes.
12. Why are nylon and Dacron polyester fibers popular for fabric gloves?
13. Of what fabrics can artificial flowers on coats and dresses be made?
14. Give the selling points of handkerchiefs.

1. Make a two-page manual for millinery salespeople showing popular styles of hats. Draw these from pictures appearing in current newspaper advertisements.

2. Prepare a 2-minute sales talk for a hat. Use a member of the class as your customer.

3. Visit a millinery department or a millinery store. Write a short theme describing how the hats were arranged, how they were grouped by style, color, and price.

4. Make a fashion count of gloves. Suggestion: sit for a half hour in a waiting room of a bus station or railroad terminal. (*a*) As women enter the terminal, count the women wearing gloves and the number not wearing gloves. (*b*) Count white, black, other colors. (*c*) Try to determine whether they are fabric or leather gloves.
Put your findings in your scrapbook.

5. (*a*) Visit a fashionable restaurant, a theater, or a hotel lobby. (*b*) Observe and record styles and fabrics of hats worn by women at these places. (*c*) Sketch the important styles in your scrapbook. (*d*) Record the material used in the hats you have sketched.

ADDITIONAL MERCHANDISE TERMS ❯❯❯❯❯❯❯❯❯❯❯❯❯❯❯❯❯❯❯❯❯

Alpaca is a fiber from a species of South American goat. Used for coating and linings of sports jackets.

Bulky knit is a coarsely constructed knitted outer garment made of large bulky yarns.

Classic suit is a woman's two-piece tailored garment made to fit the figure just as perfectly as a man's suit. A style that has recurred with slight modifications for many years.

CHAPTER 12

Men's and Boys' Apparel

In department and specialty stores, the men's apparel is usually classified into two main categories, namely, men's furnishings and men's clothing. There is often one buyer or more for each division. The former division includes such merchandise as ties, shirts, hosiery, underwear, sleepwear, robes and accessories. In some stores, there may be another buyer for sportswear. Usually all this merchandise is located in adjoining sections, and often on the main floor. Men's clothing generally includes suits, coats, and outerwear.

UNIT 31 FURNISHINGS, ACCESSORIES, UNDERWEAR, AND SLEEPWEAR

NECKTIES AND SCARFS

Why does a man wear a necktie? Is it because he wants to appear dressed up? Is it because other men wear them when they wish to appear well groomed? Or is it just a habit to put one on when "going out on a date"?

Men enjoy wearing silk accessories with a luxury look. In formal wear, for example, silk, rayon, acetate, nylon, and polyester may be used for ties and scarfs. Men also like the feeling and look of a cashmere scarf to keep out winter's chill. Wool flannel, knitted wool, and blends are used for the same purpose. Foulard and surah in silk or synthetics make lighter-weight scarfs.

While the necktie does not serve any useful function except for appearance and good grooming, a necktie may express the wearer's individuality and personality. The conservative man may indicate his type by wearing dark-colored ties in solid colors and small inconspicuous patterns. The man who is color conscious may always make sure that his socks and ties "go together." The style-conscious man may show by his choice of style, colors, and patterns in his ties that he favors those featured in men's stores and men's magazines known for style leadership. Are there styles in men's neckties? Yes, definitely. Do these styles change rapidly? Not so rapidly as styles in women's apparel.

Necktie Styles

Styles, however, have changed appreciably from the foppish age when the male wardrobe included elegant jabots with ruffles, ribbons, and braids worn at the neck. In the days of Beau Brummel, dignitaries including the Prince of Wales were invited to attend Beau's ceremony "of the tying of his white cravat." Since then the necktie has lost much of its importance and has changed greatly in appearance. If you were to compare the neckties worn today with those worn twenty years ago—even five years ago—you would be shocked to see the difference in width, color, and designs. Just a few years ago, men wore many large figured designs in painted effects, large plaids, and wide vivid stripes.

Today, the two popular forms of ties are the long tie, known as the *four-in-hand,* and the *bow*. The four-in-hand got its name from the type of coachman's knot used. When a coachman used several reins to control his horses, he tied them all together in a knot at the end.

The long tie, with straight or pointed ends, is worn for business, street, and less formal social affairs. The *bow tie* in solid colors or figured patterns is suitable for similar occasions. While the black bow tie is the traditional one worn with dinner jackets and the white bow with "the tails," there is a style trend toward wearing maroon and navy bows with dinner jackets. The *ascot* can be worn for formal or semiformal morning or afternoon wear with a cutaway coat and striped trousers. Sometimes this costume is worn at daytime weddings.

String ties made of cord are worn by ranchers and are frequently sold in western retail stores for street and casual wear. In fact, in the casual style of dress the wearing of a necktie has practically been eliminated.

Selling Points of Neckties

When you, as a customer, ask a salesman to show you a necktie, what does the salesman try to do? He tries to determine your needs—"to size you up." If you are a student, he may show you a bow tie in a bright print or a long tie in stripes or bold prints in the season's colors. He will probably demonstrate the tie's appearance in use by knotting it. He will show you the loose stitching of the back seam, which has the advantage of making the tie more elastic. The well-informed salesman will describe this tie as having *resilient construction*—meaning that the tie will stretch and spring back to shape. Hence, a resilient-constructed tie with loose stitches will hold its shape better than a machine-stitched tie with tight stitches and rigid construction. Many inexpensive ties have rigid construction.

The salesman may also tell you of what material the tie is made; he may indicate if a tie can be washed at home. Most ties, however, with the possible exception of 100 per cent Dacron polyester and 100 per cent cotton, should be dry-cleaned, because the linings of most ties are difficult to keep straight. Ties of rigid construction are especially difficult to clean satisfactorily.

Fabrics for Neckties

Following is a list of commonly used necktie fabrics:

Brocade	Foulard	Taffeta
Challis	Knitted	Texturized-nylon
Crocheted	Moiré	(spot resistant)
Faille	Rep	
Flat crepe	Shantung	

SHIRTS

The two styles of shirts we shall discuss here are dress and sport shirts. Work shirts will be covered in the section on work clothes.

Dress Shirts

Dress shirts are tailored garments worn with a necktie for street, business and semiformal wear. Collars are detachable or attached to the body of the shirt. They have a single or a pleated closing, which buttons down the front. Cuffs are single, French (double), or convertible (button in addition to buttonholes for cuff links). Collars are spread or tab. Some shirt styles have button-down collars. Colors for dress shirts are white, solid pastel shades, and fine stripes. Sizes generally run 14, 14½, 15, 15½, 16, 16½, 17 (neckband) and 32–36 length sleeves.

A well-informed customer is not only interested in correct size of a shirt to insure comfort, but also in appearance, durability, ease in care, suitability, price, and brand.

Appearance. The appearance of a shirt depends in a large part on the appearance of the fabric as well as on the neatness of workmanship, on the grade of the fabric, and on the style in which it is cut. Commercial laundries make every effort to give a good appearance to the collars and cuffs. This is why some men prefer to send their dress shirts to a commercial laundry. According to advertising and information on labels of wash-and-wear shirts,

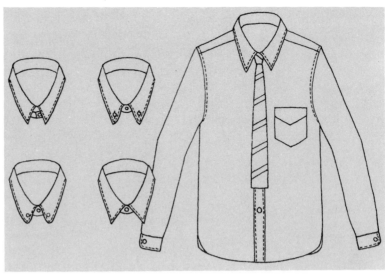

Man's dress shirt with four-in-hand tie and spread collar. **Collar Styles. Top left:** Snap-tab collar; **Right:** Button down. **Bottom left:** Round eyelet collar; **Right:** Medium spread.

customers are given to believe that shirts may be expected to "Look fresher longer" and "Slight creases will disappear when worn." Doubtless certain or perhaps most wash-and-wear shirts do have these properties. On the other hand, it has been found that polyester and cotton blends collect soil very quickly on the neckband and on the inside of the cuffs. While soil does not show in these places, the wearer would hesitate to wear the shirt a second time. Some men say that wash-and-wear white shirts turn yellow. This is because bleaches are used in washing them.

A process called "Belfast" was put on the market in 1959 by Deering Milliken and Company. It imparts a new kind of wash-and-wear property to cotton fabrics, because the process of cross-linking of molecules causes a permanent chemical change in the fibers themselves. The more common processes require the addition of a resin to the all-cotton fabric which, in some cases, makes the fabric somewhat stiff and scratchy and too hot for comfort (three characteristics that lately have been remedied noticeably). While some men will feel that the nonresin type of finish like Belfast does not require touch-up ironing, others will think a little ironing improves a shirt's appearance. For traveling men, the wash-and-wear fabric is indispensable.

Durability and Cost of Upkeep.   How long will it wear? This is a question most frequently asked by consumers. From the angle of which type of shirt will wear the longer, the American Institute of Laundering reveals that a shirt alternately worn and washed will withstand 35–50 launderings depending on the kind of wear and care it receives. Suppose a shirt averages 40 wearings and launderings. A comparison of the cost of 40 launderings of the untreated cotton in a commercial laundry with the cost of laundering it at home follows. Then a comparison of laundering a wash-and-wear cotton shirt will be made.

>> UNTREATED ALL-COTTON SHIRT <<

Laundered commercially	40 launderings = life of shirt
	$ .25 cost of each commercial laundering
	$10.00 cost to launder shirt during its life
	3.00 original cost of shirt
	$13.00 total cost of shirt to wearer

Home laundered	40 launderings = life of shirt
	$ .25 labor cost of each ironing (if it takes 15 min. per shirt and labor = $1 per hour).
	$10.00
	6.00 cost of detergent, starching & bleaching, electricity used in washing, drying, ironing, depreciation on equipment
	3.00 original cost of shirt
	$19.00 total cost of shirt to the wearer[1]

>> WASH-AND-WEAR COTTON SHIRT <<

Home laundered	$2.00 cost of laundering during life of shirt[2]
	$4.00 or $5.00 original cost of the shirt
	$6.00 or $7.00 total cost to the wearer

[1] C.U. Bulletin, January, 1960, page 9. Estimate of one government economist.
[2] Ibid. It is assumed that time spent in laundering plus cleansing ingredients, electricity, and touch-up ironing are negligible; assuming too that hand-laundering methods were used.

It will be observed that the initial cost of a wash-and-wear shirt is at least one or two dollars more than that of an untreated cotton shirt. But it will also be noted that the cost of "upkeep" is considerably less when wash-and-wear is done at home. If a wash-and-wear fabric is dried automatically, the electricity used would be a noticeable increase in total cost.

In workmanship, to insure long-wearing quality, seams should be stitched firmly without puckering (14–18 stitches to the inch). Ocean pearl buttons (plastic may melt) should be firmly stitched; buttonholes cut even and firmly bound; collar points sharp, even, and neatly sewed. Double needle (two rows of stitching) is stronger than single needle.

Ease in Care. The foregoing comparison of cost of laundering is closely related to ease in care. If a homemaker is willing to do the dress shirts at home, she may save as much as $3 during the wear-life of a $3 shirt. The fact that (1) the homemaker can wash the shirts by hand or in an automatic washer; (2) wash-and-wear shirts dry quickly; (3) they iron more easily and faster than non-wash-and-wear are selling points in favor of the wash-and-wear shirts. But for those homemakers who do not have the time or desire to launder shirts, the commercial laundry is the answer. In this case, there is no reason for putting an additional two dollars or so into a wash-and-wear shirt.

In a 6-month wear test made by Consumer's Union of 18 resin-treated white shirts (models of similar style), it was found that all sizes and dimensions were satisfactory; shrinkage was minimal. For all models tested, Consumers' Union felt appearance would be improved in restoring whiteness by bleaching after the nineteenth laundering.

If a man does not want the trouble of buying shirts, he may take advantage of a shirt-rental service. A contract with such a service may call for five laundered shirts a week at a total of $2. This is slightly higher than the usual price for laundering a shirt. If the contract says that the service agrees to keep the customer provided with shirts at all times, there is no agreement that these shirts will be new. When the customer terminates a contract, the service may require that the customer buy, at a price, the shirts he has been using. Sometimes the company merely uses the customer's shirts to replace worn ones of another.

Suitability. The principal occasions for which shirts are worn are: (1) business or everyday wear—dress shirts; (2) semiformal—white dress shirts; (3) formal—pleated or starched bosom depending on the current mode, (4) work, (5) sports.

For dress shirts, broadcloth has been for several years much more important than Oxford. A few chambray button-down styles in blue, tan, and gray are worn. White still seems to be the most desired color, although solid pastels and fine stripes are now suitable for business wear. For summer, lightweight broadcloth and batiste are popular. Best-quality domestic broadcloth is made of Pima cotton; has a count of 144 x 76; is mercerized; 2 x 2 (2-ply warp and filling). Oxford is made in 2 x 1 or 2 x 2 basket weave. The 2 x 2 should wear better, keep its size and shape better than 2 x 1 because 2 x 2 has a balanced count.

Other fabrics include madras and white-on-white broadcloth. As to fibers: all cotton, all polyester, or other synthetics, polyester or acrylic and cotton blends, the new high-strength rayons are used for shirts. Rayon stripes and figures may be woven with broadcloth or madras to make the patterns stand out.

Comfort. For comfort, a shirt should be cut full across the chest, and the garment should have tails long enough to remain tucked into the trousers. With the present reliable methods for control of shrinkage, there is relatively little need to buy a shirt a half size larger than one normally would require. Most shirts are cut from preshrunk fabrics. A smooth, soft, clean-appearing shirt fabric, both before and after laundering, is the most comfortable. Some wash-and-wear cottons feel stiff, heavy, and therefore hot.

Price. Some customers buy primarily by price. Perhaps this is more true of women than men; however, since women do buy men's shirts for their family and for gifts, the salesperson should not fail to mention price in relation to the serviceability the wearer may expect from the shirt.

Since it is difficult to see all hidden values in a shirt while in a plastic wrapping, the salesperson should know those selling points about the shirt that will interest the customer. If the salesperson can show a sample shirt, he may demonstrate selling points.

Brand Names. Some men are wedded to one brand. If a store does not carry a man's favorite, he may go elsewhere. Some national brands of men's shirts are: Arrow, Manhattan, Van Heusen, Marlboro, Truval, National, Essley, AMC, Towncraft (Penney) and Pilgrim (Sears).

SPORT SHIRTS

In general, there are two staple sport shirts: knitted and woven. The familiar polo or basque shirt with its many variations is knitted, while the woven type has a roll-down collar (it may button down); it may have a single, pleated, or fly-front closing and one or two pockets. Some shirts may be styled like jackets but be unlined and of shirting fabrics. Sport shirts are intended to be worn without neckties. Some of the knitted shirts have collars; other have round necks, crew necks, or V necks. One variation of the polo shirt is cut like a cardigan sweater with collar and is actually called a "cardigan shirt." It closes with a zipper. Another version is a pull-over with a shawl collar. This is called a "knitted shirt." Usually sport shirts are in plaids, prints, stripes, checks, or solid colors.

In this field, too, the wash-and-wear fabrics are extremely popular. Fabrics used in sport shirts include:

Cotton, wool, or viyella flannel
Corduroy
Jersey (acrylic, cotton, textured nylon)
Mesh
Madras (bleeding type)
Stretch nylon
Oxford
Percale

Sizes in sport shirts are usually small, medium, and large.

HOSIERY

Men's sizes in hose run from 9½ to 13—one or two stretch sizes will cover the whole size range. Staple colors are black, navy, gray, and brown. Fancy socks may have clocks (long embroidered designs) on the inside and outside of the leg above the ankle, all-over knitted patterns, argyle panels, or all-over argyle patterns. Lisle socks (long staple cotton in ply yarn with the amount of twist specified by the F.T.C. rules for hosiery) are plain-knitted anklets with elastic tops; others are knee length in rib knit and elastic or

Top.
Left: Short sleeved sport shirt. **Right:** Knitted polo shirt.

Center.
Left: Felt fedora with center crease. **Right:** Traditional style straw hat.

Bottom.
Man's knee-length sock, dress sock, boy's sock, small boy's sock with trim on side.

spandex tops. The same knitted constructions for everyday wear are made in all nylon, nylon wrapped around cotton, Dacron polyester, and blends. Acrylic, modacrylic, polyester, cotton, wool, and blends are used for sportswear. Usually the sports socks are made of bulky yarn; white ribbed knit with stripes at the top are popular.

ACCESSORIES

Accessories for men and boys include handkerchiefs, belts, suspenders and garters, scarfs, mufflers and gloves, sweaters, hats, and in some stores, the water-repellent windbreaker type of outer jacket, and swimming trunks. In this chapter, the water-repellent jacket and raincoat will be discussed under "Outerwear" and swimming trunks have been covered under "Beach and Resort Wear."

Handkerchiefs

Staple stocks in retail stores include plain white cotton, linen, silk, and monogrammed styles. The better grades have hand-rolled hems (hand stitched); others have hemstitched edges. For complete assortments, a store would have to carry a few fancy styles—fancy in pattern and in color.

Belts

While most belts are made of leather or plastic (nontextiles), some are made of heavy cotton with ribbed filling known as *belting*. Men in the Armed Forces wear wide cotton belting. Some belts on separate slacks are made of the same material as the article itself. The stretch belt of elasticized hemp, silk, or synthetic stretch yarn is popular for sports and casual wear. Braided, crocheted, knitted styles are textile items.

Garters and Suspenders

Even though the spandex tops on long socks eliminate the need for garters, there will be a limited sale to those men who feel more comfortable with them on. Garters and suspenders are made of webbing of very strong yarns. For much of the webbing, a core of rubber is wrapped with silk, rayon, cotton or a synthetic like nylon.

Who wears suspenders? Small boys may wear narrow elastic suspenders to hold up their dungarees; men of all ages wear them for comfort's sake.

Gloves

Leather is more popular than fabric for gloves, yet cotton and wool knits can be found in sportswear. A wool knit may line a capeskin glove, or wool may form the back of a pigskin. Driving gloves may have a chamois or pigskin palm with a crocheted or knitted wool back.

SWEATERS

As in women's sweaters, there are two classic styles for men, which retail stores must always carry to satisfy customer demand. One is the *pullover* that slips over the head, which usually has no buttons but may have a short zipper; the other is the *cardigan,* which buttons or zips all the way down the front. A variation of the cardigan is the cardigan shirt that has a collar like a sport shirt and a breast pocket.

Of the two principal styles, the pullover is the more popular. For those men who like to wear a sweater under a jacket, they may prefer a pullover without sleeves.

Necklines of these two styles vary. The pullover may have several shapes: V, round, boat, turtle, or crew. The cardigan is popularly styled with or without shawl collar and two lower pockets. For those men who like the imported flavor in sweater styles, there are Tyrolean, Italian, Israelian, Scottish, Scandinavian, and others.

Patterns in sweaters are expressed by solid colored bodies with contrasting collars and cuffs; by colored knitted designs in argyles, glen plaids, tartans, and novelties; or by knitted stitches such as the waffle, pineapple, bulky rib, splash, and cable.

In the early 1960's, the bulky textured sweaters became very popular— particularly for sportswear. The smooth textures are more comfortable under a jacket because they take less space. Ribbed and fleecy textures are fairly classic, while nubby, hairy, and shaggy are more fashion types.

Formerly sweaters were made of all wool or all cashmere. Now there are blends of wool 75 per cent and mohair 25 per cent; 100 per cent Orlon acrylic; textured nylon, and other synthetic blends.

HATS

For over thirty-five years, men have been living in a hatless era. It is said that the style of hatlessness originated at a European university. In 1921, a group of students manifestly declared their independence of headgear. Very soon, young men began to appear hatless both in Europe and in the United States. This style was copied by many older men; the next generation imitated their elders. The depression, which necessitated economy, helped to prolong this style since the elimination of the hat represented a saving of several dollars. Postwar army and navy casual styles were factors in the decline of hat sales. As a result, Allied Stores' Research Division made a survey to find out what type of customer was buying hats. The findings showed that the older men in the higher income brackets were primarily responsible for hat sales. Hat manufacturers also did research studies to improve the industry, with the result that a Hat Research Foundation and New Trade Associations were formed. These groups, individual manufacturers and retailers, are all intelligently promoting the wearing of hats (1) by creating new hat fashions, (2) by helping men to become style conscious, (3) by stressing the importance of good taste in dress, and (4) by presenting the individual correct styles for a particular use by means of advertising, store displays, and selling.

Felt Hats

For everyday wear, the felt hat in wool or fur felt has been traditionally the hat accepted by men who wear hats. For summer, the straw has been traditional. Dates were even set for wearing straws (May 15 to September 15). For town and business wear, the hat may be a status symbol representing a well-ordered substantial look of the Madison Avenue executive. But for spectator sportswear, hats represent individuality and distinctiveness.

Hats worn with traditional suits are the *felt fedora* with center dent or crease with welt edge or bound brim. Widths of brim and bands vary with style. Crowns also vary in height, width, and tapering. For more formal wear, a man wears a *homburg, bowler,* or *derby.* For very formal occasions, he might need a *top hat,* such as President Kennedy wore at his inauguration.

Cloth Hats

There has been a considerable interest in cloth (fabric) hats for casual country wear. These hats are often made of tweed in center crease and porkpie models in checks, plaids, and houndstooth patterns. Velour in solid colors with braided band is often worn with sports jackets and slacks. Also for casual wear, particularly for sports-car driving, the fabric visored cap is popular. A solid color corduroy, twilled cotton, plaid, or checked tweed or flannel fits into the sportswear picture. Boys of all ages frequently wear caps in baseball styles in cotton or flannel Eton types for fall and spring. For smaller boys, there is the rolled-brim wool or cotton fabric hat, often matching the jacket or slacks. This hat comes with ear laps for the very small child. Older boys often go hatless or pull up a hood attached to a parka for cold days. Others may wear a small, tight-fitting, bulky knitted skating cap in winter.

Sizes of Men's and Boys' Hats and Caps

To determine the size of boys' and men's hats and caps, measure around the largest part of the head above the eyebrows with a tape measure. Following are the sizes as they are marked in the hats and caps and the measurements that may be obtained from the tape measure itself.

	Size	Inches
Boys, age 3–6	Small	19–19¼
	Medium	20–20½
	Large	21–21½
Boys, age 7–15	6¼	19½
	6⅜	19⅞
	6½	20¼
	6⅝	20¾
	6¾	21⅛
	6⅞	21½
	7	21⅞
	7⅛	22¼
Men	6¾	21¼
	6⅞	21⅝
	7	22
	7⅛	22⅜
	7¼	22¾
	7⅜	23⅛
	7½	23⅝
	7⅝	24
	7¾	24⅜

In addition to the problem of head size, men's hats come in varying shapes to fit the head comfortably. These shapes are known as ovals, long ovals, and round ovals. The correct shape helps the hat to conform to the head and to keep looking neat throughout the period of use.

UNDERWEAR

Articles of men's and boys' underwear include "T" shirts, undershirts,

Men's Underwear.

Left: T-shirt.

Center top row: Boxer shorts and knit brief.

Center bottom row: Zipper-style shorts and knit mid-length drawers.

Right: Knit ankle-length drawers.

shorts, and union suits (knitted one-piece garments with sleeves and legs in varied lengths).

The most popular styles in underwear are "T" shirts or undershirts, with or without sleeves; shorts, woven boxer or gripper style (The boxer style has all-around elastic waist; the gripper has elastic side inserts.); knitted briefs or knitted shorts formerly called drawers. From elementary school through college, a male may wear the same style in underwear: "T" shirt and shorts or briefs.

"T" shirt and undershirt sizes are: small, 30–34; medium, 36–40; large, 42–44; extra large, 46–52.

Cotton fabrics are very important for men's underwear because in knitted goods, particularly, cotton absorbs perspiration better than do rayon or nylon. Cotton knitted goods expand and contract with the movements of the body. Likewise, cotton underwear can be laundered at home or in the automatic washer and dryer as well as in the commercial laundry. White cottons can be bleached.

Blends have become important in underwear. Typical ones for undershirts, are 80 per cent Orlon acrylic and 20 per cent cotton, 80 per cent cotton, 20 per cent nylon. Nylon or Dacron polyester are frequently used at the neckbands of "T" shirts to give them increased durability.

The wash-and-wear cotton broadcloth or percale are popular in boxer or gripper-style undershorts.

Since men look for comfort when they select underwear, an important selling point for cotton and for rayon underwear is that it is cool in summer. Nylon in underwear and shirting does not absorb perspiration and hence feels clammy. When nylon is mixed with cotton or rayon, the absorbent quality is improved.

SLEEP AND LOUNGING WEAR

For sleepwear, men expect comfort. Some men are discriminating in choice of color, design, fabric, and style of cut. Two staple styles of pajamas are generally sold in stores: the coat type buttoned down the front and the pullover with no front closing. For summer, the short-length pajama and the nightshirt may be sold. In addition, there are high-style pajamas for sleeping and for lounging.

Two-piece ski pajamas, similar in style to the outfit worn by the Alpine skier, have an elastic waist with a top sometimes in a different color from the trousers. Fitted wristlets and anklets may be in a contrasting color. This style is very comfortable for winter wear, yet lightweight enough for the even temperatures of the modern home or apartment. They are often made of soft balbriggan knitted cotton. They wash in the automatic home laundry and require no ironing.

Lounging pajamas, lounging robes, and smoking jackets are made of rich silk or rayon brocades and are often trimmed with satin or velvet. Flannel is another popular fabric for these uses. While a bathrobe may serve the same purposes as a lounging robe, it usually is made of less luxurious fabrics such as blanket cloth (beacon robing—a backed cloth in blanket colors), corduroy, terry cloth, flannelette (boys), and flannel.

Fabrics Used

Fabrics used for men's and boys' underwear and sleeping garments include:

Uses	Fabrics
Briefs	Mesh
Drawers	Knitted jersey
Pajamas	Balbriggan, broadcloth, flannelette, madras (woven), nylon tricot, Oxford, percale, plissé crepe, pongee
Shirts	Knitted jersey, mesh
Shorts	Broadcloth, chambray, knitted jersey, madras (woven), mesh, percale

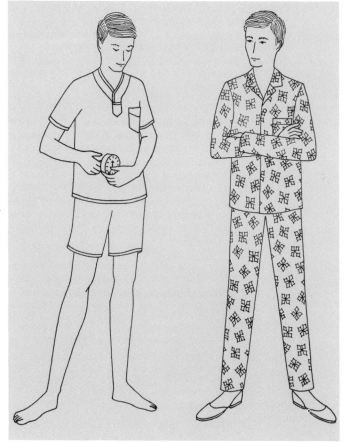

Left: Short-length pajama with pullover top. **Right:** Full-length pajama with coat top.

PUTTING THIS MERCHANDISE KNOWLEDGE TO USE ❯ ❯ ❯ ❯ ❯ ❯ ❯ ❯ ❯ ❯

1. Why is it unnecessary to buy a shirt a half size larger than one normally would require?

2. What are the selling points of a 65 per cent Dacron polyester and 35 per cent cotton dress shirt?

3. (a) What are the advantages of buying an untreated all-cotton shirt over buying a wash-and-wear shirt? (b) What are the disadvantages?

4. (a) What are the selling points of a 100 per cent Dacron polyester tie? (b) Why are all-silk ties so popular?

5. Define the following: (a) convertible cuff, (b) resilient construction, (c) tab collar, (d) French cuff, (e) pleated front closing (shirt).

6. (a) Give the selling points of men's knee-length lisle hosiery with spandex tops. (b) Give the selling points of a hand-rolled white linen handkerchief.

7. (a) For what occasion would a silk handkerchief be worn? (b) a white silk or rayon scarf? (c) a derby hat? (d) a cloth hat?

8. (a) Name two traditional styles for men's sweaters. (b) Define "bulky knit" sweaters. (c) Why and how is the hat industry promoting the wearing of hats?

9. (a) What items of apparel do men's accessories include? (b) What styles in gloves are made of textile fabrics?

10. (a) Give the selling points of ski pajamas. (b) Of what fabrics are they made? (c) Of what fabrics are the conventional pullover pajamas made?

❯ INTERESTING THINGS TO DO

1. Clip from magazines, newspapers, or mail-order catalogues illustrations to show: (a) various types of collars in men's dress shirts, (b) various styles of cuffs, (c) various types of front closings.

2. (a) Make a study of the historical periods of men's costumes to show the evolution of the modern necktie. Make sketches to illustrate the various periods. (b) Give your report in class.

3. (a) Consult a magazine, such as *Men's Wear* (Fairchild Publications) or *Esquire,* to discover the latest styles in men's sport shirts. (b) Describe or sketch these styles in your scrapbook. (c) List the latest styles in fabrics.

4. Make a study of men's sweaters to determine: (a) the prevalent styles, (b) occasions for which they would be worn, (c) fibers of which they are made, (d) colors, designs, textures, and (e) prices.

5. You and a classmate put on a demonstration sale for the class. Suggested items from your own wardrobes might include: (a) handkerchiefs, (b) fabric gloves or gloves made partially of fabric, (c) belts (with textile parts), (d) "T" shirts, (e) socks (sport or dress).

6. From shopping, reading of men's fashion magazines, and from discussion with your friends, what do you find the probable trend will be in men's hat sales: (a) at present? (b) a few years from now?

UNIT 32 SUITS AND OUTERWEAR

While it seems unlikely that men's fashions will ever change as rapidly as women's, marked changes in styles of men's suits have taken place in the past three years.

Styles

The advent of the Continental style in 1958 overwhelmed the conservative man at first. The authentic Continental's dimensions were written by clothing designers at their conventions. But this does not mean that the style is not subject to modifications. Basically, the authentic American Continental is slightly shorter than the Ivy style, which, in turn, is slightly shorter than the American Natural style. If you observe, the Continental coat is more cutaway and more rounded than the other two styles. Most of the Continental jackets are now made with peaked or notched lapels with two or three buttons. Original models in this style had no buttonholes in the lapels and no breast pockets, but customer demand restored these features. Shoulders of the Continental were more square and seemed broader than the Ivy style. Later they became either squared or natural. The jacket had short side vents with slanted pockets, and the waist had a shapely line. Trousers were originally trim and cuffless. Modified styles were made with or without cuffs and with or without vents in the jacket. The advent of the dressier Continental has challenged the Ivy look and the traditional straight-hanging suit. In line with the dressier trend, the matching vest returned for business wear. However, the modified Ivy mode, the natural shoulder, has remained a favorite with most men.

Semiformals and Formals. For evening wear, the Continental influence is noted in more cutaway jackets, in edgings, cuffs on jackets, and fancier cummerbunds.

After six, a dinner jacket of wool and spun silk or all wool; or all-silk in white for summer; black, midnight blue, or maroon can be worn at other seasons. One of the most beautiful formal fabrics for dinner jackets and for "tails" is the classic wool broadcloth. It is a smooth, silky, napped wool in twill weave. The nap is pressed in one direction.

What About Suit Fabrics?

Since worsted fabrics tailor well and look dressy, these materials fit into all three styles. Inconspicuous black or shadow stripes and muted checks are appropriate; also, the olive green, charcoal gray, and gold tones.

Inasmuch as retail stores usually carry two weights of suits—a lightweight for spring and summer and a regular weight—fabrics differ in fiber content. The strictly summer fabrics, which weigh about 4–5 ounces per square yard, have become increasingly the wash-and-wear type with treated all-cotton and blends most important.

Advantages and Disadvantages of Wash-and-Wear Fabrics. These wash-and-wear fabrics include: all-cotton woven seersucker, polyester and cotton tropicals, all-cotton gabardines. The constructions of the following four are either plain-weave or corded: polyester and cotton (75%–25% and 65%–35%); polyester and acrylic (50% of each fiber); acrylic (44%),

Men's Suits.

Left:
American natural.

Center:
Continental.

Right:
Sport jacket and slacks. In the same order, a bow tie and a four-in-hand tie.

polyester (46%), mohair (10%); polyester (55%), acrylic (35%), mohair (10%).

Consumers Union tested the blended fabrics listed above. These fabrics were made up into seventeen suits: eight models were polyester and cotton; five were polyester, acrylic, and mohair in varying percentages; the remainder were made in the other blends. Duplicate suits were bought and tested in each blend listed; one sample was worn by a tester; the other sample was laboratory tested. It was found that these suits:

1. Did not lose their creases or wrinkle as a result of rain or perspiration, but they did wrinkle at given points, such as elbows, where the fabric is sharply bent.

2. These suits did not fit so well as a good all-wool or Dacron polyester—wool tropical.

3. These suits did not shed or hang out wrinkles. Steam ironing did not remove wrinkles.

4. These suits can save the wearer money for cleaning.

5. In best grades, these suits were as good in appearance as the worsted tropicals.

6. The suits are best laundered in a modern automatic washer with slow agitation and spin speeds, short cycle, and low temperature for dryer (160°). Suit should be dried alone and should be removed from dryer as soon as it stops to avoid serious wrinkling. Suits may be hand washed.

7. Seam failures were more common than in usual suits.

8. The suits improved in appearance with touch-up ironing.

Other Lightweight Fabrics. In addition to the wash-and-wear summer suit, there are: all-wool tropicals (worsted—best grades in two-ply warp and filling yarns; plain weave), mohair, Dacron polyester, and worsted tropical, Dacron polyester and worsted (tropical or sharkskin), all-mohair tropical, worsted flannel, silk shantung, Dacron polyester, worsted, and mohair tropical, Dacron polyester and rayon tropical.

Fabrics for Year-round Wear. For climates in the same latitude as the Middle Atlantic States, regular suiting can be worn for all except the summer months. In fact, this type is sometimes advertised as a "year-round suit." As compared with summer wash-and-wear suitings, regular suitings are heavier (about 7 ozs.). For this weight, the following fabrics are used: all-wool worsteds, cheviots (woolen or worsted), flannel (woolen or worsted), sharkskin (worsted), tweed, polyester and worsted sharkskin, serge (worsted), gabardine (worsted or blend with synthetics), mill-finished worsted, whipcord (worsted).

Sizes in Men's Suitings

Chest, waist, and height measurements are the criteria for determining size of men's suits. The following chart is taken from the mail-order catalogue of Sears, Roebuck and Company. It shows the measurements needed to order a man's suit.

HOW TO ORDER SUITS. Shorts fit men 5 ft. 3 in. to 5 ft. 7 in. tall. Regulars fit men 5 ft. 7 in. to 5 ft. 11 in. Longs fit men 5 ft. 11 in. to 6 ft. 3 in. *State chest, waist, inseam, height and weight. Indicate which is waist.* Measure chest over shirt, around body, under arms, over tips of shoulder blades. Measure waist over shirt at point belt is worn. Measure inseam from crotch, along seam, to bottom of cuff of a pair of well-fitting dress slacks. Number of inches is size.

CHART "A" FOR AVERAGE BUILDS										
Chest..	35	36	37	38	39	40	42	44	46
Waist..	28 to 30	29 to 31	30 to 32	31 to 33	32 to 34	34 to 36	36 to 38	39 to 41	41 to 43

CHART "B" FOR YOUTHFUL, TRIM FIGURES									
Chest	35	36	37	38	39	40	42	44
Waist..	27 to 29	28 to 30	29 to 31	30 to 32	31 to 33	32 to 34	34 to 36	36 to 38

CHART "C" FOR SEMI-STOUTS						
Chest..	40	42	44	46	48	50
Waist..	36 to 38	38 to 40	41 to 43	43 to 45	45 to 47	47 to 49

CHART "D" FOR MEN'S SEERSUCKER SUIT, page 60	Regulars 35 to 44 in. chest; Longs 37 to 44 in.							
	Chest..	35	36	37	38	39	40	42	44
	Waist..	27 to 29	28 to 30	29 to 31	30 to 32	31 to 33	33 to 35	35 to 37	37 to 39

CHART "E" FOR MEN'S POPLIN SUIT, page 43	Regulars 35 to 44 in. chest; Longs 37 to 44 in.							
	Chest..	35	36	37	38	39	40	42	44
	Waist..	26 to 28	27 to 29	28 to 30	29 to 31	30 to 32	31 to 33	34 to 36	36 to 38

For the man who prefers individuality in styling, perfect fit, excellent tailoring, there is the custom tailor who makes a suit especially for him. The price is obviously much higher than for a suit made in mass production.

To any man, desirable features in a suit are that it be good looking, stylish, well fitting, comfortable, and suitable for the occasion for which it is worn. Following is a list of points to consider in judging good tailoring.

1. Coat front should hang smooth, not sag or buckle at the neck
2. Snug-fitting collar
3. Smooth roll of lapels
4. Good-fitting padded shoulders
5. Reinforced armholes and shields
6. Straight-hanging vent or vents
7. Buttonholes well bound and firmly sewed
8. Good grade buttons firmly attached
9. Good grade thread for stitching; reinforced stitching at points of strain
10. Wide hand-felled or silk-piped seams
11. Comfortable-fitting trousers
12. Zip-front trouser closing
13. Well-placed and securely sewed belt loops
14. Vest, if a part of suit, cut and tailored to fit smoothly

OUTERWEAR

The Outerwear Department has grown in importance as a result of our greater emphasis on outdoor living.

Slacks

Separate slacks for sports and casual wear may be sold in a department adjacent to the sport shirts, so that the customer may co-ordinate colors and fabrics. In the Continental style, slacks have been made with tapered legs and without cuffs although there are still more trousers with cuffs than without. Colors may be solid, and designs may range from small checks to large glen plaids and large lumberjack plaids. In some seasons, fine stripes and muted stripes are in style.

Sports slacks are worn with sports jackets of harmonizing colors. Recently vests have been in vogue. It is customary to wear a patterned jacket with slacks of solid color or vice versa. Two styles in jackets, the Ivy and the Continental, have been in vogue during the last few years. These two styles were described on page 233.

Jackets

The waist or hip-length jacket with zip-front closing still continues an important style for school and casual wear. These jackets come in various weights according to the season. Many of them are water-repellent and some are reversible. In fact, since the outer fabric is often cotton and is preshrunk, labels will state that the garment is machine washable. Many of these jackets are so closely woven that they serve as windbreakers.

The golf jacket is a lightweight version of the windbreaker with a lining of acetate, rayon, cotton, or wool. A separate hood may come with the jacket. We must not forget the leather or plastic hip-length jacket trimmed with knitted wool and often lined with lamb's wool or quilting.

A car coat, a type of jacket coming down below the hips, may have a fly front, buttoned, or zip closing. It can be made in cotton gabardine, cord, twilled cotton, rayon and cotton tackle twill, wool fleece. Car coats are lined with acetate, rayon, and quilted fabrics, and acrylic pile.

For boys and young men, the parka has found favor because it is warm and comfortable. It is about the length of the car coat; has a zip front, and hood attached. The garment is usually made of sateen or polished cotton twill treated for crease resistance and water repellency. The entire garment is generally lined with a furlike fabric (acrylic, modacrylic, or alpaca). Sleeves are usually quilt lined.

Boys' sizes are 6, 8, 10, 12, 14, 16, 18 and 20.

Fabrics Used

Fabrics used for sports slacks are:

Chino (cotton)—mercerized and Sanforized cotton twill
Flannel (woolen, worsted; acrylic and rayon; wool and cotton)
Hopsacking (wool)
Polished cotton
Stretch nylon (particularly for skiing)
Wash and wear (acrylic and rayon; polyester and cotton, etc.)
Whipcord (wool or cotton)

Sporting vests are made of:

Corduroy
Hopsacking
Plaid cotton
Velveteen (solid or printed)
Viyella flannel (wool and cotton)

Sports jackets are made of:

Bouclé (cotton)	Madras plaid
Camel's hair	Rayon and cotton tackle twill
Cord	Textured cotton
Cotton gabardine	Twilled cotton
Cotton knit	Wool fleece
Hopsacking (wool)	

Overcoats

Full- or three-quarter length coats come under the description of an overcoat. Usually one thinks of an overcoat as a heavy garment suitable for winter, while a topcoat or raincoat is suitable for spring and fall. To these styles should be added the three-quarter length "suburban." But exceptions must be made to this statement, because the topcoat and the raincoat may have zip-in linings, which make them suitable for winter wear.

Three-quarter length coats are appropriate for the high school or college campus and suburban wear. They can be made of water-repellent cotton gabardine, wool or cashmere fleece, tweed, hopsacking, corduroy. Some of these coats have synthetic pile or alpaca collars and linings. Full-length overcoats are made of wool or cashmere fleece, reversible double cloth, herringbone tweeds, covert (worsted), shetland (woolen), cheviot (woolen), and gabardine (worsted). Collars and/or linings may be made of furlike fabrics or knitted constructions.

Sizes in men's coats are marked short, regular, and long (lengths) and 34, 36, 38 up to 48. Boys' lightweight topcoats range from 3–10 and 11–18; overcoats come in sizes 3–10 and 11–14.

Raincoats

The trend has been to wear the raincoat for all-weather occasions. In some instances, the raincoat has replaced the topcoat in men's wardrobes. Some are double breasted, others single breasted, still others have fly fronts. Some have zip-in linings. A typical one is made of combed cotton gabardine or poplin and a cotton plaid lining. Some raincoats are finished to repel water, oil, and wrinkles; and this finish may last the life of the coat with normal washing or cleaning. Furthermore, some will be machine washable, drip dry with little or no ironing. Whatever the brand or fabric, it is well to read the label carefully to be sure what the special features of the coat are and to follow instructions for its care. Sizes are the same range as for overcoats.

Top: Bulky knit sweater and sleeveless pullover.

Center: All-weather coat with zip-out fleece lining.

Bottom: Swimming trunks with beach jacket and poplin raincoat.

WORK CLOTHES

For boys at active play and for men who do hard work, there is no more satisfactory garment than the dungaree, sometimes called "jeans." They are usually made of 10-oz. or 8-oz. cotton denim (10 oz. is heavier) and are navy-blue warps and white fillings in twill weave. Some dungarees are sold with jacket to match. Some feature as many as five pockets, a snap waist, zip fly, and double knees to increase their wear life. Nowadays they are Sanforized (shrinkage controlled), and many are vat dyed so they do not bleed onto other clothes when washed. Some feature points of durability by stressing triple-stitched main seams, rustproof zipper, snaps and buckle, bar-tack reinforcements, and reinforced bib corners.

Overalls are frequently worn by paper hangers, painters, plumbers, and small boys. One advantage of this garment is that they stay up and require no suspenders or tight-fitted waist. In short, they are comfortable for work and play. Preschool boys often wear overalls because they protect the knees from the weather and from falls.

Measurements for overalls are the same as for slacks: size of waist and inseam (from crotch to bottom of leg). Regular men's sizes are: waist, 30, 31, 32, to 42 inches; length, 30, 32, 34, 36. Boys' sizes are: 4, 6, 8, 10, 12, 14, 16, 18.

BEACH AND RESORT WEAR

A trip to the beach or resort will require swimming trunks. Two basic styles are important: the short and the bikini (abbreviated tight-fitting garment). The short is made of cotton madras in plaids or stripes, cotton gabardine, knitted cotton or wool, nylon in various weaves. The popular bikini is generally made of stretch synthetic yarn in a knitted construction.

To top the swimming trunks before and after the swim, a jacket of bouclé knitted cotton or terry cloth may be worn. These absorbent fabrics protect the skin from sun and the body from chill. Trunks and jacket are often sold as a swim set.

The ever popular cabana set for wear on the beach, sunning at the pool, or play at resorts consists of shorts and jacket usually in bright colors or prints. Cotton sailcloth, knitted cottons, crash, terry cloth are appropriate fabrics.

For resort wear, men usually include at least one sports jacket, slacks, walking or Bermuda shorts, sport shirts, sweaters, as well as more formal attire for evening.

PUTTING THIS MERCHANDISE KNOWLEDGE TO USE ❯❯❯❯❯❯❯❯❯❯❯❯

❯ DO YOU KNOW YOUR MERCHANDISE?

1. Contrast the first authentic Continental style suit with the present modified Continental.
2. (*a*) Name the common blends found in wash-and-wear fabrics. (*b*) Give selling points for wash-and-wear suits. (*c*) Give laundering instructions for this type of suit.
3. How can you distinguish (*a*) tweed from cheviot (woolen), (*b*) sharkskin from worsted flannel, (*c*) serge from gabardine, (*d*) gabardine from whipcord, (*e*) mill-finished worsted from clear-finished worsted?
4. List the points to check for good tailoring in a suit.
5. (*a*) Of what fabrics are windbreakers made? (*b*) parkas? (*c*) swimming trunks?
6. (*a*) Give the selling points of a cotton poplin, water-repellent raincoat with zip-in cotton lining; (*b*) of a man's full-length overcoat made of 70 per cent cashmere and 30 per cent wool; (*c*) of a good grade of boys' vat-dyed 10-oz blue denim dungarees.

❯ INTERESTING THINGS TO DO

1. Look at your own dungarees and check the article for points you know indicate good grade. Grade your own dungarees as to quality and give reasons for your decision.
2. (*a*) Go to a retail store where a large assortment of lightweight slacks are carried. Compare prices of slacks made of all-cotton, cotton and synthetic blends, all-synthetic blends, wool and polyester. (*b*) Which slacks are the most expensive? (*c*) the least expensive? (*d*) How do you account for differences in price? (*e*) For what purposes is each best suited?
3. Borrow from relatives or friends two or three lightweight water-repellent jackets. Bring them to class. Demonstrate the selling points and drawbacks of each garment.

ADDITIONAL MERCHANDISE TERMS ❯❯❯❯❯❯❯❯❯❯❯❯❯❯❯❯❯❯❯❯❯❯

Ascot is a scarf tie, the ends of which, being tied once, are crossed in front and fastened with a scarfpin.

Barathea is a rayon, acetate, cotton, silk, or wool with a pebbly texture. The woven-in dobby design resembles the bricks in a wall.

Barrel cuff is a synonym for a single cuff on a shirt.

Belting is a heavy cotton, rayon, silk, or nylon mixture with large fillingwise ribs.

Cravat is a synonym for necktie.

Hand felled means a hand-sewed seam finished flat by hemming one edge over another.

Rep is a heavy ribbed silk, rayon, other synthetic, or mixture. Colors are solid or striped. Used for ties and robes.

Vent is a slit at the back or sides of a jacket or coat to permit freedom of bodily movement.

Domestics

UNIT 33 TOWELS

TYPES OF TOWELS

It was the day after New Year's. Dorothy Adams had been transferred from a madly rushed toy department to a relatively quiet domestics department that was about to begin its January White Sale. She had no idea of what items her stock consisted. Fortunately there was a good-natured sponsor to give her instructions. She was first told the classification and location of various types of towels.

For Personal Use	For Household Use
1. Turkish towels	1. Dish towels
2. Guest towels (made of huck, crash or damask)	2. Dishcloths
3. Huck towels	3. Glass towels

She was told that customers are anxious to know whether a towel: (1) will absorb water quickly and easily, (2) will be durable, (3) makes an attractive appearance, and (4) is a good value.

Why Are Towels Absorbent?

Cotton is most commonly used for *Turkish towels,* although "friction towels" called "back scratchers" can be made of linen pile. The pile weave is used to form loops, which serve to absorb moisture; the greater the number of loops per square inch, the greater the absorbency of the towel.

Face cloths are ordinarily made in the Turkish type construction called *terry cloth,* and their absorbency is also determined by the number of loops

◀ Double-loop terry toweling

Huck toweling ❯

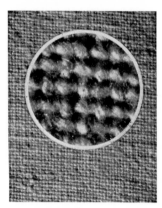

◀ Crash toweling

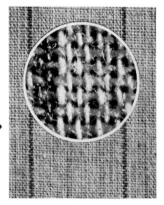

Striped glass toweling ❯

per square inch. They may also be knitted; and in that form are particularly desirable for tender skins, but they do not keep their shape.

Face towels are made of terry cloth, linen damask, all-linen huck, or cotton huck with linen filling. Huck, the short name for "huckaback," is often made in a diamond design or in a honey-combed pattern. The weave is dobby with a possible Jacquard border in white or colors. Coarse, heavy, slackly twisted yarns make for an absorbent surface.

Huck, finer crash, and damask are most frequently used for face and guest towels because absorbency is not so important a factor as it is in a fabric used for bath towels.

Glass towels, which are used for drying glasses, are generally made of linen or linen and cotton crash. Linen is better than cotton for this purpose because it does not lint. Glass towels are lighter in weight than crash dish towels. Linen crash is more absorbent than cotton crash. Linen does not feel damp so quickly, and it dries more quickly than cotton; therefore, linen dish, glass, and face towels, while more expensive than cotton, are well worth the difference.

Important Facts About the Durability of Towels

Close Weave. The more closely woven the fabric, the more durable the towel will be. This is particularly true in Turkish towels where the groundwork holds the loops in place. In Turkish towels, a twill weave in the groundwork is stronger than a basket variation. The under or ground weave can be most easily examined in the border or near the hem areas where there are no loops.

Yarns. Generally speaking, a linen huck or crash towel will outwear a cotton towel of similar grade. Yarns in warp and filling should be of the same diameter, and the tensile strength should be proportionate.

The salesperson should call the customer's attention to the label for features of performance.

Selvage and Seams. In addition to weave and yarn, the selvage will often indicate a high degree of durability if the edge is straight and the fillings bind in the warps tightly. The hems should be sewed with small, close stitches and firmly stitched at the corners.

What Factors Make a Towel Attractive?

Solid colors, colored borders, stripes, plaids, or printed patterns make towels attractive. In addition to towels in plain white, in pastel and dark colors, towels may be colored on one side only. Strong pastel colors will generally keep their color better than light pastels. Towels in very dark colors may run when washed.

Sometimes all-over Jacquard patterns or Jacquard borders enhance the beauty of towels; however, such woven-in designs often increase the price. Hemstitching is very attractive when used as a finish on face towels; however, negligence in laundering hemstitched edges may often result in ripping off the hem like a piece of perforated paper.

The salesperson should find out the color scheme of the customer's bathroom and/or bedroom in order to show harmonizing colors in towels. Color in dish towels makes the kitchen attractive. Some homemakers keep their prettiest dish towels just for show. These are called "show towels."

Hemstitching on the Edge of a Huck Towel. A hemstitched edge is attractive but may tear like perforated paper if laundered carelessly.

Often colored towels, colored bordered towels, or novelty towels may be more expensive than plain white, but this does not mean that they are better quality. Any additional decoration, such as monograms, will increase the price pf the towel. A small or medium-sized towel is often a better investment than a larger one of poorer quality. Since towels are generally classed as flatwork in the laundry and are charged for by the pound, a large-sized towel will cost more to launder. A large towel with long fine loops does seem more luxurious than a small one, however. Hence some customers are willing to spend an additional amount for this luxury even though it may not be worth the price when the utility is considered. The thrifty homemaker may prefer to buy dish and glass towelings by the yard and hem them herself. Some stores have these in 18-inch widths.

HOW TO MAKE TOWELS WEAR LONGER

Customers often ask: "Why do face towels wear out or seem to break in certain places? What can be done to prevent this?" In answering these questions, two factors must be considered. First, the durability of the towel; and second, the care and use given it by the customer. The durability of the towel has already been discussed.

Yarns often break when a towel is used to wipe a sharp knife or a razor blade. After several of such abuses, the towel will break apart entirely.

Turkish towels often become unsightly because loops are pulled out carelessly; therefore, salespeople should advise customers to take proper care in this matter.

Most colored towels are made "fast to washing." If there is any doubt

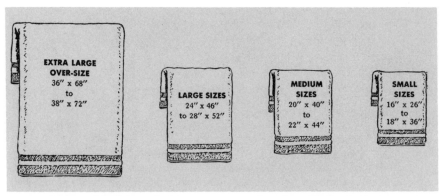

Sizes and Uses of Bath Towels. The over-size towel is often called a *bath sheet* and can be used as a wrap-around robe after bathing. Large size towels are for comfort and luxury. Hotels, clubs, and hospitals usually use medium sizes. The 20″ × 40″ towel is popular because of its ease in laundering and its convenient all-purpose size. The small sizes can be used for hands or face. They are light, easy to handle, and inexpensive to launder on the pound rate. *(Courtesy Cannon Mills, Inc.)*

about colorfastness, they should be laundered separately from the white. When dried, Turkish towels should be fluffed and not ironed. Flat borders may be ironed to even the edges. Crash, huck, and damask towels should be ironed when slightly damp.

BATH RUGS OR MATS

Bath rugs may be made of the same material as Turkish towels, but they are generally heavier. Salespeople should use the same selling points for such rugs as for Turkish towels—absorbency, durability, attractiveness, and value.

Another type of bath rug is made of *chenille* yarn, or fur, which is usually sewed or stitched onto a background of muslin in oval or oblong shape. Because of the deep pile formed by the chenille yarn, these rugs are very luxurious and absorb water readily. Bath rugs may also be made of braided strips of rag sewed or crocheted together into circular or oval shapes; or of crocheted or novelty cotton fabrics. These rugs are attractive, but they are not so absorbent as the terry cloth or chenille types.

Still another type of bath rug is the cotton tufted type with latex back to keep it from slipping.

Both rugs are made in all-over deep, rich pile or with sculptured patterns. Their backs may be covered with latex or foam rubber to be skid-resistant. Rugs come in various sizes and also wall-to-wall. Fibers for these rugs include all cotton, rayon, blends of 60 per cent acrylic and 40 per cent modacrylic pile.

Hit-or-miss rectangular rugs are an inexpensive type of bath rugs and may be purchased in some of the low-priced variety stores. They are made of various colors.

Many homemakers prefer to buy towels in attractively packaged matched sets or so-called bath ensembles. A set usually consists of bath towel, face-hand towel, washcloth, and bath mat. Not only are such sets colorful and attractive, but a different color for each set facilitates personal ease in identification.

PUTTING THIS MERCHANDISE KNOWLEDGE TO USE ❯ ❯ ❯ ❯ ❯ ❯ ❯ ❯ ❯ ❯

❯ DO YOU KNOW YOUR MERCHANDISE?

1. (*a*) Name the various kinds of towels. (*b*) Of what fabric is each type made?
2. What should a salesperson tell a customer about absorbency of: (*a*) terry towels, (*b*) crash towels, and (*c*) huck towels?
3. What should a salesperson tell a customer about durability of: (*a*) bath towels, (*b*) face towels, (*c*) dish towels, and (*d*) glass towels?
4. What factors make towels attractive?
5. What merchandise facts can a salesperson point out to show the customer that she is getting her money's worth?
6. Give concrete illustrations of how a salesperson can instruct the customer in prolonging the wear-life of a towel.

1. (*a*) Look at displays of towels in a domestics department of a store. (*b*) What proportion of bath towels are white? solid colored? printed? (*c*) What proportion of face cloths are terry cloth? huck? (*d*) Does the store carry show towels? What are they made of? in what designs?

2. (*a*) Bring two or three bath towels from home to class. (*b*) Give the selling points of each to the class.

3. (*a*) Bring two or three face towels to class. (*b*) Give the selling points of each to the class.

UNIT 34 TABLE COVERINGS

Table coverings, like sheets and pillowcases, are frequently spoken of as *linens,* even though they may also be made of cotton, rayon, or mixtures of these. Plastic place mats are textile fabrics only if they have a woven cloth or webbing as a base.

POINTS TO BE STRESSED ABOUT TABLE COVERINGS

A customer buying a table covering keeps in mind the purpose for which she is going to use the cloth, because that determines the type and size necessary.

Purpose

Is it to be for a bridge table, for a breakfast, a luncheon, or a dinner service?

For a *bridge table,* a gaily colored crash cloth may serve. Luncheon cloths and place mats may be used for bridge and luncheon settings; also embroidered or printed cottons and linens, lace cloth, basket-weave cottons, and cottons made to imitate real peasant linens that are much more expensive. Oilcloth and plastic-coated fabrics may be used for table covering as well as for shelving. These fabrics need no laundering, and dirt can be removed with a damp cloth and soap. Bridge or tea napkins are sold to match the cloth.

For *breakfast* or *luncheon,* the average size of a cloth is 54 x 54 inches. Place mats are approximately 11 x 17 inches. Matching napkins are sold. Plain and printed crash cloths also come in oblong sizes to fit long and narrow tables.

Cocktail napkins are very small (7-inch squares or 5 x 8 inches) and are made in crash (cotton or linen) or handkerchief linen.

Dinner cloths, which are used for the main meal, are usually made of cotton, linen, rayon damask, or mixtures of these. Though damask is preferred for formal occasions, dinner cloths are also made of other types of plain and embroidered cottons, linens, rayons, mixtures, and laces. Napkins come to match the dinner cloth.

What to Tell the Customer about Table Damask. Single or Double Damask

Damask is a fabric in Jacquard weave whose pattern is reversible. Its name is derived from Damascus. Linen damasks, like cotton damasks, are made single (4 float) or double (7 float). The double damask is generally more lustrous because of the longer floats, but the single damask may be more durable.

Length of the Fibers. As most linen damasks are made in combination of satin and sateen weaves, this construction will necessitate floats. If yarns are floated, the fibers in those yarns must be long so that they do not fuzz and lose their sheen. Likewise long fibers do not pull out of the yarn with friction in wear. Hence, cloths made with long fibers will be more durable than those made with short fibers.

In linen damask, the background is generally warp satin weave with the design in filling sateen construction. If the table is rectangular in shape, the cloth is properly placed when warp satin weave shows in the background as the sheen then runs the length of the table from host to hostess.

Type of Yarn. Yarns should be evenly spun. A cloth which is made up of yarns of uneven diameters—yarns with thick and thin places in them are inferior yarns—is unattractive and will not wear so well as one made from evenly spun yarns.

◀ Jacquard table damask
—white and colored

White double damask ❯

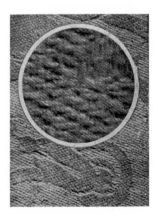

Closeness of Weave. This is very important. If a weave is loose, there is a danger of slippage of yarns. This slipping may in time wear out the float. Count of cloth should be carefully considered in buying the damask; the higher the count, the stronger and more durable the cloth.

Length of the Floats. A float may range from 4 to 20 yarns in length. A long float makes a lustrous cloth while a short float makes a more durable cloth. Long floats allow greater reflection of light and hence seem more beautiful; but they may wear out more quickly, because a greater length of yarn is exposed to friction.

Amount of Sizing. Sizing is dressing in the form of starch that gives weight and body to a material. A flimsy cloth may seem heavy if it contains much sizing. Generally, linens are not sized but have a little starch put into the fabric in finishing to give that leathery stiffness of new linen fabrics. If, when two folds of a cloth are rubbed against each other, there is a noticeable change in the stiffness and body of the fabric, then the cloth is oversized.

Amount of Bleaching. Linen damasks may be bleached pure white (full-bleach); slightly bleached (oyster bleach); deep cream color (silver bleach); or dyed in pastel shades.

From the standpoint of length of wear of a damask, cloths that are not fully bleached when new will wear longer than fully bleached cloths. Commercial laundries use a chemical bleach, which tends to overbleach the fabric if it is subjected to too many launderings. Hence the salesperson should point out the advantage of an oyster white or deep-cream-colored damask.

Size. The largest damask tablecloths are called *banquet cloths*. Cloths shorter in length are called *dinner cloths*. Napkins are sold to match the cloth.

What to Tell the Customer About Table Crash

Linen crash is a popular fabric for luncheon cloths and luncheon bridge sets, napkins, centerpieces, place mats and doilies. *Crash* is a term applied to plain-weave fabrics in linen, cotton, rayon, or mixtures thereof. It is characterized by coarse, uneven yarns, which make a fairly heavy, coarse-textured cloth. Table linen crash yarns are usually made of tow although better grades may be made of a combination of line and tow. Toweling linen crash is made with coarser yarn than table linen crash, and dress linen crash is finer than all the other crashes.

When selling crash for table linen, the well-informed salesperson will do well to know the following points:

Fiber Content. The label should be read to learn the fiber content. A mixture of linen and cotton is usually less expensive than all-linen. Rayon, in a mixture, makes an attractive cloth, but rayon often wears out first.

Count of Cloth. On the label, the count of cloth may be given. A high count (77 yarns to the inch, computed by adding warps and fillings together) is an excellent grade; 64 yarns to the inch is medium grade; and 55 yarns to the inch is poor grade. A high-count cloth makes a close construction that will insure good wearing quality.

Fast Dyes. Some crashes are yarn-dyed plaids, while others are printed or hand-blocked. If the dye is fast to sunlight and to washing, the salesperson should stress colorfastness as a selling point.

Hems. These should be even and should be stitched straight with short even stitches. A good quality thread is necessary.

What Is Art Linen?

Art linen is a fabric somewhat like crash in plain weave, in which the yarns are left round and smooth, not calendered or pressed. For this reason, art linen is often called *round-thread linen*. Since a needle may be worked more easily through art linen than through crash, it is suitable for embroidery purposes. When linen can be stocked, it is sold by the yard. It also comes made up and stamped for embroidery. A customer has a choice of unbleached, partly bleached, or fully bleached art linen.

When selling art linen, the salesperson should stress:

Yarns: even diameter and fine.

Weave: close. Count 140 is excellent grade; 60 is poor.

Bleach: a partly bleached cloth will give longer service than a fully bleached cloth. Bleaching will soften the yarns but generally weakens them.

Fancy Linens for Table Covers. Luncheon sets and place mats may be made of art linen, handkerchief linen, or crash (domestic or imported) and finished in fancy stitches, embroidery or lace such as: plain hemstitched, Puerto Rican embroidery, Appenzell (Swiss embroidery), Italian embroidery, Spanish embroidery, Mosaic embroidery, Madeira embroidery, and filet lace and cutwork.

How Can Table Coverings Be Made to Last a Long Time?

If carefully handled, table covers and napkins can be made to last a long time. Since constant folding and ironing in the same crease may cause the fabric to wear out in these places, the crease should be changed slightly with each ironing. Hand-hemmed cloths will wear more evenly than machine-hemmed cloths; because hand hemming is generally stitched more loosely than machine hemming, the stitches will not break so quickly in laundering.

Hemstitched cloths may be more expensive but will be much less durable than those that are hand hemmed, since a commercial laundry may tear a hemstitched edge like perforated paper.

PUTTING THIS MERCHANDISE KNOWLEDGE TO USE ❯ ❯ ❯ ❯ ❯ ❯ ❯ ❯ ❯ ❯

❯ DO YOU KNOW YOUR MERCHANDISE?

1. Explain how the quality of a damask tablecloth can be determined.
2. (*a*) What is oilcloth? What are its uses? (*b*) Give the specific uses of plastic-coated table coverings.
3. (*a*) Give the selling points of table damask. (*b*) For what purposes is linen damask used?
4. (*a*) Give the selling points of table crash. (*b*) For what purposes is crash used?
5. (*a*) What is art linen? (*b*) For what purposes is it suitable?
6. What fabric or fabrics would you recommend using for a table covering for a formal luncheon in your home?

❯ INTERESTING THINGS TO DO

1. Explain with diagrams how you would set the table for a formal dinner for six, and what type of tablecloth and napkins you would use.
2. Visit the fancy-linens department of a store and make a list of 15 items carried.
3. Copy labels, advertisements, or mail-order offerings for table coverings. Interpret each label.

UNIT 35 BEDDING

No sooner had Dorothy Adams learned what to tell her customers about table coverings than she was transferred to mattresses and pillows. Again the sponsor helped her learn the stock and gave her a manual outlining the essentials of a good mattress.

ESSENTIALS OF A GOOD MATTRESS

A good mattress should be made to support all parts of the body equally. It should be soft enough to permit the normal movements of the body, yet hard enough to afford complete relaxation. It should be resilient (able to return to its original shape). As a mattress is not changed very frequently, it should be durable and buoyant.

How can the durability and the comfort of a mattress be determined?

Type of Spring or Filling

Inner-spring Mattress. Inner-spring mattresses are one of the most popular types in use today because they keep their buoyancy. In this type, as its names suggests, a series of wire coil springs is padded at both top and bottom with layers of filling. The filling or padding may be cotton felt, kapok, hair, or lamb's wool. The coil springs and padding are then covered by a ticking, which is tufted to keep the filling in place. Mattresses made with a relatively few well-placed large springs, if correctly designed, properly tied, and combined with good padding and insulation, can make a mattress as firm and comfortable as many small springs. The durability of the mattress depends more on the quality of the steel used in the springs than on the number of springs used. The coil springs are generally tied together with twine, hinged clips, wire, or metal straps in such a way to allow a relatively independent up-and-down movement of individual springs. The number of coils may vary from 200 to 850. Poor grades become rusty and noisy in a very short time.

Fiber-filled Mattresses. The most durable, resilient, and expensive filling is made of South American horsehair. However, since horsehair is an animal fiber, it tends to produce heat; it also gradually becomes hard packed, and therefore requires occasional renovating. The quality increases with the length of the hair: the longer the hair, the better the filling. Horsehair is frequently mixed with hog hair which is stiff and short, or with cattle hair, which frequently retains an odor. Labels should state the percentage of each type of hair, for example, 25 per cent hog hair and 75 per cent horsehair, because the quality of the mattress is affected by the types of hair used.

Mattresses filled with kapok, a vegetable pod fiber, are resilient when new but, within four or five years, may lose their flexibility because the fibers begin to pulverize. This type of fiber-filled mattress is moisture-resistant and dries quickly.

Cotton-filled mattresses may be made of new, long-staple cotton which has been carded, combed, and placed in layers or felted and called *cotton-felt*. This is the best type of cotton-filled mattress and is only slightly less resilient than kapok. Inexpensive cotton-filled mattresses are stuffed with cotton that has not been carded, and becomes lumpy in a short while. The poorest grade of cotton mattress is made with cotton linters, which have little or no resiliency.

The cheapest grades of fiber-filled mattresses can be made of substitutes for cotton, such as excelsior, shredded cocoanut fiber, and corn husks. These have no resiliency and mat in a short time.

Foam rubber (a nontextile) is also used for mattresses. Its covering is the same fabric that is used on the inner-spring and fiber-filled types.

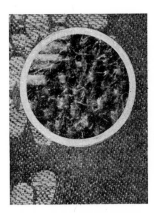

◀ Jacquard damask ticking

Heavy twilled striped ticking ❯

Type of Covering

The covering of a mattress is usually a heavy twilled cotton in blue and white stripes called *ticking*. The covering will also affect the durability of the mattress. Closely woven tickings are desirable because they do not permit stuffings to come through. The strongest quality is made of closely woven yarn-dyed cotton in the twill weave. Pillows are also covered with this type of ticking. Coverings are also made of figured cotton damask, sateen, and of sheeting materials with a printed design. The latter is the poorest grade.

Workmanship

The workmanship of a mattress should also be examined. *Tufting* is used to prevent the filling from becoming lumpy or shifting to one side. The tufting yarn, of which the tufts, buttons or eyelets are the visible part, should go from one side of the mattress to the other. In the better mattresses, the tufts are at regular and frequent intervals, and are directly opposite each other on each side of the mattress, and not merely on the surface of the ticking. The *edges* of the mattress should be firm and strong. Cotton-felt mattresses of the better grade have several rows of stitching on the side walls to reinforce the filling. The better inner-spring mattresses have small screened holes that are used as ventilators. These holes create suction by compressing and releasing air and thereby aid in keeping the mattress sanitary.

How to Make Mattresses Wear Longer

Mattresses, with the exception of foam rubber, should be turned from side to side, end to end, and top to bottom frequently in order to prevent sagging in one place. Inner-spring mattresses should be turned about three or four times a year. To keep them clean and fresh, they should be sunned occasionally as well as dusted and vacuumed. Mattress pads and covers keep the mattress clean and sanitary and add to the comfort of the bed.

PILLOWS

Pillows also play an important part in the comfort of a bed. Some people prefer a plump and well-filled pillow, while others like one that is softer and less tightly packed. Pillows should be light in weight, resilient, bouyant, and free from odor, stiff feathers, and lumps. Like mattresses, they should be covered with a tightly woven ticking that will prevent the filling from coming through. Zip-in pillow covers protect the pillow, can be removed and laundered frequently.

Fillings for Pillows

The comfort, durability, and price of pillows depend on the type of filling as well as on the ticking. Pillows may be filled with *down* (the soft under-coating from the breasts of geese or ducks), goose, chicken, and turkey feathers, mixed feathers, kapok, silk floss or waste (often confused with kapok), or cotton.

Pillows filled with down are very comfortable since they are light in weight, resilient and soft (because they have no quills). Down is the most expensive of all types of fillings. Feather fibers that have been stripped from the quills of feathers are sometimes substituted for down. The label should tell whether the pillow is stuffed with *down, feathers,* or *feather fiber.* Goose feathers are next in order of desirability. These have more body than down and are therefore more buoyant. The quills may be felt through the casing unless the ticking is very closely woven. Duck feathers have less arch to their quills and are therefore less buoyant and resilient. An excellent combination is made of 75 per cent down with 25 per cent goose or duck feathers, which add body and prevent gradual wadding of the soft down. Pillows made of chicken or turkey feathers are not so desirable because they are much heavier, stiffer, and harder. Though there is no difference in buoyancy, the white chicken feathers are more expensive.

Less expensive pillows are stuffed with kapok, cotton, or cotton linters. These will get hard and lumpy in a short time. Since cotton and kapok are vegetable fibers, they have very little resiliency. Dacron polyester fibers make nonallergic and resilient stuffing.

Some people who are sensitive to feathers can sleep comfortably on kapok-filled pillows that will not irritate them. Kapok pillows are also suitable for the seashore, since they do not get damp quickly and will float if they fall into the water. It is for this reason that they are used as cushions for canoes and boats and also for life preservers.

The ticking on pillows may be the same as that used on mattresses.

Care of Pillows

Pillows should be kept well aired and exposed occasionally to the direct rays of the sun to keep them fresh. When the pillows become dirty, they can be washed satisfactorily in a renovating factory where they can be sterilized.

Dorothy Adams had a chance to sell pillows but not mattresses; however, her knowledge of them will be helpful to her when she has occasion to buy them.

Bed-sheet sales were mounting, so extra salespeople were needed in that department. While Dorothy had never bought a sheet in her life and had never thought much about them until now, her sponsor gave her enough information so she could give customers intelligent advice on what to buy.

BED COVERINGS

Although many of the articles in this classification may be made of fibers other than cottons, cottons are used to a greater extent.

Sheets and pillowcases, for example, are often spoken of as "linens." This is an incorrect usage of the word "linen," for most of the "bed linens" are made of cotton muslin. Real linen bed sheets and cases are more expensive than the average grade of cotton; they wrinkle much more than the cottons and are more leathery to the touch. They are very cool, smooth, and attractive, but are really luxury items. The average person who buys "bed linen" buys cotton, either muslin or percale.

Nylon sheets in white and in colors are being sold in many stores. Women can wash them at home in their automatic washer, dry them in a dryer, or drip dry them without ironing. If they are sent to a commercial laundry, they 'do not shrink out of fit and weigh little on the pound rate.

SHEETS

In purchasing sheets, a customer often makes her choice on the basis of a brand name that has become familiar to her or on the basis of the salesperson's recommendations. She may not understand why the sheets do not fit her bed after they are laundered or why they do not last as long as she had expected. Reliance on brand names may not always lead to a satisfactory choice, for each manufacturer may make several grades.

What questions may a customer ask about sheets and pillowcases before she purchases them?

1. Durability—how long will they wear?
2. Launderability—how will washing affect them?
3. Size—will they be the correct size?
4. Colorfastness—will colored sheets be fast color?
5. Value—will the purchase be a good value?

Durability—How Long Will They Wear?

Length of Fibers and Twist of Yarn. The best sheets are made from combed cotton fibers that are at least one inch long and are evenly and tightly spun into yarn. An unevenly spun yarn consists of thick and thin places and, therefore, will not wear well. A loosely twisted yarn may pull apart with wear, and the short ends of the fibers may protrude after washing, giving a fuzzy appearance. The length of fibers and twist of yarn are, therefore, important factors in durability of a sheet.

Count of Cloth or Thread Count. The closeness of the weave of a sheet should also be considered by wise customers. A closely woven (high count) cloth with a good balance between the warp and filling threads will be stronger than a cloth with a low count.

Cotton sheets are made of two kinds of fabrics: (1) percale, (2) muslin. Percales have a minimum count of 180 yarns per square inch; while muslins come in counts of 140, 128, and 112. The largest selling fabric in the United States is 180-count percale (40 per cent of the market); 128-count muslin (30 per cent); 140-count muslin (18 per cent); 200-count percale (5 per cent). Some sheets are finished to give a no-iron feature.

Fine-quality percale sheets are made of fine, combed yarn. Hence they are very smooth and appear to soil less easily than coarser sheets. A percale that is not quite so fine and smooth is made of carded yarn.

A muslin sheet of 140 count is not so smooth as a percale sheet, but it is usually less expensive and can be sold on the basis of economy as well as on durability.

The muslin sheets of 128 and 112 counts are made of shorter fibers and yarns, which are more loosely woven than the 140 type. The lower-count muslins are low priced, and in Consumers' Union tests were approximately equal in durability to the high-count muslins. The luxurious percales were less durable than the muslins. According to these test results, it would appear that muslins, generally cheaper than percales, are better buys from the standpoint of durability. Percales, however, are lighter weight: flat type—1.4 lbs.; low-count muslin—1.6 lbs.; high-count muslin—1.8 lbs. Fitted sheets weigh about ½ lb. less than flats of similar sizes. Fitted sheets are sheets whose corners are made to fit the corners of the mattress. They are made for both top and bottom sheets, the latter selling more.

Tensile Strength. The answer to the question "How long will they wear?" depends not only on the fibers, yarns, and count, but also on the strength a sheet retains in use and the care it receives. The information about performance as well as thread count should be found on the label.

Selvages. Plain selvages will not wear so well as tape selvages, which resemble a modified basket weave. Since the selvages are apt to show wear first, they should be examined carefully to see that the edges are firm.

Hems. Hems may be either plain or hemstitched; however, the hemstitched hems are less durable since they tear very easily.

When the average customer buys sheets and pillowcases, she wants not only those that will be most durable but also the ones that give the most comfort. All sheets are quite smooth when they are new because of the calendering and, sometimes, the sizing used as finishing processes. Those sheets and cases, however, that are closely woven will retain their original smoothness after being washed. The sizing, which is used to give body and smoothness by covering up the imperfections in construction, will come out in laundering, leaving the material light in weight and fuzzy. Sheets with little or no sizing will naturally be much smoother after washing than those with much sizing.

Shrinkage. Most sheets will shrink from 1 per cent to 4 per cent in washing (the majority are limited to 2 per cent). Shrinkage is more serious in a fitted than in a flat sheet, because excessive shrinkage can make the fitted sheet utterly useless. It would be advisable in buying fitted sheets that the customer reserve the right to return them if they do not fit after washing. Consumers' Union tests also revealed the differences in length and widths between brands and models of the same and different brands.

Size—Will the Sheets Be the Correct Size?

Sheets may be durable, smooth, and satisfactory in all ways; but, if they are not the correct size, they will soon prove most unsatisfactory. Sheets are made in crib, single, twin, double, queen, and king sizes.

In deciding on the size of sheet to buy for a bed, the housewife may know what width she wants but frequently fails to analyze the best length to protect the bed and the sleeper. By buying sheets that are too short she may save some money, but she will pay for the saving in discomfort and needless strain on the sheets. Salespeople should know the correct size to recommend in order to satisfy their customers.

How to Compute Necessary Length of Flat Sheets. Sheets are sold in lengths from 92–108 inches, which is the measurement *before hemming*. Many people wonder why a 92- or 99-inch sheet is entirely too short. The salesperson can determine the proper length of a flat sheet from the following table:

Standard mattress length	74 inches
Allowance of 6 inches at each end for thickness of mattress	12 inches
Allowance for shrinkage	5 inches
Hems (3 inches at top and 2 at bottom)	5 inches
Total so far	96 inches

In this case, the 96 inches has not yet allowed for any tuck-in. If a tuck-in of 4 inches is allowed at both ends, 8 inches will be added to the total so far.

Total so far	96 inches
Tuck-in	8 inches
Total length required	104 inches

A sheet that is 92 inches long will therefore be too short after washing to cover the ends of the mattress. It also does not allow for tucking in or folding over.

A 99-inch sheet, used for the bottom sheet, allows only 1½ inches for tucking in at either end. Used for the top sheet, it will not allow a sufficient turn-back over the blanket. Hence the 108-inch-length sheet is the length to be suggested, for it will give the most comfort, wear, and protection.

Colorfastness—Will Colored Sheets Be Colorfast?

Sheets and cases come not only in all white, but in solid colors, in stripes, and in white with colored or printed borders and all-over designs to harmonize with the color scheme of a room. Colored sheets should be colorfast to washing and to sunlight and should be so labeled.

Value—Will the Purchase Be a Good Value?

Value is judged not only by the original price paid, but by the amount of wear or the expected durability. A sheet that is very inexpensive may become an expensive purchase if it does not wear well or give satisfaction. In some bargain sheets, there may be defects in the weave that will lessen the durability. Others, such as 90-inch-length sheets, will prove unsatisfactory after they are washed since they will be too short for the bed and may wear out sooner because they are subjected to much pulling. Another factor to be considered in the value of the purchase is the cost of laundering. If sheets are paid for by the pound, the lighter-weight sheets, such as percales, will cost less, hence the price will prove less in the long run.

How to Make Sheets Wear Longer

No matter what quality sheet is purchased, the care which the customer gives it in use will affect its durability. The following are some recommendations for making sheets wear longer.

1. Sheets should be bought in the correct size for the bed. A fitted sheet should fit when it is first put on. Consumers would do well to get a money-back guarantee should a sheet not fit after washing. Shrinkage should not exceed 2%.

2. The use of a smooth mattress pad, especially with a tufted mattress, may save wear on the sheets.

3. Broken springs, loose nails, or a projecting sliver of wood, which may catch and tear the sheets, should be avoided.

4. Torn places should be mended before the sheets are laundered.

5. The use of strong bleaches should be avoided in laundering.

6. Ironing creases or folds should be avoided, since they tend to weaken the fabric.

7. If ironing is required, the corners of pillowcases should be ironed first, and the hems last for greater wear.

8. Too hot an iron, which may scorch and weaken sheets, should not be used.

9. The top and bottom of sheets should be reversed frequently to equalize wear.

10. Beds should be made with a light touch, not with forcible pulling.

11. If the household supply of sheets is rotated so that the same sheets are never used twice in succession, the fibers can dry out thoroughly and hence give longer wear.

PILLOWCASES

The same standards that govern the quality of sheets should be applied to pillowcases. In fact, since cases usually become more soiled than sheets and require more vigorous washing and more frequent bleaching, their durability should be considered even more carefully.

Pillowcases should measure 2 inches larger around than the pillow on which they are to be used and about 10 inches longer. A pillow, therefore, which is 20 inches wide measures 40 inches around, and should have a 42-inch case. Common sizes are 42 x 36 inches and 42 x 38½ inches.

BLANKETS, COMFORTERS, AND BEDSPREADS

These three items come in different weights and styles for the different seasons of the year.

Blankets

Cotton or rayon blankets are desirable for summer, for they are cooler, easier to wash, and less expensive than all-wool blankets. Whereas wool blankets have to be protected from moths when stored, cotton, rayon, and acrylic blankets are unaffected by moths.

Cotton blankets are sold on the basis of the comfort, attractiveness, durability, correct size, price, and ease in caring for them.

Woolen Blankets. On the first really cold night of winter, however, the homemaker goes to her cedar chest and brings out a heavy wool blanket. To insure the maximum warmth, with the minimum amount of weight, many homemakers prefer an all-wool blanket to a wool-and-cotton mixture, a wool-and-rayon mixture, a 100 per cent acrylic, or a 70 per cent rayon, 15 per cent

Orlon acrylic, 15 per cent cotton blend. When a customer buys a blanket for use in cold weather she wants:

1. Warmth
2. Comfort—no undue weight
3. Beauty—soft, fluffy texture and rich colors
4. Durability

A customer can make a thoroughly happy purchase when she buys a wool blanket because of the inherent qualities of the wool fiber.

A wool blanket is *warm* because wool fibers retain the warmth of the sleeper's body. Wool fibers have air pockets holding still, dry air through which cool outer air must pass, thus being warmed before it strikes the body. The napping of the blanket (whether it is made of wool or other fibers) will increase the number and size of the air pockets, hence increasing the blanket's insulating value. Laundering a blanket will tend to close these air pockets and prevent ventilation and the escape of evaporated moisture. Wool absorbs a good deal of moisture without feeling damp and provides evaporation of the moisture from the body. Campers and outdoor sleepers need fear no chill from dew or light showers when they are covered by a wool blanket. Because wool fiber is a poor conductor of heat (keeps the heat near the body), a wool blanket is warmer than a cotton or rayon blanket of the same thickness.

Comfort depends on the warmth and the weight and size of a blanket. The weight of a blanket is no real indication of its warmth. A lightweight wool blanket may be as warm as, or warmer than, a heavy, closely woven, felted wool blanket. A thick, lightweight blanket is more comfortable on the sleeper than a heavy one. Furthermore, a blanket with only a very small percentage (less than 5 per cent) of wool feels no warmer than an all-cotton blanket.

Blanket Bindings. Bindings should be of materials that will not shrink more than the blanket when laundered. The ends should be neatly finished and the threads well fastened. Satin and sateen are commonly used for bindings, as in the two on the left. The blanket stitch on lightweight blankets, as in the two on the right, wears well if the threads are secure. *(Courtesy Consumers' Guide)*

The size of a blanket is important to the comfort of the sleeper. A blanket should be large enough to tuck in sufficiently at the sides and foot. A safe rule is that a blanket should be 10 inches longer and 18 inches wider than the mattress.

A blanket should be *attractive*. New wool blankets, if they are properly cared for, are soft, fluffy in texture, and rich in color. The color of the blanket should harmonize with the color of the room.

The binding or finishing of the edges of a blanket affect the beauty and the wearing quality of the blanket. The ends may be finished by a blanket stitch, which is a kind of scalloped embroidery (machine done or hand done), or they may have a turned hem. For real beauty, ends are bound with silk, rayon, acetate, or nylon satin. Sateen (all cotton) and nylon are more durable for bindings, however, because silk or rayon bindings may wear out before the blanket.

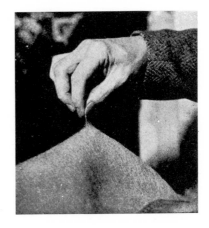

Testing Nap of a Blanket. *(Courtesy Consumers' Guide)*

A wool blanket can be *durable,* but not all wool blankets are always good. For durability, a wool blanket should have long, strong fibers, good tensile strength of yarn, firm weave, and a moderately thick strong nap. To test a nap for strength, take hold of a little bit of nap between the thumb and forefinger, and lift the blanket. If the blanket can be lifted by the nap, the nap is strong.

CARE OF WOOL BLANKETS   Wool blankets can be washed at home by hand or in a washing machine. They may also be dry-cleaned. Some commercial laundries specialize in washing blankets.

If laundering is to be done at home, choose a clear, dry day when there is air stirring. It is better to launder one blanket at a time. Bindings should be first washed by hand by applying soap suds made from a flake soap to the binding with a brush.

Most city homemakers store heavy wool blankets during the summer, unless they use them in the mountains or at the seashore. Since moths like to feed on wool blankets, they should be cleaned before they are stored by washing or dry cleaning and then wrapped in heavy paper. The package should be sealed, for moths are adept at finding the tiniest opening. Some homemakers sprinkle moth flakes or moth balls in the folds of the blanket before wrapping it.

Blankets Made of Synthetics and Blends.   Some apartment dwellers and homeowners do not own a 100 per cent wool blanket. These are usually young homemakers who find their homes heated so well that they do not require warm bed coverings. Laboratory tests on the thermostatic quality of

HOW TO LAUNDER A BLANKET IN A WASHING MACHINE

Use cool or lukewarm water (as much water as the machine will hold).

Put in neutral soap.

Run machine to make foam before blanket is put into it.

Run machine set to "modern" or "delicate" fabrics.

Use moderate temperature for drying.

Hang blanket over line evenly (half on each side of line) to distribute the weight.

Brush softly to raise nap.

Press binding with warm iron.

HOW TO LAUNDER A BLANKET BY HAND

Use cool or lukewarm water.

Make suds with neutral soap.

Fill tub with as much soapy water as possible.

Squeeze suds through blanket by cupping the hands. Use enough fresh suds to be sure blanket is clean.

Rinse in clear water of the same temperature as the suds. The number of rinses depends on the number required to cleanse blanket of suds.

Squeeze suds out gently by hand.

Hang over line evenly to distribute weight. Dry in moderately warm room or out-of-doors.

Brush softly to raise nap.

Press binding with warm iron.

wool blankets vs. synthetic-fibered blankets reveal that a 100 per cent wool blanket is warmer than a 100 per cent acrylic fiber blanket of the same weight. The latter type and blends have the advantage that they can be washed in an automatic laundry; that they have a pleasing comfortable feeling, and that they are usually less expensive than all-wool. The new synthetics are nonallergic, mothproof (what moth would want to eat a plastic?),and made in all sizes, in solid colors, plaids, and prints.

Blankets come in sizes for:

Cribs	Single Beds	Twin Beds	Double Beds
36 × 54	54 × 76	66 × 76	70 × 80
42 × 60	60 × 76	66 × 80	72 × 84
	60 × 80	66 × 84	80 × 90
	60 × 84	66 × 90	

Comforters

Stuffed or quilted bed coverings are called *comforters*. They are used on a bed for both attractiveness and warmth. The covering makes it attractive, and the filling gives it warmth. Rayons, acetates, and silks in matelassé and brocade make the most luxurious-appearing comforters; while sateen, polished cotton, and challis are generally more durable. Fabrics with long floats do not adhere to the bed as well as short-float fabrics or twills. Coverings should be made in washable or dry-cleanable fabrics.

Stuffing should be soft, light, and resilient. Australian wool makes a soft filling; however, domestic scoured and carded wool, reused wool, and short fibers of wool waste can be used. Cotton and kapok particularly may become lumpy in use. Polyester fibers are common and do not mat down. Down from the eider sea duck is quite warm; it is the softest, most resilient, lightest, and also the most expensive stuffing. Chicken feathers are often substituted for down. Unless the quills are carefully chopped, they may work their way through the outer covering.

Patchwork quilts, in designs imitating the antique ones, are really a type of comforter. The antique patchwork quilt is made of small pieces of fabric cut in various shapes and sewed together to form designs. Modern types may be printed to resemble the handmade antique ones. Modern quilts are filled with cotton batting and are quilted or tufted. They can be laundered, but antique quilts should be dry-cleaned.

Bedspreads

Bedspreads are made of tufted cotton, rayon and nylon chenille, candle-wick, cotton Jacquards, woven madras, seersuckers, chintz, cretonne, embossed cotton, dotted swiss, organdies, and sailcloth. In selling them salespeople stress:

1. Washability or ease in cleaning
2. Correct size
3. Attractive appearance—to harmonize with other furnishings of the room
4. Texture—a rough, tufted, or crinkled surface will not crush readily
5. Easy care, including wrinkle resistance, shrinkage control, machine washability

PUTTING THIS MERCHANDISE KNOWLEDGE TO USE ❯ ❯ ❯ ❯ ❯ ❯ ❯ ❯ ❯ ❯

❯ DO YOU KNOW YOUR MERCHANDISE?

1. What questions may a customer ask a salesperson about sheets and pillowcases?
2. You, as salesperson, answer the questions in No. 1.
3. What recommendations can you give your customer regarding wear-life of sheets?
4. (a) Of what fibers are blankets made? (b) What are the advantages and disadvantages of all-wool blankets? (c) of a 100 per cent acrylic-fibered blanket?
5. (a) Give instructions for laundering an all-wool blanket in an automatic washer at home. (b) Give instructions for laundering a 70 per cent rayon, 15 per cent acrylic, 15 per cent cotton blanket in an automatic washer at home. The blanket is shrinkage controlled; lilac color; binding is acetate satin.
6. (a) Give the selling points of a kapok-filled comforter with an acetate satin covering. (b) What are its chief drawbacks?

1. (*a*) Go to an antique shop in your community. Ask to see antique patchwork quilts. Estimate sizes and ask the prices. Note the designs, colors, and workmanship (stitching). (*b*) Compare prices, sizes, designs, colors, and workmanship on modern quilts in department stores.

2. (*a*) Make a study of the fashions in bed sheets to find out what percentage is flat compared with fitted. How many stores carry fitted bottom sheets but not fitted top sheets? Why? (*b*) What are the most popular sizes? (*c*) the most popular fashion colors?

3. (*a*) Make a study of the styles, colors, fabrics, textures in bedspreads carried by stores in your neighborhood. (*b*) What seems to be the style trend in bedspreads?

ADDITIONAL MERCHANDISE TERMS ❯

Candlewick is a cotton tufted fabric used as a bedspread. The tufts are spaced (as coin dots).

Contour sheet is synonymous with *fitted sheet*.

Domestic means a classification of household textiles consisting of towels, bedding, and table coverings.

Quilt is a bedcovering usually thinner and less soft and resilient than a comforter.

Silence cloth is a cotton-felt or quilted pad placed under the tablecloth on a dining table to diminish noise and also protect the wood against heat and dampness.

Tufting is a brushlike button of clipped cotton yarn. Tufts may appear at regular intervals on mattresses, on some comforters, bedspreads, and quilts.

Curtains, Draperies, and Upholsteries

CHAPTER 14

UNIT 36 CURTAINS

TYPES OF CURTAINS

Have you ever studied an advertisement of draperies and curtains? Has the wording confused you—curtains, cafés, draw curtains, sash curtains—some lined, others not; some lightweight, some heavyweight, some sheer, some opaque, some pleated, others to be shirred over a rod, of many different lengths and widths? It sounds confusing, yet these different styles can be classified easily into four groups.

1. Glass Curtains. These curtains are hung next to the window pane or glass. This type of curtain is made of thin, lacy fabrics such as ninon, marquisette, organdy, or dotted swiss. *Casement* curtains are glass curtains made of heavy lace, net or casement cloth (often with a fringed edge) suitable for out-swinging, leaded windows or large picture windows. A very popular type of glass curtain is a heavily embroidered Swiss batiste, lawn, or net. It is called a *tambour curtain* because the fabric, when hand embroidered, is stretched over a drum called a *tambour* in French. Curtains often have a strip of fabric across the top of the window called a *valance*. This may be flat, shirred, pleated, or festooned. Valances are used also with draperies.

2. Draw Curtains. These curtains are used as window shades to insure privacy or to shut out bright light. A pulley or draw cord opens and closes these curtains. When made of opaque fabrics and lined, they may be called *draperies.*

3. Sash Curtains. These curtains cover the lower half of kitchen or

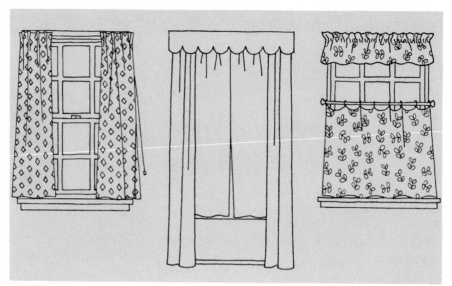

Left: Draw curtains. **Center:** Floor-length side draperies with glass curtains. **Right:** Café curtains with valance at top.

bathroom windows. The curtain is of thin material hung from a rod attached to the lower window sash or to the lower half of the window casing. Sheer curtains for French doors also come in this category. The curtains are held fast at the top and bottom of each door.

4. The Café Curtain. Originally used in France in cafés, this curtain is a kind of sash curtain because one tier covers the lower half of the window. Another tier may cover the upper half. Sometimes cafés are sold in sets of three tiers. One tier overlaps the next by about 3 inches. These curtains can be made of sheer fabrics, such as embroidered batiste (tambour), marquisette, or heavy fabrics like cretonne, sailcloth, or chintz.

Wash-and-Hang Curtain Fabrics

Time was when glass curtains were all made of thin cotton fabrics. They had to be washed, bleached, and starched each time they were laundered. Then they had to be stretched and dried on pin frames. After that, it was still necessary to press them. Then they were hung at the windows. When soiled and often yellowish with age, they were taken down. To the surprise of their owner, they often literally fell apart. Consequently, when nylon and Orlon acrylic fibers came into use as glass curtaining, the homemaker thought she would be relieved of all hand laundering and labor.

But alas! Acetate, rayon, and then nylon did not solve her laundering problem. Rayon had about the same resistance to light as cotton, and acetate only a little more resistance than cotton. Rayon, like cotton, was subject to shrinkage; acetate was more stable but would not stand a hot iron. Nylon curtains grayed in use; strong sunlight or long exposure to ordinary light injured them.

Then came Orlon acrylic curtains, but these fibers proved unsuitable for making into sheer white yarn. After that came glass fibers. These fibers seemed to be the answer to the homemaker's prayer for a wash-and-hang glass curtain. Glass fabrics will not burn, will wash by "dunking" in soap and water, rinsing in clear water, then hanging at the window to dry. They dry quickly and require *no* ironing. But experience of homemakers showed that glass fibers shifted in the weave (yarns slipped) because yarns are so smooth and slippery. Dry cleaners disliked cleaning glass-fiber curtains because short fibers "came off" in the process and, in time, have been known to clog the machine.

Next came Dacron polyester fibers in glass curtaining. Instructions on the labels claimed they could be washed by hand or by machine with the "modern fabrics" or "wash-and-wear" setting; no ironing was required. For the most part, ironing was unnecessary, but many discriminating homemakers preferred to "touch up" the curtains.

According to Consumers Union, the most satisfactory of all fibers for glass curtains is Dacron polyester. Consumers Union found it strong, durable, and unaffected by sunlight. The best Dacrons tested approached the wash-and-hang performance of Fiberglas, while the poorest Dacrons responded well to touch-up ironing. Consumers Union also found that Fiberglas curtains deserve the wash-and-hang label. But the careless pulling by a child or abrasion caused by constant friction may cause the fibers to break and therefore make them a poor buy. They are also sensitive to light.

While nylon curtains tested were found to cost less than Fiberglas or Dacron, they made a poor appearance, even after ironing. A resin-finished rayon curtain in the same price group as the lower priced Dacron, was similar to the less satisfactory Dacron curtains in its wash-and-hang characteristics.

PUTTING THIS MERCHANDISE KNOWLEDGE TO USE ❯ ❯ ❯ ❯ ❯ ❯ ❯ ❯ ❯ ❯

❯ DO YOU KNOW YOUR MERCHANDISE?

1. Why was it difficult to find a synthetic fiber that would be satisfactory for use in glass curtains?
2. Define (*a*) draw curtains, (*b*) sash curtains, (*c*) café curtains, (*d*) glass curtains.
3. (*a*) What is meant by a wash-and-hang curtain? (*b*) Which fibers are best suited for wash-and-hang types?
4. What are the selling points of resin-finished rayon glass curtains?
5. (*a*) What fabrics would you recommend for curtaining the lower half of kitchen windows? (*b*) What style of curtains would you suggest?
6. (*a*) Give the selling points of glass fibers for curtains. (*b*) What are their possible disadvantages?

❯ INTERESTING THINGS TO DO

1. Copy newspaper and magazine advertisements pertaining to any of the facts discussed in this unit. Interpret and analyze each advertisement.
2. (*a*) Find out from your relatives or friends their experiences with laundering glass curtains. (*b*) Which fibers and fabrics do they find most satisfactory? Why?
3. (*a*) Visit model rooms in a furniture or department store. (*b*) Make notes of the style of glass curtains used in the various rooms. (*c*) List fabrics in each style and use.

UNIT 37 DRAPERIES

Draperies, like curtains, may be bought ready-made or the material may be bought by the yard. The ready-mades are the most popular, even though a homemaker can save herself the price of the workmanship if she makes her own.

FABRICS USED

An elderly housewife was admiring a pair of ready-made, good-quality silk damask draperies in a large retail store. The salesperson remarked upon the attractiveness of the design (merchandise approach). "Yes," replied the homemaker, "the design stands out so beautifully and the cloth is so rich-looking." "That's because the design is silk," replied the well-informed salesperson, "and has a satin float."

The draping quality of pure *silk,* its strength, and its quality of elasticity make silk fabrics particularly adapted for draperies, curtains, and upholstery. Damasks, taffetas, satins, brocades, and marquisette are some of the fabrics frequently used. In addition, there are armure, chenille, habutai, faille, silk gauze, grosgrain, moiré, pongee, shantung, voile, and velvet. These fabrics will be described later in this chapter.

While *linens* are less frequently used for draperies than are the other fibers, they are quite appropriate for more informal rooms, such as dens, studies, boys' rooms, recreation rooms, halls, and sun porches. They are also suited to formal living rooms in the summer, replacing heavy fabrics such as velours, damasks, and brocatelles. Linen fabrics suitable for draperies include crash, theatrical gauze, chintz, damask, homespun, velour, and velvet.

Cotton or *blends* with rayon and polyester fibers are exceedingly popular for informal draperies. Cretonne and chintz are staples sold in drapery departments, for use in rooms such as sun porches, dens, dinettes, and nurseries. Chintz is a plain-weave muslin fabric usually with glazed finish. Cretonne is heavier than chintz. It usually has large printed designs and no glazing. Other fabrics in cotton include corduroy, crash, gingham, homespun, marquisette, organdy, percale, sateen, dotted swiss, toile de Jouy, and velveteen.

Wool is well suited especially for formal draperies because it (1) holds its shape in draperies; (2) is resilient—wrinkles hang out or steam out; (3) is strong and wears well; (4) burns slowly when lighted cigarettes touch it; and (5) has deep, rich coloring.

Mohair is also suitable for draperies because it (1) is more lustrous than wool; (2) sheds dirt more readily; (3) is easy to clean; (4) shrinks little if laundered; and (5) is more durable than wool. Wool or mohair drapery fabrics can be made of friezé, a looped, springy, heavy pile fabric with crosswise rows or small looped pile.

All the above-mentioned fabrics may be used for draperies. There are a few additional wool fabrics which are used for draperies. They are *whipcord, casement cloth* (wool or mohair), synthetic fibers, *homespun,* and *tweed.*

Wool fringes, edgings, braids, balls, and tassels are used to trim draperies and upholstery.

Glass fibers are used extensively for draperies because they do not shrink or sag, do not wrinkle, and consequently do not require ironing. They do not mildew or rot, and do not catch fire. As draperies of glass fiber are water-repellent as well as stain-resistant, they stay clean longer and can be washed and rehung in a short time.

Since the advent of the newer synthetic fibers, the vinyls, polyesters, acrylics, and the "strong" rayons in particular, such as Fortisan, the drapery department is now able to offer new textures in drapery fabrics with minimum-care features. A wider selection of patterns and colors is now possible.

SELLING POINTS OF DRAPERIES AND CURTAINS

In selecting draperies and curtains, ready-made or by the yard, it is important to consider these points:

1. The purpose of the room where they are to be hung.
2. The color scheme in the room—the colors and patterns of upholstery and rugs.
3. The style of furniture in the room.
4. The amount of direct sunlight in the room.

Fabrics Suitable for Specific Styles

Some of the principles of interior decoration were discussed in Chapter 7. The points to consider in choice of color and size of patterns are the same

◄ Brocatelle, right side with corner turned to show reverse side

Silk brocade with the same treatment ❯

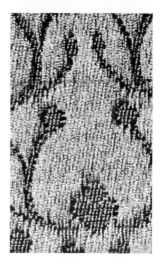

◄ Rayon matelassé

Rayon brocade ❯
(Courtesy American Viscose Corp.)

for all fabrics. As a general rule, a salesperson can recommend:

Antique satin—a drapery fabric with a warp satin weave on the right side and slub filling yarns on the back; suitable for a formal room in contemporary style.

Armure—a drapery fabric in a fancy twill weave to produce a pebbled surface. It may be made of wool, silk, cotton, synthetic fibers or blends; suitable for a formal room in contemporary style.

Brocade—a luxurious fabric with a slightly raised Jacquard design. It looks appropriate when used in Italian or Spanish Renaissance; French Louis XIV, XV, XVI, Directoire, Empire; English Jacobean, Queen Anne, Georgian, Sheraton, Adam, and Victorian styles.

Brocatelle—a double cloth with a padded-looking Jacquard design which stands up from the background. It is intended for the same type of room as that for which brocade is appropriate.

Casement curtaining or *cloth*—a fabric of light weight such as lace, net, gauze, openwork dobby weave; suitable for casement windows (particularly the leaded type and picture windows).

Chenille refers to fabrics made of chenille yarn. The fuzzy pile (chenille) yarn is made with short ends protruding from all sides. Used for chenille bedspreads and carpets of the same name.

Damask—a fabric woven in Jacquard—made of silk, cotton, synthetics or mixtures. It is suitable for the same type of room as brocade is appropriate.

Gauze—a fairly sheer, loosely woven, plain-weave fabric, suitable for summer when heavy draperies are stored.

Lace—an openwork fabric whose design is made by a network of threads; appropriate for glass curtains and panels.

Marquisette—a sheer glass curtaining in leno weave. It is made in cotton, rayon, acetate, polyester, acrylic, and Saran fibers.

Ninon—a glass curtaining made in plain weave with its warp yarns spaced in pairs.

Moiré—a ribbed fabric with watered (moiré) design. It is suitable for draperies with French Louis XV, Empire, English Hepplewhite, and Adam styles.

Rep—a stiff, ribbed fabric made of silk, wool, and/or synthetics. It is suited to rooms decorated in Jacobean and modern styles.

Plush—a heavy pile fabric. The pile is longer than in velour or velvet. It can be made of mohair, silk, or synthetic fibers and is suitable for formal draperies, particularly in Victorian style.

Satin—a stiff, plain-weave silk or synthetic fabric; suitable for rooms in which brocade is appropriate.

Taffeta—a crisp plain-weave silk, or synthetic fabric; appropriate for formal rooms in Louis XV, XVI, Empire styles.

Velvet—a pile fabric in cotton, silk, or synthetic fibers; appropriate in Italian and Spanish Renaissance, Louis XIV, XV, XVI, Directoire, Jacobean, Georgian, Victorian, and American Federal styles.

Velour—a smooth, closely woven pile fabric, heavier than velvet. It is made of cotton, wool, mohair, or mixtures.

Voile—a sheer, plain-weave fabric for glass curtains.

CARE OF DRAPERIES AND CURTAINS

A customer often asks, "Can I wash these draperies in my automatic washer?" The safest answer to that question is, "Read the label." If instructions for care are given on a label, the consumer should save them and follow them implicitly whenever draperies or curtains need cleansing. In general, silk curtains are best dry-cleaned by a reliable cleaner. Draperies of rayon brocade, damask, or satin should be dry-cleaned only.

Cottons, particularly those blended with polyester or acrylic fibers, can usually be washed at home in an automatic washer. They should be pressed or not, as their appearance after laundering may vary with the washing and drying process used.

It should be remembered that nearly all cottons used for draperies, curtains, and upholstery are washable, except velveteen, velour, and tapestry, which should be dry-cleaned. While there are permanently glazed chintzes that can be wiped off like oilcloth, many inexpensive qualities lose their glazing when laundered or cleaned; therefore, it is wise to use the permanently finished chintz. The permanent starchless-finished organdy will keep its stiffness after laundering.

Linen draperies can be laundered in an automatic washer if colors are fast to washing. They will probably need pressing, which should be done while the fabric is damp.

If a homemaker has wool or mohair fibers in her draperies, a good rule to follow is always to remove a soiled spot as soon as it appears. If the spot has a greasy base, a dry-cleaning fluid will suffice. If not, soapy foam like that used to clean rugs may work. When draperies show all-over soil, they should be sent to a reliable cleaner.

Frequent brushing and vacuum cleaning with a nozzle attachment will delay the need for all-over cleaning. Also frequent cleaning and spraying with insecticide prevents the invasion of moths.

Before curtains and draperies are packed away, they should be thoroughly cleaned or laundered. They may then be wrapped in white paper and placed in a dry place in a closet or chest. If fabrics contain wool, a spraying with insecticide or a scattering of paradichlorobenzene crystals or even the old-fashioned moth balls will prevent moth damage.

SHOWER CURTAINS

Some shower curtains are made of plastic film, a synthetic substance somewhat like cellophane—not woven and therefore not a textile fabric. Many better-grade shower curtains are made of rayon or silk taffeta, satin, or moiré fabrics. These cloths are waterproofed by dipping the fabric into a plastic substance or by pressing a sheet of plastic against the fabric. The latter method closes the pores of the fibers, hence making the fabric waterproof. A layer of sheet rubber instead of plastic can be used on the back of the fabric. A more expensive and durable process than either of those mentioned is treating a silk fabric with a solution of rubber and oil which impregnates the fibers, thus becoming part of the fabric itself. Accordingly, the fabric remains waterproof during its entire wear-life.

Designs and colors in shower curtains are now as attractive as those in draperies. Stores may offer the same design for shower curtains, window curtains, towel sets, tank toppers, bath mats, and lid covers. A consumer may select whichever items she wishes; however, she should remember one of the principles of interior decoration, namely, to avoid too many designs in a room, particularly a small bathroom.

PUTTING THIS MERCHANDISE KNOWLEDGE TO USE ❯❯❯❯❯❯❯❯❯❯❯

❯ DO YOU KNOW YOUR MERCHANDISE?

1. (*a*) What are the selling points of wool draperies? (*b*) of mohair draperies?
2. How can you tell (*a*) homespun from tweed, (*b*) antique satin from satin, (*c*) velvet from velour, (*d*) ninon from voile, (*e*) plush from velvet?
3. (*a*) What style of drapery would you recommend for a picture window in a living room decorated in contemporary style? (*b*) What fabrics would be appropriate?
4. What principles of interior decoration did you apply in answering the previous question?
5. (*a*) How are shower curtains made to shed water? (*b*) Can you think of any advantages of a plastic-coated textile shower curtain over a nontextile plastic film type?
6. (*a*) How can moths be prevented from attacking wool drapery fabrics? (*b*) Should you mothproof draperies made of rayon and cotton? Why?

❯ INTERESTING THINGS TO DO

1. (*a*) Compare the prices, fabrics, colors, and styles of ready-made draperies with those of homemade draperies. (*b*) Does it pay to make your own draperies?
2. (*a*) Make a study of current styles and fabrics sold for draperies for bedrooms. Suggestion: Shop three stores: a high-fashion department store, a semipromotional department store, a promotional store or discount house.
3. (*a*) Draw the windows in one room of your house or apartment. (*b*) Indicate the type of furniture and floor covering in this room. (*c*) Disregarding the draperies in the present room, describe the styles and fabrics which you think would be most appropriate. Why?

UNIT 38 UPHOLSTERIES AND SLIPCOVERS

UPHOLSTERY

Upholstery fabrics are those used to cover stuffed furniture and cushions. Slipcovers also fall into this classification.

Upholstery fabrics should harmonize with the rest of the furnishings of the room and be suitable for the use to which the room is put. For example, fabrics containing rayon, acetate, and silk give an attractive, decorative effect, but they should not be used in rooms where young children may soil or tear these fine fabrics. Slipcovers may be used over fine upholstery until the children are old enough to appreciate and take care of fine fabrics.

Suitability of Fabric

Almost any textile fiber can be used in upholstery. Cotton alone or in blends with the synthetics are relatively inexpensive and easy to care for. Bright, attractive designs in cotton chintzes and cretonnes can make an otherwise drab-looking room seem cheerful. Cotton denim now styled in plaids, stripes, and novelty textures (some of which are shot through with metallic yarn) makes excellent upholstery material for contemporary-style rooms. Bouclés in cotton or blends with synthetics are used in similar decors.

Tapestry is attractive for upholstering furniture in traditional styles such as the French Louis periods, Directoire, Empire, Jacobean, Queen Anne, Georgian, Sheraton, Adam, and Victorian. Linen tapestry wears very well and can be sponged with soap and water when soiled spots appear.

Wool tapestries made by hand are antique masterpieces of the art of weaving. Large pictorial designs are typical of handmade wool tapestry. The handmade tapestries are made by a bobbin which is worked into the warp yarn from the wrong side. The warp yarns may be made of wool, linen, or cotton, but linen or cotton is preferable because it is stiffer. Wool is so elastic that an all-wool tapestry would not keep its shape. However, wool is preferable for the filling because it gives a depth to the pictorial designs which silk or cotton cannot do. In weaving a tapestry by hand, the bobbin is carried only to the edge of a pattern and not way across the cloth as in the plain, twill, or satin weaves. The warps may be stretched on the hand loom vertically or horizontally. When the warps are stretched vertically, the design is outlined in ink on the warp for the weaver to follow. When the warp is stretched horizontally, the outline of a cartoon is placed under and close to the warp for the weaver to follow. There is no need for inking the warp in this case.

Rare museum pieces depict historical events, mythological characters, pastoral scenes. While handmade tapestries are very expensive and even priceless, the modern Jacquard loom can make good reproductions of cotton—not so exquisite, but less expensive.

Brocade, damask, brocatelle, matelassé are also suited for rooms of formal style; but as upholstery fabrics they are inappropriate for very informal rooms, especially for rooms used by small children.

Natural Fibers

For upholstery, mohair will give the longest wear of all natural fibers;

and wool, the next longest. Mohair is quite lustrous and sheds dirt. Both mohair and wool are very resilient; as a result they do not crease or muss. Sometimes pile fabrics made of mohair mat, but if this happens, apply a hot, damp cloth to the cloth for 10 minutes. The fabric should then be dried and brushed lightly. Steaming will also accomplish the same result. Hence, wool upholstery fabrics will not be so quickly injured by cigarette sparks or ashes as other fabrics.

Upholstery fabrics often made of wool or mohair include armure, tapestry, rep, damask, brocade, whipcord, homespun, bouclé, and tweed.

For upholstery, linen can be used satisfactorily with contemporary furniture, Early American, French Provincial, Queen Anne, and Sheraton period styles. Linen fabrics used for upholstery and slipcovers include chintz, homespun, linen crash. A better grade of brocatelle may have a linen back.

Synthetic Fibers

One of the most satisfactory of the synthetic fibers for upholstery has proved to be nylon. It is resistant to abrasion; strong in close weaves; it does not pick up soil readily, and it can be easily cleaned, usually with a brush and a soap-and-water solution, or with an upholstery cleaning fluid.

Velon and Saran have proved very satisfactory for coverings and webbing of beach chairs.

Care of Upholstery

One of the main problems of the homemaker is to keep moths out of *wool and mohair* drapery and upholstery fabrics. If moths once get into the crevices of upholstered furniture, it is a Herculean feat to dislodge them.

To guard against moths:

1. Use mothproofed fabrics. There are cloths on the market that have been chemically treated and are guaranteed mothproof.

2. Use furniture with inside muslin (cotton) covering to keep moths out of the inside of the furniture.

3. Use slipcovers in summer for moderate protection against moths, but remove covers once a week to brush and vacuum the upholstery.

If upholstered furniture is attacked by moths, it can be fumigated at home by spreading paradichlorobenzene crystals (2 to 3 pounds to a chair) over it. Wrap the chair in wrapping paper to keep in the odor.

Rayon, acetate, and silk upholstery can be vacuum cleaned with a nozzle attachment without the brush. Spots of soil should be removed from all fabrics immediately. Soap and water can be used on rayon and acetate when the fabric is washable, or a dry-cleaning fluid (containing no chloroform or acetone when the fabric is acetate). A dry-cleaning fluid or a chalk type of cleaner will often be effective on silk. When the upholstery is badly soiled, home-cleaning methods are not recommended. The piece of furniture should be sent to a reliable upholsterer for cleaning.

‹ Cretonne

Tapestry, showing right and wrong side ›

‹ Chintz

Monk's cloth ›

Spots on *cotton and linen upholstery* can often be sponged or scrubbed with soap and water if the fabric is fast color; however, if the whole fabric is badly soiled, a ring may result.

If an upholstery is a blend of fibers, it is advisable for the owner to know what they are because their proper care will be determined on the basis of what you have learned about each kind of fiber. For example, should an upholstery damask contain rayon and cotton, it would be inadvisable to scrub it with a brush and hot soap and water. A brush might break or roughen the floated satin yarns.

SLIPCOVERS

Slipcovers are used to cover badly worn pieces of furniture, to make them feel more comfortable in summer, or to protect fine upholstery fabric until the children are old enough to take proper care of it.

A consumer may buy a slipcover custom made for her particular chair or sofa, of the fabric she selects, and tailored especially for her piece of furniture. Obviously, this is the most expensive type. Stores and mail-order houses offer ready-made slipcovers to fit certain standard style chairs and sofas in standard measurements. Choice of color and fabrics is limited.

The knitted type of stretch cover is also sold for standard styles of furniture. Unless the piece is exactly standard in style and measurement, a stretch knit looks unsightly.

A very inexpensive way to cover and to protect furniture is to use a "throw." This is usually a minimum-care knitted or a woven tweedlike textured fabric made in different sizes so it can serve as a fabric to throw over a chair, sofa, bed, car seat, or outdoor furniture. It can even be used as a rug for children to play on or to watch television.

When purchasing slipcovers, it is often desirable to get draperies to match, working out a pleasing color scheme.

Fabrics for Slipcovers

The more expensive custom-made slipcovers should be made of good-quality fabrics. It is not worthwhile to pay for the workmanship on a poor-quality fabric that will give only limited use.

Linen or cotton crash, sailcloth, cretonne, permanent-finished chintz, bark cloth, denim, and drill are all sturdy fabrics. These fabrics are often crease resistant, shrinkage controlled and minimum care. Such fabrics are very desirable where there are small children.

The more luxurious-appearing fabrics and those made to resemble upholstery fabrics are often made of nubby, ribbed, slub, or tweedy textures and antique satin.

PUTTING THIS MERCHANDISE KNOWLEDGE TO USE ❯ ❯ ❯ ❯ ❯ ❯ ❯ ❯ ❯ ❯

❯ DO YOU KNOW YOUR MERCHANDISE?
1. What instructions would you give a customer on how to keep moths out of upholstery fabrics?
2. How would you recommend that rayon and cotton upholstery be cleaned?
3. How can you distinguish (a) armure from rep, (b) tapestry from damask, (c) brocade from brocatelle, (d) matelassé from brocatelle, and (e) damask from brocade?
4. What are the selling points of linen crash for a slipcover?
5. (a) Name the types of slipcovers sold by retail stores. (b) What textures and styles are now popular? (c) What fabrics are popular?
6. (a) Recommend a fabric for upholstering a Louis XVI armchair. (b) Recommend a fabric for upholstering a Victorian sofa.

1. (*a*) Visit model rooms in a department or furniture store. (*b*) List all the fabrics used for upholstery in these rooms. (*c*) On what period piece of furniture is each fabric used?

2. From reading magazines, such as *House and Garden, Good Housekeeping,* or *House Beautiful,* name and describe styles, textures, and fabrics recommended for upholstery in living rooms in contemporary decor.

3. (*a*) Find out from your parents the approximate age of each upholstery fabric in your living room. You may substitute slipcovers if you wish. (*b*) Which fabrics seem to be giving the best service? How do you account for this?

ADDITIONAL MERCHANDISE TERMS ❯❯❯❯❯❯❯❯❯❯❯❯❯❯❯❯❯❯❯❯❯❯❯❯

Matelassé is a heavy double cloth with Jacquard designs. In the background, one may observe small stitching in the form of patterns like a patchwork quilt. Used for draperies and upholstery.

Sailcloth is a heavy carded cotton fabric in plain weave and often with a basket variation. Made to resemble cloth sails for ships. It is often printed in gay colors for use in draperies and slipcovers.

Theatrical gauze is a sheer linen made of tow yarn in plain weave with a low count. The fabric is colored, somewhat stiff and may be embroidered with wool.

Toile de Jouy is a cotton fabric which is printed in pictorial designs. The original toile was printed in France in 1759.

Carpets and Rugs

UNIT 39 CARPET FIBERS

LOOKING BACKWARD

In your grandmother's day, a rug was selected on the primary basis of its wearing quality. It had to last until the children were grown up, and many of the hand-tied Orientals were handed down from one generation to the next. Those were the days of the family homestead. People stayed in their native towns to grow up, marry, and rear their children in the same environment in which they had been raised. In those days, it was seldom that an entire room was "done over." New pieces of furniture were added when the old ones wore out or when the family became larger. In fact, the living room was not the room most lived in. It was one that was used for special occasions such as weddings, christenings, funerals, and other important family gatherings.

The carpet or rug, therefore, was the heart of the room. The investment in a textile floor covering represented a major investment. Hence it had to be durable because its wear life was planned to be long.

MORES OF TODAY

Nowadays, family life is quite different from "the good old days." Young married couples are very mobile. If the husband works for a large corporation that has branches in several cities or towns throughout the country or abroad, he will be expected to pull up stakes and move to another branch as he is needed.

Certainly there seems to be very little of the nostalgic feeling about an apartment one must vacate as there was for the old family homestead. Likewise, furnishings of a present-day home are sold, at least in part, when the family must move a great distance. It is too costly, as a general rule, to move all one's household effects.

Our modern homemaker is very conscious of style. She knows that she must have current fashion in her home decoration as a status symbol. To "keep up" with style changes in decoration, she knows she must change her home furnishings every few years. Obviously a textile floor covering is not expected to wear a lifetime. Yet it must be made in a fashionable color that can be co-ordinated with draperies, curtains, and upholstery. Textures and fabric must be suitable to the use to which they are to be put. And they must be *style right*.

The emphasis on style, color, and texture in carpets and rugs has increased in the last five years. New synthetics, used alone or in combination with other synthetics or with wool, have helped to give the vivid, cheerful, stylish colors and the varied textures so much desired by the modern homemaker.

TODAY'S CARPET SALESMAN

Times have also changed in the salesman's method of presenting a carpet to a prospective customer.

The salesman used to "talk up" his merchandise on the basis of its being a "Wilton," an "Axminster" or a handmade Oriental rug. The modern salesman tries to determine the customer's needs by finding out as much as he can about her mode of living and her likes and dislikes. Ideally, he tries to visit her home with samples of his line of carpets. He prefers to have the husband and wife see the line together, so that a final decision can be reached at once. Salesmen find that, when the husband is present, he may approve the purchase of a more expensive floor covering than the wife would dare to decide upon alone. By going to the home, the husband and wife can see how colors, textures, and fabrics "go with" other furnishings. These points are current sales clinchers rather than the name of a rug construction such as Wilton, Axminster or Oriental. In fact, there are salesmen who do not mention these constructions unless the customer asks.

MACHINE-MADE DOMESTIC FLOOR COVERINGS

Up to this point, we have used the terms "rugs" and "carpets" interchangeably. Is there a difference? Yes, a considerable one. A *carpet* is really yard goods cut from a bolt. Should the customer desire a wall-to-wall installation, she would buy broadloom (woven wide). It would be cut to the shape of the room and would be installed by the store. Rugs are woven in definite sizes: 9x12 feet, 5x7 feet, 4x6 feet or 2x3 feet. The last two sizes, classed as "scatter rugs," are placed in front of stairs, doors, or large pieces of furniture.

When rugs are used to identify different functions of a room, these rugs are called *area rugs*. They may be woven in a pattern or solid color and in different types of weaves.

Over the past decade, the broadloom carpet has been most popular. In fact, if floors are unattractive, a wall-to-wall carpeting is advisable.

FIBERS FOR CARPETS AND RUGS

We should remember that until very recently, wool was most widely used for pile in rugs and carpets.

There are many reasons for this:

1. Wool cushions footfalls and so is less tiring to walk on.

2. Wool absorbs noise, which is an especial advantage in apartments where children live.

3. Wool wears well, because it is resilient and soft; hence wool rugs will not wear out quickly from having heels dug into them.

4. A rug with deep wool pile will break a fall and prevent a person from hurting himself badly when he falls.

5. Wool is warm to sit on. When children play on the floor, a wool rug prevents a chill in cold weather.

6. Wool takes deep, rich dyes. The Oriental rug is an example of exquisite coloring and intricacy of design.

Kinds of Wool Used for Rugs and Carpets

Sheep's wool and mohair are used for rugs and carpets. Mohair makes a more lustrous carpet than sheep's wool, but eventually mohair pile mats down more than wool pile. When dirt gets down deep into the pile, it is difficult to remove.

Rugs can be made of either worsted or woolen yarns. But the length of fibers of woolen and worsted yarns in rugs differs from that of woolen and worsted yarns used for clothing. Woolen fibers for clothing range up to 2 inches in length, whereas woolen fibers used for rugs average 3 inches in length. Woolen yarns used in rugs are purposely made of fibers intertwined or interlocked when the sliver is carded. Ply yarns (2 ply to 6 ply) are commonly used for rugs.

Worsted yarns have to have more processing than woolen yarns. A chart for comparison follows:

	Woolen Yarn for Rugs	Worsted Yarn for Rugs
Fibers	3″ average. Carded only. Fibers intertwined in carding.	15″—coarse and resilient. Carded and combed; slack twist.
Yarns	2 ply to 6 ply	More wiry, stronger, and shinier than woolen.

Worsted yarn is used for the pile of the so-called *worsted Wilton*. The wool

Wilton is made with woolen yarn. The pile for Axminster can be made of woolen yarn, not worsted. Woolen yarn can also make the pile for the luxurious chenille rug, which is so popular in theater and hotel lobbies and stairs. American Orientals, sometimes called "domestic Oriental" or "sheen-type rugs," are machine-made either on the Wilton, Axminster, or the velvet construction. Consequently, the kind of wool yarn selected will depend on the construction used. Since hand-tied Oriental rugs are made by hand, the type of yarn selected depends on the choice of the weaver. Frequently, goat's hair is used for the webbing at the ends (fringe) and to bind the edges of the rug. It has a characteristic animal odor when the rug is damp.

Fleece from the wire-haired sheep is used for the *druggets* and rugs made in India. The best grade of drugget is all wool. Poorer grades of druggets have pile of wool mixed with cow's hair and a groundwork of jute. Druggets are used extensively on sun porches and in summer cottages because they are very colorful.

The numdah rug, also from India, is made of goat's hair which is felted and not woven. Floral or vinelike designs are often embroidered by hand on the felted cloth.

Carpet wool comes from northern India, the mountains of Siberia, Tibet, Chile, Argentina, China, the Nile Valley, the Near East, Scotland, and southwestern Europe. We are getting most of our carpet wool from Argentina.

Other Natural Fibers

Cotton has become increasingly important as a fiber for rugs. In 1946, cotton was used primarily for bath mats. By 1949, one carpet mill was weaving cotton on regular carpet looms; whereas in 1955, over 100 large and small companies were producing cotton floor coverings. Cotton rugs are inexpensive, fashionable, and easy to care for. Broadloom carpets, room-size rugs, and scatter rugs can be made of cotton.

Linen is not an important fiber in rug construction. Wool, cotton, jute, and synthetic fibers are the leaders in this field.

Linen was used as a backing for antique handmade hooked rugs. The modern hand-hooked rugs use a burlap back, which breaks and disintegrates much more quickly than linen.

Synthetic Fibers

The United States has to import its carpet wools. An increase in the number of new families would require a step-up in carpet production. If all rugs for new families had to be made of 100 per cent carpet wool, there could be a very grave shortage of carpet wool with the resultant increase in price. Carpet manufacturers, however, have not been faced with this problem because of the improvement of our new synthetic fibers for use in carpets. While the use of good quality nylon, Orlon, or Acrilan acrylic fibers has not been accepted as a universal replacement for all wool, these fibers have advantages when used in floor coverings alone or in blends with wool. A list of some of the new synthetics together with their selling points follows.

Fiber	Selling Points
Nylon	Strong, cleans easily, does not mildew, resists moths and upholstery worms. Flameproof. (Does melt, so would be damaged by fire.)
Acrylics (Orlon and Acrilan)	Strong, cleans easily, does not mildew, resists moths. When Acrilan is blended with at least 20 per cent Verel modacrylic, the carpet is flameproof. Orlon acrylic with 45 per cent wool is also satisfactory in this regard.
Modacrylic (Verel)	Wool-like texture; not flammable. Often blended with wools or one of the acrylics.
Rayon (high-strength carpet variety)	Inexpensive, mothproof. Will burn unless treated for flammability. A dense pile is less flammable than a short, sparse pile because there is less access of air necessary to support flame.

The Textile Fiber Products Identification Act requires that a tag or label giving fiber content of carpets and rugs be attached to them.

Following are some typical synthetic fiber blends used for floor coverings:

100 per cent Acrilan acrylic fibers
⌈80 per cent Acrilan acrylic and
⌊20 per cent Verel modacrylic fibers
⌈70 per cent Orlon acrylic fibers
⌊30 per cent wool

⌈70 per cent Orlon acrylic
⌊30 per cent Verel modacrylic
⌈55 per cent Orlon acrylic
⌊45 per cent wool
⌈79 per cent Acrilan acrylic
⌊21 per cent Verel modacrylic

Since 100 per cent nylon pile, nylon and wool, 100 per cent carpet rayon, and rayon and cotton have been used satisfactorily for rugs for several years, their performance in this use is pretty well known. The acrylics and modacrylics, however, have only been in this use for a short time; therefore, the above list covers these new fiber combinations. Polypro entered this field in 1962.

PUTTING THIS MERCHANDISE KNOWLEDGE TO USE ❯ ❯ ❯ ❯ ❯ ❯ ❯ ❯ ❯ ❯

❯ DO YOU KNOW YOUR MERCHANDISE?

1. How does carpet wool differ from clothing wool?
2. (a) What is the difference between woolen yarns used for rugs and woolen yarns used for clothing? (b) between worsted yarns used for rugs and worsted yarns used for clothing?
3. Contrast styles in carpets and rugs used in the United States (a) in the early 1900's and (b) today.
4. How does the selling of carpets and rugs differ in these two periods?
5. Give the advantages of the newer synthetic fibers in textile floor coverings.
6. Define the following: broadloom, carpet, rug, wall-to-wall installation, carpet wool.

1. (*a*) Make a list of the homes you have visited recently. (*b*) Give name (use) of the room. (*c*) Type of floor covering, that is, color, texture, style. (*d*) Which style, color, texture is most used in your friends' living rooms? (*e*) Is the floor covering appropriate for purpose of room?

2. (*a*) Ask your parents, relatives, and friends what has been their experience with carpets made of synthetic pile. (*b*) Do they wear well? Does the pile mat down? (*c*) Do they clean satisfactorily?

3. Find out from a retail store selling carpets what percentage of the stock is wool pile; synthetic pile; cotton pile; broadloom; rugs.

UNIT 40 RUG AND CARPET CONSTRUCTIONS

We have said that the names of carpet construction, such as Wilton, Axminster, and chenille, for example, are not used as specific selling points as they once were. Consumers are primarily color, texture, style, synthetic fiber, and suitability conscious. However, one will often see in advertising the old terms such as velvet twist, carved "Wilton," and cotton "tufted" rugs.

The modern homemaker, through her shopping experience and reading of advertising, is familiar with terms used for certain classes of rugs. In the next section, we shall discuss them according to present classifications.

TUFTED RUGS AND CARPETS

In the chapter on "Domestics" we talked about tufted bedspreads made on sewing machines which tuft the yarn into a cotton muslin backing. The same principle is used for tufted rugs and carpets. In the early 1950's, cotton was the fiber used. Later, Verel modacrylic 70 per cent and wool 30 per cent; Acrilan acrylic 71 per cent and 29 per cent Verel modacrylic; 55 per cent Orlon, 45 per cent wool; 80 per cent Acrilan acrylic and 20 per cent Verel modacrylic came into use. With a giant sewing machine, having more than 1,000 needles, over two yards of 15-foot broadloom can be produced in one minute.

The tufts of pile are punched through a backing fabric of jute or canvas. The pile may be either cut or uncut. If uncut, the retailer will advertise these rugs as tufted, loop pile, and fiber content in percentages. If cut pile, he will advertise them as tufted, cut pile, and fiber content.

Cross-sections of Axminster, Velvet, and Wilton weaves showing the backing fabric. (Courtesy Alexander Smith)

The selling points of this type of rug construction are so appealing to the thrifty homemaker that this type has become increasingly important. Of thirty-three representative carpets using Acrilan, Orlon, and Verel fibers, studied for flammability by Consumers Union, seventeen were listed as "tufted."

Usually these tufted carpets have a preparation of rubber on the back so that they will not slip; others have thick foam rubber permanently bonded to the back.

Tufted rugs are inexpensive and, in small sizes, are easy to care for. Cotton tufted rugs in scatter size can be sent to a commercial laundry or can be washed in an automatic washer at home. Wall-to-wall carpets should be cleaned by a professional. Tweed textures using colored yarn to give a tweed-like effect, hi-lo pile (two or more lengths of pile), and fashionable colors all make for attractive tufted rugs.

KNITTED RUGS AND CARPETS

Those who have had experience with knitted Turkish towels know how soft and absorbent they are. Knitting has recently been employed for constructing carpets and rugs. In the Consumers Union study mentioned previously, six of the thirty-three carpets were knitted.

Unless a customer is told that a carpet is knitted, he will have trouble identifying the construction; however, the back looks something like an enlarged construction of a knitted towel. Backing is similar to tufted types. Fiber combinations, colors, and textures are similar to tufted carpets.

Again, this type of construction is less expensive than woven rugs. They are fashionable, resilient, cushiony. The pile is looped.

WOVEN CARPETS AND RUGS

This classification includes the traditional types of carpets like Wilton,

Axminster, velvet, and chenille. Wool or nylon fibers or combinations with synthetics are used for the pile of woven rugs. The pile may be looped or cut. The surface may be sculptured (designs made by use of varied depths of pile); ridged with rows of pile of varied depths; or random pile (loops in different lengths but not intended to form designs).

Wilton Rugs

Wilton is a traditional woven construction. Wilton rugs are of two types: wool Wiltons and worsted Wiltons, the name depending on the type of yarn used in the pile. Worsted Wiltons are firmer in design and texture than the wool Wiltons, but they are not so soft. Wiltons are made on a Jacquard loom and may have cut or uncut pile. On account of their construction, they are generally limited to only five or six colors. Wiltons are recognized as the longest wearing type of machine-made domestic rugs, and they rank next to chenille rugs in fineness. *Domestic rugs* are those manufactured in the United States.

Axminster Rugs

Axminster rugs have pile which, when pulled out, resembles the letter "V." This woolen pile is not knotted into the groundwork as in Orientals. Neither is the pile yarn concealed inside the rug as in the Wilton. Axminster rugs come in unlimited colors and are often found in Oriental patterns. The back of the rug is jute. Axminster rugs can be distinguished from other domestic rugs by the fact that Axminsters can be rolled lengthwise and not crosswise.

Axminster rugs are usually popularly priced, but they cannot be expected to give such hard service as the Wiltons.

Chenille Rugs

Chenille rugs are considered rug aristocrats; first, because chenilles have the deepest pile of any rug; second, because they may have any number of colors or designs; third, because they have soft, beautiful colorings; fourth, because they are the highest priced machine-made rugs. While there are inexpensive chenille rugs on the market, their wearing quality is uncertain. Chenille rugs are made by two looms: one that weaves a fabric called a chenille blanket, which is cut apart into narrow strips lengthwise of the fabric. These strips resemble a caterpillar (hence the term *chenille,* the French derivative). The second loom uses this chenille strip as a filling in weaving the rug proper. Their backing is jute or cotton.

Velvet Rugs

Velvet rugs will come within the budget of the most budget-minded customers, for velvet rugs, as a group, are inexpensive. Velvet rugs are colorful; they are not woven on a Jacquard loom. While most of them are solid color, it is possible to print designs on warp yarns either before weaving or by copper rollers after weaving. They commonly have a jute backing.

Velvets are inexpensive not only because of the simplicity of the weave, but also because they do not require as much pile yarn as Wiltons do, since the pile yarns can all lie on the surface and are not buried under the surface as they are in Wiltons.

One type of velvet construction is called the "velvet twist." It is sold in two-ply and three-ply—the three-ply pile yarn is more durable than two-ply. Recently a long, dense pile like plush has been developed in velvet construction and is sold as "plush velvet." Its luxurious texture has made it especially popular in the New York area. In all-wool or all-nylon pile, it is a good seller.

Velvets with definite rows of short, even, looped pile are particularly suited to rooms and halls where there is heavy traffic. Some aisles in department stores and theaters use this construction. Again, all-wool or all-nylon pile have proved durable.

Luster Rugs

Luster rugs are sometimes called *American Orientals* or *domestic Orientals*. The last two terms are really misnomers, although the designs of these rugs are adaptations of Oriental designs and colors. They are made not by hand but by machine on the Wilton, Axminster, or velvet construction. Customers who do not wish to pay the price of the hand-tied Oriental rug will do well to choose the luster rug. It is particularly appropriate for living rooms and dining rooms. Karastan and Gulistan are examples of this type.

Fiber Rugs

The term *fiber* usually denotes *paper* when it is applied to a rug. Strips

Hand Shearing or Carving of a Plain Chenille Carpet. Carving adds to its beauty and enhances its value. *(Courtesy Mohawk Carpet Mills, Inc.)*

from fir or spruce wood are cut, then twisted into yarn and woven into a fabric on a flat loom. Color for the rug is introduced into the paper pulp. These rugs are fine for use in summer cottages and sun porches.

Sometimes a wool yarn and twisted paper strips are woven in simple weaves—the wool usually showing on the right side and the fiber on the wrong side.

Other fiber rugs are made of sisal, a fiber from the leaf of a plant grown in the West Indies and in Central America. Still other fiber rugs are woven of coconut fibers which are dyed and then woven by hand.

Grass and Rush Rugs

Prairie grass, which has been cured, and straws are bound together with cotton strands to form "ropes" of grass. These ropes are woven or bound together by cotton yarn running both vertically and diagonally to the rug. The design is either stenciled on the finished rug after it is woven, or painted on it.

Rush rugs, which are generally made of reeds grown in the sluggish waters of the Far East and Europe, come in the same sizes and have the same uses as grass rugs; namely, for porches sun-rooms, and summer cottages.

Rag and Hooked Rugs

Rag rugs, woven with a filling yarn of twisted, braided, or crocheted rags and a cotton warp, are also in this classification. Rugs with designs simulating the hand-hooked pattern are made on a Jacquard loom with looped pile.

POINTS TO EMPHASIZE IN SELLING DOMESTIC RUGS AND CARPETS

1. Look at the back of the rug. Stiff backs, if brown in color, are probably jute. Jute backs do not wear as long as wool or cotton backs. Rubber preparations may be applied to the back to keep the rug from slipping. Sometimes this backing flakes off if rubbed. The closer together the horizontal or vertical ridges are, the closer is the weave, and the more durable will be the rug.

2. Look at the pile. It should be erect and stiff and thick enough to hide the groundwork of the rug.

3. Walk on the rug to determine its softness and resilience. Does it show footprints? Be sure white lines do not show through the pile.

❯ DO YOU KNOW YOUR MERCHANDISE?

1. Define the following: hi-lo pile; random pile; tweed texture; knitted rug; chenille rug; velvet twist; plush velvet; luster rug; fiber rug.
2. Give the selling points of domestic rugs and carpets.
3. What are the reasons why tufted rugs have become so popular?
4. How can you identify the following rug constructions: (*a*) velvet twist, (*b*) Wilton, (*c*) Axminster, (*d*) chenille, and (*e*) tufted?
5. (*a*) Why are chenille rugs as a class expensive? (*b*) Why are Wilton rugs more expensive than tufted rugs?
6. (*a*) Name the rugs made in Jacquard weave. (*b*) Name the rugs which are not Jacquard weave.

❯ INTERESTING THINGS TO DO

1. You have just clipped the following advertisement from your daily newspaper. It is an ad for a chain of carpet stores that claims never to sell seconds. Assume you are looking for a carpet for your living room which is in contemporary decor.
   (*a*) Study each offering carefully to determine (1) which is the best offering as far as fibers in pile are concerned; (2) the probable wearing quality; (3) most stylish and appropriate texture.

BROADLOOM CARPETING FROM FAMOUS MILLS
Sale Priced at 50% Savings
It's Like Getting 2 Yards for the Price of 1

Completely Installed	Completely Installed	Completely Installed
All Wool Pile RIB TEXTURED **7**99	100% Continuous Filament Nylon **7**99	All Wool Pile 3-PLY TWIST **8**99
Orig. 15.98 sq. yd.	10 yr. guar. Orig. 15.98 sq. yd.	Orig. 17.98 sq. yd.
Completely Installed	Completely Installed	Completely Installed
100% Nylon Pile PLUSH VELVET **5**99	Sculptured All WOOL WILTON **8**99	100% Nylon Pile TEXT. TWEED **4**99
Orig. 11.98 sq. yd.	Orig. 17.98 sq. yd.	Orig. 9.98 sq. yd.

(*b*) Write up your choice in your scrapbook, giving reasons for your decision.

2. Shop two or three rug or department stores to discover if the offerings really saved the purchaser 50 per cent. Write up your findings in your scrapbook.

UNIT 41 HANDMADE RUGS

Hand-woven rugs include hand-tied, hand-hooked, hand-crocheted, hand-braided rugs. Hand-tied rugs are made on a vertical loom. The warp yarns are stretched vertically on a loom facing the weaver. Wool or silk yarns that form the pile are tied by hand around two warp yarns. These pile yarns are cut with a knife by hand according to the depth of pile desired. Rugs made by tying the pile by hand include Chinese, Near East Orientals, and some Indian (Lahore) varieties. In the hand-hooked rugs, wool, cotton, silk rags, or wool yarn is pulled through the mesh (weave) of a piece of burlap by means of a metal hook similar to a crochet needle. The maker of a hooked rug follows the design which is drawn or printed on the burlap. The antique hooked rug may be differentiated from the modern hooked rug by the linen backing. Backs of old hooked rugs have generally turned rusty.

Hand-crocheted rugs are made by crocheting strips of rags of various colors and fibers into an oblong or round rug. Hit-or-miss rugs are made of vari-colored twisted strips of rags sewed together. Braided rugs are made similarly except that the strips used are braided before they are sewed together. Hit-or-miss rugs are generally oblong, while braided rugs are usually round or elliptical.

SELLING POINTS OF ORIENTAL RUGS

The term *Oriental rug* implies that the rug was made in the Orient—Near East or in China. While antique Chinese rugs may be sold at auction, China, as a market, now lies behind the "Iron Curtain." The customer expects an Oriental rug to be made by hand; that is, hand-tied. Domestic Orientals, American Orientals, sheentype or luster rugs are made by machine on a Jacquard loom in Oriental designs. They are sold under the brand name of the maker.

If a rug is made by machine, even though it has an Oriental design, it should be labeled clearly, so that the customer may know she is not buying a hand-tied Oriental.

Hand-tied Oriental rugs can be purchased from a rug specialty store or in a department store. Many used rugs are sold at auction. They come mostly from estates and dealers. At present, there seem to be relatively few old Oriental rugs of fine workmanship and beautiful design for sale. Dealers claim that European importers come here to buy these works of art. They forecast that, if this continues, Europe will be the market for antique Orientals—not the United States. It has been true in the past fifteen years that Americans have, by and large, preferred broadloom domestic carpeting to Orientals in their contemporary decors. But those who own luxurious Kirmans, Sarouks, or Bokharas will testify to their beauty and long life. These rugs are works of art.

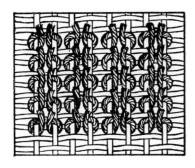

◀ Hand-tied knot used in Oriental rugs

Portion of a finished Oriental rug ▶

When selling or buying Oriental rugs one should look for:

1. *Closeness of weave.* Turn the rug over on the back to see the number of knots to the inch, the more knots to the inch, the more durable the rug.

2. *Evenness of weave.* If a rug is woven evenly, it will lie flat on the floor. Many consumers complain that Oriental rugs curl at the ends from puckers caused by uneven weaving. A heavy rubber strip sewed to the corner of the rug will keep it from curling.

3. *The pile.* The pile should be the same depth throughout the rug. A deep pile does not make a rug any stronger than a short pile. Nor does the thickness of a rug affect its strength. A thin, closely woven rug with short pile may wear longer than a thick, loosely woven rug with long pile.

4. *The color.* If the rug is new, the color at the surface of the rug should be the same depth of color as it is at the knot. This rule does not apply to antique rugs.

5. *The design.* Outlines of the design should be clear cut. There should be no running or bleeding of colors. White designs should be clear white—untinged.

To become an expert judge of Oriental rugs is a career in itself. Many more factors than the five given above are considered by a rug expert. But those five are important and can be observed with some ease by the customer. Nevertheless, a customer will do well to purchase an Oriental rug from a reliable retailer.

HOW TO GET THE MAXIMUM OF SERVICE FROM CARPETS AND RUGS

Vacuuming. Carpet manufacturers now recommend that a vacuum cleaner should be used twice a week in most rooms and daily in entrance halls and areas of heavy traffic. A vacuum cleaner should be chosen that has good dirt-removing ability. A carpet sweeper is intended to pick up surface lint, crumbs, and other soil, but a good vacuum gets right down deep into the body of the rug.

Rug Cushioning. Consumers' Research has found that a waffle-pattern rubber floor pad, when laid under a rug, improves the effectiveness of the

Persian Oriental rug.

vacuum cleaner in removing dirt from a rug. Consumers' Research also found that a rug cushion makes a floor covering more pleasant to walk on and contributes appreciably to the wear-life of any carpet.

Rug cushions or "underlays" are made of hair felt, jute and hair mixtures, and rubber. Consumers' Research advises a good-quality hair-felt underlay because it wears well and provides an adequate cushion for the carpet. A poor quality of hair felt is not a good buy, because fibers tend to break off and to be reduced to powder after a while.

Rug cushions made of good-grade, dense, foam or sponge rubber are quite satisfactory from the angle of service and are also unattractive to carpet beetles and moths. Spike heels and metal toes are a menace to cut-pile carpeting and also to a deep, porous (not dense) foam-rubber cushion or pad. Heels in this style cut the pile of the carpet and puncture the backing, causing snags, rips, and loops—both unsightly and hazardous.

Cleaning.   When the newer synthetics entered the carpet field in the tufted rugs, some homemakers had sad experiences in cleaning them. Some rugs showed extensive discoloration; others, excessive shrinkage; and still others, a crushed appearance after cleaning. It seems that tufts act like lamp wicks. When the moisture of the cleaning fluid is applied, soluble coloring material and certain impurities are brought to the surface of the carpet. When the moisture evaporates, discoloration or even permanent stains may be evident. Consequently, the National Institute of Rug Cleaning recommended cleaning new tufted rugs with "dry foam" only.

How can a customer know whether a rug cleaner knows all the fine points about the reaction of her rug to his cleaning methods? The rug salesman should call the customer's attention to the label, which may say that the rug is "certified cleanable" by an organization such as the National Institute of Rug Cleaning. Rugs which pass a battery of tests to determine their resistance to approved cleaning methods used by commercial rug cleaners are given a "Seal of Cleanability" by the Institute.

A rug-cleaning plant is recommended for its service in cleaning thoroughly

A Navajo Indian weaving a rug.

and efficiently soil embedded in carpets and rugs. If the carpet can be removed from the floor (once every two years—depending on the traffic over it), it can be more efficiently cleaned professionally at a plant than at home. If one does not know a reliable cleaning plant, one may inquire of the retailer who sold the carpet or write to National Institute of Rug Cleaning, 7355 Wisconsin Ave., Bethesda, Maryland 20014, who will supply names of member cleaning plants.

Spots or stains should be removed as soon as possible after they are discovered. If information for this type of care is on a label attached to your rug, you will do well to save it and refer to it as needed. If this information is not on the label, American Carpet Institute's booklet on *How to Care for Your Carpets and Rugs* should prove helpful.

The young homemaker who has to make payments on a house, a car, home appliances, and taxes may not feel financially able to pay for services of rug cleaning in a plant, which may cost $9 to $11 for a 9 x 12 ft. rug. Accordingly she invests in a $9.95 shampooing device plus $1.98 for a 22-oz. can of shampoo. The device looks somewhat like an upright vacuum cleaner—its bag is plastic, which feeds the liquid to a sponge roller when a trigger on the handle is squeezed. Above the roller is a plastic strip with small holes that distributes the liquid shampoo on the roller. Care should be taken to wet only the surface of the carpet in cleaning. This will avoid possible staining, mentioned previously, and drying will be much faster than if the rug were soaked through to the back. Those who object to this home method of cleaning claim that it is hard work and, at best, the results do not measure up to good commercial cleaning.

CLEANING ORIENTAL RUGS.   Hand-tied Oriental rugs will stand vacuum cleaning, sweeping with broom or carpet sweeper, and shampooing. A vacuum cleaner will draw the dirt from the center of the pile quite satisfactorily. In the dining room, a carpet sweeper can be run over the rug after each meal. As virtually all modern hand-tied Oriental rugs are dyed with aniline dyes, they can be successfully shampooed at home with a neutral soap and scrubbing brush or a shampooing device. It is wise to scrub a corner of the rug first to see whether the colors run. If they do, then the rug should be sent to a reliable dry cleaner. To shampoo a wool rug manually at home, make thick foamy suds with neutral soap flakes and warm water. With the scrubbing brush, take off the suds from the top and scrub the rug with it—doing a place about a foot square at a time. When the rug is entirely scrubbed, then wipe the surface with a rag wrung out in clear water. The pile should be wiped in the direction in which it is supposed to lie.

Prevention of Moths.   The best way to prevent moths from getting into wool or hair rugs is to use the rug constantly. Sunlight and walking on a rug discourage moths. A frequent spraying with insecticide is also helpful. All rugs should be either dry-cleaned or shampooed before they are stored for the summer. Frequently, a dry cleaner will store a rug for the summer, after he has dry-cleaned it. If the rug is stored at home, moth balls, flakes, or other moth repellent should be scattered over it before it is wrapped in heavy paper. If the rug is free of moths when it is put away, and if the wrapping paper is sealed tightly, no moths can enter the rug. Cedar chests are satisfactory provided they can be tightly closed. The aroma of the cedar oil will kill any newly hatched moth larvae.

PUTTING THIS MERCHANDISE KNOWLEDGE TO USE ❯ ❯ ❯ ❯ ❯ ❯ ❯ ❯ ❯ ❯

❯ DO YOU KNOW YOUR MERCHANDISE?

1. (*a*) What instructions would you give a customer for removing grease spots on rugs? (*b*) How should hooked rugs be cleaned?
2. (*a*) What is the best way of preventing moths from getting into rugs? (*b*) How should wool rugs be stored for the summer?
3. What are the ways of determining whether an Oriental rug is of good quality?
4. (*a*) What is the best type of vacuum to use on rugs and carpets? (*b*) What are the advantages of rug cushions?
5. (*a*) When and how may rugs be effectively cleaned at home? (*b*) When should they be sent to a rug-cleaning plant?
6. How may a consumer know whether a rug is cleanable and how it should be done?

❯ INTERESTING THINGS TO DO

1. After studying this chapter, make a list of rugs by name in each room of your home. Check for accuracy the names of the rugs by consulting your textbook or asking your parents what the salesman called the rug when he sold it to them. Find out from your parents the approximate age of each rug and write down the present condition of the rug. A form like the following may be used: Which rugs seem to be giving the best service? How do you account for this?

Room	Name of the Rugs	Approximate Ages	Present Condition (Worn, Fair, Good)

2. (*a*) A living room 22 feet x 12 feet is to be furnished. You are to choose the style of furniture you wish. Make a floor plan of the room. Fit in the furniture to scale. (*b*) Completely furnish this living room with rugs, draperies, curtains, and upholsteries. (*c*) Secure fabrics or pictures of fabrics which you would use for each article of furnishing.

ADDITIONAL MERCHANDISE TERMS ❯ ❯ ❯ ❯ ❯ ❯ ❯ ❯ ❯ ❯ ❯ ❯ ❯ ❯ ❯ ❯ ❯ ❯ ❯

Druggets are rugs made in India of fleece from the wire-haired sheep.
Navajo rugs are made of wool by the Navajo Indians in the western part of our country. Warp yarns are hung between two horizontal sticks. A pointed stick serves to carry the filling over and under the warps. Designs are geometrical, and red, white, and gray are favorite colors.
Numdah rugs are made of felted goats' hair. They come from India.

PART TWO: NONTEXTILES

Plastics—New, Important Materials

CHAPTER 16

UNIT 42 WHY ARE PLASTICS IMPORTANT?

Do you know that there are many kinds of plastics? Some plastics are hard, others are soft; some melt, others don't, but they may burn as wood does; some are smooth, others are rough; some are transparent, others are opaque; some are stretchable, others are rigid; some break, others are unbreakable; some are used in "fine" products, others are "work horses" for industry.

HOW TO LEARN ABOUT PLASTICS

At first, plastics may seem confusing because of their many strange names. The chemicals that make up the plastic are usually the basis for the odd names. Manufacturers, however, often do not like to use those chemical names when they make their products for consumers. They prefer trade names, which the consumer will recognize as a certain manufacturer's products; consequently, there may be dozens of trade names for each plastic. We shall study basic chemical names; however, some of the better known trade names will also be mentioned.

Although there are about thirty different kinds of plastics (many more if you count plastic combinations), our study will be confined to the fourteen that are really important for retailers and consumers to know.

Plastics are a whole family of products having different ways of looking, feeling, and reacting in use. Like metals, no one plastic can satisfy all needs. A man buys platinum or gold for his wife's jewelry, but steel for the supports for his house. He chooses chromium or aluminum for the trim on his automobile, but copper for the electric wiring. Yet, all these materials are called *metals*. In a similar manner, plastics must be chosen for the services they can give in use. Knowing what plastics will do and what they will not do is the job of the retailer who stocks these products. The plastic used for dishes would be hard and rigid and unusable for slipcovers. Likewise, the flexible, meltable plastic in slipcovers could not be used for serviceable dishes.

Plastic materials may be used alone to make products such as the dishes and slipcovers just mentioned. Plastics may be mixed with other materials—such as fibers, wood, or glass—to give added strength to the plastic or to give it other wanted qualities. Some plastics may be used just as a surface finish on other materials, such as shiny finishes on notebook covers or mar-resistant finishes on tops of furniture. This further complicates learning about these plastic products.

BACKGROUND OF PLASTICS

Since plastics are used in so many products, it is surprising to learn that they are only about one hundred years old! The first plastic, *nitrocellulose,* was made by an English science teacher. An exhibition of products made from nitrocellulose was held in London in 1860. In America, this material was first used while searching for a substitute for the genuine ivory used in billiard balls. In 1868, ivory from elephant tusks was becoming scarce. A young printer, John Wesley Hyatt, mixed nitrocellulose with camphor and alcohol. The product he created became famous under the trade name of *Celluloid.* Billiard balls, false teeth, men's high Celluloid collars, women's "bone" hairpins, combs, dice, buttons, dolls, rattles, umbrella handles, piano keys, fountain-pen cases, and camera film were made from nitrocellulose. Because this material was available, we were able to make motion-picture film by the year 1882. However, during the showing of the film, it caught fire easily from the lighted bulbs behind it; and entire reels would burn before the fire could be put out. Newer plastics that do not flame so easily are used today.

After the development of nitrocellulose, it took almost thirty years before a chemist in Germany developed the second plastic, *casein.* A preservative, formaldehyde (a gas mixed with water), accidentally tipped over and splashed into some milk that had soured (casein) when the chemist's cat had failed to drink it. Before the chemist threw out the mixture, he noticed that a strange chemical reaction was taking place; he experimented with the mixture and finally developed a new plastic. Some buttons, buckles, and knitting needles are available today made from this plastic. It is also used as glue.

Regenerated cellulose, used in the making of rayon, was developed as a packaging film about 1900. It is best known by the name *cellophane.*

The three plastics mentioned above were all easily affected by heat. An entirely different kind of plastic that was highly resistant to heat was developed in 1909. It was known as *phenol-formaldehyde* or just as a *phenolic.* Developed by Dr. Baekeland, an American chemist, this plastic was made from phenol (carbolic acid) and formaldehyde (a gas mixed with water). Dr. Baekeland used his name as the basis for the first trade name of this plastic, *Bakelite*. This new kind of plastic resisted heat and did not melt at any temperature. It was the first of our "heat setting" plastics—plastics that could be used safely around fairly high degrees of heat and electricity.

Since 1914, new plastics have appeared frequently. Following is a list of the fourteen plastics you are going to study, their dates of development, and a few of today's uses of these materials.

Date	Name of Plastic	Some Common Uses
1868	Nitrocellulose (pyroxylin)	Toys, piano keys, eyeglass frames, fingernail polish
1898	Casein	Knitting needles, buttons, buckles, glue
1900	Regenerated cellulose (cellophane)	Transparent packaging film
1909	Phenol formaldehyde	Handles for electrical appliances, electrical housings
1914	Cellulose acetate	Coatings, packaging, combs, fabrics
1927	Vinyl	Safety-glass interlayer, waterproof materials for shower curtains, table covers, raincoats, umbrellas, leatherlike upholstery materials, floor tiles
1929	Urea formaldehyde	Lamp fixtures, housings for products
1931	Acrylic	Brush sets, rigid handbag cases, dentures, edge lighting fixtures, jewelry
1938	Nylon	Parachutes, tow ropes, fishing leaders, bristles for brushes, cases
1938	Styrene (polystyrene)	Toys, combs, kitchen gadgets
1939	Melamine formaldehyde	Dishes, table tops
1942	Ethylene (polyethylene)	Squeeze bottles, refrigerator jars, packaging film, wastebaskets, pails
1947	Epoxy	Glues
1955	Urethane (polyurethane)	Foam cushions, sponges, mop heads

As you can see from this shortened list of plastics, developments of new plastics have been made every few years; furthermore, plastics are constantly being improved, and new uses for them are occurring almost daily.

Plastics today are "big business." From their humble beginnings a century ago, they are today a multibillion-dollar industry. Billions of pounds of raw plastic materials are produced annually for products for American use. The industry is over twice as large as it was just ten years ago!

In 1940, the average family used about 9 pounds of plastics a year.
In 1950, the average family used about 74 pounds of plastics a year.
In 1960, the average family used about 152 pounds of plastics a year.

The future is indeed bright for plastic products. They are not considered to be "substitute" materials, but are used where they perform better than natural products, where they are less expensive, or where, combined with natural products, they can improve usefulness, attractiveness, or durability.

We write with plastic pens, carry plastic flashlights, sit on plastic chairs, walk on plastic floor tiles, use plastic wall coverings and shower curtains. We use plastic measuring devices in cooking, serve on plastic trays, eat with plastic-handled cutlery from plastic dishes set on plastic table coverings, and store food in plastic containers. We clean our teeth with plastic bristles set in plastic handles, wear plastic jewelry, listen to music encased in a plastic box, or to music recorded on a plastic record or a plastic tape, talk to our friends over a plastic-encased telephone, ride in cars upholstered in plastic, or in boats that have been bonded with plastic. These are just a few of our frequent contacts with plastics. And yet, plastics will become even more important in the years to come. As you can now see, these are important materials to get to know.

PUTTING THIS MERCHANDISE KNOWLEDGE TO USE ❯❯❯❯❯❯❯❯❯❯❯

❯ DO YOU KNOW YOUR MERCHANDISE?

1. Can all kinds of plastics be used for the same products? Give reasons for your answers.
2. Why are plastics complicated to study?
3. How long ago were plastics first made available to consumers? Are plastics developments still continuing? Use examples from the book or from your daily reading of newspapers or magazines to explain your answers.
4. What two important plastics were developed before 1900? What are some of the uses of these plastics today?
5. What was the trade name of the first plastic made that resisted heat?
6. Why do chemists still experiment with plastics?

❯ INTERESTING THINGS TO DO

1. Make a list of 20 items made of or containing plastic that you have in your home.
2. Bring a plastic item to school and tell the class why you enjoy using it.
3. Make a list of words or phrases that tell about plastics such as, "colorful," "warm to the touch," and so forth.

UNIT 43 TYPES OF PLASTICS MATERIALS AND HOW THEY ARE MADE INTO PRODUCTS

WHAT ARE PLASTICS?

Now that you have some idea of how plastics were developed and how some of them are used, you are ready to learn the terms related to them.

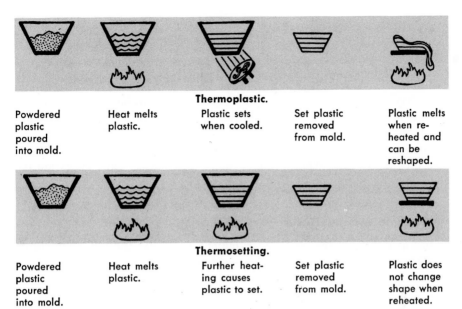

Thermoplastic.

| Powdered plastic poured into mold. | Heat melts plastic. | Plastic sets when cooled. | Set plastic removed from mold. | Plastic melts when re-heated and can be reshaped. |

Thermosetting.

| Powdered plastic poured into mold. | Heat melts plastic. | Further heating causes plastic to set. | Set plastic removed from mold. | Plastic does not change shape when reheated. |

The word *plastic* means the quality of being shaped or molded; however, many other articles that are not plastics may be made by shaping or molding, such as iron used for skillets or clay used for dishes. *Plastic,* therefore, means more than just the ability of being shaped or molded. Specific characteristics of plastics are: (1) Plastics are made by man from various chemicals. They are not natural substances although some contain natural substances. (2) Plastics are shaped or molded into their finished form. (3) After being formed, plastics cannot be changed back to the original chemicals from which they were made.

The word *synthetic* is used to describe plastics. This means they are built up from various chemicals by man—they are artificial, not natural substances.

TWO BASIC TYPES OF PLASTICS

The fourteen plastics that we are going to study may be separated into two groups—those that melt when brought into contact with heat and those that never melt but may burn like wood when brought into contact with a direct flame. We have two well-known words for these two kinds of plastics—*thermoplastic* and *thermosetting*.

Thermoplastic means that the material softens or melts or becomes plastic in the presence of heat. The prefix *thermo* means heat. If you reverse the parts of the word, you will see how easy it is to remember—plastic thermo, shapable under heat.

The great bulk of the commonly known plastics for household and personal use comes under this classification: the cellulose plastics, caseins, acrylics, vinyls, styrenes, ethylenes, nylons, and urethanes. Some of these products resist boiling water (212° F) and even higher temperatures, but they will melt at some point. Nylon, for example, in some forms will not melt until heated to about 400° F.

Thermosetting means that the material once shaped by the use of heat cannot be softened or melted at any temperature. It has been set or fixed into that shape permanently by the heat. This does not mean that it cannot be burned if it comes into contact with an open flame or with very high heat. It may char like wood, but it will not melt.

While fewer home products are made from these plastics, they have extensive uses in industry. The phenolics, ureas, melamines, and epoxies are the thermosetting plastics you will study.

Ingredients Used in Making Plastics

Just as mother mixes flour, sugar, butter, eggs, milk, and other ingredients in making a cake, so the chemist mixes different chemicals in varying amounts in making plastics. If he varies the amounts of these chemicals or adds a dash of a new ingredient, he alters the appearance and the working properties of the plastic. Plastics are made by combining binders, fillers, coloring materials, and other substances. This makes up the plastics raw materials that later will be shaped into finished products.

Binders. Binders are the main materials used in the plastic. For example, in the phenol-formaldehyde plastic, the binder is made from phenol (carbolic acid) and formaldehyde (a gas combined with water). In the nitrocellulose plastic, the binder is nitric acid and other acids plus cellulose (purified cotton or wood fibers). If the plastic is to be clear and colorless, like some wrapping materials, buttons, or combs, only the binder may be used to make the entire product.

Fillers. Fillers are added to binders in most plastics. These may be finely ground wood pulp (called wood flour), asbestos, mica, cellulose, or just paper. The fillers give body to the plastic and may add other desirable properties, by making them fire-resistant, decreasing their cost, increasing the amount of the plastic, or strengthening the plastic. Some fillers also give some color to the plastic.

Coloring Materials. Coloring materials are added to most plastics unless they are to be colorless. Since dyes are costly, they add considerably to the price of the plastic; however, attractive colors also add to the salability of the plastics products.

Other Chemicals. Other chemicals may be needed to soften or to harden a product, to make ingredients unite with one another, or to make the plastic more workable and pliable.

Plastics raw materials are made mostly by a few large chemical companies, such as DuPont, Rohm & Haas, Catalin Corporation, and Celanese Corporation of America. These companies ship the raw material as powder, sheet, tube, or liquid to the manufacturers who shape the plastic into desired forms and package it ready for the consumer. Plastics may be molded, extruded, cast, laminated, blown, or foamed into shape.

Molding. Some plastics are molded into shape by pressure, like waffles made in a waffle iron. This is known as *compression molding*. The raw materials arrive at the factory in powder form. This powder is poured into steel molds, on which tremendous pressure is exerted and the right degree of heat is applied. The heat causes the molding powder to melt into a solid mass taking the shape of the mold into which it has been forced. The molded plastics when removed are ready for sanding, polishing, hole drilling, or any other operations necessary to make an attractive and salable product. Both thermoplastic and thermosetting plastics may be shaped in this manner. Molds to make these items often cost thousands of dollars, but some may be used over and over again for years.

Refrigerator parts, radio cabinets, boxes, buttons, screw caps, knobs, handles, toys, camera cases, and dishes are a few of the products shaped in this way.

Some thermoplastics may be heated first and then shaped in a cold mold. This is known as *injection molding*. This is a rapid and inexpensive method of molding and manufacture. This machine has a chamber for heating the plastic, which is then forced (injected) into a cold steel mold. In just a few seconds the plastic is shaped, and a puff of air forces it out of the now open mold. A little smoothing of one edge, and the plastic is ready for the consumer.

Buttons, typewriter keys, combs, parts of toys, bowls, and parts for musical instruments, such as bugles, are products made by injection molding.

Making Buttons. Left: Pellets are placed on tray of compression molding machine. *(Courtesy Sickles Photo-Reporting Service)* **Right:** The buttons on the hand at left have not yet been deflashed. The buttons on the hand at right have been deflashed. *(Courtesy Plaskon Division, Libby-Owens-Ford Glass Co.)*

Upper left: A drill press bores into a transparent plastic rod. *(Courtesy E. I. duPont de Nemours & Co.)* **Upper right:** Various shapes may easily be formed by revolving the plastic on a lathe much in the way wood is turned. Chess men are being formed by this workman. **Left:** The prepared liquid plastic is poured into lead molds. The molds are then placed in bake ovens until the resin has hardened. The hardened castings are removed from the molds by an air hammer. *(Courtesy Catalin Corp.)*

Extrusion. Just as tooth paste is forced from a tube, so plastics may be shaped by continuously forcing them through a nozzle. This is known as *extrusion.* The softened thermoplastic is forced through a shaped die. This is similar to the method of extruding rayon and acetate filaments through tiny holes in a spinneret.

Thermoplastics may be extruded in the form of flat sheets, rods, tubes, or filaments of varying thickness and length. Packaging films, napkin rings, tubing, water hose, and moldings may be made in this manner.

Casting. When plastics do not need to be very strong or to support heavy weight, they may be formed by pouring them into lead-covered steel molds. Both thermoplastic and thermosetting plastics may be made this way. These molds are less expensive than those for compression or injection molding as they do not have to withstand any pressure.

Hangers for clothing, furniture trim, mirror and brush backs, inexpensive buttons, and jewelry stones may be made by casting.

Laminating. Sheets of thermoplastics or thermosettings may be pressed against materials such as fabrics, paper, or wood and fused or melted, thus permanently bonding them together. This is called *laminating*. Shower curtains, raincoat materials, artificial leather, imitation veneers for furniture, and safety glass are examples of articles made by laminating plastics with other materials.

Blowing. Hollow thermoplastic products may be shaped by blowing air into plastics placed in molds. Bottles, tumblers, balls, and floating toys are examples of plastics that may be formed in this manner.

Foaming. A few plastic materials may be filled with air bubbles either by first whipping with giant beaters or by using chemicals that cause the plastics to bubble. After the plastic has been filled with air bubbles, it is poured into a mold to set in the desired shape. Ornaments such as snow men, sponges, floor-mop heads, cushioning materials, and imitation leather (expanded vinyls) are made in this manner. The following thermoplastics may be formed in this way: vinyls, styrenes, and urethanes.

FINISHING PLASTICS

After being formed, the plastic may be sawed, drilled, carved, sanded, or polished to finish the edges or to give a decorative effect. Plastics may also be stenciled, printed, painted, or metal plated to impart attractive appearance.

CARE OF PLASTICS

Plastic articles in general are easily cared for—one of their most important selling points. Most of them have smooth surfaces, which may be washed or wiped with a damp cloth, then rubbed dry. Mild soap suds or detergents may be used, if necessary, to remove grease and dirt. Gritty cleaners, however, should never be used on plastic articles, for these may scratch the surface. Fine scratches on the surface of plastics may be removed with furniture wax.

While moderate to fairly high heat is not harmful to the thermosetting plastics, little or no heat should come into contact with thermoplastics unless directions on the products state what temperatures they will withstand.

Most plastics are resistant to breakage, but they can be cracked or chipped if abused; they therefore should be handled with care.

PUTTING THIS MERCHANDISE KNOWLEDGE TO USE

❯ DO YOU KNOW YOUR MERCHANDISE?

1. What are the two basic types of plastics? Explain how they differ.
2. What do people mean when they say a product is "plastic"?
3. What is the binder used in making plastics? Why is filler used? How would you recognize a plastic that had no filler?

4. Why are plastics shaped in different ways? Which is the least costly method of molding plastics? Why would a manufacturer use a more costly method?
5. How does compression molding differ from injection molding? What type of plastic cannot be shaped by injection molding?
6. Explain what is meant by extrusion.
7. How are plastics made by casting?
8. What kinds of products are shaped by blowing?
9. What kinds of plastics products are shaped by foaming?
10. What are three important rules in caring for plastics?

> INTERESTING THINGS TO DO

1. Bring a plastic article to class and give a sales talk for it. Be sure you tell what advantages the plastic has for the user.
2. Visit a store and list ten different departments (such as the china department, handbag department, and so forth) that carry some plastic merchandise. Do you think they carry mainly thermoplastic or thermosetting products?
3. Prepare a chart for ten plastic articles with which you are familiar or which you have in your home. Use the following headings as a guide: Article; Use; Thermoplastic or thermosetting; Probable shaping method; Color; Finish; Transparent, translucent, or opaque.

UNIT 44   THE THERMOPLASTICS

Now that you know that plastics are of two types—heat softening (thermoplastic) and heat setting (thermosetting)—and that they are shaped, finished, and cared for by various methods, you are ready to learn about the ten thermoplastics.

What do you and other users want to know about these materials? Customers want to know what they will and will not do in use. If there is any caution to be taken in their use, that is important to know. Do you think customers want to know about the chemicals used to make them? Very few, if any, will ever ask such a question. The chemicals have therefore been listed in parentheses in the following discussion, and you need not study them unless you are a chemistry student.

The ten familiar thermoplastic products include three basic cellulose plastics, caseins, acrylic resins, vinyls, styrenes, nylons, ethylenes, and urethanes.

All cellulose plastics have purified cotton or wood pulp (known as *cellulose*) as part of the binder, and all are classed as thermoplastics. Since most of the cellulosics are affected by temperatures of about 160°F, their uses are somewhat limited. There are several varieties of cellulosics, the most common being *nitrocellulose, cellulose acetate,* and *regenerated cellulose* or *cellophane.*

Nitrocellulose Plastics or Pyroxylin

These are the oldest commercially important plastics. They are made from cellulose treated with acids (nitric and sulfuric) and mixed with softeners (camphor and alcohol).

A liquid solution of this plastic is colored and sold as nail polish. Nitrocellulose has countless other uses in the form of fountain-pen barrels, toothbrush handles, unbreakable watch crystals, piano keys, dominoes, coating on fabric to make artificial leather, buttons, eyeglass frames, Ping-Pong balls, toe boxes, and counters for shoes.

Nitrocellulose has many advantages for use in these articles because it is very tough, water-resistant, takes clear vivid colors, may be transparent, translucent, or opaque, is easily shaped, and parts can be cemented together readily. Because nitrocellulose plastics maintain their shape unusually well (known as dimensional stability), they are ideal materials for eyeglass frames.

The main disadvantage of this plastic is its high degree of inflammability. If you coat a piece of paper with fingernail polish, you can test the burning property of nitrocellulose. Since the coated paper will burn very readily, this experiment should be performed with the greatest caution, preferably over the kitchen sink. Nitrocellulose also scratches rather easily and is discolored by sunlight and heat. A child's cowboy outfit coated with nitrocellulose lacquer to resemble leather is dangerous if the child, while wearing it, gets near a fire or match flame. It is because of this danger that motion-picture films for schools are no longer developed on nitrocellulose. For safety, some other plastics (usually cellulose acetate or similar plastics) are used.

Familiar trade names for this plastic are *Celluloid* (now discontinued), *Herculoid, Kodaloid, Nitron, Nixon C/N, Pyralin.*

Cellulose Acetate Plastics

During World War I, cellulose acetate coatings were used for the protection of fabric and wooden airplane wings. This syrupy material is made from cellulose plus acids (acetic acid and acetic anhydride). Its best-known use today is in the form of acetate fibers for fabrics; however, it has many other uses. It is popular in jewelry in imitation mother-of-pearl, tortoise shell, and onyx, in addition to the popular transparent stones. Translucent lamp shades, watch crystals, fountain pens, combs, toothbrush handles, table mats, toys, and plastic containers for cosmetics are made from cellulose acetate. A large proportion of camera and projection film is also made from this plastic. By coating colored acetate film over aluminum, nontarnishable yarns for dress and upholstery fabrics are available. These yarns are washable, so that they can be used even in cotton fabrics.

Although this plastic has many of the advantages of cellulose nitrate, it tends to warp and deform more readily in the presence of moisture. It also melts at fairly low temperatures (160°F), so that acetate spoons will droop if used to stir hot drinks, and acetate buttons will melt if touched by a hot iron. The fact that it burns slowly and thus is not a fire hazard offsets some of these disadvantages and permits it to be used where the nitrocellulose plastic might be dangerous. Familiar trade names of this plastic are *Lumarith, Nixon C/A, Tenite Acetate, Vuepak.*

Regenerated Cellulose

This material is best known in its fiber form as *rayon;* however, it is also used as a packaging material in the form of transparent sheets and is known by the term, *cellophane.*

The transparent cellophane sheets are formed by forcing the cellulose solution through a long slit and extruding it in continuous sheet form. The sheets may be extruded in any thickness. When used for packaging, cellophane keeps the product clean, yet allows the customer to see clearly what he is purchasing. It is the most transparent packaging material in use. Cigarettes, lamp shades, boxed grocery items, and cosmetic products are examples of products commonly wrapped in cellophane. One firm increased its sale of coal by packaging it in cellophane for use in outdoor grills.

Cellophane tends to shrink somewhat. If used to cover a flat piece of paper or thin cardboard, it will cause the paper or cardboard to buckle out of shape. If wound too tightly around the frame, it has been known to distort lamp shades.

Cellophane is not a true thermoplastic nor is it moistureproof unless a special lacquer coating is applied on its surface.

In addition to packaging, cellophane is a popular decorating material, as in bows on Easter baskets. Shredded cellophane is used as the imitation grass for nesting Easter eggs or around jars and bottles to prevent breakage.

Familiar trade names for this plastic are *Sylphwrap* and *Cellophane* (with maker's name attached).

CASEIN

This plastic is composed of the curd of milk (casein) plus another material (formaldehyde). It has been used for products in the United States since 1919. It is used today primarily to make buttons, buckles, beads, knitting needles, and crochet hooks. It has a high luster; it is not harmed by dry-cleaning fluids; nor do the buttons made from casein plastic melt under the heat of the pressing iron as do those made from cellulose acetate. Casein buttons and buckles may, however, warp out of shape when soaked in water. Casein is also used for glues that are easy to use and that hold tenaciously.

Familiar trade names for products made from this plastic are *Ameroid* and *Galorn.* Trade names for glues are *Ad-A-Grip, Elmer's,* and *Sobo.*

ACRYLIC

Acrylic plastics are made by using the chemicals obtained from commonly used materials (petroleum, water, and chlorine).

Clear plastic furniture, decorative ornaments mounted on furniture, jewelry with a silken sheen characteristic of moonstone, handbag trim, cosmetic and cigarette cases, comb-and-brush sets, and lenses for auto and highway stop signals are some of the important uses of this water-clear plastic. Fabrics impregnated with an acrylic solution have a permanent stiffness imparted to them. The fabrics may also be made water-resistant.

Acrylic resins have proved to be a boon to science because rods or sheets of this plastic carry light around curves. This is useful in medicine because it gives a cool light for operating and can therefore be placed near the patient. Decorative signs also make use of this reflecting ability. A technique of carving the plastic from the bottom and then filling the carved areas with coloring material has created the illusion that flowers, fish, or other forms are imbedded in the plastic. Such ornamentation is used for jewelry, paperweights, book ends, and umbrella handles.

Acrylic plastics are more transparent than glass, and they have a brilliant, gemlike sparkle. Acrylic resins are half the weight of glass and warm rather than cold to the touch. They are shatterproof and thus are especially desirable for use in airplanes. Since they have the clearness of glass and are weather resistant, they are popular for windshields and enclosures. The main disadvantage of these plastics is that they scratch easily. The two best-known trade names for this plastic are *Lucite* and *Plexiglas. Orlon* and *Creslan* are trade names for fibers extruded from acrylic resin.

VINYL

This "elastic plastic" is also made from chemicals present in well-known substances (air, natural gas, water, salt, and coal). Vinyls have many and varied uses. For home use, these plastics have been popular in the form of transparent, waterproof kitchen aprons, table covers, refrigerator-bowl covers, and shower curtains. Sturdy backyard swimming pools are also made from this material, as are beach balls and inflatable toys and rafts. Both fabric-backed (supported film) and nonfabric-backed (unsupported film) materials that resemble leather are used for upholstery materials on living-room furniture, and seats in cars, airplanes, and boats. Vinyl does not "breathe," however, as leather does. This limits its uses as an imitation of leather in such products as shoe uppers where breathing quality is desirable. Vinyl is used, however, for molded soles on inexpensive shoes. In one of its variations, vinyl is used between layers of glass to make "safety glass," discussed in Chapter 28.

Some other uses of this popular material are as unbreakable watch crystals, combs, packaging films, draperies, and wall coverings. Another extensive use is in the hard-surface floor-covering field as tiles or in place of linoleum. Its hardy surface resists scratches and wear, and it is easy to care for.

Vinyl resins are tough, odorless, tasteless, noninflammable, and many are resistant to warping, moisture absorption, and shrinkage. This plastic in certain forms, in addition to being waterproof and oilproof, can be stretched two and one half times its normal size, yet return to its original shape. With age, however, it loses some of its elasticity and tends to stiffen and crack.

Since vinyl plastics, especially when made as nonbacked film, are subject to "creep tear" whenever a hole or a v-shaped cut is made, they are more successfully joined by heat sealing than by sewing. By this method, two layers are melted (fused) together with a heated bar. Thus the joined portion, which is double in thickness, is stronger than any other part of the product.

The same properties that permit the vinyl plastics to be fused by moderate temperatures also place restrictions on their use. For example, a woman wearing one of these aprons should not lean over a hot stove, nor should a hot dish or pan be placed on a vinyl tablecloth.

Foamed vinyls known as *expanded vinyls* have been used as insulation in household products and in clothing as protection against cold weather. They are currently popular as imitation leather for handbags, slippers, and jackets.

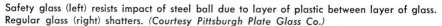

Safety glass (left) resists impact of steel ball due to layer of plastic between layer of glass. Regular glass (right) shatters. *(Courtesy Pittsburgh Plate Glass Co.)*

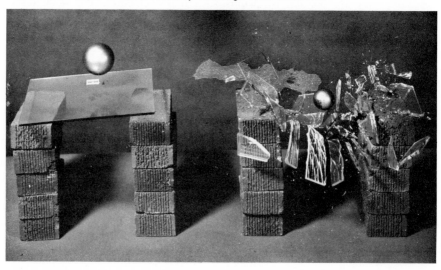

Familiar trade names for the many varieties of this plastic are *Butacite, Duran, Geon, Koroseal, Naugahyde, Saflex, Vinylite*. Trade names for fibers used in woven fabrics are *Vinyon* and *Velon*. As an extruded strawlike filament, one variety of the vinyl plastics is known as *saran*. This is a basic, not a trade, name.

STYRENE

In 1938, this plastic was perfected for commercial production. It is also obtained from well-known chemicals (ethyl chloride and benzene). Because it is resistant to concentrated acids, it is used as a packaging material for these substances. Like the acrylics, this plastic has the quality of carrying light around curved sections. Since styrene reproduces tiny details on a mold, it is particularly useful for bottle and jar caps where threading is required. Because it resists breakage even when bounced on a hard surface, it is used as salt-cellar caps in place of glass. It is also used for costume jewelry stones, magnifiers, wall tiles, refrigerator parts, and countless household gadgets. Its low price and sturdy qualities have made it a desirable plastic for children's toys where it is commonly seen in model cars, planes, and ships that young people assemble. This plastic is readily identified by a metallic sound when tapped and a dense black smoke and chemical odor when burned.

Styrene is one of the plastics that can be foamed before shaping. When filled with air bubbles, it makes a material that is quite rigid, strong, and light in weight. In that form, it is used for molded chair frames. The uncolored foamed plastic resembles snow, so that it is a popular material for ornamental decorations at Christmastime and as a backing material in jeweler's cases.

The plastic is most commonly known by its product name, *styrene,* but a few familiar trade names are *Lustron, Lustrez, Styrofoam,* and *Styron.*

NYLON

This is a general term for a large group of materials made by complicated procedures from the chemicals contained in well-known natural materials (coal, air, and water). Nylon is so familiar to everyone in its textile form that few realize its other important uses. Nylon is used in molded form in such articles as slide fasteners, buttons, combs, tableware, and tumblers (where it may even resist boiling temperatures) and in filament form for bristles in tooth- and paintbrushes and as strings for tennis rackets, leaders for fishermen's lines and for tow ropes for airplane gliders. Bristles made of nylon wear well, are uniform in length, and resist strong chemicals. They are versatile because, unlike natural bristles, they may be made any length and thickness. The generic term *nylon* is used for all these products.

One of the problems of using nylon as a plastic has been in the difficulty of coloring the resin, but even this has been effectively solved.

ETHYLENE (Polyethylene)

This plastic has had a phenomenal sales growth since its introduction in 1942. It is made by a complicated process from chemicals (ethylene which is derived either from petroleum or from natural gas). The resulting plastic that may be either flexible or rigid has a waxlike feel.

Its most common uses are in the form of film for packaging of all kinds; in tablecloths, aprons, covers for containers; and in its molded form for closures, containers, ice-cube trays, wastebaskets, garbage containers, and flexible bottles.

Ethylene is noted for its toughness, its resistance to solvents and other chemicals, and its flexible form which requires no chemical softener as most other flexible plastics do.

Its disadvantages are mainly its resistance to inks and its difficulty of being heat sealed or bonded by solvents or the usual heat bars. Oils and greases also tend to cling to this plastic, and it must therefore be washed thoroughly if these oily products are to be completely removed from its surface.

In 1959 thin ethylene bags suffocated several babies that accidentally sucked the film against their noses and mouths. Dry cleaners and manufacturers who used such thin films for packaging were advised to print a warning on each bag to guard against its being left around carelessly where a baby could reach it.

Trade names for the plastic are *Dylan* and *Polythene*. The basic term *ethylene* or *polyethylene* is also used.

URETHANE

A new and different kind of plastic became available in 1955 in this country. Made from complicated chemicals (isocyanates and polyesters), it needs no whipping to foam but puffs like bread dough to 25 times its original size when the liquid mixture is poured into a mold. This swelling occurs because the plastic releases carbon dioxide, the gas that makes soda pop bubble. The foamed plastics that result are creamy tan in color, flexible, light in weight, inexpensive, long wearing, and do not disintegrate like foam rubber when repeatedly exposed to air.

Urethane's popular uses since its introduction are as foamed cushioning in upholstered furniture, pillows, and mattresses where it always looks plump because it never sags. As kitchen sponges and spongelike mops, it is ideal because it holds nearly twenty times its weight in water. It is also used for cushiony toys, for cushioning under rugs, and laminated to fabric for insulation. It is easily cleaned with soap and water and is not affected by dry-cleaning solvents; but it is not so luxuriously soft as good quality foam rubber.

By changing the chemical formula slightly, chemists can prevent the foaming action of the plastic. This permits it to be made in ordinary rigid forms. Trade names for the plastic are *Fomrez, Isofoam,* and *Polyether*.

❯ DO YOU KNOW YOUR MERCHANDISE?

1. Nitrocellulose plastics have not grown in volume as have the other plastics. Can you explain this fact?

2. Can you use foamed styrene and urethane foams for the same purposes? Explain your answer.

3. What, in your opinion, is the reason that vinyl is being used in place of leather for car and furniture upholstery? Why is it little used for shoe uppers?

4. Which plastics will carry light around curved surfaces? How can this feature be put to use?

5. How does cellulose acetate plastic react to moderate heat? How does that restrict its use?

6. What plastic is used to make "safety glass"? What is *heat sealing?*

7. What plastic has a waxlike feel? How can this plastic be dangerous to infants?

❯ INTERESTING THINGS TO DO

1. Look through a magazine and see how many advertisements are written about plastics products. Make a list of the trade names or basic names they give the plastics. How many of those names were familiar to you? How many advantages did the advertisers list for the plastic products?

2. Visit a toy department, housewares department, or dinnerware department. How many products did you see that appeared to be made from plastics? Can you name a natural material that would serve just as well or better for those products?

3. If you have a plastic item around your house that you have broken or that you are throwing out, put it on a warm radiator and see if it changes shape. Drop it and see if it breaks. Use a harsh cleanser or steel wool on its surface. Write a short report telling the results of your experiments.

UNIT 45 THE THERMOSETTING PLASTICS

The last four plastics you will study are thermosetting plastics. The most important difference between these and the thermoplastics is in their reaction to heat. Once having been set by heat into any given form, the thermosetting plastics can never again be melted; however, open flames or high-oven heat may char and burn them. The four thermosetting plastics are *phenol formaldehyde, urea, melamine,* and *epoxy.*

PHENOL FORMALDEHYDE (Phenolics)

These plastics products are named for their two basic ingredients, phenol (carbolic acid) and formaldehyde (a gas obtained from coke then mixed with water). They are shaped by two methods, either by compression molding or by casting. Because they have different characteristics and uses depending on how they are shaped, the two types of phenolics will be discussed separately.

Molded Phenolics

Molded phenolics that go into huge presses to be shaped require filler materials to give them extra strength. These filler materials are dark in color. The resulting plastics are, therefore, dark in color—dark purple, red, navy blue, dark brown, dark green, and the most frequently used, black. These plastics are also opaque. While the dark colors and the opacity do not lessen their usefulness, these plastics have less eye appeal for customers than do the other more colorful ones. However, they are useful plastics for products that come into contact with heat and electricity.

Because they do not conduct heat or electricity and thus remain cool to the touch, they are used as handles and bases for many products such as irons, toasters, waffle irons, electric griddles, electric plugs and as housings for radio and television sets and telephones. Because of their strength, and the fact that neither water nor household chemicals affect them, they are used as agitators for washing machines. Camera cases, and ash trays are also popularly made from these plastics.

Familiar trade names are *Bakelite, Durite, Durez, Kys-Ite.*

Cast Phenolics

Cast phenolics, which are not so strong as the molded products, require no dark filler and thus may have delicate to vivid colors; and they may be transparent, translucent, or opaque. They, like the molded phenolics, do not absorb water or chemicals and are therefore usable for products such as cutlery handles that may be washed in boiling water.

Because of their color range, mah jongg tiles, radio and clock cases, jewelry and other attractive items are made from these plastics; however, clear plastics and white colors tend to yellow with age.

Familiar trade names are *Gemstone, Catalin,* and *Marblette.*

UREA (Urea Formaldehyde)

Urea resins are made from urea (derived from ammonia and carbon dioxide) and formaldehyde. The resulting resin is mixed with cellulose to yield a translucent plastic that may be given any desired color. Urea plastics have no noticeable odor. They have hard, durable, scratch-resistant surfaces and

The first batch of new disposable thermoplastic bowls comes off the line. (Courtesy Sweetheart Plastics, Inc.)

are not affected by boiling water. Light in weight, they are resistant to breaking but may crack if dropped from a considerable height. They are used for bottle closures, toys, buttons, cutlery handles, cosmetic containers, and lamp fixtures. As a resin, ureas are useful for bonding plywood and wood joints.

Familiar trade names for these plastics are *Beetle, Urac,* and *Uformite.*

MELAMINE (Melamine Formaldehyde)

Like the ureas mentioned above, these plastics made from different chemicals (calcium cyanamide mixed with formaldehyde) have unlimited color possibilities and an unusually tough surface when compared with many other plastics. The fact that this plastic has no odor and is completely tasteless is important, inasmuch as it is used extensively for dishes. For further discussion of melamine, see Chapter 27.

Familiar trade names are *Boontonware, Melmac, Plaskon.*

❯ ❯ THERMOSETTING CHART OF TRADE NAMES ❮ ❮

PHENOL FORMALDEHYE			UREA FORMALDEHYDE	MELAMINE FORMALDEHYDE	EPOXIES
Molded	Cast	Laminates			
Bakelite	Catalin	Formica	Beetle	Boontonware	Apco
Durez	Gemstone	Micarta	Foramine	Cymel	D.E.R.
Durite	Kaston		Plyamine	Lenoxware	Devcon 2-Ton
Indur	Marblette		Rhonite	Melantine	Epocast
Kys-Ite	Plyophen		Sylplast	Melmac	Epon
Pyrotex			Urac	Melurac	E-Pox-E
Resinox			Uformite	Plaskon	Epoxy Weld
Varcum				Permelite	Plastic Steel
				Resimene	Resinfoam
				Texasware	Rezolin

CELLULOSE PLASTICS			CASEIN	ACRYLIC	VINYL
Nitrocellulose (Pyroxylin)	**Cellulose Acetate**	**Regenerated Cellulose**			
Celluloid[1]	Arnel[3]	Cellophane[2]	Ad-A-Grip	Acrylite	Boltaflex
Herculoid	Chromspun[3]	Sylphwrap	Ameroid	Butaprene	Butacite
Kodaloid	Lumarith		Elmer's Glue	Creslan[3]	Contact
Nitron	Nixon C/A		Galorn	Lucite	Duran
Nixon C/N	Tenite Acetate		Sobo	Orlon[3]	Elvacet
Pyralin	Vuepak			Plexiglas	Exon
Pyroxoloid				Zerlon	Geon
Rowland CN					Koroseal
					Marvinol
					Naugahyde
					Opalon
					Pliovic
					Saflex
					Saran[2]
					Velon[3]
					Vinylite
					Vinyon[3]
					Ultron
					Vinafoam

NYLON	STYRENE	ETHYLENE	URETHANE
Caprolan	Butaprene	Dylan	Adiprene
Nylon[2]	Dylene	Irrathene	Fomrez
Nylasint	Dylite	Marlex	Hylene
Zytel	Lustrex	Poly-eth	Isofoam
	Lustron	Polythene	Nacconate
	Plyton		Paraplex
	Polyco		Polyether
	Polystyrene[2]		
	Styrafil		
	Styrofoam		
	Styron		

[1] Trade name discontinued but term is still commonly used.

[2] Generic name—may be used by any firm manufacturing the product.

[3] Fiber made from this plastic.

EPOXY

Epoxy resins are thermosetting materials made from the condensing of certain chemicals (phenol, acetone and epichlorohydrin). These resins were introduced in America in 1947. Their main consumer use is as bonding material for china and glass, metal, wood, plastics, marble, and other difficult-to-join products. Epoxies make the most powerful glues known. In recent years, these adhesives have been packaged for consumers. All these adhesives consist of two separate parts, the epoxy resin and a hardener. These two parts must be mixed together just before use in exactly right proportions. Once properly mixed, they are so strong that they are used to bond bathroom fixtures to walls, to repair holes or cracks in metal tanks. Once an epoxy glue has dried, water, gasoline or oil have no effect on it. It takes about 24 hours to dry to complete hardness.

Familiar trade names for this plastic glue are *Plastic Steel, Devcon 2-Ton, Epoxy Weld, E-Pox-E.*

SELLING PLASTICS

If you have read advertisements, looked through catalogues, analyzed merchandise in your home, or looked at merchandise shown on television and in stores, you know how extensively plastics are being used. Yet, judging by their constant rate of growth, many new items will be made from plastics in years to come. Chemists are talking about plastic houses, plastic cars, and many more plastic products for your future! Through study of these products, you will have a better knowledge of the world you are and will be living in.

In selling plastics, the durability, usefulness, appropriate shape, ease of care, and attractive, serviceable color will be important selling points. The fact that plastics are light in weight, easy to handle, comfortable to use, and resistant to breakage make them particularly salable. Be sure to remind your customers to keep thermoplastics away from excessive heat! You will find that, because you know about them, you will enjoy selling plastics, and your customers will enjoy buying and using them.

PUTTING THIS MERCHANDISE KNOWLEDGE TO USE ❯❯❯❯❯❯❯❯❯❯

❯ DO YOU KNOW YOUR MERCHANDISE?

1. Define thermosetting. Would cement be described as being thermosetting or thermoplastic? iron rails? glass? china dishes?
2. Why is urea a desirable plastic for cutlery handles?
3. What is the difficulty in using an epoxy resin glue?
4. Why aren't molded phenolics available in pastel colors?
5. Explain why *molded* phenolics look different from *cast* phenolics.
6. Why is *melamine* a desirable material for dishes?

❯ INTERESTING THINGS TO DO

1. Copy the information from a label on a plastic article. What kinds of information does the label give the customer? Could you identify the plastic and know its advantages and disadvantages from the label? Was there a trade name on the label?

2. Write a label for a plastic article that you have in your home. Give information to the customer that will assure him of maximum use and enjoyment from the plastic. Warn him of any misuse that will harm the plastic.

ADDITIONAL MERCHANDISE TERMS ⟩⟩⟩⟩⟩⟩⟩⟩⟩⟩⟩⟩⟩⟩⟩⟩⟩⟩⟩⟩⟩⟩

Amino is a classification that includes *urea* and *melamine formaldehyde* plastics.

Asbestos is a gray-colored, fiberlike mineral that occurs in fibrous masses. It is fireproof and is used in some plastics to give a fire-resistant quality.

Calendering is a method of making thin sheets of plastic by pressing the plastic through heavy rollers. Plastic may be laminated onto cloth or paper by this method.

Catalyst is a substance which hastens a chemical change in other chemical mixtures, but may be recovered practically unchanged at the end of the experiment. Distilled water, caustic soda, sulfuric acid, alcohol, and acetone are popular catalysts used in the making of plastics.

Condensation is the process of separating off or evaporating one substance from something, as condensed milk is made by separating off water. Some plastics are made this way.

Dimensional stability is the ability of a substance to be stretched and then to return to the exact size it was before the stretching took place.

Flash is the leftover plastic material squeezed outside the rim of the mold when it is closed. This flash later has to be removed from the product and the edges smoothed.

Formaldehyde is a preservative and a disinfectant. It is made from a colorless gas called formalin that is obtained from methanol (wool alcohol). It is used in a water solution.

High impact is the ability of a plastic to withstand hard blows. It refers to strength.

Hydrocarbon is a compound which contains hydrogen and carbon. Acetylene and benzene are hydrocarbons.

Mylar is a trade name for a polyester film thermoplastic. It is unusually strong and may be printed, laminated, or coated. It is used for packaging, magnetic recording tapes, apparel stays, and metalized fabrics.

Natural resin is a natural substance found in nature such as *rosin,* used in varnishes, soaps, and driers for oils; *lac* from an insect used to make shellac. These are brittle substances, which have a waxy luster, and are insoluble in water.

Organic solvents are compounds of carbon. Acetone is an organic solvent.

Phenol is commonly known as carbolic acid. This is obtained from coal tar. It is a crystalline compound that is used in solution as an antiseptic.

Plasticizers are chemicals which are added to plastics to increase their workability. They are particularly important for use with the thermoplastics. Some chemicals used as plasticizers are camphor, high-boiling esters, and polynaphthalenes.

Polymerization is a chemical change which causes the formation of large molecules from single molecules. Some plastics are made in this way.

Resins, natural or synthetic, are the base of many plastics. See *Natural resin.*

Silicones are unusually strong materials of the thermosetting class that are used as adhesives, laminating resins, electrical insulation, and as protective coating.

Synthetic resins are chemically formed resins which have properties resembling natural resins. For example, the combination of phenol plus formaldehyde forms a synthetic resin which is the basis for the plastics by that name.

Tar is a dark brown, thick liquid obtained by distilling bituminous coal, to make coal tar used in some plastic substances and from which explosive materials, flavoring extracts, dyes, and medicines may be made.

Rubber, Automotive Products, and Paints

CHAPTER

17

UNIT 46 RUBBER—NATURAL AND SYNTHETIC

Rubber contributes comfort to the lives of everyone. We sleep on it; ride on tires made from it; walk on heels made from it; use it for protection from rain in the form of galoshes and rubbers; play with it in the form of rubber balls, golf balls, and bowling balls; and find hundreds of household uses for it in the form of hot water bottles, rubber gloves, stoppers, glue, elastic bands, jar rings, and so forth. Rubber and rubberlike products have gone through experimental and developmental stages and have emerged with new, better properties as a result of chemical discoveries. The extensive development of the synthetic rubbers under government sponsorship during World War II has increased the source of our raw materials for rubber and increased the uses of these products.

IMPORTANCE OF RUBBER

The annual use of rubber in the United States has grown from less than a pound per person in 1900 to almost 16½ pounds per person in 1950 and nearly 20 pounds per person today. Its extensive use is due to its versatility. Chemists can make rubber hard enough for bowling balls, combs, buttons; durable enough to resist thousands of miles of abrasive wear on highways; thin enough to be transparent; soft enough to be used for pillows, cushions, and mattresses; sticky enough to be used for adhesive tape or self-sealing envelopes; versatile enough to be formed into sheets or tiny filaments; waterproof for use as a raincoat; absorbent for use as a sponge; airtight to use in a balloon or tire or tube; or filled with air when made into foam rubber for cushions and mattresses.

ORIGIN AND HISTORY OF RUBBER

Some trees, plants, and shrubs when cut exude a gummy, milky-looking liquid similar to the substance from the stem of the milkweed. This white liquid, which is composed largely of water and a chemical known as *rubber hydrocarbon,* is known as *latex,* a Latin word meaning *liquid.* Many people think latex is the sap from the tree, but that is not true. The sap flows inside the woody part of the tree. The latex is found only in the bark.

When this milky-looking latex is allowed to stand, the water evaporates from it, the latex coagulates, as milk curdles, and forms a gummy, resilient material that we call *rubber.* The name *rubber* was first used about the year 1770 by an English chemist when he found it would "rub" pencil marks off paper.

Rubber was known to the natives of South America as long ago as the eleventh century. They called it *caoutchouc* (pronounced koo′ chook) and knew about some of its interesting characteristics long before Europeans saw them bouncing balls made from it.

The Europeans were delighted with the newly found substance. Not only did it bounce and rub pencil marks off paper, but it could be used to waterproof clothing and shoes; and when formed into a bottle or bowl, it would hold liquids. But their delight was short-lived. This remarkable material had some limitations—it became sticky in the summer and cracked and stiffened in the winter months, and so was practically useless.

Experimenters worked with the rubber. They spent money and time trying to produce rubber goods. A man named Charles Macintosh in 1823 evolved a method of putting a layer of rubber mixed with coal tar naphtha between two layers of cloth, like a sandwich. The coats and jackets made in this way

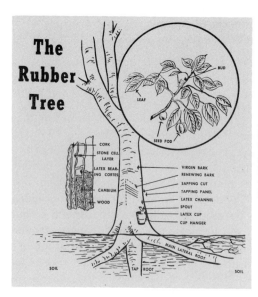

A full-grown "hevea brasiliensis" (rubber) tree averages 30 to 60 feet in height. Its useful life is 25 years or more. In full yield, a mature tree gives between 4 and 15 or more pounds a year. This is a cross section of the rubber tree. (*Courtesy U. S. Rubber Co.*)

are known as *mackintoshes*. But they, too, became sticky when warm and stiff when cold.

Charles Goodyear, an American inventor and experimenter, heard that the addition of sulfur aided in hardening rubber. His experiments were all a failure until accidentally in 1839 a piece of rubber that had sulfur mixed with it was left too near the hot stove. Ordinarily rubber became sticky, but this rubber did not melt. It acted like a new, different substance. That accident was the forerunner of his method of curing rubber, which he patented, known as *vulcanization,* named for Vulcan, the god of fire.

This new product, *vulcanized rubber,* lost none of its original fine qualities and, regardless of the season of the year, was a durable, useful material. Rubber today has been greatly improved by the addition of many other chemicals, but the formula, rubber + sulfur + heat, is still the basic method of vulcanizing rubber and preparing it for use.

England, realizing the growing market for this improved product, sent Sir Henry Wickham to South America to study the various species of rubber trees and to obtain seeds. He selected the seeds from the tree known as *Hevea* (Hee'-vea) *Brasiliensis* because it produced quality rubber in quantity. Over 2,000 of these seeds sprouted when planted in Kew Gardens, in England, and these seedlings were transplanted to the Botanical Gardens in Ceylon and the Malay States and later to Java, Borneo, Sumatra, India, and the Philippine Islands, where the moist, warm climate is ideally suited to the growth of the trees. Before the invasion of these countries by Japan, they were the sources of about 97 per cent of the total world production of rubber.

The plantations in the Far East are again yielding 92% of the natural rubber used. These areas are like well-kept orchards where nothing hampers the daily routine of collecting the precious latex.

Some natural rubber is obtained from Brazil. Liberia and Nigeria in West Africa have also developed a rubber industry.

During the 1950's and early 60's scientific development improved rubber production by increasing the yield from 400 pounds per acre to as much as 3,000 pounds per acre. This permits rubber to continue to compete in the world markets with the newer synthetic rubbers.

HOW LATEX IS OBTAINED FROM RUBBER TREES

At daybreak the workers depart to cut the bark of the tree—a delicate and skillful operation known as *tapping*. A tree is not ready for tapping until it has reached 5 years of age. As the tree gets older, its supply of latex increases somewhat. The tree continues to supply latex until it is about 45 years old.

Each tapper can take care of about 300 trees a day. About one-fifteenth of an inch of bark cut at an angle half way round the tree is removed. As the bark is cut, the tubes holding the latex are severed, and they begin to *bleed* the milk-white fluid. This latex flows down the trough formed by the cut in the bark into a porcelain cup placed by the tapper at the base of the cut. Then the tapper continues his rounds and returns before noon to empty the cup. The latex by this time has ceased dripping. The next time he returns, he makes a cut directly below the one he first made. He may tap the same tree on alternate days, weeks, or months. Each tree is tapped six months out of the year. It takes approximately six years for the bark to grow sufficiently thick before it can be cut away again. Each mature tree supplies from 6 to 10 pounds of crude rubber a year. One tire uses 10 or more pounds of rubber. The year's supply of one and a half to two trees is required to make one tire of all-new natural rubber.

By noon the latex has been gathered and brought to the central station where it is weighed and strained to remove impurities. It may then either be curdled with acetic acid (the acid in vinegar) or formic acid to form rubber, or it may be preserved in its liquid form with ammonia and shipped in tanks.

SYNTHETIC RUBBER

World War II, which began in 1939, caused a demand for rubber for vehicles of all types. All countries involved in the war were forced to develop rubber substitutes. Most substitutes are used because they are less expensive than the real product. When first produced, the rubber imitations, however, were not less expensive but actually several times more expensive. But real rubber was not available, so substitutes had to be used regardless of price.

During the 1950's and early 1960's synthetic rubbers were produced in great quantities, so that their price dipped until today they sell for slightly less than natural rubber. Because of its availability and quality, almost two-thirds of the rubber in use in the United States today is synthetic rubber.

Kinds of Synthetic Rubber. Several kinds of synthetic rubber are made. They are known as *Styrene Butadiene Rubber* or *SBR* (formerly known as Buna S), *Buna N* or *Perbunan, Chloroprene, Isobutylene, Polyisoprene.*

Styrene Butadiene Rubber (SBR)

This synthetic rubber, which wears approximately 30 per cent longer than natural rubber in tire treads, has become the most important of the chemical man-made rubbers. *Butadiene,* the main chemical from which this rubber is made, is a gas that can be derived from alcohol or petroleum. *Styrene,* the other important ingredient, is a colorless liquid derived from petroleum. After processing, these chemicals become a milky latex, which is then converted into a rubber crumb. These crumbs are baled ready for the manufacturing plants, where they must be vulcanized, like natural rubber.

SBR rubber is noted for its resistance to oil, heat, and abrasion; however, it is not as resilient as natural rubber. Its main disadvantage is that it tends to heat up more rapidly than natural rubber when subjected to abrasion and thus may crack more readily. A cold process of producing this rubber, developed in 1948, provided greater durability to this synthetic. SBR rubber may be used alone or combined with some natural rubber in making tires.

Buna-N or Perbunan Rubber

The *Buna-N* or *Perbunan* synthetic rubber is particularly noted for extreme resistance to oil, heat, abrasion, dyes, and paints. It is used for such products as "bullet sealing" fuel tanks and fuel hose. This synthetic operates successfully in temperatures below freezing, so that tires made from it are better in extremely cold climates than natural rubber.

Chloroprene Rubber

This product made from acetylene gas is processed and later vulcanized (without sulfur) in a manner similar to rubber. It also resembles rubber in its elasticity and strength and is superior to rubber in its resistance to oils and other chemicals, to sunlight, and to general aging. Because of its high resistance to chemical attack, it is particularly useful for gasoline hose and tank linings. In addition to being more expensive than Buna types of synthetic rubber, it also heats up more rapidly when used for tires on trucks carrying heavy loads. It is used for rubber gloves, foam-rubber cushioning, rubber tiles for floors, crib sheets, baby pants, and sporting equipment. There is only one commonly used name for this type of rubber: Neoprene, the generic term given it by the E. I. duPont de Nemours and Co., Inc.

Isobutylene

Another of the synthetic rubber products, invented in 1937, known as *Isobutylene,* is produced economically and has some advantages over rubber. It is made from chemicals derived from petroleum and turpentine. It is particularly noted for its resistance to high temperatures and strong chemicals. It is successful when used for inner tubes since it has high tear resistance. It is also less porous than natural rubber and, therefore, holds air better. Tires and tubes of Butyl rubber do not require inflation as often as those made from natural rubber or other synthetic rubbers. Even helium is encased without leakage in tubes of this rubber.

In 1957 further development of this synthetic rubber made it suitable for truck tires that met army specifications. Such tires hug the road, are quiet, and do not squeak on turns. Now used for passenger car tires, manufacturers have successfully overcome heating and softness of this rubber. When used in tires, this rubber is known as *Butyl* or *Butylaire.*

Polyisoprene

This synthetic rubber more nearly corresponds to natural rubber in chemical composition and molecular structure than any of the other synthetics discussed. Because it duplicates the long-wearing and heat-resistant qualities of natural rubber, it is used for tires and for pale crepe rubber used in shoes. It can also be used to make white side walls of tires that require a particularly fine quality of rubber.

In 1954 polyisoprene was introduced by Goodrich Gulf. Firestone introduced it in 1955. The Shell Chemical Corporation and the U. S. Rubber Company then found a way to produce it less expensively in 1959. *Coral* is one trade name for this rubber.

PUTTING THIS MERCHANDISE KNOWLEDGE TO USE ❯❯❯❯❯❯❯❯❯❯

❯ DO YOU KNOW YOUR MERCHANDISE?

1. What is latex? Where did we get the word *rubber?*
2. Why wasn't rubber used extensively as soon as it was discovered?
3. What is a *mackintosh?* What is meant by *vulcanization?* How and by whom was it discovered?
4. How did England aid in the development of rubber?
5. What was our main source of rubber before World War II? Now?
6. Explain briefly how trees are *tapped.*
7. How may rubber be shipped to America?
8. What is meant by *synthetic* rubber?
9. Why were synthetic rubbers produced originally?
10. Which is the most important synthetic rubber from the standpoint of volume? Which synthetic resembles rubber most closely?
11. What are some of the advantages synthetic rubber has over natural rubber?

❯ INTERESTING THINGS TO DO

1. On a map of the world indicate the countries where rubber is grown.
2. In the library, look up information on the life of Charles Goodyear and write a short theme about his contribution to rubber chemistry.
3. Analyze advertisements for rubber products. What features do they talk about?

UNIT 47 HOW RUBBER IS MANUFACTURED AND CARE OF RUBBER

KINDS OF RUBBER SENT TO AMERICA

After the natural latex is formed into the curdled or coagulated rubber, it must be air-dried or smoked. If it is air-dried, a chemical (sodium bisulfite) is added to prevent the rubber from rotting or getting moldy. By passing the rubber through rollers, the liquid is squeezed from it, and a continuous sheet is formed. This is hung to dry in a well-ventilated room. This rubber is light yellow in color and has a pleasant odor. It is known as *pale crepe*. This is used for light-colored rubber products such as white or light-colored rubbers or overshoes and white sidewalls on tires.

Most solid rubber is prepared by smoking it. Rubber that is smoked does not need any other substance to keep it from molding or rotting. After having the moisture pressed out, the sheets are hung over a smoking fire to dry. The smoke changes the color to a reddish brown and imparts a smoky odor to the rubber. This rubber, known as *smoked sheet,* dries in less time and is stronger than *pale crepe.* The natives of Brazil for many years have prepared rubber by rolling it into a ball and smoking it over a fire. This smoked rubber, known as *Para* (pronounced *Pah-rah'*), is considered to be one of the finest of rubbers.

The crude rubber, either in liquid form or in solid form as *pale crepe* or *smoked sheet,* is now shipped for manufacture. The natural rubber may be used alone or from 2 per cent to 79 per cent of it may be compounded with synthetic rubber.

MANUFACTURE OF RUBBER

Many operations are involved in the manufacture of rubber from the raw to the finished product.

Solid Rubber

The manufacture of rubber is like the making of bread or cake, for rubber must be "mixed, shaped, and baked." When you put a piece of chewing gum into your mouth, it is firm and dry. Chewing the gum makes it pliable and sticky. Rubber, either natural or synthetic, when it arrives at the mill is hard and dry and has to be broken up by a machine known as a *plasticator*. This huge contrivance tears the rubber and actually chews it until the rubber is broken down and becomes doughy and plastic. Some of the energy of the rubber, however, is removed by this process; and the life of rubber articles is therefore shortened to some extent.

Rubber in this state is known as *unvulcanized* rubber, and it has few uses because it becomes soft and sticky when heated and stiff when cold. It is used for electrical insulating tape to wind around copper wires which would be corroded by the sulfur in vulcanized rubber. It is also used for adhesive tape and rubber cement.

Rubber to be used for other purposes is now ready for the mixture of chemicals that will add durability, hardness, toughness, and color. These are added in a machine known as a *Banbury Mixer,* which kneads and squeezes the batch in a water-cooled chamber; or the chemicals are added in a *rubber mill,* which compresses the rubber and chemicals between big steel rollers.

After thorough mixing, the rubber is ready to be shaped. It may be formed into sheets by being run through rollers, or it may be extruded through a tubing machine from which it emerges like a long hose, or it may be forced into molds to be shaped into various well-known forms—sink stoppers, water bottles, halves of rubber balls.

The shaped rubber mixture containing sulfur plus other chemicals is now ready for the last important change caused by baking, known as *vulcanization* or *curing.* This may take place in a mold under pressure that shapes the article which is softened by heat; or rubber may be cured by placing it in a large container where heat is applied, but where there is no pressure to change the shape of the rubber.

Vulcanization

Vulcanization, we now know, is the curing of rubber by mixing it with 1 to 5 per cent sulfur and subjecting it to about 245°–300° F. of heat. A chemical change takes place that gives the rubber added strength, resistance to wearing away, greater ability to return to its original shape after being stretched, and resistance to extremes of temperature changes. Vulcanized rubber is also a nonconductor of electricity and gases, and it is waterproof. It is not soluble in ordinary solvents such as gasoline and chloroform; and it keeps its shape under pressure, heat, and strain.

Reclaimed Rubber

Used or worn-out rubber articles may be ground up, cleansed thoroughly, softened, and combined with crude rubber to facilitate reprocessing and manufacturing of new articles, such as tires, shoe soles and heels, and rubber clothing articles. Excessive amounts of reclaimed rubber will impair the wearing qualities of the articles made from it.

Liquid Latex

Many of the familiar household articles we use are formed directly from the liquid latex rather than from the coagulated rubber. After the discovery that ammonia would prevent latex from coagulating, and that latex could be creamed and thus lose some of the water weight, it became economically advisable to import it and use it for some articles. It is, however, more costly to use than solid rubber. In 1920 the first commercial quantities of latex were sent to America.

Synthetic latex as well as natural latex is used in manufacturing products today. Because latex is in liquid form, it is easy to stir in the required ingredients; this increases the life of the rubber which is somewhat reduced by the

◀ After these forms, modeled from a hand, have received their deposit of latex, they will be vulcanized by heat; then stripped off and packed.

Hot-water bottles are made of rubber molded under heat and pressure. Here they are being removed from the molds to be trimmed and hung on the rods near the worker. *(Courtesy B. F. Goodrich Co.)* ▶

Left: Golf balls coming from the special molds where they get those regular dimples that give them long, straight, true flight. **Right:** The parts of a golf ball. **Left to right:** rubber core containing liquid silicone center, core with rubber thread wound around it, and the tough cover which goes over all. *(Courtesy U. S. Rubber Co.)*

Bowling Balls. Top row, left: Core stock material before compaction. Inner core is cork and rubber, outer core is rubber. **Center:** Compacted core components in raw state prior to curing in high-temperature ovens. **Right:** The fully cured core—unbuffed. **Bottom row, left:** Rough turned core ready for cover molding. **Center:** Hard rubber core molded over the rough turned cover. **Right:** After ball is ground to perfect spherical shape, it is polished and finished. *(Courtesy AMF Pinspotters)*

plasticating machine. Such articles as balloons, gloves, and nipples can be formed by dipping a mold into the liquid mixture, just as you might dip a finger or spoon into cream, which adheres in a thin layer. Repeated dippings make the article thick enough to use.

Molds may also be rubber plated by running an electric current through the liquid causing the negatively charged rubber particles to adhere to the metal molds. Thus rubber girdles, bathing suits, and bathing slippers may be formed. This is called *electro-deposition*. Liquid latex is used to impregnate the backs of carpets and rugs to make them nonskid. It may also be used with paper or fabric to make simulated leather products.

Lastex is a trade name for a rubber thread made by pouring latex through a glass nozzle and coagulating the thread as it comes out. The round thread is more durable than elastic that is cut from a tube of rubber that has been through the plasticating process. Lastex is vulcanized after being formed.

In making latex sponge, the latex is whipped like cream until the air mixed with it makes a foamy, frothy mass. This mass, while still stiff, is vulcanized in molds having fingerlike posts which give added resilience to the finished cushion. This foam rubber, which is springy and lightweight, may be used for mattresses, car and furniture upholstery filling material, and pillows.

MISCELLANEOUS ARTICLES MADE FROM RUBBER AND LATEX

Airplane deicers are tubes of rubber attached to the wings of planes. These can be inflated with air and deflated by controls in the plane. This causes the ice that forms on the wings to crack and to drop off as the plane soars along.

Elastic bands and jar rings are made by slicing a tube of vulcanized rubber into thin sections.

Football bladders are made of flat pieces of rubber cut to shape, with the ends pressed together. Talcum powder is used to keep the pieces from sticking to each other. They are then vulcanized.

Garden hose is made by a hollow core of rubber with several layers of fabric coated with rubber wound around it. It is vulcanized inside and out so it will be properly cured.

Golf balls are very intricate to manufacture. The weight must be concentrated in the center of the ball. This is accomplished by the addition of finely ground lead to a rubber core or by a liquid weighted with lead. After vulcanization, the core is frozen and wound with a row of wide tape and then covered with narrow stretched elastic. *Balata* and *gutta percha,* tougher inelastic substances from other types of trees, are used as the covers of golf balls.

Hard rubber articles such as bowling balls, buttons, combs, fountain pens, and telephone instruments, are made by addition of a larger percentage of sulfur to the rubber. The more sulfur, the harder the product becomes after vulcanization. For black coloring, carbon black is also added to the mixture.

Ink erasers have powdered glass or pumice added to wear down the surface of the paper until the ink is removed.

Pencil erasers are made by adding a certain proportion of oil to make the rubber soft and pliable.

Pliofilm is the trade name for rubber products made by adding a chemical (hydrogen chloride) to the rubber. This chemical makes the rubber resistant to oil and grease and tearing. Pliofilm is moistureproof. It is made into a thin, transparent sheet for use in such things as raincoats, shower curtains, and umbrellas. It needs no stitching, since it can be sealed together by heating.

Rubber balls are molded in spherical halves, pressed together with a tiny ball of a chemical inside. When heated by the vulcanization process, a gas, such as nitrogen, is produced which presses the ball against the mold from the inside. If you shake a rubber ball, you can probably hear the residue from this chemical rattle inside.

Rubber cement is made by adding a solvent such as ether to rubber. When the ether evaporates, the rubber acts as an adhesive. If two surfaces are covered with rubber cement and permitted to dry until tacky, then pressed together, it is virtually impossible, after the cement has set, to tear them apart. Thus, rubber cement is used for bonding such things as parts of cemented shoes, handbags, and other leather and paper products.

Self-sealing envelopes and *sticky tapes* are made by oxidizing unvulcanized rubber. This forms a sticky rubber substance which adheres to other substances.

CARE OF RUBBER

Natural rubber even though it is vulcanized is affected by oil, which causes it to soften and swell. Rubber mats and rubber floors should therefore never be oiled. Synthetic rubber is generally more resistant to the adverse effects of oils or soaps.

Water left on a bathing cap or on rubber gloves will cause the rubber to become sticky and eventually rot. After drying rubber articles thoroughly by wiping and blowing into them, it is wise to sprinkle talcum powder over them. Hot-water bottles should have the stopper placed in so that the air is retained as in a balloon. This prevents the sides of the bottle from sticking together.

Since sunlight and heat deteriorate rubber articles, they should never be dried near a radiator or in the sunlight. Extremely cold weather may cause rubber to stiffen and crack. Rubber tubing should not be bent, as it may eventually crack.

If you stretch a rubber band around some papers and leave it for several months, you will notice when the band is removed that it has lost its resiliency and may even be sticky and worn out. This wearing out can be tested by stretching a rubber band and placing it quickly near the cheek. The warmth noticeable by this test is energy being given off by the stretched rubber.

Because rubber is acid resistant, it may be used for aprons worn in chemical laboratories.

❯ DO YOU KNOW YOUR MERCHANDISE?

1. Explain briefly how rubber is made into useful articles.
2. What qualities does vulcanization add?
3. Explain briefly the method of forming rubber articles from latex. What is *Lastex?* How is foam rubber formed?
4. Explain briefly how the following articles are made: bowling balls, telephone instruments, erasers, elastic bands, rubber balls, golf balls, airplane deicers, sticky tape.
5. What is *Pliofilm?* How is it used?
6. Why is care of rubber articles important? Give rules for their care.

❯ INTERESTING THINGS TO DO

1. If you have an old ball around your house, cut it in half and examine the inside. What did you find? Mount the halves and label all parts.
2. Flex a rubber band repeatedly against your hand. What did you feel? Why did you get this reaction?
3. Prepare a 2-minute sales talk for a rubber product. Be sure also to explain its proper care.

UNIT 48 RUBBER TIRES AND TUBES AND OTHER AUTOMOTIVE PRODUCTS

TIRES AND TUBES

Over 70 million automobiles and trucks transport people and goods on American roads today; as a result, these moving vehicles have become the greatest users of rubber products, both natural and synthetic. The tire manufacturers, prepared for a constantly increasing demand for rubber tires, have improved their products so that today tires give good service for 40,000 or more miles; they may be puncture resistant, blowout safe, and soft riding. New developments and constant research have made these improvements possible. Everything that goes into a tire determines its strength and the satisfaction it will give in use.

Composition of Tires

About one-sixth of the tire is nylon, rayon, or cotton fabric; one-third is wire and chemicals added to the rubber; and the balance consists of natural and synthetic crude rubber mixed, in some cases, with a small percentage of reclaimed rubber.

Passenger car tires have two plies to six plies, while truck tires may have from four to ten plies. Until 1961, only four-ply and six-ply tires were used for automobiles. Two-ply tires were introduced to make the purchase of compact cars more economical. These tires, by proper distribution of rubber, were made to give adequate service for small cars.

The term *ply* refers to the layer of fabric cord coated with rubber and made into sheets. Each sheet (or ply) of cord fabric is cut on the bias and placed to form a complete circle over a drum. Then another layer of fabric is placed on top with the cords running at right angles to the previous layer of fabric. The greater the number of these plies, all other factors being equal, the more durable the tire.

Nylon has proved repeatedly in tests to be the strongest material for serviceability in tires. High-strength rayon is second, and cotton is last.

Durability is also affected by the rubber used and by the manner in which it is distributed across the tread part of the tire. According to tire manufacturers, a tire gives 25 per cent better service by reinforcing the outer rim where load and wear on a tire are heaviest than by applying the same amount of rubber evenly.

Steel wires known as the *bead* hold the tire on the wheel rim. The rubber that is to form the side wall and tread of the tires is placed over a cushion strip or breaker, which binds the tread to the body of the tire. The entire tire is rolled under pressure to be sure that all parts adhere together securely. This tire, in the form of a circular band, is next put over an air bag and placed in a shaping machine that molds it into the form of a huge doughnut. The tire is now ready to have the tread design impressed on it during the vulcanizing process.

The curing or vulcanization process takes from 45 minutes to 60 minutes for ordinary auto and truck tires. On its completion a finished tire emerges. The heat of the vulcanization mold causes the rubber to soften and take the form of the metal against which it is pressed. Treads with zig-zag markings are good for regular driving and for resisting skids on wet or icy streets. Deeper treads are formed in tires that are to be used in snow or mud.

Tires may be *tubeless* or may include tubes. Tubeless tires introduced in 1956 use strong cord such as nylon and require rims that permit locking air into the tire. Premium tubeless tires may have a double chamber to hold air if the outer casing is ripped. Regular tubeless tires, however, rely on the slow release of air from the tire to protect riders until the car has been brought to a stop should the tire be punctured. A tubeless tire costs about the same as an ordinary tire together with its tube.

Classification of Tires

Tires are classed as premium or super, first, second, or third line tires.

Premium or *super* tires give maximum wear and safety. These are the most costly tires, and they are not used by automobile manufacturers on new cars.

First line tires are the regular fine-quality tires embodying all up-to-date quality features necessary for passenger cars.

Second line tires are less expensive and give adequate mileage to the motorist who drives at average speeds over regular highways.

Third line tires are advisable only for those people who use their cars very little and who are very cautious in their care of the tires.

Second hand or used tires may be retreaded, recapped, or regrooved. *Retreading* puts a new cushion and breaker strip and new top tread of rubber over the old tire. If properly done, this can result in a tire with about 60 to 70 per cent of the service of a new tire.

Recapping is the addition of a top layer of rubber cemented to the old worn-down tread. It is less expensive than retreading and does not give as long service, but it may be done as many as three or four times if the rest of the tire is in good condition.

Regrooving merely removes some of the tread by cutting out part of the rubber after the tread has become smooth. This temporarily improves the grip of the tire, but may shorten its wearing qualities.

Inner tubes are formed by a tubing machine. The rubber is cut to the required length, joined, and the entire tube inflated and vulcanized.

Tire Sizes

As car styles, shapes, and sizes have changed through the years, so tires also have changed in size and shape. Narrow tires on wheels with large diameters have become unfashionable. Tires today are squat appearing, and the center diameter is less than on cars of the 1920's and 1930's.

Tire sizes are stated by the use of two numbers, as 7.50–14. The first number means that the tire is 7.5 inches wide at its widest point. The second number means that the tire has an inside diameter of 14 inches. This is the most popular size in tires for mass-produced cars like the regular Chevrolets, Fords, and Plymouths. Compacts made in the United States have tires ranging from 6 to 6½ inches wide with an inside diameter of 13 to 15 inches. Imported small cars have tires that range from 5 to 5.6 inches wide with diameters of 13 to 15 inches. Truck tires may be as small as 6 inches in width and 16 inches in diameter to 8¼ inches by 20 inches.

Care of Tires

A few precautions for the care of tires that will increase their wearing qualities are important to all of us. The correct pressure of air is important. Underinflation seriously reduces the life of the tire. Overinflation may cause a blowout.

Tires do not wear out evenly on the four wheels. The rear-wheel tires wear

◀ When tire is built on a revolving drum, two plies are locked around the bead, then two more plies are added. The operator is shown here applying the fourth and last ply while building a tubeless tire. ▶ Curing, or vulcanizing, is started by the operator placing the barrel-like tire in a mold. An inflated "shaping bag" is forced inside the tire. The mold gives the tire its permanent shape and tread design.

◀ The mold which "cured" the tire and applied the tread is opened to release the tire. The finished tire is inspected and placed on a conveyor that carries it to the wrapping section. ▶ (Courtesy U. S. Rubber Co.)

out first. Spare tires that are not used deteriorate. Changing tires and shifting them from one wheel to another occasionally will even up the wear.

High speeds, slamming on brakes, fast turns around corners, bumping tires against curbs, wheels not correctly aligned are all causes for unnecessary wear and tear on tires.

GASOLINE

Gasoline, an essential to automotive and truck travel, is a product obtained from *petroleum*. Petroleum, it is believed, was produced millions of years ago in the earth by heat and pressure exerted on layers of marine plant and animal life deposited in the beds of seas. Chemical changes caused by the heat and pressure together with bacterial action are believed to have transformed these remains of the marine plants and animals into petroleum and natural gas. By the shifts of land masses, petroleum and gas became caught in "traps" where today geologists uncover them.

When oil and gas are brought to the surface by drilling, they are separated mechanically; the oil goes to a storage tank, while the gas is processed and then piped into lines for distribution to consumers. The crude oil must then be moved to refineries. At the refinery, further processing converts the crude oil into gasoline, kerosene, fuel oil, lubricants, and asphalt.

Modern processes of refining petroleum, known as *cracking,* make it possible to obtain larger percentages of gasoline than were obtained heretofore. Today almost 50 per cent of crude oil may be converted to gasoline as compared with 15 per cent before cracking. Cracking also makes possible the development of finer gasolines, such as those used for aviation motors.

Petroleum, in addition to providing gasoline and oils, is used as the raw material for many plastics and for waxes for milk containers and bread wrappers. Detergents, insecticides, medicines, dyes, and paints may all contain petroleum materials.

Qualities in Gasoline

When people buy gasoline for their cars, they seek several features:

1. The gasoline should vaporize easily to give quick starts and fast engine warm-up.
2. The gasoline should not boil in fuel lines in hot weather thus causing stalling.
3. The gasoline should not knock. *Knocking* is a sudden explosion caused by the last bit of gasoline to burn in the engine's combustion chambers.

Octane Rating of Gasoline

There are two basic types of gasoline: *iso-octane* and *heptane.* The iso-octane gasoline will give a 100 *octane rating* (no-knock rating), while heptane gasoline provides a zero rating. The highest octane is given the number 100, while the lowest octane is represented by zero. If 80 per cent iso-octane gasoline is used with 20 per cent of heptane, a rating of 80 octane is achieved. Octane, therefore, is the term used to designate the antiknock features of gasoline. The higher the octane, the less chance of engine knock.

Another method has also been found to increase the antiknock performance of gasoline. In 1922, an American chemist, Dr. Thomas Midgley, found that adding *tetraethyl lead* to gasoline would decrease engine knock. As little as a teaspoon of this chemical in a gallon of gasoline raises the octane rating considerably. Since more powerful, high-compression engines could not be made until the knocking in gasoline was overcome, the entire automotive industry was improved when higher octane ratings in gasoline were devised. High-compression engines give better service, use less gasoline, and provide more power.

While the addition of tetraethyl lead changes the octane ratings in most gasolines, gasolines differ from one another because of other chemical additives used.

Service stations sell *regular gasoline,* with lower octane ratings, for regular engines. These have octane ratings around 90 today. The service stations sell premium or special-grade higher octane gasoline for high-compression engines. These premium gasolines at present have octane ratings around 98. Gasoline for airplane engines has an octane rating as high as 130.

If a car does not need the special octane gasolines, there is no reason to buy them. High-compression engines, however, will knock if they do not have the proper gasoline; this knocking causes engine wear and poor performance.

How Gasoline Works in Engines

Power is obtained in an engine from gasoline by vaporizing the gas in the carburetor and then compressing it in the engine's cylinders. The gas is mixed with air; and the more it is compressed, the more power the engine has. The mixture of gas and air has to burn smoothly to prevent knocking. If it burns too fast, the driver gets a knock that reduces the power and efficiency of the engine. The octane scale determines how much a particular mixture of gasoline and air can be compressed and ignited without knocking.

MOTOR OIL

Oils, which are liquid lubricants, are used in automobiles to perform several functions. They lubricate various moving parts by providing a protective film that reduces friction when the car is in use. Oil also protects the engines from rust and from acid attack. Acids are formed in engines when water is condensed from the steam formed when gasoline burns and mixes with some of the other by-products of combustion. These acids cause corrosion of rings, pistons, cylinders, and rusting of other parts. In addition to acid-forming materials, the by-products of fuel combustion form sludge and varnishlike deposits that clog parts and make operation of the car sluggish. Quality oils minimize the formation of such sludge and varnish deposits.

As with gasoline, oil varies in quality. The American Petroleum Institute (API), has established letter symbols for various grades and types of oil:

API Service MS is the oil for all types of automotive use. It is made for recently designed cars, for all cars for stop-and-go city driving, and for cars used for short trips and for high-speed, long-distance driving particularly in hot weather. This is also the best oil for cold-weather driving.

API Service MM is the oil for older-model cars to be driven at high speed for short distances, at moderate speeds in warm weather, or for long and short trips in cool weather.

API Service ML is the oil for minimum protection for old-design cars driven at moderate speeds in above-freezing weather.

The Society of Automotive Engineers (SAE) has set the standards for the *viscosity*—thickness or thinness—of the oils. Thick oils, which flow slowly, have high numbers while thin oils, which flow freely, have low numbers. "W" denotes oils for winter service. Following are the numbers used:

Thinnest—(5W	20)	Warm-weather
Cold-weather (10W	30)	driving
driving (20W	40)	
	50)—Thickest	

For wintertime driving, the following are recommended:

20W or less for temperatures to 10° F.
10W or less for temperatures to 10° below zero.
5W for temperatures below 10° below zero.

For summertime driving, heavier grades of oil are recommended.

Some oils have viscosities that do double duty. These may be marked, for example, SAE 5W–20. Such an oil will perform for both winter and warmer weather driving.

AIR FILTERS

Air filters are metal strainers that catch the dirt from the air that flows through the motor of the automobile. About 9,000 gallons of air flow through an engine for each gallon of gasoline used. Air brings dust and sand with it. These combine in the engine with other waste material to form harmful sludge. Clean air filters catch most of this harmful dirt. Clogged air filters, however, permit more abrasives to get into the oil and then to damage engines. To assure the smoothest trouble-free performance in an engine, filters should be changed regularly.

GREASE

Grease used for lubricating the moving parts of cars is a solid or semisolid material that has a slick feel and that cuts down on friction which wears out metal parts. Grease is usually made by blending lubricating oils with soaps containing sodium.

DISTILLATE FUELS

Diesel engines, airplane jet engines, boats, busses, tractors, and trucks use materials heavier than regular gasoline for their power. These are called *distillate* fuels and are obtained by vaporization and condensation of petroleum.

Automobile batteries are known as *"dry-charged"* batteries because they are not ready for use until seals that keep out moisture are removed and sulfuric acid is added. Dry-charged batteries can be stored for a long time without deterioration. The outer case of the battery is made of hard rubber.

Batteries generate current by having a positive metal plate coated with lead peroxide and a negative plate coated with lead submerged in a dilute solution of sulfuric acid. The lead peroxide plate changes to lead sulfate on discharge and changes back when charged. A fully charged battery has a sulfuric acid content a little over one-third. When the acid content is reduced to about one-fifth, the battery is discharged.

Testing Batteries

Batteries may be tested by two different devices known as *hydrometers* and *volt meters*. The *hydrometer* measures the specific gravity of the acid and water mixture. Since the acid is heavier in weight than water, a measurement of the specific gravity indicates the amount of acid present. The hydrometer syringe is filled with the fluid in each battery cell. The glass sides of the hydrometer have markings that permit a specific gravity reading to be taken. Each cell must be checked separately.

The *volt meter* has prongs that are attached to the battery. The indicator on the volt meter is marked to show when the battery is satisfactorily charged and when it needs recharging or replacement.

PUTTING THIS MERCHANDISE KNOWLEDGE TO USE ❯ ❯ ❯ ❯ ❯ ❯ ❯ ❯ ❯ ❯

❯ DO YOU KNOW YOUR MERCHANDISE?

1. What is a tire ply? How many plies do automobile tires usually have? Why are better tires made with more plies? What fiber is the best for plies?
2. What are the differences between tubeless and regular tires?
3. What are the different qualities of tires? What advantages do the better tires offer the motorist?
4. What rules of tire care are important for a motorist to observe?
5. What is meant by an octane rating in gasoline? What chemical additive changes the octane rating of gasoline? What octane is regular gasoline?
6. What are the three grades of oil products? Which would be the best grade for all cars? What is meant by 5W oil? 50 oil?
7. What function does an air filter perform? How often should it be replaced?
8. How may batteries be tested to determine if they are properly charged?

❯ INTERESTING THINGS TO DO

1. Analyze five advertisements on gasoline appearing in magazines or

newspapers. (*a*) Does the gasoline in each advertisement have a trade name? If so, list the trade names for each. (*b*) List and explain the features the advertisers claim are superior about the gasoline they are advertising. (*c*) What technical terms have they used in the advertisements? Are any of these terms explained? If so, which ones?

2. Interview a service-station attendant. Write a report about his answers to the following questions: (*a*) Does he sell to more women customers or to more men customers? (*b*) Which demand more service generally? (*c*) Which ask more questions usually about the products the service station has available? (*d*) Does the service-station attendant use any suggestion selling? If so, do men or women buy more of the products he suggests?

3. Write a short sales talk for one of the following products: a high octane gasoline; tubeless tires; oil filters.

UNIT 49 PAINT AND ALLIED PRODUCTS

"Save the surface and you save all." This slogan of one paint manufacturer explains the value of surface coatings. Paint brushed, sprayed, or dipped onto wood or metal keeps the surface from imbedded soil; it protects wood from rotting and iron and steel from rusting.

Paint and paint products have always been used extensively, but they became of noticeable importance to individual consumers during the "do-it-yourself" era following World War II. Paint is not a new fad, however. Tracing the use of paint products through the ages, we find references that indicate that they were employed over 20 thousand years ago! If you visit a museum, you will see ancient Egyptian pottery and mummy cases that were decorated with paint. The early Greeks and Romans were among others who left us a heritage of colorfully decorated products. Natural substances such as vermilion (mercuric sulfide), colored clays, red iron oxide, ochre (iron ore such as hematite or limonite), and white lead were used. These are still the ingredients used for certain types of paints. Recent developments of new synthetic products have extended the types of paints available and have improved the ease with which paint may be applied.

MATERIALS USED IN PAINTS

Paint is a thin, protective film applied to a surface. Paint may be opaque or transparent. Opaque paints contain *pigments* or solid coloring material. When these are not present, the material is transparent. Opaque paints are composed of pigment, a binder that holds the pigment together, and a solvent or thinner that makes the paint thin enough to spread over a surface easily. Manufacturers also add other ingredients to give their products certain other featured advantages.

Pigments that provide the color are usually in powder form. For white color, white lead, zinc oxide, and titanium dioxide are commonly used. Red colors are obtained from iron oxides; yellow colors, from siennas (oxides of iron and manganese) and ochres; brown, from manganese; green, from chromic oxide; blue, from iron, cobalt, and coal-tar derivatives; and black, from burned animal bones or carbon. Lead oxides should not be used in paints that are applied to children's toys or furniture, as they are dangerous to health if eaten.

Binders for most paints are some type of oil. For oil-base paints, vegetable oils such as linseed oil (from flax), tung oil (from seeds of a Chinese tree), soybean oil, and castor oil are used. Fish oils have also been used for a few paints. These oils form a hard, resinous coat when dry and help to protect the surface.

Thinners are mostly volatile liquids that evaporate after the paint is applied. Turpentine from pine trees, benzene and naphtha from petroleum are the usual thinners employed. For water-base paints such as casein, emulsion paints (latex and acrylate types), and calcimine (essentially chalk and glue), water is the thinning agent used. With the exception of calcimine, however, once these paints are dry they are unaffected by water.

TYPES OF PAINTS, STAINS, AND SHINY COATINGS

Different kinds of coloring materials serve various needs.

Paints

Calcimine (sometimes spelled *kalsomine*) is a white ceiling paint composed essentially of chalk and glue. This paint is not washable.

Enamel, a smooth, hard-surfaced, usually shiny paint material, is made by adding a pigment to varnish and linseed oil. Enamels wash well. *Epoxy,* a plastic enamel, is very smooth and hard, but difficult to use.

Luminous paints are made by the addition of chemicals that glow under ultraviolet light (known as *fluorescent* paints) or that glow in the dark (known as *phosphorescent* paints).

Metallic paints use as pigment tiny flakes of the desired metal. Aluminum, copper, and other metals may be used in such paints. These metal flakes provide particularly protective surface coatings.

Latex base paints (synthetic rubber) and *plastic base paints* (polyvinyl acetate and acrylates such as Lucite) are paints that form an emulsion in water. That means that the pigment and binder are held in tiny droplets in water until they are spread on a surface to dry. When the water evaporates, the paint is not solvent in water and thus becomes waterproof. These paints are much easier to apply than traditional oil-base paints and have made painting far easier for the amateur do-it-yourselfer. These paints can be applied easily without showing joining marks; they dry quickly; and fresh splashes may be wiped off with a damp cloth. The brushes and rollers used for application are restored to their original state by merely washing in soap and water. When thoroughly dry these paints have a tough but resilient finish that resists scuffs and does not separate from plaster walls or woodwork. These paints are almost odorless.

Stains

Stains differ from paints because they do not cover or protect the surface but merely change its color. When used on woods, the grain of the wood is visible through the stain. The colors are mostly derived from aniline today. Stains may be *water* stains, *oil* stains, and *spirit* (alcohol) stains. The water stain is the most resistant to fading. The oil stain accentuates ornate grains, but it bleeds or runs when covered with varnish or lacquer necessitating a sealer coat. Spirit stains dry fast but penetrate only slightly and are rarely used except for touch-up work.

Shiny Coatings

Shellac is a durable, transparent coating made from *lac,* a resinous secretion of a scale insect from India. The thin sheets of lac are dissolved in alcohol

Left: Easy clean-up of brushes and rollers after painting is one advantage new acrylic wall paint shares with other water emulsion finishes. Wet paint is quickly removed from hands and tools with soap and water. A damp sponge also whisks away accidental spills. *(Courtesy E. I. duPont de Nemours & Co.)* **Right:** All good bristles have "flag" ends; that is, the end of each bristle is slightly fuzzed. These flags spread the paint evenly over the working surface. Hog bristles are naturally flagged, while synthetic bristles are artificially flagged. *(Courtesy Home Modernizing Guide)*

to make a durable finish used for floors and other wood surfaces. *Orange shellac* is the natural color, while *white shellac* has been bleached. This product has never been duplicated synthetically.

Varnish is a transparent coating that contains no pigment. It is made from natural resins, such as insect excretions and oozings from certain types of trees; or newer types are made from synthetic resins (phenolics and alkyds). *Oil varnish,* which is the better quality, uses linseed or tung oil; while *spirit varnish* uses alcohol as the solvent. Varnish is used as a protective coating for furniture and other wood products.

Lacquer is a fast drying, tough, durable finish. While lacquer was extensively used by the ancient Chinese, modern formulas have little relationship to those of ancient times. Lacquer today is made from cellulose nitrate resins (one of the cellulosic plastic substances) plus plasticizers for flexibility, and solvents that evaporate quickly when exposed to air. Clear lacquer is often used as the final finish for furniture. Pigmented lacquers are used for metal coatings. These fast evaporating solvents made lacquers the desirable coatings for mass-produced automobiles during the 1920's and 1930's and helped to speed production on the assembly lines. The necessity, however, for several coats for durability made these nitrocellulose lacquers lose their popularity during the 1940's; since then, they have been replaced in the automotive trade by the alkyds.

Alkyd lacquer paints have replaced the nitrocellulose lacquers for automobiles. These synthetic resins dry harder and tougher than the former lacquers used and necessitate fewer coats, thus speeding the cars on the assembly line. When silicones are added to the formula, the lacquers maintain their shine permanently without waxing.

PAINTBRUSHES

Paintbrushes affect both the ease of application of the paint and the finished appearance of the surface painted. Brushes, therefore, must be selected with care.

Hog bristles from China are the traditional materials used for fine quality brushes. These have natural elasticity, and they wear well. In addition, the end of each bristle is split, making it slightly fuzzy, known as *flagged.* This enables the brush to hold the paint and to spread it evenly. Hog bristles from India and Korea are not considered as fine as the Chinese bristles. These natural bristle brushes are used with oil-base paints.

Nylon bristles, used first when hog bristles were scarce, but now appreciated for their fine qualities, also make good brushes, and they are considerably less expensive than good natural bristles. Nylon, of course, can be cut to the desired length, while hog bristles have to be sorted for length and then matched. To give nylon bristles some of the characteristics of the hog bristles, they are split or flagged on the ends. Nylon brushes are used with any type of paint. These bristles wear several times longer than do natural bristles.

All good quality brushes have tapered ends. This permits painting in corners and in small places. Brushes should be chosen to fit easily into the paint-can opening and to be large enough to do the work with a minimum of strokes.

The best quality brushes have the bristles solidly set in rubber or epoxy cement. This prevents the brush from shedding its bristles. Good brushes also flex easily, and the bristles feel springy yet do not fan out excessively when pressed against a surface. Harsh, stiff brushes are less expensive and less desirable.

Care of Brushes

Brush care is important. Brushes must be kept soft at all times. They should be thoroughly cleaned in the proper thinner immediately after use. After a thorough washing, they should be allowed to dry, then wrapped in paper to keep them in good condition until used again. Never allow the bristles to dry in a bent position. Suspend the bristles so they dry straight.

AEROSOL CONTAINERS

Aerosol paints, stains and lacquers are packaged in airtight cans with a compressed or liquefied gas that permits the contents to be sprayed on the surface rather than painted in the usual fashion. Aerosol paints leave no brush marks, get at hard-to-reach spots, and may be used for touch-up with a minimum of care. These paints dry fast; and since the can is airtight, no film is formed in the can itself. This method of packaging makes the paint several times more costly than traditional packaging methods, and care must be taken while applying the paint to avoid "overspray."

PUTTING THIS MERCHANDISE KNOWLEDGE TO USE ❯ ❯ ❯ ❯ ❯ ❯ ❯ ❯ ❯ ❯

❯ DO YOU KNOW YOUR MERCHANDISE?

1. What is paint? How do opaque paints differ from transparent paints?
2. What are the three basic ingredients used in paints? Explain what role each plays in making paint.
3. What is the difference between enamel and lacquer?
4. What are the advantages of metallic paints?
5. What paint is used in the automotive industry today?
6. How do stains and paints differ?
7. What are the characteristics of good brushes? Which brushes give the longest wear?
8. What are the advantages of aerosol paints?

❯ INTERESTING THINGS TO DO

1. Visit a local paint store and notice how many kinds of paint, how many sizes of paint cans, and how many different colors are carried.

2. Analyze five paint advertisements. Did the advertisements tell you what kind of paint was being sold? What advantages were stated for the paint?
3. Prepare a 2-minute sales talk for a certain type of paint. Present your talk for the class.

ADDITIONAL MERCHANDISE TERMS ❯

Balata is a somewhat elastic gum exuded from a type of tree similar to the rubber tree.

Bristle refers to the hair of pigs, or hogs. This term is not properly applied to the hair of other animals or to fibers.

Butadiene is a gas made commercially from petroleum.

Chisel is a symmetrically curved point to the working edge of a paintbrush. This enables the paint to flow smoothly.

Cold rubber is a synthetic rubber made at lower temperatures than most man-made rubber.

Ebonite is rubber that contains a great deal of sulfur and is very hard and quite tough. It is black in color and hence resembles ebony, from which it gets this name.

Elasticity is the quality of being stretched and recovering size and shape readily.

Flamenol is a trade name of the General Electric Company for a rubberlike substance used for electrical insulation.

Gutta percha, a substance resembling rubber, is also obtained from the bark of certain types of trees. It is tough, inelastic, and very resistant to effect by water. It is used for the coating on some golf balls, for lining containers for acid.

Koroseal, see *Vinyl.*

Lucite is a trade name for an acrylic emulsion paint.

Oxidation is a chemical change that takes place in a substance combined with oxygen in the air. The surface of rubber becomes sticky by oxidation.

Resiliency is the quality of a stretched article to recover its size and shape.

Vinyl is the "elastic plastic" that requires no vulcanization and that is not useful for tires or tubes. It is a rubber substitute made from the chemicals present in air, natural gas, water, salt, and coal. Products made from this plastic may be stretched to about 300 per cent of their length, yet return slowly to shape. This elongation does not seem to affect the wearing quality of the article, regardless of how often it is stretched. It is also a useful material because of its resistance to oils and greases. It is used as unsupported film (no backing) or as a coating over fabric or paper. Familiar trade names for this product are: Koroseal and Vinylite.

Vinylite, see *Vinyl.*

Vulcanite is hard rubber. See *Ebonite.*

Paper and Stationery Products

UNIT 50 THE ART OF PAPERMAKING

Our most common material, paper, has many uses for the individual, for business, for industry, and for the government. Today, manufacture of paper is the nation's fifth largest industry. Our consumption per capita of paper is now 420 pounds each year, and experts predict that it will be 600 pounds for each person yearly by 1975.

SOME USES FOR PAPER

When the cave man wanted to write history, he had to use a sharp rock and scratch his symbols or characters on stone or bone. He would have regarded paper and pencil as a miracle. To us, however, paper is a commonplace everyday necessity with a thousand varied uses. Paper towels and tissues aid cleanliness and comfort and prevent the spread of cold infection. Paper cups and cartons, coated so they are leakproof, are sanitary and inexpensive. Many kinds of food are wrapped in waxed paper to protect the food and bring it to our homes fresh and ready for use. If we look around our homes, we may find walls covered with paper; windows may be framed with paper drapes; tightly twisted paper coated with enamel is used for fiber furniture. Even "fiber" rugs are made of paper.

Pyroxylin and vinyl-coated paper are used for imitation-leather notebooks, wastebaskets, book covers. Pictures painted on paper adorn our walls, papier-mâché masks or decorations add a festive note in the house. Economical and safe transportation of merchandise is accomplished by packing in paper cartons. Even furniture is successfully delivered this way, in contrast to the old-time wooden crates. Lamp shades, wastebaskets, and numerous other household articles are made of paper.

Probably one of the most important features of paper is that its low cost permits its use for conveying the printed word daily in newspaper, magazine, and book form to almost every home in the world. Printed greeting cards for all occasions bring cheer or solace yearly to millions of people.

In retail stores paper is used for sales checks, for order blanks, for salesmanship manuals, for record keeping, for wrapping merchandise, for decorative backgrounds in windows and showcases, and for hundreds of other uses. The tons of waste paper that large stores accumulate weekly are baled and sold as scrap. Enough money is obtained this way to pay for the running of several elevators yearly.

HOW PAPERS DIFFER

Collect a few pieces of paper available in your house. Probably one of the most noticeable ways in which they vary is in color. Papers are bleached white, dyed, or printed to give them varying colors and qualities of color. Fold the paper and notice if the two edges are the same color. Evenness of color is an important quality. Unfold the paper and hold it to the light. Are there pin-point holes where the paper was folded? If so, the paper is inferior in quality. Notice any defects—dark spots, tiny holes (other than the ones made by the fold) or thin places in the paper.

Now examine the finish. Blotters have a dull, linty appearance on one side and often a glossy finish on the back. The paper wrapped around the butter or other food has a smooth translucent appearance. Put a sheet of writing paper and a section of paper from a bread or butter wrapper in water. Notice that the writing paper absorbs the water and the wrapping paper sheds water. Write with ink on regular stationery. The pen flows smoothly, and the ink line is fine and sharp. Now write with ink on newspaper or pencil paper. If you are using a fountain pen, the ink smudges and flows unevenly and makes fuzzy-looking letters.

Examine the morning or evening newspaper. Notice the color, texture, appearance. Contrast this with the paper used in magazines and books. Look through some old books in the library. Are some of the sheets yellow at the edges from age?

All these and many other facts are characteristics of paper. The raw materials used and the methods of manufacture are responsible for the many differences you have noticed.

PAPER THROUGH THE AGES

The Egyptians 4,000 years ago developed a writing material from a plant known as *papyrus,* which grew in the region of the Nile River. They used the pithy center of the stalk, which was sliced and pressed into sheets.

Later the skins of goats and sheep were made into *parchment,* and the skins of calves into *vellum* by a process similar to the making of ordinary leather. The skins were then polished to give them a fine, permanent writing surface. This was a long, tedious process and required many skins just for one document. Unless we had progressed beyond that stage, large Sunday editions of metropolitan newspapers would be unheard of today, as there are not enough animals in the world to supply the needed quantity of material.

The beating of wood and fabric fibers into pulp for papermaking is credited to the Chinese Emperor Hoti and his subject, Ts'ai-Lun, who are generally believed to have developed this method about 2,000 years ago. They used silk, the core of the mulberry tree, and bamboo stems. Then they beat the fibers and mixed them with water. The water they shook out through a screen, leaving the dried matted fibers in the form of paper. Linen was later used in place of silk and mulberry-tree fibers by the Arabs, who by 105 A.D. had learned the art from captured Chinese.

Slowly this method of papermaking spread to Europe, but not until the invention of movable type around 1450 was there any stimulus to the development of the paper industry. Cotton and linen were the chief materials then used in Europe. Hemp, jute, and straw were also used experimentally. Wood, the most common material today, was not used as raw material until a Frenchman, Rene de Reaumur, discovered its value about the year 1719. It is believed that the paper wasp which chews the wood and then builds its nest of the paper substance was the inspiration for the new discovery. Wood, the new material, was slow in being accepted, for it was approximately 1854 before commercial use was made of this fiber by a German who read of Reaumur's discovery.

MATERIALS USED IN PAPERMAKING

Today paper is made from linen and cotton rags; and from grasses, plants, and woods—mainly the softwoods, spruce, pine, hemlock, and fir. Cellulose, the cell structure of all these materials, is the basic substance used for paper.

Preparing Wood for Papermaking

Since most paper is made from soft wood, we are primarily interested in its methods of manufacture. After the logs are brought from the forests to the mills, the bark is removed, and knots are cut out of the wood. The wood is then reduced to *pulp*. This is done by two general processes known as *mechanical* and *chemical*. The *mechanical* method is the least expensive because none of the wood is wasted. The log is pressed against a grindstone which reduces it to minute sliverlike fibers. Of course, substances other than *cellulose* (the cell wall of the fibers) are left in by this method; and these other substances cause discolorations and impurities in the paper made from this pulp. This type of pulp is used mostly for newspapers, pencil pads, some tissue papers, and building and insulating papers. These papers (unless coated with other substances) will yellow with age and become brittle. This pulp is known as *groundwood*. Paper made from it is speckled and somewhat gray.

For *chemical* pulp, the logs are first "chipped" into small pieces by rotating knives. These cut chips permit the ends of the cellulose fibers to absorb water and chemicals. The chips are then put into a large tank; various chemicals are added plus water or steam, and the chips are cooked for 8 to 16 hours. The chemicals cause all substances except the cellulose to dissolve. About 50 per cent of the wood is made up of these binding substances. Subsequent washings in pure water remove the dissolved substances, leaving pure cellulose.

Commonly used names for the two most used chemical pulps are *sulfate* and *kraft*. These chemical pulps are used for better qualities of paper than the mechanical or groundwood pulps. They may be combined with groundwood in the making of newsprint, which is usually about 85 per cent groundwood and 15 per cent chemical pulp. The chemical pulps may be used in their natural state for sacks and wrapping papers, bleached for writing paper, or further refined and used as the base for *rayon*. The wood pulp is now ready for papermaking.

Preparing Rags for Papermaking

Rags are used in making the longest lasting papers. For paper for wills or documents that must be good indefinitely, 100 per cent fine-quality new white rags are used. Some poor-quality rag paper may be made by using worn-out rags. Some papers contain 10 per cent to 90 per cent rags and the balance wood pulp.

Linen and cotton rags from worn-out clothing are gathered by ragpickers. Cuttings from shirt and underwear mills are collected. They are cleaned and sorted, all hooks, eyes, buttons removed. The rags are cut into pieces about 4 inches long and 2 inches wide. They are then boiled in a lime solution that removes all substances other than the cellulose fiber. The lime is washed out, and the rags are frayed and reduced to a pulp by steel knives attached to a large roller. The pulp is then bleached in *chlorine* for about a week to 10 days. The rag pulp is known now as *half stock* and is ready to be made into paper.

FROM PULP TO PAPER

Some paper mills buy the pulp already prepared. Other mills buy the logs and prepare the pulp in their own plant. At this point the pulp, however prepared, resembles a blotter.

The first step in the papermaking process is known as *beating*. This process is so important that most paper manufacturers claim that "Paper is made in the beaters." Here the cellulose fibers are flayed until they are separated from each other and reduced to the desired length. The amount of beating varies with the quality and type of paper desired.

If the paper is to have a smooth surface for writing or printing, sizing in the form of starch, glue, casein, clay, or other material is now added. Coloring may also be put in while the stock is in the *beaters*.

A further refining is given in a *Jordan* machine. The stock is then carefully cleansed and is now ready for the papermaking machine known as the *Fourdrinier,* a giant, block-long contrivance that takes in the watery pulp at one end and delivers the finished dry sheet at the other end, even cut to the desired width.

Not until the year 1801 was paper made by machine. Until that time each sheet was laboriously formed by hand from the prepared pulp. A screen was dipped into the watery pulp and, as the water drained out, the screen was shaken so that the fibers would mat together. The sheet of paper, so formed, was dried and removed. In 1799 a Frenchman conceived the idea of making a machine that would mechanically shake the water out and form the sheet. This idea was adopted and developed in England by two brothers named Fourdrinier, who patented the machine in 1807, thereby giving to the world the revolutionary improvement that not only speeded up papermaking, but also made available greater quantities of paper for printing newspapers, books, and magazines. Today the Fourdrinier machine is still the papermaking machine in use in most paper factories.

When the pulp flows onto this machine it is approximately 99½ per cent water and ½ of 1 per cent cellulose fiber. By suction and a shaking movement, some of the water content is drawn through a fine screen, thus reducing the moisture to about 80 per cent. The shaking movement also tends to make the ends of the fibers interlace and mat together. The faster the machine travels, the thinner will be the resulting sheet of paper; and likewise the closer the mesh of the screen, the finer the paper.

The wet sheet is then carried between felt wringers that gently press out from 10 to 15 per cent of the moisture. Next the sheet is carried through warm drying rolls that remove most of the remaining moisture. Ironing by large metal rollers known as *calenders* and slitting by rotating knives may also be done by this machine. The paper emerges from the machine in a huge roll ready for any one of many uses to which it may be put.

SPECIAL FINISHES ON PAPER

In order to sell paper goods enthusiastically, you will want to know how some of the unusual textures are achieved.

Watermarks

You have seen watermarked paper. Hold a sheet of bond paper with a watermark to the light. Observe how much thinner the paper is where the lettering appears. That occurs because the lettering is pressed on the paper while it is still wet. Small wire letters are raised on a wire roller known as the *dandy roll;* and as they press against the wet sheet, they separate the

The dandy roll impresses the watermark on the wet sheet of paper that has just been formed. *(Courtesy Eaton Paper Corp.)*

fibers, causing a thin impression. Sometimes these watermarks are in the form of a design, such as wood grain; rather than letters. Watermarks are generally used only on good quality paper.

Another design known as *laid* may be impressed into the paper by the dandy roll. A few heavy wires run vertically and many finer wires run horizontally and press against the paper, making a typical design. If this design is not apparent, the paper is said to be a *wove* paper. This book is printed on wove paper.

Embossing

Designs may be pressed or embossed on the paper to give it a linenlike crash or ripple finish. Sheets of paper are laid against heavy linen fabric and tremendous pressure in a hydraulic press is exerted to transfer the appearance of the texture of the fabric to the surface of the paper.

To achieve a leatherlike texture known as *vellum finish,* the paper is pressed against smooth sheets of cardboard.

Coating

Paper that has a high, glossy shine is known as *coated* paper. Materials such as clay, aluminum sulfate, slaked lime, and casein are used to coat the paper. The paper is then run through calenders that apply a high gloss.

Metal Finishes

These finishes are applied by gluing very thin sheets of the metal to the paper. Aluminum, which may or may not be colored, is the most popular metal for this purpose. Aluminum paper, called *foil,* is used for wrapping food and tobacco products, for various kitchen uses, and for decorative papers and wrappings.

Plastic Finishes

Many types of plastic are coated over paper to give it special qualities. Plastics may make the paper more attractive, may give it leatherlike textures, may improve its durability, may make it waterproof, and may make it suitable for use as coffee cups or hot-food plates. Vinyl resins, cellulosics, melamines, ethylenes, and silicones are among the plastics commonly used to coat paper.

Carbon Paper

This paper, invented in England in 1803, is made by coating one side of thin tissue paper with lampblack mixed with oil or wax.

Waxed and Grease-resistant Papers

A translucent paper that is grease resistant is known as *vegetable parchment*. This is made by passing the paper through a bath of sulfuric acid, then washing and drying it. This paper is used for wrapping foods and also for greeting cards.

Paper that is coated with *wax* is used for such things as bread wrappers and cartons for butter and milk.

Edges and Borders

Edges of paper may be made more attractive by various processes. The *deckle edge* is a rough or uneven edge, a characteristic of handmade sheets of paper. It is artificially put on some writing paper today by a sort of embossing machine. *Beveled* or *sloping* edges are placed on greeting and announcement cards by pressing or embossing. *Colored borders* are applied by fanning out the edges of the paper and stenciling the color on by hand or by airbrush.

PUTTING THIS MERCHANDISE KNOWLEDGE TO USE ❯❯❯❯❯❯❯❯❯❯

❯ DO YOU KNOW YOUR MERCHANDISE?

1. List various articles made of paper. What qualities make paper desirable for these items?
2. What basic raw materials are used for paper?
3. Explain what is meant by *mechanical* pulp? *chemical* pulp?
4. Trace briefly the steps in making paper.
5. What is a watermark? How is it applied? What is meant by *laid* paper?
6. How are the following papers finished: metal-coated paper, carbon paper, shiny paper, vegetable parchment, wax paper?
7. What is meant by a *deckle edge,* a *beveled edge?* How are colored borders applied to paper?

1. Collect samples of various types of paper. Mount these in a notebook, and write below each the various uses of the paper.
2. Make a list of all articles in your home and school made of paper.
3. Several people have suggested that clothes be made from paper. Write a short theme telling why you do or do not think paper will ever be used for some articles of clothing.

UNIT 51 THE STATIONERY DEPARTMENT

Jack Murphy and Jeffrey Black decided to apply for summer jobs at a large department store. Each sent a letter requesting an appointment for an interview. Only Jeffrey received a reply requesting him to come in the following day at 10 a.m. to see the employment manager. Jack thought it very unfair that he, too, did not receive an appointment. Both boys were the same age, had similar grades in schoolwork and had done odd jobs before. What Jack did not know was that the employment manager always judged an applicant first by the appearance of the letter sent to ask for an appointment. Jack's letter was written on a piece of his mother's social stationery. Since there were no lines to guide him, Jack's handwriting went slightly downhill. He enclosed the letter in an envelope which was too long and narrow for the folded paper.

Jeffrey's letter was quite different. He selected plain white single-sheet bond paper and a matching envelope. He borrowed a friend's typewriter which he could use, having had one term of typing in school. His finished letter looked neat and businesslike. It impressed the employment manager favorably enough to secure the interview.

In the business world many people are known by the letters they write. They can be judged only by their choice of words, the neatness of the letter, and by the quality of the paper they use. Because of this, the selection of writing paper is very important.

Friendly letters should reflect the writer's personality and are usually written on paper that is much less formal in appearance than the stationery selected for a job application letter.

It is also important that envelopes match the color and the quality of the letter paper.

SPECIFICATIONS FOR STATIONERY

Stationery comes in various sizes and shapes. Men usually prefer large single sheets for their stationery. Women usually prefer smaller single sheets or folded sheets that have four pages for writing. *Informals,* which are small note-sized single or folded sheets, are used for "thank you" notes and similar purposes. Commonly used sizes are:

Single	Folded
6⅛ × 8"	4¼ × 3"
6½ × 7"	3⅛ × 6"
7½ × 10⅛"	3 × 4"
8½ × 11" (Bond)	5½ × 8½"

Business stationery and formal stationery for personal use are usually white. Informal stationery may be any color to suit the personality of the writer.

Envelopes

Envelopes should match the stationery both in color and texture. The paper should also, when properly folded, fit neatly into the envelope. Lined envelopes are attractive for social stationery. When envelopes are very thin, linings protect the contents from being read through the envelope.

Since January, 1963, the United States Post Office Department has banned the use of envelopes less than 4¼ inches long and 3 inches wide. Mail of unusual shape, such as post cards in the shape of autos and animals, was also prohibited. These regulations were necessary in order to permit efficient use of mechanization in handling mail in the post offices throughout the country.

Envelopes were first made in 1841. Before that, letters were just rolled up or folded and sealed in the manner of some airmail stationery today.

Weight of Paper

Years ago heavy paper was regarded as a mark of quality. The lighter-weight papers, which save space and postage, became popular for airmail.

This machine folds and seals three sides of the envelopes automatically after they have been cut to shape by a steel die. The machine also places the adhesive glue on the top flap of the envelope. (Courtesy Eaton Paper Corp.)

Stationery is considered by many people the appropriate gift for many occasions. Boxed papers containing 24 sheets and 24 matching envelopes are available. Paper is also sold by the pound. Each pound generally contains 3 quires, or 72 sheets. Envelopes to match are purchased in packages of 25. Some manufacturers call the pound paper "open stock," since the same weights and colors are available year after year in these papers.

PERSONALIZING

People like to see their names, initials, addresses, or nicknames in print. Consequently, personalizing stationery, calling cards, invitations, announcements, and Christmas cards is an important part of the stationery business.

Engraving

The most expensive and finest method of imprinting paper is by means of *engraving*. The desired lettering is first engraved (scratched out of the metal by an artisan) on a copper plate. Because it is harder than copper, steel may be used if several thousand imprints are to be made, since it will give a sharper impression throughout the entire run. The ink is rubbed into the depression, then transferred to the paper leaving a slightly raised impression. The plate is the property of the customer and may be used repeatedly for other personalizing.

Imitation engraving (called thermography or embossing). Raised lettering is produced by printing with a special ink and then running the paper over heated rollers to set the ink. While this method lacks the character and fineness of engraving, it is suitable for less costly articles.

Printing

Printing is the least expensive method of personalizing merchandise. Raised letters, placed into position, rub against an inked roller; then the design is transferred to the paper leaving a flat, smooth finish similar to the printing in this book.

GREETING CARDS

Greeting cards for birthdays, anniversaries, and holidays have become a half-billion dollar industry. About five billion cards a year are sent in the United States alone. To staff this industry, many different types of workers are needed. Among these are designers who create the motifs; verse writers to compose the ditties printed on the cards; stylists to select the paper stock,

Silk inserts are being placed over soft cotton pads for Christmas cards. (Courtesy Rust Craft Publishers)

shapes, and sizes and, in addition, the inks to be used. Cards vary in price according to the uniqueness of the design, the quality of the paper used, and the kind and number of colors and the quality of ink used. Raised designs, embossed motifs, special engraving, and hand coloring increase the price of the cards considerably.

PENCILS

One of the most commonly used "tools" is the ordinary pencil. Americans use a billion and a half yearly—almost a pencil a month for every individual in the country.

Although men throughout the ages have devised ways and means of recording history, it was not until approximately the year 1400 that graphite, the material we have in modern pencils, was used. It was incorrectly referred to then as "lead" and this name has clung to the pencil. By 1560 the graphite was wound and held by string, tubes, or metal. About 1686 graphite was placed between two pieces of wood and the forerunner of our modern pencil was developed.

Today graphite is mixed with clay, shaped, cut, baked at a high temperature, and dipped in wax. It is then placed in a narrow groove cut into a thin section of cedar wood. Another grooved slat covered with glue is pressed against this to give the impression of a solid rod with the lead inserted into a drilled hole.

Pencils are then smoothed and painted. If desired, brass tips and rubber erasers are pinched onto one end of the pencil.

It takes approximately 125 factory operations to make an ordinary pencil. There are 17 degrees of hardness in pencils and 72 shades. Hardness in pencils depends on the proportion of clay to graphite. A soft and popularly used number-2 pencil has about two-thirds graphite and one-third clay, while harder pencils contain more clay. A number-9 hard lead pencil contains about one-third graphite and two-thirds clay.

A pencil point can withstand over a ton of pressure per square inch before the point breaks. Special pencils have been developed that write on glass, cloth, and plastics.

Mechanical Pencils

Mechanical pencils, first developed in 1921, are also available and may match fountain pens. The best quality mechanical pencils work backwards and forwards, not only drawing the inserted rod of lead (graphite, etc.) into the body of the pencil, but also extending the lead to any desired length for writing or drawing.

Some pencils are equipped with two or more lead holders for varying colored leads. These may be extended as desired.

FOUNTAIN PENS

An insurance salesman in the 1880's lost an important sale because the pen and ink with which he provided his client did not work smoothly at the moment the client had said "yes." Determined to overcome these "pen and ink" difficulties, Lewis Edson Waterman invented the automatic-feeding fountain pen.

W. A. Sheaffer, a jeweler of Fort Madison, Iowa, in the year 1908 invented the lever-filling mechanism which depressed a rubber sac with a metal bar. This is still a common mechanism for filling fountain pens.

Conventional Pens

Fountain pens consist of *pen points* or *nibs* which in better quality pens are made of 14-karat gold tipped with an alloy containing iridium, a very durable, rare, and expensive metal. On less expensive pens, steel is used. This, however, may stain, and it may corrode if used with inks containing acid. Steel nibs become scratchy and do not write as smoothly as do the gold alloy or iridium points. *Caps* which protect the nibs and *barrels* which hold the sac for the ink are usually made of colored plastic materials. The *grip* or *point* section which holds the pen to the barrel is generally made of hard rubber. The *inner sac* which holds the ink may be made of rubber or a transparent plastic substance. The *ink feed,* just under the pen point, is a small rod with cut channels for the ink, made of hard rubber or plastic.

Ordinary fountain pens are filled with ink by a metal *lever* which presses against the sac creating a vacuum, or by a metal *plunger* which creates a vacuum when pressed down and draws ink into the pen when released. The plunger type usually holds more ink than does the lever type.

When the customer purchases this type of fountain pen, the correct method of filling the pen with ink should be demonstrated. The nib or point should be completely immersed in the ink during this process. After filling the pen it should be carefully wiped before the cap is adjusted.

Advise the customer that air inside the sac sometimes expands and causes the pen to leak. To avoid this, the pen should be kept as full of ink as possible.

Rubber-sac pens should be flushed occasionally with clean water to prevent ink from causing the rubber sac to rot.

Cartridge-filled Fountain Pens

The competition of the ball-point pen described below forced manufacturers to develop another type of ink filler for fountain pens. This is a separate cartridge or holder already filled with ink, which may be easily inserted into the pen and avoids the need to fill it in the old-fashioned way.

Ball-point Pens

The *ball-point pen* with a pencil-like writing action, which was introduced through sensational sales and advertising campaigns during 1945–1947, represents almost 90 per cent of all fountain pens sold in America today. Approximately 800 million ball-point pens are manufactured annually.

The nib, having a round or ball-like point that rotates in a socket, differs in shape and writing quality from that of the regular pen. When writing, the ball rotates and transfers the ink to the paper. Because of its pencil-like action, carbon copies may successfully be made with it.

This pen is not filled with ordinary ink, but a special ink is provided in a cartridge to be inserted when needed. This cartridge, which may be purchased separately, consists of a hollow tube tapered at one end. Into this end is fitted a socket and a ball, which rotates during writing. The ink feeds into the socket and against the ball by gravity. The ball which determines the smoothness of the writing is made of stainless steel, jeweled sapphire, or it may be impregnated with diamond dust.

INK

Ancient Egyptians and Chinese living about 2500 B.C. developed colored writing fluids from various vegetable sources as well as from soot and charcoal mixed with gum. Today's ink is made from wood, aniline, iron, tannin, or carbon dissolved in water.

Wood from the logwood trees of Central America and the West Indies is chipped and steeped to give a purple-black fairly permanent ink that is popular for school use.

Aniline, a coal-tar substance which is oily and colorless, is used with other chemicals to produce all colors in inks. These inks will wash out of fabrics and will fade in sunlight.

A colorless solution containing an *iron salt* (ferrous sulfate) is mixed with *tannic acid*. The ink is temporarily dyed blue, but it turns black when exposed to the air. This is a permanent, waterproof ink known as *blue-black ink*.

Carbon in the form of sticks shipped from China is ground up and mixed with chemicals to make a black permanent ink, such as *India ink*.

Since the chemicals in these various types of inks for regular pens may react with chemicals in other inks, pens should not be filled with another type of ink until the sac has been thoroughly flushed with water. Otherwise the pen may clog.

Ink for ball-point pens is provided in cartridges which are replaced when the ink runs dry. These inks are more like printing inks since they use oils and resins, rather than water, to carry the color. Extensive research has resulted in inks that flow freely, write smoothly and evenly; and some of the inks are even fast to sunlight and water. The oily base, however, may penetrate the paper, making it possible to write on one side only. The ink in the ball-point pen is concentrated as these pens are expected to write many more words than ordinary pens without inserting new cartridges.

PUTTING THIS MERCHANDISE KNOWLEDGE TO USE ❯ ❯ ❯ ❯ ❯ ❯ ❯ ❯ ❯ ❯

❯ DO YOU KNOW YOUR MERCHANDISE?

1. Why is it important to choose business stationery carefully? Why is personalizing an important selling aid?
2. A customer wants business stationery. What color would you suggest?
3. What is the smallest size envelope that the U. S. Post Office will accept? Why?
4. Of what is the *lead* in pencils composed?
5. Who invented the fountain pen? What materials are used for pen points; caps and barrels; grip or point section; inner sac of fountain pens? What are the selling features of the ball-point pens?
6. How do ball-point pen inks differ from other inks?
7. Explain the action of ball-point pens.
8. Why are some greeting cards more costly than others?

❯ INTERESTING THINGS TO DO

1. Prepare a 2-minute sales talk on stationery. If possible, bring some stationery to class to illustrate your sales talk.
2. Repeat project 1, selling a pencil or a pen.
3. Write your name on a piece of paper with an ordinary pencil, a mechanical pencil, a regular fountain pen, and a ball-point. Analyze the differences in the ease of writing, the smoothness of appearance, the ease of reading. Look at the back of the paper to see if any of the writing penetrated. Rub your finger over the writing to see if any of the markings smear. Explain the results of this experiment.

ADDITIONAL MERCHANDISE TERMS ≫ ≫ ≫ ≫ ≫ ≫ ≫ ≫ ≫ ≫ ≫ ≫ ≫ ≫ ≫ ≫ ≫ ≫ ≫

Absorbent paper, a soft paper made to absorb water or other liquids, is unsized and loosely felted. It may be used for blotting paper, toweling, and facial tissues.

Abrasive papers are made rough by a coating of glue and abrasives (aluminum oxide, sand, garnet). May be sandpaper, emery paper, emery board.

Asbestos paper is made by adding a rock or mineral substance to the wood pulp, producing fireproof paper. Used for mats and for wrapping pipes.

Bond is a good quality paper for writing, typewriting, or printing, made from rag or bleached wood pulp. The paper has a hard smooth surface, good erasing, qualities, folds well, and is translucent.

Bristol board (name comes from Bristol, England, where it was first made), is laminated paper—glued together in layers. Carboard 0.006 of an inch thick or over.

Cellophane is the generic name for a viscose rayon solution which has been solidified in thin sheets or strips. These are waterproofed by a coating of lacquer.

Cigarette paper is unsized, strong tissue paper specially prepared from linen rags or flax or hemp. It is odorless, tasteless, and resists sticking to the lips.

Corrugated board is made of a fluted piece of cardboard sandwiched between two plain sheets; it acts as a cushion for the merchandise wrapped inside.

Currency paper is rag paper sized with animal glue—has silk or nylon threads running through it.

Crepe paper is made by crowding the wet sheet on the roller, causing creping. Used for wrapping, novelties, weaving, decorations, and costumes.

Film paper is a sheet of cellulose covered with gelatin and chemicals sensitive to light.

Glassine is a glossy, transparent paper made by extra beating of sulfate pulp. Fibers become almost gelatinous from this beating. Used in window envelopes, bags, and wrapping material.

Linen paper is made entirely of linen rags and is very expensive.

Linen-finished paper has the pattern of linen cloth embossed on the paper.

Onionskin is thin, translucent paper. So called because it resembles the skin of an onion when peeled. Made of rags or sulfate.

Papier-mâché is made of sheets of specially prepared paper moistened, molded, dried, and covered with linseed oil. It is used for stage decorations, ornaments, and masks.

Parchment is a paperlike substance, prepared from the skins of animals.

Parchment finish or *vegetable parchment paper* is made of wood pulp passed through a bath of sulfuric acid, washed, and dried. It is grease resistant. Used for wrapping foods, or for menus, or cards.

Quire is the term used to refer to the usual amount of paper in a box which consists of 24 sheets and 24 matching envelopes. This is known as a "quire box." When buying sheets of paper only, the term means 24 (or 25) sheets.

Safety paper is made by adding chemicals to paper, or by printing it with an all-over design which is sensitive to moisture or erasure. Used for bank checks, postal money orders, traveler's checks.

Stencil paper is tissuelike paper covered with paraffin, used to cut the impression for mimeographing.

Vellum is a leather used in ancient times as a writing material. Paper with this finish is rich, dull, and leatherlike.

Leather—
The Versatile Material

CHAPTER
19

UNIT 52 **WHAT YOU NEED TO KNOW ABOUT LEATHER**

Any young person hoping for a job in a store during the holiday seasons may have an opportunity to sell handbags, wallets, notebooks, brief cases, gloves, sport jackets, shoes, or luggage. Have you ever wondered or thought about the animals whose skins have been used for the merchandise; or the handling, workmanship, and transportation necessary to bring those items to the stores for sale? Have you ever bought leather or leatherlike articles? If so, you may have wondered what such terms as *top-grain cowhide, genuine Morocco, patent leather, glacé kid, simulated leather, box calf, pig-grained pig, capeskin,* and many others mean.

Whether you sell such products or buy them for your own use, knowing about leathers will prove interesting and helpful.

WHAT IS LEATHER?

The use of skins of animals for articles of clothing dates back to the time of primitive man. He slew the beast, ate the meat, and threw the remaining skin across his shoulders. He tore strips of the skin and bound his feet for protection against rocks, thistles, and thorns. Thus attired, he sallied forth, having unknowingly discovered one of our most important natural clothing materials.

After he wore the skin for a while, however, the odor became very disagreeable. If he continued to wear the skin, it slowly began to decay.

Many years later, although man knew nothing of chemistry, he discovered ways to treat skins so they would be useful but not perishable. Since he kept no records of his progress in preserving skins, we can only imagine how his

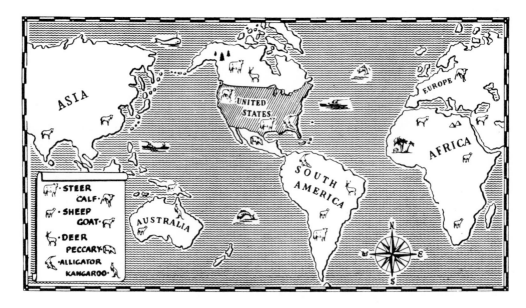

Sources of Leather. *(Courtesy Leather Industries of America)*

first discoveries were made. Perhaps he noticed that the oil from the animal's body when rubbed into the skin made it soft and durable. Maybe at another time he accidentally tossed a skin at the base of an oak tree. The skin later was covered by the falling oak bark, and then by rain and snow. In the spring, he saw the skin he had tossed away changed strangely. It had a different appearance and feel, and it had no disagreeable odor. It had been transformed into what we call *leather*. The oak-bark method, which may have been accidentally used by the cave man, was later developed by the ancient Hebrews.

MODERN METHODS OF LEATHER PRODUCTION

Today, leather is still made by rubbing oil into the skin or by soaking it in the acid made from oak bark. Other means of preserving skins have also been developed. These methods of preserving skins are known as *tanning*. The word *tanning* comes from the medieval Latin term *tannare* meaning *oak bark*.

Although some skins were valued for the attractive hair covering they had and were therefore worn as furs, other skins were more desirable with the hair removed. A few leather products, such as sheepskin for ear muffs and slipper linings, have the wool or hair covering left on the skin. Most leather, however, has the hair covering removed. Animals such as snakes, alligators, and lizards have no hair covering. After the tanning process, leather goes through finishing processes that give it varying textures and colors to make it more attractive for leather articles.

Leather is notable for many outstanding qualities. Examine your shoes, gloves, belt, wallet, or football. The long list of advantages or "selling points" you can name will include the *durability* of the leather, the *strength* of the article, the *comfort* due to leather's breathing quality, called *porosity,* its *softness,* its *elasticity* which aids leather articles to keep their shape yet conform to the movements of your hands or feet, and its *attractiveness.* For such a fine product, many kinds of leather are also fairly *inexpensive.*

THE GRAIN OF LEATHER

The markings that make leathers look different are known as the *grain* of the leather. In leathers from animals that grow hair or wool, the grain is caused by the hole left in the skin when the hair is removed. These holes, called hair-follicle openings, form patterns that make each animal's skin easy to identify. Notice the hole at the base of each hair on your wrist. That is the grain of your skin! If the hair of the animal is coarse, the hole will be larger and more noticeable. In ostrich leather, the hole is made by the removal of a quill, so it is about $\frac{1}{16}$ of an inch large! The hole left by the removal of the hair on a calfskin is so tiny it can hardly be seen except under magnification.

On animals such as alligators, snakes, and lizards that have no hair, the scale form becomes the grain. All kinds of leathers are valued for their natural grain markings.

When the grain side of the leather has not been altered in any way, the leather is known as *top grain,* which indicates the best quality of leather from that animal with all the natural beauty of the animal's skin markings intact.

The grain side of the leather is the right side. The other side, next to the flesh of the animal, is known as the *flesh* side. The grain side in addition to its attractive appearance is more durable, firmer, and smoother than the flesh side.

On the flesh side, neither holes nor scale markings will show. Only little fibers that make up leather are visible. By raising all these fibers to a uniform height, the leather worker produces *suede.*

HIDES, KIPS, SKINS

No doubt you have noticed that you say *cowhide* and *calfskin, horsehide* and *coltskin, goatskin* and *kidskin;* but have you ever wondered why?

In the leather trade, animals whose skins weigh 15 pounds or less when they are shipped to the tannery are referred to as *skins.* Calves, goats, sheep, deer, alligators are some of the animals so named. For the few animals whose skins weigh between 15 and 25 pounds there is a classification known as *kips.* This term is used mainly in referring to oversize calves, whose skins are called *kipskins.* The word *hide* is used to refer to large animals whose skins weigh over 25 pounds. Cows, oxen, buffalo, walrus, and horses all come under this classification.

Best Part of the Hide or Skin

The center back section of most animals produces the best leather. That is where the animal develops a tough, thick hide to protect himself from snow, wind, rain, and sun, and from his enemies. This section of leather in cowhide is known as the *bend,* and it gives the firmest, most durable, best quality sole leather for shoes. Toward the belly section, the leather becomes spongier, looser in texture and softer. Soles made from this section of the animal's hide will not wear so well, nor resist water so well as will "bend" leather soles. Some animals that crawl instead of walk, such as the alligator, lizard, and snake, develop fine-quality belly section leathers.

REASONS FOR THE INEXPENSIVE PRICE OF LEATHER

Leather is known as a by-product. That means it is obtained after the animals have been used for their milk, meat, or wool. Thus leather is lower in cost than it would be if the animals were raised just for their skins, as are some alligators.

The cost of leather is further reduced by the fact that leather has its own by-products. The hair scraped from the skin is used in plaster, hair felts, and rug pads. The flesh scraped from the skin is used as fertilizer, glue, and the best qualities, for gelatin.

LEATHER IMITATIONS

Imitations of leather are frequently made from plastic materials, such as nitrocellulose lacquer which is coated over fabric or paper, or from vinyl

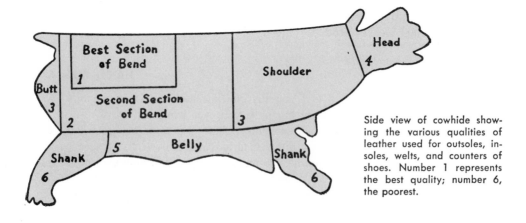

Side view of cowhide showing the various qualities of leather used for outsoles, insoles, welts, and counters of shoes. Number 1 represents the best quality; number 6, the poorest.

plastic which may be used alone or coated over fabric or paper. Although these materials may be made to look like leather and may be as durable in some cases as leather, they are not so good as leather for some uses. *Expanded vinyl* is one of the most leatherlike in appearance. Since most of them are not porous, they are seldom used in place of leather in shoes or gloves where porosity is important. *Corfam,* a DuPont material, however, does have some porosity. These imitations do not become richer and more attractive with use and care, however, as most top quality leather products do.

Imitations of leather are called *simulated leather, plastic calf, plastic kid, plastic patent,* and so forth. The Better Business Bureau asks retailers not to use the term "leatherette" for such imitations, as this word really means "little (or diminutive) leather."

PUTTING THIS MERCHANDISE KNOWLEDGE TO USE ❯❯❯❯❯❯❯❯❯❯

❯ DO YOU KNOW YOUR MERCHANDISE?

1. Why do skins of animals need to be preserved? What is this preservation called?
2. What important word do we obtain from the ancient word for oak bark?
3. What are the basic changes necessary to change a skin into leather?
4. What is meant by the "grain" of leather? Name some animals whose grain is formed by hair removal. Name some animals whose grain is formed by scales.
5. What is the right side of leather called? What is the inside of leather called?
6. How is suede made?
7. When do we use the words hide, kip, skin?
8. What does the word "bend" mean when referring to a cowhide?
9. What animals produce good quality leather from the belly section?
10. Why are leather articles relatively inexpensive?
11. What is simulated leather? How does it differ from leather?
12. Why should retailers not call imitation leather "leatherette"?

❯ INTERESTING THINGS TO DO

1. Make a list of all your wearing apparel that is made of or contains some leather.
2. Explain the reasons that leather is an ideal shoe material.
3. Make a list of words or phrases that describe leather, such as, "comfortable," "breathes" and so forth.

UNIT 53 FROM SKIN TO LEATHER

PREPARING SKINS FOR TANNING

Skins of animals come from the far corners of the world to American tanneries. To keep the skins from spoiling while en route, they are either salted or dried. When they reach the tannery, they must go through many processes before they are ready to be preserved or tanned.

Since only the *dermis* or *true skin* is tanned, the *epidermis* or *outer layer* of dead skin, plus all the natural liquids and oils in the skin, must be removed. All that is left of the dermis are the tiny short bundles of fibers, which will be converted into leather. These fibers are interlaced at various angles in groups or bundles. They give the characteristic strength to leather, and the spaces around them permit leather to breathe.

In order to remove everything from the skin but these fiber bundles, the skins must first be washed; then they are soaked in chemicals that loosen the hair or outer-scale layer. After scraping off hair or scales, adhering bits of flesh from the inside of the skin are scraped off with sharp knives. The skin, now denuded of all substances that are not to be part of the finished leather, is ready for the tanning operation. In this condition, the skin is creamy off-white in color.

TANNING

As you read before, the word *tan* comes from the Latin word meaning *oak bark*. Today, however, many other substances have been found that will preserve the skin and make it durable and useful. Tanning in modern tanneries is done by oil or vegetable substances that the ancients used, by mineral salts such as chrome and alum and, more recently, by formaldehyde, a chemical. Some tanneries have even used synthetic tanning materials made from coal tar.

Oil Tannage

Oil tannage is believed by many to have been the first type of tannage ever

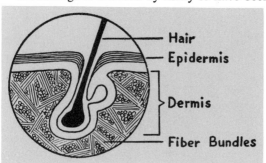

Enlarged view of cross section of animal's skin before being converted into leather.

discovered—older even than vegetable tannage. The American Indians rubbed oil into deerskin, then smoked the skin in a tepee over a fire. Thus was developed the characteristic *buckskin tan* with its gray color and smoky odor.

Today cod oil is mainly used for oil tannage. The solution is poured over the skins, then mechanical kickers knead the oil into the skin. This process is repeated until a chemical reaction takes place that changes the skin to leather. The excess oil is then removed, leaving a soft, yellow-colored skin. Chamois skins used for gloves and cleaning purposes are tanned by this method. Doeskin and buckskin may also be oil tanned. Place a piece of chamois leather in a glass of cold water. Notice the slimy, oily feel of the skin, yet no oil comes off the skin when it is used to polish windows or mirrors.

Vegetable Tannage

This is one of the oldest methods of tanning known. It is a method, as explained before, that was developed by the ancient Hebrews several thousand years ago and still in use today for much of our finest leather. Today, however, *tannic acid,* the substance that causes the chemical change that converts the skin into leather, is found in many types of trees, shrubs, and nuts. Even tea is a mild vegetable-tanning material.

The tanning solution is made by grinding the wood or other material used into a sawdust. Hot water is poured over it to extract the tannic acid. The prepared skins are then soaked in this solution for a period of two weeks to six months until they are converted into leather. The thicker the skins, the longer it takes for them to become leather.

When the skins come out of the tanning solution, they are tan in color. This helps you to identify vegetable tannage. If you look at the cut edge of a piece of leather, or if you see shoe soles that have not been dyed, you will see this familiar tan color that tells you vegetable tannage has been used.

This method of tanning makes a firm, durable, attractive leather. Vegetable-tanned leather is porous yet resistant to moisture. It is often spongeable or even, when properly dyed, washable.

Because of the long period of time required for the actual tanning, the vegetable method is, however, slightly more costly than other tannages. Any leather may be vegetable tanned. Shoe soles, heavy leathers for upholstery, belting leathers, alligator, lizard, and saddle leathers are typical of vegetable-tanned products.

Mineral Tannage

Alum Tanning. This was the tannage used by the ancient Egyptians for vellum and other materials used as writing surfaces. This ancient tannage has come down through the ages mainly for leathers to be used in gloves.

In this tannage, skins are tumbled around in an alum solution that changes them to leather in a few hours, but they must be laid away for seasoning for several weeks or even months before they are ready to be made into gloves or other leather articles.

Alum-tanned leather is soft and pliable to the touch and when it emerges from the tanning process is white in color. Both of these factors are desirable qualities for gloves. The main disadvantage of alum tanning, however, is the fact that it is not washable. Even rain spots may cause the gloves that have been alum tanned to become stiff and harsh. If you have ever tried to wash leather gloves that became stiff and shriveled, they were probably alum tanned. Alum-tanned articles must be carefully dry-cleaned. Because these leathers are ruined when soaked in water, other tannages are used for them today.

Chrome Tanning. This process of changing skins into leather was perfected in 1893. In this method, the skins are tumbled in a huge revolving drum containing the chrome liquid until every fiber is thoroughly saturated. When this method was first developed, tanners scoffed at the leather produced, for it was grayish-blue in color rather than the tan with which they were familiar. However, the use of the metal, chromium, in the form of a solution of chrome salts revolutionized leather production; instead of requiring from two weeks to six months to change skins to leather, as vegetable tanning does, chromium salts take only from five to eight hours. This, of course, reduces the cost of the finished leather. Today, two-thirds of our leather is chrome tanned.

If you examine the cut edge of a piece of leather, or the inside of a pair of dark-colored kid gloves, you may be able to see a pale bluish-gray color. This indicates that the leather has been chrome tanned.

Chrome-tanned leather is extremely durable—even slightly more durable than vegetable-tanned leather. It tends, however, to become somewhat slippery when wet and is not so moisture resistant as vegetable-tanned leather; for this reason it is not often used for shoe soles. This leather is generally washable; therefore, articles so labeled may be carefully sponged when soiled.

Chrome-tanned leather is considered ideal for shoe uppers, gloves, handbags, and many other articles.

Formaldehyde Tannage

The colorless gas, formaldehyde, is used in solution with water to preserve skins. The skins which are tanned in a few hours by formaldehyde are also very soft and supple and like alum-tanned skins are white in color. Formaldehyde-tanned leathers, however, may be washable, a fact that makes this tannage superior for glove leathers and children's shoe-upper leathers.

Combination Tanning

To combine the good qualities of two tannages, some leathers are tanned first by one tannage and then receive a light tannage by the second material. Some leathers are tanned by chrome and then vegetable substances. This is called *combination* or *retanning* and produces leather particularly desirable for heavy-duty work shoes, armed-services shoes, and farm shoes. When formaldehyde and alum are combined, good glove leather results. Chrome and oil also makes a desirable glove leather.

FINISHING SKINS AFTER TANNING

Customers would never stop to admire leather articles if leather were used as it emerges from the tanning operation. The skins at this stage are wrinkled, dull, and unattractive. Processes that make the skins pliable and beautiful are known as *finishing processes*.

The tanned skins are first straightened, then stretched, and then tacked on a board so they will dry properly.

Splitting

Skins too thick for certain articles have to be split. In 1809, Samuel Parker of Massachusetts patented a machine to split leather to any thickness. By means of this machine that looks like a washing-machine wringer equipped with sharp knives, skins may be split into two or sometimes three, four, or five layers. All these layers may subsequently be used to make leather articles.

Because the top layer that contains the natural grain is the strongest and the most attractive, it is the most desirable and the most costly. Like whole skin leathers, it is spoken of as *top grain*. It will wear for many years and merely become shiny and lustrous with age if properly cared for. All remaining layers from that skin are called *splits*. Tanners, however, in order to know which layer is referred to, have given each separate layer a different name: *top grain, deep buff, split, slab*. These lower layers may have artificial grains stamped on them, so it is not always possible to tell at a glance whether or not an article is made of top-grain leather. Split leather usually has a rougher, coarser appearance than top grain; it does not wear so well and sells for considerably less money. The splits may not be called "genuine leather." Top grain, however, may be so labeled and sold, since it represents a quality product.

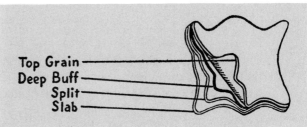

Split Leather. Heavy hides may be split into as many as four layers of leather. Only the top grain has the natural grain pattern. All the other splits may be sueded or may have artificial grains embossed. The splits may not be sold as "genuine leather."

Top Grain
Deep Buff
Split
Slab

Fat Liquoring

Just as a woman rubs creams into her skin to soften it and to keep it smooth and attractive looking, so finishers soften leather by the addition of animal or fish oils to replace the natural oils removed by the tanning processes. When you polish your shoes, you are really *fat liquoring* them. Leather that has sufficient oil rubbed into it stays mellow and supple; without oil, leather dries out and cracks.

Coloring

Today shoes, gloves, bags, and most other leather articles may be purchased in various attractive colors, an important beauty aid for leather. Dye that penetrates the skin deeply and that colors both sides is applied by *dip dyeing*. This is a costly process that uses a good deal of dye. Such leather articles keep their rich color well. *Brush dyeing* applies the dye on the surface only, leaving the original tannage color showing on the inside of the article. Gloves so dyed may become gray at the finger tips as the thin layer of dye is rubbed away. *Spraying* the dye on with air guns permits two-tone or shaded effects, which are often novel in appearance.

Metallic surfaces may be applied by affixing a thin sheet of the desired metal to the leather and then pressing it until it is firmly bonded to the surface. Gold leaf is used for gold finish, and thin sheets of aluminum impart a silver finish.

Glazing

When you examine leather articles, you will notice that the leather may have a shiny, smooth surface. By coating the grain side of the leather with a condensed milk and water solution, called *seasoning,* then placing the leather under a glass cylinder which strikes it and presses it with a great deal of force, a high shine is imparted to the leather. This finish is known as *glazing* and is popular for leathers used for accessories. The term *glacé* is used to describe this finish.

Boarding

To give the leather a dull, creased, and rather bumpy surface, a process known as *boarding* is applied. Notice the leather across the toe of your shoe where the creases show. As you bend your foot you are performing part of the boarding operation. The grain side of the leather is folded over and creased by a cork-covered wooden board that is attached to the workman's arm. This results in thousands of creases, which account for the bumpy appearance of *boarded calf, pin seal,* and *morocco* leather.

Boarded Leathers. Left to right: Morocco, calf, pin seal.

Napping

When a nap is raised on leather, it is usually done on the flesh side. A buffing wheel revolves against the fibers of the leather. The tiny fibers are raised by the abrasive action of the wheel, and the result is a soft, velvety surface on the flesh side known as *suede*.

Sometimes the nap is raised on the grain side of the leather. This makes a durable, coarser appearing nap that does not mat down and become shiny as easily as does flesh-side napping. Doeskin-finished lambskin and *mocha* leathers are napped on the grain side.

Embossing

If you pass a handbag counter, you may see an alligator handbag for $35 and near it a bag that looks similar for only $10. The second bag, however, is probably not real alligator, but some other leather made to look like it. The artificial grain is put on the leather by a process known as *embossing*. The desired grain is first etched on a large steel plate, then placed against the dampened leather in a hydraulic press where tremendous pressure and heat stamp the grain permanently on the leather.

Alligator, lizard, snake grains, and pin-seal grains are popular designs. By embossing, inexpensive leathers are made to look like more expensive leathers—split leathers are made to look like top-grain leathers; and marks and scars are covered by this process. Such leathers must be correctly labeled as *alligator-grain calfskin* or *lizard-grain sheepskin* or *pressed calf*.

Patent Finish

Shiny patent-leather shoes and handbags have been popular for many years as accessories in springtime. This shiny finish may be put on any smooth-surfaced leather, whether cowhide, calfskin, kidskin, or coltskin.

Patent leather is made by putting a lacquer coating on leather, much as fingernail polish is coated on a woman's nails. Since the lacquer coatings are put on the right side of the leather, the grain is visible. The more distinct the grain surface is, the better quality the finished leather is likely to be. Since this nonporous coating does not expand at the same rate as the leather, it may eventually crack. New urethane-coated leathers are superior to other patent leathers.

Patent leather has limited use because it lacks the porosity and elasticity that are important features of other leathers. Imitations of this leather are made today in vinyl plastic substances and in a new material, *Pattina*.

CARE OF LEATHER

A customer purchased a patent-leather handbag in a department store. Just as she was leaving the department, she asked the salesgirl how she should care for the bag. The clerk said, "Well, I don't know. We don't have any polish for patent leather, but why don't you do what most people do—just use Vaseline on it."

The customer followed the salesclerk's suggestion but noticed that her handbag looked gray, collected dust very easily, and was not so attractive as it should be. The next time she was in the store, she complained to the head of the department. He said, "I regret that you were given incorrect information. Patent leather should never have grease applied to it. The best way to care for patent is to use a damp cloth and a little hand soap or put a few drops of vinegar in the water. Wipe off finger marks and other dirt, then wipe with a damp cloth wrung out in clean water and polish with a dry cloth." The customer was very pleased with the appearance of the handbag after she followed these instructions.

Patent leather must be treated carefully, for the surface often cracks rather easily. Taking patent-leather articles from a warm house to freezing temperatures outdoors may cause the leather to crack, as will creasing the leather. Salespeople should never guarantee patent leather against cracking.

Other smooth-surfaced leathers require "oiling" from time to time. The life of shoes may be greatly prolonged by applying polish to them often.

Some glacé or shiny leathers blister slightly when rain spotted. A good rubbing with wax before using the article will reduce this blistering effect.

Suede articles should be brushed with a rubber sponge or a bristle brush (preferably not wire) in a circular movement to remove dust. When suede becomes shiny, a fine emery board may be used gently to brush up the nap. There are also colored dressings, which restore color to suede articles that have become grayed.

Leather articles marked "washable" may be washed carefully in a mild suds of lukewarm water. After rinsing, the articles so washed should be carefully rolled in a towel to press out excess water, then placed away from sunlight and heat to dry slowly.

As the leather dries it feels rather stiff. By pulling it gently between the fingers, the soft, supple feel is restored. This is called *finger pressing*.

Leather articles, such as jackets and gloves, not marked washable, and leather-trimmed apparel should be dry-cleaned by cleaners who specialize in handling leather.

Proper handling and care of leather articles can prolong their life and beauty. It is important to find out how best to care for a leather article when purchasing it.

PUTTING THIS MERCHANDISE KNOWLEDGE TO USE ❯❯❯❯❯❯❯❯❯❯

❯ DO YOU KNOW YOUR MERCHANDISE?

1. What part of the skin remains to be tanned after pretanning is complete?
2. What are the advantages of oil tannage? of vegetable tannage? of chrome tannage? of formaldehyde tannage?
3. Why is alum tannage little used today?
4. Why do tanners use combination tannages?
5. Explain the differences between top-grain leather and split leather.
6. Why can't a person always recognize a top-grain leather from a split leather?
7. What is fat liquoring and why is it used on leather? Why do you fat liquor leather products?
8. Which method of dyeing leather applies the most dye and therefore gives the longest lasting color to leather?
9. If a tanner wants a novelty or two-tone color on leather, what dye method will he use?
10. Explain the difference between a patent finish and a glazed (or glacé) finish on leather. What advice would you give a customer about care of each?

❯ INTERESTING THINGS TO DO

1. Look through the daily newspaper and make a list of all terms referring to leather that you can find in the advertisements. What proportion of the terms are finishes?
2. Bring a leather article to class and explain its advantages to the students.
3. Collect samples of various kinds of leather which may be obtained from worn-out leather articles or from scraps from shoe-repair shops or tanneries. Paste them neatly in your notebook and label them. Examine the cut edges. If possible, tell what kind of tannage was used on each leather. Tell what finishing processes were used on each leather.
4. Write three selling sentences about leather.

UNIT 54 THE EVERYDAY LEATHERS

The general word "leather" covers all animals used for this product. Because each group of leather from different animals varies in appearance, use, and wearing quality, customers like to know what kind of leather they are buying. Thus, the salesperson needs to know all the various terms used for each group of leathers. The most common terms are included here. Since all leathers from one family of animals will have similar qualities, the leathers have been listed in family groups.

COWHIDES AND CALFSKINS

A majority of all leathers used in the United States comes from the cow and the calf. These leathers are the by-products of the large meat-packing industries of North and South America. The skin from the young calf a few days to a few weeks old produces a smooth-surfaced, fine-grained, firm leather that makes up beautifully into shoe-upper leather, handbags, luggage, and many other articles. Calfskin may also have a patent or a suede finish. Calf suede is the most common type used for shoes. The grain of calfskin may be made more attractive by *boarding,* and it is then called *boarded calf.* Coarser calf suede is known by the trade name *Bucko* or as *reversed calf.*

Saddle leather, popular for handbags and shoes, is vegetable-tanned calfskin or cowhide. Calf with an embossed alligator grain, known as *alligator-grain calf* or *alligator-embossed calf,* is also popular. Calfskin is durable and does not scuff easily. It stretches only moderately, cleans well, and takes a lustrous polish.

As the calf grows older, the grain of the skin becomes more distinct; and the skin itself becomes thicker, heavier, and larger. These large hides, known as cowhides, make durable, pliable leathers that are used largely for shoe-sole and durable shoe-upper leather. Cowhide is also used for belts, luggage, briefcases, upholstery leather, and footballs.

Rawhide is the name for cowhide that is stuffed with oils but not actually tanned. It is particularly tough and thus is used for drumheads and for luggage. It must be kept dry, however, as it can mildew or rot if not properly cared for.

Scotch grain is a bumpy, embossed leather used for men's heavy-duty sport and walking shoes.

Side leather is a general term used to refer to all cowhides. Since the hide is large, it is cut in half, and each half is a "side." Thus, *elk side* means cowhide finished to look like elk.

GOATSKINS AND KIDSKINS

The second most important group of leathers used in the United States is imported. Kids and goats are raised in Europe, Asia, Africa, and South America primarily for their milk and meat. Their skins are by-products mainly of the milk industry of those countries. The young kid has a fine, thin, smooth skin with tiny holes on the grain side that look under a magnifying glass like little pinholes arranged in tiny groups. As the animal grows older, these grain marks become coarser and more noticeable. The finer the grain of the kidskin, the better the quality.

Kidskin is unusually strong; and being porous, it is excellent for gloves and shoes, permitting the hands and feet to breathe. It is noted as being the most healthful leather for shoe uppers. These leathers, because of their fineness and softness, require careful handling in contact with harsh objects to prevent scratching or peeling. Being a fine, soft leather, it is easily wrinkled. Textured or bumpy finishes keep the wrinkles from showing. Another attribute of kidskin, which makes it desirable for gloves, is that it takes a high glaze. Glove leathers with such a shiny finish are called *glacé kid* or *smooth kid*. Kidskin can also be buffed on the flesh side to produce a fine quality suede for shoes.

Kidskin is useful for shoe uppers and linings, gloves, handbags, bookcovers, wallets, and belts. *Gold kid* is produced by pounding thin sheets of real gold into the grain side of the skin until the gold becomes part of the leather. Since the gold is very thin, it requires careful handling and should only be used for special-occasion wear. *Silver kid* is made similarly by applying nontarnishing aluminum sheets; *bronze kid* is produced by coating with a metallic powder.

Morocco leather refers to vegetable-tanned goatskin that has been creased (boarded) to give it a fine, pebbly surface. This leather is used for wallets and bookbindings. Many other leathers imitate genuine morocco leather.

Crushed kid is creased in many different directions to impart a bumpy, uneven texture. It is ideal for casual shoes as it does not show wrinkles or scratches.

KANGAROO

This animal is new to the leather group, for its skin has been successfully tanned only since the latter part of the nineteenth century. Kangaroo skins, which are chiefly imported from Australia, resemble kidskins. The leather is even stronger than kid, and it does not scuff as easily as kidskin. It may have either a sueded or a glazed finish. It is used for men's street and athletic shoes where comfort and durability are desired.

While kangaroo is not a commonly used leather, it is tanned by the same tanners who handle kidskin and is used for the same kinds of shoes. Its limited quantity makes it slightly more expensive than kidskin.

SHEEP AND LAMB

The third most used leather comes from both domestic and imported sheep

 Alligator-embossed calf

Sheepskin >

and lambs. Sheepskin leather is generally inexpensive. It is less durable than many other leathers and tends to stretch easily. It has many important uses, however, as linings, jackets, handbags, gloves, house slippers, sweatbands for hats, and inexpensive baseballs, mitts, and footballs. It is sueded successfully for jackets and gloves. Fine qualities are buffed on the grain side to imitate doeskin and are known as *doeskin-finished lambskins*. American tanners are specializing in a washable tannage for this leather. These leathers are sometimes tanned with some of the wool left on and are then known as *sheepskin* or *shearling leather* and used as linings in men's and women's jackets. By use of a chemical that straightens the hair, a fine velvety-textured wool pile may result. This is called *electrified sheepskin*.

Parchment is made from specially tanned and prepared sheepskin. The famous *chamois skins* are made from the undersplit or "flesher" of the sheepskin which has been oil tanned. *Chamois* was formerly leather from a goat-like antelope, called a *chamoisgoat*.

Mocha leather, used especially for men's fine quality gloves, comes from a hair sheep. This leather is buffed on the grain side and is usually dyed gray, black, or brown.

Imported capeskin is also from a type of hair sheep from South Africa near Capetown where the name originated. This leather is more durable than ordinary sheepskin. It has a glazed finish and is used mainly for gloves and handbags. Imitations from domestic sheep are sometimes called *capeskin*. They are also advertised merely as *glacé leather*.

PUTTING THIS MERCHANDISE KNOWLEDGE TO USE ❯❯❯❯❯❯❯❯❯❯

❯ DO YOU KNOW YOUR MERCHANDISE?

1. Why is cowhide our most used leather?
2. Define reversed calf, saddle leather, alligator-grain calf, rawhide, scotch grain, side leather.
3. What are some outstanding advantages of kidskin?
4. What finishes keep wrinkles from showing in kidskin?
5. Define glacé kid, kid suede, gold kid, morocco leather, crushed kid.
6. What are the unique features about kangaroo leather?

7. Why is sheepskin not used as a leather for shoe uppers and soles?
8. Define shearling leather, doeskin-finished lambskin, parchment, mocha, imported capeskin, glacé leather.

❯ INTERESTING THINGS TO DO

1. Make a study of the cattle industry in Texas or in Argentina and write a short theme telling the interesting things you learned.
2. Write selling sentences for five leather terms used in this unit.

UNIT 55 THE UNUSUAL LEATHERS

Although the cowhide, goatskin, and sheepskin leathers make up the bulk of those used in leather shoes, gloves, handbags, luggage, and apparel, other leathers add variety, varying desirable qualities and fashion importance. These leathers are not so readily available, nor do they come from animals raised primarily for meat, milk, or wool bearing; consequently they are usually somewhat more costly. You will recognize many of these leathers even though they are not so frequently used.

BUFFALO HIDE

These hides, imported from Asia and Eastern Europe, are coarser than cowhides and are nearly always so badly scarred when they reach the tannery that they must be embossed with an artificial grain. They are used for shoe uppers, heavy work gloves, and durable handbags and luggage.

HORSEHIDE

Most young men are familiar with horsehide, for the best baseball covers and the finest baseball mitts are made from this leather. Horsehide is not so available for use in America as it is in parts of Europe, however, because we do not eat horsemeat as people in those countries do.

Cordovan, a term originating in the city of Cordova, Spain, is now applied to leather from the hind quarters of the horse known as the *shell.* The leather is nonporous, durable, and resistant to scuffing. It is particularly valuable for the tips of small boys' and girls' shoes, because it is so resistant to scuffing. It is also a heavy-duty leather for boys' and men's shoes.

Coltskin, when available, makes fine leather articles.

DEER, ELK, AND ANTELOPE SKINS

Skins from these animals were tanned by the Indians long before Columbus discovered America. Today, when they are available, deerskin and elkskin make porous, fine-textured leathers, which have a good deal of stretch. They are suitable for shoe uppers, jackets, and gloves. Calfskin and cowhide are often tanned to resemble elk. Since deer, elk, and antelope live in the forest, their skins are usually scarred; and the grain side must often be napped when used for leather.

Antelope, a suede-finished, fine-textured leather, is rarely available commercially. Instead, lambskins are buffed on the grain side and finished to resemble antelope. They are then used for trimmings, handbags, and gloves, and are known generally as *doeskin-finished lambskin* or *antelope-finished lambskin*. Because the manufacturers are proud of the real deerskins, they label those leathers as *genuine deerskin, genuine elkskin,* and so forth.

PIGSKIN

The peccary, a wild hog from Mexico and South America, and the carpincho, which in reality is not a pig at all but a member of the rodent (rat) family, are the main sources of *pigskin*. The peccary produces the better quality leather, and the carpincho produces a heavier leather. Both of these animals have bristles which when removed leave visible holes in groups of three's. These holes, which go right through the skin, act as both beauty marks for the grain side of the skin and as ventilators. The leather itself is quite durable, but it tends to stretch. It is particularly desirable for driving gloves, luggage, small leather articles, and is also used occasionally for shoe uppers. Most real pigskin articles will have a few scars on the surface. Of course, if there are too many scars, the leather will be embossed and sold as "pig-grained pig." Domestic pigskin is used only for heavy work gloves.

SEAL

This animal's skin makes a smooth, soft leather which, when boarded, has a beautiful pebbly grain. The finest boarded skins from young seals are known as *pin seal* and are used for handbags and small leather items.

WALRUS

This leather may be several inches thick. A thick hide may be used for the polishing wheels in buffing gold and silver jewelry. Split walrus hide, which is almost always embossed, is used for luggage.

SHARKSKIN

This leather is noted for its scuff resistance. It has an interesting diamond-

Left to right: Snake, alligator-lizard, lizard.

Left to right: Genuine alligator, Brazilian tannage; genuine alligator, domestic tannage; shark. *(Courtesy Tanner's Council of America)*

Left to right: Walrus, buffalo, ostrich.

shaped grain. Tips for children's shoes are sometimes reinforced with shark-skin.

ALLIGATOR

It takes about fifteen years for an alligator to mature and become large enough to be commercially valuable. Part of the high cost of alligator leather results from the great danger and risk to the men who actually kill the animals. The alligator skins are noted for the beauty of their markings, the almost square markings from the belly section being the most valuable part. Mexican alligator, which has a tiny pore mark in the center top of each scale, is the finest quality. Less attractive alligator comes from Argentina. The skill necessary in the matching of the scales that vary from tiny oval and round marks to large squares and rectangles also makes these leather articles expensive.

Because the horny back section of the skin cannot be used for shoes and is desirable only for decoration on some handbags and luggage, the alligator skin is usually slit down the back and the valuable belly portion left intact.

Some manufacturers make pieced alligator accessories by sewing scraps of alligator leather together to form artistic designs. These finished articles are, of course, much less expensive than whole-skin accessories are.

Alligator, because it is so popular, has been imitated by embossed calfskin and sheepskin. It is possible to identify real alligator, however, either by its rich appearance, or by catching some of the scales with the fingernail. Embossed scales cannot be lifted. While this test does not always work, it is sometimes helpful in identifying real alligator.

LIZARD

Lizards are found in jungles throughout the world. The leather from these animals is prized for the unique appearance of the skin. The markings of lizard resemble small grains of uncooked rice. Some species of lizard have tiny rectangular scales that resemble miniature alligator markings. These are known as *alligator lizards* or by the trade name *Lizagator*. The skins make long-wearing leathers.

SNAKE

Snakes have very thin skins with loose scales. Most snakeskins have to be backed with fabric because they are so thin. Any kind of snake may be used for leather products: diamond back, cobra, watersnake, and so forth. They are used for shoe uppers, for handbags, and for decorative accessories.

OSTRICH

The ostrich is the only bird whose skin is frequently used for leather articles. The ostrich plumes are pulled from the skin leaving "rosettes," spiral-shaped markings with a hole near the edge of the marking. The beauty of the skin depends on these markings. Ostrich skins are quite expensive because of their rarity. This leather is used mainly for small items such as key cases, billfolds, men's shaving kits, and bookcovers. Calfskin and sheepskin are sometimes embossed to imitate the rosette of ostrich. The rosettes, however, when embossed, look quite regular and cannot be lifted, as can real rosettes, with the edge of the fingernail.

PUTTING THIS MERCHANDISE KNOWLEDGE TO USE ❯ ❯ ❯ ❯ ❯ ❯ ❯ ❯ ❯ ❯

❯ DO YOU KNOW YOUR MERCHANDISE?

1. Why is horsehide not so popular as cowhide in the United States?
2. What is the difference between genuine deerskin and doeskin-finished lambskin?
3. Explain why pigskin usually has small scars on the finished skins.
4. Define peccary, carpincho, cordovan, pin seal.
5. How can alligator articles be made inexpensively?
6. What part of the alligator's skin yields the most attractive leather?

7. What is one method of identifying alligator from leathers embossed to resemble it?
8. What is the only bird commonly used for leather articles? How would you identify that leather?

> INTERESTING THINGS TO DO

1. Make a study of the methods of catching alligators, lizards, or snakes and write a short theme explaining where and how the animals are caught.
2. Make a chart for the leather articles you own. In the first column list the article, in the second column on the same line list the length of time you have had the article. In the third column list the price of the article. In the fourth column write your comments about the wear, comfort, appearance, or other qualities as selling points of that article.

ADDITIONAL MERCHANDISE TERMS ❯❯❯❯❯❯❯❯❯❯❯❯❯❯❯❯❯❯❯❯❯

Aniline dye is a transparent dye that can only be used on the best qualities of leather. Every mark and scar shows through this dye, but it also reveals the natural grain and texture of the leather. Aniline-dyed products darken with age and may waterspot if not thoroughly waxed.

Boroso is the name for a tough outer layer of sharkskin with a beadlike grain sometimes used in novelty leather items. It is extremely durable.

Corrected grain means that scratches or slight damages in the leather, which mar its appearance, have been removed. To accomplish this, a gentle buffing is given the entire grain side of the skin to remove a thin top layer. The skin is then coated with seasoning and coloring materials. The finished leather is useful for inexpensive shoes and accessories. It may not be advertised as "genuine leather."

Elk-finished cowhide is cowhide tanned and finished to resemble elk or buckskin. Sometimes called *elk side* or *smoked elk*. These, however, are misleading terms.

French kid formerly denoted a fine quality kidskin from France, which was used in gloves and shoes. Today the term is loosely used to apply to good quality kidskins.

Galuchat, like boroso, refers to the tough outer layer of sharkskin. The beadlike grain on galuchat is somewhat larger than that of boroso. It is used for small clutch bags and other novelty items and may be dyed in attractive colors.

Genuine leather is a term properly used for any whole-grain or top-grain leather.

Machine buff is the split of leather remaining after a thin layer of the top grain is removed. It is used in upholstered articles.

Parchment is sheepskin that has been alum-tanned and specially finished so that the surface is smooth. Parchment was once used for scrolls. Today paper is used successfully to imitate real parchment for documents, diplomas, etc. Real parchment is still used for some documents and scrolls, for lamp shades, and for drumheads.

Pigment dye is an opaque dye used on most leathers. It helps to cover minor scars, and it hides to some extent the natural markings on the leather. It does not darken with age except from soil, and it usually does not waterspot.

Retanned cowhide is heavy leather for boots and work shoes that is given a combination of chrome and vegetable tannage and then stuffed with grease to make it resistant to moisture and barnyard acids.

Skiver is the thin top-grain layer of sheepskin that is used mainly for linings, sweatbands for men's hats, and small leather items.

Vellum is calfskin prepared for use in the same way as parchment.

Vici kid is a trade name for a chrome-tanned, glazed kidskin.

Shoes for Men, Women, and Children

CHAPTER 20

UNIT 56   WHAT YOU NEED TO KNOW ABOUT FEET AND SHOE FITTING

Do you know that together with the increased height of the average American has come an increased shoe size? Many young girls have larger feet than their mothers had when they were young; and, in a similar manner, young men often have larger feet than their fathers. Today's young person is more sensible about proper fit and comfort than many young people were a few decades ago. Comfortable shoes affect our health, our appearance, our disposition, and the length of time we can remain on our feet. Properly fitted shoes, therefore, are important to everyone.

The shoe salesman needs to sell more than just a pair of shoes. He sells the customer a special service by selecting the shoe that will best fit her foot as well as her needs and her pocketbook. He should do his utmost to satisfy the desires of the customer as to color and style, but he should stress throughout the transaction the importance of the correct fit. Sometimes a customer doesn't realize when she merely steps into a shoe in the store that it is too short or too narrow. It is the salesman who can give her expert advice about the fit of the shoe.

A knowledge of the construction of the shoe enables the shoe salesman to speak with authority about the unseen values in the shoe. Inexpensive shoes cannot possibly embody all features of more expensive shoes, but they may serve a person's purpose just as well. The salesman should be prepared to point out these differences to the interested customer.

In the shoe department, he will find that his first problem will be to learn to locate the stock. Some shoe departments arrange the stock according to color, some according to size, and some according to style of shoe. He will need to learn the code letters which some manufacturers use for marking the size of the shoe. Today, however, most sizes are plainly marked: 5½ A, 7 C, and so on.

An interest in the customer's problems in caring for the shoe will also be an aid in selling of the shoes.

The shoe salesman must always remember that he is selling more than just the shoes—he is selling comfort and enjoyment in the use of the shoes, and these are the factors that determine his selling ability.

FOOT STRUCTURE AND SHOE FITTING

Customers may start their requests for a new pair of shoes with a complaint: "My last pair of shoes pinched," or "These shoes burned my feet," or "I have calluses on the bottom of my feet."

Most of these ills are caused by incorrectly fitted shoes. If the shoe is too long, too short, too narrow, or just shaped incorrectly, it may be the cause of one of these discomforts. Since every person's foot differs in some manner from every other person's foot, and since even a pair of feet may vary in size, you can see what a difficult job the shoe salesman faces.

Every normal foot has 26 bones. Fourteen are toe bones; five, instep bones; and seven, heel bones. These bones are all necessary to permit flexibility in the use of the feet; otherwise we would walk like ducks. Not only are these bones useful for walking, but they hold our body weight and must absorb sudden shocks when we run or jump. If these bones are crowded in the shoe, normal movement is restricted.

In order to perform all these tasks, the bones form arches that have been likened to bridges. The arches are suspended, yet they hold great weight and permit elasticity and spring, making it possible for us to move with ease and grace.

In addition to the bones and arches of the feet, there are muscles, tendons, and ligaments that permit proper foot movements; blood vessels that carry nourishment to the feet; and nerves that inform the brain when the foot is strained or shoes are incorrectly fitted.

Feet differ in size, shape, amount of flesh, and height of arches. Most people's feet are normal at birth. If a normal foot is correctly fitted to shoes

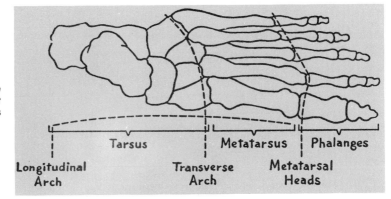

Skeleton Structure of a Human Foot Showing Bones and Arches.

Tarsus   Metatarsus   Phalanges

Longitudinal Arch   Transverse Arch   Metatarsal Heads

throughout life, the person will have little or no foot discomfort. Incorrectly fitted shoes, however, may ruin feet. Bunions, calluses, blisters, and corns may be caused by poorly fitted shoes.

CARE OF THE FEET

A suit or gloves that are too small may be uncomfortable but they will not cause pain. Incorrectly fitted shoes, however, not only cause temporary pain, but may also deform the feet permanently. Painful feet often cause a person to feel fatigued, and they can spoil an otherwise enjoyable day or evening. When a young girl spends an evening in a new pair of dancing slippers, you may notice that she slips her feet out of her shoes when she sits down to give her feet a momentary rest.

The first item of importance, therefore, in caring for feet is to select shoes and hose that are sufficiently large and comfortable.

Cleanliness is also important for comfort and health of the feet. Perspiration is irritating. Circulation in the feet is generally poorer than in any other part of the body; therefore, feet should be bathed and massaged daily.

Shoes and stockings should be changed daily if possible. Toenails protect toes, so they should not be cut too short. If corns, calluses, or bunions are developing on the feet, they are danger signals that your shoes are not properly fitted. Exercises, alternate hot and cold plunges, massaging, and resting the feet are helpful in keeping them normal. If the person is suffering from foot ailments, a doctor should be consulted.

For women, the height of the heel on the shoe is important to foot health. Heels over two inches in height throw the body off balance. Extra weight rests on the ball of the foot, and calluses may result, Constant wearing of high heels causes the back leg muscles to shorten. Consequently, when an older person changes to low heels, she usually feels pains in the back of her legs.

Shoes that are too tight or that have been outgrown should be discarded. This may not seem an economic measure at the time, but it will eventually save money by dispensing with future foot treatments for ailing feet.

SIZE RANGES OF SHOES

Shoe sizes are computed on a scale with two size ranges. The first size range is used for infants and children and runs from 0, which is approximately 4 inches in length, to 13½. The second size range begins at 1 and goes up to 15. This range is used for older boys and girls and adults. Each half size is approximately $\frac{1}{6}$ of an inch in length along the sole. Size 5 therefore is $\frac{1}{6}$ of an inch longer than size 4½.

Sizes in widths run from quadruple A to quintuple E. There is no exact number of inches that determines a size in width. The width of the shoe is entirely dependent on its relationship to the length of the shoe. The entire

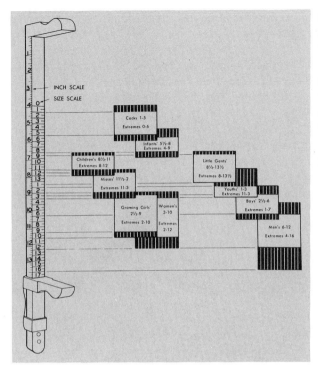

circumference of the foot at the ball portion amounts to about $\frac{1}{4}$ of an inch between each width. Size AAA, therefore, is about $\frac{1}{4}$ of an inch narrower than size AA, but across the sole it appears to be only about $\frac{1}{12}$ to $\frac{1}{16}$ of an inch narrower.

Classification of Shoe Sizes. *(Courtesy United Shoe Machinery Corp.)*

SHOE FITTING

The next time you purchase a pair of shoes notice the procedure used to take measurements of your feet. Some salesmen look inside your old shoe and use that as a gauge for the size to show you. Other salesmen ask you to step on their size indicators to see what size your foot measures. Formerly X ray machines were used to show how the bone structure of the foot conformed to the shape of the shoes, until many states restricted use of such machines that could be harmful to the feet if they were overexposed to the rays or exposed too frequently.

With an ordinary measuring stick, the shoe salesman can do a thorough size analysis by:

1. Measuring both feet. One foot (usually the left) may be larger than the other. The larger foot should be fitted unless different size shoes can be ordered to fit each foot.

2. Measuring feet in standing as well as sitting position. Some feet elongate, others widen when standing; and properly fitted shoes should allow for this spread.

3. Measuring heel to ball in addition to heel to toe. Some people have longer toes than others. Since the ball of the foot is the widest part, it should be fitted to the widest part of the shoe. Heel-to-toe measurement is not sufficient to detect this characteristic.

4. Measuring width of the foot in both a sitting and standing position.

After measuring the customer's feet, the salesman should check the shoe he has selected to be sure that:

1. The ball of the foot fits into the widest part of the sole of the shoe.
2. The shoe is at least ½ inch longer than the end of the big toe. Children should be fitted ¾" to 1" longer than the foot measures.
3. The heel of the shoe fits snugly and does not permit the person's heel to slip up and down.
4. Open-toe shoes are fitted shorter, because toes show at the opening of the shoe and movement of the toes is not restricted. Conversely, extremely pointed toes should extend 1 to 1½ inches from the end of the big toe to assure proper fit.
5. The shoe feels comfortable on the foot. Shoes that fit properly need little or no "breaking in."
6. The customer has actually tried the shoe on and is not buying just by size.

It is possible to determine if the shoe is the same general shape as the foot by tracing an outline of the foot with a stocking or sock on and making a tracing of the bottom of the shoe directly over the first outline.

PUTTING THIS MERCHANDISE KNOWLEDGE TO USE ❯❯❯❯❯❯❯❯❯❯❯

❯ DO YOU KNOW YOUR MERCHANDISE?

1. Why is it important to purchase shoes that fit our feet properly?
2. How many bones does the normal foot have? Why are all of these bones necessary?
3. What function do the muscles of the foot perform? the blood vessels? the nerves? the arches?
4. What ailments of the feet may be caused by incorrectly fitted shoes?
5. Why should shoes be changed daily?
6. Why should feet be measured in both a sitting and a standing position?

❯ INTERESTING THINGS TO DO

1. Draw an outline of your foot on a blank sheet of paper in your stocking or sock. Compare the outline to the bottom of your shoe. Which appears to be larger? Did you learn anything about the fit of your shoes from this experiment?
2. Plan a sales demonstration with another member of the class. Show the correct method of measuring the customer's feet and trying on the shoes. Advise the customer on the proper care of the feet.
3. Analyze five shoe advertisements. What size and fit information did they give?

UNIT 57 PARTS OF SHOES, MATERIALS USED, AND LABELING GUIDES

Before customers can buy shoes, or before salespeople can find the shoes that will fit customers' feet correctly, a great deal of work must be done by designers and manufacturers to make sure that the shoes will conform to the thousands of types and sizes of feet for which they are made. The fact that shoes are a fashion item further complicates this problem since customers seek changes not only in color and material but also in shape to follow a new and different fashion trend.

Shoes are scientifically built over a last. The *last* is a wooden form in the shape of a foot modified to adapt to current style characteristics. The last has been carefully made according to exact measurements. Since feet that measure the same length and width vary considerably however in shape, lasts of many different shapes may bear the same size markings. Perhaps you have had the experience of trying on a shoe marked with your size, yet the shoe may not have fitted you at all. Thus, many different shapes of shoes are needed for people whose feet measure the same length and width.

The shape of the wooden last is determined by the size and shape of the foot, by the type of shoe to be constructed (street shoe, dress shoe, sport shoe, etc.); by the shape of the toe (open toe, pointed toe, rounded toe, square toe, etc.); and by the height of the heel to be placed on the shoe.

PARTS OF THE SHOE

If you listen to the shoe salesmen in a shoe department you may hear a number of strange words. One says, "That vamp is too short." Another mentions the "open shank," and still a third talks of the "counter" that needs

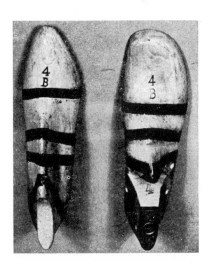

Lasts that are the same size may be shaped differently. The shoes built over the second last will fit a different type of foot from those shaped over the first last.

softening. To the shoeman all these are familiar terms that refer to parts of the shoe.

The parts of the shoe are divided into two groups: the upper and the sole.

The Upper—Outside

The upper includes all parts of the shoe above the sole and heel. Uppers are made from leather, plastic, or fabric. Outside sections of the upper are:

1. *Vamp*—the front part of the shoe from the toe to the instep.

2. *Tip*—a separate piece of material covering the toe section of the vamp. It may be used on men's, boys', and girls' oxford type shoes.

3. *Quarter*—the section of the shoe from the instep to the center back of the heel.

4. *Saddle*—a separate piece of material covering the instep section of some sport oxfords.

5. *Tongue*—the reinforcement behind the lacings that protects the foot. The tongue may be part of the vamp or a separate stitched-on piece.

The Upper—Inside

Inside sections of the shoe that are not visible or that form the lining of the shoe are:

1. *Toe box*—the stiff reinforcement used under the top of some shoes to protect the toes and to help the shoe retain its shape. Toe boxes are made from leather, plastic, or in some inexpensive shoes, stiffened paper. The

(Courtesy United Shoe Machinery Corp.)

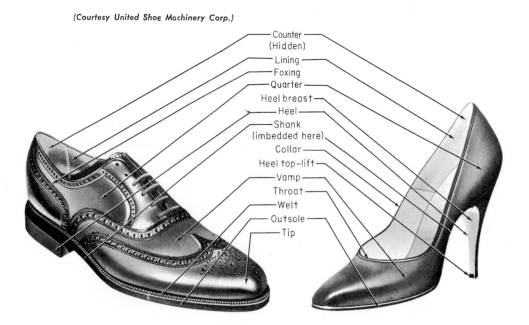

Italian influence that emphasized a softer appearance in shoes has virtually eliminated the toe box in men's and women's dressy shoes.

2. *Counter*—the stiff reinforcement at the heel under the quarter of the shoe. The counter preserves the shape of the shoe and aids in making the shoe fit snugly at the heel. The counter is made from leather in better shoes, from plastic or stiffened fabric in medium quality shoes, and from stiffened paper in inexpensive shoes. Some soft-back shoes have eliminated the counter.

3. *Linings*—cloth, plastic, or leather inside layers that aid in absorbing perspiration and that cover the joinings and seams and make the insides of the shoes more comfortable and attractive. The best linings are made of kidskin, sheepskin, or good quality cotton drill. Inexpensive linings are split leather, plastic made to look like leather, or heavily sized cotton fabric.

4. *Doubler*—cotton-felt interlining between the outer material and inside lining of the upper part of the shoe. It makes the shoe look richer, and adds to comfort by acting as an insulating material.

The Sole

The sole of the shoe is made of one or more layers of leather, plastic, or rubber, depending on the quality and type of shoe and its construction. Parts of the sole are:

1. *Outsole*—the outside sole on the bottom of the shoe. In the best quality shoes, this is usually made of top-grain leather so that it will be durable, flexible, water-resistant, not slippery when wet, yet porous enough to permit the foot to breathe. Since vegetable-tanned cowhide leathers that are cut from the "bend" incorporate all these qualities, they are most desirable for soles. Chrome-tanned soles are usually given a "tread" to keep them from becoming slippery when wet. Other products that resemble leather, such as Neolite or Searosole, make long-wearing shoe bottoms, but they lack the porosity of leather soles. Outsoles may also be made from crepe rubber or plain rubber. Crepe rubber provides a soft, comfortable, flexible sole. Ridged rubber soles vary in thickness and depth of the ridges. The ridges add flexibility to the movement of the feet and may reduce fatigue. The newest soles for inexpensive shoes are made from a nonporous form of vinyl and are long wearing but not resoleable.

The thickness of the leather sole is measured by irons. Each *iron* is equal to $\frac{1}{48}$ of an inch in thickness. Men's shoes usually have soles 9 to 12 irons thick; women's, usually 2 to 6 irons.

2. *Insole*—an innersole that is under the foot inside the shoe. This innersole acts as a foundation for the shoe and also adds comfort and durability. Good quality insoles are made of leather. Less expensive insoles are made of plastic materials, and in inexpensive shoes a specially prepared cardboard (fiberboard) may be used.

3. *Filler*—the space between the insole and the outsole, which is filled with cork, felt, rubber, polyurethane, or leather. This adds to comfort, makes the

sole of the shoe more water-resistant, and eliminates squeaks. Foam rubber or polyurethane foam impart buoyancy that is often featured in advertising the shoes.

4. *Shank*—wood, leather, or tempered steel bridge between the heel and ball of the shoe that gives added support to the arch of the foot and helps keep the shape of the shoe.

5. *Welt*—a narrow strip of leather approximately ⅛ to ½ of an inch in width, used on oxford-type or heavy-duty shoes to hold the sole to the upper part of the shoe. The welt is sometimes decorative in effect. It may be seen around the upper edge of the sole on men's shoes. If the welt is shaped so that it rests against the upper leather of the shoe along the seam that joins the upper and sole, it aids in making the shoe water-resistant.

6. *Sock lining*—cloth, plastic, or leather linings, sole shaped to provide a smooth inside surface for the sole of the foot to fit against.

7. *Heels*—various sized and shaped supports under the heel portion of the foot. Heels are made from wood, leather, leatherboard (waste leather ground up and bonded with a special glue), plastic, or wood reinforced with metal. Wooden or plastic heels may be covered with the material used to make the shoe upper, or they may be sprayed with an enamel paint that matches the color of the shoe upper material. This enamel may chip rather easily.

8. *Heel lifts*—metal, nylon, leather, or rubber protectors that are attached to the base of the heel. These are usually replaceable when worn.

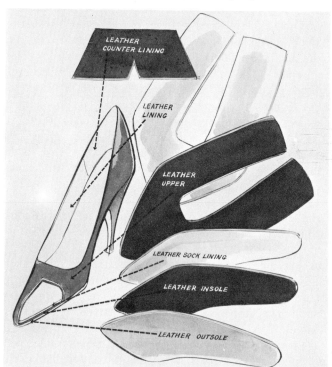

WHAT'S IN A SHOE? According to the Federal Trade Commission, the illustrated parts of a shoe should be labeled if they imitate leather. (Courtesy Leather Industries of America)

Leather continues to be used for uppers, linings, soles, and heels by manufacturers of better quality street, sport, dress, and casual shoes. Manufacturers of medium quality and economy shoes also use leather for some parts of the shoe such as the vamp, quarter, and outsole. For purposes of fashion, the leather may have a smooth, textured, patent, metallic, or suede finish; and it comes in a wide array of colors.

The use of leather for shoes began with prehistoric man who wrapped his feet in leather to protect them. Leather even today is considered to be the finest basic shoe material. Many United States foot specialists, according to the American Foot Care Institute, believe that leather provides the healthiest foot-covering material and that conditions such as athlete's foot, chafing, and irritation are less likely to occur in leather shoes.

However, the increasing use of nonleather substances in shoes for over a decade expanded extensively during the early 1960's. Leather substitutes appeared not only in sneakers and dress shoes, but also in shoes for street wear, school, sports, and casual wear. The popular sneaker is made of cotton canvas, duck, and corduroy; beach sandals, of linen, cotton crash, cretonne, and webbing. An expanded vinyl (vinyl filled with tiny air bubbles that makes it feel and look leatherlike), tough, with little or no porosity, made its appearance in children's shoes. Plastics that look like patent leather or that resemble suede have been increasingly accepted as shoe-upper materials. For example, in 1962, under the trade name, Pattina, a plastic material by Du Pont resembling patent leather but not cracking, peeling, or chipping, was introduced for women's and misses' street and dress shoes. Other nonleather substances used for shoes included wool and cotton gabardine, silk, rayon, lamé, nylon, vinyl, and other synthetics, cotton, linen, and sisal (a straw). Evening slippers may be made of rayon brocade, satin, metal cloth, faille, moiré, or taffeta. *Corfam,* a DuPont plastic introduced in 1963, is the first leather imitation to have breathing characteristics.

These new materials have become popular because they are available, easy to use because of their uniformity, less expensive than good quality leather yet often equal in durability, and easier to care for. Their low-cost advantages often offset the slightly greater comfort the customer may have experienced in all-leather shoes.

Federal Trade Commission Guide for Shoe-content Labeling and Advertising

With the widespread use of leather substitutes for various parts of shoes and slippers came the need for proper labeling of the materials so that customers would know what was actually used. Through accurate labeling, the consumer can be informed about the shoe materials, and any misrepresentation due to the appearance of the shoe can be avoided. Labels that accomplish this must be securely attached so that they remain in place until the products are bought by the ultimate user. The following rules that apply to labeling and advertising were adopted on October 2, 1962, and became effective in January, 1963.

1. The word "leather" may be used in labeling and advertising shoes and slippers only when the products (except for heels, inside stiffenings, and ornamentation) are entirely composed of top-grain leather. This means that split leather and ground or shredded leather may not use the unqualified term "leather." Also, coined names or trade names such as "Duraleather," or "Barkhyde" that suggest leather may not be used unless the product is actually top-grain leather.

2. Split leather, which simulates top-grain leather, must be clearly labeled as "split."

3. If shoes or slippers are made of an embossed, dyed, or other type of processed leather that simulates the appearance of a different kind of leather, the label must disclose the kind of leather of which they are actually made. For example, "Simulated alligator made of split cowhide."

4. If shoes or slippers are composed either wholly or partly of ground or shredded leather that appears to be leather, the label must clearly identify the parts as: "Upper material made from shredded leather."

5. If the shoes or slippers appear to be made from leather but are made from nonleather material, they must be labeled and advertised in such manner that the customer will know they are not leather. For example: "vinyl linings" or "outersole and linings made from imitation leather."

6. If the shoes contain visible parts of leather, but the innersoles concealed from view are made from nonleather materials, the label must clearly inform the customer of this fact.

7. If shoes or slippers pictured for advertising appear to be made of leather but are made from split leather or some imitation leather, the true composition of the material must be stated.

PUTTING THIS MERCHANDISE KNOWLEDGE TO USE ❯❯❯❯❯❯❯❯❯❯

❯ DO YOU KNOW YOUR MERCHANDISE?

1. What is a last? How is a last used in the making of shoes?
2. Explain the following terms: vamp, quarter, toe box, counter, iron thickness, welt. How does knowing these terms help a shoe salesman?
3. Explain how fashion might affect the actual fit of a pair of shoes.
4. Is leather becoming more or less generally used for shoes?
5. In what quality shoes are you likely to find top-grain leather?
6. What advantages do some of the new materials used in shoes possess?
7. How do the new Federal Trade Commission rules on shoes and slippers help the consumer?
8. How should the following pairs of shoes be labeled? (a) top-grain leather shoes with vinyl counters and toe boxes, (b) split-leather uppers, vinyl innersoles, and enameled wooden heels, (c) calfskin leather shoes embossed to look like lizard.

❯ INTERESTING THINGS TO DO

1. Take a worn-out shoe or slipper, cut it in half and label the parts.
2. Analyze three advertisements for shoes. What statements were made about the materials used in the shoes? Did the shoes appear to be leather? Do you think the labeling met the F. T. C. requirements?
3. Give a demonstration on the parts of the shoe for your class.

UNIT 58 CONSTRUCTION OF SHOES

PRESENT-DAY METHODS

The making of shoes was entirely a handcraft at first. Development of machinery during the Industrial Revolution was responsible for the great advancement in shoe manufacture and prepared the way for the present-day mass-production, assembly-line methods. Even these highly mechanized methods are, however, giving way to newer developments begun in the 1960's. Shoes today may require as many as 200 to 300 operations, or some all-plastic shoes may be made with as few as 1 or 2 operations. For the shoes that take many operations, skilled workmen stand at their benches or machines and repeat one operation over and over again with precision and accuracy. In such shoe factories, it takes from a few days to a week or more for one pair of shoes to pass through all necessary steps. In the manufacture of the best quality shoes, the shoe may stay on the last from two to three weeks.

For such complicated processes, the shoes first have to be designed; then patterns for each part of the shoe are cut to scale and prepared for use. When manufacturing expensive shoes, each slight variation in the shape or size of the last means that a new pattern must be cut for that particular size. In less expensive shoe manufacture, one pattern may serve for two or three sizes by "pulling" the leather to fit the last.

Shoe uppers, soles, and linings are then cut by hand or machine from the patterns, and the various parts of the shoe uppers are stitched together on sewing machines. The completed uppers then go to the section of the factory where the "lasting" operation takes place.

The wooden last first has the insole tacked on it. The completed upper is then pulled snugly over this wooden form and attached to the insole. Counters and toe boxes are inserted in their correct positions. Filler is pasted on the bottom of the insole, and the outsole is then attached to the shoe.

Methods of Attaching Outsoles

Outsoles are attached either to a welt or directly to the insole. There are many methods for making the outsole adhere permanently to the upper part of the shoe. The construction at this point also determines to a large extent the comfort and durability of the shoe. Some of the more important methods of attaching outsoles are by stitching, cementing, pegging or nailing or a combination of any of these; by vulcanizing, molding, or injection molding.

Stitching. The *stitchdown* is the simplest stitching method. This is used on inexpensive children's shoes such as "barefoot sandals." The upper is turned out and a machine stitches the upper to the outsole.

Steps in Making a Shoe. Top row, left: The upper parts of the shoe are stamped out. Vamps have been cut out, and the operator is stamping out matching quarters. **Right:** Vamps, quarters, and linings are stitched together. **Center, left:** Completely sewed uppers are pulled over the last by an ingenious machine that grips and tugs the leather into place and there tacks it until permanent stitching or cementing takes place. **Right:** Soles are attached by stitching or cementing and are then rolled to conform to the shape of the last bottom. **Bottom row, left:** Heels are tacked to sole bottoms by special machines. *(Courtesy Melville Shoe Corp.)*

TURNED METHOD. The *turned* method of construction is one of the most expensive ways of making shoes. It is a little-used method for making high-grade women's and children's shoes. This construction uses only one sole—and the shoe gets its name from the fact that it is made inside out. The upper is stitched to the sole by hand or by machine and when that has been completed, the dampened shoe is turned right side out and the heel is attached. Only the sock lining covers the seam where the upper and sole were joined. Because only one sole is used, this shoe is extremely flexible and light in weight.

THE GOODYEAR WELT. This is generally considered the best construction for men's, women's, and children's oxfords. This shoe requires no sock lining as there are no stitches or seams visible on the inside of the shoe. In this construction there are neither tacks nor stitches on the insole bottom to press against the wearer's feet. The welt is attached to a channel, cut in the bottom of the insole, by a thread which is stitched with a curved needle. The vacant space between the insole and outsole is filled with cork, and the outsole is stitched to the welt around the outside of the shoe. This shoe is easily repaired, is flexible and comfortable, and has durability and strength.

THE TRUE MOCCASIN. The Indians when discovered in America had developed a sacklike shoe known as a *moccasin*. The principles of construction of this shoe have been adapted to present-day sport shoes for men and women and to house slippers. The upper, instead of covering just the top of the foot, begins on the side of the foot and goes *under* the foot in place of the insole. The outsole is then stitched directly to the upper material. Hand stitching attaches the parts of the upper together on the top of the shoe in the form of a "U."

THE CALIFORNIA SLIP LAST. This shoe, which was developed during 1942–43, has an accurately cut upper. A fabric insole, which is made in several layers, is then stitched to the upper and a platform covering before the shoe is placed on the last. The platform is then cemented in position, shank, heel, and outsole added, and the play shoe or dress shoe is completed in a fraction of the time needed for the ordinary shoemaking methods. This speedily made shoe, constructed by a combination of stitching and cementing, has become one of the most popular for inexpensive women's and girls' casual wear.

Cementing. The cementing method of joining outsoles to shoes is a newer method than stitching. With the development of rubber and plastic cements, which are waterproof, this type of construction has become practical. Cement is used in the place of stitching, staples, or tacks.

SINGLE-SOLE CEMENTED. Extremely lightweight women's shoes may be made by cutting an outsole in half and using the upper part as the insole while lasting the shoe. The other half of the outsole is cemented on after the shoe has been pulled over the last. Cement is also used frequently for resoling turned, stitchdown, and cement-type shoes.

Pegging or Nailing. The first shoes to be made by mechanized means were made by pegging or nailing. Today, however, this method is little used except for work shoes, ski boots, and other heavy-type shoes. The upper is attached to the insole by tacks which hit against the steel bottom of a specially prepared last and thus are turned over so they do not press against the foot of the wearer. One or two outsoles are then attached to the insole by wooden pegs, nails, or screws. The construction is not flexible, but very durable.

Vulcanizing. This is a method of joining rubber soles with canvas uppers, as in tennis shoes and sneakers. The various parts of the shoe, the canvas upper, rubber mudguard, and the rubber sole, are placed over a metal last, then put into an oven and baked under pressure. This vulcanizes (cures and hardens) the rubber and joins the various parts permanently.

Molding. This is a recently developed method of making fabric or leather uppers with rubber soles for street and casual-wear shoes. Synthetic rubber is often used for this type of shoe sole. The parts of the shoe are first cemented together, the shoe is placed over a metal form, and the rubber sole is attached by hydraulic pressure and heat, which vulcanizes the rubber and affixes the sole permanently. If a waterproof finish is applied to the leather, these shoes are "weatherproof." Such shoes, however, are difficult to resole.

INJECTION MOLDING. Vinyl shoe soles may be attached by injection molding. In this process, the softened vinyl material is forced under pressure against the shoe in a mold, and the heel and sole are shaped from the vinyl and cooled and hardened in one operation. Shoes so constructed cannot be resoled, but these soles are tough and usually wear for several months. These soles are black in color and have a tread embossed on them.

In 1961, for the first time, entire shoes were made by forcing vinyl into a mold to shape the upper and outsole all in one operation. Only the shoelaces had to be attached separately. Such shoes sell for a low price; however, because they are made from a solid plastic, they encase the foot without any air unless holes are cut into the uppers. Sandals so formed were sold in some low-price shoe chain stores in 1962. In 1963, some department stores featured these as all-purpose sandals.

Joining Heels and Finishing the Shoes

Separate heels may be attached to the back part of the shoe by pegs, nails, screws, or glue. Top lifts of leather or rubber are then nailed to the heels.

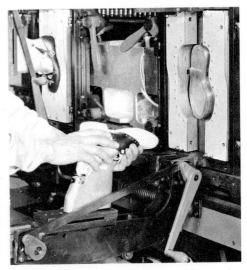

Injection Molding Process. Left: Upper part of shoe is inserted into the sole-forming mold. **Right:** The finished shoe with its sole affixed is removed from the form. *(Courtesy United Shoe Machinery Corp.)*

After the shoe has been completely assembled, it is removed from the last, sock linings where needed are put in, all edges are trimmed, the shoe is cleaned or polished, inspected, wrapped carefully in tissue paper, and placed in appropriately labeled shoe boxes. The shoes are now ready for delivery to the stores—and to customers desirous of comfort, style, and durability.

PUTTING THIS MERCHANDISE KNOWLEDGE TO USE ❯❯❯❯❯❯❯❯❯❯

❯ DO YOU KNOW YOUR MERCHANDISE?

1. Is any other article of clothing as complicated to construct as shoes made in a traditional way? Give reasons for your answer.
2. What construction would most likely be used on the following shoes? Men's street and dress-wear oxfords, children's barefoot sandals, women's inexpensive summer casual shoes, women's lightweight, expensive dress shoes, heavy-duty boots, and sneakers.
3. What does vulcanization accomplish?
4. What are the advantages of the vinyl injection-molded shoe soles? What is the main disadvantage?
5. By what method are shoes made in just one or two operations? How does this affect the price of the shoes?

❯ INTERESTING THINGS TO DO

1. Write a 2-page manual for new salespeople explaining how to sell a Goodyear welt oxford for a young boy.
2. Prepare a sales talk about the importance of good construction in a pair of shoes to be worn by a person who stands on his feet all day.
3. Analyze five shoe advertisements. What construction terms (if any) did you find?

UNIT 59   SHOE AND HEEL TYPES AND SHOE CARE

TYPES OF SHOES

When a new salesman enters the shoe department to sell shoes, he is especially perplexed by the variety of shoe types. He is familiar with the oxford, because he wears one, but he often dreads approaching the first woman customer for fear she will want some queer-sounding shoe about which he knows nothing.

Styles of shoes throughout the ages have varied. Toes have been narrow at one period, broad at another, have turned up to protect the toe or have been cut out to reveal the toe. Shoes have had high tops or have been cut low. Jewels and embroidery have adorned shoes in various ages, or the shoes have been severely plain. Heels have become stiltlike or pencil thin; and thickness of soles has also varied widely.

Most shoes, however, may be classified into five basic types: sandals, pumps, step-ins, oxfords, and high-top shoes or boots. There are also subdivisions of each of these that salespeople learn as they sell shoes. In addition to shoes, boots, house slippers, rubbers, and galoshes may also be carried in the shoe department.

Shoes

Sandal.   The *sandal* was originally just a slab of leather held to the foot by means of straps. Sandals now vary in shape—some covering the foot, some revealing the foot, but all make use of straps in some form to hold the shoe on the foot. Familiar types of sandals are the *T strap, Mary Jane* (for children), *open toe, open shank,* and *open quarter.*

Pump.   The *pump* is the most popular style for women's and girls' street and dress shoes. It is low cut but is not held to the foot by means of any straps. The *opera* pump is a classic, plain-type pump. Pattern pumps have fancy cut-out sections, bows, buckles, or other trim. The *D'orsay* pump is low cut on the sides. The *sling pump* has an open back.

Step-in.   The *step-in* is as high around the ankle as an oxford, but it has no laces. For ease in slipping this shoe on, it is either made with an elasticized upper, or it has elastic gores that expand when needed. This type of shoe is used for men's and women's dress and street shoes.

Oxford.   The *oxford* is a shoe cut below the ankle that is held on the foot by means of laces in the center of the instep or at the side of the shoe. The oxford supports the foot well. Oxfords are popular for children, men, and women. Women's and girls' oxfords may have any height heel. Saddle oxfords for boys and girls have low heels, and the section of the shoe across the instep has a contrasting color material.

High-top Shoes. These shoes, which lace above the ankle, or which have some other type of closure, are used today for workmen's shoes, for people who wish extra support around the ankle when walking, for some athletic shoes, and for lined footwear for winter comfort for people of all ages.

Boots

Boots may be any heavy type of high-top shoe used for sports or work purposes. There are ski boots, riding boots, hiking boots, fishing boots. These are carried often in the sporting goods sections of stores. Dressy boots with medium and high heels came into vogue for women in the 1960's. *Chukka boots* and *pacs* are also popular for street and heavy-duty wear respectively.

Slippers

These are one of the most important Christmas items for men, women, and children. Customers usually ask for "low-cut slippers" that resemble pumps, or "high-cut slippers" that resemble ankle-high boots. Some commonly known types of slippers are mules, Everetts, opera slippers, scuffs.

Sheepskin leather, various fabrics, and plastics are used for most slipper uppers. Either stiff or soft soles made from leather, plastic, or rubber may be used. Some slippers fold for ease of packing and carrying.

Rubbers and Galoshes

For rainy seasons, rubbers are necessary to keep shoes and feet dry and in good condition. Galoshes protect the shoes and feet during the snowy winter season. Leather and fabric shoes that are properly protected from rain and snow wear much better, because constant soaking of shoes dries out the oils, making the leather stiff and uncomfortable, or soaks through fabric so that it wears out more quickly.

All rubber, all vinyl, or fabric uppers with rubber soles are used for rubbers and galoshes. Some have fancy trim, such as fur, and some are lined with cotton fleece or synthetic pile fabrics for warmth.

Boots and rubbers require special heel-reinforced sections for pencil-slim metal-tipped heels that poke holes into them otherwise.

TYPES OF HEELS ON SHOES

Heels on shoes are generally classified as *flat, medium, high,* and *novelty.*

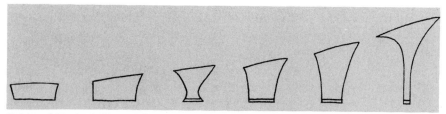

Types of Heels. Left to right: Spring, military, Baby Louis, Cuban, high Cuban, breasted high.

There are, however, some well-known types of heels that are often referred to in advertisements and by people purchasing shoes as the *Cuban, military,* and *spring* heels.

Covered heels for women's shoes also may be made either plain or breasted. A *breasted* heel has an extension that fits under the arch of the shoe to give it a more graceful line. Since these are more expensive to attach than plain heels, they are more frequently used on good quality shoes.

Heel heights are measured in eighths of inches. A heel that is $1\frac{3}{4}$ inches high would be referred to as a $1\frac{4}{8}$ths heel. Heel heights range approximately from $\frac{2}{8}$ths to $2\frac{8}{8}$ths.

Although men do not wear heels of varying heights, a construction known as an *elevator* may be used to give them additional height. This is a special construction with a cork addition inside the shoe that builds the heel section in height between an inch and two inches. The back of the quarter is raised slightly, and when the man's foot is in the shoe, he gives outwardly the appearance of wearing just an ordinary oxford, but in reality he is standing one to two inches taller because of this inner wedgelike construction inside his shoes.

Platforms that form part of the sole on women's shoes achieve the same feature of added height. Heels on these shoes must be made taller to accommodate the higher sole. These are rarely used, however, except when they are in fashion.

CARE OF SHOES

After purchasing a pair of gabardine shoes, a customer asked for a cleaner for the shoes. The salesman said he did not know whether such a cleaner was carried in the department, but he would ask the buyer. It took several minutes before he could locate the buyer. During that time the customer picked up a bottle of shoe cleaner that was displayed on a nearby counter. She read on the label the words "Especially made for use on gabardine shoes." When the flustered clerk finally returned, the customer was able to tell him about the cleaner he should have been prepared to sell.

The proper care of shoes can lengthen their life as well as aid in keeping them properly shaped for utmost comfort and support. If possible, shoes should be changed daily to permit them to regain their shape and to allow time for perspiration to evaporate completely between wearings. Thus, it is wise to suggest that the customer purchase two pairs of shoes to wear on alternate days.

When shoes are not being worn, they may be kept on shoe trees. These make the shoes hold their shape better. For the care of leather shoes, see page 370.

Run-over heels not only make shoes unattractive, but also give incorrect support of the feet. Heel lifts should, therefore, be repaired promptly when they wear down.

PUTTING THIS MERCHANDISE KNOWLEDGE TO USE ❯❯❯❯❯❯❯❯❯❯

❯ DO YOU KNOW YOUR MERCHANDISE?

1. What are the basic differences between pumps and sandals? step-ins and oxfords?
2. What kind of shoe would you recommend for the following occasions and outfits: (*a*) dressy afternoon-tea outfit for a young girl, (*b*) man's business suit, (*c*) young boy's casual school outfit, (*d*) farmer's work clothes, and (*e*) little girl's afternoon birthday party? Give reasons for your answers.
3. What item carried in most shoe departments makes a thoughtful gift? Why aren't shoes given as gifts commonly?
4. How are heel heights measured? How would you express the heights of the following heels: ¼ inch high? 1 inch high? 2 inches high? 1½ inches high?
5. Give suggestions for the care of the following kinds of shoes: smooth calf, patent leather, gabardine, silver kid, suede.
6. Why should people avoid wearing the same shoes day after day?

❯ INTERESTING THINGS TO DO

1. Set up a one-page manual for new shoe salespeople explaining the different kinds of shoes worn by men and women students. Use the students' shoes in your own class as models.
2. If you are purchasing a pair of shoes or can accompany some relative or friend who is buying shoes, make a record of this for a shoe-shopping report. Include in your record the following information: (*a*) How many customers did the salesclerk wait on while serving you? (*b*) How did he measure your feet? (Make this a very detailed account.) (*c*) When he tried the shoe on, how did he check it to make sure it fitted correctly? (*d*) How many pairs of shoes did he show you? (*e*) What did he tell you about the quality of the leather and how to care for the shoes? (*f*) Make suggestions for improvement of his selling technique.

ADDITIONAL MERCHANDISE TERMS ❯❯❯❯❯❯❯❯❯❯❯❯❯❯❯❯❯❯❯❯

Bal (Balmoral) is an oxford that has the tongue of the shoe stitched to the vamp. Thus, the closed throat does not expand to accommodate plump feet. Looks trim and neat, however.

Blucher is an oxford that has the tongue of the shoe as part of the vamp. This open throat readily expands to adjust to any foot thickness at the instep. Especially good for child's foot.

Chukka boots are ankle-high, loose-fitting boots for everyday casual wear. May have lace or buckle closings.

Clogs are thick-soled, heavy-looking shoes for beach wear and play use.

Combination last is a wooden last made with a heel section two sizes narrower in proportion to the rest of the shoe. It fits most people snugly at the heel and prevents heel slippage.

Crepe sole is a cream-colored, spongy-looking rubber sole used on school oxfords, play shoes, and street shoes.

Espadrilles are play shoes with thick, rope soles and cotton uppers.

Everett slipper is shaped like a pump, but a protruding tongue covers the instep. This is especially popular in men's slippers.

Ghillies are low-cut shoes held to the foot by means of laces that may tie around the ankle. The laces on the ghillie pass through loops instead of eyelets.

Heels, built-up, are made of layers of leatherboard that resemble lifts glued one on top of another. This heel is used on spectator sport and street shoes.

Heels, Cuban, may be the same height as the military heel, or somewhat higher. This heel has more curve in the back than the military and is therefore more shapely, but gives its wearer a narrower base on which to stand.

Heels, flat or spring, are very low heels that are used on tots' and children's shoes.

Heels, high, vary in height from about 2½ to 3½ inches. They also vary in shape. Common names for high heels are: French, square back, Spanish, built up, spike, novelty high.

Heels, military, are broad heels that are slightly higher than the common-sense heel. They have a slight curve at the back of the heel. They are desirable for girls' and women's walking and street shoes.

Huarachos are shoes on which the tops are made of strips of leather braided or woven together. These are stitched or laced to the sole, making a comfortable, sporty-looking shoe or house slipper for men's, women's, or children's wear. Real huarachos are made of horsehide by the peons in Mexico.

Jodhpur is a low-cut riding boot.

Mary Jane is the term applied to a flat-heeled, plain sandal with a single strap across the instep. This sandal is popular for little girls to wear for dress-up occasions.

Mules are backless slippers that cover just the top of the toes. Heights of heels may range from no heel at all, which is popular for men, to a very high heel, which is popularly worn by many women. Also called *scuffs.*

Open-shank sandal has sides cut out to the sole at the sides of the shoe.

Opera slippers are shaped like an ordinary pump, but are cut low on either side so that the foot can be slipped into the slipper without any difficulty.

Pacs are above-ankle-high lace boots for outdoor workers and sportsmen. Waterproof features are especially desirable in these shoes.

Platform sole is a built-up sole usually made of a lightweight material such as cork or wood. It may have a leather outsole attached. Used on some beach and play shoes and when fashionable for some evening and daytime shoes for women.

Rubbers. *Toe rubbers* are made especially for women's high-heeled shoes. They cover only the toe part of the shoe and have a back strap that holds the rubber on at the heel.

Scuffs, (see *Mules*).

Slippers, high cut, may have various names such as *Hi-Lo, Cavalier, Romeo, Juliet.* See also *Mules, Opera slippers, Everett slipper.*

Storm rubbers have a tongue that covers the instep of the shoe or foot.

T-strap sandal is made with a strap that comes up the instep to form the shape of the letter T with the regular strap from the sides of the shoe.

Gloves, Handbags, Luggage, and Umbrellas

CHAPTER

21

GLOVES FOR MEN, WOMEN, AND CHILDREN

For Christmas, Easter, and vacation selling seasons, small-wares departments offer young people salesmanship opportunities. Gloves, handbags, briefcases, wallets, belts, luggage, and umbrellas are all ideal gift-giving items. In addition, many people shop for these items for their own use. Knowledge of styles, leathers, fabrics, and construction of these products enables the young person to sell them with confidence.

GLOVES THROUGH THE AGES

The word "glove" is believed to come from the old Saxon word *glofe,* meaning *to hide* or *to cover.* We know that primitive man early learned to cover his hands with animal skins to keep them warm and to protect them from scratches, bruises, or cuts. Mittens were the next hand covering developed, and centuries later, gloves with individual although somewhat bulky fingers were made.

Gloves at one time were used as a good-luck charm. A knight would wear his lady's glove on his arm when he fared forth to battle. As a legal symbol denoting good faith, the glove was given in property transactions.

The use of gloves as a style factor developed early. At various periods gloves were lavishly embroidered or trimmed with stones, lace, fringe, and tassels. Today the glove is an indispensable item for the well-dressed man or woman, and the correct color and type of glove is available for every occasion. The salesperson, therefore, needs to be a fashion as well as merchandise adviser to the glove customer.

MATERIALS USED IN GLOVES

Gloves are made both from leathers and from fabrics. They are also made from combinations of leathers and fabrics. The leathers used (which were discussed in the leather chapter) must be thin enough for comfort, sturdy enough for durability, yet soft and supple. Familiar glove leathers you have already learned about are kidskin, capeskin, mocha, pigskin, doeskin-finished lambskin, cabretta, and chamois. Men's gloves and sport gloves may be made from heavier leathers such as top-grain and split cowhide, deerskin, and horsehide.

These leathers may be used in all-leather gloves or as the backs of gloves with fabric palms or the palms of gloves with fabric backs. Leather gloves may also have fur or wool linings for wear in cold climates. Women's leather gloves for dress wear may have thin silk linings. The furs used for lining gloves are usually rabbit skins, but sheepskin (with the wool attached), muskrat, and even mink have been used.

Special Features of Leather Gloves

Many customers today are interested in the washability of leather gloves. Few dark-colored leather gloves will wash, but since these do not readily show soil customers do not demand that they be washable. Lined gloves also are rarely washable. Both the method of tanning the leather and the kind of dye used to color the glove affect its washability. Only leathers stamped *washable* may safely be laundered, and even then the utmost care in following directions must be taken.

Another important consideration of customers today is whether or not a leather glove will *crock*. The color of a dip-dyed glove may rub off on the hand when the hand perspires. This is known as *crocking*. On gloves that have been brush-dyed the coloring matter is applied only on the outside of the glove. The inside remains white or gray-blue (the color of the original tannage), and thus cannot crock on the hands. However, the fingertips of brush-dyed gloves may become somewhat grayed and appear worn, when actually only the surface color has rubbed away.

Special Features of Fabric Gloves

Glove fabrics include cotton poplin, canvas, cotton jersey, Durene cotton, cotton flannel, cotton fleece, nylon, stretch nylon, hi-bulk acrylic, wool, cashmere, brushed rayon, as well as meshes, tricots, and crocheted lace. These fabrics were discussed in Part I—Textiles.

PARTS OF A GLOVE

Gloves, unlike shoes, have few "hidden" parts. If you put on a glove, stretch your fingers, and then examine the glove, you can see all parts with

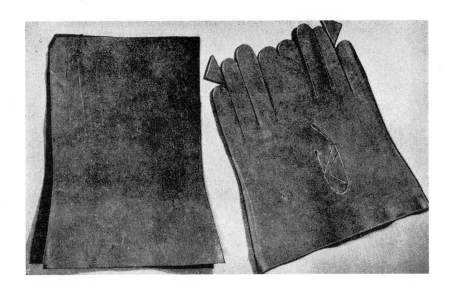

Trank, table cut, slit trank, and three quirks. (Note quirk in cutout for thumb piece.) Quirks will be used between fingers for added freedom of movement. *(Courtesy Boys' Outfitter)*

the exception of the lining and small reinforcements. In selling gloves, it is important to know the purpose of the various small sections of gloves, in order to be able to explain to the customer how to make the glove fit properly.

The *trank* of the glove is the general outline that forms the palm, back, and fingers of the glove. It resembles an oblong, before the fingers are slit.

The *thumb* of the glove is made from a separate piece of material, and later stitched around a hole that was cut in the glove trank. The *Bolton* thumb is bulkier in appearance but provides complete freedom of movement and is thus used on men's gloves and women's sport and street gloves. For a daintier, sleeker fit for women's dress gloves, the *quirk* thumb that fits more snugly but restricts movement somewhat is used.

Some of the fingers of gloves are made in four sections. The front and back sections are part of the trank. The side pieces are known as *fourchettes* or *forks*. They are small oblong pieces, the length of the fingers, which provide ample space for finger width.

At the base of some fourchettes are tiny triangular sections. These are known as *quirks*. They are used for extra give between the fingers. The presence of quirks indicates quality workmanship.

Linings may be used in gloves. They are made of silk, rayon, cotton, nylon, acrylic fiber, fur, or blends of two or more of these materials. While skeleton linings cover only the trank, full linings which are more costly provide a complete glove within a glove.

MAKING LEATHER GLOVES

A trip to a leather-glove factory provides quite a contrast to the vastness

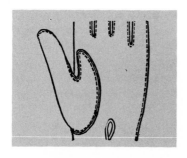

◄ Bolton Thumb.

Quirk Thumb. ➤

and complicated operations and machinery of a shoe factory. Very few machines are necessary, and comparatively few workmen may be employed in any one factory. In glove manufacture there are about 20 to 30 operations in contrast to 200 to 300 involved in traditional shoemaking.

Some parts of glovemaking may be "farmed" out. One small factory may not have proper equipment for one operation, so the owner packs up a few hundred pairs of gloves and takes them next door, or up the street to another small factory that specializes in that particular operation. This procedure reduces equipment necessary in each factory and means that skilled operators may concentrate on just one process. Most glove operations are "hand guided" or in some cases completely "hand" done.

Preparing and Cutting the Material

Taxing. The first operation, known as *taxing,* is the job of deciding how many pairs of gloves should be cut from a skin. After the *taxer* has marked the number of pairs on the skin, he sends it to the cutter, who prepares the leather for *trank cutting.*

Trank Cutting. The most expensive method of cutting is known as *table cut.* The leather is dampened slightly and worked (pulled over the edge of the table, stretched and pulled) until it is in the correct shape for cutting. Then the workman, who has spent years learning to judge the feel and give of the leather, measures the space for the specified size trank. He then uses a large pair of shears to cut this oblong section. Since every piece of leather differs in feel, thickness, and give, and since scars and cuts on the leather must be avoided, his is a complicated job. Most table-cut gloves are stamped inside the wrist section of the glove with the Glover's Guild symbol denoting quality, or have the words *table cut* stamped in the glove. Table-cut gloves fit well, and give with the hand to permit maximum flexibility of movement.

Less expensive leather gloves are made by a modified method of this cut, known as a *pull-down* cut. This, however, does not give the customer the same assurance of fit and comfort that she gets with table cutting. The leather is not worked and cut by such expert glovemakers, and no attempt is made to create a perfect fit.

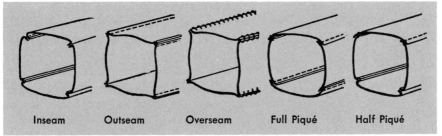

| Inseam | Outseam | Overseam | Full Piqué | Half Piqué |

Inexpensive leather gloves, work gloves, and bulky lined gloves may be cut by the *die* or *block-cut* method. Here, a metal trank-shaped knife cuts the leather in a manner resembling a cookie cutter. No allowance is made by this method for avoiding scars on the leather or for a sleek fit of the finished glove.

Slitting. The next step in glovemaking is known as *finger slitting.* This is done by steel dies which, when pressed down on several layers of tranks placed face to face in pairs, cut fingers, holes for thumbs, and the tiny triangles known as *quirks* in one operation.

Seams Used on Gloves

There are two uses of seams on gloves. One use is decoration on the back, known as *pointing;* and the second is the closing of the glove.

Pointing. The cut and slit trank is now ready for the decorative stitching. This may be done with contrasting colored threads, braids, or beads and can be hand or machine stitched.

Closing. Attaching the thumb, stitching the fingers together with the fourchettes and quirks, and stitching the sides of the trank is known as *closing* the glove. The seams used for this closing determine to some extent the quality of the glove.

Examine your friends' and your own gloves. You will notice undoubtedly that the edges of the fingers and sides of the gloves have been put together in different ways. These various *stitches* are important selling points in gloves. They affect the appearance, durability, and price of the glove.

INSEAM. The least expensive seam, and the one easiest to make, is known as the *inseam.* The edges of the glove are stitched together on the inside. When turned on the right side, no stitches or edges of the leather are seen. This seam is used on some inexpensive leather gloves and some fabric gloves.

OUTSEAM. The outseam stitch is just the opposite of the *inseam* in appearance. Both raw edges of the glove are visible on the outside of this glove. A visible running stitch is used. Often hand stitching or simulated hand stitching is used to give a decorative effect. Since the fingers are bulkier in appearance, this stitch is used mainly on men's gloves and sportswear gloves for women. The extra finishing operations that are required make this a more expensive seam than the inseam.

OVERSEAM. In the overseam method, both raw edges of leather are visible on the outside of the glove, but the stitches go over and over the edges, reinforcing them and making a fine or deep seam as desired. If only a narrow strip of leather is caught into this seam, it is not very durable. Its sleek attractive appearance, however, makes it desirable for dressy gloves. Coarser stitching is used on men's gloves and women's sport gloves.

PIQUÉ. The *piqué* or P. K. is the most durable stitch for street and dress gloves. One edge of leather is lapped over the other edge so that only one raw edge shows on the outside. The glove is then stitched carefully. This is the most difficult stitch to put on gloves. In addition to a specially designed sewing machine, which is necessary to sew inside the tubelike fingers of the glove, operators with special skills are needed. The piqué stitch is, therefore used only on good quality gloves. It makes the slimmest, trimmest appearing glove.

The *half piqué* is a seam that is made by using an ordinary sewing machine. Only the seams on the back are overlapped, those on the palm side being inseam or outseam sewed. This seam imitates the more costly piqué (P.K.) sewed gloves but does not give the same sleek fit on the hand.

Pressing

After stitching, the gloves are ready for pressing. They are shaped and smoothed from the inside by a hot metal plate shaped like a stiff, narrow hand. Grooves along the sides of the fingers permit the fourchettes to be folded in like a bellows. After removal from this ironing form, the gloves are packed for shipment to the store.

MAKING FABRIC GLOVES

Woven and warp-knit fabrics for gloves are shaped by die cutting. The pointing and closing seams are done in the same manner as the leather gloves described above. The term *double woven* really refers to warp-knit materials of double thickness. This double-woven fabric makes the most durable of fabric glove materials. Single-knit materials are thinner and have less body.

Regular knit gloves are made in woolen, hi-bulk acrylic yarns, or cotton string yarns. These are knitted to shape either by hand or more commonly on knitting machines that are similar to hosiery knitting machines. Tips of fingers after knitting are closed by hand or by machine stitching.

TYPES OF GLOVES

An advertisement for gloves appeared in the newspaper the day before

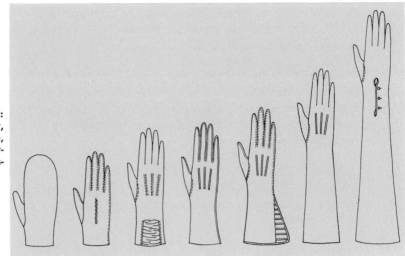

Types of Gloves.
Left to right: Mitten, shorty, novelty, slip-on, gauntlet, 8-button length, mousquetaire.

Betty Ann was to begin her Christmas selling job in a glove department. The advertisement said, "Slip-ons and mousquetaires in popular 8-, 12-, and 16-button lengths." As she read the advertisement, Betty Ann suddenly realized that even though she had always worn gloves, she needed to learn many terms before she could explain such words to customers.

Length of women's gloves is referred to by the term *button length*. This term is confusing, because today it has nothing at all to do with buttons. Each button refers to one inch of length, which is measured from the base of the thumb to the edge of the arm section of the glove. A twelve-button length glove, therefore, would be approximately elbow length; while four-button gloves would extend just a couple of inches beyond the wrist; and eight buttons, to the middle of the forearm. Popular types of gloves, which may or may not vary in length, are the following.

Mittens. Mittens are a covering for the hand having a separate sheath only for the thumb. These may be made of any usual glove material. They are used primarily for warmth for children's wear and sportswear for men and women.

Slip-on. This is a popular type of glove for women. The average slip-on is a two-button or a four-button length glove. Slip-ons are, however, also available in eight- to sixteen-button lengths. No fasteners or openings are used on this glove. It actually just "slips on."

Mousquetaire. This looks like a slip-on when you see only the back of the glove. It is a long, dressy-type glove that is worn with a short-sleeved afternoon or dinner dress. It has an opening at the wrist that permits the wearer to remove the hand from the glove, turning the hand portion under at the wrist while the arm is still covered by the upper part of the glove. Most people today, instead of asking for a mousquetaire, request an eight-, twelve-, or sixteen-button length glove.

Gauntlet. This resembles the slip-on, except that it has a much wider flare above the wrist. To give this effect, a separate gore in the shape of a triangle is set in above the wrist of the glove. This type of glove is seen in most western pictures. The cowboys use gauntlets with elaborate beading and fringe as decoration.

Shorty. This is the name of most sports and men's gloves. These are wrist-length gloves that may have a side or center opening or that fasten at the wrist with clasps, buttons, or straps. Men's shorties are known as *clasp* or *pull-on* models.

Novelty Gloves. These include other types that have unusual combinations of material, shirring, cuffs, or trimmings.

USES OF GLOVES

In addition to dress and street gloves carried in regular glove departments, sports gloves are usually carried in the sportswear department of a store. Specially designed gloves are made for archery, baseball, bowling, boxing, golf, handball, ice hockey, and skiing.

Work gloves for farmers and others who work out of doors and around heavy machinery are also specially designed and made from sturdy materials.

SIZES IN GLOVES

A glove that is too small will wear out at the seams and fingertips much more quickly than one that fits correctly. The wrong size in a glove may also cause some discomfort and annoyance to the wearer.

Sizes of gloves are determined when the trank is cut. Naturally, the table-cut trank will give the customer the best fit in leather gloves. Fabric gloves have considerable elasticity and therefore are not sized so precisely. The nylon

❯ ❯ GLOVE SIZES ❮ ❮

		Small					Medium				Large		
Women	Leather	5^2	5^3	6	6^1	6^2	6^3	7	7^1	7^2	7^3	8		
	Fabric	5^2		6		6^2		7		7^2		8		
Men	Leather	7	7^1	7^2	7^3	8	8^1	8^2	8^3	9	9^1	9^2	9^3	10
	Fabric	7		7^2		8		8^2		9		9^2		10
Children														
Size		0	1	2	3	4	5	6	7					
Age		1	2	4	6	8	10	12	14					

stretch gloves enable people with different size hands to wear the same size glove comfortably.

Sizes in men's and women's leather gloves range by quarter inches. In fabric gloves the sizes range by half inches. Women's glove sizes range from 5½ to 8, with the average 6½. Men's sizes range from 7 to 10. The average is about 9. Children's glove sizes usually run by one-half the age of the child. Size 0 is for the one-year-old, size four for the eight-year-old, and so on.

Fitting Gloves

To determine the size of a customer's hand, the measurement is taken around the knuckles, the widest part of the hand. Because the glove has some stretch, the measurement is usually one size larger than the glove needed.

If a leather glove is being put on for the first time, it should be "worked" on. The customer's hand is put into the glove and each finger is worked on separately, until the glove has been eased over the entire hand and is smooth and sleek in appearance. It is very interesting to watch an expert fitter's technique. Her fingers are like an artist's molding the leather onto the hand. Both gloves should be worked on the customer's hands in this manner.

After the gloves have once been adjusted to the customer's hands, she should have no further difficulty in getting them on. She must, however, take good care of the gloves both in putting them on and in removing them, if she is to have maximum wear from the gloves.

In removing the gloves, the salesperson should first loosen the finger tips by pulling them slightly. The glove is then turned inside-out and eased off the customer's hand. The glove is turned right side out, the fingers straightened, and the glove looks almost as sleek as it did before it was tried on.

CARE OF GLOVES

The customer should be advised that the method used in trying on the gloves is the correct one for putting them on and removing them. Gloves handled in this manner never have a "crumpled up" look. Some people are careless with their gloves. They remove the glove by yanking at it, then crumple it up and stuff it in the coat pocket where it remains without any opportunity to air out, or to resume its original shape. Perspiration from hands is harmful to gloves unless it is permitted to evaporate.

Many leather gloves today are washable, but unless they are so marked, washing may ruin them. Washing leather gloves requires care and a certain amount of working with the glove. Lukewarm mild soapsuds should be used. If the gloves are made of firm smooth leather, they may be washed on the hand. Doeskin-finished lambskin and other suede-finished gloves should, however, be washed carefully off the hands. This prevents tearing the leather, which is softened by the moisture. After the gloves are washed thoroughly,

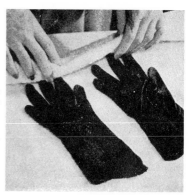

Tell the Customer How to Wash Her Gloves. Upper left: Wash gloves, before they become badly soiled, on the hands (except suede-finished leather gloves). **Upper right**: Rinse thoroughly, then roll in a Turkish towel to knead out excess moisture. **Lower left**: Unroll immediately and puff gloves into shape. Dry away from heat. **Lower right**: When gloves are almost dry, finger press gently. *(Courtesy Lever Brothers Co.)*

they should be rinsed; then the excess moisture should be pressed out in a towel. The gloves should be blown up like a balloon, to shape the fingers and to prevent the leather from sticking together. Then the gloves should be smoothed out, and placed on a towel to dry in a cool, shady place. Gloves should never be dried over a radiator or in the sun. When the glove is almost dry, it should be finger-pressed. The glove salesperson should demonstrate this procedure to the customer by grasping the glove with both thumbs and forefingers and massaging gently. This loosens the leather fibers and prevents the leather from feeling harsh and brittle after it dries. It also causes the leather to absorb some of the natural oil from your fingers, thus making it soft and pliable.

Washable gloves should not be allowed to become too soiled before washing as this necessitates extra rubbing to remove the dirt, which may tear the gloves. Gloves not marked washable should be dry-cleaned by an approved dry-cleaning concern. Fabric gloves that are washable should be pulled smoothly into shape while still damp or dried over plastic hand forms.

PUTTING THIS MERCHANDISE KNOWLEDGE TO USE ❯❯❯❯❯❯❯❯❯❯

❯ DO YOU KNOW YOUR MERCHANDISE?

1. What are the qualities that are desirable in glove leathers?
2. Explain how you can tell the method by which a glove is dyed.
3. What is meant by *crocking?* Compare the crocking of leather with the crocking of a textile fabric.
4. Explain the meaning of the following: trank; fourchette; quirk; taxing; trank cutting; finger slitting; four-button glove; gauntlet; pointing; closing; inseam; outseam; overseam; piqué seam; slip-on; cadet.
5. Explain how you would measure a customer's hand to fit a pair of gloves.
6. Explain the correct method of "trying" on a glove.
7. What is the correct method of removing gloves?
8. Tell how to care for gloves that are not marked "washable."
9. Explain how to wash leather gloves for best results.
10. What are the advantages of stretch nylon gloves?
11. What is meant by double-woven gloves? Why are they desirable?

❯ INTERESTING THINGS TO DO

1. Prepare a demonstration showing the correct method of measuring and fitting a pair of gloves.
2. Bring some dress gloves, everyday gloves, or active-sports gloves to class and give a 2-minute sales talk for your class.
3. List all terms that appear in an advertisement for gloves. Classify the terms as material terms, glove-style terms, size terms, construction terms, finish terms. Look up any terms that you do not understand and explain what they mean.

UNIT 61 HANDBAGS, OTHER SMALL LEATHER GOODS, AND GARMENTS

HANDBAGS

Purses to hold money have been used ever since man first devised coins as a medium of exchange. Handbags such as the modern woman carries, however, are of rather recent vintage. As women's responsibilities have increased they have found more and more need for sizable carry-alls. Rather than having pockets bulging with odds and ends, they assemble keys, compacts, lipsticks, combs, wallets, and miscellaneous items into a handy handbag.

The handbag today, however, is much more than just a carry-all. It is a smart addition to the well-dressed woman's attire. She selects her handbag to harmonize with, or dramatize, her outfit. She also considers the ease with which it can be carried and the amount of space it provides for the items she usually takes with her.

As in glove selling, the salesperson becomes a fashion adviser as well as a quality adviser to the customer.

Materials Used for Handbags

Leather, once the most important handbag material, has lost its pre-eminent position except for fine quality handbags and for some heavy tote bags. The unique properties of leather, so essential for comfortable gloves and shoes, are not so necessary to the handbag field. Fine calfskins, goatskins, cowhides, alligators, lizards, and some patent leathers are, however, still made by manufacturers who cater to the woman who wants fine quality handbags.

Bonded leather fibers (also known as "shredded" leather), made by matting the fibers of leftover scraps of leather and holding them together with plastic materials, make a serviceable product for medium-priced handbags. These are marketed under trade names such as "Lavalize" and "Nouveau." While these materials have a similar appearance to leather, they have no true grain and do not become richer looking with age as top-grain leather does.

Plastic materials have emerged as the most important handbag materials in the volume-priced handbags during the past decade. Some of these handbags are made to simulate leather and are called "plastic calf," "plastic kid," "plastic patent," or "plastic suede." Since these materials are used in less expensive bags, they are not so well constructed and do not give so many years of service as do fine leather bags. *Vinyl* (discussed in the Plastics chapter) is the most commonly used handbag plastic. It may be given a surface texture to resemble leather, straw, lace, or corded fabrics. It is usually washable and very durable. When the vinyl material is foamed slightly (like whipping cream) its texture is similar to that of a marshmallow. Such plastics have been eagerly accepted by customers for their attractive appearance and texture.

Acrylic plastics have been used to make box-type bags with glasslike appearance. These bags, however, are considered as novelties and have never become extensive sellers.

Handbags are also made from fabrics such as piqué, gingham, bouclé, wool broadcloth, felt, taffeta, velvet, petit point, tapestry, linen crash, and metallic cloth. Evening bags, which are usually tiny enough to be held in the hand or to dangle daintily from a wrist strap, may be decorated with beads, embroidery, rhinestones, sequins, or marcasites. Straw bags and strawlike bags (toyo) are used in the summer.

Parts of a Handbag

Handbags consist of the outside material plus frame, fasteners or zippers, linings, inside coin purse, compartments, or pockets, plus paddings and reinforcements to give the outside material a plump feel and rich appearance and to make the bag keep its shape.

Handbag frames are usually made of brass or steel and may be gold, silver, or chromium plated, or covered with leather or fabric. Inexpensive bags may have frames that have been sprayed with enamel to match the material used on the bag and to simulate a covered frame. Such enameled frames chip easily and make the handbag appear worn out even though it has been used only a few times.

Gussets or side gores are used to allow a bag to expand to hold more paraphernalia.

Handles are used on many handbags. They may be small to hold in the hand, medium length to fit over the arm, or long to hang over the shoulder. These three types, which extend across the top of the bag, are known as *top handles*. Occasionally, a handbag may have a handle that allows the bag to be held on the back. This is known as a *side* handle. Handles may be made from the same material as the bag itself, or they may be made from chains, bone, or rigid plastic.

Coin purses inside the handbag may swing from the frame in the center of the bag permitting easy access. Attached coin purses are sewed to the lining at the side of the bag. Loose coin purses are also provided in some handbags. They may or may not have a chain or elastic that attaches to the bag and prevents their loss. *Zipper pockets* in handbags are popular to carry important small items and to prevent their being lost when the bag is opened. Travel bags may have attached sections to hold passports, identification cards, tickets, and other necessities. Hidden pockets are also built into some expensive handbags. These permit a person to carry jewelry or large sums of money without fear of detection when the handbag is opened.

Linings in handbags may be made from leather, leatherlike plastic, or fabric.

Hidden parts of a handbag contain such things as cardboard, stiff plastic, cotton felt, paper, muslin, and heavy duck fabric. These are glued to the bag and help to give it a firm shape.

Manufacturing Handbags

Since the handbag does not have to be made to fit, as gloves and shoes do, the designer of handbags can allow his imagination free rein. In factories that manufacture expensive handbags, the designer's drawing is worked out in muslin to show the effect of the finished bag without wasting expensive materials. After approval, the muslin becomes the basic pattern from which the cardboard or metal patterns for the 30 to 40 different parts of the bag are cut.

The leather or other material is then cut with dies or by hand, much as shoe parts are cut. From that point on, the job of assembling and sewing the parts of the bag proceeds. Most of the equipment consists of various types of sewing machines where workmen stitch parts together. Other workmen glue linings, filler, and stay materials into the bags. When the lining and outside are completed, the bag goes to the frame worker, who inserts all the parts skillfully into the required frame or applies the necessary fasteners to the bag. Framing is the most difficult and the most costly construction feature.

The final step in making a handbag is the inspection of the finished bag. It is then stuffed with tissue paper to hold its shape and packed ready for the retail store.

Types of Handbags

Because handbags may be large or small, long and thin, short and wide, big and bulky, or dainty and trim, there seem to be dozens of different types of these products. Regardless of size, however, they may be classified into four groups: envelope, pouch, box, and novelty. Of course, there are subdivisions under these groupings.

❯ ❯ **Types of Handbags** ❮ ❮

ENVELOPE BAG   SHIRRED POUCH   ZIPPER POUCH   SWAGGER POUCH

BRACELET BAG   PANNIER HANDLE BAG   HAND TOOLED   TAILORED VANITY

BOX BAG   FEED BAG   VAGABOND POUCH   BARREL SHAPE

Envelope. The envelope bag gets its name from the fact that it resembles an ordinary envelope with a top flap. It usually has no handle, although it may have a small one on the back of the bag. These bags are either carried in the hand or under the arm. The *clutch* bag is an envelope bag that has been popular for evening and daytime wear.

Pouch. The most popular bag used for every type of occasion is the pouch. Any type of handbag with a zipper top closing or a frame or a top handle is called a pouch bag. There are underarm pouches, zipper pouches, swagger pouches (with two handles and ample space), shoulder-strap pouches, tote bags, and dressy pouches.

Box Bag. Any rigid bag that does not expand to accommodate contents is a box bag. Since they have limited carrying space, they are usually in fashion for short periods of time only. Most box bags have built-in mirrors, and many have space for certain items such as lipsticks, compacts, and coins.

Novelty. Unusual bags for special occasions may be referred to as novelty bags. Belt bags for sportswear, muff bags for winter use, beach bags, and knitting bags are examples of novelty bags.

Selling Handbags

In addition to helping the customer select the correct color and style of handbag, the salesperson can stress many other points. Look for these "talking points" in the handbags you sell:

1. Inform the customer of the quality of the leather or other material used. If so labeled, assure her that the leather is colorfast to handling, sunlight, or rain, and show her by rubbing the leather with a white cloth that it will not crock. Show her the beauty of the grain of the leather, or the richness of the velvety finish, if it is suede.

2. Point out the finish of the handle and the way it is attached to the bag.

3. Demonstrate the "roominess" of the bag itself.

4. Show her the lining, the extra pockets, the hidden compartments, and how the coin purse is attached to the bag.

5. Ask the customer to hold the bag as she would when using it to get the effect of its appearance.

SMALL OR FANCY LEATHER GOODS ITEMS

Christmas, graduation, and birthday gifts abound in the "small leather goods" departments. Here tricky, handy cases for every possible occasion have been devised to keep women's handbags neat and orderly and men's pockets from bulging with too many miscellaneous, hard-to-find articles.

Two basic types of wallets are the *flat* and the *folding* type. The folding type is more popular for young men; but older men often prefer the flat wallet, which does not have so many compartments and will not hold so much as the folding type but which is neater appearing when carried in a breast pocket.

The cost of most of these items depends on the quality and kind of leather used, the amount of "extras," such as zippers and pockets, the workmanship used, and reinforcements. Beads and imitation stones may trim women's wallets. Inexpensive wallets, key cases, and other small items may also be made from imitation leathers. Vinyl plastic is most commonly used for these products.

Jewelry cases, traveling cases, card holders, belts, and name holders are a few of the items also classed as small leather goods.

LEATHER AND LEATHERLIKE GARMENTS

In selecting clothing made of leather, the quality of the leather itself will determine to a large extent the durability, beauty, and price of the garment. The customer, however, will be especially interested in the fit of the garment and its appearance.

In order for jackets to be comfortable, the leather used in them must be soft and supple. All leather jackets need ample shoulder and elbow room to prevent wear at those two vital points of strain. Dry cleaning by a reputable cleaner is recommended for all leather garments. Horsehide, deerskin, and sheepskin are the commonly used garment leathers. The natural insulating properties of leather make it ideal for fall, winter, or spring wear.

Finishes on the leathers used for garments are glacé, crushed or textured, and suede.

Vinyl plastics that resemble leather have proved to be serviceable, long-wearing, easily cleaned materials also for garments. Since these plastic materials lack the natural porosity of leather, they may become too warm except in the coldest weather.

PUTTING THIS MERCHANDISE KNOWLEDGE TO USE ❯❯❯❯❯❯❯❯❯❯

❯ DO YOU KNOW YOUR MERCHANDISE?

1. What materials are used for (a) the outside of handbags; (b) the linings of handbags; (c) the trim and frames of handbags?
2. Explain briefly the steps necessary in making a handbag.
3. What advantage does real leather have over bonded leather fibers for handbags?
4. Name and describe five important parts of a handbag.
5. Define envelope, pouch, box bag, novelty bag.
6. What are the important selling points for salespeople of handbags?
7. What items are classified as "small leather goods"?
8. What advice would you give a customer about the care of a leather garment?

1. If your mother or sister has an old, discarded handbag, take it apart carefully. Mount the various sections of the bag on cardboard neatly. Label each section. Bring it to class as a demonstration.
2. Prepare a 2-minute sales talk for handbags or small leather items.
3. Make a chart showing the advantages and disadvantages of leather garments and leather imitation (plastic) garments.

UNIT 62 LUGGAGE

TYPES OF LUGGAGE

Americans have developed "travelmania." Every person wants to go on a plane or train trip, a cruise or ocean voyage, or a bus or automobile excursion. Luggage requirements for these many types of trips are so varied that manufacturers design numerous containers with just the right space and extra accessories to fit each traveler's specific requirements. In addition, each new case is given a different name by each manufacturer.

However, with all these varying styles in luggage, the basic types may be classified as:

Hand Luggage

Any kind of luggage that a porter or the traveler can carry and can keep with him in a train, auto, bus, or plane is known as *hand luggage*. Included in this list are soft-side luggage, hard-side luggage, travel bags that fold for carrying like a suitcase and unfold like a garment bag to hold clothes on hangers. Toilet kits, attaché cases, brief cases, zipper tote bags, two-suiters, and pullman cases are also included in this group.

Trunks

Large rigid cases that are too bulky to be carried by the traveler, and may be checked, are classified as trunks. The two types are the *box,* which is convenient for packing bedding, linens, and clothing for storage or long journeys, and the *wardrobe trunk,* which has hangers for clothes in one section and drawers for underwear, accessory items, shoes, hats, and cosmetics in the

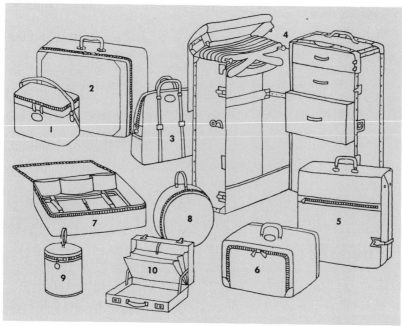

Types of Luggage.
1. Trip kit
2. Air pullman
3. Tote bag
4. Wardrobe trunk
5. Ladies dress-pak
6. Carry-on
7. 2-suiter
8. Hatbox
9. Hat and wig bag
10. Attaché case

other section. During ship travel, these trunks may serve as a closet for clothes and accessories.

SELLING LUGGAGE

The salesman of luggage can, in his imagination, travel the "four corners of the earth." His is a romantic and interesting job because every customer who walks into the luggage department is contemplating a journey at some time for himself, some member of his family, or a friend. Perhaps he is only taking a short trip, or sending his son or daughter to college, or he may be planning a vacation. This customer wants more than just a pleasant salesperson to wait on him. He wants a salesperson who can aid him to select luggage that will be adequate and appropriate for his needs. The salesperson should also know luggage requirements for travel by train, bus, boat, or plane so that he can advise the customer about the approximate packed weight of the luggage being shown.

Luggage today has style quality just as do other articles; it is built for economy of space and ease of packing and unpacking. Customers are particularly interested in lightweight luggage designed for ease of packing that eliminates extra folds in clothing.

Durability of luggage presents a problem different from that of any other article, for its care and life depend on the porters, expressmen, checking-room clerks and bellboys who will handle the luggage. This is an important feature in selling good-quality, well-built luggage that can better withstand rough treatment than can inexpensive, poorly constructed cases.

MATERIALS USED IN LUGGAGE

Because leather makes luggage somewhat heavy, it has lost its important place as the most used covering material.

Leather

Some customers continue to seek luggage made from leather, and many manufacturers continue to make some leather items. Top-grain leathers are used for expensive luggage, and split leathers are used for less costly articles. Cattle hide leather, including rawhide, steerhide, and cowhide, are the most usual leathers used, although alligator, ostrich, pigskin, walrus, sealskin, and shark are also available.

Split leathers do not withstand rough handling nearly so well as do top-grain leathers. The Federal Trade Commission therefore issued rules in September, 1941, that require that such luggage or fancy leather-goods articles (wallets, billfolds, etc.) state on a label or tag attached to the article that split leather has been used, as for example: "Split cowhide."

Sometimes only small sections of the luggage, such as the gussets, are made of the split leather. The label then should read: "Top-grain cowhide with split cowhide gussets." These labels aid salespeople to give the customers correct information about quality and expected durability.

The Federal Trade Commission rules also require that the true name of the leather be used, as: "Split cowhide embossed to imitate walrus."

Other Materials

Airplane travel has created a need for lighter-weight materials for the covering of luggage. Because *vinyl* is a tough, lightweight plastic material that may be used in film form to resemble leather, or coated over fabrics to add surface strength and resistance to abrasion, it has supplanted leather in many manufacturers' lines. Tough, molded-side luggage is made from glass fibers bonded with vinyl plastic. Soft-side luggage with zipper openings is made sturdy with strong nylon fabrics. Nylon is also used as a coating for other materials used in luggage.

When carpetbags become fashionable, as they did in the early 1960's, wool becomes a useful luggage material.

Canvas that has been vinyl coated to resemble leather is popular in less expensive luggage. The best quality of this type of luggage has a two-ply canvas base. Cheaply constructed luggage is made of paper-covered cardboard. Leather and sometimes metal strips are used for the reinforcements of corners and edges of luggage. Some luggage has been made of aluminum in

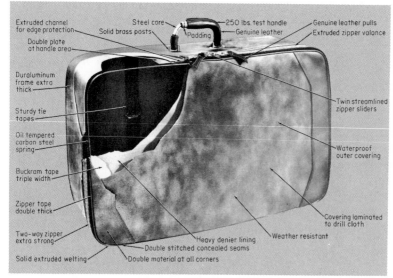

Extruded channel for edge protection
Double plate at handle area
Steel core
Solid brass posts
Padding
250 lbs. test handle
Genuine leather
Genuine leather pulls
Extruded zipper valance
Duraluminum frame extra thick
Sturdy tie tapes
Oil tempered carbon steel spring
Buckram tape triple width
Zipper tape double thick
Two-way zipper extra strong
Solid extruded welting
Twin streamlined zipper sliders
Waterproof outer covering
Covering laminated to drill cloth
Weather resistant
Heavy denier lining
Double stitched concealed seams
Double material at all corners

Construction Features of a Modern Piece of Luggage. *(Courtesy Lark Luggage)*

sheet form, but since the metal dents easily in use, it has not been widely accepted. As the covering material on inexpensive trunks, enameled sheet metal may be used.

The two most usual materials for the base of luggage underneath the outside covering are fiber and basswood. Fiber, which is just cardboard, may vary in quality from a fine rag content, specially treated fiberboard, to a cheap, common cardboard. Fiberboard, however, does not compare to three-ply basswood used in quality luggage. Basswood, which comes from the linden tree, is light in weight, soft, close grained, and strong. Since it is three ply, there is little danger of the wood warping or cracking.

Inside the luggage, the lining materials may be made of sheepskin or other thin leather, nylon, or rayon. Less expensive cases may have cotton or even paper linings.

The hardware (clasps, hinges, rings to hold handles, and locks) is another important feature of luggage. The best hardware is made of polished brass, or stainless steel which does not rust. Other luggage has nickel or brass-plated steel hardware. If scratched, these latter types may rust.

SELLING POINTS IN CONSTRUCTION

If you look around a luggage department and see the bewildering variety of items, you can appreciate the job the salesperson has in knowing the outstanding features of each bag, case, and trunk on display. Since no two types of luggage embody the same construction methods, it is almost impossible for the salesperson to know all about them. But there are certain features of workmanship and detail that should be pointed out to the customer.

1. Explain the differences in the wearing quality of the materials used.

For example, top-grain leather will wear longer and look richer and more luxurious than split leather; vinyl luggage will outlast ordinary fabric luggage; molded luggage will give longer service than canvas luggage.

2. Examine the edges of the luggage. The best quality has rounded, leather-reinforced edges that resist handling and wear.

3. Point out the number of catches or locks used to hold the case closed, the quality of the hardware, and the ease with which it works.

4. Tap the side of the case. If it resounds sharply you can assure the customer a wooden base has been used, while cardboard has a muffled sound.

5. Point out the extra pockets in the lining, which are useful for hosiery, handkerchiefs, and other small articles. Discuss the quality of the lining material used, reminding the customer that rayon and nylon linings are very resistant to abrasive wear.

6. In selling luggage for airplane travel, stress the lighter-weight nylon or vinyl-coated fabrics that are used. These are water-repellent and wear resistant. The coating prevents the fabric from sagging or snagging.

7. Mention the luggage wardrobe. It is smart to have matching pieces of luggage that can accommodate clothing for any type of trip.

8. Show the customers the "extras" on the bags—hangers, dust-resistant curtains, partitions, pockets that provide means of packing various articles.

9. Ask the customer to visualize his belongings packed in the particular case you are displaying. This gives him a personal interest in the luggage.

10. Some luggage is sized so that one case fits into another when storing. Be sure if the luggage "nests" that you point out this feature to the customer.

RULES FOR PACKING

Customers welcome instructions on how to pack clothes most efficiently and compactly. While different cases provide different space for articles, the following general rules are helpful to the traveler:

1. Travel advisers recommend two pieces of luggage for trips of any duration in preference to one big carry-all. One bag may then be used for daily needs, while the other is reserved for arrival outfits. This saves packing and repacking en route and simplifies travel.

2. In unfitted cases that do not provide special spaces for articles of clothing and accessories, heavy articles like shoes, irons, and small radios should be placed on the bottom. Cosmetics should be in leakproof, unbreakable containers.

3. Jackets and coats are folded inside out and placed neatly over the heavy articles.

4. Underwear, nighties, or pajamas may be rolled together and fitted into spaces in the case.

5. Lighter-weight dresses, blouses, shirts are packed with the collar against the end of the case. Sleeves should be folded over, and the entire article made as smooth as possible.

6. Small accessory items such as jewelry, hosiery or socks, ties, neckwear, handkerchiefs, and gloves should be tucked into pockets in the luggage or in the toes of shoes. Men's ties remain in shape if placed inside a magazine laid flat on the bottom of the suitcase.

7. If hats are to be packed, crowns may be kept in shape with tissue paper stuffed inside. Belts, handbags, wallets, and other small items may be placed in pockets or tucked into open spaces in the luggage.

8. Tie tapes provided in many luggage items may be tied to prevent shifting when the bag is closed and carried.

PUTTING THIS MERCHANDISE KNOWLEDGE TO USE ❯ ❯ ❯ ❯ ❯ ❯ ❯ ❯ ❯ ❯ ❯

❯ DO YOU KNOW YOUR MERCHANDISE?

1. What are the Federal Trade Commission rulings about labels on leather luggage? Explain how this aids the salesperson in selling such luggage.
2. Why is polished brass or stainless steel preferable to plated steel for locks and catches on luggage?
3. Explain the selling points of the following luggage materials: top-grain leather, imitation leather made from vinyl, nylon for soft-side luggage, vinyl-coated two-ply canvas, paper-covered cardboard.
4. Explain four features that you would look for if you were selecting luggage for a friend.
5. Give at least six important rules for packing luggage efficiently with a minimum of wrinkles.
6. Explain the difference between hand luggage and trunks.

❯ INTERESTING THINGS TO DO

1. Visit a local airline terminal or travel bureau to find out the weight limits for luggage on domestic flights and on overseas flights. Prepare to explain these weight allowances to the class.
2. Repeat this assignment for train, bus, or steamship travel for places in the United States and Canada.
3. Bring a piece of luggage to class and demonstrate correct packing techniques.

UNIT 63 UMBRELLAS

The umbrella was originally used as a protector from the sun's rays. The word, *umbrella,* came from the Latin word *umbra* meaning shade or shadow.

These shade protectors were popular in ancient times in Asiatic countries. By the 1700's they were being used in Europe. It was during that century in England that umbrellas were first used for protection from rain.

Today the utility of the umbrella in protecting its user from rain and snow is its most important feature; however, when a person is attired in a smart outfit, the umbrella, as an accessory, may add to the overall attractive appearance. Thus, the umbrella, even though a utility item, may also be a smart addition to the well-dressed person's wardrobe during rainy or snowy seasons. As a protector from the sun, the lightweight, portable parasol may also serve as an attractive dress accessory. Beach or yard umbrellas add a colorful note while they serve as sun protectors.

PARTS OF THE UMBRELLA

Rarely are users of umbrellas familiar with the various parts of these utility items. Umbrellas are composed primarily of three sections, the canopy, the shank, and the handle.

The Canopy Parts

The *canopy* is that part of the umbrella that spreads and protects the user from rain or sun. The material from which the canopy is made is stretched over metal *ribs* that form the frame for the canopy. These ribs arch radially and impart the desired shape to the canopy. The ends of the canopy are stitched to *tips,* which are rounded to prevent injury to anyone bumping into the umbrella when it is open. These tips slip over the ends of the ribs and

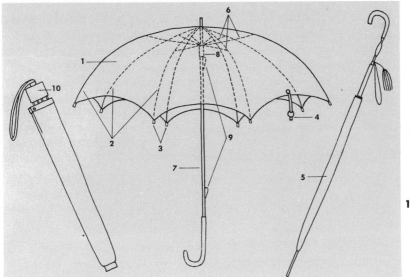

Parts of an Umbrella.
1. Canopy
2. Ribs
3. Tips
4. Tape
5. Sheath
6. Spreader
7. Shank
8. Sleeve
9. Springs
10. Cup

hold the canopy firmly in place whether the umbrella is open or closed. To keep the umbrella slender in appearance when it is closed, a *tape* attached to the canopy may be wound around it and fastened; or a *sheath* or *case* may be slipped over the umbrella to give it a trim shape.

Spreaders are attached to the center of the ribs. These enable the canopy to be opened or closed as desired.

The Shank Parts

Between the canopy and the handle is a shaft known as the *shank* or *rod*. Over this shank is a metal *sleeve* which slides up and down and enables the spreaders to which it is attached to be opened for use or collapsed for carrying. Two small *springs,* which can be depressed into the shank by slight finger pressure, hold the sleeve in position when the umbrella is open or closed. Some umbrellas have push-button, self-opener spreaders that operate with a special hidden spring. A metal *cup* that fits over the tips of a closed umbrella may also be affixed to the shank.

The Handle Parts

Handles enable the umbrella's user to hold it comfortably either when it is open or when it is closed. Handles themselves are rigid. Additional *straps* or *cords* are usually attached, however, to women's umbrellas. This permits the umbrella to hang from the wrist when carried, thus freeing the hands.

SPECIAL CONSTRUCTION FEATURES

The number of ribs in an umbrella differs depending on the size of the umbrella, its construction, and its shape. The sturdiness, rather than the number of ribs, determines the quality of the umbrella. Self-opening umbrellas have 7 ribs, small umbrellas for young people usually have 8 ribs, slim umbrellas usually have 10 ribs, while other styles may have 16 ribs.

To shorten umbrellas when they are not in use, some have ribs and spreaders that fold in half while others have detachable handles.

MATERIALS USED FOR UMBRELLAS

Many types of materials are used for the various parts and different qualities of umbrellas.

Materials for the Canopy

For protection from the elements, the canopy is made from fabrics or plastics that are water-repellent. Frequently these are cotton. The cotton must be closely woven and may or may not have a plastic finish that increases its protective qualities. *Gloria,* originally a cotton and worsted combination, is now usually a silk and cotton lustrous fabric. This is a tightly woven, plain-weave material used commonly in men's black umbrellas. *Drill,* a twill-weave cotton, is often used for beach umbrellas. When it is coated with vinyl plastic, an enduring sun and rain protector is provided. These materials are often colorfully dyed or printed.

In addition to cotton materials, silk, acetate, rayon, and nylon make desirable rain- and sun-resistant fabrics for umbrellas. Transparent umbrellas may be made from sheets of vinyl plastic. Although waterproof, these must be treated with care to avoid cracks or tears.

When a parasol is to provide sun protection only, its fabric does not need to have water-repellent qualities and may be organdy, lace, or other attractive dress material.

Outer cases, or sheaths, may be made from the same material as the canopy or from leather or plastic. Some elaborate sheaths are fur trimmed or jeweled.

Materials for Ribs, Spreaders, and Shanks

The ribs and spreaders are usually made of grooved metal. Steel, being strong and inexpensive, is most commonly used for these parts. If too thin, however, these may bend easily and thus quickly lose their shape. Better umbrellas have sturdier steel ribs and spreaders. Brass plating for inexpensive umbrellas and chromium plating or enameling for more costly umbrellas keep the steel from rusting. Solid brass ribs and spreaders add to the sturdiness of the frame. The shank is made from wood; if made from metal, it is called a rod.

The tips are made from metal or plastic.

Materials for Handles

Handles of umbrellas are made in the widest range of materials. They are made from inexpensive woods and plastics; or they are made from costly woods, bone, horn, cane, bamboo, leather, or metal. They may be carved, studded with jewels, engraved, or hand painted. The most common shapes for handles are the *crook* (shaped like a question mark), the *straight,* and the *golf* or *opera* (which is a modified crook). Other handles may have fancy twists and curlicues.

In addition to the rigid handle, women's umbrellas have braided cord, leather, or plastic straps, beads, or chains that permit easy carrying.

TYPES AND STYLES OF UMBRELLAS

Ballerina umbrellas have a dainty appearance with a ruffled edge that makes them resemble a dancer's skirt.

Beach umbrellas vary in size from 5 to 8 feet in diameter. They are made from waterproof materials and may have gaily colored stripes or figured patterns. Center poles are usually made of wood or aluminum, and they are pointed on one end to fit easily into sand or soil.

Clamp umbrellas are large umbrellas that serve the same purpose as the beach umbrella, but they are made to be portable and to clamp on to golf carts, chairs, or other furniture. The shank may be equipped with a swivel device to permit tilting the canopy.

Cocktail umbrellas are dainty, dress-up umbrellas that have a tiny canopy just large enough to shield one person.

Extension-handle umbrellas have a handle that telescopes for carrying or for ease in packing in a suitcase. When in use, the handle extends to regular length.

Folding umbrellas are made to tuck into a brief case or other carryall, yet to be ready for use instantly as needed. The umbrella canopy folds to half its length, the handle telescopes, and a case is used to hold the folded umbrella in a compact form.

Garden umbrellas are large beach-type umbrellas that fit into an outdoor table. They have a 7- or 8-foot spread when open and are gaily colored and usually trimmed with fringe. A huge aluminum pole permits them to tilt as needed. Some are also equipped with lights attached to the center pole for use in the evening.

India umbrellas have a flat, shallow, saucerlike shape.

Men's umbrellas are usually black in color, and they have a wider spread than ladies' umbrellas.

Pagoda shaped umbrellas have "S" shaped canopies in contrast to the usual bell or mushroom shapes of regular umbrellas.

Regular umbrellas are approximately 24 inches in length. They may have 8, 10, or 16 ribs.

Self-opening umbrellas have a push button that works a hidden spring that releases the sleeve, pushing the ribs into place. When closed, the tip ends of the ribs are held in a metal cup.

Slim-jims are 30 inches or over in length and usually have 10 ribs to make them less bulky when folded.

Windproof umbrellas can be snapped back into shape if accidentally blown inside out. Regular umbrellas are usually so badly bent when blown inside out that they are unusable afterward. Windproof umbrellas may have a spring between the spreaders and ribs just under the canopy, which help to keep the umbrella in shape, or they may have hinges at the point where the spreaders and the ribs join. These hinges permit the umbrella to have the ribs turned back without bending them out of shape.

CARE OF UMBRELLAS

Umbrellas require very little care. When wet, it is desirable to open the umbrella after use to allow it to dry thoroughly. This keeps the fabric from spotting and from wrinkling excessively. When dry, the umbrella may be rolled neatly and secured with the case or with a ribbon tape.

PUTTING THIS MERCHANDISE KNOWLEDGE TO USE ❯❯❯❯❯❯❯❯❯❯

❯ DO YOU KNOW YOUR MERCHANDISE?

1. From what word is the word "umbrella" derived? What was the original purpose of the umbrella?
2. What materials are used for the canopy portion of the umbrella? What purpose do the ribs of the umbrella serve? What materials are commonly used for these ribs?
3. Explain the following terms: shank, tip ends, sleeve, rigid handle, flexible handle, cups.
4. Explain the advantages of the following types of umbrellas: beach, clamp, extension handle, folding, garden, self-opening, windproof.
5. What rules for care would you give a customer about an umbrella he is purchasing?

❯ INTERESTING THINGS TO DO

1. Bring an umbrella to class and make a sales presentation to the class.
2. Draw a picture of an umbrella and label all parts on your drawing.
3. Visit two or three stores that carry umbrellas. Where do they regularly sell umbrellas? What changes, if any, do they make on rainy days? Write a short theme telling what you would do on a rainy day if you ran an umbrella department to make umbrellas easily accessible for customers.

ADDITIONAL MERCHANDISE TERMS ❯❯❯❯❯❯❯❯❯❯❯❯❯❯❯❯❯❯❯

Attaché case is a small, hard-sided case for carrying legal papers, order blanks, or other business or personal documents. These cases may contain handy dividers and some may serve as a writing desk en route.

Biarritz is a term synonymous with *slip-on* glove.

Camp trunk is a small trunk which is packed flat. It is small enough to be used at the foot of a cot when camping or vacationing.

Club bag is a small piece of luggage. It differs from the suitcase inasmuch as it has flexible rather than rigid sides and is packed upright, the way it is carried. This makes it convenient for packing containers of liquids without danger of the contents spilling while the case is being carried.

Dressing case is a small piece of hand luggage with tray or fittings in the lid. The fittings consist of comb, brush, mirror, bottles, and jars for necessary cosmetics.

English thumb—see *Bolton thumb,* page 404.

Finger-free gloves is a trade name for gloves with specially designed fourchettes that go across the end of the fingers, thus permitting extra room and freedom of movement.

Fur lining, used for warm winter gloves, is made of rabbit fur or occasionally squirrel fur. Fourchettes are lined with wool jersey to keep the fingers of the gloves from looking too bulky.

Gore is the triangular insert sewed in the glove above the wrist to give a flared effect. Gores are used in gauntlet-type gloves.

Jewelry case is a boxlike case, small enough to be carried as a handbag, usually fitted with a tray, and often velvet lined. It is suitable for carrying jewelry and other small valuables while traveling.

Kid seam is the piqué type seam applied to good quality fabric gloves. The raw edge, on the outside of the glove, however, is turned under to prevent raveling before being stitched.

Men's fitted or dressing case is a small compact leather container holding brushes, comb, mirror, shaving soap, brush and razor, and file.

Overnight case is a small suitcase that holds just enough clothing for a short trip or visit. Men's overnight cases are often called **one-suiters**. They accommodate one suit, underwear, shirts, and other accessories yet are small enough to fit under a plane or train seat.

Portfolio is a small, flat, convenient container resembling a brief case; however, the portfolio has only a single pocket in contrast to the two or three pockets usual in the brief case. The portfolio is used to carry legal papers, documents, and students' papers.

Pullman is a large suitcase that has hangers for dresses and suits in the lid and compartments in the bottom for shoes, hose, accessories, and toilet articles.

Salesman's case is a rigid case large enough to carry samples, catalogues, and order books.

Service-Pak was designed by the U. S. Army Air Corps. It is a combination portable bag for three uniforms with places for shirts, socks, toilet goods. It extends full length so that garments may be hung as in a closet and folds over for carrying into a neat sectioned case.

Shoe case is a large, compactly arranged case with compartments for shoes. May be combined with a hatbox.

Shoulder-strap pouch is a handbag with long top straps that fit over the shoulder, providing convenience and freedom of the hands for work.

Suitcase is the original name applied to the rigid-type case that is flat and rectangular in appearance. While the word implies that the case be large enough to hold a suit, smaller cases are also generally known by this name.

Swagger pouch is a handbag with two top handles and open sides with a zipper-closed center section.

Tote bag is a large handbag made with a drawstring top, an envelope flap, or a bucket-shaped top. It is useful to carry books, papers, or other paraphernalia needed during the day.

Two-suiter is a suitcase with a tray designed to hold two men's suits. Ties may hang in the lid section, and under the suits are compartments for accessories, shirts, etc. A *three-suiter* has space for three suits plus accessories and other items.

Underarm pouch is a long, narrow bag with a frame or zipper top, easily carried under the arm.

Vagabond pouch is a pouch-style handbag with a back handle.

Wardrobe case is smaller than a Fortniter. It contains hangers in the lid for dresses and suits, but necessitates extra folds in the garments because of its smaller size.

Wardrobe trunk, full size, has ten hangers on one side and four large drawers on the other.

Wigcase is shaped like a hatbox and has a head form inside to hold the wig in shape during transport.

Zipper pouch is a handbag that dispenses with the frame top and uses a zipper closing instead.

Zipper luggage is shaped like a suitcase, but instead of the usual center opening, the case has a side zipper that opens permitting packing and unpacking. This is soft-sided luggage that can be made with a minimum of weight and is therefore popular for plane travel and for all-purpose carrying use.

Furs for Glamour and Beauty

CHAPTER
22

UNIT 64 THE FUR INDUSTRY

Furs are not necessities. They are bought for their attractiveness, their look of luxury, their downy-soft, warm, cuddly texture, or their dramatic appearance. Furs are among the products classified as "luxury" items by the United States government. They are, therefore, subject to a 10 per cent excise tax. Products, such as furs, that are not bought frequently, that carry an excise tax, and that are not actually needed are the most difficult to sell skillfully. Most fur salespeople are mature, experienced people. Years of training are necessary to become an expert fur salesperson.

The advertising and selling of fur garments is subject to the regulations of the Fur Products Labeling Act, which became effective August 9, 1952. This law requires that certain information be given on the label that must be attached to every fur garment or item having a value of over $5. While this label helps both the salesperson and the customer to know what the fur is and what finishes, if any, have been applied to it, a tremendous amount of knowledge is required to interpret this information in terms of what the product will do for the customer.

Furs have been worn throughout history and, as with any fashion item, constant changes and improvements are being made in these luxury products, which both men and women are interested in studying.

FASHION INTEREST IN FURS

Americans come by their interest in furs naturally. North America was largely developed because of the fur industry. Although we import many furs that are not raised here, we actually have a major part of the world's fur-bearing animals roaming the wilds or being raised on ranches in North

America. In the days of the Indians, traders bartered beads for the precious furs. Trading posts were established, and later some of them grew into such large cities as Chicago, St. Paul, Detroit, and Spokane. St. Louis and New Orleans were early centers for fur collection.

Because furs are purchased more for their becomingness than their warmth and durability, there is no standard for judging fur prices. If a certain type of fur is in fashion it may be far more expensive than a fur that will give more warmth and better service. In years when brown furs are in fashion, some black furs may lose prestige and thus can usually be purchased at comparatively lower prices. When flat furs are in vogue, manufacturers find that no amount of promotion will make customers want bulky, fluffy furs so they become relatively inexpensive. In contrast, when long-haired furs are fashion right, short-haired furs lose their value.

FUR FARMING

An important development occurred in the fur industry in the year 1880 when silver-fox *fur farming* (raising and breeding the animals under controlled conditions) was begun in Prince Edward Island off the eastern coast of Canada. This project was just getting well under way when World War I brought a slump in the fur business. Following the war, American women became very fur-fashion conscious; and the lovely silver fox, which was plentiful because of the established fur farms, became one of fashion's pets and remained so until the 1940's when women lost interest in its long, silvery-colored fur.

Chinchilla farms, mink ranches, Persian lamb farms, fox farms, and nutria farms have developed throughout America in the past fifty years. These fur farms have made it possible to supply manufacturers with furs that were in demand. By careful breeding, fur farmers have improved the textures and colors of the fur-bearing animals. The sensational *mutation* mink furs are also the result of fur farming. When an animal was born with an odd-colored fur, by carefully breeding the animal to close relatives, called *inbreeding,* and to other minks from nonrelated families called *crossbreeding,* these unique colors were developed in a sufficient number of animals to be made into many garments. Thus, fur farming has literally revolutionized the fur industry.

IMPORTANT FUR TERMS

To talk about furs intelligently and to interpret labels, it is first necessary to understand all frequently used terms.

Furs have been defined by the Fur Products Labeling Act as any animal skin or part thereof with hair, fleece, or fur fibers attached, either in its raw or processed state; but it shall not include such skins as are to be converted into leather.

The skin of the animal with hair, fleece, or fur fibers attached may be

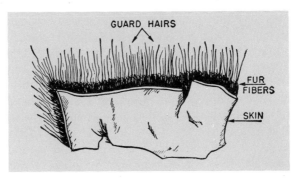

Fur Fibers and Guard Hairs of Long-Haired Animal.

explained as follows: Most animals have two kinds of hair covering—soft, downlike hair next to their skin, used for warmth as we use an overcoat. These downlike hairs are known as *fur fibers.* Usually protruding beyond these, and somewhat stiffer, are the hairs known as *guard hairs,* which the animal uses as a raincoat to shed rain and moisture.

The definition says only "hair, fleece, or fur fibers attached." Sometimes, to beautify a fur, the guard hairs may be shaved down, a process known as *shearing.* This is the process used on sheared, dyed muskrats and a number of other furs to give them a rich, velvety pile texture. In some furs such as *beaver* and *fur seal* from Alaska, the *guard hairs* are plucked out completely so that only the *fur fiber* which is sheared remains. In contrast to these sheared furs are the minks and fox furs, which depend on the length and beauty of the guard hairs for the attractiveness of the fur.

Other definitions of importance include the terms "used fur" and "waste fur." If a fur has previously been used in a garment that has been worn, and is then cut up and placed in another garment, it must be revealed as "used fur." Odds and ends like ears, throats, and leftover pieces when cut from new fur are referred to as "waste fur." These may be used in some inexpensive fur or fur-trimmed products, but they must be labeled properly.

JUDGING QUALITY IN FURS

The quality of the animal's skin and hair covering varies with the season of the year, the altitude, the amount of moisture, sunlight, food available, and many other factors. Since animals in colder climates grow more fur fiber to act as an overcoat, the animals that live farther north usually have the fullest fur fibers. This is important also to the beauty of the fur, because thick fur fibers cause the guard hairs to stand erect and make the fur look fluffy and luxurious. Animals living in water or in a rainy climate will develop more guard hair. On furs where the guard hair is the beauty mark, this factor is important.

When the winter is at its coldest, the animal's skin and fur, known as the *peltry,* are at their best. A fur taken at this time is known as a *prime fur* or a first quality fur. In a prime fur, the animal has a thin supple skin, dense fur fiber, and silky guard hair. As the season becomes warmer, the animal begins to molt or shed his fur fibers. His skin becomes tougher, and his hair has a straggly appearance. These furs are not so suitable for fur garments and are known as *seconds* or, if very poor quality, as *thirds,* or *fourths.* Furs taken in the fall before the development of the best quality fur fiber and guard hair are also known as seconds, thirds, or fourths. The government tries to regulate the trapping seasons so that animals are caught only during the prime season. If a fur garment has a soft supple skin, luxurious fur fiber, and glossy guard hair, it is undoubtedly a prime fur. By looking at the skin side of the fur, you can determine whether the skin is prime or unprime. If the hairs extrude through the back of the skin, or if the skin has heavy tough leather, it is an unprime skin.

The color of the fur will also be affected by the season, the climate, and the place where the animal lives. Some animals that live in the frozen north are white in color like the surrounding country—such as the fox and the wolf from the Arctic region. If the animals live in swamps or forest land, their protective coloring is usually darker than that of animals living in more open country. The majority of animals have yellow-brown to blue-brown fur. A few have black fur, which is a concentration of brown hair pigment. Tinges of yellow or red color in brown furs usually indicate that the furs are of inferior quality. Fine quality undyed brown furs have a bluish cast.

Male animal skins, being larger and more luxurious looking than female skins, are more desirable and thus more costly.

CATCHING FUR-BEARING ANIMALS

Obtaining the wild animals just at the prime season presents a problem. Many are caught by the use of judiciously placed traps. Often, however, the trapper returns to the trap to find that another animal has made a meal of the one that was caught.

When an animal's home is discovered, the animals may be clubbed as they emerge from their hiding place. Some animals are shot, although the danger of damaging small furs makes this practice undesirable.

Animals raised on fur farms lead vastly better lives. They are fed adequate diets at regular intervals. On the farms animals are carefully bred, so that only the finest strains are developed. They are protected against disease and receive all the care that newborn babies do. Not only are they protected, well fed, and carefully bred on fur farms, but they also can be raised in the climate and altitude best suited for their particular needs. When prime, the animals are rounded up and dispatched by a quick and painless death.

After the animals have been killed, their skins are removed. These may be taken off inside out as a slip-on sweater is removed, known as *case handled,* or slit up the belly section and removed as one would take off a coat, known as *open handled.*

The furs are now collected at some central place and sent to the auction houses, where they are sorted in bundles according to quality and size. The various manufacturers then bid for the bundles of furs.

Few women would want the furs, however, in their native state. Many processes are necessary to change the skins into leather and to make the fur desirable for luxurious garments. For the manufacturers, then, obtaining the skins is just the initial step. How the fur is transformed will be discussed in the next unit.

PUTTING THIS MERCHANDISE KNOWLEDGE TO USE ❯ ❯ ❯ ❯ ❯ ❯ ❯ ❯ ❯ ❯

❯ DO YOU KNOW YOUR MERCHANDISE?

1. Why is there an excise tax on furs?
2. Explain why fur selling is not effective when done by amateurs.
3. How have furs played a part in the development of America?
4. What factors affect the price of furs?
5. When was fur farming begun? How has it affected the fur industry? What furs are farmed today?
6. Define furs, fur fibers, guard hair, shearing, plucking, used fur, waste fur, peltry, prime fur.
7. Explain the difference between the methods used to catch wild animals for furs and the methods used on fur farms.

❯ INTERESTING THINGS TO DO

1. Visit your local zoo. Write a description of one animal whose pelt is used for fur. What quality fur do you think the pelt would make? Why?
2. Ask among your friends to find someone who traps animals. What methods does he use to catch the animals? What animals does he catch? Are the skins worth very much money?
3. Read fur advertisements in newspapers and magazines. How many of the advertisements mention mutation furs? How many mentioned ranch furs? Did any state that the furs were "wild"?

UNIT 65 DRESSING AND DYEING FURS

After purchasing the furs, the manufacturers send them to a firm that specializes in the dressing and dyeing of furs. *Dressing* is synonymous with *tanning* in the leather industry. It means the treatment of the skins so that they will not putrefy and disintegrate. Dressing also beautifies the fur and includes the removal of any unnecessary guard hair or fur fiber. *Dyeing* refers to the darkening or changing of the color of the fur.

DRESSING FURS

The peltries are first washed in salt water to remove dirt. Excess flesh and fat are scraped off the skin side by sharp knives. If guard hairs are not wanted, they may be sheared the way tall grass is cut by a lawn mower, or plucked out.

The cleaned and scraped skins are now ready for the tramping machine. Large machines known as *kickers* are used. Huge wooden blocks kick the furs against one another with a great deal of force and break up all the fibers in the skin so they will be pliable and soft.

Following this tramping operation, the skins are put into a huge revolving drum filled with sawdust. The skins and sawdust are revolved together for several hours, the sawdust taking all the dirt, grease, and grime from the fur and making it shiny and clean. The sawdust is removed, and the skins are ready for the chemicals that will preserve them and turn them into leather. The skin side usually has some chemicals applied that are made from a salt-acid pickle, vegetable materials, oils, or mineral salts such as chrome or alum. The thin skins are packed together overnight, and by the following day they have been converted into leather.

The tanned leather on the skin side is then lubricated by the application of oil in a process similar to the fat liquoring of leather, and the skins are again drummed with sawdust. After removal of all sawdust, the skins are stretched and the fur beaten with a rattan stick or blown with compressed air to fluff it and increase its beauty.

CHANGING THE COLOR OF FURS

The color of a finished fur garment may be *natural, dyed, tip-dyed, bleached,* or *bleached and then dyed.*

Natural

When a fur is used in its natural coloring, only the pigments present in the animal's skin are responsible for the color. Since natural color will remain attractive for a long time, and since harsh dyes or bleaches have not been used on the fur, such fur, when it is rich looking, is the most desirable of all. Many fur-bearing animals, however, are not attractive in their natural colors; chemists have therefore developed various methods of changing and improving the appearance of drab-looking furs.

Dyeing

Dyeing was originally used to make less expensive furs, such as rabbit, look like better furs. Today, however, dyeing is an art used not for imitation so much as to beautify the fur. The Fur Products Labeling Act has definite rules about labeling dyed furs. When the natural color of a fur has been changed, the customer must be informed of this fact by a label or tag attached to the

Left: Natural dressed (tanned) rabbit. **Center:** Sheared and brown-dyed rabbit. **Right:** Dyed and striped rabbit.

Left: White rabbit's fur may be used for evening jackets or trimmings on garments. **Center:** White rabbit dyed and stenciled. **Right:** White rabbit dyed and stenciled.

garment. If the change has taken place because the entire fur has been immersed in a dye bath, the fur is specified as being dyed. A muskrat that has been dyed black must be labeled "dyed muskrat." A squirrel that has been dyed brown must be labeled "dyed squirrel." The color of the dye may be mentioned also as, "brown-dyed muskrat," "honey-dyed squirrel."

Unless the animal's skin has been shaved after dyeing, you may be able to tell that it has been dip-dyed, for the skin side will be dark. Some undyed furs, however, have the skins darkened so that they will not reveal white streaks when the fur separates while being worn. Gray Persian lamb, for example, always has a dyed skin although the fur is usually naturally gray. This is called *tipping* in the fur trade and need not be mentioned on the label.

Tip-Dyeing

Some furs are not *dip-dyed* to change the color, but rather have color brushed on the fur side of the garment to darken the natural color. Since this method changes the color of the fur but does not affect the skin, these furs are known as *tip-dyed*. In some cases a feather is actually used for the tip-dyeing. The workman dips the feather into the coloring matter and brushes it over the tips of the guard hairs, artistically shading the fur to the desired color. Tip-dyeing is less harmful to a peltry than dyeing. Often pale, off-colored furs are enhanced by tip-dyeing to resemble a better color quality of that same fur, such as *tip-dyed mink*. The skin side of tip-dyed fur does not show any change in color, but may be light cream as it was before any coloring matter had been applied. Tip-dyeing will eventually fade if the garment is worn much in the sunlight.

Stencil Dyeing

When a less expensive fur is used to imitate a spotted fur such as leopard, a stenciling process must be used to apply the spots. *Dyed rabbit* is transformed in this manner.

Bleaching

White furs that have a yellow tinge or dark furs that are to be made attractive by being dyed pale shades may first be bleached. Bleaching chemicals are used in a manner similar to that of bleaching a woman's hair. Bleached furs may become tinged with yellow or tan as they are exposed to the sun.

GLAZING

Natural furs and those that have undergone a color change should appear sleek and glossy. The final beauty treatment is known as *glazing*. This may be accomplished by spraying the furs with a chemical that imparts a sheen; but in most dressing plants, merely spraying the skins with water and then pressing them skillfully with a specially padded iron makes the fur smooth and lustrous by bringing the oil from the hair to the surface.

The furs now looking very different from the way they did before the beauty treatment are ready for manufacture into various kinds of garments.

❯ DO YOU KNOW YOUR MERCHANDISE?

1. What is meant by the dressing of furs? Give briefly the steps necessary in dressing furs.
2. Why are furs dyed? Which is better: a natural mink or a dyed mink? Give reasons for your answer.
3. Define natural fur, dyed fur, tip-dyed fur, tipped fur, stenciled fur, bleached fur.
4. Why are furs glazed? Explain the glazing process.
5. If you were advertising a muskrat that had been dyed dark brown and given a black stripe down the center back, how would you describe the fur in the advertisement?

❯ INTERESTING THINGS TO DO

1. Analyze five fur advertisements. How many mentioned dyed furs? How many mentioned natural furs? Were the dyed or the natural furs more expensive?
2. Prepare a 2-minute sales talk for a natural fur.
3. Prepare a 2-minute sales talk for a dyed fur.

UNIT 66 CONSTRUCTION OF FUR GARMENTS

The construction of a fur coat or jacket is indeed an intricate process, as those who have ever seen the skin side of a fur garment know. Some coats have relatively few seams inside. Some garments are made of tiny strips of fur no larger than ⅛ of an inch in width and 1½ inches in length, yet from the outside, the garment looks as though it were made of long strips of handsomely matched fur. Other coats resemble from the inside a jig-saw puzzle with tiny jagged sections dovetailing perfectly. All this work, which is fitted by hand and stitched on a special type of sewing machine, takes many hours and much skill and adds considerably to the beauty, sleek appearance, good fit, and cost of the finished coat.

MUSLIN PATTERN

Before a fur garment is begun, a muslin garment is made, fitted on a form, and analyzed. Any mistakes in the fit of the coat or any details that are not just right may be changed easily at this stage; whereas, if the garment were made up originally in fur, the errors would indeed be costly. After the muslin garment is approved, the shape is translated into a heavyweight paper pattern. This resembles any ordinary coat pattern and is used as the guide for the cutting and arranging of the furs.

MATCHING FURS

The man who selects the furs for the different sections of the garment must be highly skilled. Choice pelts are used for those areas of the garment that are most noticeable, such as the collar, center back, center front, and sleeve sections. The pelts that are placed under the arms and along the sides of the garment need not be so choice.

Matching the furs that are to adjoin one another must be done with care. The matcher must consider the length and texture of the hair and fur, the color, any markings on the fur, and the size of the peltries. He places the furs in order on the pattern and hands them to the cutter.

CUTTING

The fur cutter is an important person in the making of a fur garment. His tools consist only of a sharp knife that resembles a razor blade with a handle attached, a ruler, and pincers. His skill and knowledge, however, are valuable to the finished beauty of the fur. He arranges the skins that have been given him to fit the various parts of the pattern. Any markings on the fur must be

Methods of Damaging Out. Left: Peltry showing damages on skin side. **Center:** Peltry with cuts made preparatory to repairing damages. **Right:** Damaged sections removed, and cut sections closed and sewed.

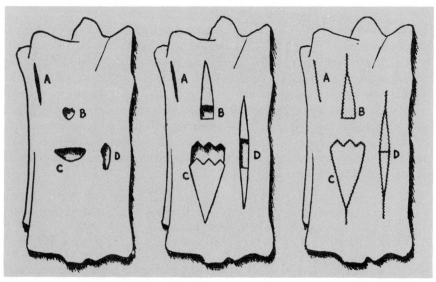

matched perfectly. Then, using the fur as economically as possible, he cuts the skins so that one part will match the color and pattern of the fur next to it. He must also see that stronger sections of fur are used in those places on the coat that will get the most wear. As he cuts and fits these tiny pieces of fur together, he also removes any small holes or imperfections in the skins by cutting them out in zig-zag fashion so that they can later be drawn together by the sewer without any noticeable loss. This process is known as *damaging out*. If skins are inferior, there may be several of these damaged-out spots visible on the inside of the skins.

The cutter also cuts the skins in different ways depending on the manner in which the skins will be joined together. He may be using *whole skins* for the length of the garment, *skin-on-skin* construction, *let-out* construction, *semi-let-out* construction, or *split-skin* construction. He may also make *plated, leathered,* and *reset* garments.

Whole Skins

Only a few fur pelts are large enough to be made into garments without joining the peltries together lengthwise. Some lambs are large enough to be used from neckline to hemline of a garment.

Skin-on-Skin Construction

The majority of fur-bearing animal skins such as the mink, muskrat, and rabbit are too short to be used for the full length of even short garments. They are joined one below the other in a method known as *skin-on-skin construction*. Since it is difficult except with wavy or curly haired furs to hide these seams, they are almost always visible.

Three types of skin-on-skin seams are used: *straight, wavy,* and *zig-zag.* For the *straight* seam, which is the easiest to cut and sew, the least expensive, and the least durable, the skins are simply cut straight across and joined in blocklike form to the one above and below. These inexpensive seams are seen on some rabbit and some kidskin coats.

Wavy seams are more difficult to cut and sew, are more secure, and are commonly used on slightly better quality kidskins, patterned furs such as wavy haired lambs, and on spotted furs.

The *zig-zag* seam is the strongest of all the skin-on-skin seams. The tail section of the fur is cut into a "v" shape and the head of the fur to be placed below it is cut to receive the "v". These seams are popular on muskrat, squirrel, marmot, and other flat-haired fur garments.

Since all these skin-on-skin seams produce a horizontal marking around the fur garment, some women dislike this type of construction because it makes them appear somewhat shorter as they wear the garment. They seek a more costly construction that eliminates these horizontal markings.

Leathering: Skin side of fur showing strips of leather or ribbon sewed between strips of fur.

Letting-Out

A costlier method of constructing garments that eliminates the horizontal markings is known as *letting-out*. Each skin is cut down the center of the dark vertical stripe running the length of the skin. Narrow strips are cut at an angle. For fine quality mink, these cuts are often ⅛ of an inch apart. Each tiny strip is now resewed to the strip above it and below it at a different angle to make the skin longer and narrower. The other half of the skin is resewed in a like manner; and when the two halves are later joined, the short, broad skin has become long and narrow. These long narrow strips may be used to give lengthwise grace to a garment; or for some styling, horizontal strips of these narrowed furs are used.

Variations of this letting-out process are used on muskrat, silver fox, platinum fox, ermine, sable, gray Persian lamb, beaver, sheared raccoon, and chinchilla.

Since letting-out not only takes a great deal of time, effort, and skill, but also uses more fur than would otherwise be necessary, it adds considerably to the cost of the garment. In advertisements, this construction is often referred to as *fully let-out.*

Semi-Let-Out. When a fur garment is to be made from skins that are broad and short, and a narrower, somewhat longer skin would be more attractive, a modified cutting and resewing of the skins as described under the "letting-out" section are performed. Instead of making one skin run the length of the garment, semi-let-out construction merely increases each skin's length slightly. This gives more attractive lines to the garment. Since only two or three cuts are made in each half skin, the process is not very costly. It is used primarily on squirrel skins and occasionally on chinchilla skins.

Split-Skin Construction

All through the 1950's mink grew in popularity until few other kinds of fur were in demand at any price. The costly let-out process used on the minks, added to the high price of the furs themselves, however, made the finished garments too expensive for people with only modest incomes. In 1953 some furriers introduced a new method of handling mink skins that resembled to some degree the appearance of let-out skins, costing however but a fraction of the price to construct. The process, however, could only be used on short garments such as jackets, capelets, or stoles. Instead of cutting and restitching each skin so the center dark mark on each mink remained in the center of each narrower strip, the skin is simply cut in half right through the dark stripe. Each half is then turned on end and placed side by side with the dark stripe at the bottom of the peltry running crosswise across the back of the garment. While let-out garments may also have the skins running crosswise, the darker center stripe is always in the center of the skin instead of being on the edge of each skin as in the split-skin construction. Since the term "split skin" is not a good selling term and since the construction is an inexpensive one, furriers do not use the term in advertising or selling garments so made. Such garments may, however, not be misrepresented by indicating that they are made by a more costly method such as the let-out method.

Plates

Inexpensive garments are made from "waste fur." Sections of the peltry such as the neck (gills), paws, sides (flank), and parts of the belly, which are not used in good-quality garments, are stitched together like pieces in a patchwork quilt. The finished oblong or square is called a *plate*. This plate is then used as cloth would be. A pattern for a coat or jacket is laid on it and various sections cut ready for joining. The finished garment made from these pieces must have an attached label that tells the customer the garment was made from leftover pieces, as "Persian paw," "mink gill," or "muskrat flank."

Leathering

Bulky furs such as fox, skunk, and raccoon may have strips of leather or ribbon sewed at intervals between strips of fur. This process, known as *leathering,* reduces the amount of fur needed and gives the garment a slenderizing effect.

Sections of the Peltry.
1. Gill
2. Head
3. Back
4. Rump
5. Flank
6. Paws
7. Tail

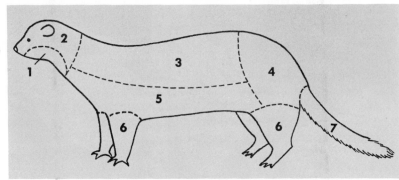

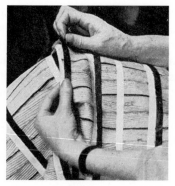

Making a Let-Out Mink Coat. Left: Nailing. After the pelts are dampened, fine nails are used to hold each seam in place until the skins are dry. The strips of fur are thus evenly spaced and hang perfectly straight. **Right: Taping.** Rows of tape sewed on the inside of the pelts protect them from strain. *(Courtesy Trencher Furs)*

Resetting

A large, bulky skin may be made to look like two smaller skins by a process called *resetting*. Parallel, vertical cuts are made in the skin, then every other strip is assembled to make one skin, and those remaining form the second skin. Since these are cut from the same skin, any marks are the same on both the smaller skins.

SEWING AND ASSEMBLING

The cut sections of fur are carefully marked and handed in groups to the

Left: High-Grade Sewmanship. This machine operator is patiently sewing together strips of fur into a long "let-out" skin. Original skin, sliced by cutter but not finally separated, is seen at left of sewing machine. Almost complete let-out skin, more than twice as long as original, is in operator's hands. Letting-out results in supple graceful skins of great beauty. **Right: Closing Time.** Sections of a Persian lamb coat are being sewed together in the important "closing" operation. Each section is made of skins that have been expertly worked into uniform, perfectly matched areas. Closing transforms the individual parts—body, sleeves, cuffs and collar—into a whole garment. *(Courtesy Ruder & Finn, Inc.)*

operator who stitches them together. A machine that stitches a seam similar to the overseam stitch on leather gloves is used. The sewer holds the two edges of the leather side of the fur together, and stitches row after row without a moment's hesitation. Cut-out sections of damage, long or short strips, or large sections of fur are sewed together, the seam stretched by pulling to make the fur lie flat, and the next section attached. In a fitted type the garment emerges from his machine in several separate sections—the sleeves, the back, the collar and lapels, and two front sections. In a swagger or box model the sections consist of the body, the sleeves, and the collar.

NAILING, STAYING, AND FINISHING

Fur coats cannot be pressed, as can woolen coats, to make seams straight and to make the coat hang correctly; however, a process known as *nailing* performs this operation. A large wooden board has the pattern of the sleeves, back, front pieces, collar, and lapels traced on it in chalk. These various pieces as they come from the sewer are dampened and stretched to fit the chalked pattern on the board. They are then nailed on the board with the leather side out (in most furs) and left to dry. In let-out coats, every seam the length of the garment has nails holding it firmly in place to assure that the finished coat will hang and drape gracefully. Thousands of nails are necessary for this operation.

After the fur is dry, it is removed from the board and all edges are closed and taped, the lining is sewed in, and buttons, loops, and snaps are attached.

Some thin-skinned furs, such as broadtail lamb, kolinsky, rabbit, before being made up into garments, may have a thin piece of fabric stitched or glued to the leather side to reinforce the skin and prevent it from ripping. This is known as *staying*.

SCARFS

Sable, mink, fox, stone marten, baum marten, bassarisk, and squirrel are some of the popular furs used for scarfs. These furs have the heads mounted by special companies. The scarf itself is made of full skins unless specified as a "pieced-skin scarf" or a "brown-dyed squirrel scarf with mink tail."

PUTTING THIS MERCHANDISE KNOWLEDGE TO USE ❯ ❯ ❯ ❯ ❯ ❯ ❯ ❯ ❯ ❯

❯ DO YOU KNOW YOUR MERCHANDISE?

1. Why is a muslin pattern (garment) made up before a fur garment is begun?
2. What is the function of the matcher of furs?
3. Why are fur garments not made from whole skins without further manipulation?
4. Explain skin-on-skin construction, let-out construction, semi-let-out construction, split-skin construction, plated garments, leathering, resetting.

5. What are the three methods by which skin-on-skin construction can be made? Which is the best? Why? What are the disadvantages of skin-on-skin construction?
6. When would you suggest that a person seek let-out construction? What are its advantages? What are its disadvantages?
7. What is the advantage of having furs semi-let-out?
8. Why is the term "split-skin" not used in advertising fur garments?
9. What is the main advantage of a "plated" garment? the main disadvantage?
10. Why is nailing necessary for fur garments?

> INTERESTING THINGS TO DO

1. Prepare a sales demonstration telling a customer about the construction of the garment she is considering for purchase.
2. Read several fur advertisements. List all construction terms you could find in those advertisements. Why do you think your results were not impressive?

UNIT 67   THE FUR-BEARING ANIMALS

FEDERAL TRADE COMMISSION RULES AND REGULATIONS UNDER THE FUR PRODUCTS LABELING ACT

For many years furs were sold under names which would make the customer feel that she was getting some rare or expensive fur instead of an ordinary, inexpensive fur. *Brown-dyed marmot* masqueraded as a *marmink;* rabbit was called anything but its own name. Such terms as *lapin, chinchillette, ermeline, northern seal,* and *coney* were frequently used to intimate that the customer was purchasing something other than rabbit.

Today, however, such imaginative names are no longer allowed, for the Fur Products Labeling Act which became effective August 9, 1952, designated that the true English name of the animal must be used and must be as prominently printed in advertisements and labels as the other words used. No other animal's name may be used to describe any dye or process. Thus what used to be called "Hudson-seal dyed muskrat" today is known simply as "dyed muskrat" or "sheared and dyed muskrat" or "black-dyed muskrat."

The Federal Trade Commission insists that the geographic origin of the fur be accurate. Thus mink from Asia must not be represented as coming from Canada. Persian lambs, however, need not come from Iran, since the term "Persian" means a special type of lamb rather than a geographic location.

The fur origin of all imported furs must be noted on the label which must be 1¾ inches by 2¾ inches in size. Also any *waste fur* or *used fur* must be mentioned.

If a fur has been made a different color by dyeing or if it has been made darker or richer looking by tip-dyeing, the fur must be labeled as "dyed rabbit," or "tip-dyed mink," or whatever the process may have been.

The Fur Products Labeling Act has made customers want to know more about the various furs. The salesperson, therefore, has to meet a real challenge by knowing the characteristics of the more usual furs.

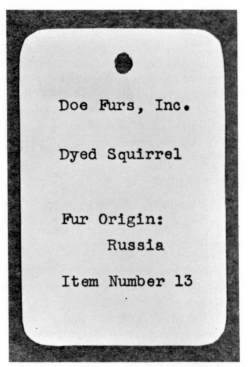

Doe Furs, Inc.

Dyed Squirrel

Fur Origin:
Russia

Item Number 13

FUR-BEARING ANIMALS

Furs appeal to all women. They come to the fur department with their many problems: "I want a coat that gives me a slender line," "I want a coat that will wear well," "I want a jacket that will be appropriate with both daytime and evening clothes," "I want a jacket that will not make me look shorter," "Show me something inexpensive for sportswear." These and thousands of other problems face the fur salesperson.

Some customers when they enter the fur department express a preference for a particular fur. Often this is because they have seen that fur worn by a friend, or have seen it displayed in windows, or read about it in advertisements. If that particular fur is too expensive, or does not come in the style the customer wants, the salesperson usually shows her a similar-appearing fur—one with the same general coloring, texture, and appearance. Thus if a customer specifies a beaver coat, but none in stock suits her purpose or her pocketbook, nutria, sheared raccoon, mouton-processed lamb, and brown-dyed rabbit or any other brown-colored furs may also be shown.

To answer the customer's questions, aid her in selecting the correct garment, and be able to explain variations in price, quality, and workmanship, the salesman must be informed about the varying characteristics of the furs themselves as well as about the methods of dressing, dyeing, and assembling them.

The only way to learn about the various furs is to study them by looking at them, stroking them, analyzing them, and comparing them with similar furs.

Furs may be divided into any number of classifications—color, type of fur and general character, or by family groupings. Although customers purchase furs because of their flatness, their fluffiness, their beautiful markings, their beauty of coloring, or their price, it is easier to learn about the furs in their family groups. Often furs in one family will show related characteristics. Furs may be classified in the following family groups: rodent family, weasel family, cat family, canine or dog family, hoofed animals, and miscellaneous group, which includes those animals that are not members of the other families.

THE RODENT FAMILY

This family consists of a number of the most popular fur animals.

Beaver

Outstanding among them is the *beaver*. This animal is very ambitious. He chews through logs many times his size and drags them long distances to build dams in which he and his family can hide during the winter. He then builds a large hut which he enters through the water to be safe from other animals. Because his dams flood the surrounding country, the beaver cannot be farmed successfully.

Beaver fur has always been useful because of its warmth and serviceability. However, stylish women disliked the beaver fur because it made a heavy, bulky-looking coat with thick leather and long shaggy guard hairs. In 1935 a new process was developed to make the skin thinner, to pluck the guard hairs, and to shear the remaining fur fibers. In addition, by extra low shearing on the sides of the peltry and by letting-out the skins, wide silvery stripes were revealed between areas of dark blue-brown fur. Sheared beaver fur does not mat nearly so badly as it did before the long fur fibers were sheared. The fur may, however, mat slightly when wet. Glazing the fur gives it a smooth appearance.

Canada, Alaska, and the Rocky Mountain states are the beaver's native habitat. The bluish-brown fur from the Eastern Canadian beaver is considered the finest quality.

Nutria

This South American animal, also raised in Louisiana, is a relative of the northern beaver. The fur is not shaded, however, so no stripes are revealed when it is sheared. The guard hair of the nutria is not plucked as is the beaver, so these shiny hairs are visible when the pile of fur is examined closely.

The nutria spends a great deal of time in the water, but he differs from the other animals because his belly section contains the best quality fur. Although nutria may be as costly as beaver, it does not wear quite so well. It has a somewhat shorter, flatter, less bulky-appearing pile surface. A rich, blue-brown is the best color.

Muskrat

Muskrats live in practically all regions of the United States and Canada. There are two general types: the northern muskrat and the southern muskrat. The best qualities in both hair covering and leather texture come from the Great Lakes region, but the largest production region of the northern variety is New Jersey and the Chesapeake Bay river marshes in Maryland and Delaware. The southern variety comes only from the delta of the Mississippi River. The latter are not so well furred as the northern variety, hence have a flatter appearance. The durability of muskrat coats depends chiefly on the thickness of the fur fiber and guard hair.

Many different types of coats are made from the muskrat. The vogue that began during the latter part of the 1930's for mink furs caused dyers to experiment again with the muskrat. When a dark ground color and a darker stripe were applied, the muskrat emerged resembling mink, sable, or baum marten. The long guard hair is silky looking, and the rich brown coloring makes the coat appear luxurious. The fur wears fairly well and is useful for most occasions.

Many years ago, furriers experimented with the northern muskrat to make it resemble fur seal. They sheared the guard hair and dyed the fur a rich black. Since it was just called *Hudson seal,* women did not know they were wearing a muskrat coat. The Fur Products Labeling Act now does not permit any reference to the seal that is imitated. There is no such animal as a Hudson seal. That term was created to apply only to the sheared, black-dyed muskrat before the labeling laws made it obsolete. This fur is velvety in texture, has a deep, luxurious looking pile, and when it is in fashion, makes sturdy, durable coats and capes for all occasions.

Muskrats are also made up into natural muskrat coats. The dark brown center back sections are used for the better quality; the golden sides of the muskrat for a medium quality; and the silver belly for inexpensive muskrat-flank coats. The serviceability of these coats depends on the section of the fur used. The back section from good-quality muskrats will wear much better than will the belly section.

Squirrel

The little squirrel you see in forests and parks is an important fur-bearing animal. Squirrels grow in almost all sections of the world. Siberian squirrels are considered to produce the best fur. The peltries have soft, dense fur fiber and guard hair. The best quality are a clear gray color. These are made up into natural squirrel coats. The red- or yellow-streaked peltries may be dyed brown in imitation of more costly brown furs.

The white belly sections are sewed into plates, dyed, and used as *squirrel belly* coats and jackets. The fur of the squirrel is luxuriously soft, but it is not very durable. Its silky sheen and softness make it desirable for dressy type garments, especially jackets, capes, stoles, and scarfs.

Marmot

The marmot is a land rodent, which burrows under the earth's surface. His fur is used to imitate costlier brown furs, but the fur is coarser and harsher in appearance and has an almost glassy luster. This fur is inferior in wearing qualities to the muskrat.

Chinchilla

The chinchilla, in spite of its poor wearing quality, is one of the more expensive luxury furs because of its rarity and exquisite softness. It is a native of the South American Andes Mountains. In 1923, eleven chinchillas, bundled in blankets and surrounded with hot-water bottles because of the changing temperatures, were brought from their native South American home to a chinchilla farm in California. Here they were carefully tended and reared. Today there are several dozen chinchilla fur farms in the United States all populated by descendants of the original eleven. The availability of the farmed furs has reduced the chinchilla's price somewhat, but it is still rare enough to be a luxury fur.

The fur fiber and guard hair are both "soft as silk," about three-fourths of an inch to one inch in length and luxurious to the touch. The best color is a bluish gray with white guard hairs that are black tipped. Less expensive varieties have yellowish coloring.

Because of their perishable nature, chinchilla garments are only suitable for dressy wear.

Rabbit

The rabbit, which is a common garden pet, multiplies rapidly, so there is rarely a scarcity of rabbit fur. Although the rabbit grows on most continents, the Australian rabbits and those from surrounding islands have the best texture of guard hair and fur fiber. Rabbit fur, which was known before the Labeling Act commonly as "coney" fur, may be used to imitate almost any other fur. Sturdy rabbit pelts may be sheared and dyed to resemble seal. These furs used to be called by the misleading term *sealine,* but today according to Federal Trade Commission rulings they must be called *dyed rabbit.* Lighter-weight rabbit skins, by blending, spotting, or dyeing, may be made to imitate chinchilla, mink, sable, ermine, leopard, or beaver. The French term *lapin,* once used as synonymous with *rabbit,* now may not be used, as only

English words are acceptable. The rabbit fur is attractive and soft to the touch, but it is not durable.

Since rabbit can be used to imitate almost any fur, it is useful for all types of garments. It may be seen as an evening jacket in the form of a white-dyed rabbit, or it may be spotted yellow and black and worn as a sports jacket under the guise of spot-dyed rabbit. Dyed dark brown and striped, it resembles mink and is popular for street and dress wear. Fur from the bucks (males) gives better service than fur from the does (females).

THE WEASEL FAMILY

Most of the expensive furs belong to this group of animals, which includes the *sables, minks,* and *ermines.* Most of the animals in this family are killers. Some of them also have unpleasant odors which keep their enemies from attacking them. These odors, however, are not noticeable on the finished fur garment, even though some people seem to imagine they are.

Sable

The sable, a native of Siberia, and for many years a leading quality fur, was long used for Russian royalty. The best quality sables have dark bluish-brown fur fiber and a lustrous sheen to the short dark brown guard hair which always appears fluffy. Most sables are used for scarfs. The very wealthy may have a sable cape for evening wear or a sable coat for street wear. Single skins sell from a low price of $50 a skin to a high price of several hundred dollars for one skin.

American Sable

Similar in appearance, but considerably less expensive, is the American marten or American sable which lives in Alaska and Canada. The darker these furs, the higher their value. The light-colored peltries are tip-dyed.

Ermine

The ermine, long thought of as the fur for royalty, is famous for its lustrous brown coat which turns white when the animal lives in the frozen north. Only the black tip of its long tail snares its prey into attempting to follow it over the snow-covered country. These ermine tails are used as trimming on various types of garments.

The finest ermine, pure white in color, with silky guard hair and fur fiber, comes from Siberia. The further south the animal lives, the shorter is the fur fiber and the coarser is the guard hair. In some sections of America, the ermine, called the *American weasel,* does not change color, but remains brown throughout the year. Before the Federal Trade Commission rulings, this

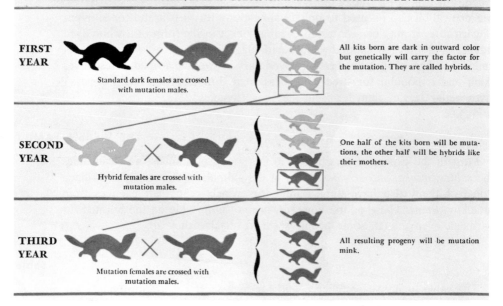

FIRST YEAR

Standard dark females are crossed with mutation males.

All kits born are dark in outward color but genetically will carry the factor for the mutation. They are called hybrids.

SECOND YEAR

Hybrid females are crossed with mutation males.

One half of the kits born will be mutations, the other half will be hybrids like their mothers.

THIRD YEAR

Mutation females are crossed with mutation males.

All resulting progeny will be mutation mink.

(Courtesy Emba Mink Breeders Assoc.)

animal was called *summer ermine,* but that term obviously is incorrect, because a fur taken in the summer would not be prime. The American weasel does not have as luxurious and long fur as does the Siberian ermine. Ermine is traditionally used for evening capes or jackets. Dyed ermine makes a lustrous, soft, and luxurious street and dress-wear garment.

Mink

The fur from the vicious, bloodthirsty mink has been one of the most popular and durable when it is converted into a coat, cape, or scarf for street or dress wear. This animal's fur has been imitated by the fur of the muskrat, marmot, rabbit, fitch, and squirrel, but there is no question which is the mink and which is the imitation when they are placed side by side. Confusion might occur, however, between the varying qualities of the mink itself. The finest mink peltries, which come from eastern Canada and the United States, have short, dense, soft, blue-brown fur fiber and slightly longer shiny guard hair. The center back of the mink has a narrow dark stripe which is its beauty mark. In *letting-out* mink garments, this stripe is always preserved down the center of the peltry. Imitations of mink have this black stripe dyed on the fur.

Fine ranch mink are usually darker in color than most wild mink because of more selective breeding. Wild mink that are quite pale in color are often blended to look darker and richer.

The animals called *mutation minks* are minks with unusual color achieved by crossbreeding and inbreeding. In this way some of today's most fashionable mink furs have been developed. The *silverblu* mink (gray-blue) when first bred was made into a coat selling for $25,000. Today, because increased numbers of these furs are available, silverblu mink coats are available for less than one-fifth of their former price. Over twenty additional shades in mink have been developed through the years ranging from white through pale to deeper tan and thence to brown and black. Pearl gray to gun-metal gray colors and pale blue through to dark gray-blue are also available. As each new mutation color is introduced, its rarity makes it costly. As other minks of this color are successfully raised, the price gradually becomes more and more reasonable.

Less expensive mink garments than those made from the whole skins of either wild or ranch animals are those made from mink paws, throats, and sides which are sewed together into plates.

Skunk

The skunk, until the Federal Trade Commission rulings prohibited it, long masqueraded under false names. That was because women, knowing the fur was skunk, always felt that an odor was noticeable when the garment was worn. This, of course, is not true. The skunk has two large glands that hold an ill-smelling liquid that can be sprayed on its enemies from a distance of six to eight feet, but the odor does not cling to his own fur.

The skunk's long hair and fur fiber are dark brown in color. Two white stripes which vary in width and length on the various animals run along the skunk's back. Since these white stripes consist of coarser hair that does not absorb dye well, they are often cut out and a group of them used for less expensive *dyed skunk stripe* coats. Skunk coats sold as *natural skunk* really have the leather side dipped into dye to prevent the white skin from showing through the dark brown hair. "Tip-dyed skunk" means that both the fur and leather have color applied, and "dyed skunk" means that the white stripe has been left in and the entire coat dipped in dyestuff strong enough to make the entire fur alike in color. Skunk coats are worn for sports, street, and dress wear. They are often let out to give them an elongated, flattering line and leathered to make them appear less bulky.

Spotted Skunk The *spotted skunk* (often incorrectly called "civet cat") is a smaller animal which has many of the characteristics of the skunk. It has an unusual marking of white in the shape of a lyre against a dark black-brown background. Both the fur fiber and guard hair are medium in length and soft to the touch. The fur is used for inexpensive sport and street-wear coats, jackets, and trimmings. The quality of the fur is determined by the clearness of coloring and the beauty of the markings.

Badger

The badger, which has a pale yellow color enhanced by guard hairs with brown and white tips, is used mostly for collars on women's sport coats. The long brown and white guard hair is also occasionally glued to a black fox skin to make it resemble silver fox. This is known as *pointing*. Men are familiar with badger hair, because the guard hairs from coarse-haired peltries are used for shaving brushes.

THE CAT FAMILY

This family is famous for its unusual spotted furs.

Leopard

The leopard is the most valuable member of this family. The sleek appearance of this fur is caused by the short flat guard hair of this animal. The black, rosette-shaped marks of the leopard skin are sharply contrasted with the creamy yellow background coloring of the fur. The smaller the spots, the more desirable the fur. The best quality of these come from Somaliland in Africa. Sports and street-wear coats and jackets are popular in this fur and its imitations.

Ocelot

The ocelot is the South American relative of the leopard. It is, however, considerably less valuable. The markings are in the shape of elongated ovals rather than rosette-shaped, and the fur is somewhat fluffier than the leopard's. The quality of this fur is determined by the flat, sleek appearance and sharply visible markings of the fur.

Lynx

Lynx, a long-haired, fluffy, light-colored fur with attractive shadings from creamy white to a light brown, is used for trim on dress and sports coats and for short bulky jackets. Its light color and fluffy almost foxlike appearance are particularly becoming to brunettes. Canadian lynx is considered the best quality. The fur requires great care because it sometimes sheds rather badly.

THE CANINE FAMILY

Some beautiful furs come from animals in this family. These furs are noted for the luxurious length of the guard hair and the fullness of the fur fiber. The fluffier and richer the appearance of the fox fur, the better the quality. Fox furs are commonly considered rather perishable, but many people have worn fox-trimmed winter and spring garments for four or five years without noticeable wear on the fur. Of course, a poor quality fox fur with little fur fiber and straggly guard hair would not wear very well.

Fox is suitable for scarfs or collars for dressy street wear and for capes and jackets for evening wear.

Red Fox

The red fox is the animal whose offspring may be either expensive cross fox, silver fox, or black fox, as well as red fox. In seasons when the rich orange-yellow to brown-red fur is not popular, it is dyed to represent other fox furs. The pale-colored furs are less valuable and are almost always dyed.

Silver Fox

The silver fox is noted for the rich beauty of the fur and guard hair. Most silver foxes are raised today on fur farms, which flourish in many sections of North America. The quality of the silver fox depends on the amount of silver guard hairs and the blue-black color of the thick underfur. Silver foxes that are completely covered with long silvery guard hair are known as "full silver." These have a dark stripe in the center back and a black tail with a snowy white tip. Mutations of silver fox that have a pearl-gray background or white neck portion have outmoded the darker silver fox.

Platinum Fox

The platina, or platinum, fox, a new addition to the fox family in 1933, is a

Furs from All Parts of the World. Foxes, mink, Persian lamb are being inspected by a fur buyer. *(Courtesy Ruder & Finn, Inc.)*

color phase of the silver fox. It was developed in Norway. This fox has the distinction of having brought the highest price ever paid at auction—$11,000 for one exquisitely beautiful platina fox in 1940. In its early years, when it was very scarce, the Duchess of Windsor and Sonja Henie each owned one of the lovely platina scarfs. The name comes from the platinum color of the fur which is a shaded cream to light blue with a silvery hue.

Cross Fox

The cross fox gets its name from a dark crosslike mark at the back of the neck. The color of this fur varies from that of the red fox to the silver fox. The better qualities resemble the latter in appearance.

White Fox

The white fox comes from the far north where there is ice and snow the year around. The furs with snow-white coloring and long silky guard hairs are the best quality. This fur is popular for evening capes. For daytime wear it is often dyed to resemble lynx and is known as *dyed white fox*.

Blue Fox

The blue fox is not blue at all, but a rather rich dark brown with a blue tinge to the fur. Since this brownish color has not been fashionable for many years, a really blue colored mutation fox was developed. This is known as *Norwegian blue fox*. It has a silvery blue color that is very flattering to most women.

Gray Fox

The gray fox is the inexpensive, less attractive member of the fox group. The fur, being gray with reddish undertones of color, is almost always dyed to resemble silver fox, and the tips of the guard hair are left silvery white. The fur and guard hair, however, are shorter and flatter than silver fox, and give but a poor imitation of the better fur. It is used for inexpensive jackets and trimmings on cloth coats.

Wolf

The wolf is another branch of the canine family, but one that is less important to the fur industry than the fox group. The finest wolves come from the arctic region and are known as *timber* wolves. These have a pale almost white fur which is very soft, with long, flowing guard hairs. Less expensive and less attractive wolf fur is known as *Canadian* and *prairie*. These have coarser hair which is flatter and shorter in appearance, and blue to yellow-gray in color. Wolf garments, when popular, are used for sports and street wear.

This family, known as the *ungulates,* includes the lamb, kid, guanaco, and pony.

The Persian lamb is one of the best-known furs of this group. Although this animal does not come from Persia, it retains its name of "Persian" by special permission of the Federal Trade Commission rulings, because customers have come to think of the Persian lamb in reference to that type of fur. This lamb comes mainly from Central Asia, Bokhara, and Afghanistan. It is noted for its tightly curled fur and beautiful luster. The more beautiful and tighter the "bean" or "knuckle" curl, the better the quality. The kinky, dull-looking fur is inferior in quality because it is crossbred. It is used on less expensive garments.

The Persian lamb may be naturally gray, brown, or black. The black are more plentiful and usually more attractive. In order to keep the light-colored skin from showing through the creases in the fur, the gray, brown, and black furred skins are tipped. But this, according to Federal Trade Commission rulings, does not have to be specified on the fur's label or in advertising. This fur is quite durable. It is used for dressy coats and as trimming on cloth coats. In selling this fur, the salesman should point out to the customer the beauty of the pattern, the lovely sheen of the fur, and the richness of the coloring. It is not difficult to tell differences in quality of Persian lambs, as the better quality have more beautiful markings and are much more lustrous.

Some Persian lambs are dyed. Often the black fur or the brown fur is made more lustrous by dip-dyeing the entire skin. This is then labeled as "black-dyed Persian lamb" or "brown-dyed Persian lamb." When attractive, gray Persian lamb furs are not dyed. These are sold as "natural gray Persian lamb."

Persian Paw is a familiar term for a plated garment made from the sections left over from whole-skin coats. These are considerably less expensive than Persian lamb garments. *Persian head* and *pieced Persian* are also plated garments.

Broadtail Lamb. This is the peltry from a newly-born lamb of the Persian group. The hair is not long enough to form curls but has a beautiful and very fine moiré effect. The quality of the fur depends on the design and the natural sheen of the fur. The fur, which is used for dressy coats, capes, jackets, and as trimming, is expensive, but not very durable. *Persian broadtail lamb* is made from the same kinds of lambs that are two to three days old and have slightly more curl than the broadtail lamb.

One of the most serviceable of all furs is that of a South American lamb which is sheared, processed to straighten the hair (called *plasticized* and *electrified*), and dyed. This short-pile, rather stiff, fur is particularly popular for campus wear. It is moderately low in price and is noted both for its warmth and durability. Although it is much bulkier and stiffer than beaver, some resemblance to the more expensive fur may be noticeable.

Broadtail-processed Lamb

Another variety of South American lamb is specially selected and sheared to reveal a moiré design somewhat resembling that of the more costly broadtail lamb. The leather is rather stiff, but the fur is made into attractive jackets, capes, and three-quarter-length coats for fall and spring wear. The midnight-blue dye has proved popular on this fur in recent seasons.

Kidskin

This skin comes mainly from China. A few have a wavy moiré appearance and somewhat resemble caracul lamb, but this fur is not popular at the present time. In recent years many of these skins have come from western India. Kidskin is a fairly perishable and inexpensive fur. The more beautiful the markings and the greater the sheen, the better the quality of the fur. It is occasionally used for dressy and street-wear coats and jackets.

Others

Pony skins from Poland and Russia resemble kidskin, but have much heavier skins. The best quality have a decided moiré pattern. When available, they are used for inexpensive sports coats, jackets, and trimmings.

The *guanaco,* a member of the camel family from South America, when very young produces fur suitable for dressy and sportswear jackets, coats, and trimming. The wool, which is yellow-red, resembles the red fox, but it is much coarser and duller in appearance. It is used in its natural color or is often dyed to resemble the blue fox. The young is known as a *guanaquito.*

MISCELLANEOUS

There are a number of other animals which are in no way related to one another.

Opossum

The opossum, which inhabits the North American continent, is famous for playing "dead" when about to be attacked by an enemy. The expression "playing 'possum" has come from this animal. The American opossum is gray-white in color and has long guard hair with a black tip. The fur is often dyed black to resemble the skunk; however, the fur and guard hair are coarser and lack the sheen of the skunk fur. Sporty-looking garments are popularly made from this bulky fur.

Australian Opossum

The Australian opossum, which has a pouch for carrying its young, has a very different appearance. This animal's fur is blue-gray in color. The guard hair is fairly short, and it is much softer than is the other opossum fur. The bluer the color of the fur, the better the quality. This fur is used mainly for bulky sports coats. It has recently been sheared and dyed to resemble beaver.

Raccoon

The raccoon lives in sections of North America. It was used years ago for college men's "rah-rah" coats, and thus it was not considered desirable for better quality women's garments. During the 1950's there was a revival of interest in this fur for sportswear.

Today, however, raccoon may also be sheared, let-out, and made to look like beaver or nutria. In its natural state, the raccoon fur has long guard hairs and medium-length fur fiber. Its color varies from light silvery to dark brown. The darker, fuller-furred peltries are the better quality and are the only ones that can successfully be sheared. When the guard hair is left intact, raccoon wears exceptionally well. Even sheared raccoon gives serviceable wear.

Fur Seal

The fur seal has been a very popular fur ever since great grandmother had her coat made of, or trimmed with this fur. This seal, which is controlled by the United States government, comes from the Pribilof Islands off the coast of Alaska. Each year, when the mating season begins, young male seals are caught for their peltries. The older males are busy fighting with one another over the harem of females each is gathering. The vicious battles they engage in make their pelts worthless for fur use. The fur is called *Alaska fur seal*.

The guard hairs are removed from the peltries, leaving only the beautifully soft, lustrous fur fibers. Sealskins are dyed black or in a rich, dark-brown color known as "matara" or a gray-black color known as "kitovi." Seals are difficult to dye so the fur side has the dye laboriously applied.

The skins are stamped with the United States government label. Other varieties, not bearing the United States government label, are obtained from South Africa, South America, Siberia, and Japan. These furs are durable, and good qualities are quite expensive. Seal coats and capes are worn for dress and street wear.

SELLING A FUR GARMENT

When you show a fur coat, stole, or jacket to a customer, her first interest is in the color, the beauty, and pattern of the fur. If the pile of the fur is deep and rich, stroke against the course of the fur to show her the luxuriousness of the fur fiber. Point out the characteristic markings and tell her how to recognize quality in that particular fur by the fullness of the fur fiber, the erectness of the guard hair, the depth of color, and the fineness and suppleness of the leather.

The customer will then want to try on the garment. She will be interested in its suitability for certain occasions, its becomingness to her, its style, and its serviceability. Show her how the richness of the fur frames her face. Call attention to the luster and sheen of the fur as she walks. Show her how well the garment fits across the shoulders and in the sleeves, yet how ample it is to wear over a heavy dress or suit. Explain that the fur, being the natural covering of an animal, is warm and comfortable to wear, and that a serviceable fur is in reality inexpensive when the length of wear and comfort are considered.

Turn the coat inside out and show the customer the 1½- to 2-inch facings, the attractive long-wearing lining. Point out the good quality of fur that has been used at the points of wear such as the back of the coat, the cuffs, the back of the neck, and the outer sections of the sleeves.

All these selling points are the buying points which will build the customer's confidence in your knowledge, and her appreciation for the coat she is planning to purchase.

Be sure in selling fur garments that you consider the height and weight of the customer. A short stout woman usually looks better in a flat, sleek-looking fur coat than she does in a short bulky fur jacket. A tall thin person may carry a bulky jacket with ease and grace and also wear a fully furred full-length or three-quarter-length coat. The customer, of course, must be the final judge of the type of fur and garment she is choosing, but she will appreciate your honest opinion and advice.

CARE OF FURS

A vain young lady proudly showed her new fur seal coat from Alaska to a number of envious friends in early November. By February, none of her friends would have worn the coat. It had holes in the seams, cigarette burns and singed places on the fur. Those who had seen her toss it near a radiator, or stand by an open fire in the coat, or leave it crumpled in a chair after wearing it in the rain or snow, knew why it looked so worn out. She had violated every rule of caring for a beautiful fur garment, because she was too lazy to give her coat a little special attention.

Care of fur garments is essential to their serviceability as well as their beauty. Every customer should be told a few simple rules:

1. Always hang a fur garment on a hanger in a cool closet. Be sure there are no hot-water or heat pipes running through the closet.

2. If coat is wet, shake off the water, and hang the garment to dry away from heat. The fur may mat if it is crushed with other things in a closet while it is still damp.

3. When possible, avoid sitting on the fur coat. Always open the coat before sitting down so that there will be no pull on the buttons or hooks which hold the coat closed.

4. Have the fur cleaned and glazed by a furrier at least once a year. This restores beauty and luster to the fur. Furs should never be dry-cleaned as this removes oils from the leather and the fur and causes the skin to crack.

5. Although she may think it rather costly, the customer who employs cold storage each summer is assured that her fur garment will not be attacked by moths or have the oils in the skins dried out by the hot summer weather.

6. Damages should be repaired as quickly as possible to prevent their becoming larger and more difficult to fix.

7. Restyling when fashion changes occur is desirable for a garment if such work does not cost more than one-fourth of the original cost of the garment. Of course, restyling may cost much less than that also.

PUTTING THIS MERCHANDISE KNOWLEDGE TO USE ❯ ❯ ❯ ❯ ❯ ❯ ❯ ❯ ❯ ❯

❯ DO YOU KNOW YOUR MERCHANDISE?

1. What service does the Fur Products Labeling Act perform for the customer?
2. Explain three important provisions of the Act.
3. Tell what family or group the following furs belong to and give two distinguishing features of each:

beaver	rabbit	platinum fox	opossum
muskrat	sable	Norwegian blue fox	raccoon
squirrel	ermine	Persian lamb	fur seal
marmot	mink	broadtail lamb	
chinchilla	leopard	mouton-processed lamb	

4. Give five rules for the care of a fur garment.
5. Explain what steps a good salesperson will take in showing a fur garment to a customer.

❯ INTERESTING THINGS TO DO

1. On a map of the world, locate all fur-bearing animals discussed in this chapter.
2. Make a study of one particular animal, and write a short theme telling about his manner of living, where he lives, how he obtains his food, how he is caught, and the use of his peltry in fur garments.
3. With another member of the class, prepare a sales demonstration for a fur garment. Include information about the fur used, the quality of the fur, workmanship, style of the garment, and proper care.

4. Read fur advertisements in newspapers. Make a list of any statements not in accordance with Federal Trade Commission rulings.
5. Make a chart of the furs studied in this chapter. Classify them under the following headings: flat furs, medium-length furs, patterned furs, long-haired or bulky furs.
6. Make a chart of furs studied in this chapter. Classify them under the following headings: furs suitable for evening capes and jackets, daytime dress wear, street wear, school wear, sportswear.

ADDITIONAL MERCHANDISE TERMS ＞

Baum marten (weasel family), a native of Europe, resembles the Siberian sable, but it is usually lighter in color and has to be tip-dyed or dyed to obtain the deep rich coloring of the sable. Baum marten is popular for use in scarfs and capes and jackets for evening and dressy street wear.

Boa is a plain fur neckpiece, rounded in effect. Boas became fashionable in the 60's replacing scarfs. Boas are worn with coats, suits, and dresses. Matching fur hats make an attractive ensemble.

Burunduk (also spelled baronduki) (rodent family) has a most unusual looking fur. This little animal comes from Russia and Siberia and resembles the American chipmunk. He has a small peltry that is noted for the five to seven long dark stripes against a light yellow background. Because the guard hair is short, flat, and rather coarse, and because there is little fur fiber and the animal's skin is thin, the fur is not warm. It is used mainly for the trimming on street and sports outfits, or as the lining on a reversible jacket.

Caracul lamb. This lamb which comes from Russia and China is noted for the beauty of its flat, wavy, or moiré patterned fur. The animal's fur is usually white, although some are brown in color and a few are black. The white peltries are sometimes dyed light colors.

Civet cat is an incorrect term for the animal known as the "spotted skunk."

Electrifying is a chemical process to straighten out curly-haired furs. It is particularly associated with mouton-processed lamb.

Fisher (weasel family) is a large marten with long, black-tipped guard hairs that are accented against the fur fiber which is medium to dark brown in color. The best quality comes from eastern Canada. This fur is used as a scarf or may be made into a coat or other garment. It is considered very durable, and is usually quite expensive.

Fitch (weasel family) has fur and guard hair somewhat longer than the other furs in the weasel family, but like them it is lustrous and soft to the touch. The natural coloring is yellow to white fur fiber in sharp contrast to black guard hair.

Hair seal (miscellaneous), which differs radically from the fur seal, is caught mainly around the coast of Labrador and Greenland. The fur from the young seals is woolly in texture and is commonly known as wool seal. The older hair seal has a short, wiry-looking straight hair covering. The fur, which is dyed and used for sports- and street-wear coats and as trimming, is inexpensive.

India lamb is a white, flat-curled, coarse-haired lamb which sheds rather badly. The fur is dyed in various colors.

Kolinsky (weasel family) is the best quality Asiatic mink. Because it has an unattractive yellow-brown color, it is always dyed to resemble better quality mink or sable.

Lapin is a French term meaning *rabbit*. Under the Fur Labeling Act, the Federal Trade Commission requires that the word "rabbit" be used so that customers will not think they are buying something other than rabbit fur.

Lynx cat (cat family) resembles the lynx in coloring but it has slight spots on the sides and belly sections. These furs are used as are the lynx, but they are somewhat less expensive.

Monkey (miscellaneous), caught on the African coast, has a long coat of guard hair with no fur fiber. The fur is usually long, black, and glossy, although white monkey fur is also obtainable. The skin of the black fur must be colored so that it does not show when being worn. It is used for dressy jackets and trimmings.

Otter (weasel family) has the distinction of producing the most durable fur. The fur, which may be used plucked or unplucked, resembles that of the beaver when plucked. It is very thick and is a deep shiny brown. *River otter* has a short hair with very sparse fur fiber. This flat fur, which is never plucked or sheared, resembles kidskin or hair seal. It is brown in color and is used for casual garments and sportswear.

Plasticizing is the name of a process that uses a plastic chemical to straighten kinky fur. This process is used on some furs, such as mouton-processed lamb, and some long-haired sheep. Plasticizing also makes the fur water-repellent and moth-resistant.

Scarf is fur used in its original shape with mounted head affixed, and paws, tail, etc., left attached to the peltry. These scarfs are worn by women over suits and untrimmed coats for warmth and beauty.

Spotted cats (cat family) from South America have small dash-shaped marks against a cream-tan-colored background. They are used for inexpensive garments and for trim on cloth coats.

Stole is a short fur cape that fits across the back and shoulders and extends in long panels down the front. It is worn over evening gowns, suits, or coats.

Stone marten (weasel family) is usually less expensive than the baum marten. Its coloring resembles the stone for which it is named. The fur fiber is a pale gray in contrast to the darker color of the brown guard hair. Stone martens are usually worn as scarfs, although occasionally expensive dressy jackets and capes are made of this fur.

Wolverine (weasel family) ranks as one of the most durable of furs, and it claims the distinction of being the only fur on which moisture does not congeal. For both of these qualities, it is valuable for use by arctic explorers. It is a coarse-textured, long-haired fur, with a wide dark-brown center stripe along the back and light-brown streaks along the sides. This characteristic marking is enhanced by the way the fur is made up into a garment. It is used mainly for trimming on sports coats, and for bulky jackets and coats for street and sportswear.

Jewelry

UNIT 68 METALS USED IN JEWELRY

Jewelry is worn by men and women; by the old and the young; by those who use it as a symbol of some important event, such as an engagement or a wedding, and by those who merely want an eye-catching ornament; by those who can afford costly gems and by those who have made their purchases in variety stores; by those who need the item for a special purpose, such as timekeeping, and by those who are seeking merely a conversation piece. Virtually everyone owns one or more pieces of jewelry. This product is, however, considered a luxury item and is so taxed by the Federal government.

TYPES OF JEWELRY

Jewelry is divided by its value into two general groups: the *inexpensive,* known as *costume* or *fashion jewelry;* and the *expensive,* known as *fine jewelry.* Men's jewelry, if inexpensive, is a type of costume jewelry. When made from costly materials, men's jewelry may be fine jewelry. Similarly, some watches are classified as inexpensive ones and sold in costume jewelry departments, while others are classified as fine jewelry and sold alongside diamonds, rubies, emeralds, and pearls.

Jewelry that is inexpensive may be attractively styled but made from materials such as plastics, imitation pearls, wood, glass, brass, or other base metals which are coated with more costly metals such as gold, rhodium, or silver. The potential in colors and shapes possible with these materials is a never-ending source of inspiration for designers who always have some enticing new bangle to catch the looker's eye. The prices are attractive, too, ranging from ten-cent-store prices to as high as $50 or more.

❯ ❯ Types of Jewelry ❮ ❮

Right, top to bottom: A charm bracelet; a sautoir; synthetic star rubies and sapphires set into rings and stickpins for men and women. **Left, top:** A bib necklace in Cleopatra style. **Bottom:** Two-strand choker, button earrings, and bee-shaped pin. *(Courtesy Coro Jewelry Co. and Linde Air Products Co.)*

Good quality or "fine" jewelry has true value. The customer for this jewelry is interested in its durability, its style importance, its intrinsic worth as well as its appropriateness for the individual for whom it is selected and the occasion that it commemorates.

In such a sale, there is a real challenge to the ambitious salesperson, for he must be ready to answer the customer's queries, assure him of value, and be able to explain various technical terms. This type of jewelry usually will be made from gold, platinum, or palladium; and if it contains stones, they will be semiprecious or precious gems, or synthetic stones having similar properties.

TYPES OF METALS USED IN JEWELRY

In glancing through an advertisement for a jewelry department, you will undoubtedly notice some of these terms: *sterling silver, 14K gold, 1/20 10K gold filled, 1/40 14K rolled gold, gold plated.* The salesperson must be thoroughly familiar with the exact meaning of these phrases in order to be able to explain their relative values.

Metals are divided into two groups: precious metals and base metals. Gold and all members of the platinum family (palladium, rhodium, and iridium) are the *precious metals* that are used in *fine jewelry*. Silver, which is also classed as a precious metal, is much less expensive and does not hold stones successfully. It is used in fashion jewelry.

The *base metals* are aluminum, copper, tin, lead, zinc, chromium, nickel, and iron. While precious metals are desirable for jewelry manufacture, each has some disadvantage which prevents it from being used alone. To add sufficient hardness, two or more metals must be combined by being melted and mixed together into one different metal. The resulting metal is known as an *alloy,* a combination of two or more metals that results in a different metal having added characteristics. Alloying may change the price of metals. Some alloys, such as platinum mixed with its family metal *iridium,* are higher in price than pure platinum. Well-known alloys used for jewelry are sterling silver, karat gold, brass, bronze, stainless steel, nickel silver.

Another term often used is *plating.* This is a process of coating one metal or alloy with another metal. It might be likened to a woman's coating her fingernails with a layer of nail polish. This coating just covers the outside of the article (top, bottom, and sides) and unless it is sufficiently thick, it may wear off rather quickly. (This process is explained in detail on page 466.) Silver, gold, rhodium (a member of the platinum family), and chromium-plated articles are frequently used for jewelry.

Anodizing is one of the newest finishes on metal. This finish, used only on fine quality aluminum, may impart a permanent shine and luster as well as a different color. Anodizing is done by forming an oxide film on the surface of the metal by a method similar to electroplating. Special colors are then sealed under this oxide film so they cannot wear away. Gold is the most popular color used for jewelry, but blue, pink, and lavender have also been used in anodized aluminum. Aluminum with this finish is used for metal necklaces, bracelets, earrings, pins, and watchcases for inexpensive watches. The anodized metal is light in weight, does not tarnish, cannot have the surface color scratched or worn away, and remains bright and shiny in use; however, it has a rather "tinny" feel.

PLATINUM AND ITS FAMILY METALS

Of all the metals, *platinum* is considered the most desirable for settings for diamonds. The main source of platinum is the Ural Mountains of Russia. Some is also available in South America, Canada, and South Africa. Like gold, it is found in veins or nuggets. It is usually in combination with one of the rare members of the platinum family of which iridium, rhodium, ruthenium, and palladium are the best known.

Platinum was not always considered a precious metal. When it was first discovered in Russia, the peasants thought it was poor quality silver; and they used it for buttons on their peasant blouses. Subsequently the qualities of platinum were discovered, and today it is classed as a precious metal.

Platinum is much heavier than gold. This is noticeable when you hold a gold ring in one hand and a platinum ring in the other. They may look the same size, but the platinum one weighs considerably more. Even though it is so heavy, it can easily be shaped into jewelry, because it can be hammered into thin sheets, or drawn out to a fine wire suitable for making tiny links for chains. Both of these qualities are important in jewelry manufacture.

The silvery color of platinum is also desirable for jewelry. It serves as an attractive setting for precious stones, especially the diamond.

Platinum is not hard enough to be used successfully by itself; it must be combined or alloyed with another metal. *Iridium,* a platinum-family metal that is rare and often more costly than platinum, is commonly used to harden platinum used in jewelry. The usual percentage is platinum 90 per cent and iridium 10 per cent. The label inside rings then reads: *10% Irid. Plat.*

Platinum does not tarnish and it holds gem stones securely; it therefore is much more desirable than silver for jewelry. Since it is not affected by body acids, platinum does not darken the skin. It cannot be used, however, for plating as are gold and silver. Platinum may be replaced by *palladium* which is similar in appearance and jewelry characteristics, but lighter in weight and considerably less expensive.

Rhodium, also a white-colored metal, is usually the most costly of all the platinum-family metals. It is used for plating both fine and costume jewelry pieces. Its bright luster, durability, and nontarnishing qualities have proved most desirable. Platinum, white gold, and even base metals may be plated with rhodium to make them sparkling white. Although rhodium is very expensive, as little as three ten-millionths of an inch may be used in plating any single piece of jewelry.

GOLD

Lust for gold has had an important effect on the growth of America, for civilization followed in the footsteps of the fortune seekers who rushed to California's gold mines in 1849.

Gold occurs in nearly every part of the world and turns up at the most surprising places. This glittering metal in its native state has limited uses because it is much too soft; it must be combined with another metal to give it the necessary hardness. In this combined, or "alloyed" state, gold becomes hard enough to be useful. Copper is the usual metal added to gold to make it hard.

Gold itself has a beautiful, pale, yellow color with a bright luster. It does not tarnish or change color, nor is it affected by acids. Real gold jewelry will not turn the skin green unless an excess of copper has been mixed with it.

Gold can be hammered into sheets so thin that they cannot be picked up except by an electrical or a magnetic attraction, which a worker obtains by rubbing a paintbrush through his hair and then touching the paintbrush to the finer-than-tissue sheet of gold. This gold leaf, as it is called, is used mostly for lettering. It takes nearly 300,000 of them to make a pile an inch high. Gold can also be drawn into a very fine wire which can be used for many intricate designs in fine jewelry.

Karat Gold. The quantity of gold present with another metal in an alloy is referred to by the term *karat*. Twenty-four karat gold would be 100 per cent gold or *solid gold*. This, however, is never used commercially. Twenty-two karat is the finest quality gold used in jewelry. This means 22/24 of the article is gold and 2/24 is composed of some other metal to give the needed hardness. The usual karat-gold qualities are 22k, 18k, 14k, 12k, 10k. Any proportion of gold less than 10/24ths or 10 karat, may not use the term *karat*.

Gold-plating Methods

The beauty of gold may be imparted to base metals by plating either with a sheet of alloyed metal or by coating the base with gold by electroplating.

Gold Filled. This is a frequently used term. A thin sheet of karat gold (10–22k) is securely attached on all sides of some metal by fusing. Base metals such as brass or nickel silver are used. In order to be called *gold filled* the layer of karat gold must weigh at least 1/20 of the weight of the entire metal used. The finer quality of gold filled is 1/10. Thus the term "1/10 14k gold filled" stamped inside a ring means that a layer of 14k gold has been used to cover the base metal and the weight of this gold layer is 1/10 of the weight of the metal in the ring. Gold-filled articles give good service.

Rolled Gold. This is a less expensive method of combining base metals by the same process as the gold filled explained above. The only difference in the two methods is that in rolled gold the gold layer is only 1/30 to 1/40 the total weight of the metal in the jewelry. For that reason the layer is thinner and, thus, less durable. Gold-filled jewelry gives twice to four times the wear of rolled-gold items.

Gold Electroplate. This term means that the article has had a layer of pure gold applied to it by an electroplating process. The quality of gold plate depends on the thickness of the coating, which is thinner than filled or rolled gold and thus does not give as good service.

SILVER

This plentiful precious metal is much less expensive than gold. The beauty of silver has long been the subject for poetic phrases such as "the silvery moon," "the silvery hue," and the "gleam of silver." The lovely soft luster of silver makes it attractive for use in jewelry.

Silver is not so heavy as gold or platinum, but it is somewhat harder. It is, however, not hard enough to be used alone, but must have some metal (usually copper) mixed with it.

The great disadvantage of silver is that it tarnishes. Tarnishing qualities of silver may be used advantageously, however, to highlight silver designs by darkening the background areas. This type of coloration is known as *oxidation*.

The term *solid silver* does not mean pure silver as it does when referring to gold. Instead, it is used to refer to the popular silver alloy commonly known as *sterling silver,* which contains 925 parts of silver and 75 parts of copper, a standard set by law. The quality of sterling silver is judged by its thickness.

Coin silver, which is also used in the manufacture of jewelry, is 90 per cent silver and 10 per cent copper.

Pure silver may be used for electroplating over base materials.

Engine Turning. This is a process of engraving metal by a machine-operated cutting tool controlled by a craftsman.
(Courtesy Swank, Inc.)

SHAPING AND DECORATING METAL FOR JEWELRY

The jewelry to be made may be cut from a thin sheet of the metal by *hand,* or it may be shaped by a *die* that stamps out the metal and presses it into the desired form, or it may be *cast* by melting the metal and pouring it into molds. Jewelry made by hand is the most expensive.

Metal jewelry may be decorated by scratching a pattern known as *engraving,* or by tapping tiny designs onto the metal known as *chasing.* Sometimes the design is painted on with colored enamel. Silver, copper, and brass articles, which are affected by acid, may have *etched* designs.

Settings

Preparing metal jewelry to be used as a setting for stones entails a great deal of labor. Some settings have long prongs that press against the stone and hold it in place. For small diamonds (called *melees*) set in platinum or gold, tiny rolls of metal are grooved out by the workmen and pressed against the stone to hold it securely, without hiding any of the stone from view.

Settings with a plain band of metal around the edges of the stone are known as *flush settings.* These are used on school insignia rings, large stones for men, and some flat stones in women's rings. High prong settings are known as *Tiffany settings.* *Square settings* are popular for diamond rings today. These have tiny corner prongs, or rolls of metal that hold the stone in place just on the corners, giving a "square" effect. Inexpensive stones may be glued into the setting. This is known as a *paste setting.*

The quality of a setting is judged by the metal used, the size of the setting, the way it enhances the beauty of the stone, and the ornamentation or decoration of the setting itself. Of course, in good quality jewelry all edges will be well polished and no sharp edge will "catch" on clothing.

❯ ❯ Types of Settings ❮ ❮

| Fishtail (Motif derived from fish's tail) | Prong | Channel (Stones are held in groove) | Flush |

❯ DO YOU KNOW YOUR MERCHANDISE?

1. Distinguish between costume jewelry and fine jewelry. How would you classify the following: inexpensive silver-plated cufflinks; 14 K gold wedding band; gold electroplated locket for a little girl; boy's ring found in a box of popcorn as a prize; platinum alloy tie clasp?
2. Name the precious jewelry metals.
3. Define alloy, plating.
4. Give the outstanding characteristics for use in jewelry of platinum, gold, silver.
5. Explain what is meant by the following: solid gold, karat, 14 karat gold, gold filled, rolled gold, gold plated, sterling silver, solid silver, coin silver, tarnish, silver plated, handmade jewelry, die stamped, cast metal, etching, oxidizing, anodizing.
6. Explain how to judge the quality of a piece of metal jewelry.

❯ INTERESTING THINGS TO DO

1. On a map of the world, mark the countries from which the various jewelry metals come.
2. Copy technical metal terms in your notebook from jewelry advertisements. Be prepared to explain the meanings of the terms.
3. Prepare a 1-page sales manual for new costume jewelry salespeople about the metals used in jewelry that they are likely to sell.

UNIT 69 STONES USED IN JEWELRY

Although all metal jewelry is attractive, the color and luster, or sparkle, of stones do much to enhance the article. We know ancient peoples valued stones for ornamentation, inasmuch as cut stones have been found in excavations of early civilizations. Superstitious people often believed stones possessed supernatural powers, and they revered stones as symbolic of certain virtues and attributes. The ruby symbolized love; the sapphire, truth; the emerald, faith; and the diamond, joy. Today we, too, use jewelry symbolically for our wedding and engagement ceremonies.

KINDS OF STONES

The many attractive stones used today are known as *natural,* either precious or semiprecious; *synthetic;* and *imitation* or *simulated.*

The *precious stones* are those natural stones that are beautiful to look at, durable enough to be worn constantly, and rare enough to be valuable. The diamond, emerald, ruby, sapphire, and pearl are known as the precious stones.

The *semiprecious stones* are all other natural stones that are attractive, and suitable for ornamental purposes.

The ability of the chemist to mix the chemicals on his shelf and transform them into all manner of interesting objects extends to the jewelry field in what are known as *synthetic stones*. The chemist takes the exact proportions of the actual chemical ingredients that nature has used, creates with these chemicals a boule, or tubelike form, and presto! a synthetic jewel has been formed and is ready for cutting.

It is difficult to tell the synthetic stones from the real ones, unless jewelry instruments are used, although the true color of the natural stone is almost impossible to duplicate. The stones that can be made synthetically are the ruby, the sapphire, star ruby, star sapphire, the spinel (a semiprecious stone), quartz (which is so plentiful in its natural state that the synthetics are not needed for jewelry items), and more recently, the emerald. Another product known as *rutile* is made by subjecting titanium dioxide to intense heat, yielding a sparkling, white stone that has a great deal of brilliance, but that is not very hard. Diamonds have been made synthetically since 1957, but none has yet been made large enough and flawless enough for jewelry use. Now that the process for making them has been developed, jewelry-size stones may, however, be created if a shortage of diamonds ever occurs.

Imitation or *simulated stones* are found in inexpensive or costume jewelry. These have none of the properties of the real stones except surface appearance. They may be made from clay, glass (as rhinestones are), or plastic substances.

Interesting Facts About Stones

To the person who has made a study of stones, it is just as easy to tell one natural stone from another as it is to tell one's friends apart. Each type of stone possesses definite characteristics. Without the aid of delicate jewelry equipment, however, it is often difficult for the average person to tell some stones apart. Some of the ways by which a jeweler can tell stones are:

Shape.   When stones are discovered, they usually have a definite shape or form by which they may be recognized. The diamond, for example, is generally octahedron in shape (having eight faces). The zircon is found in a four-sided form known as tetragonal, and the quartz, ruby, and emerald are six-sided, or hexagonal. This is known as the *crystalline* structure of the stone. A few stones, such as the turquoise and the opal, do not have any definite shape. These are known as being *amorphous*.

Resistance to Scratching.   A young man entered a jewelry store and expressed interest in a ring he saw on display. "Is it a diamond?" he asked.

"Certainly," said the salesman reaching into the show window to remove the ring. "I'll prove it. See how it scratches this glass window!" and as he said that he drew the edge of the stone sharply across the glass leaving a scratch. "That proves it is a diamond."

Unfortunately, that test does *not* prove the stone is a diamond, because other colorless stones that resemble the diamond, such as the zircon and colorless topaz, will also scratch glass.

The quality of resisting scratching is known as the hardness of the stone. The diamond is the hardest known substance. Only a diamond can be used to scratch another diamond. A diamond will scratch any other stone. The ruby and sapphire are next in hardness. While they will not scratch a diamond, they will scratch all other stones. The following chart shows relative resistance to scratching of well-known stones. Stones are placed in order of hardness beginning with the diamond. Only stones above or on the same line in the list with any given stone will mar the surface of that stone. Notice how many stones will scratch glass.

Hard Stones	Stones Easily Scratched
Diamond (hardest known substance)	Garnet, quartz, jade
Ruby and sapphire	Marcasite
Oriental cat's-eye (chrysoberyl)	Opal, moonstone, and turquoise
Topaz and spinel	Glass
Emerald, aquamarine, and zircon	Lapis lazuli
Tourmaline	Pearl
	Coral
	Amber

The Chemical Composition of Stones. While natural stones themselves are found only in certain sections and are rare in comparison to ordinary rocks, the stones consist of the most ordinary chemicals. The diamond, for example, is practically pure carbon, the main substance in coal and in pencil lead. The ruby and sapphire are composed of alumina, similar to the metal from which pots and pans are made. The opal and quartz stones contain mostly silica, the chief ingredient of common sand. Stones often have little flaws, inclusion of chemicals not part of the stone, or cracks and holes that mar the beauty and value of the stone.

The Color of Stones. Most people think of stones in terms of certain colors. We say, for instance, that the diamond is white or colorless, yet there are also pink, blue, red, black, brown, and yellow diamonds. The color of a stone is usually caused by some minute chemical impurity. Thus the beautiful green of the valuable emerald is caused by a tiny bit of chromium. Without the vivid green color which chromium imparts to the stone, the precious emerald becomes the much less sought after and rather pale semiprecious aquamarine.

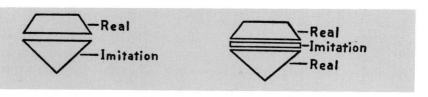

At left: doublet; **at right:** triplet. To make a stone appear larger or to enhance the color of pale stones, a real stone may be glued to an imitation stone.

Some stones reflect color due to moisture being trapped in tiny cracks in the stone itself. Thus the opal seems to consist of myriad colors.

Some stones may be artificially colored by heat or chemicals. The yellow zircon is often made colorless by heat treatment. Some agates are artificially colored with chemicals. Atomic bombardment has imparted a green color to otherwise white diamonds.

Another method of enriching the color of stones is by gluing a pale stone over a deeper colored stone or a colored piece of glass. This is called a *doublet*. When a piece of glass is inserted between two layers of stone, it is known as a *triplet*.

Transparency, Translucence, Opaqueness. You can see through some stones as you can through a glass window. These are known as *transparent* stones. The diamond, emerald, and zircon are examples of transparent stones. Other stones, such as some quartz stones and moonstone, are like frosted glass that reflects light and shadow. These are called *translucent* stones. Such stones as the pearl, lapis lazuli, and turquoise are *opaque* and allow no light to pass through.

HOW ARE STONES CUT?

Although stones possess all the characteristics for beauty when they are found, they need the handwork of polishing and cutting before their beauty is visible. You could easily pass up a diamond "in the rough" because it is dull, gray looking, and has no sparkle or luster. The cutter, or *lapidary,* as he is known, changes the dull-looking stone into a brilliant, sparkling gem. Stones are cut in different ways depending on the size of the stone, the type of setting in which it is to be used, and its ability to reflect light.

Faceted Stones

Transparent stones are usually *faceted.* That means they are cut with little flat places or planes at angles to other planes. Each little facet or plane then reflects like a mirror against the other facets and makes a great deal of sparkle. The more of these facets there are, the more expensive is the cutting, because each requires accurate measuring and careful handling to be cut

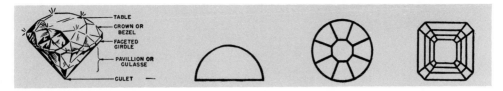

From left to right: brilliant cut; side view of cabochon; top view of single cut; top view of emerald or square cut.

perfectly. This cutting, which reduces the stone 40 to 50 per cent in size from the original, also adds to the cost of the stone.

Familiar types of facetings are the brilliant or full cut, single cut, and emerald or step cut.

The *brilliant cut* is expensive. It is used for some diamonds, rubies, sapphires, and transparent semiprecious stones, synthetic and imitation stones. This cut has 58 facets. The stone may be round, oval, marquise, or pear shaped. More stones lend themselves to cutting in the round brilliant shape than in odd shapes. The shape of the stone is determined by the shape of the original "rough" stone. The final cut shape is selected to make the largest possible stone from this unfinished "rough."

The single cut is used on small stones and less expensive stones and may have as few as 18 facets. Melees, the tiny diamonds used around larger stones, are usually cut in this manner.

The step or emerald cut is useful for stones such as the emerald that do not have sparkle or fire as does the diamond. Diamonds are sometimes cut in this manner, too, but it reduces considerably the sparkle of the diamond. The facets in the emerald cut, instead of being diamond or triangular in shape, are oblong and are placed in horizontal position. *Baguettes,* rectangular-shaped small diamonds set around larger stones, are cut by this method.

Cabochon Cut

Translucent and opaque stones and those stones showing a "star" or "cat's-eye" light are cut *en cabochon.* The distinguishing feature of this cut is that the stone resembles a bald head. The cabochon is a simple and much less expensive cut than the faceted one. Some cabochon-cut stones are very flat, others have a high curve. Moonstone, turquoise, some garnets, agates, star rubies, and star sapphires are a few of the many stones cut in this manner.

Decorative Cutting

To enhance the beauty of some opaque and translucent stones, they are carved with decorative designs. The most popular form of this type of cutting is known as the *cameo.* Raised figures or heads are carved in relief against a background which is usually a different color. Stones and shells that have layers of different colors are adapted to this type of cutting. Thus the woman's head on a cameo is light in color against a dark background.

> > **Steps in Cutting and Polishing the Brilliant Cut Diamond** < <

Upper left: Marking. The rough diamond is marked with India ink for cutting. **Upper right:** Marked rough stones are ready for cleaning or sawing. **Center left:** Splitting or "cleaving." A gentle tap against the knife placed in a tiny groove scratched in the diamond splits it in half. **Center right:** Sawing. This is a 35 carat diamond being sawed in half by a thick metal disk covered with oil and diamond powder. **Lower left:** Cutting. It takes a diamond to cut a diamond. One diamond is held by the worker as the other revolves in a lathe against it. The diamond dust from the cutting is saved. **Lower right:** Polishing. The diamond is held in a metal holder and polished against a revolving wheel charged with diamond dust. *(Courtesy Baumgold Bros., Inc.)*

Actual Size of Diamonds. Left to right: ¼ carat, ½ carat, 1 carat, 2 carats. *(Courtesy N. W. Ayer & Sons, Inc.)*

The opposite effect caused by grooving out the design is known as *intaglio* cutting. This is popular in some men's rings.

JUDGING SIZES OF STONES

Advertisements of diamonds and other expensive stones often use such terms as ¾ carat, or 1½ carat, or 80 point stone. This refers to the weight and size of the stone. In ancient times tiny dried seeds were used to determine the weight of a stone. The seeds, however, were not always exactly the same size, and therefore weights were not accurate. The term *carat* comes from the name of these seeds. Today delicate jeweler's scales are used to weigh the stone exactly.

Most stones are measured by the *carat* weight. Do not confuse this term with *karat* referring to proportion in jewelry metals. The carat weighs 3.165 grains troy, but most jewelers speak of a carat as being 4 grains which is its avoirdupois weight. The table below will give you a better idea of the meaning of *carat*. This table is according to troy weight used to measure precious metals, precious and semiprecious stones, and drugs.

1 pound troy	=	12 ounces troy
1 ounce troy	=	20 pennyweight
1 pennyweight	=	24 grains
3.165 grains	=	1 carat
1 carat	=	100 points

Some semiprecious stones are measured in millimeters. Each millimeter is approximately $\frac{1}{25}$ of an inch.

The value of a certain quality stone increases with the size of the stone. If a ½-carat diamond sold for $160, a 1-carat stone of the same quality would sell for about $450, and a 2-carat diamond would be about $1,000. The larger the stone, the rarer and more valuable it becomes and consequently the more expensive.

PUTTING THIS MERCHANDISE KNOWLEDGE TO USE ❯❯❯❯❯❯❯❯❯❯❯

❯ DO YOU KNOW YOUR MERCHANDISE?

1. Name the precious stones. What qualities make them precious?
2. What are semiprecious stones? What are synthetic stones? How do they differ from imitation stones?

3. Explain how stones vary and can be told apart by experts.
4. What is meant by the hardness of a stone? Which stone is the hardest?
5. Explain how color of stones may affect their value.
6. Explain what is meant by the terms transparent, translucent, and opaque. Give examples of each as available in stones.
7. (*a*) What is meant by faceting, brilliant cut, single cut, melee, step cut, emerald cut, baguette, cabochon cut, cameo cut, intaglio cut? (*b*) Give an example of a stone used for each type of cut.
8. Which is larger: a ¾ carat or an 80 point stone?

❯ INTERESTING THINGS TO DO

1. Copy technical stone terms in your notebook from jewelry advertisements. Be prepared to explain the meanings of the terms.
2. Draw the outlines of the following stone shapes on drawing paper with crayon. (Make the drawings large enough to be seen from the back of your classroom.) Round brilliant, marquise, pear shape, baguette, emerald cut, cabochon, cameo.

UNIT 70 STONE FAMILIES

A tour of a museum where jewelry stones are on display, or a visit to any jewelry department or store, is a fascinating experience. All the shimmering beauty of a stone is visible as it resides inside a glass case with artificial light enlivening its sparkle and sheen.

The natural stones used in jewelry are known as *gem stones* in contrast to those that are less attractive and can only be used in industry. These natural stones are grouped by families; that is, those that have the same chemical composition (except for impurities that may affect clarity and color) and the same properties are grouped together even though, in appearance, they may seem to be quite different. Thus, for example, we find that the red ruby and the blue sapphire are both *corundum* stones.

The following families of stones are usually carried in jewelry departments or jewelry stores:

Amber	Diamond
Beryl—aquamarine, emerald, golden beryl	Feldspar—moonstone, sunstone
Coral	Garnet—green garnet, red garnet
	Jade—jadeite and nephrite
Corundum—ruby, sapphire, star ruby, star sapphire	Lapis lazuli
	Marcasites

Opal
Pearls—fresh water, oriental, baroque
Quartz—agate, amethyst, bloodstone, carnelian, cat's-eye, citrine, onyx, rock crystal, sardonyx, tiger's-eye
Spinel
Topaz
Turquoise
Zircon

AMBER

The semiprecious, nonmineral amber is a fossil resin secreted from the trunks of trees that were buried in the earth and covered with water many ages ago. The resin, which is occasionally found now in the form of amber, is a transparent, translucent, or opaque substance that varies in color from honey yellow, its most usual color, to white or brown. Amber is extremely light in weight and in contrast to mineral jewelry stones is warm rather than cold to the touch. When rubbed, amber has strong electrical attraction.

Bakelite and Celluloid plastics, being light in weight and capable of a variety of colors, are often used in imitation of amber. They lack, however, the electrical property and lasting beauty of amber.

BERYL—AQUAMARINE AND EMERALD

The green *emerald,* a precious and extremely valuable as well as beautiful stone, and the pale blue-green semiprecious *aquamarine* differ chemically only in the substance that gives the color to the emerald; yet there is no comparison in the beauty, rarity, and desirability of the two.

South America is the main source of the emerald. A tiny bit of chromium, in reality an impurity in the stone, gives the emerald its rich green color.

Emeralds are transparent unless badly flawed, when they appear translucent. If the stone is large and free from flaws, it undoubtedly is not a true emerald. Because the emerald does not reflect light, as does the diamond, the step-cut method of faceting is the popular cutting used. Emeralds are brittle and, as a result, difficult to cut and set. Translucent emeralds are cabochon cut. The synthetic emerald was developed in this country in 1948. It has a good color and is less brittle than the genuine emerald.

The transparent *aquamarine* is the color of the sea water from which it derives its name. The deeper the color of the stone, the greater is its value. The main sources of aquamarines are South America and Russia. Greenish-colored aquamarines may be heat-treated to yield a more desirable blue color.

The aquamarine may be made to have the color of the more expensive emerald by placing a layer of green glass between two sections of the aquamarine and gluing them together securely. This is correctly known as an *aquamarine triplet.* (See illustration, page 472.)

CORAL

The coral, like amber, is not really a stone, but a deposit in the ocean of a tiny jellylike organism known as the coral polyp. The coral is deposited in formation resembling the branches of a tree. It is red, white, or yellow in color. The oxblood color is the most desirable. Since coral is often carved, the value of the jewelry using it depends on the amount of handwork. Coral comes from many places, but mainly is found in the Mediterranean area and around Japan. Real coral effervesces when acid is applied to it.

CORUNDUM—RUBY AND SAPPHIRE

The red *ruby* and the blue *sapphire* differ from each other only in color. The red color is much rarer than the blue, and therefore the ruby is more valuable than the sapphire. These two stones since 1904 have been made synthetically.

Most rubies are found in Burma. Flawless rubies are very rare, and thus extremely valuable. The color of the ruby is best when it resembles the color of a drop of pigeon's blood. Since the stone is transparent, it is usually faceted. Because of the stone's hardness (it is second only to the diamond in this quality), it is ideally suited for use in delicate watch parts that need it to resist friction and wear. Tiny rubies are used for the jeweled movement in good quality watches. Since real rubies are rare, synthetic rubies are used for the majority of watches made today.

The transparent sapphire comes in many different colors, but the cornflower-blue color is rarest and most valuable. Sapphires may also be colorless, yellow, green, purple, or pink. Ceylon, Burma, and Australia are the important sources of the sapphire. The synthetic colorless sapphire has been sold under the trade name "Diamondite" as an imitation diamond.

Some rubies and sapphires are famous for an unusual light resembling a star that is reflected on the surface of the stones. These stones are known as *star rubies* and *star sapphires* and are opaque rather than transparent. Star rubies are very rare. They are a rich reddish pink in color. These also have been developed synthetically and usually have a better-formed star than do the natural star stones.

Synthetic rubies and sapphires are formed in a specially built furnace in the shape of an upside-down bottle called a *boule. (Courtesy Linde Air Products Co.)*

This best-known of all stones is, surprisingly, in its white color, not the most valuable. Although it is expensive, it usually costs less than rubies or emeralds of the same size and perfection. Since 1867, South Africa has been the main source of supply for diamonds.

Because the diamond is the hardest substance known, it was not appreciated until the thirteenth century, when it was discovered that a diamond could be cut and polished by another diamond. In spite of its hardness, which makes it useful in industrial work for drawing wire and cutting parts of machinery, the diamond is brittle and will break if it is hit at a certain angle. This property of *cleavage* is important in separating a large stone into smaller stones for cutting. It may prove disastrous, though, as it did for two boys in South Africa. The story tells us that they found a large red stone, and determined to test it with a hammer, "because if it is a diamond," they said, "it will be so hard it won't break." They struck the stone a blow that fractured it into a thousand fragments. Later they were told that the stone they had "cleaved" into almost worthless sections had been a large, very rare red diamond.

The value of diamonds is determined by their size, color, perfection, and quality of cut. Diamonds advertised as *perfect* are stones that magnified ten times their size (under a ten-power jeweler's loupe) show no flaws when a trained diamond expert examines them. A stone is called "perfect" regardless of *color* or *cut* if it meets these standards. The best color is a *fine white*. Diamonds this color are sometimes known as being "of the first water." The pure-white diamond is difficult to designate, however, because a stone may appear to have a white cast when placed next to an inferior dull-appearing diamond, yet actually not be fine white next to another with a truly fine color. Occasionally diamonds are also found in yellow, pink, red-orange, green, and blue. These fancy-colored stones are collector's items and are very costly. Black diamonds unless they are of unusual quality are mostly used by industry.

The term "blue-white" in reference to the diamond is frowned upon by the Better Business Bureau since no two jewelers are in agreement as to what color it designates. Unfortunately the term is so commonly used that most customers believe it signifies quality.

Synthetic diamonds were developed in the United States in 1957. Pure graphite under superpressure and high heat is transformed into the diamond; however, only tiny, industrial type stones have been created so far.

FELDSPAR—MOONSTONE AND SUNSTONE

Moonstones, which are translucent, milky colored stones with a glow or reflection that gives them an attractive sheen, come from Switzerland and Ceylon. The bluer the stone, the better the quality. By cutting the stone cabochon shape, its sheen is enhanced. The stone is easily scratched and thus must be treated with care. Lucite, a plastic, is used successfully to make attractive imitations of moonstone.

Sunstones, found mainly in Norway, have rich red or orange reflections caused by inclusions of a glittering iron oxide.

GARNET

The transparent garnet, which is a very common stone, is generally thought to be red in color, but it also comes in emerald green. In its translucent and opaque varieties, it resembles jade and is pale green, blue and white. While the garnet is very attractive, it is too soft for use in jewelry such as rings that receive hard wear.

Inexpensive watches use the red garnet which resembles the ruby for the "jeweled" movement; however, being softer than the ruby, these stones do not work so effectively. Garnets are found in many countries, notably Czechoslovakia, Italy, United States, and India. They are faceted, or cut cabochon, and some are even carved.

JADE—JADEITE AND NEPHRITE

The fine quality *jadeite,* which comes from Burma, Tibet, and China, is translucent to opaque and varies in color from pale to rich green. Some pink, violet, and pale blue jade have also been found. Those of rich green color are the most valuable. Exquisite carving further enhances the value.

Nephrite, a less expensive variety of jade, is found in colors ranging from white to gray-green to dark green and even black.

LAPIS LAZULI

This stone from Afghanistan and Siberia is opaque, with a rich almost royal blue coloring. The less expensive stones have a lighter color and streaks of white, gray and yellow. Lapis may be cut cabochon shape or it may be carved.

MARCASITES

These stones, which are used frequently today in costume jewelry, are composed of iron pyrites, a pale brass-yellow colored mineral, which was called "fool's gold." Marcasites, which are faceted, reflect light and are used in inexpensive jewelry to resemble tiny diamonds.

OPAL

People often look at this stone and then exclaim, "Oh, what a beautiful stone—What is it?"

It is a mysterious stone depending for its beautiful play of colors on tiny invisible cracks within the stone itself that are filled with moisture. The opal varies from transparent to opaque and, because of the myriad fiery colors reflected from it, may be any color of the rainbow. The opal is cut cabochon to allow the greatest span of surface to show its fiery light. Australia is the source of some of the most valuable opals. Mexico and the United States are also the source of some of these stones. Opals may be formed in doublets to deepen their color.

The opal is quite soft and therefore easily scratched. Since it is porous, an opal ring should be removed before washing one's hands. When put away, the opal should have olive oil smeared over it for protection from becoming dry.

PEARLS

These do not truly come under the classification of stones, as they are the product of the oyster. The oyster lines his shell with a "nacreous" solution which is composed of carbonate of lime. It is this same substance which is used to make the expensive pearl.

The pearl starts as a tiny irritant to the soft body of the oyster—a tiny grain of sand perhaps, which has been washed in between the two halves of the oyster's shell. To keep this irritating substance from annoying him, he covers it with the nacreous solution used to line his shell, and thus a pearl is formed. If the pearl is formed next to the oyster's body, it may be round in shape. These pearls are the most valuable. Pearls formed against the shell have an oblong shape and do not bring so high a price as the round ones. They are known as *baroque* pearls.

Pearls also come in various colors—white, yellow, pink, red, blue, brown, green, and even black pearls have been found. The most expensive pearls have a rosy sheen, a beautiful luster, and no flaws or irregularities.

Saltwater pearls, known as *oriental pearls,* come from the Persian Gulf, Australia, Venezuela, Japan, Panama, and the Pacific isles.

Freshwater pearls, obtained from mussels that abound in rivers in the United States, have a matte or dull finish and a chalk-white color.

Pearls need no cutting, but often they have a hole drilled in them so they can be strung for necklaces or used as earrings. The perfect matching of pearls for a necklace is a long and tedious job which increases the cost of the necklace considerably.

Cultured Pearls. Cultured pearls which were introduced in 1921 are akin to synthetic stones in value. Man was not satisfied with the rate at which oysters produced real or oriental pearls so this method was devised for "stepping up" production. A tiny fragment of mother-of-pearl (the lining of shells) is inserted into the shell of an oyster. The oyster is then placed in a cage which is lowered into the water where it is left for several years. The oyster, irritated by this foreign substance, begins the process of coating it

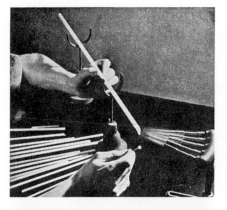

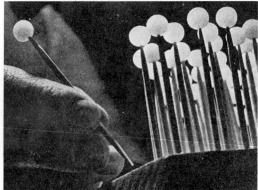

Forming Artificial Pearls. Top left:
The glass blower forms the ball of
white glass which is the base of the
man-made pearl. **Right:** The white balls
of glass are mounted on toothpicks and
stuck into racks. **Lower left:** The glass
balls are dipped into the lustrous pearl
solution, then dried in thermostatically
controlled rooms. *(Courtesy Weinreich
Bros.)*

with layers of his nacreous solution. The longer the oyster is allowed to coat
this irritation, the more valuable becomes the pearl so formed. Only about 60
per cent of the oysters so treated produce pearls of commercial value. Being
artificially stimulated these pearls have much less value than do the real pearls.
The irritant used is often large, and the layers of coating are not nearly so
thick as they are on the real pearl. The natural pearls retain their sheen and
beauty much better than do the cultured ones. However, only by X ray tests
can the real pearl be differentiated from the cultured pearl. In the cultured
pearl, a shadow shows where the pearl essence joins the inserted bead.

Imitation Pearls. *Imitation* or *simulated* pearls are entirely man-made.
Either an opaque white glass or a cellulose acetate plastic base is covered
with a solution called *pearl essence,* which is made of the lustrous material
from the scales of fish mixed with a plastic material to make it adhesive.
These imitations may vary in beauty and price depending on the base used
(glass is considered the best) and the number and attractiveness of the coatings of pearl essence applied.

This comes in so many forms and colors that it is very difficult to describe. It comes in almost every color and in combinations, and it ranges from transparent to translucent and opaque. It may sparkle or be satiny in luster, it may have a "cat's-eye" gleam, or be completely dull. Some well-known quartz stones are:

Agate. This is a translucent-to-opaque stone varying from milky white to red or yellow brown. The *moss agate* has dark mosslike markings from which it gets its name. The *onyx,* an opaque form of agate, is famous for its black color which is alternated with bands of white. The *sardonyx,* also an opaque form of the agate, has alternate brown and white bands.

Amethyst. This stone which comes mainly from South America is one of the best-known members of the quartz family. It is a transparent stone, lilac-to-purple in color, and the deeper and richer the color, the better the quality. It is faceted to bring out the beauty of the stone.

Bloodstone. This stone from Russia and India is well named. It is a dark green opaque stone spotted with bright red. It is cut in cabochon shape.

Carnelian. This translucent stone from South America is reddish in color. It is often carved to add to its attractiveness.

Cat's-Eye. This comes from India, and is an opaque greenish-to-brown colored stone cut cabochon so the curious light or gleam of the cat's-eye will show as the light strikes the stone at various angles.

Citrine. This amber-colored variety of quartz is often mistaken for real topaz. It is a transparent stone that is faceted like the more expensive topaz. It is properly sold as *citrine* or *topaz quartz.* Some jewelers incorrectly call it citrine topaz or just topaz.

Rock Crystal. This colorless, glassy-looking stone that is used for crystal balls, artwork figures and beads, comes from Brazil. It lacks fire but has considerable life when faceted. Rock crystal is colder to the touch than glass and shows double images rather than single as does glass when you look through it.

Tiger's-Eye. This stone from South Africa is a golden brown to blue color. It also has a gleam or light that moves vertically along its surface. Many tiger's-eyes are used in men's rings and have intaglio cutting.

SPINEL

These fairly inexpensive, semiprecious stones have the distinction of having been worn in crowns and carried in scepters under the mistaken idea that they were the more valuable rubies. The spinel is a transparent stone that varies in color, being ruby red, purple, sapphire blue, or orange. These stones come mainly from Burma and Ceylon. In contrast to the ruby, they rarely have flaws. The spinel is made synthetically and, as such, is used in place of the diamond, the amethyst, and various other stones.

TOPAZ

This transparent stone is one of the finest of the semiprecious stones. It is very hard and quite rare and beautiful. It ranges in color from the yellow attributed to it, to colorless, pale blue, and green; and pink and red topazes have also been found. The stones are faceted, but since they have little "fire" the colorless ones do not really resemble the diamond. South America, Russia, and the United States are some of the countries where the genuine topaz is found. Topaz is fairly expensive. Most stones sold as topaz are citrine, a quartz stone that resembles the yellow-brown variety of topaz.

TURQUOISE

This stone, found in Persia, Egypt, and Mexico, is opaque, and ranges from the rather expensive sky blue to the less desired apple green in color. It has a waxy luster and a soft surface that scratches rather easily. The stone is cut cabochon. Inexpensive turquoise may be cut with the brown rock in which it was found as part of the finished stone. This mother rock is known as a *matrix* and the finished stone is known as a *turquoise matrix*. The turquoise is often imitated by stones made of colored clay or glass.

ZIRCON

Many people have the mistaken idea that this is not a natural stone because it has been displayed in a colorless variety in imitation of the diamond. It ranges in price from very inexpensive to fairly expensive. It is famous today because of its sparkle which more nearly resembles the sparkle of the diamond than that of any other natural stone.

Zircons also come in pale yellow, blue, and reddish-brown colors. Since colorless stones are most popular and since they are rare, some yellow stones are given a heat treatment which makes them white. The blue shades are also popular. The main source of supply of zircons is Ceylon.

BIRTH-MONTH STONES

Customers often purchase gifts of stones that symbolize traditionally each month of the year. This makes an excellent suggestion list for the jewelry salesperson in aiding the undecided customer:

MONTH	STONE	MONTH	STONE
January	Garnet	July	Ruby
February	Amethyst	August	Sardonyx or peridot
March	Bloodstone or aquamarine	September	Sapphire
		October	Opal or tourmaline
April	Diamond	November	Topaz or yellow quartz
May	Emerald		
June	Pearl, moonstone, or alexandrite	December	Turquoise or lapis lazuli

PUTTING THIS MERCHANDISE KNOWLEDGE TO USE ❯ ❯ ❯ ❯ ❯ ❯ ❯ ❯ ❯

❯ DO YOU KNOW YOUR MERCHANDISE?

1. Explain what features the following groups of stones have in common: (*a*) ruby and sapphire, (*b*) aquamarine and emerald, (*c*) moonstone and sunstone, (*d*) jadeite and nephrite, (*e*) natural and cultured pearls, (*f*) onyx and sardonyx, (*g*) cat's-eye and tiger's-eye, (*h*) amethyst and rock crystal.
2. Name the stones that are used in place of the diamond.
3. How do salt-water and fresh-water pearls differ? cultured and imitation pearls?
4. Which stone is very light in weight?
5. What is meant by a doublet? a triplet? Which stones are used as doublets? as triplets?
6. Which stones are not made from minerals but are really organic materials? Which stone is made from a type of iron?
7. Name stones that are available in the following colors: (*a*) red; (*b*) blue; (*c*) yellow to orange; (*d*) green; (*e*) violet; (*f*) colorless. Which stones come in more than one color?

❯ INTERESTING THINGS TO DO

1. On a map of the world, chart the countries from which the various jewelry stones come.
2. Prepare a birthstone chart by drawing pictures of the various stones and mounting the pictures by the names of the stones for each month.
3. Copy technical terms in your notebook from jewelry advertisements about jewelry stones. Be prepared to explain the meanings of the terms.

UNIT 71 TYPES OF JEWELRY

Since jewelry is a personal item that will be worn by the owner, it has distinctive characteristics that make it quite different in appearance when made for men, women, or children. Fine and costume jewelry are available for both males and females in all age groups. The salesperson for jewelry must not only be familiar with jewelry metals and stones, but must also know jewelry items and style trends.

WOMEN'S JEWELRY

Necklaces, bracelets, clips, earrings, and rings are some of the common items included in women's jewelry. See page 463 for illustrations of some types of men's and women's jewelry.

Types of Necklaces

Necklaces may be worn with any type of collarless dress, with some collared dresses, and with any low-neckline dress. Since they are so versatile and so flattering to women of all ages, they are found in a wide variety of styles, lengths, and widths. Beads for necklaces may be *uniform* in size or *graduated* from large in the center front to small at the nape of the neck.

The *collar* is a flat necklace that fits the neck closely.

The *choker* is made from uniform or graduated beads or from metal links. It fits snugly around the base of the neck. It may be single or multistrand, and it may be adjustable to fit various size necks.

Two-to-twelve-strand necklaces that fit over the collarbone of the neck or that fit like a *bib* are also fashionable from time to time.

A *lavaliere* is a pendant or ornament that hangs from a fine chain or cord.

A *locket* is a small case, held by a chain or cord or ribbon, in which may be placed pictures or other mementos.

Matinee lengths are a single row of graduated or uniform bead necklaces 30 to 35 inches long.

Opera lengths are uniform necklaces from 48 to 120 inches in length.

Sautoir is a matinee-length chain with a tassel of metal links and/or beads.

Bracelets

Bracelets are decorative arm ornaments that are especially popular when sleeve lengths are three-quarter or shorter.

Bangle bracelets are round hoops of any width that just slip over the hand. They are made of any alloy, plated metal, or plastic and may or may not be set with stones.

Chain, link, or *flexible* bracelets are made of mesh or links fastened together.

Charm bracelets are usually link type with tiny curios of metal or stone which are attached and dangle from the chain.

Hinge bracelets are bangle bracelets with a center hinge and clasp closing for ease in putting on and removing.

Clips and Brooches

The brooch, which is a development from the safety pin, is used ornamentally on dresses, suits, or blouses. It may be any shape or size, and be made of any material and set with any type of stone.

Clips are ornaments that are "clipped" on by a hinge and spring attachment instead of being pinned. They are sometimes worn in pairs. Some clips are made with a special attachment that permits them to be made into a brooch. Clips are worn at the neckline, on hats, and even at the wrists as ornaments on long-sleeved dresses.

Lapel pins, which vary from the costliest fine jewelry to carved wood initials, are popular for wear on suits, coats, and dresses.

Chatelaine is an ornamental piece made from one or two brooches with a long, looped chain.

Earrings

Earrings, which are considered appropriate with any type of outfit, fit the ear in various ways. Special attachments are made for women with pierced ears. Those without pierced ears may hold earrings on with *screw backs, clips* that grip the ear lobe, *wing backs* that have wing-shaped wires that fit inside the ear and grip the earring, and *magnets* in the shape of buttons that fit behind the ear holding the earring on the front.

Button earrings fit against the ear and may be small or large. They are appropriate for casual wear and with street-wear clothing.

Drop earrings have a button at the lobe of the ear and a pendant which hangs down. These earrings are used mainly for evening and dressy wear. They are also called *chandelier* earrings when they are extra long.

Debonnaire earrings are a newer style that fit upward against the line of the ear.

Rings

Rings have long been associated with symbolism. Engagement and wedding rings are traditional.

Cocktail rings are rings with stones which may or may not be colored. They are usually fancy shapes and appropriate for evening and dress-up wear.

Cluster rings have stones set in groups. All small stones may be used or one or more large stones may be surrounded by small stones.

Dinner rings are usually long narrow rings made to fit the little finger.

Signet rings are used as seals. They contain initials or a crest which may be used to stamp against a wax seal.

Solitaires are rings containing a single stone. The term is often used in reference to the diamond engagement ring.

Hair Ornaments

Hair ornaments that may or may not be functional are stylish when the type of coiffure that is fashionable permits their use.

Barettes of metal or plastic with or without stones act like big, blunt pins to hold the hair in place.

Combs with decoration may be used in various ways to hold the hair and add a decorative accent.

Tiaras that may be elaborately jeweled are worn like small crowns atop the head or over the forehead.

MEN'S JEWELRY

Various types of functional and ornamental jewelry items are sold by men's haberdashers, jewelers, and in department stores. Functional uses are:

To hold ties in place, men may use tie bars, tie holders, tiepins, or tie tacks
To hold watches in place, men may use watch bands, chains, or fobs
To keep keys together, there are key chains and key rings
To wear with shirts, there are collar pins, cufflinks, and studs
To wear on lapels, there are various types of lodge and emblematic pins

As ornaments, men wear finger rings that may be wedding rings, signet rings, or stone-set rings. Men may wear identification bracelets and watch bands.

Miscellaneous items for men include fancy cigarette lighters, cigarette cases, belt buckles, pocketknives, mechanical pens and pencils, and money clips.

CHILDREN'S JEWELRY

While miniature styles listed under men's and women's jewelry may be available for children, there are a few items created just for children:

Teething rings are made of sterling, mother-of-pearl, or plastic.

Add-on-necklaces may be made with pearls or other stones that may have additional stones added to commemorate various occasions until the necklace is complete.

CARE OF JEWELRY

The sparkle and sheen of beautiful jewelry should never be allowed to become dull by lack of care and disuse. Whether a person has purchased fine or novelty jewelry, proper care should be taken to keep it looking attractive.

Sometimes inexpensive brass or other metal jewelry causes the skin to darken where the metal touches. To eliminate this difficulty, a colorless liquid nail polish or lacquer may be applied to the sections that touch the skin. Good quality gold, silver, and platinum jewelry will not darken the skin.

It is wise to remove a ring before washing the hands, being sure to put it in a safe place, because rings are often lost when left on washbasins in theaters, schools, or other public places.

Ring settings should be examined often to see that they are secure, as stones are easily lost when a prong or section of the setting comes loose. Soap and dirt often collect underneath a stone and cause it to appear dull. One may be tempted to use the sharp point of a pin to remove the accumulation. This, however, may loosen the stone, and is never advisable. A soft brush and mild soap and water or water with a little ammonia in it may be used to remove the film. Dry the ring carefully with a smooth-surfaced towel after washing. Soft stones that have scratches on them may be "buffed" slightly by jewelers.

Beads should be examined frequently to see if the thread on which they are strung is fraying or wearing thin. Heavy beads, such as rock crystal or other cut stones, will wear through the thread much faster than will lightweight beads such as amber. Pearl necklaces should be restrung regularly to prevent the thread from breaking unexpectedly. Knots between beads in a necklace will eliminate the chance of losing more than one or two beads at a time. Pearls should be wiped with a soft damp cloth after being worn to remove grease and perspiration which may have accumulated on the beads. They should be worn often, as they lose their luster when left in a jewelry box for any period of time.

Jewelry that is not being worn should be kept in a jewelry box, or wrapped carefully so that different pieces will not scratch one another.

WATCHES

Like other jewelry items, watches may cost a few dollars or many hundreds of dollars depending on the quality of the movement used and the kind of case that surrounds it. Inexpensive movements may be mass produced by stamping them from inexpensive metal, and inserted moving parts cannot be assured to give accurate or enduring timekeeping service. Precision-made watches, however, with each part machined to exacting tolerance, assure many years of accurate timekeeping. In inexpensive watches, known as *pin lever* watches, metal revolves against metal causing noise and inaccuracy of timekeeping in a relatively short time. Better quality watches are known as *jeweled movement* watches. Moving parts revolve in jeweled bearings that resist friction and wear, make less noise, and assure better timekeeping accuracy. Less expensive jeweled watches may have 7 jewels or reinforcements. Better watches have 14, 15, 17, or 21 jewels. Special watches with calendars, timers, or other

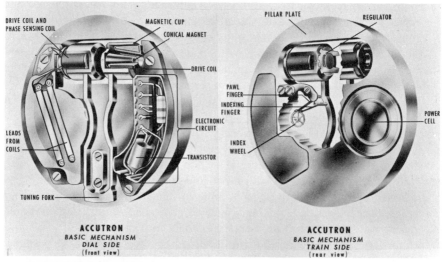

DRIVE COIL AND
PHASE SENSING COIL

MAGNETIC CUP

CONICAL MAGNET

DRIVE COIL

LEADS
FROM
COILS

ELECTRONIC
CIRCUIT

TRANSISTOR

TUNING FORK

ACCUTRON
BASIC MECHANISM
DIAL SIDE
(front view)

PILLAR PLATE

REGULATOR

PAWL
FINGER

INDEXING
FINGER

INDEX
WHEEL

POWER
CELL

ACCUTRON
BASIC MECHANISM
TRAIN SIDE
(rear view)

❰ The cell that powers the watch for at least one year is smaller than a dime. *(Courtesy Bulova Watch Corp.)*

devices may have 23 or more jewels. While originally natural rubies or sapphires were used for jeweled bearings, today synthetic jewels are used in almost all jeweled movements.

Recent developments in watches include self-winding watches that are powered by the movement of the wearer's wrist, or battery-powered watches that have tiny batteries to supply the power formerly achieved by winding the mainspring of the watch. The most recent battery-powered watch, trade named "Accutron," dispenses with the mainspring and makes use of a minute tuning fork to give the motive power to the watch. These watches "hum" rather than "tick." They are extremely accurate timekeepers.

While the movement is all important for timekeeping, the case may be the most costly part of the watch. Inexpensive cases may be made from stainless steel, anodized aluminum, or plated brass. Better cases may be made from karat gold, palladium, or platinum. These latter may be set with precious stones to make them still more costly. The case should be sturdy enough to protect the delicate mechanism.

Care of Watches

For best results, regular-movement watches should be wound at the same time each day, being careful not to overwind them. Self-winding watches should be worn daily to be kept in good condition. Battery-powered watches will run until the battery itself needs replacement. If a watch does not run, it should not be shaken since this may dislocate some of the tiny mechanism and necessitate a costly repair job. Watches should be thoroughly cleaned and examined once a year by a watch repair expert.

SELLING JEWELRY

The way you hold a piece of jewelry which a customer wishes to see may greatly increase its value in his estimation. If you hold it daintily, and allow it to be shown off to its best advantage, it takes on added value in the eyes of the customer. Bright lights, of course, are useful in enhancing the glitter and fire of both inexpensive and expensive stones.

As you show the customer the jewelry, point out the workmanship, the fine detail of the setting, and the unusual color, sparkle, or cut of the stone. This builds customer appreciation for the merchandise you are showing. In displaying expensive diamond or other precious stone jewelry, it is wise not to have more than three pieces on the counter at the same time. This avoids confusion, and also prevents the customer from having to decide among too many articles at once. When he shows a lack of interest in one item, put it away and bring out another which might suit his purpose or taste better. If he indicates a definite interest in one item, stress selling points of that jewelry, being careful not to "talk down" the other items you have shown him. Don't be afraid to show expensive items. Fine jewelry is bought rarely, and a person is often willing to pay a little more than he had planned if he can obtain an unusually fine or beautiful piece. Show the customer the markings on the metal which assure him of value. Explain how the stones are set, and tell him how the jewelry should be cared for. If the jewelry is to be sold in a jeweler's box, place it in the box to illustrate how it will look when received.

PUTTING THIS MERCHANDISE KNOWLEDGE TO USE ❯ ❯ ❯ ❯ ❯ ❯ ❯ ❯ ❯ ❯

❯ DO YOU KNOW YOUR MERCHANDISE?

1. Differentiate between (*a*) collar and choker necklace, (*b*) lavaliere and locket, (*c*) opera and matinee-length necklace, (*d*) bangle and charm bracelet, (*e*) drop earrings and chandelier earrings.
2. Explain the following terms: cluster ring, signet ring, solitaire ring, tiara, chatelaine, pin lever watch, jeweled movement watch.
3. Explain what factors affect the price of a watch.
4. What are the jewels that are used in jeweled movements today? Why are jewels used in watches? How many jewels are used in inexpensive watches?
5. What care should a customer be advised to take of a ring? a watch? beads? pearls?
6. How many pieces of jewelry should you show a customer at a time to avoid confusing him and to assure keeping track of the jewelry being shown?

1. Prepare a manual for salespeople who are to sell either women's costume jewelry or men's jewelry in a haberdashery store.
2. Visit a local jewelry store. Make a list of all types of jewelry in the case. What items did you find that you had not studied in your class?
3. Make a list of all jewelry items owned by various members of your family. Who has the most jewelry in your family?

ADDITIONAL MERCHANDISE TERMS ➤➤➤➤➤➤➤➤➤➤➤➤➤➤➤➤➤➤➤➤

Alexandrite is a form of chrysoberyl, a durable and beautiful stone. It comes from Russia and Ceylon. In daylight, the stone appears to be green, but in artificial light, the stone looks red-violet. It was named for Czar Alexander II of Russia.

Asterism is the starlike effect present in star rubies and star sapphires.

Balas rubies are rose-tinted spinels.

Base metals are metals other than precious ones. Aluminum, copper, zinc, tin, lead, nickel, chromium, steel are usual base metals used in jewelry manufacture.

Brass is the most commonly used metal alloy for inexpensive jewelry. It is a mixture of copper and zinc and has been a popular metal throughout the ages. When polished, it has a luster and color resembling gold. Brass jewelry darkens, however, with use and turns the skin of some people green where it touches. It is also used as a material for the base of gold-filled and rolled gold-plated jewelry.

Cape rubies is an incorrect term for blood-red garnets from South Africa.

Chased design consists of fine lines indented in the metal to outline the shape of flowers, leaves, or other design motifs. This is a popular type of design in silver, copper, and gold jewelry.

Chips are tiny uncut diamonds. These are not used in jewelry because they lack the fire of cut stones. See *Melees.*

Chromium resembles silver in color except that it has a blue cast and a more metallic sheen. It is very durable and is used mainly for plating over brass or copper. Chromium does not tarnish, therefore many people prefer it to silver-plated articles.

Cinnabar is an inexpensive, opaque red stone, which is elaborately carved by the Chinese and used in brooches, necklaces, and rings.

Copper is a red-orange metal, soft and easily worked. It is extensively used with other metals for jewelry manufacture. Jewelry articles made of copper may be plated with silver, gold, rhodium or chromium.

Jet is a black stone made from a very hard type of coal that takes a high polish.

Melees are tiny, single or full-cut diamonds, usually 12 points or smaller in size (⅛ of a carat). These are sometimes erroneously called *chip diamonds.* They are used in settings around larger stones.

Mohs' scale is a scale of hardness, denoting resistance to scratching of stones ranging from the diamond, which rates 10 as the standard for the hardest known substance, down to talc, the soft stone ground and screened and used for talcum powders, which rates 1.

Mother-of-pearl is the nacreous coating on the shell of the oyster, used for ornaments and inexpensive jewelry. It is often carved and has an iridescent, changeable milky-white coloring.

Nickel silver is an alloy containing no silver, but composed of nickel, zinc, and copper. The nickel and zinc give the alloy its characteristic silver color. It is used mainly as a base for silver- and gold-plated jewelry.

Oriental cat's-eye is a greenish-colored chrysoberyl with a band of light running vertically along the stone's surface. This stone is better quality than the quartz cat's-eye.

Oriental emerald is an incorrect term for a green sapphire.

Oriental topaz is an incorrect term for a yellow sapphire.

Paste stones are imitation stones usually made of lead glass which has brilliance and sparkle.

Peridot is a dark green transparent stone known as the olivine. It has an oily appearance and scratches rather easily. It is usually step cut.

Reconstructed stones are made of dust and chips from such stones as the ruby or amber, which are melted or fused and compressed to make a good sized reconstructed ruby or compressed amber stone. These stones are practically nonexistent today because synthetic stones are easier to make.

Rhinestone is a glass stone cut to resemble the diamond and often backed with tin foil to give it more brilliance and sparkle.

Rhodium is a metal resembling silver in appearance, but lacking the soft luster characteristic of silver. Rhodium-plated articles wear very well, but since rhodium is expensive, it is used in extremely small amounts when plating fashion jewelry items.

Rose cut is a common type of faceted cut for beads and marcasites. The stone comes to a point at the top and the facets are triangular in shape.

Scotch topaz is a yellow quartz transparent stone.

Soft solder is made of lead and tin and is used to hold catches on pins and brooches, and other parts of inexpensive jewelry items together.

Solid gold is a term used in referring to pure gold, which is not used commercially except for plating, therefore, according to the Federal Trade Commission rulings, the term should *never* be used.

South American jade is the incorrect term for translucent to opaque pale green, white, blue, and pink garnets.

Specific gravity of a stone is the ratio of its weight to the weight of an equal volume of liquid. If the stone sinks in certain liquids, it is known to have a higher specific gravity than that liquid. If it floats, it has a lower specific gravity. One cc of pure water at 4° C has a specific gravity of 1. Amber has a S. G. of 1.08, the diamond 3.52, the zircon 4.20 and the marcasite 5.00. Since the S. G. for stones differs, this can be used as a test to determine what a stone is. It also affects the size of a stone. The denser the material, the smaller the stone of a given carat weight will be.

Stainless steel is a white alloy composed of steel, nickel, and chromium. It has become popular for watchcases and the underportion of watch bands, especially for those used for sports and other activities. Stainless steel wears very well, and does not tarnish or become discolored with wear.

Swiss lapis is an opaque, dark red, quartz stone which has been stained blue to resemble lapis lazuli.

Ten-power loupe is a jeweler's magnifying glass that enlarges a stone 10 times.

Tourmaline is a translucent-to-opaque stone, which may shade in color from red at one end of the crystal to green at the other end.

White gold, green gold, and **red gold** are alloys made in different colors by varying the proportions and kinds of metals mixed with the gold. Red gold is a mixture of gold and copper, green gold has a little silver added, and white gold also adds nickel and zinc. These may vary in karat quality.

Soaps and Cosmetics, the Cleansing and Glamourizing Products

UNIT 72 COSMETICS AND THEIR USE

WHAT ARE COSMETICS?

Cosmetics have been in use by both men and women since time immemorial. Today their use is almost universal. Everyone has daily need for cosmetics to cleanse, to beautify, or to promote attractiveness. In the United States consumers spend almost a billion and a half dollars yearly on these products. Yet cosmetics cannot be tried on as are clothes, nor examined with a jeweler's loupe as are fine gems, nor stroked as are fine furs. Customers who seek cosmetics are desirous of the effects that can be achieved by their use. Being able to hold a tube, jar, or bottle in front of the customer and explain how she will benefit by using its contents, takes skillful selling ability.

As one buyer stated at a meeting of cosmetic department executives, "It takes real skill to sell a customer a jar of hope!" The customer purchasing cosmetics is interested in their effect—in what the cosmetics will accomplish in use. The customer is truly purchasing a jar of "hope."

While some people mean make-up (rouge, lipstick, eye shadow) when they say "cosmetics," a host of other products also come under this classification, such as tooth pastes, lotions, talcum powders, shaving creams, deodorants, sun-tan lotions, and perfumes.

According to the Federal Trade Commission, cosmetics are:

1. Articles intended to be rubbed, poured, sprinkled, or sprayed on, introduced into, or otherwise applied to the human body or any part thereof for cleansing, beautifying, promoting attractiveness, or altering the appearance, and

2. Articles intended for use as a component of any such articles; *except* that such term shall not include soap.

Accordingly, we find that men need cosmetics just as women do!

Before the Federal Food, Drug and Cosmetic Act, which was passed June 25, 1938, and became effective June 25, 1939, some cosmetic manufacturers were making fantastic claims for their cosmetics. Cosmetics were the magic solutions (so they said) which restored youth to the aging, beauty to the unattractive, hair to the bald, and glamour to the mousy types. All manner of infectious germs, body odors, and sluggishness were eradicated by the use of various cosmetics according to claims.

The passage of the Federal Food, Drug and Cosmetic Act resulted in a new truthfulness and a reduction in exaggerated claims. Contrary to the expectations of the advertisers, sales did not fall off even though cosmetics were no longer claiming magical prowess.

Aid to the Advertiser and Salesperson of Cosmetics

If you have confidence in the quality of the merchandise you sell, you can convince the customer of its worth. The Federal law assures you that the cosmetics you sell will be:

1. Made of clean, fresh, nonpoisonous substances, packaged under sanitary conditions in harmless containers. (Hair dyes are the only cosmetics which may contain coal-tar substances that may be harmful even when used as intended.) All coloring materials must be certified by the U. S. Department of Agriculture. In 1960 certain of these colors were withdrawn from the market because in large doses they had proved to be harmful to rats in laboratory tests. Most of the colors were quickly restored for use since the quantities needed to be harmful to human beings were found to be so great that a lifetime of continuous use could not provide enough of the dye to be dangerous.

2. Accurately labeled with cautions against their misuse. The label must not claim exaggerated benefits to be derived from use of the cosmetic; the label itself must contain the name and address of the manufacturer, and an accurate statement of the weight or contents of the package. Containers may not have false bottoms or sides which make them appear to contain more than they do. If the name of the cosmetic suggests an ingredient such as *cucumber cream,* the cucumber must be the active and important ingredient used.

As a result of this law, the salesperson can talk with conviction, assuring the customer that so long as he or she follows the directions on the package the cosmetics will be harmless.

Before the Federal act, heavy containers like this were sometimes used to misrepresent the actual amount of contents shown at the right. ❯

ALLERGIES

We hear many people today complain about hay fever, or rashes they get from certain trees, weeds, or some ingredients in food or cosmetics. These people have an *allergy* (or sensitivity) to the irritating substances. Such cases, however, are rare, and if the cosmetic ingredient is at fault, simply stopping the use of that product will effect a cure. If the customer has been adversely affected by one type of cosmetic because she is sensitive to some ingredient used in it, another type should be tried. Always, of course, suggest that the customer so afflicted consult her physician, as he can often determine the cause of her ailment by skin tests. In this way she can in the future avoid cosmetics containing that ingredient to which she is allergic.

WHAT CAN COSMETICS DO FOR THE SKIN?

Before the Federal Trade Commission was empowered to check cosmetic advertisers, some of them were telling customers that their products would:

eliminate wrinkles	close pores
nourish underlying	disinfect the mouth
layers of tissue	remove freckles
stimulate sluggish	permanently remove hair
muscles in the face	restore youth

An understanding of the truth about these statements depends on a knowledge of the skin which every cosmetic salesperson should acquire.

Parts of the Skin

The covering of the body is known as *the skin*. This is composed of the top layer or *epidermis* and the underlying layers known as the *dermis*. The epidermis has as its outside covering a layer of dead cells which eventually flake off. If you rub your skin briskly with a harsh towel after bathing, you may see some of these scales peeling off. A few days after being sunburned, you can usually peel this dried epidermis. When the flakes accumulate in the hair, they are known as dandruff. Part of the epidermis has living cells which replace the dead cells as soon as they flake away.

Protected by this epidermis section is the lower layer of the skin known as the *dermis* or *true skin*. Contained in the dermis are blood vessels, nerves, hair roots, fat, sweat and oil glands. The hair grows through an opening or shaft to the outside of the epidermis. When one hair is plucked from that hole, another usually grows in its place. Sebaceous oil glands surround the hair root and coat it with oil that keeps the hair shiny and healthy. If the action of the oil glands is not normal, the hair becomes dry and brittle.

Since the entire body, except the palms of the hands and soles of the feet, is covered with a downlike fuzz of hair, the holes through which the hair grows are visible over the entire surface. Although the hole provided for the hair may not contain a hair, the oil is still present and may collect and form

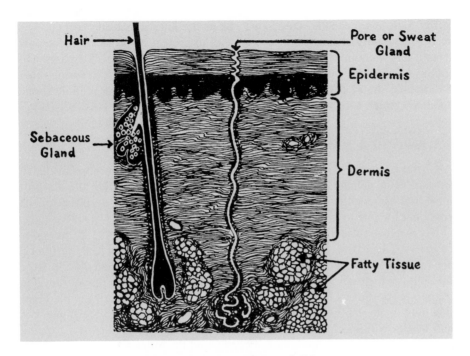

> > Magnified Cross Section of Skin < <

a blackhead on the surface of the skin. Cosmetic advertisers, before the Federal Food, Drug and Cosmetic Act was passed, referred to the holes as the *pores of the skin,* and effectively used fear advertising to stimulate purchase of their cosmetics to "remove the secreted oil and close the pores of the skin." Obviously, no cosmetic can do this. Careful cleansing will keep blackheads from forming, but no known substance can eliminate these natural passageways for the hair nor close them as one would close his mouth. The real pores of the skin are microscopic openings on the surface through which waste materials in the form of perspiration are exuded from the skin and through which the natural oils of the body are secreted to lubricate and nourish the surface of the skin. If they were all closed, suffocation would ensue.

The lower layer of the dermis is composed of fatty tissue that plumps the skin and makes it look smooth and attractive. As a person grows older, this fatty tissue becomes very thin in spots. As a result, grimacing, eyebrow raising, pouting, and laughing eventually form permanent wrinkles in the face. No substance applied to the outside of the skin can rebuild this fatty tissue.

Since it is the duty of the epidermis to protect the lower layer of skin, it must keep gases and liquids from penetrating below its surface. Although some substances can get into the body by being rubbed on the skin's surface, no known cosmetic can in any way penetrate underneath and benefit any part of the dermis. Cosmetics applied to the skin, teeth, hair, and nails serve only to keep them smooth, clean, and attractive. That is the function of cosmetics, and that is how they should be presented to the customer.

Dry Skin, Normal Skin, Oily Skin. Skins are known as being normal, dry, or oily. The normal skin requires cosmetics to protect it and to aid in keeping it soft and smooth. The dry skin needs external appliances of creams and lotions to supplant nature's lack. The oily skin needs thorough cleansing often and application of drying substances such as talcum powder or mild alcoholic solutions which give temporary aid.

COSMETICS AND THEIR MANUFACTURE

Chemistry is the basis of all cosmetic products. The chemist mixes available substances in definite proportions as a cook mixes a cake. With the aid of a little beating, cooking, and sifting, the cosmetic is ready to be placed in its container for sale to the consumer.

No magical substances are used in cosmetics; there are no rare new discoveries; only a few expensive and valuable ingredients, such as perfumes, are used. In a cosmetic factory, white-robed workers deftly handle the large machines which are stirring the ingredients; chemists are measuring the proper proportions of each item to be used and experimenting with other mixtures in the laboratory; large automatic bottling machines are filling jars and bottles with mechanically measured proportions of ingredients, a capping machine clamps the lid on the jar or bottle, and the articles are placed in plain or fancy wrappers or cartons by hand or machine.

Often you read or hear statements about the comparative cost of cosmetic ingredients and their retail price. Examples are given, such as a powder with ingredients costing 7 cents selling for $1 a box. Some analyzers add the cost of the package and inform you that ingredients and package or container cost 15 cents and sell for $1. They admit in analyzing this price statement that they are not including the labor costs, the costs for chemical research, or the cost of dermatology tests, or overhead expenses, or allowances for costly machines used for mixing or sifting, or the mark-up of the retailer or advertising costs.

For the customers who consider price uppermost, cosmetics are available in 20-, 50-, and 75-cent price lines. These cosmetics may not have been made from the finest ingredients, nor have they gone through extra refining processes in their manufacture. They may, however, serve the customer's purpose very well. In some cases, the less expensive cosmetics have been found to be equal in quality to more expensive ones.

Since the ingredients in cosmetics consist mainly of fats, waxes, oils, talc, alkalies, alcohol, glycerine, borax, and dyes, there is little sales appeal in listing them for the customer. It is impossible to know every ingredient in all cosmetics, since every manufacturer has a secret formula and strives to have some advantage over his competitors. The basic ingredients used will be mentioned here, so that you will have some idea of cosmetic formulas and what results may be expected from their use.

In small stores where a cosmetic department consists of one or two counters, each salesperson is responsible for selling every item. In larger stores, where many counters are devoted to the various articles, the toothpastes, mouthwashes, shaving creams, and soaps may be in one section of the department. Creams and lotions occupy a space, hand beauty aids and hair beauty aids each have their counters; and lipstick, rouge, and powder are grouped for the convenience of the customer. Perfumes, toilet waters, and colognes usually occupy another counter. Men's toiletries may be grouped together and sold in separate sections in large stores.

Many of the leading cosmetic houses hire and train their own salespeople, who are known as *demonstrators*. Special counters are devoted to these complete lines, so that the customer who wants all of a certain manufacturer's line need not go to every counter to obtain it. For the customers' information the *demonstrators* are identified by buttons or other designation.

PACKAGING COSMETICS

Cosmetics may be packaged in regular bottles, cans, tubes, or cardboard containers. Containers may be constructed to permit pouring or sprinkling the contents, rolling on liquids by means of a glass ball, squeezing the contents, or spraying the contents from squeeze bottles or from the newest containers called the *aerosols*. This latter type of packaging introduced in the early 50's is used for many products in addition to cosmetics. Today it is one of the leading ways of packaging perfumes, toilet waters, colognes, hair sprays, shaving creams, shampoos, and lotions.

Aerosols. The aerosols dispense their contents from a container by means of a compressed or liquefied gas. Contents are expelled in a fine mist, spray, foam, or powder form. These holders are noted for their ease of application by means of a push button, for their airtight, spillproof containers, which preserve contents, maintain cleanliness, and assure an even application. Certain cautions are needed, however, with aerosol containers: (1) They must not be stored near heat nor should the container be punctured or thrown into a fire or incinerator. (2) Light pressure is all that is needed to assure that the right amount of contents will be released. Advise the customer to hold the container in the position and at the distance recommended by the manufacturer and to use short, light bursts of pressure.

PUTTING THIS MERCHANDISE KNOWLEDGE TO USE ❯ ❯ ❯ ❯ ❯ ❯ ❯ ❯ ❯ ❯

❯ DO YOU KNOW YOUR MERCHANDISE?

      1. Explain the fact that men *do* use cosmetics.

2. How has the Federal Food, Drug and Cosmetic Act affected (*a*) the cosmetic manufacturer, (*b*) the cosmetic advertiser, (*c*) the cosmetic salesperson, (*d*) the cosmetic consumer?
3. What are allergies? What would you recommend for the customer who said she was sensitive to a certain cosmetic?
4. Explain epidermis, dermis, hair shaft, pore, wrinkles.
5. What can cosmetics do for the skin, hair, teeth, nails?
6. Explain what is meant by a dry skin, a normal skin, an oily skin.
7. Explain briefly how cosmetics are manufactured.
8. What is meant by a demonstrator in a cosmetic department?
9. What are the features of the new aerosol containers?

> INTERESTING THINGS TO DO

1. Copy in your notebook any comments of the cosmetic advertisers that are not in accordance with the actual purpose of the cosmetic. (For example: "closes the pores of the skin," "whitens the teeth," "eliminates halitosis")
2. Copy in your notebook statements from the cosmetic advertisements that tell what the product will do to benefit the customer. Why do cosmetic products have so many of these "selling sentences"?

UNIT 73 SOAPS AND DETERGENTS, SHAMPOOS, AND DENTIFRICES

SOAPS

Although soap is not considered to be a cosmetic and, therefore, is not subject to any cosmetic tax, it is an important item for use in beautifying oneself, for it is the true cleanser for the skin. With all its importance, soap is a comparatively recent discovery. Some crude types were made about A. D. 200; by A. D. 700, Spanish soapmakers made a type of castile soap. Until 1800, however, soap was expensive and therefore available only to the wealthy. A method of making soda from salt inexpensively permitted people to make soap in their homes and widespread use of this product then became possible.

The basic formula for soap is *oil* plus *alkali* = *soap* and *glycerine*. The kinds of oil and alkali used make the different types of soaps, and other processes and materials used also vary the soaps and their uses.

The usual oils or fats used in soaps are coconut, olive, palm, peanut, linseed, cottonseed, soybean, and lanolin. The alkalis are sodium hydroxide or potassium hydroxide. The oil and lye are mixed together in huge metal vats which may be twenty or thirty feet tall. They are cooked for a long period of time, until all the particles have been completely united, and no free alkali is present. The glycerine separates out and is drawn off leaving the soap which is ready to be made into various types.

Soaps that are white in color and have little or no perfume are made of pure ingredients. Colored and perfumed soaps are usually more expensive; they generally are made of the finest ingredients, but it is possible to mask poor quality substances by the added color and perfume.

Soaps are made either as *floating soaps* or *milled soaps*.

Floating Soap

Soap after being cooked may be whipped like cream into a foaming, frothy mass. The air bubbles present in the soap then cause the soap to become lighter than water and to float. Floating soaps are usually white in color and have no perfume added, as processes necessary to add color and perfume would remove the air bubbles.

Milled Soaps

Colored and perfumed soaps are made by a process known as *milling*. Depending on its quality, the perfume can add greatly to the cost of the soap. This soap is not whipped, but is chipped and run between heavy metal rollers that press the ingredients tightly together. Color and perfume are added, and the rollers blend these substances evenly with the soap. The soap is then forced into a long tube that shapes it, and it is cut into bars, stamped, and wrapped. Most toilet soaps are milled. These soaps do not float because they have no air whipped into them.

Soaps, whether floating or milled, cleanse the skin by surrounding particles

Continuous Soap-Making Process. Left: Warm, creamy floating soap is mixed in high-speed equipment; from there it goes to a freezer (center) which works the same as an ice-cream-making machine. This machine whips and congeals the warm soap mixture to a smooth-as-silk consistency and turns out an endless oblong of white soap. The soap is then solid enough to be cut into cakes. **Right:** The cakes are trimmed, stamped, and wrapped. *(Courtesy The Procter & Gamble Co.)*

Making Milled Soaps. Left: The huge hopper is opened; and the measured load of solid soap pellets, already mixed with perfume, is dumped between the heavy rollers or mills. **Right:** Soap pellets are compressed into a hard cylinder and cut and shaped into bars of soap. Milled soaps get their name from the heavy rolls or mills that mix and knead the soap during the soap-making process. *(Courtesy The Procter & Gamble Co.)*

of dirt, freeing them from the surface, and then rinsing away. Since different people seek various features in soaps, many types are made to suit all fancies. Following are some familiar types of soap carried in drugstores, supermarkets, specialty, and department stores.

Castile Soap. The term *castile* means that olive oil has been used in the soap. Olive oil has long been considered an ideal ingredient for soap used on babies' skins and for people with sensitive skins. However, the soap becomes quite hard and brittle after standing for a while and needs the addition of other oils to keep it from becoming dry. Glycerine is also added to castile soaps.

Cold-cream Soap. Soap with a cream (fats plus borax) base that aids in keeping the soap from drying out the skin.

Deodorant Soap. While soap rinses surface dirt, bacteria soon collect again causing odors in perspiration that may be offensive. Deodorant soaps contain mildly antiseptic substances that deter the growth of the bacteria. The most famous of these is *hexachlorophene,* developed during World War II by a German-born chemist. This chemical kills bacteria and continues to act for a considerable time after it has been used. Other similar chemicals are also used with similar effects.

Grit Soaps. Some soaps for cleansing and scrubbing mechanics' greasy hands contain gritty substances such as pumice or sand. Naphtha may also be present in the soap to aid in dissolving the grease.

Hard-water Soaps. To aid in obtaining a lather in hard water, special soaps are made with coconut oil which lathers readily.

Laundry Soaps. Few laundry soaps contain such fine fats and oils as do the toilet soaps. Many laundry soaps may also have some free alkali present, which will not harm cotton, linen, and many man-made fibers, but which are very hard on silk and woolen fabrics. Most strong laundry soaps contain "builders" for dirt removal and the softening of the water. These are usually alkalies such as soda ash and borax. Laundry soaps may be purchased in bar, chip, flake, or bead form.

Shaving Soaps or Creams. In addition to a mild soap, shaving soaps and creams usually contain glycerine and stearic acid that aid in producing creamy, lasting lather. These soap products are all the lathering type. The brushless types are made from synthetic detergents, which are discussed below.

Superfatted Soaps. People with sensitive skins often find it advisable to use soaps that have additional oils added during the milling process. The added oils overcome any alkalinity in the soap.

Transparent Soaps. Many people believe that the purity of the ingredients makes these soaps transparent. Any soap may be made transparent by the addition of alcohol and sometimes more glycerine.

Synthetic Detergents or Syndets

Products that clean without using the usual fats and oils are known as "soapless soaps" or *detergents*. The word "detergent" comes from the Latin "detergere," which means to wipe off. Their cleansing action is due to their ability to make water "wetter" and thus to release dirt easily.

Some of these products proved to be so drying to the skin that manufacturers added cold cream to their detergent bars to permit some oil to be left on the surface of the skin. Detergents used in washing machines have removed grease from the working parts of the machines and caused them to get out of order. Care should, therefore, be used not to have these products overflow onto the moving parts of a washer or other machinery.

Hard detergents, presently in use, are mainly obtained from a petroleum derivative called *ABS* (alkyl benzene sulfonate) that is not easily decomposed. Thus foam or suds from waste of detergents often seep through the ground or remain in the water and reappear in fresh water. New *soft* detergents that are decomposed more easily are being developed to offset this disadvantage. An alkylate sulfonate that will decompose will be used in soft detergents.

SHAMPOOS

Although shampoos are regarded by most people as a product closely related to soap, shampoos are considered cosmetics (and subject to cosmetic taxes), while soaps are not included in the cosmetic classification.

Shampoo, being filled into bottles, is moving along the packing line. (Courtesy The Procter & Gamble Co.)

Keeping the hair and scalp clean is important to the health and beauty of the hair. Both soap and soapless (detergent-type) shampoos are available.

It is always wise to follow the directions given on the package for the best results in shampooing the hair. Loose surface dirt can be removed by brushing the hair before the shampoo. At least two and preferably three soapings are necessary to remove all dirt from the hair. Careful rinsing to remove every particle of soap and dirt is most important in shampooing. If possible, a spray such as that used in beauty parlors or barbershops is desirable, because it permits lengthy freshwater rinsings which remove all soap particles.

Types of Shampoos

Cream shampoos are soap or oil emulsions that have a thick, creamy appearance.

Dry shampoos consist of substances such as rice starch, sodium bicarbonate, and powdered borax. They remove dirt when they are brushed from the hair.

Dandruff remover shampoos usually contain some antiseptic product, such as hexachlorophene, to prevent bacterial growth on the skin. The dandruff, which is caused by dried epidermis flakes in the hair, is removed by ordinary washing.

Egg shampoos contain one-half per cent or more of dehydrated egg, which aids in emulsifying dirt for removal from the hair.

Soap Shampoos. These are solutions of soap containing 20–30% soap (oil + alkali) mixed with water. A cake of soap is more difficult to use in shampooing the hair than is the soap solution, but the latter is more costly. Coconut oil, which gives a rich lather, leaves a high shine on the hair. It is considered somewhat drying, however, and so should be used only by people with normal or oily-type hair. Olive oil is considered very good for the hair, although it does not lather so well as does the coconut oil. Lanolin, an animal fat, is also considered a very good substance for use in shampoos.

Soapless Shampoos. These detergent shampoos are made in both the lathering and nonlathering types. *Lathering types* of *soapless* shampoos are made from sulfated alcohol which forms a good lather and does an effective cleansing job. They leave the hair lustrous and shiny, but are somewhat drying. *Nonlathering types* made from sulfonated oils that form no lather are useful for people with dry scalps. They are somewhat difficult to use and must be rinsed out thoroughly to prevent the hair from feeling sticky.

BATH SALTS AND WATER SOFTENERS

Hard water makes bathing and washing difficult because it retards the lathering action of the soap and causes the soap plus the minerals in the water to unite and form a scum on the surface of the water. Certain chemicals added to the water neutralize the minerals present. Sodium hexametaphosphate, commercially known as *Calgon,* helps to soften water for the bath or for laundry purposes. Other sodium substances are also used in bath salts and have a similar action.

Scented bath salts perform two functions—impart a delightful aroma to the bath and soften the water. When detergents are used, water softeners are not necessary.

DENTIFRICES

Cleanliness of the mouth is as important as cleanliness of the body. You can assure the interested customer that most dentifrices are completely harmless; powder, paste, or liquid are equally effective in cleaning the teeth.

After years of dentifrice advertising which appealed to the emotions by such phrases as: "If it's kissin' you're missin'," "The smile of beauty," and "Four out of five have it," *ammoniated dentifrices* which assured better teeth cleansing action were introduced. The public response to the advantages of these dentifrices proved that the desire for clean, healthy teeth was far more important in the public's mind than the desire for allure.

Using Soap in Hard and Soft Water. The same amount of soap is used in each solution. The hard water at left becomes cloudy and gray, and a scum of insoluble soap forms on the surface. The water at the right, which is soft or has water softener added, remains clear and makes a deep frothy suds with excellent cleansing action. *(Courtesy Textiles Education Bureau—Calgon, Inc.)*

A second proof of the customer's interest in mouth hygiene came in 1960 when dentifrices containing *fluorine* chemicals that deter tooth decay were introduced and endorsed by the American Dental Association.

Dentifrices are made in powder, paste, and liquid form. *Tooth powders* are generally composed of mild abrasives such as chalk, plus salt, or baking soda, a sweetener and flavoring.

Tooth pastes are made in paste form by the addition of glycerine to the tooth powder.

Liquid dentifrices are mainly soap substitutes (alkyl sulfates) with coloring matter and flavoring added.

The customer should be informed that dentifrices will not prevent bad breath odors, except those caused by food particles lodged between the teeth. Suggest dental floss or toothpicks for use between teeth to dislodge these food particles. Odors resulting from other causes are not prevented by dentifrices.

Since people's teeth naturally vary somewhat in color, it is important to understand that dentifrices cannot whiten the teeth any more than is natural. *Tooth whiteners* may contain acids harmful to the tooth enamel.

TOOTHBRUSHES

While not part of the cosmetic classification, toothbrushes are an important adjunct to mouth hygiene. Brushes are made of natural or synthetic bristles. Natural bristles are less apt to abrade gums than the harsher synthetic bristles. Rubber tips on the handles of many brushes are useful in dislodging food particles and in gum massage.

PUTTING THIS MERCHANDISE KNOWLEDGE TO USE ❯ ❯ ❯ ❯ ❯ ❯ ❯ ❯ ❯ ❯

❯ DO YOU KNOW YOUR MERCHANDISE?

1. What is the basic formula for soap?
2. What is the difference between floating soap and milled soap?
3. Explain the advantages of the following: castile soap, cold-cream soap, deodorant soap, grit soap, hard-water soap, laundry soap, superfatted soaps.
4. What does *detergent* mean? Why are these called "soapless soaps"?
5. What are the differences in coconut-oil shampoos, olive-oil shampoos, and lanolin shampoos? How do the lathering and nonlathering types of soapless shampoos differ?
6. What is the primary function of dentifrices?

❯ INTERESTING THINGS TO DO

1. Analyze five advertisements for soap products. What benefits do they claim?
2. Analyze five advertisements for dentifrices. What benefits do they claim?
3. Prepare a 2-minute sales talk for a bath soap, a detergent bar, a water softener, or a dentifrice.

UNIT 74 PERFUMES, DEODORANTS, AND ANTIPERSPIRANTS

Perfume, the subtle, alluring product that may be purchased for its own delightful aroma, or diluted to become a toilet water or cologne, or used by the chemist as a costly addition in soaps and cosmetics, has been important to mankind since earliest times. From the odors of burning wood and incense, we get the word "perfume," which means *through smoke*. Perfume in addition to its pleasant odor is a powerful antiseptic—more so even than carbolic acid. In recent years, scientists have confirmed the benefits of perfume oils in killing both bacteria and fungi, either when applied to the skin or when inhaled.

SUBSTANCES USED IN PERFUMES

Secrecy pervades the perfumer's industry. The perfumer has over 3,000 products from which to select in the blending of perfumes and as many as 60 to 100 may be used in obtaining one lovely fragrance. These products are both natural and synthetic substances. Most perfumes sold today are mixtures of natural and synthetic ingredients.

Essential Oils

Essential oils extracted from flowers, fruits, leaves, nuts, and woods, which are grown and gathered in all parts of the world, form the natural odors used in perfumes. Since the latter part of the twelfth century, France has been renowned as the center of the perfume industry. In the south of France are the flower gardens that produce the rose, jasmine, orange, lavender, and numerous other flowers. The famous attar of roses is obtained both from France and from Bulgaria. This is one of the most costly and desirable of perfume substances. All these essential oils when extracted are costly and are valued up to several thousand dollars a pound.

Fixatives

The odors of these natural oils or essences would not be lasting if used alone, however; so other ingredients known as *fixatives* must be added. These scarcely sound like perfume ingredients in their natural state, for they are scent bags or other products from animals that exude unpleasant odors. Most expensive of these is *ambergris,* which whaling parties hope to find floating in the water or in the body of a sick sperm whale. The substance resembles amber, from which it gets its name, although it is gray in color; and it is literally worth its weight in gold. *Civet* from the Abyssinian civet cat, *musk* from the musk deer from Tibet, and *castor* from the Canadian and Russian beaver are the valuable fixatives available for use in perfumes. These, greatly diluted, add a fragrant, delightful body to the scent of the perfume, and make the fleeting flower odors remain for hours. Synthetic fixatives are also available.

Synthetic Fragrances

The synthetic ingredients are products of the chemist's research and are made from coal-tar substances to improve or supplant natural flower, fruit, and animal odors. While these synthetic products do make perfumes more available and less expensive, they in no way lessen the fragrance or pleasure in the use of the perfume. There are still a few odors which the chemist has never been able to imitate.

Alcohol

The natural and synthetic oils together with fixatives are diluted slightly with alcohol to make commercial perfumes. These have a lasting fragrance and may be applied behind the ears, on the neck, hair, and hands. To demonstrate the odor of perfume to a customer, the bottle stopper may be waved underneath her nose, or a tiny bit rubbed on the back of her hand. Allow the alcohol to evaporate before the customer smells the perfume.

Perfumes are sold in "bulk" by the dram or already packaged. When sold in bulk, the perfume is carefully measured into a measuring device, then poured into a small bottle provided for that purpose. Purchasing perfumes in "bulk" is usually less expensive than purchasing them in prepackaged containers; however, most customers prefer to purchase perfumes prepackaged.

TYPES OF PERFUME ODORS

While thousands of blends of odors are available, perfumers classify them into seven main types:

Single florals which have a carnation, rose, lilac, gardenia or other flower aroma
Floral bouquet which has a mixture of flower scents
Oriental which has exotic odors unlike flower scents
Forest or *woody* which resemble sandalwood, balsam, cedar, ferns, or other woodsy products
Spicy which are reminiscent of cinnamon, clove, vanilla, or other sharp, tangy aromas
Fruity which have lemon, orange, peach, or similar fragrances
Modern which is usually composed of a mixture of two or more of the above-mentioned groups

TOILET WATERS

These are perfumes that have been diluted with a considerable amount of alcohol and distilled water. They are useful for spraying in a room and are refreshing to use after bathing. The odor of toilet water is not very lasting.

Some perfume "bootleggers" have bottled toilet waters and falsely labeled them as perfumes.

EAU DE COLOGNE

While similar to toilet water in formulation, eau de cologne has a spicy odor that comes from the citrus and lavender oils often used. It is especially cooling and refreshing after a bath or after shaving.

Cologne sticks combine the alcohol and perfume with a wax base. The alcohol evaporates when it touches the skin leaving a cool, tingling feeling.

CARE OF PERFUMES, TOILET WATERS, COLOGNES

Since these articles all evaporate quickly, stoppers should always be replaced securely in the bottles immediately after they are used. Aerosol containers are airtight. Strong sunlight deteriorates the color of perfume. The oils in perfume may stain fabrics; therefore it is wise to apply the perfume to the body to avoid staining clothing.

DEODORANTS AND ANTIPERSPIRANTS

Perspiration is a normal, healthy function of the body by which it rids itself of waste material. Bacteria on the skin may give perspiration an unpleasant odor. Two precautions may be used by the individual in addition to bathing: deodorants to mask the odor and antiperspirants to mask the odor and deflect the perspiration to other parts of the body.

Deodorants

Since every person perspires to some extent, everyone is in need of some deodorizing material to use under the arms. Most of these deodorants remove the odor without affecting the person in any way. They come in paste, dry, or liquid form and usually contain such chemicals as boric acid, benzoic acid, zinc stearate, or zinc oxide slightly perfumed. These do not harm clothing and can be easily and quickly applied. Many advertisements appeal to men as well as women to use a safe, harmless deodorant.

Antiperspirants

Chemicals that deflect perspiration to some other area of the body, as well as serving as deodorants, are known as *antiperspirants*. At one time these products were harmful to cotton, linen, and rayon clothes. Today, since their acidic reaction has been changed, they are less harmful to use. Pressing clothes before dry-cleaning them or washing them, however, may cause the fabric to deteriorate where the chemical has been rubbed against it. Armpits therefore should be dried thoroughly before dressing.

The essential ingredient of antiperspirants is a 10–15 per cent solution of a salt of aluminum, such as aluminum chlorhydroxide, aluminum sulfate, or aluminum formate. Directions for their use should be followed carefully. If any skin irritation results, their use should be discontinued immediately. One product containing a salt of zirconium has been known to cause an allergic reaction in some users.

The *styptic pencil* men use on cuts after shaving contains aluminum chloride, which acts to close the cut and keep it from bleeding.

PUTTING THIS MERCHANDISE KNOWLEDGE TO USE ❯❯❯❯❯❯❯❯❯❯

❯ DO YOU KNOW YOUR MERCHANDISE?

1. What is meant by the term *perfume?*
2. What are the three basic types of ingredients used in making perfumes?
3. Why are fixatives used in perfume manufacture?
4. Why are synthetic fragrances used?
5. How many basic types of perfume odors do perfumers use?
6. How does perfume differ from toilet water and cologne?
7. How would you advise a customer to care for perfume products?
8. Explain the difference between deodorants and antiperspirants.
9. Which product might be harmful to clothing?

❯ INTERESTING THINGS TO DO

1. Rub an antiperspirant and a deodorant on a piece of cloth in separate spots. Allow it to dry, then iron the cloth. Did either affect the tensile strength of the cloth? Did either stain the cloth?
2. Make a "fashion count" of the girls in your class who used perfume, toilet water, or cologne before coming to school. Report the results by percentage to the class.
3. Prepare a 2-minute sales talk on perfumed products for your class.

FACE CREAMS, LOTIONS, AND MAKE-UP COSMETICS

Face creams are among the most used cosmetics. Many people who use no coloring cosmetics will use face creams. Creams are pleasant to use both because of their odor and the pleasant feeling resulting as the cream is rubbed into the skin. The massage that accompanies the rubbing on of the cream is also stimulating to the skin. Creams also aid nature in keeping the epidermis soft and smooth.

Creams will not nourish the underlying layers of skin, nor will they erase wrinkles, or bring the glow of youth to the users' cheeks, although claims of this type are made by certain manufacturers of these products.

MATERIALS USED IN CREAMS

Creams consist mainly of fats, oils, waxes, water, and a binder (borax), plus a delicate perfume. From time to time products are introduced that claim special attributes for a given cream. For example, *polyunsaturated* oils were found to increase the moisture-holding capacity of the skin, thus keeping it from becoming dry. *Royal jelly,* produced by nurse bees to nourish the queen bee and assure her a long life, has been used as an ingredient in some face creams. *Plankton,* a substance that grows in sea water, has been added to some creams that claim youth-giving qualities. *Sulfur,* held in fine dispersion (known as colloidal), has also been added to creams to reduce the oiliness of skins.

FAMILIAR TYPES OF CREAMS

These may be broken down into two broad classifications: cleansing and beautifying creams.

Cleansing Creams

Cold creams are white, thick, opaque-looking creams that are pleasant and smooth to apply. These are used mainly as cleansing creams.

Liquefying creams have a translucent appearance. They liquefy at body temperature; hence when one rubs this cream on the face it becomes just a thin, watery film. Liquid petrolatum (from which Vaseline is made) is used to give the cream its low melting point. They are not emulsified (mixed) with water as other creams are. These creams are also used for cleansing.

Beautifying Creams

Bleaching creams are used by many young girls who are unhappy about their freckles caused by spots of pigment in the skin. They seek a bleach that will fade these spots, or a cream or powder that will cover them. Lemon juice, hydrogen peroxide, and ammoniated mercury creams are available. The lemon juice creams are fair in their action. Since the pigment lies between the dermis and the epidermis, it is practically impossible to remove. Hydrogen peroxide tends to dry the skin, and since it loses its strength rapidly, it cannot be depended on to be effective over a period of time. Ammoniated mercury creams may irritate the skin if the concentration is too strong or if the cream is used too often. Be sure to warn the customer about care in the use of creams containing this chemical.

Protective creams, such as vanishing creams and make-up base creams, are applied to the skin just before the application of rouge and powder. The vanishing cream, which has a soap base, acts to hold the powder to the skin. The make-up base cream in addition masks defects in the skin such as blotches and freckles. It is similar in appearance and texture to theatrical grease paints.

Emollient creams are ordinary cold creams that have been *superfatted* by the addition of lanolin or other animal oil. They are used for massage around the eyes and on the forehead. They are also referred to as *night creams.* They are somewhat stickier than cold creams so they are not useful for cleansing. They do, however, aid in keeping the outer skin soft.

Hormone creams are regular creams with an estrogenic hormone added. This substance is administered by doctors for some diseases of aging people, and it is questionable whether such hormones should be rubbed indiscriminately on the skin. These are advertised as imparting a more youthful appearance to users, but this claim has never been substantiated by actual proof.

LOTIONS

In addition to creams, lotions are used to soften the surface of the skin. Lotions may be made by thinning some creams. This results in a creamy lotion that may be used much as creams are used.

Popular Lotions

After-shave lotions are astringent lotions containing alcohol (which has an antiseptic action), alum, menthol, boric acid, glycerine, coloring matter, water, and perfume.

Astringent lotions usually contain alcohol, glycerine, borax, and water. They are patted on the face after cream is removed; because of the alcohol in them, they have a tingling, drying effect.

Hand lotions protect the hands by leaving a smooth, nongreasy film. They generally contain glycerine, alcohol, water, and perfume. Since glycerine is drying to the skin, hand lotions may need to be used sparingly by people with dry skin.

Silicone lotions form an invisible coating on the skin that prevents moisture from drying them out and keeps them soft.

Tanning Agents

Tanning agents include sun-tan oils, sun-tan preventives, and tanning liquids.

Sun-tan oils merely keep the skin from drying out during the time that the pigment in the body is allowed to react to the ultraviolet rays of the sun.

Sun-tan preventives usually contain some chemical substance and some vegetable oil. The chemical acts to deter the ultraviolet rays of the sun from harming the skin, and the oil keeps the surface of the skin from becoming dry. These also come in cream form. If the product prevents sunburn, it is a drug; if it only aids in acquiring a tan, it is a cosmetic.

Tanning liquids and creams (a fermentation product of glycerol), introduced in 1959, were made from chemicals that reacted with the protein in the skin to produce a brown stain, somewhat resembling a sun-tanned skin. There were two disadvantages to these products: they did not produce an even color, and many people reported severe allergic reactions to these chemicals. In addition, if spilled on a carpet or clothing, they left a brown, nonwashable stain.

MAKE-UP PRODUCTS

The number of items needed for a complete make-up has grown by leaps and bounds since grandmother's day. Powder, rouge, lipstick, eye make-up, nail polish are but a few of the items.

Powder

Women everywhere seem to have attempted to improve their faces by whitening them. White lead, chalk, powdered rice, and many other substances have been used for this purpose. The base of most powders in use today is *talc,* which is a soft mineral found in the earth. California supplies us with a good quality of this substance which, after being mined, is ground and purified.

Talcum powder (dusting powder, or bath powder) is usually pure talc with a little perfume added. For babies' use and for men's after-shaving powders, boric acid or zinc stearate may be added for their antiseptic qualities. Slight coloring may also be added to talc for men's use. Advise customers not to "dust" talc on or cause tiny particles to fly, as they may be harmful if breathed into the lungs.

Face powder is quite different from *talcum powder*. Smear a little talc over the back of your hand. Notice that it absorbs moisture, but it leaves the skin looking shiny. For this reason, other ingredients are necessary in making face powder. Substances added may be zinc oxide, chalk, China clay, titanium dioxide, starch, perfume, and coloring matter. Some powders may have a cold-cream base. Too much starch in a powder may cause it to "cake" on the face. Powders are sifted repeatedly through fine silk screens, or they are blown about in a chamber to reduce the size of the particles. The more they are sifted, the finer and more uniform the powder will be. Naturally, this adds to the cost of the product.

Since powder looks different under electric light than in daylight, it is wise to use another shade for evening wear. Most boxes of powder have cellophane covered "windows" to show the customer the shade of the powder.

Powders come in dry, cake, cream and liquid form. The *cake* or *compact* powders may be made by adding tragacanth mucilage to the powder and drying and compressing it. *Liquid* powder, which has an adhesive effect, is made by adding oxide of zinc, alcohol, and glycerine to the powder. These come in varying shades and are useful for face, neck, arms, and legs. *Cream* powder is made by adding coloring matter and powder to a vanishing cream base.

Powder or Make-up Bases

The desire for a smooth, satiny effect on the skin has been achieved by the use of powder or make-up bases. These come in three types: cake make-up, cream base, and liquid base.

Cake make-up consists mainly of pigmented powder in a dehydrated cream (cream with all the water removed). When this is applied to the skin with a moist sponge, it forms a film covering which is quite lasting. Various pigments give the required color to the make-up base. *Cream-base make-up* consists mainly of pigmented powder in a thick cream. *Liquid-base make-up* is an oil suspension of coloring matter.

Rouge

Grandmother secretly applied a tiny bit of red cake coloring to her cheeks to give her a healthy look. Granddaughter prefers the "pale look" and may use little or no rouge.

Rouge, like powder, comes in dry cake form. It also comes in cream form. *Dry rouge* varies from powder only in that coloring is added. All dyes used in rouge are certified by the Department of Agriculture. *Cream rouge* is essentially cold cream mixed with approved coloring matter.

While the cake rouge is easier to apply, it does not adhere as well as the paste rouge does. To apply cream rouge so that it will be even and attractive takes a little practice. Advise the customer to take just a tiny bit of the rouge on the end of her finger and apply it in triangle form beginning at a point directly under the center of the eyes working out and up. Blend it in carefully with the finger tips to avoid producing a painted look.

It has been estimated that 95 per cent of women use lipsticks. They own at least two and a half lipsticks at a time! Lipsticks, which are often used by many women who use no other make-up, are basically stiff creams to which have been added coloring substances certified by the Department of Agriculture. The lipsticks to which some people might be allergic are those known as "permanent." They often contain bromo-acid dyes which in some cases have proved irritating.

Even though only approved colors are used, some of the coal-tar dyes used in lipsticks have proved harmful to rats in laboratory tests. It was found, however, that the amounts necessary to be harmful to people would be greater than any woman could possibly use in a lifetime. It is wise to avoid licking lipstick, and the lips should be wiped before eating to prevent small amounts of lipstick from being eaten with food.

In selling lipsticks, it is important to know that shades not only vary in the tubes, but also may look different on various skins. Lipsticks are usually tested for color by marking the back of the customer's hand with a few different shades so she can compare their effect on her skin and select the desired one.

Eye Make-up

The year 1950 marked the introduction of exotic eye make-up reminiscent of the "flapper era." The advent of the Cleopatra fad in 1963 created further demand for dramatic eye make-up.

Mascara, used to darken and lengthen eyelashes, may have carbon (lampblack) or other approved coloring ingredients added to a soap base, which smarts if it gets in the eye; or the colors may be mixed with waxes, which do not smart. Mascara comes in solid or semiliquid form, and a brush is used for application. The liquid mascara is insoluble in water.

Eyebrow pencils are made by adding carbon to wax or paraffin. These may be sharpened as pencils are to produce fine lines.

Eye shadow, which comes in blue, green, lavender, and brown, and also in exotic gold and silver shades, has coloring materials mixed with a cream base.

Eye liners are varicolored liquids similar in formula to mascara.

Nail Preparations

Nail Polish. Colored liquid nail polish, which became a vogue many years ago, was frowned upon by many as being gaudy and unattractive. Men especially disliked seeing deep red or pink fingernails. Advertising and availability, however, were strong factors, and today colored nail polish, which sells from 25 cents to $1.50 a bottle, is an accepted cosmetic used by a great many women. The polish itself is nitrocellulose lacquer, which also is used to make Celluloid. This is dissolved in acetone or a similar solvent. Plasticizers (chemicals that add flexibility) and coloring materials are added. When the polish is applied to the nails, the acetone evaporates leaving a hard, colorful coating on the nails. For best results all oil should be removed from the nails before applying the polish. Two coats are generally more lasting and more attractive than a single coat of the polish.

Since the nails are merely a horny substance similar to the epidermis and to hair, they are rarely harmed by this coating. A person, however, may have allergic reactions to these polishes when she touches her face with her nails when coated with these lacquers.

Nitrocellulose lacquer is highly flammable. The customer should, therefore, be advised not to smoke while applying nail polish nor to apply it near an open flame.

Polish Remover. To remove nail polish, acetone, ethyl acetate, or a similar solvent is used. To this may be added a little oil, coloring matter, and perfume. Like cleaning fluid, polish remover evaporates very quickly when the cork is removed from the bottle and when in use. Solvents also dry the skin wherever they touch. Advise the customer to rub oil around the nails after using polish remover. Nail-polish remover dissolves acetate fabric and is also harmful to the finish on wooden furniture.

Cuticle Remover. Customers should be advised to read very carefully the directions on cuticle-remover bottles before using them. Anything strong enough to eat the dead skin of the cuticle may be strong enough to irritate the rest of the epidermis. Cuticle removers consist of dilute potash lye and glycerine and perhaps a little perfume. It is wise to wash the hands with soap and water and apply oil after using cuticle remover.

PUTTING THIS MERCHANDISE KNOWLEDGE TO USE ❯❯❯❯❯❯❯❯❯❯

❯ DO YOU KNOW YOUR MERCHANDISE?

1. What is the main function of face cream?
2. Do creams nourish the dermis or true skin? Do they eliminate wrinkles? Explain your answers.
3. What is the difference between talcum powder and face powder?
4. In selling talcum powder for babies, what precautions would you give the customer?
5. Which make-up product is almost universally used by American women?
6. What cautions should users of lipsticks be given? of polish removers?
7. What are the basic ingredients of nail polish? What cautions should customers observe in their use?

❯ INTERESTING THINGS TO DO

1. Analyze five ads for face creams. What benefits are claimed by the manufacturer?
2. Analyze five lipstick advertisements. How many different colors did each manufacturer feature?

COSMETICS FOR THE HAIR AND FOR HAIR REMOVAL

Since the advent of "do-it-yourself" hair dyes, these products have become popular. Many women, however, find that home hair dyeing is not always satisfactory, and eventually they seek beauty operators who are skilled in applying these coloring materials.

Dyes

Since manufacturers of hair dyes are permitted to use substances which are *not* approved by the Department of Agriculture, all hair dyes containing ingredients that might be harmful to some people must be labeled with appropriate warnings. The salesperson should stress these warnings because customers often believe every product sold by a certain store has been approved by that store, and they may not bother to read the warning labels! These labels advise that patch tests (application of the dye on a small control area of the body) should be made 24 to 48 hours before the application of the dye to the hair.

Vegetable dyes are on the whole harmless. Henna, a leaf from an Egyptian plant known as the "flower of paradise," coats the hair, making it somewhat gummy to the feel. If it is used constantly, it may cause the hair to become brittle. Other vegetable substances, such as sage for dark gray and camomile for yellow coloring, may be used on the hair. These vegetable dyes tend to streak, and they do not color evenly so that in recent years they have lost their popularity.

Metal dyes, such as the salts of silver, copper, or lead, coat the hair and become darker with each application. They fade after being applied and sometimes leave hair with purple, green, or orange colors.

Tints

Hair tints, which really change the color of the hair but which work inside the shaft of the hair instead of coating it on the outside as the vegetable and metal dyes do, are made from coal-tar substances. These are known as "para" dyes because paraphenylenediamine is the base in general use. Hydrogen peroxide is combined with these dyes to make the hair more absorbent and to bleach the natural pigment. The dye then penetrates the hair shaft with the desired color.

Since these tints are made from synthetic substances that may or may not be harmful to users, directions for their use should be carefully followed and patch tests made 24 hours in advance to determine if the user is allergic to these dyes.

Hair-tint shampoos, which tint the hair while it is shampooed, incorporate these coal-tar dyes in the shampoo.

Bleaches or *lighteners* are drying to the hair and are best applied by experts. Most hair bleaches contain hydrogen peroxide and ammonia.

Color restorers are misnamed. The pigment that colors the hair forms at the root of the hair. If this pigment-forming mechanism is not functioning, the hair is colorless or white when it comes out. Any products that claim they can restore color would have to be able to stimulate the pigment-forming mechanism. This, of course, is impossible. Color restorers are merely hair dyes and should be sold as such. Because their action is slow, often requiring two or three applications before any change is noted, they may seem to be restoring color.

Color Rinses

While dyes are permanent and can be retained by touching up new hair that continually grows in, rinses are temporary and will .wash out of the hair at the next shampoo. These are pigments that are carried in soap-and-water soluble fixatives. Vegetable and coal-tar pigments are used. Some people are so sensitive to the coal-tar pigments that they have reactions to these rinses. If such an allergic reaction occurs, the use of the rinse should be discontinued. A rinse, unlike a dye, can merely deepen the color of the hair slightly or add highlight colors to it. Sometimes the rinse stains the hair, and several shampooings are necessary to restore it to its original color.

HOME WAVE KITS

These permanent wave kits for use in the home were advertised and sold on an extensive scale for the first time in 1947. The active ingredient in the cold wave is ammonium thioglycollate or sodium thioglycollate, a strong alkaline solution. Both these substances and the acid neutralizer are poisonous if taken internally, and care must be taken even if a cut or scrape is present on the hands or head, since application of these solutions may cause an unpleasant irritation.

The curl is accomplished by the alkaline thioglycollate, which softens the hair fibers while holding them in a curled position. The hair is then set in that form by the neutralizer. If the alkaline solution is left on the hair too long, it may result in disintegration of some of the hair. The solution is also harmful to the nails, and therefore, as a precaution, rubber gloves should be worn during application of the solution.

WAVE-SET PRODUCTS

The *wave lotion* used for setting finger waves or bouffant hair-dos is a honeylike liquid made from acacia gum, karaya gum, tragacanth gum, quince-

or flaxseed, water, alcohol, and borax. Some liquid plastic substances are also being used for hair setting.

Aerosol spray lacquers, which are soluble in water, may also be sprayed on fancy hair settings to hold the hair in place. The older sprays were made from shellac, while the newer ones have a PVP (polyvinyl pyrrolidone) base. This is a white powder that is soluble in water, is very stable, is compatible with the skin, and forms an excellent film. It is also soluble in alcohol which is used to carry the chemical onto the hair. Bleached shellac may be added to reduce brittleness of this material.

Since these products are highly inflammable, they must be so labeled and care should be taken to keep them away from any lighted cigarettes or open flames.

HAIR RESTORERS

Although these products are always being announced and developed, no known cosmetic can restore or grow hair.

HAIR LOTIONS

Mineral oils, such as petrolatum, give the highest gloss to the hair; the vegetable oils are second; and the animal oils (lanolin) give little shine. The latter, however, do nourish the hair better than the other two types. Some hair lotions claim they contain no oil or grease. These usually have a high alcohol content and perfume ingredients.

HAIR REMOVERS

Common methods of removing hair are:

Mechanical

An abrasive such as sandpaper or pumice may be used in the form of mitten or pad for use in rubbing the hair away. Care must be taken not to rub so hard that the skin is harmed.

Wax is melted and applied to the area where the hair is to be removed. When the wax has set, it is yanked off like adhesive tape, bringing embedded hairs with it. Constant use of the wax may cause the skin to become irritated.

Shaving is considered entirely safe and is especially recommended for large areas, such as legs and arms. Shaving does not stimulate the growth of more hair as some people seem to believe it does. If it did, men's shaved heads would become the fashion. Hair feels stiff as it grows out because it is all the same length, like the bristles on a brush. Shaving creams, soaps, powders, or lotions prevent irritation when applied before using a razor or electric shaver.

Tweezing is harmless as long as it is done cautiously with a clean tweezer.

Tweezing is somewhat painful, but for small areas such as eyebrows, it is successful. Since the hair is pulled out by the root, it takes a little longer for it to be replaced than it does when the area is merely shaved. Tweezing does not stop or retard the growth of hair. Care must be taken to avoid infection when hair is removed by this method.

Chemical

A sulfide, such as sodium, which is used for removal of hair from animal hides during pretanning, is the usual chemical packaged for use in removing hair from arms, legs, and face. This chemical is easily recognized by its odor resembling rotten eggs. Since it can cause serious irritation and burns on the skin, it must be used cautiously. Advise the customer to test it on a small area before spreading it over legs, arms, and face.

A newer chemical which is replacing the older sulfides and which has a more pleasant odor is being used today. This chemical is known as *calcium thioglycollate*.

Since the hair is composed of substances similar to the epidermis, any article strong enough to eat unwanted hair if left on long enough will eat the skin too. In selling depilatories, one must always caution the customer about their use, and warn them to read labels and follow directions.

Electrolysis

The only method known to remove unwanted hair permanently is electrolysis. By this method a trained nurse or electrolysis expert inserts a fine wire into the hair follicle opening, turns on the electric current and burns the hair root. A small blister forms after several hours, and, if broken, a scar may result.

PUTTING THIS MERCHANDISE KNOWLEDGE TO USE ❯❯❯❯❯❯❯❯❯❯

❯ DO YOU KNOW YOUR MERCHANDISE?

1. What cautions should you give the customer concerning hair dyes?
2. Explain the different results to be obtained from metal dyes, vegetable dyes, and coal-tar hair dyes.
3. What cautions should you give a customer who buys bleach material for the hair?
4. How do color rinses differ from hair dyes?
5. How does the chemical work to make hair wavy in home wave kits?
6. What cautions should you give the customer who buys an aerosol hair spray?
7. For chemical removal of hair, what cautions should be given the customer?
8. What is the only method by which hair may be removed permanently?

1. Analyze five advertisements for hair-coloring products. What claims did these products make? Did any advertisements for hair dyes suggest patch tests 24 hours in advance?
2. Prepare a 2-minute sales talk for a hair-coloring or hair-wave product.
3. Make a "fashion count" among the girls in your class. How many use hair sprays? hair bleaches or lighteners? color rinses? hair dyes?

ADDITIONAL MERCHANDISE TERMS ❯

Acetone is a colorless inflammable liquid that evaporates readily. It is used to dissolve nail polish (made of nitrocellulose lacquer). It has a drying effect on the skin.

Alcohol is a colorless liquid, resulting from fermentation of grain, starch, or sugar, which evaporates readily and has a cooling effect. It is used as a solvent in some cosmetics, but it is drying to the skin.

Alkalies are bases that are formed by combining a metal with hydrogen or oxygen. Alkalies in combination with acids form a neutral substance known as a salt. The word "alkali" comes from an Arabic word meaning "ashes" from which alkali was once obtained.

Alkyl sulfates are soap substitutes used in liquid dentifrices.

Aluminum chloride is a white powder, soluble in water, which has astringent and antiseptic properties that are useful in antiperspirants and styptic pencils. If the solution is not carefully dried when applied under the arms, it may harm fabrics. Some people find it irritating to the skin.

Ammoniated mercury is a white powder which is used in some freckle remover and bleach creams. It should be used with caution, however, as it may be irritating and may form dark splotches on the skin.

Alum (ammonium alum or potassium alum) is an astringent white powder used in lotions, deodorants, styptic pencils, and antiperspirants.

Antiseptic is a substance that inhibits the growth of germs on the body.

Astringent is a substance that shrinks, contracts, and drives the blood from the tissues.

Borax is a mild alkaline substance in the form of a white powder. It has a slight antiseptic value and is widely used in bath salts, some soaps, tooth paste, brushless shaving cream, and other creams.

Boric acid is a white powder with antiseptic qualities, used in astringents, cleansing and other creams, deodorants, some talcum powders, shaving creams, and antiperspirants.

Bromo-acid dye is an orange-red powder that is mixed with fats and waxes in lipsticks. Some people are sensitive to bromo-acid, which is used in some indelible and changeable lipsticks.

Coal-tar dyes are made of coal tar, which results when bituminous coal is distilled. This is useful for dyes, explosives, flavorings, etc. Some coal-tar dyes are harmless, others may irritate people allergic to them.

Coconut oil is a white butterylike oil from coconuts, useful in soaps and shampoos because of the foamy lather which it induces. It may be irritating to some people and tends to have a drying effect on skin and hair.

Cottonseed oil is a pale yellow oil from the seed in the cotton boll, used in some inexpensive creams and soaps.

Emulsion is an oil and water mixture with oil held in suspension in water, or water held in oil.

Fluoride is a salt of the element *fluorine* which has been found to be helpful in retarding tooth decay when used in small quantities in drinking water. When added to dentifrices it is supposed to have the same beneficial results.

Glycerine, a clear, colorless liquid of about the consistency of syrup, is a by-product from the manufacture of soap. It is extensively used in cosmetics and some soaps.

Hydrogen peroxide is a watery appearing liquid that has antiseptic value and also bleaches by oxidizing color. It is used in some bleach creams and lotions and in white henna, a hair bleach. It has a drying effect on the hair, and continued use may make hair very brittle.

Hexachlorophene is a chemical that eliminates skin bacteria.

Menthol is a colorless liquid from the oil of peppermint. It has antiseptic action, reduces pain when applied on the skin, and has a very cooling effect. Useful in after-shave lotions.

Olive oil is a light yellow or greenish oil pressed from ripe olives. It is antiseptic and astringent and may be used in any cosmetics that use oils. It is particularly valued for use in castile and other types of soap and shampoos.

Lanolin is a yellow or white butterlike fat obtained from the shorn wool of sheep during the washing and cleansing processes. The fat is then cleansed and purified. The sticky substance is mixed with liquid petrolatum and used in soaps, creams, and shampoos.

Palm oil is a hard or butterlike orange-colored substance from the palm seed or fruit, used especially in soaps and shampoos.

Peanut oil is a yellowish-color oil from the seeds (nuts) of the peanut plant, used in soaps, sunburn oils, and some creams.

Petrolatum is a greasy substance prepared from petroleum. *Vaseline* is a trade name for petrolatum.

Potassium hydroxide (caustic potash—potash lye) is a powerful alkali in the form of brittle white chunks that are neutralized when combined with acid in oils and fats. Used in some soaps, creams, and lotions.

Pumice is a gray, powdered, volcanic, glasslike substance useful as a gritty ingredient for polishing nails and also in grit soaps for greasy hands.

Quinine is a white powder from the bark of the cinchona tree used as an antiseptic substance in sun-tan preparations. Some people, however, are allergic to quinine.

Sodium hydroxide (caustic soda—lye) is a powerful alkali in the form of brittle white chunks that are neutralized when combined with acid in oils and fats in the manufacture of some creams and soaps.

Sodium sulfide is a clear colorless salt crystal that is a compound of sulfur. The crystals are effective in hair removal, but may be harmful to the skin. They are distinguished by the odor of rotten eggs, which they impart when moistened. Hair removed by this chemical grows back again just as it does when shaved off.

Sulfated alcohol is a soap substitute used in some shampoos. It leaves hair glossy, but may have drying effect.

Titanium dioxide is a fine, white powder with very fine covering properties that make it desirable for use in face and liquid powders.

Wax is a viscous-to-solid substance that is insoluble in water and has a waxy luster. Examples: beeswax, paraffin.

Zinc oxide is a fine, white powder, extremely absorbent, which is used in face powder, depilatories, bleaches, cleansing lotions, etc.

Zinc stearate is a white chemical powder. It has an astringent action and may be used in face and talcum powders, skin whiteners, and deodorants. It may be irritating and dangerous if breathed into the lungs.

Foods

CHAPTER 25

UNIT 77 THE FOOD STORE AND ITS DEPARTMENTS

The classes of foods necessary for health are commonly grouped as follows in the supermarket which now accounts for nearly three-quarters of the country's grocery business. A supermarket is a self-service food store with annual sales of $500,000 or more. Selling here largely takes the form of arrangement and display with special emphasis on new items and interesting food combinations. Allowance is made for the nonfood departments that usually carry health and beauty aids and housewares.

	Approximate % of Total Sales
Grocery	40
Meats	25
Produce	10
Dairy	8
Frozen Foods	5
Baked Goods	5
Nonfoods	5
Miscellaneous	2
Total	100

GROCERY DEPARTMENT

This major department of the supermarket sells prepared foods of many kinds: canned, bottled, and packaged. No special refrigeration or humidity control is required to keep the food in good shape for weeks or even months.

The fastest sellers in this department are coffee, canned vegetables, canned and dry packaged fruits, sugar and sugar products, and cereal products including cookies and crackers. Some important nonfood items are also carried in this department: soaps and detergents, paper goods, and cigarettes and tobacco.

A current problem in connection with packaged foods of all kinds grows out of the practice of packing food slackly and using bulky containers to give the impression that the quantity of the contents is larger than it actually is. While weights must be accurately stated by law, packages often contain an odd number of pounds and ounces and it becomes a difficult mathematical problem for the customer to determine the cost per pound or ounce.

Cereals

Most packaged foods in the grocery department are made primarily from cereals, that is the seeds or grains of grasses. The cereals—wheat, rice, corn, oats, rye and barley—are the world's chief staple diet. An excellent source of carbohydrates, most prepared cereals today are fortified with vitamins.

Wheat contains starch, a carbohydrate, and gluten, a protein. The chief wheat products available in the grocery department are flour, semolina, macaroni, spaghetti, and breakfast foods. Whole-wheat flour utilizes the entire grain; while white flour, only the kernel. The former is more nutritious but does not keep well. With people doing less and less home-baking, flour today accounts for less than a half of one per cent of supermarket sales, whereas prepared foods in which flour is a major ingredient account for nearly 10 per cent.

Rice is the world's leading cereal but is used less than wheat in America. It is 80 per cent starch with less protein and fat than wheat. Rice is sold polished and unpolished. The latter has more nutritional value but tends to mush in cooking. Precooked rice, which can be prepared in a few minutes without boiling, is now a major item. Popular breakfast cereals are also made of puffed rice.

Corn, the third most important cereal, has a wide variety of uses. Corn oil is used for cooking and for salads; it is also contained in some kinds of oleomargarine. Corn is used in the production of corn syrup, corn flakes, corn meal and cornstarch.

Sugar

Like the cereals, sugar is a carbohydrate but in immediately digestible form. Chemically there are many types—sucrose (ordinary kind), fructose (in fruits), glucose (in grapes and starchy foods), lactose (in milk) and maltose (in beer). The two principal sources of sucrose are cane sugar and beet sugar. In this country, we have depended largely on the former. When refined, the two are hard to distinguish. Other important sources of sugar commercially are corn, sorghum (a fodder grass), maple, and honey. These are usually processed as syrup.

Sucrose sugar is sold in many forms: granulated, fine granulated, powdered granulated, confectioner's powdered (cornstarch added), brown (light and dark), cake and tablet, and mixed (with flavoring). It is also a major ingredient in soft drinks, candy, and many prepared foods. In fact, the retail sales of candy, chewing gum, and soft drinks are over four times the sale of plain sugar.

While sugar is high in calories, providing quick energy, nutritionists tell us that most Americans consume too much, about 100 pounds a year. Sugar lacks the natural proteins, minerals, vitamins and fatty acids essential for health. As the consumption of sugar and starch is increased, the intake of proteins decreases almost automatically.

Overconsumption of fats and carbohydrates is associated with both tooth decay and overweight, leading sometimes to coronary troubles.

Where the retail salesman has the opportunity, he should suggest to his customers greater purchase and consumption of meats and vegetables and relatively less sugar and starchy foods.

Beverages

In terms of dollar sales volume, coffee is the most important item in the grocery department. Coffee is the ripe fruit of a plant of African origin that is now grown mostly in Brazil, Colombia, and the East Indies. Coffee is roasted and may be sold in the bean to be ground by the customer or by the grocer at the time of sale. Today's demand for the quick and easy transaction has, however, led to the sale of packaged coffee, ready for use. To retain flavor, vacuum-packed coffee is most satisfactory. Various grinds are available for percolator, drip, and silex.

Instant, completely soluble coffee has become the most popular form because of convenience in preparation. While it does not match fresh-roasted and ground coffee in aroma, many persons cannot distinguish the difference.

Other beverages, considerably less important saleswise, are tea and chocolate. Tea consists of the tender shoots, leaf buds, and leaves of a plant. Black tea is fermented; green tea, not; and Oolong tea is semifermented. Much of the tea sold in this country is blended.

Chocolate is made from the seeds or beans of the fruit of the tropical cacao tree. When the butterfat is removed, the product is called *cocoa*.

Soft drinks and beer both outsell tea, but not coffee. Much of the discussion above about sugar applies also to soft drinks.

Condiments

Among the less important grocery department items, which are nevertheless essential to good eating, are *condiments*. These are flavoring extracts (alcoholic preparations) and spices. Extracts of natural ingredients are called true extracts in contrast with imitation extracts that use synthetic flavoring. Spices come from the berries, bark, pits, seeds, and roots of various plants. Examples are pepper, cinnamon, mustard, and nutmeg.

MEAT DEPARTMENT

Meat consists of the flesh, edible glands, and organs of animals. It is one of the most complete and best sources of protein. It also contains much fat and important minerals. A high protein diet has been found to provide protection against colds and to assist the body in warding off poisons.

The chief kinds of meats are:

Beef—from cattle (steer, ox, or cow)
Veal—from calves (6–8 weeks old)
Pork—from hogs
Mutton—from sheep
Lamb—from young sheep or lambs, 3–12 weeks old
Poultry—from fowl, particularly chickens, turkeys, ducks
Seafood—fish, scallops, oysters, clams, lobsters, shrimp, an excellent source of iodine and of vitamins A and D
Variety meats—brains, kidneys, sweetbreads, heart, liver, tongue, rich in minerals and vitamins, low in fats

Most meat is graded according to conformation, finish, and quality.

Conformation covers the general build, shape, and plumpness of the carcass, side or cut. *Finish* refers to the quality, color and distribution of the fat.

Tender meats are fine grained and have less connective tissue than is found in the muscles that receive most exercise. They are *well-marbled,* that is the fat and lean is minutely intermingled. Fatty meats are, however, to be avoided by those with heart disease in the family history. Lean meat, often the cheaper cuts, is to be preferred.

In some localities, beef has to be sold by Federal grades, but the big meat packers also have their own grading systems. However, all meat sold between states has to bear a Federal inspection stamp to guarantee not the quality but the wholesomeness of the meat. More than half of the beef on the market is medium grade as the following table shows:

Federal Grades of Beef		
U. S. 1A	(Prime)	very little on market
U. S. 1	(Choice)	10%
U. S. 2	(Good)	25%
U. S. 3	(Medium)	50% plus
U. S. 4	(Plain)	lowest on retail market
U. S. 5	(Cutter)	for sausage, dried beef, and canning
U. S. 6	(Canner)	for canning

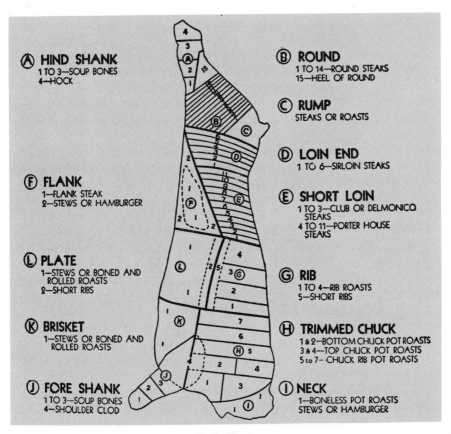

Ⓐ HIND SHANK
1 TO 3—SOUP BONES
4—HOCK

Ⓑ ROUND
1 TO 14—ROUND STEAKS
15—HEEL OF ROUND

Ⓒ RUMP
STEAKS OR ROASTS

Ⓓ LOIN END
1 TO 6—SIRLOIN STEAKS

Ⓕ FLANK
1—FLANK STEAK
2—STEWS OR HAMBURGER

Ⓔ SHORT LOIN
1 TO 3—CLUB OR DELMONICO
STEAKS
4 TO 11—PORTER HOUSE
STEAKS

Ⓛ PLATE
1—STEWS OR BONED AND
ROLLED ROASTS
2—SHORT RIBS

Ⓖ RIB
1 TO 4—RIB ROASTS
5—SHORT RIBS

Ⓚ BRISKET
1—STEWS OR BONED AND
ROLLED ROASTS

Ⓗ TRIMMED CHUCK
1 & 2—BOTTOM CHUCK POT ROASTS
3 & 4—TOP CHUCK POT ROASTS
5 to 7—CHUCK RIB POT ROASTS

Ⓙ FORE SHANK
1 TO 3—SOUP BONES
4—SHOULDER CLOD

Ⓘ NECK
1—BONELESS POT ROASTS
STEWS OR HAMBURGER

❯ ❯ Beef Chart ❰ ❰

Quality of Meat

Since the customer is seldom able to judge meat quality at the time of purchase and yet recognizes quality keenly at the time of eating, it is important that the seller be able to recognize quality and select cuts suited to a customer's needs.

Beef, of top quality, should be well marbled, fine grained, firm, and velvety in appearance. *Veal* should be light grayish-pink in color, fine grained, fairly firm, and velvety. It should have little fat and no marbling.

Lamb should be medium pink to light red in color, whereas *mutton* is darker red. Age can best be judged by the break-joint, the point at which the forefeet are taken off. In young lambs, this has four ridges that are smooth, moist, and red. When the mutton stage is reached, the joint cannot be broken, and the forefeet are taken off at the round joint, just below the break-joint.

Pork should be relatively firm, fine grained, well marbled, and free from excessive moisture. The fat is firm and white. Federal regulations call for precooked hams to be held at the original weight of the fresh, uncured meat plus 10 per cent added moisture. But local plants, selling in one state, sometimes increase the weight of smoked ham 30 per cent by adding moisture in curing. State legislation is being formulated to protect the consumer from paying ham prices for water.

Poultry should be plump and have no objectionable odor. A young tender chicken can be distinguished from a fowl, or hen, by feeling the end of the breastbone. In the chicken, this is soft gristle, in the hen it is hard bone. Again, the legs of the chicken break easily at the joint, whereas the hen's legs are harder to break and the bone above the joint often breaks before the joint itself.

Fish should be free of sharp, objectionable odor; and the flesh should be firm, the skin shiny with scales adhering tightly and the eyes transparent and bulging. Great care should be taken to insure that shellfish, often eaten raw, has been caught in uncontaminated waters.

Revolution in the Sale of Meats. Since World War II, there has been a revolution in the retailing of meat. Formerly, a butcher prepared the cuts desired upon order from the customer. Today, most meats are precut under standardized conditions; wrapped in cellophane; carefully labeled with weight, price per pound, per piece and the nature of the cut; and displayed in refrigerated storage and dispensing bins. This development has greatly speeded up the meat sale transaction. Labor cost to the store has been reduced, and the customer can see in advance just what she is buying. A butcher is still available in many markets to handle special cuts and unusually large quantities. Many young customers today much prefer to buy packaged fresh meats. They would find it difficult to explain to the butcher just what cut they wanted, and the transaction would take too much time.

Another revolution is now in sight. A new freeze-dry process has been developed that freezes meat, and then, by means of a vacuum process, removes 98 per cent of the moisture. The resultant product is light and dry. The soluble salts, sugars, and proteins are held in their natural positions and not drawn to the surface of the food as in conventional drying processes. Consequently, there is little shrinkage, shriveling, or change in nutritional value or palatability.

The dehydrated product weighs only one-sixth to one-third of its original weight and can readily be stored indefinitely like other packaged food. When ready to use, it is soaked for a few minutes by the housewife to regain its moisture and then cooked like fresh meat. Many users cannot distinguish this product from fresh meat. Ultimately this development may eliminate much of today's fresh-meat business, but today it is of special interest to campers and those with inadequate refrigeration facilities.

PUTTING THIS MERCHANDISE KNOWLEDGE TO USE ❯ ❯ ❯ ❯ ❯ ❯ ❯ ❯ ❯ ❯

❯ DO YOU KNOW YOUR MERCHANDISE?

    1. (*a*) In the typical supermarket, how are the eight classes of goods grouped or departmentalized? (*b*) Discuss the variety carried.

2. (*a*) What are the best sellers in the grocery department? (*b*) What is a current problem in connection with packaging?

3. (*a*) What are cereal foods? (*b*) What is their importance in nutrition? (*c*) What products are made from wheat? from rice? from corn?

4. (*a*) Give the sources of sugar. (*b*) In what forms is it sold? (*c*) What are your conclusions about the amount of sugar and sugar products consumed?

5. (*a*) From what countries is coffee obtained? (*b*) Why is coffee roasted? (*c*) Is instant coffee as good as freshly ground coffee? (*d*) Differentiate between chocolate and cocoa.

6. (*a*) What are condiments? (*b*) Differentiate between a spice and an extract.

7. (*a*) Give the sources of beef, veal, pork, mutton, lamb, poultry. (*b*) Define conformation, finish, marbling. (*c*) Explain the grading of meats. (*d*) How may the quality of the different meats be determined?

8. (*a*) What revolution has taken place in the meat retailing business? (*b*) What second revolution is in sight?

> INTERESTING THINGS TO DO

1. The label on brand A of potato chips reads as follows: "Potatoes cooked in pure vegetable oil or shortening, salt added."

   The label on competing brand B reads: "Potatoes, vegetable oil, salt, citric acid, propylene glycol, tricalcium phosphate, antioxidant added to preserve quality: butylated hydroxyanisole, butylated hydroxytoluene, propyl gallate and guaranteed fresh."

   (*a*) Ask three people to read these two labels and indicate which potato chips they would prefer to try. (*b*) Ask them why they think manufacturer B puts in so many chemicals. (*c*) Discuss findings with others in class. To what conclusions do you come?

2. Shop for a turkey in your local supermarket.
   (*a*) Do you find A, B and C grades? Does the best quality offered meet the following government standards for A grade?
   (1) Goodly amount of flesh on the breast
   (2) Conformation of carcass free from deformities
   (3) A well-developed covering of flesh
   (4) A well-developed layer of fat in the skin
   (5) Defeathered with a clean appearance, especially on the breast
   (6) Free from cuts, tears, and missing skin
   (7) Free from disjointed and broken bones and missing parts, not more than one disjointed bone
   (8) Free from discolorations of skin and flesh
   (9) Free of freezer burns, except for an occasional pockmark
   (*b*) There are five classes of turkeys on the market. How many do you find in your store and what are the particular selling points of each?
   (1) Fryer or roaster (under 16 weeks of age)
   (2) Young hen turkey (under 8 months of age)
   (3) Young tom turkey (under 8 months of age)
   (4) Yearling hen or tom (under 15 months of age)
   (5) Mature hen or tom (in excess of 15 months of age)
   (*c*) As a result of the study what conclusions do you arrive at in regard to buying turkeys?

UNIT 78 THE FOODS WE BUY

PRODUCE

Produce consists of fresh fruits and vegetables. These have advantages in flavor and in unimpaired vitamins and salts as compared with processed foods, but they lose their advantages if improperly stored or cooked or if the liquids accumulated in cooking are wasted.

The ten items of produce that account for over three-fourths of all produce sales in dollars are in order: potatoes, bananas, oranges, apples, tomatoes, lettuce, grapes, grapefruit, onions and celery.

The grocery trade classifies produce as follows:

Garden Vegetables, such as tomatoes, peas, and celery. Tomatoes are rich in vitamin C, a good source of vitamin A, and rich in minerals. From a dietetic standpoint they are similar to oranges but cheaper. They are graded A, B and C according to flavor, color, and freedom from defects; but from a nutritional standpoint, grade C is wholesome and desirable. Green peas are a good source of riboflavin. The two major types are early or Alaska peas and the sweet pea.

Root Vegetables, such as potatoes and onions. The potato is three-fourths water and most of the rest is starch. The potato is one of the most important energy foods and one of the cheapest. It also contains potash and other salts which are mostly in the skin; it is wise therefore to cook potatoes with their jackets on. Potatoes can be stored for a long time if kept in a cool, dry, and dark place; otherwise, they will sprout and decay.

Leafy Green Vegetables, such as lettuce and spinach. These are important sources of vitamins and salt. Their high cellulose content provides bulk as an aid in avoiding constipation.

Berries, such as blueberries and strawberries. Most of these come on the market for a short period; and careful shoppers buy them in quantity, both to can and to add variety to the diet when prices are low. The table below indicates the peak months to buy berries. Salespeople of produce should learn the seasons in their locality so that they will be sure to promote not only berries but other seasonal fruits and vegetables at a time when they are cheapest and best. This is a service both to the customer and to the grower.

Citrus Fruits, such as oranges and grapefruit. Oranges, like tomatoes, are rich in vitamin C and certain important mineral salts. There are two major

Blackberries	June–July
Blueberries	July
Cranberries	October–December
Currants	July
Gooseberries	July
Raspberries	June–July
Strawberries	April–June

kinds, (1) sour, such as Seville and (2) sweet, from California, Arizona, and Florida. Sweet oranges are further classified as navel (dessert), Valencia (juice), and mandarin (loose skinned). The mandarin includes the tangerine and the temple. The United States government has grades for oranges based on appearance and freedom from damage, dryness, and defects that may lead to decay. The grades, however, do not measure nutritional values. Oranges are also classified by size. The large—80—means that there are about 80 oranges in the standard crate. The smallest are 350. In relation to weight, the smaller oranges have more juice. Other citrus fruits are the lemon and the lime.

Hand Fruits, such as apples and grapes. Apples and grapes are good sources for certain mineral salts and are much desired for flavor. Apples sell the year round, but principally in the fall. Most apples on the market today are prepacked. The McIntosh is the most popular.

Melons, such as cantaloupes and watermelons. While mostly water, the sweet juice is very palatable to many. There are many varieties of melons on the market including the casaba, the cranshaw, honeyball, honeydew, and Persian. A big problem in selling is to learn when melons are ripe or will be ripe. The best test for ripeness of the cantaloupe is the scent and softness at

Mushrooms grown in an air-conditioned plant are hand-picked with the aid of a miner's lamp. (Courtesy Chef Boy-Ar-Dee®)

the stem end and well-developed veining, which stands out prominently with yellowish or gray-green color showing through the veining. Softness should not be tested with the fingers, but with gentle palm pressure.

Tropical Fruits, such as bananas and dates. Bananas are similar to the potato in carbohydrate content, but they are among the most digestible of foods, rich in vitamins and minerals. They are often the first solid food given to babies; with milk, they provide a balanced meal.

Storage of Produce

Most fruits and vegetables should be kept cool and dry in both store and home, but there are important exceptions.

Keep wet: cabbage, carrots, celery, endive, escarole, kale, kohlrabi, lettuce, mint.

Keep moist: bamboo shoots, broccoli, brussels sprouts, cauliflower, chervil, chicory, chives, collards, dandelions, leeks, mustard, peas, rhubarb.

Keep moist with tops dry: asparagus, beets, green onions, poke, radishes, rutabagas, turnips.

DAIRY PRODUCTS

As used in grocery stores, the term "dairy products" includes not only milk and milk products, such as butter and cheese, but also butter substitutes and eggs.

Milk

Milk consists of casein, butterfat, water, and certain salts and vitamins. Casein, a protein, contains also calcium and phosphorus. Whole milk contains about 4 per cent butterfat.

Federal, state, and city governments have set standards of bacterial and butterfat content for milk and cream. For example, the Food and Drug Administration requires that coffee cream have not less than 18 per cent butterfat, and light whipping cream not less than 30 per cent. Half-and-half— 10 per cent butterfat—is very popular today. Milk grades vary. In one large city, Grade A indicates a butterfat content of 4 per cent and only 30,000 bacteria per cubic centimeter. Grade B has a butterfat content of 3.8 per cent and as much as 50,000 bacteria.

Pasteurization. The pasteurization of milk is a major safeguard to health. It is a process of heating milk to a point that kills harmful bacteria without injuring the useful lactic-acid bacteria. While the process causes a slight reduction in the nutritional value of milk, the insurance against disease more than offsets this disadvantage. Raw milk obtained from certified cows is generally safe but is expensive and does not keep so well as pasteurized milk. Furthermore, raw milk from cows not subjected to the highest standards may be a cause of tuberculosis and of undulant fever.

Homogenization, a recent process of reducing the size of fat particles in milk and cream and distributing them evenly, has become popular. Homogenized milk contains no cream line; that is, the cream will not separate from the milk. There is no evidence that the milk is more digestible.

THIS MUCH WATER
IS REMOVED

IN MAKING

EVAPORATED
MILK

WATER

MILK SOLIDS

Preserving. Milk may be preserved by sterilizing or adding sugar and canning. In evaporated milk about half the bulk is removed by evaporation—it must contain at least 7.9 per cent milk fat and 25.9 per cent milk solids. It is sterilized and canned. There is considerable loss of vitamin B in evaporating and canning; evaporated milk, therefore, is not a complete substitute for fresh milk.

Condensed milk is whole or skimmed milk with added sugar, evaporated to the point where it contains at least 8.5 per cent milk fat and 28 per cent milk solids. It is preserved by its sugar content and is not sterilized, as is evaporated milk.

There is still another way to preserve milk: to dry it. Skim milk is dried to a powder. It can take the place of fresh milk for most cooking purposes and is handier than evaporated milk for some. Its chief advantage, however, is its cost which is about 60 per cent of that of an equivalent amount of fresh milk and 80 per cent of that of evaporated milk, even after allowing for enough margin to make up the loss of butterfat.

Butter

More milk goes into butter each year than is used for fluid consumption. Butter is the solidified fat of milk. The only additions permitted by law are salt and certain harmless coloring matter. Not less than 82.5 per cent should be butterfat, with water not more than 16 per cent and the remainder the salt and coloring matter mentioned. It takes about 10½ quarts of average rich milk to make a pound of butter.

Butter is generally made by separating the cream from the milk, heating it to destroy bacteria, and then treating it with a prepared culture of useful bacteria which causes the cream to "ripen." The cream is then churned (beaten and shaken) until the tiny fat globules form a mass. Since it is not possible to separate all the milk from the cream earlier, it is now necessary to drain off some excess liquid, the buttermilk. The butter is placed between wooden rollers to reduce moisture and to produce a smooth even texture. If no salt is added, butter is called *sweet butter*. This does not keep as well as salt butter.

Butter made on the farm is called *dairy butter,* whereas butter made in a factory is called *creamery butter*. If cut up and packaged, the butter is called *print*. If packed in a large container, it is called *tub butter*. The latter is generally slightly less expensive because of saving in packaging costs.

Butter is graded or scored according to flavor, body consistency, color, salt content, and packaging, flavor being the most important factor. The best butter, AA, scores 93 or better out of a perfect score of 100. Grade A has a score of 92. The lowest permissible score is 85; and butter scoring 85–89 is suitable for cooking, whereas 89–93 is suitable for table use.

In the store, it is important to keep butter at a low temperature and protected from strong odors, for it absorbs the odors of the foods quickly. It should be wrapped separately before being included in the customer's package with other purchases.

Oleomargarine

Oleomargarine is an economical substitute for butter, and its consumption per capita now exceeds that of butter. It is a mixture of one or more refined food fats or oils, sour milk, and salt. The most commonly used fats are soybean, cottonseed, safflower, and corn, often in combinations. The product is wholesome and has a taste similar to that of butter, since it contains milk, sugar, and citric acid, the same ingredients that give butter its distinctive flavor. Most oleomargarine is now reinforced with vitamin A.

Cheese

Cheese, like butter, is made from milk. It is made by adding rennet to slightly sour milk to coagulate it. *Rennet* is an extract from the stomach of the calf. The curdled mass becomes semisolid. The solid part is called the *curd;* and the liquid, the *whey*. The whey is removed; and the curd, which is largely casein and fat, is allowed to become acid. The curd is then cut up, minced and shredded, pressed into molds, and stored to mature so as to produce the desired flavor. *Ripe* or well-matured cheese is easier to digest than new cheese, because the casein gradually assumes a fatty character and becomes softer and more soluble. It is leathery when new.

There are several hundred kinds of cheese differing in details of manufacture and place of origin. These may be classified under three heads: hard, soft, and semisoft. The best known hard cheeses are the Cheddar (American), Swiss, and Gruyère. The leading soft cheeses are Camembert, Limburger, cream, and cottage. Roquefort and Gorgonzola are examples of semisoft cheeses.

Process cheese is made by grinding up cheese and combining it with coloring matter, salt, water, and a chemical emulsifier. Its smooth texture and keeping qualities appeal to many.

Eggs are an important source of proteins, fats, and vitamins. Freshness is a major factor, since eggs lose their flavor quickly. Even more important than freshness—the length of time between laying and eating—is proper handling and refrigeration.

The Federal government has set up grades for eggs, although in normal times it is not mandatory that eggs be sold by grades. The finest is called Retail Grade AA; only a few of them are on the market. The top grade in most stores is Retail Grade A, desirable for breakfast eggs. For cooking purposes, Retail Grade B is satisfactory and cheaper. A fourth grade, U. S. Trade, is also good for cooking when the egg flavor is not a factor.

These grades may be applied to storage as well as fresh eggs, so long as the former are clearly identified in the case of the top grades.

The quality of an egg is determined by *candling,* that is, by holding the egg to a strong light. This shows how much air space there is at the round end of the egg, how firm and clear the white is, whether the yolk is in the proper position and free from blemishes. When opened, the yolk of Grade A stands up round like a ball and the white holds firmly around the yolk. In poorer qualities, the yolk is flatter and the white is thinner, spreading out more.

Eggs are also classified by size. Large eggs must weigh 24 ounces to the dozen, medium eggs 20½ ounces, and small or pullet eggs 17 ounces. Thus large eggs are worth in nutritional value about 40 per cent more than small ones. On the other hand, since the consumer of an egg is likely to be satisfied by the number rather than the bulk of eggs consumed, the small eggs are likely to prove more economical.

FROZEN FOODS

The sale of frozen foods has increased tremendously in recent years as customers seek to reduce their food preparation and cooking chores. What made this development possible was, first, the perfection of a quick-freeze process that retained the natural flavor and nutrients; and second, the construction of deep-freeze units open at the top, from which the customer makes her own selection.

The most popular frozen foods are vegetables of many kinds, fruits and fruit juices, pies (both meat and sweet), soups, frozen fish sticks, and complete dinner entrees.

Frozen dinners are today the biggest of the frozen food items. They include fried chicken, roast turkey, pot roast, ham, fillet of haddock and other meat dishes. Their popularity can partly be explained by the lowering of price made possible by expanding volume. Today's frozen food platter offers a very satisfactory menu in a convenient form. All the customer has to do is pop it into the oven in its own aluminum container and serve when hot.

A first-class frozen dinner meets the following standards: (1) The meat portion is tender and succulent, top quality in flavor and appearance, and free of excessive fat, cartilage, and tendon. (2) The vegetables taste good and are firm but tender, free of blemishes and other defects, and bright in color. (3) The bacterial count is low.

The great problem in the marketing of frozen foods is to keep them continually at $0°$ F temperature from packer to consumer, although temperatures up to $10°$ F can be tolerated for a short time. If this degree of coldness is not maintained, the food deteriorates and bacteria multiply. Unfortunately, some present equipment does not maintain a $0°$ F temperature, and loading and unloading are not always properly controlled. All retail personnel should be trained in the importance of keeping frozen foods in adequate freezers at all times.

BAKED GOODS

Bread is the most important item in baked-goods departments and the most important form in which cereals are consumed. Much of the information already presented about cereals applies to fresh bread as well.

Bread

Bread can be made simply by mixing flour and water and baking the dough. This is called *unleavened bread* and is sold in some stores as matzoth. Most bread is leavened bread, that is, the dough has been treated to make it rise into a light, porous, spongy mass before baking. Bread may be leavened by thorough kneading, by adding baking powder, or by adding yeast to cause fermentation. The last is the usual process.

While leavened bread, then, may be baked from flour, water, and yeast, good bread generally includes milk, shortening (fat), sugar, and salt as well. The milk adds essential elements not found in the flour; the shortening gives a finer texture, keeps the bread moist and also keeps it from spoiling fast; the sugar supplies gas to raise the dough, gives color to the crust, and adds sweetness.

Many commercial bakeries use a chemical as a "softener" so that the bread will stay soft and thus seem fresh for a long time. Certain of these softeners have been outlawed by the Food and Drug Administration as harmful; also formulas have been drawn up for bread, rolls, and buns entering interstate commerce.

Bread should be handled carefully, particularly in the store, to avoid crushing or contamination by strong odors.

Other Baked Goods

Consumers are interested in purchasing a wide variety of fresh baked goods other than bread. Among these are cakes, pies, rolls, buns, and cookies.

Daily store deliveries are a must, since these foods go stale quickly. For fancy baked goods, cellophane packaging is important so that the customer can see just what she is buying.

Bakers display their products on enclosed shelves and wrap them after the customer has selected. With the general acceptance of self-service, however, baked goods must be prewrapped for customer handling and convenience.

GOVERNMENT SUPERVISION

Federal, state, and local governments carefully supervise our food supply and maintain minimum standards to safeguard health. Under the Federal Food, Drug and Cosmetic Act, adulteration and misbranding are illegal; and foods are carefully checked.

Meats have to be inspected for wholesomeness; for many other food products, a voluntary inspection and grading service is made available by the Federal government. When this service is employed, the producer may grade his product U. S. Grade A, B, or C, as the case may be.

In the case of packaged foods sold under brand names, it is also required that the label reveal the manufacturer, packer, and distributor, the quantity of contents, and the ingredients. Foods for special dietary use must also reveal vitamin and mineral content. Unfortunately, the size, conspicuousness, and clearness of statements about ingredients are sometimes misleading. Technical terms for chemical additives often are unintelligible to the consumer.

The United States Bureau of Agricultural Economics has established standard grades for many canned fruits and vegetables. For example, Grade A fruits (fancy) consist of physically perfect and the best obtainable quality, packed in heavy syrup. Grade B (choice) is fruit of good quality also packed in heavy syrup. Grade C (standard) is uniform and wholesome, packed in medium syrup. Substandard fruit (second grade) is wholesome but not uniform in size or color and is packed in light syrup. Substandard fruit is sometimes packed in water with no sugar. It is then known as *water grade* or *pie grade,* is packed in large cans, and is used largely by bakeries.

Although the use of these grades is not mandatory, more and more packers are using informative labels that describe the product in the can in considerable detail.

Treating Foods with Chemicals

While one of the major reasons for the use of chemical additives is to keep food fresh from deterioration during transportation and storage, there are also the following reasons:

1. To promote the health and growth of food plants, accomplished by the application of chemicals either directly to the plant or to the soil.

2. To speed up the growth of meat animals, accomplished by adding chemicals to their feed or even injecting it into their veins.

3. To speed up a natural process, such as coagulation, or jelling or fermentation.

4. To make the product more palatable, more tender, sweeter or thicker.

5. To improve the appearance of the produce, accomplished by the application of chemical dyes.

6. To make the product cheaper, often at the expense of good nutrition. For example, chemical purple pellets have been substituted for blueberries in a certain preparation.

While the above reasons, except the last perhaps, seem legitimate ones, the chemicals that bring about the desired results are not all safe. Many are dangerous to some people, at least, causing toxic, allergic, and even cancer-inciting effects. Sometimes the harm does not become evident for many years.

Protection for the Consumer. In 1958 a Federal Food Additive Law was passed that provides considerable protection against chemical additives not known to be safe. A producer who wants to use a questionable chemical must petition the Food and Drug Administration for a regulation stating the conditions under which it may be used. Adequate enforcement of this law is difficult and very costly, and further legislation may be required, particularly on the state level.

PUTTING THIS MERCHANDISE KNOWLEDGE TO USE ❯❯❯❯❯❯❯❯❯❯

❯ DO YOU KNOW YOUR MERCHANDISE?

1. (*a*) What are the 10 best sellers in the produce line? (*b*) How is produce classified in the store?
2. (*a*) Of what value are garden vegetables in the daily diet? (*b*) root vegetables? (*c*) leafy green vegetables? (*d*) What is the importance of the potato in diet?
3. What is the season for blackberries, blueberries, cranberries, currants, strawberries?
4. (*a*) How are the kinds of oranges classified? (*b*) How are they classified by size? (*c*) Why are citrus fruits important in nutrition?
5. (*a*) Differentiate hand fruits, melons, and tropical fruits. (*b*) What are the values of each as food?
6. Explain how to store carrots, cauliflower, asparagus, lettuce, peas, and radishes.
7. (*a*) What are the food elements in milk? (*b*) Explain the grading system for milk. (*c*) What are the reasons for pasteurization? homogenization? (*d*) How may milk be preserved?
8. (*a*) How is butter made? (*b*) Distinguish between dairy and creamery butter. (*c*) between print and tub butter. (*d*) Explain the grades of butter. (*e*) Why is oleomargarine a good butter substitute?
9. (*a*) In what respects does cheese differ from butter? (*b*) How are cheeses classified?
10. (*a*) Why are eggs important in the diet? (*b*) How are eggs graded? Describe candling.
11. (*a*) Why are frozen foods so important today? (*b*) How may frozen dinners be graded? (*c*) What temperature should be maintained?
12. (*a*) Differentiate between leavened and unleavened bread. (*b*) Explain the use of "softeners."

13. How does the Federal government try to protect the consumer against (*a*) adulteration, (*b*) use of dangerous chemicals, (*c*) improper labeling, (*d*) misrepresentation of quality?

❯ INTERESTING THINGS TO DO

1. Ask your grocer how he can tell when the following produce is ripe: watermelon, pears, honeydew melon, peaches, bananas.
2. Ask your family to buy two brands of frozen dinners for the same meal—differing somewhat in price, if possible, but containing the same types of meat. When ready to eat, check both brands against the meat and vegetable standards suggested in the text and compare the size of the portions. Which is the better in quality? Which is the better buy for the money?
3. Make an inventory of all kinds of baked goods sold in your favorite supermarket. How does the assortment compare with that of a local bakery?
4. How many brands of dog food are there in a local supermarket? Which are labeled as meeting recognized standards of nutrition? What special features does each seem to have?

ADDITIONAL MERCHANDISE TERMS ❯❯❯❯❯❯❯❯❯❯❯❯❯❯❯❯❯❯❯❯❯

Calcium is a soft, silver-white metallic element, occurring only in combination.

Dextrose is a quick-energy sugar derived from corn. It has less sweetening value than *sucrose*. It is used in the manufacture of foods but not much is sold direct to the consumer.

Iodine is a nonmetallic element—a shining, blackish-gray crystalline solid with a chlorinelike odor. Traces are necessary to protect against goiter.

Phosphorus is a nonmetallic element of the nitrogen group. While poisonous in a separate state, it is an essential element of bone structure.

Household Utensils and Gadgets

CHAPTER 26

UNIT 79 MATERIALS USED IN UTENSILS

Surprisingly, household utensils are truly as romantic and historic as any product. Man has always eaten food; and since heat improves many foods, he has sought materials to hold the foods while they are cooking. The development of household utensils involves the discovery and isolation of metals and the creation of other products such as Pyroceram, plastic linings, and ceramics that are used for utensils. Ingenious manufacturers are constantly changing and improving the design and materials used in order to provide greater utility and eye appeal in these products.

To cook his food, primitive man, since he did not have stoves or pots and pans, heated stones in the open fire, then dropped them into a leather bag containing water and the food to be cooked. The Indians, at the time America was discovered, were using a similar method of heating food.

As fireplaces, ovens, and stoves developed, man's cooking utensils also were improved. Vessels of bronze (an alloy of copper and tin) were developed during the Bronze Age, and iron vessels were in use early in history. Today, aluminum, iron, steel, copper, chromium, nickel, tin, and zinc are all important metals used in utensils. In addition to these, heat-resistant glass and fire-clay utensils are available for certain cooking uses.

CAST-IRON UTENSILS

Iron is one of the most useful of all metals, and it makes excellent cooking utensils. The iron obtained from iron ore by smelting is impure and not easily worked. It can, however, be shaped by being poured into a sand mold while it is still molten. Cooking utensils formed in this manner are known as *cast iron*. Heavy looking, dark, gunmetal-colored baking pans, frying pans, and

Dutch ovens are made in this way. Cast iron is acclaimed by many cooks who think that the natural food flavors are all retained by cooking food in an iron utensil.

Iron heats slowly, but it heats evenly without danger of scorching if it is used over the proper sized burner or in an oven. Iron distributes the heat slowly, but it retains heat for a long time. Cast iron becomes smoother and finer and improves with age and use if it is well cared for.

The greatest disadvantage of iron cooking utensils is that they rust unless properly cared for. If they are in constant use, there is little danger of their rusting as long as they are thoroughly dried after each using. Utensils of iron that are kept in summer homes or camps may rust during the damp winter and spring months unless they are well covered with wax or grease. To prevent rusting while the utensil is still in the store, most manufacturers coat them with lacquer. This lacquer must be completely removed before the pan is used for cooking. Thorough scouring with hot water and soap will remove the lacquer.

Food tends to stick to an iron pan when it is new unless it is properly prepared. This is known as *seasoning*. Most iron pans have directions for seasoning on the attached label. Instructions for seasoning show it is not difficult to do:

1. After removing lacquer, fill pan with water and some washing soda or potato peelings.
2. Boil slowly for two hours.
3. Rinse well and dry thoroughly.
4. Rub a thick layer of suet around inside of pan, and allow this to cook into the pores of the utensil slowly for about three hours. Be sure the fire is turned low so that the fat does not burn.
5. After cooking, remove excess fat with clean paper. The pan is now ready for use.

Not all iron utensils include seasoning instructions because some have been preseasoned by the manufacturer and are so labeled. Preseasoned pans merely need to have the lacquer removed.

Iron utensils are heavy to lift and some women object to handling them for this reason.

SHEET-STEEL UTENSILS

Lighter weight frying pans are made from ordinary steel. When pig iron has more of the impurities removed and carbon added, the resulting harder metal is known as *steel*. This metal does not have to be cast as does the impure iron, but can be rolled into sheets from which thin utensils may be shaped by stamping. These steel pans have a smoother surface than cast iron, are thinner, conduct heat more quickly, and may also warp and bend out of shape. Being thinner, they are also much lighter in weight. They rust, however, in the same manner as the cast-iron pans.

PLATED IRON AND STEEL PANS

To prevent a cast-iron or a steel pan from rusting, a plated finish of nickel or chromium may be put on it. Both of these metals give a silvery color to the pan. The nickel finish may wear off rather easily, but the chromium finish that is placed over a nickel finish is very durable. Even if the finish wears off, the iron or steel pan is still useful.

Steel garbage pails are also coated with zinc. They are known as *galvanized iron*. Zinc is never coated over cooking utensils, however, because zinc may combine with some of the acids in foods to form a poisonous compound. The zinc coating is not costly and it does have an attractive silvery color; it keeps the iron from rusting until it wears off. That is why it is used for washtubs, water pails, and other useful items.

STAINLESS STEEL

In 1915, an important discovery was made about steel. If a minimum of 11½ per cent of chromium were mixed with the molten steel, the steel would no longer rust. When experimenters subjected this new mixture to acids that stained ordinary steel, they found this new mixture resisted staining. It was, therefore, named *stainless steel*. There are many formulas for stainless steel today, but they all contain chromium. Better quality stainless steels also contain some nickel. The best stainless steel for pots and pans is known as 18–8, which means it contains 18 per cent chromium and 8 per cent nickel. Such a stainless steel stays bright and white throughout a lifetime of use. And stainless steel is not plated, so there is no surface layer to wear away!

While stainless steel has many advantages over ordinary steel, it does not have the reputation of cast iron for imparting flavor to food, nor does it heat as evenly. It is possible to scorch foods cooked in plain stainless-steel pots when using high heat.

ALUMINUM on the outside for even cooking
STAINLESS on the inside for easy cleaning

Aluminum and stainless steel in the right place make for good cooking and easy cleaning. (Courtesy Aluminum Co. of America)

Copper, which is not used for the insides of utensils because it imparts a metallic flavor to food, is excellent as a heat conductor. Consequently, by plating a thick coating of copper on the bottom of a stainless-steel utensil, the poor heating qualities of stainless steel are offset and the copper-clad pans heat quickly and evenly. The copper diffuses the heat evenly, speeds cooking time, and prevents scorching.

Aluminum is almost as good a heat conductor as copper; so aluminum-clad stainless steel also makes a good, useful utensil; however, both copper and aluminum stain.

Instead of placing the copper on the outside of the pan, some manufacturers make a three-layer pan with stainless steel inside and outside and a core of copper for heat conductivity. In this manner, the copper is not exposed to the air to turn dark and to require cleaning when used. Yet all the heat-conducting properties of the copper are retained in these pans.

PORCELAIN ENAMELWARE

Porcelain-enamel pans come in attractive colors such as white, red, yellow, pink, dark blue, and speckled varieties. Their colors make them a cheerful as well as a practical addition to any kitchen. Enamelware is made with a regular steel base. In inexpensive lines, the base is thin and the finished pan light in weight. Better quality pans have a much heavier base, which wears better and gives more body to the ware. Very heavy wares are made with cast-iron bases that permit excellent cooking.

The porcelain-enamel coating is similar to glass and ceramics in its construction. The steel or iron base is dipped into a liquid solution made from the glass and clay. The dipped piece is then baked in a hot furnace. The best quality enamelware is dipped and baked three times. Medium quality ware has two coats, and inexpensive ware has but one coat. Since the first coat, because of the chemicals used to make it adhere to the iron or steel base, is dark in color, all single-coated ware is either dark gray, black, or dark blue. Such ware may be speckled with white to give it a granitelike appearance. The additional work and materials needed for the triple-coated ware add to its cost, but they prolong the life, durability, and beauty of the article.

Porcelain enamelware gives good service if the customer knows how to care for it. The article is coated with a layer similar to glass and should be handled as though it were glass. However, like glass, it chips and cracks easily when banged against the sink or other pans and may even be chipped by stacking pans one inside the other. When cooking in these pans, the customer has to be sure that the flame is not turned too high, as the food scorches rather easily; and if the water in the pan boils away, the porcelain enamel may crack.

With reasonable care, however, enamelware has many advantages: its attractiveness, ease of cleaning, tastelessness, and nonporosity. In use, extremes of temperature must be avoided or the inside as well as the outside surface may crack and chip. Once the inside surface is cracked, the pan should not be used as some chips may then come off in the food.

ALUMINUM UTENSILS

Although aluminum is prevalent in the earth's crust, as recently as 1852 it was considered more precious than gold or silver and sold for $545 a pound. Knives and forks of aluminum were luxuries for kings and queens to use! Then in 1886, a young American, Charles Martin Hall, discovered the secret of isolating aluminum! With the development of his new process, aluminum became available not only to kings and queens but to all mankind; and it sells now for a few cents a pound! Aluminum is only a little over seventy years old commercially, yet it has become one of our most important metals. Recently aluminum has begun to replace tin cans for packaging canned goods.

The outstanding quality for its use in kitchenware is the attractive appearance of the aluminum. It has a silvery color, which is easily kept bright and shiny. Probably the second advantage is its light weight. The lightness of the metal is one of its natural properties. It weighs only about a third as much as iron and copper: that means a pan can be made as thick as an iron pan, yet weigh a third as much!

It conducts heat quickly and evenly too. While it does not scorch food because of uneven heating, it may scorch because it heats so quickly. It is usually wise when using aluminum to have the gas or electricity turned low when the pan is first placed on the stove. The thicker the aluminum pan is, the better the cooking job it will do. The heavier pans are cast as the iron skillets are. Heavy stamped ware is as good for cooking purposes as the cast aluminum is.

Thin aluminum dents rather easily and, of course, once dented it no longer heats food evenly. It also warps out of shape somewhat if it is thin. Even heavier pieces must not be plunged into cold water as they come from the stove, because they too can be warped out of shape. Aluminum does discolor, but most stains on the metal can be removed by boiling a weak solution of vinegar in the pan. Since alkalies stain aluminum, strong soap should not be used on aluminum. The aluminum companies advise us that soda should not be added to foods cooked in aluminum utensils. Aluminum needs to be dried thoroughly before storing because hard water may pit the metal. Foods left standing in aluminum for a prolonged period also will cause pitting.

TIN UTENSILS

Tin is a silver-colored metal that melts at a very low temperature. It is usually used as a coating or plating over iron and steel. That is what tin cans are—steel cans with a tin coating inside and outside that keeps them from rusting. The tin-plated ware is approximately 98 per cent steel and 2 per cent

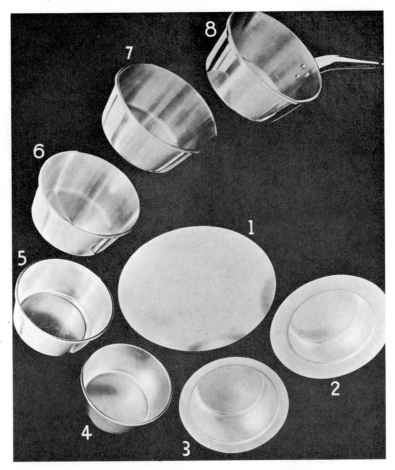

Steps in Making a Utensil. 1. Blank is cut from the metal sheet. **2.** Stamping operation with a die starts to form the utensil. **3.** Another stamping operation gives the required depth. **4.** The edge is trimmed and rolled, called "beading." **5.** The outside is polished. **6.** The inside is smoothed. **7.** The pouring lip is formed. **8.** The handle is riveted to the pan. *(Courtesy Wear-Ever Aluminum, Inc.)*

tin. Of course, you have seen the gold-colored lining in some cans. This is an enamel lining that protects the color of tomatoes, red cabbage, and also fish and prevents foods containing sulfur from discoloring the tin. Lids and baking pans are often made from tin coated over steel bases.

Heavily coated pieces are called *retinned* or *block tinware*. Naturally they are a little more expensive than the thinly coated lids and pans, but they wear much better.

Tin is soft, so it scratches readily. When scratched down to the steel base the pan is no longer rustproof.

Tin stains rather badly when used for cooking. Boiling in strong washing soda may remove the stains. Because tin melts at the low temperature of 450° F., it should not be used for frying as frying temperatures are often over 500°. Hot foods containing acids (vinegar, tomatoes, apples, and so on) should not be cooked in these utensils because the acid attacks the tin. When cold, these acids do not affect it.

NONSTICK COATINGS ON METAL PANS

Industry, desirous of making housework easier through new developments, has now created substances that keep food from sticking to pans. Two such products are currently on the market—silicones and Teflon (a chemical known as tetrafluoroethylene). The silicone chemicals have been applied primarily in the silver holloware field, and they are colorless and transparent. The Teflon chemical is coated on frying pans and other household utensils used for cooking. It is applied over aluminum and cast iron. The coating is a dull, pale gray in color and is so easily scratched that it is necessary to use wooden spatulas or rubber tools for handling food in these pans. The pans also must not be overheated, as high heat destroys the coating and may also be dangerous. They may be safely used with temperatures up to about 350° F. This means the customer should be advised to use only low heat when cooking with such pans. Since the coating is easily scratched, a soft dishcloth and mild soap or detergent are all that can be used in cleaning the pan. While fat is not needed in cooking foods in such pans, some foods are too dry without any grease; the user is therefore advised occasionally to add a little cooking oil or fat to the foods being cooked.

GLASSWARE AND EARTHENWARE UTENSILS

Glassware used for cooking is commonly known as *Pyrex* and *Glassbake*—two trade names. Rather thick items are used for baking and as lids while some thinner glass can be used on the top of the stove. The bluish color in the top-of-stove ware is caused by the chemicals used that make the glass withstand high temperatures.

Glass has many advantages for cooking. First, you can see the food cook without lifting the lid to see if the article is scorching or the water boiling away. Being nonporous, glass does not absorb any greases or odors from the food. It does not combine with any chemicals in the food itself. Food can be served in the same glass dish in which it has been cooked keeping the food hot and eliminating extra dishwashing! Glass is also easy to clean by soaking food loose, then washing with soap or detergent and water.

Certain precautions must be taken with glass. Instructions for care include the following:

1. Preheat any glass item to be used over a flame or in the oven by running hot water over its surface.
2. Have the flame turned low when you first place the glass on the stove. This will allow the glass to expand evenly and not cause strains that might crack the glass. Never allow water to boil away completely.
3. Handle hot glass utensils with a dry (never a wet) holder when removing from the stove.
4. After removal from the oven or top of the stove, do not set the glass on a cold sink or other cold or wet surface.
5. Never place ovenware type glass directly over a flame on the top of the stove.

For baking, special ceramic products, made with clays that withstand very high heat, are available. They have glazed interiors to protect the food and thus have the same advantages in cooking and serving that glassware has. They come in a wide range of lovely colors from white to russet terra cotta. Care needs to be taken, of course, to avoid breakage and to avoid exposing these pans to extremes of temperature without first preheating or precooling them.

Pyroceram, the trade name for a "super-glass-ceramic," developed by Corning Glass Company originally for guided missiles, has proved to be a useful and attractive ware for baking or for use directly over flames on the top of the stove. Pure white in color, this material also comes to the table as an attractive serving piece. Tea and coffee pots, casseroles, frying pans, and baking dishes, with and without cradles on which they may be placed at the table, are available. While these products can be broken if they are dropped on a hard surface, they are not subject to breaking due to extremes of temperature and therefore require much less care than glass or ordinary ceramics utensils.

PUTTING THIS MERCHANDISE KNOWLEDGE TO USE ❯ ❯ ❯ ❯ ❯ ❯ ❯ ❯ ❯ ❯

❯ DO YOU KNOW YOUR MERCHANDISE?

1. Why is iron cast to shape it rather than rolled as steel is?
2. How does steel differ from iron? What are the advantages of each?
3. What makes steel stainless? What is the best quality stainless steel for pots and pans? Why do qualities of stainless steel differ?
4. Why are some stainless-steel pans coated with copper or aluminum?
5. What is galvanized iron? Why is it not used for cooking utensils?
6. What are the advantages and disadvantages of porcelain enamelware? What is meant by single-, double-, and triple-coated ware? Which is best? Why?
7. What are the advantages and disadvantages of aluminum ware?
8. How is tin used for household utensils? What is a tin can?
9. What precautions should a customer take with nonstick coatings on pans?
10. How are glassware and earthenware used in cooking? What are their advantages and disadvantages? What is Pyroceram? Why is it better than glass or ceramics for utensils?

❯ INTERESTING THINGS TO DO

1. Assume you are a head salesman for the housefurnishings department. Explain the advantages and disadvantages of any one material used in utensils, so that new salespeople will have selling points for it.
2. Talk to three housewives whom you know. Ask them which material they prefer to cook in and why. Write a short theme in which you summarize their replies.

UNIT 80 TYPES OF UTENSILS

Every person who cooks refers to "pots 'n pans." The two words have become almost inseparable so that we rarely wonder about the meaning of the terms. Yet each applies to a specific type of utensil. The terms are abbreviations for "saucepot and saucepan."

POTS AND PANS

A *saucepan* is a rather deep utensil with a long handle attached to one side. Saucepans regularly range in size from 1 quart to 4 quarts. They may be used without lids as *open saucepans* or have lids and become *covered saucepans*.

Sometimes two or three saucepans are made to fit against one another over one burner; thus small quantities of two or three different foods can be cooked at the same time. Sometimes these pans have removable handles that are used only to take the hot pan from the stove. These are known as *duplicate* or *triplicate saucepans*. Saucepans are used for cooking small vegetables, sauces, syrups, and fruits, and warming leftovers.

Saucepots have no long handle, but rather a small "ear" handle on each side of the utensil. Some people prefer saucepots, some saucepans. The former are available in larger sizes than are the saucepans, and are useful for cooking soup, stew, jams and jellies, and pot roasts.

Double boilers consist of a smaller top vessel that fits into a larger bottom vessel used for boiling water to heat the food in the top vessel. These pans are used for cooking creamy foods, puddings, custards, and cereals, and warming leftovers. There is no danger of scorching the food when it is cooked in these utensils.

Utility or *double-purpose pots and pans* are a type of double boiler that may be used in many different ways: as a double boiler (complete); as a saucepan (bottom only); as a saucepot (top only); as a baking dish (top only); as a casserole (top plus lid). Some have a skillet-type cover and permit extra use as a frying pan!

KETTLES

Kettles are usually large vessels that have an overhead or "bail" handle. They are used for cooking jelly, preserves, and large quantities of foods. They range in size from 6 to 16 or more quarts.

Teakettles are used for heating water. They are used primarily when hot or boiling water is needed for pouring over such foods as cereals, rice, and spaghetti; for making "instant" cereals, coffee, and tea; or for brewing tea or making drip coffee.

The spout on a teakettle should be easy to clean; and if the lid is large enough, it is possible to remove the lime deposits that sometimes accumulate. *Whistling teakettles* have a tiny mechanism connected to the spout. The steam from the boiling water presses against this mechanism causing a whistling sound that informs the user that the water is boiling.

FRYING, ROASTING, AND BAKING UTENSILS

Skillets or *frying pans* (called *spiders* in some cookbooks) are wide, shallow pans with a long side handle. They are used for frying foods. Some skillets are somewhat deeper and have covers that fit tightly and permit "steaming" of food. These are known as *covered skillets,* and some of them are called *chicken fryers.*

Griddles are flat frying pans with only a tiny lip or ridge around the edge. They are used for cooking griddlecakes and for making such things as grilled sandwiches.

Deep-fry pans are saucepans with a wire-net pan that fits inside. These are used for French fried potatoes, doughnuts, fritters, and croquettes.

Roasting pans may be square, oval, or round in shape. They often have covers that permit the vapors from the meat to rise, be condensed, and fall back over the meat. Inside the roaster may be a wire rack or pan that keeps the meat from touching the bottom of the pan and scorching.

Dutch ovens are large saucepots with close-fitting lids that hold 5 quarts or more. They may be used over an open flame or in an oven.

Casseroles are covered saucepots used for baking scalloped foods, pud-

Pots 'n Pans. Standing in the back is a skillet. Clockwise next is a Dutch oven, double boiler, covered chicken fryer, open saucepan, and deep-fat fryer. *(Courtesy Wear-Ever Aluminum, Inc.)*

dings, and a variety of dishes that are to be served hot. Casseroles are usually made from attractive materials that can be used at the table for serving as well as for cooking. Glass, Pyroceram, ceramics, and porcelain enamelware are frequently used in making casseroles.

Cake pans are made in any shape—round, square, loaf shape, or oblong—but are usually rather shallow. Some cake pans have removable bottoms for ease in taking the cake out after baking. Angel food cake pans have a tube in the center which permits the heat to reach the center of the cake and bake it at the same time the outside is being baked.

Muffin tins that have 6, 8, or 12 cups, *cookie tins* that are a flat sheet of metal, and *pie pans* that are shallow and round are popular baking dishes.

COFFEEPOTS AND TEAPOTS

Coffeepots are no longer simple contrivances to be filled with water to which the coffee is added. They come in a wide range of types:

Percolators are made so that boiling water in the bottom of the pot rises through a metal tube and filters back through the coffee held in the top of the pot in a perforated cup.

Dripolators require that the water be heated separately and poured into a cup at the top of the dripolator. This cup has perforations in the bottom that permit the hot water to drip through onto the coffee, held in a "coffee well" (also perforated) immediately under it. The water slowly seeps through the coffee into the lower section of the pot.

"Silex" coffee makers are heat-resistant double glass pots permitting the coffee-making process to be watched closely. The bottom pot contains water which, when boiling, rises through a tube and thence is forced by steam pressure through the coffee funnel at the base of the top glass section. The coffee is filtered, and as it cooks slightly, it drops back into the lower bowl. In this bowl it may be kept hot, or it may be served immediately. These coffee makers may be kept on top of the stove or may have an electric attachment. Restaurants and lunch counters use these coffee makers extensively.

Teapots, short, squat pots with a spout and handle, are made in metal,

Left: Percolator. Center: Dripolator. Right: Silex.

glass, or ceramic materials. Tea may be brewed in them by pouring hot water over tea leaves, and they are then used as servers.

MISCELLANEOUS UTENSILS

Pressure cookers are a unique type of cooker that reduces cooking time from hours and half hours to minutes. Very little water is used in these pans. The covers are adjusted carefully, the timers set and within a few minutes the pressure and steam have cooked the food that normally requires much more time. These cookers develop tremendous pressure and when not handled properly have been known to "blow up" and throw hot vegetables all over the kitchen. Advise the customer to follow the printed directions concerning their use exactly!

In addition to pots and pans used for cooking, there are many types of vessels used in the preparation and serving of food. These include *pitchers* for serving all types of hot and cold liquids; *mixing bowls* that come in a variety of shapes and sizes for stirring and mixing foods; and *colanders,* bowl-shaped sieves or strainers made from metal or plastic, used to drain vegetables or boiled foods, such as noodles.

SELLING POINTS OF UTENSILS

When a customer looks at a pot or a pan, little does she realize that she may be handling that article almost daily for the rest of her life. She notices that the pots and pans come in various price ranges, and often she figures it an economy to purchase the less expensive pan. She may never realize how much money she might have saved by investing a little more money for a better quality pan. Spread over the many years the pan will be used, this initial purchase difference may only amount to a few cents more a year, yet it can save dollars in fuel economy, besides saving food values for the family. Here are a few important factors to explain to the customer:

Fuel Economy

1. Heavy pans may be slower to heat, but they require less water and thus enhance the taste of the food. They heat evenly and retain heat longer, so that after the first heating, the flame may be turned low and the temperature will be maintained. They do not warp or dent so easily as thinner utensils and therefore give longer, more efficient service.

2. Pans that have flat bottoms that cover the burner do not waste fuel. Straight sides on pans permit space to be used economically and pans to heat evenly.

3. Covers that fit snugly and do not permit steam to escape cook food more quickly, thus economizing on fuel.

4. Shiny metal reflects heat away. Dull bottoms or black bottoms on pans absorb heat more quickly.

Fuel Economy. Straight-sided pans that fit over the burner correctly do not waste heat.

Laborsaving

    1. Smooth, rounded edges clean more easily than do square, sharp corners.

    2. Plain shapes in baking pans are simpler to keep clean than the fancy grooved kinds.

    3. There should be no tiny grooves, or open spaces around rivets, as these are difficult to clean.

Quality in Workmanship and Design

    Handles. 1. Pans or coffeepots with handles sometimes tip when empty. This indicates inferior design. The pan should stand upright even when empty.

    2. Handles should be firmly attached to the pan and the joining should be smooth. Rivets inside the pan are difficult to clean thoroughly.

    3. Wooden handles should be so placed that the flame cannot char or burn them.

    4. Plastic handles do not burn, but they may crack; however, they can be handled comfortably even though the pan itself is very hot.

    5. Metal handles do not crack or burn, but they conduct heat readily and may be uncomfortable to handle without a pad for protection.

    Spouts. Spouts should be placed and shaped so that contents will pour easily without dripping. They should be high enough on the pot to keep contents from spilling over when the pot itself is full.

    Lips. Most pots, pans, and skillets have lips on one or both sides. Lips on both sides facilitate pouring out contents in either direction. Lips, of course, allow steam to escape from a covered pan unless the lid fits over the lips.

GENERAL RULES FOR CARE

    By pouring water into pans after food is removed, the food particles can be prevented from sticking and are readily removed at dishwashing time.

    Utensils plated with chromium, tin, or nickel, should not be cleaned with cleaning powders or metal scrapers, for these will scratch off the surface plating and expose the metal underneath. Enamelware may be scratched by using metal scrapers.

    Avoid burning foods in pans. Keep sufficient water to cover the bottom of the pan.

Avoid stacking glass or enamel pans, for this may cause them to be broken easily.

Glass, pottery, plastics, wood, steel, chrome plating, and tin are among the familiar materials used for cutlery and gadgets.

The housewife might be able to do without some gadgets, but a sharp *knife* is indispensable in the kitchen. Knives that have the best cutting edge are made of high content carbon steel. These are rarely used nowadays except for commercial cookery as they require extra care to prevent staining and rusting. *Stainless-steel knives* that are kept in good condition with a sharpening steel will have a sharp cutting blade; furthermore, they will not rust or stain.

The best blades of knives are *forged* rather than *stamped*. Forged blades are made individually from a round bar of metal, which is rolled under tremendous pressure and shaped. At the bolster (the section of the knife that fits into the handle), the forged blade is thick, reinforcing that part of the blade, and it tapers to the thin cutting edge of the blade. (See illustration page 607, for steps in making forged blades.) *Hollow-ground blades* hold a keener cutting edge than regular blades.

Other less expensive blades are simply stamped from a thin piece of metal and ground down to a sharp edge. Knives have handles of wood, metal, bone, and plastic materials. Handles are made in one and two pieces. It is important in purchasing a knife to see that the blade is securely held in the handle. Rivets are often seen on the outside of the handle. There should be at least three rivets to hold the knife firmly.

The amount of time needed to prepare food for cooking can be cut considerably by having the proper cutlery and by keeping knife blades well sharpened. The following items are indispensable for the well-managed home.

A *paring knife* is a short, thin-bladed knife used for peeling and sectioning vegetables and fruits.

A *utility knife* is somewhat larger than a paring knife. It is suitable for slicing larger vegetables, cutting through grapefruit, cantaloupe, and larger fruits.

A *hot-meat knife* is either a *butcher knife* or a *French cook's knife* having a large, firm, broad blade for cutting hot meat, slicing watermelon, and other heavy-duty cutting. The wide blade aids in keeping the hot meat from shredding as it is cut. These knives are also handy for chopping foods because the knuckles fit comfortably around the handle as the chopping of the food proceeds.

A *cold-meat knife* or a *ham slicer* has a long, thin-bladed, flexible knife for slicing cold meats and for other slicing duties. The fat on the cold meat has coagulated and a thin-bladed knife makes a smoother cut than the heavier butcher knife.

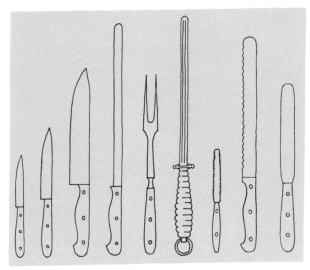

Left to right: A paring knife, a utility knife, a hot-meat knife, a cold-meat knife, a pot fork, a steel, a grapefruit knife, a bread knife, a spatula.

A *pot fork* has a long handle and two or three tines. It is used to hold meat and vegetables steady while they are being cut. It is also used to turn foods while cooking, and to aid in lifting hot foods onto a serving dish. When used with a hot-meat knife, it forms a carving set.

A *steel* is a tubular bar with tiny ridges to aid in straightening the edges of knives. These edges which, like razor blades, are very thin, are easily turned over. The proper use of the steel keeps the edge straight and razor sharp. In a meat market, the butcher uses the steel after every few cuts with the knife to assure a keen cutting edge.

In addition to the necessities listed above, customers may also be interested in *grapefruit knives* that have a curved blade to aid in coring the fruit; *bread knives* that have sawlike (serrated) edges that prevent the knife from crushing hot bread while cutting it; *spatulas* that have dull blades with rounded edges that are not meant for cutting but which are used for spreading fillings and icings, and used for turning foods while cooking; *poultry shears* for cutting joints of chicken and other poultry; *grape shears* for cutting stems of fruits; *mixing spoons* for stirring foods during preparation and cooking; *measuring spoons; bottle openers; corkscrews; egg beaters; sandwich spreaders,* and so forth.

Proper care of knives will prolong their life and usefulness. Suggest that the customer purchase a convenient wooden knife rack. This holds the knife blade in a specially provided slit and prevents blades from being dulled by hitting against other objects in a drawer. The sharpening steel should be used frequently to keep the blade ready for cutting.

❯ DO YOU KNOW YOUR MERCHANDISE?

1. What is meant by saucepan, saucepot, triplicate saucepan, percolator, dripolator?
2. Explain the purpose of double boilers; utility pots and pans; pressure cookers.
3. Explain what is meant by fuel economy. What are fuel-saving qualities of pots and pans?
4. What qualities in pots and pans make for convenience and ease in using?
5. What are some general rules for caring for pots and pans that the customer should be informed about?
6. Differentiate between a forged and stamped knife blade. Which is better?
7. Which takes a sharper cutting edge: high content carbon steel or stainless steel?
8. Explain the difference between paring knife and grapefruit knife; bread knife and carving knife.
9. If a young bride wanted to purchase basic cutlery needs, what items would you suggest as essential for efficiency and convenience?

❯ INTERESTING THINGS TO DO

1. Assume you are a salesman for the housefurnishings department. Bring a utensil to class and explain its merits and methods of care.
2. Talk to three housewives whom you know. Ask them which of their kitchen utensils they prefer to use and why. Write a short theme in which you summarize their replies.

UNIT 81 ELECTRICAL APPLIANCES

Great-grandmother's work would have been almost a pleasure had she been suddenly transported into a modern kitchen with all its up-to-date electrical equipment. She would be amazed by the electric toaster that automatically pops up the browned toast, the electric waffle iron that bakes the waffles a crisp golden brown as you sit leisurely at the table eating previously cooked waffles. The mixing machine, with countless gadgets attached to it, which is useful for every whipping operation from cream to cakes and in its spare time can be used as a fruit-juice extractor, would have left her gasping. Electric clocks, irons, vacuum cleaners, refrigerators, sewing machines, fans, air conditioners, combination toaster ovens, electric frying pans, grills, rotisseries that revolve meats and may even cook them with infrared heat for speed and thorough heat penetration, and countless other electric devices would have seemed like dreamland wonders. Many of these appliances we accept as being essential to efficient housekeeping duties.

SELLING POINTS

The salesperson selling these items should stress proper care. Electrical goods are made for AC (alternating current) or DC (direct current). Some items may be used with either. If there is any chance whatever of the customer's having DC in her home, be sure to advise her to check with her electric light company before attempting to use an appliance designed for AC use and vice versa. To be assured of safety in use, look for the Underwriters' Laboratories seal of approval present on all tested, approved electrical appliances. Those can be bought and sold with assurance.

Small appliances use 110–120 volts of electricity. Most homes are wired for such voltage. Larger appliances, such as electric stoves, refrigerators and freezers, usually require 220–240 volts. This necessitates special wiring in some older homes.

Explain to the customer that the proper handling and care of electrical appliances can prolong their life and permit them to give trouble-free performance. The following instructions will be helpful.

1. Never allow an electrical unit to get wet. In washing such things as electric coffeepots, the pot must *never* be placed in the water, but rather it should be washed carefully by placing the wet dishcloth inside the pot to rub away any coffee stains or grounds. Rinse with a damp rag, clean the outside with a damp rag, and wipe dry. Toasters, irons, etc., may be cleaned with damp rags, then polished dry.

2. Never *bend* cords or allow them to be tangled or knotted as this may break the fine, soft copper wires inside the cord.

3. If a cord is frayed, it should be repaired immediately by being wrapped with friction tape. Badly worn cords should be replaced, since they can cause a short circuit that may prove dangerous.

4. If the appliance needs to be oiled, as do mixers, vacuums, sewing machines, and some other electrical equipment, follow the directions for oiling given in the booklet that comes with the article. This is important to the length of life and smooth, efficient working of the machine.

5. Do not overload the electrical capacity of the wiring of the home or apartment in which you live. Dangerous fires may result by using too many electrical products at one time. If a light dims slightly when an appliance is turned on, that is a warning that there is an overload on the wire and some item should be disconnected.

6. Small electrical appliances such as toasters, grills, waffle irons, and so forth, are made from chromium plated over steel. The chromium surface is bright and shiny and will wear well as long as no abrasive is used on its surface. It should merely be wiped off with a damp cloth but never scoured.

PUTTING THIS MERCHANDISE KNOWLEDGE TO USE ❯❯❯❯❯❯❯❯❯❯

❯ DO YOU KNOW YOUR MERCHANDISE?

1. Name the two kinds of current used in homes. Why should a customer be advised when buying electrical goods to check the kind of current used in her home?
2. What significance does the Underwriters' Laboratories seal have?
3. What electrical voltage is common in most homes? If the voltage needed for large appliances is higher, what advice should be given the customer?
4. Why should cords be kept as straight as possible?
5. What danger is there from frayed electrical cords?
6. What may result from electrical overload in a home or apartment? What test can be made to determine if there is an overload?
7. How should the chromium-plate on electrical appliances be cleaned?

❯ INTERESTING THINGS TO DO

1. Make a list of all electrical appliances both small and large that you have in your home. Next to each item write how often it is used. Which appliances are used most frequently? Why?
2. Ask three married women what electrical appliances they would like to have if they were to win them on a give-away show. List their answers.
3. Prepare a 2-minute sales talk on a small electrical appliance.

ADDITIONAL MERCHANDISE TERMS ❯❯❯❯❯❯❯❯❯❯❯❯❯❯❯❯❯❯❯❯

Alloy is the mixture of two or more metals to make another metal with added characteristics. Brass, bronze, and stainless steel are well-known alloys.

Brass is an alloy containing copper and zinc, used for clock cases, some hardware, and trimmings on furniture.

Bronze is an alloy containing copper and tin, used for lamp bases, hardware, and trim on clocks and furniture.

Canister set consists of varying sized cans which are used for storage of sugar, flour, and so on. Cans are usually enameled and may have decalcomania designs. Sets are also made of plastic or aluminum.

Condiment shakers are containers with perforated tops appropriate for salt, pepper, and spices.

Crockery is an earthenware dish that is rather heavy in appearance.

Ductile metals are metals that can be drawn out into a fine wire by passing them repeatedly through smaller and smaller hole openings. Gold, silver, copper, and aluminum are noted for this quality. Cast iron, tin, and lead are not ductile.

Forging means that metals are shaped by heating and hammering.

Gauge is the measurement of the thickness of metals. The smaller the gauge, the thicker the metal: 26 gauge is a thin metal, 18 is medium, and 12 heavier still.

Malleable metals are metals that can be pressed into sheets of varying thickness. Gold, silver, and aluminum are noted for this quality. Cast iron is not malleable.

Monel metal is a stainless alloy consisting mainly of nickel and copper. It is used for such things as sinks and fountains in kitchens and drugstores.

Ore is material from which metallic ingredients may be extracted. Bauxite is the ore from which aluminum is extracted.

Smelting is the process of separating metals from their ores.

Welding is the joining by heat and pressure or hammering of two sections of metal.

Wrought iron is iron from which most of the impurities have been removed. It is malleable and can be shaped by hammering and forging.

China, Earthenware, and Plastics for Dinnerware

CHAPTER 27

UNIT 82   DISHES—MATERIALS USED IN THEIR MANUFACTURE

Even though every young person in the United States eats from some type of dish, young girls about to select dinnerware for their homes often find that they do not know whether they want earthenware, chinaware, melamine, or what kinds of decorations are best for continuous use. The product is commonplace, but only those who make a study of these products really know what they are buying.

TYPES OF DISHES

Not all dishes sold in the chinaware department are china! Usually, there are three basic kinds of products sold in that department: *earthenware, chinaware,* and *plastic.* Two other terms are also used frequently, *pottery* and *ceramics.* These latter terms, pottery and ceramics, are general words referring to any dishes or other products made from clay and baked. We speak, for example, of *the pottery,* meaning the factory where dishes are made; *the potter,* meaning the man who makes the dishes; *the potter's wheel,* meaning the turntable upon which he shapes the clay. *Ceramics* refers to the art of pottery making. Thus we speak of ceramic vases, ceramic tiles, and ceramic ornaments or dishes.

Earthenware

Earthenware is a term that informs us that such dishes are made from earthy materials—clay and other ingredients dug from the ground. Two kinds of earthenware dishes are available in most dinnerware departments: pottery and semivitreous ware. Used in this way, the word "pottery" has a slightly different meaning from the one used above. Dishes that are colorful, heavy, and crude looking and are made by hand in most countries are called *pottery*. The clays used are not purified; the dishes are baked at a low temperature, and thus they are neither very strong nor durable. The clay body is coated with a glassy layer that makes it sanitary, but if the glassy layer is chipped off, the clay underneath absorbs any liquid that touches it.

Most of us in our homes use dishes known as fine earthenware or *semi-vitreous ware*. This means the body under the glassy coating is somewhat porous, but not so porous as pottery dishes. These dishes are daintier looking and better wearing than the pottery dishes. They do not chip nearly as easily, but when chipped they are somewhat absorbent and therefore not sanitary to use.

Chinaware

The more expensive and durable dishes, although the most fragile looking, are called *chinaware*. In addition to being durable, these dishes, being non-porous under the glassy coating, are also sanitary even when chipped. Such dishes are known as being *vitrified*. The process of making these dishes was *first* perfected by the Chinese about the year A.D. 1000, after they had discovered and experimented with a fine white clay named *kaolin,* meaning *high hill,* for the place where it was found. With this clay they developed a new type of dish, ornamented it beautifully, and exported it to other countries. Because it came from China the people in England referred to it as *chinaware*. Italians noticed the gloss of this ware which they compared to the polished surface of a shell known as *porcellana*. So we have the two words for this fine type of dish: Americans generally call it *china* and Europeans call it *porcelain*.

The fashion for drinking tea, coffee, and chocolate became the vogue in England about 1650, and the clumsy pewter tankards were outmoded. Fashionable society demanded dainty cups and saucers, and soon people all over Europe and America were trying to get chinaware or porcelain. This demand caused many attempts at imitation; and finally, John Frederic Böttger, the man who failed to make gold out of brass, discovered fine china or *kaolin* clay in Germany and made true chinaware.

In the meantime, the English also were experimenting, and they discovered that when bone ash pulverized from the bones of oxen was added to the kaolin, they could make a fine quality of chinaware. In 1800, Josiah Spode perfected and began to use this method. Some of the other leading English manufacturers also added the bone ash to their wares, and their dishes became known as *bone china*.

Earthenware is still made all over the world, bone china is still made almost exclusively in England, and the regular china is made in the other European countries, in Japan, and in the United States. In 1963 one United States manufacturer introduced a line of bone china trade named *Oxford*.

Plastic

Although dishes have been made from various types of plastics ever since they became popular in the early 1900's, it was not until World War II that a plastic was discovered to have the attributes needed for dishes. The United States Navy, seeking materials that would be light in weight, resistant to breakage, sanitary in use, and attractive enough for food service, developed the first melamine plastic dishes. *Melamine* is a thermosetting (heat resistant) plastic, so that dishes made of this material can be used to serve hot foods and drinks and can be washed in the hottest water without damage. In 1946, manufacturers introduced melamine plastic dishes for consumers. They were accepted so eagerly that within a short time one-fifth of the dishes sold in the country were melamine plastic. Less desirable dishes of thermoplastic that cannot hold hot foods or that melt when placed near a hot stove are sometimes made by manufacturers. These types of plastic dishes are not satisfactory in use. Customers should make sure that the plastic dishes they are buying are made from melamine plastic.

MATERIALS USED IN CERAMIC DISHES

Look at several different dishes or ornaments. Notice that some of them are thicker than others. Some have entirely different shapes. Notice that the finish on some is much shinier than the finish on others. Some of the dishes have just a little decoration, and some have a great deal. Now hold the dishes to the light. If any of the dishes are china, you can see the shadow of your fingers through the dish. If the dishes are opaque, they are probably earthenware. Hold the dish *carefully* by the base and tap the edge *gently* with a pencil. Notice the difference in the tonal quality of the dishes. Those with a bell-like ring are known as *chinaware,* and those with a dull sound are known as *earthenware.* If any of the dishes are chipped, put a drop of ink on the fractured section. If you can wipe off the ink, the dish is nonporous or "vitrified" and is chinaware. If the ink soaks into the fracture, the material is porous and is earthenware.

These differences in appearance, translucency, sound, and absorbency depend on the kinds of clays and other raw materials used, the way the dishes are shaped, the heat of the oven in which the dishes are baked or fired, and the method of decorating them.

Clay

The cave man was probably the first manufacturer of clay dishes. Perhaps he noticed that his footprint hardened in the clay when a fire was built nearby. By experimenting with this clay after it hardened, he found it would hold liquids and foods. Thus, the first clay dish had been made.

For centuries man continued to make clumsy-looking clay dishes and to decorate them in a crude manner. Ovens were substituted for open fires for

A Chinaware Plate Showing Translucency. The shadow of leaves is seen through the plate held to the light. *(Courtesy Syracuse China Corp.)*

the baking of the clayware. Some Indian tribes still make pottery in this primitive manner, baking it in ovens.

Today in the large factories that manufacture dishes, the basic material for all ceramic ware is *clay,* the essential ingredient the cave man used.

Clay is a kind of earth or soil which, when moist, is plastic and can be molded. We used clay in our kindergarten days to mold various objects. For pottery, common clay like that used for ordinary modeling is used. Semi-vitreous ware is made from a combination of china clay and ball or blue clay, which adds plasticity and strength to the body. For china dishes the china clay (kaolin) used is the finest, purest, whitest, strongest clay available. Because of its whiteness and fineness it was used to powder wigs in the days of George Washington; and is used today as an ingredient in some face powders. This clay is found in certain sections of the United States, China, England, Germany, France, and some of the other European countries.

Other Ingredients

Since clay will not melt at any temperature, *feldspar,* a crystalline mineral substance which melts at a rather low temperature, is used to hold the clay particles together. Before being added to the clay, it has to be crushed into a fine powder. When combined with fine ingredients and heated at a high enough temperature, the feldspar gives the translucency to the chinaware.

Flint, a hard stone, is another commonly used ingredient of ceramic wares. It is first heated, and when it turns white, it is also ground into a powder and mixed with the clay to aid in holding the body of the ware in shape and to add strength.

Ox bones from South America are fired at a great heat and crushed into a fine powder. They are then used in place of flint in making *bone china.* They aid in fusing the clay particles together and add whiteness and strength to the body.

Coloring materials used to color clay or to apply designs on ceramic products are metallic oxides. No other coloring materials can withstand the high heats used to fire clay products.

MAKING CERAMIC DISHES

After the clays are washed and filtered to remove stones and dirt, the powdered ingredients are stirred together with water until the mixture resembles thick cream, known as *slip.*

For fine chinaware or earthenware, all impurities must be removed, so this slip is poured through a fine screen and run over magnets that attract and remove all iron particles that will make brown spots in the dishes.

The slip is then pumped into filter cloths and the water is drained off, leaving slabs of plastic clay. These slabs are stored for several weeks to permit ripening or aging, which makes the clay much easier to work.

Next, bubbles are beaten and pressed out of the clay by a machine known as a "pug" mill. The clay mixture is then ready to be shaped.

Shaping the Clay

Shaping the clay by hand is the most expensive method. It is a fascinating sight to see a man take a piece of common-looking clay, throw it on the fast-revolving turntable called the *potter's wheel,* press his hands deftly against the clay, and, as the clay whirls around, press and form it in a few seconds into a beautiful cylindrical vase or bowl.

In most factories today, however, machines known as *jollies* or *jiggers* are used to press the outside or inside of the clay against a mold while the clay revolves on the turntable, thus shaping both the inside and outside of the dish at the same time. Little chunks of clay may be shaped into handles, spouts, or knobs by being sandwiched between two parts of a mold. The object may be "cast" by pouring slip into a porous plaster-of-Paris mold just as jello is poured into a mold and left to set. After the slip sets around the edges, the center liquid then is poured out to make the hollow center in the dish.

Joining Handles and Spouts

After the clay articles are shaped, any mold marks are smoothed away by brushing with a small brush and water. Then previously molded handles, spouts, or knobs are pasted on. The edges of these pieces are covered with slip, pressed against the body of the ware, and the joinings are smoothed with a brush till all marks are removed. The completed pieces, which are still moist, are now approximately one-fifth larger in size than they will be when baked. This increase in size allows for the shrinkage which will occur during the firing process.

Shaping a vase by hand on the potter's wheel, which revolves as the moist clay is shaped.

The plaster of Paris mold, jigger, and finished plate.

Jollying a bowl in a mold made of plaster of Paris.

Casting slip in plaster of Paris molds. (Courtesy Paul A. Straub & Co., Inc.)

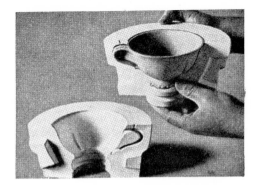

Cup formed by pouring slip into the mold shown.

Attaching handles with slip used as paste.

Placing ware in saggers preparatory to first or "biscuit" firing.

Glazing the biscuit ware. (Courtesy Paul A. Straub & Co., Inc.)

By the simple act of subjecting this fragile molded clay to intense heat, the easily broken, unattractive-looking clay object will be transformed into a thing of usefulness, durability, and beauty. The temperature at which the clay is fired also makes a difference in the finished product. The higher the temperature, the more durable, less porous, and finer the finished ware will be. Earthenware is fired at approximately 1,000° C (approximately 1,800° F) and china is fired at approximately 1,250° C–1,600° C (approximately 2,280° F–2,900° F).

The dishes are stacked in fire-clay racks and then placed on moving belts to travel slowly through a tunnel-shaped *kiln* (oven). In this oven, temperatures are gradually increased until at the center of the oven the heat is intense enough to fire the products. Gradually diminishing temperatures, as the ware progresses through the kiln, cool the ware so that it may easily be handled after emerging from the open end. Modern kilns fire and cool the ware in 24 to 48 hours.

The ware that is removed from the cooled oven is known as *biscuit* ware. It has a dull appearance and a rather rough texture. This biscuit ware is sometimes used for such things as medallions, sculptured figures, flowerpots, or tiles. Such ware is often called *bisque*.

The earthenware bisque is porous and will absorb liquids, while the china-ware bisque is nonporous or vitrified.

In order to make earthenware nonporous and to put a shiny finish on it and on chinaware that will make the dishes pleasant to eat from and easy to clean, the ware is now smoothed by sanding and then covered with a glassy coating called a *glaze*. This glaze is made by different formulas but usually contains very finely ground glass. The glaze may be sprayed or painted on, or the article may be dipped into it. As long as this glaze remains on the ware, earthenware is as sanitary as chinaware. To achieve modern effects, some glazes are made dull. These are known as *mat* glazes.

The glazed dishes are prepared for a second firing at a lower temperature than the biscuit firing. This time no two pieces may be allowed to touch or the melting glaze would weld them together! Dishes are balanced on small clay triangles, or the glaze is wiped from the bottom rim of the dish. Notice the tiny unglazed marks left on the bottom of a dish or the rough bottom of the foot of a cup or plate where there is no glaze! That is where the dish rested during the second or *glost* firing. On fine chinaware, these marks are ground away so they do not show, or the foot on which it rests is left unglazed during the firing.

Sometimes glazes on earthenware crack or "craze" rather badly. This is caused by the uneven expansion of the porous body and the nonporous glaze.

These fine hairlike cracks collect dirt and make the dishes not only unsightly, but also unsanitary. Today, the crazing of the glaze has been overcome to a great extent. China dishes are not subject to crazing because the body and glaze are both nonporous and they expand and contract together.

CHARACTERISTICS OF EARTHENWARE AND CHINAWARE

The manufacture of chinaware and earthenware is now complete. Since these two products, although made in a similar manner, are really very different, the following chart explains their varying characteristics:

Earthenware	Chinaware
1. Opaque	Translucent—unless the ware is very thick
2. Porous to slightly porous under the glaze	Not porous—sanitary even when chipped
3. Dull tone when struck	Bell-like tone when struck
4. Colored to creamy-white body with opaque or transparent glaze	Usually white or cream-colored body with transparent glaze
5. May break if subjected to extremes of temperature	Very resistant to temperature changes
6. Glaze may chip off rather easily and ware is subject to breakage	Glaze is difficult to separate from the body of the ware; the dishes are very durable
7. Inexpensive to fairly expensive, depending on the amount of handwork, country of origin, and the fame of the manufacturer	Fairly inexpensive to expensive depending on the country of origin, quality, decoration, and reputation of the manufacturer

Because of its resistance to breakage and its sanitary qualities even when chipped, chinaware is used by most restaurants and cafeterias. Heavier ware is made for this purpose; it may, therefore appear to be opaque instead of translucent.

MAKING PLASTIC DISHES

Melamine plastic dishes are named for the basic plastic compound, melamine, of which they are made. The melamine is combined with other chemicals and made into a syrup. To give strength to the plastic, cellulose fiber is mixed with it. When the mixture has dried, it is ground into a powder to which color may be added.

This melamine powder is next formed into large pellets with just the amount of powder needed to form a given size dish. These pellets then are placed into a press and molded into shape with heat. The heat and pressure harden the melamine permanently. Since the walls of the molds are very shiny, a glossy finish is imparted to the dishes; and no added glaze is needed. The edges, however, need to be polished when the piece is removed from the mold.

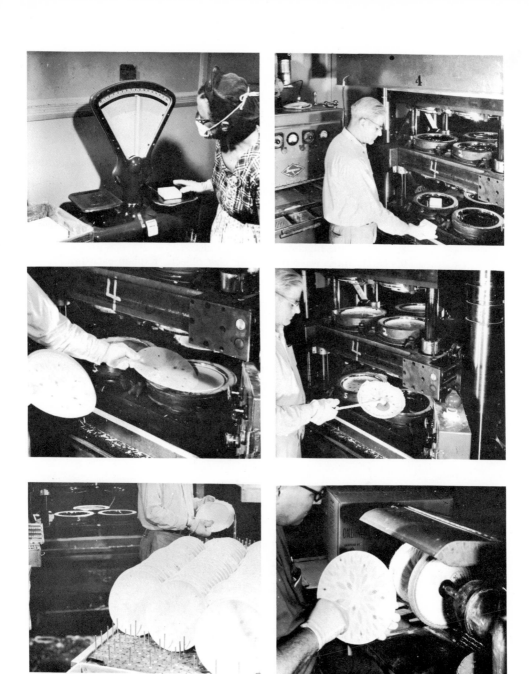

Steps in the Formation of Melamine Dishes. Top row, left: The melamine preformed material is weighed. **Right:** The preform is placed in the mold. **Center row, left:** The decorating foil (also made from melamine) is placed on the plate. **Right:** After foil and body are united, the plate with excess material (flash) is removed from the mold. **Bottom row, left:** Cleaning the "flash." **Right:** Buffing the finished plate. *(Courtesy The Melamine Council)*

> DO YOU KNOW YOUR MERCHANDISE?

1. List five differences apparent between earthenware and chinaware.
2. What is meant by *peasant pottery?* Explain its appearance, durability, and degree of porosity.
3. What are the differences between *vitreous* and *semivitreous* ware?
4. (*a*) What is meant by the term *chinaware?* Where did the name originate? (*b*) What is meant by the term *bone china?* What country is famous for its manufacture?
5. What is the basic ingredient of all dishes? Why is feldspar added? Why is flint added?
6. What is slip? How is it used?
7. What will specks of iron left in the slip do to the finished dish?
8. Explain the function of the pug mill.
9. Name three ways of shaping clay objects. Explain each briefly.
10. Explain how handles, spouts, etc., are formed. How are they joined to the dishes?
11. How large is the clay object before it is fired in comparison to its size after firing?
12. What is the main advantage of plastic dishes over ceramic dishes?

> INTERESTING THINGS TO DO

1. Collect samples of the raw materials used in making ceramics, place in bottles and label neatly.
2. Draw a diagram showing the various steps in the manufacture of a dish.
3. Write a letter to an imaginary friend telling him how to determine whether his dishes are earthenware, chinaware, or plastic.

UNIT 83 DECORATING CERAMIC AND PLASTIC DISHES

When you walk through a chinaware department you may notice that the dishes range in price from a few dollars to hundreds of dollars for the same number of pieces. Sometimes earthenware sets may be more expensive than chinaware sets. Some plastic sets are almost as costly as some china sets, while others sell for only a few dollars. These price differences are due not only to the differences in the ingredients used and the amount of care put into the making of the dishes but primarily to the amount and kind of decoration applied.

Ceramic dishes show the greatest range of prices due to decoration. Two plates, for example, made by the same manufacturer using identical materials can vary from a few dollars for the plate to $15, $20 or more depending on the differences in decoration alone.

WHEN TO APPLY DESIGNS ON CERAMIC WARES

Since decorations on ceramic dishes vary so greatly, salespeople need to know why they affect the price of the wares so much. Decoration on ceramic dishes may be applied while the dishes are being shaped (*in the clay*), after the first or biscuit firing (*underglaze*), or after the second or glost firing (*overglaze*), or the glaze itself may be colored (*in the glaze*).

In the Clay.   In-the-clay decorations have designs made on the moist clay by hand or by pressing designs on with molds. Some designs are molded separately and then pressed against the dishes using *slip* as the glue to hold them in place. Some famous Wedgwood pieces are made this way. For color, metallic oxides may be added to the slip and painted on the wet clay. If hand-work is needed, these designs may be quite costly. After the decoration is applied, the ware must be fired.

Underglaze.   Underglaze decorations refer to colors applied on the biscuit after the first firing. Colors are easier to apply, and many more details may be worked in than by using colored slip. This is, therefore, one of the commonly used methods of decorating dishes; and colors so applied are very durable since the designs are protected by the glaze applied later. The colors, how-ever, are limited because the intense heat needed to melt the glaze over them burns out several commonly used colors. Gold, for example, turns brown when put on underglaze. Usually only a few colors are used in underglaze designs. Blue, pink, yellow, russet, green, and black are colors that have been used underglaze. Once applied, however, these colors become permanent when the glaze covers them. They cannot be washed off or worn away.

In the Glaze.   In-the-glaze decorating is done by coloring the glaze which is applied over the clay body. Most glazes are transparent and show the clay body through the glaze. Some, however, are opaque and hide the color of the clay. Perhaps you have seen vases with two different colored glazes which are used to give the vase or dish a two-tone effect. When the dish has a metallic luster, made by using silver or copper or some other metallic substance in the glaze, the decoration is known as *lusterware*. Sometimes the glazed ware is cooled quickly causing tiny cracks in the glaze which give a decorative *crackled* effect.

Overglaze.   Overglaze decorations are applied over the glassy coating. These may rub off in time, so they are not considered as durable as underglaze decorations. All overglaze decoration must be given added firings in decorating kilns for permanency. Each added firing raises the cost of the decoration. Since the temperature of these kilns is much lower than the heat of the glost oven, the colors retain their beauty. Gold and platinum, which become unattractive when applied underglaze, are always applied overglaze for this reason. Delicate tints and shades also may be achieved through overglaze decoration.

HOW TO IDENTIFY UNDERGLAZE AND OVERGLAZE DECORATION. While it is not always possible to determine whether decoration is underglaze or overglaze unless it is labeled, the following are helpful clues:

Underglaze decoration is usually limited to a few colors in the design. No gold or platinum will be present in underglaze portions of the design. When the fingertips are passed over the design area, the glaze is even to the touch. Light also reflects smoothly over the design area because of the superimposed glassy surface.

Overglaze decoration may have many colors and minor variations of color in the pattern. Gold or platinum is frequently used in part of the decoration or for lining (banding) around the edges. When the fingertips are passed over the design area, a slight dullness in texture may be noticed in contrast to the glazed portion that has no design. When light is reflected along the surface, the design will interfere with its gleam.

HOW DESIGNS ARE APPLIED TO CERAMIC WARES

Engraved lines may be scratched into the clay. Holes may be *carved out* of the clay and later filled in with glaze, or left open to make a lacy-appearing pattern.

Raised decorations may be painted on the clay with slip. The clay may be formed in a mold having a carved-out design that will make a raised pattern on the dish, or small molded pieces may be applied on the clay in cameo fashion. Such decoration is called *bas relief,* meaning a low, raised design.

Colored designs may be made by using varicolored clays, coloring the glaze, putting colored designs on the biscuit, or over the glaze. They may be applied by any one of the following methods:

Hand painting is the oldest and one of the most expensive methods. Colors are applied by hand, or designs are touched up by hand. Fine lines or bandings around the edges of plates, cups, saucers, bowls, and so on are put on by skilled workers who twirl the circular dish on a turntable. By holding their paintbrush against the article as it turns, the line miraculously appears—perfect in proportion and placement. The more lines on an article, the more expensive that dish will be.

Decalcomania is a colorful transfer design that is used to imitate hand painting. The design is first printed on thin tissue paper. A sticky varnishlike material is applied to the dish, and then the tissue is pressed against the dish. After the tissue is rubbed carefully, the design adheres to this sticky substance. The

Application of decalcomania on a glazed plate. *(Courtesy Edwin M. Knowles)*

tissue is then washed off and the design that remains is fired onto the dish. This process lacks the quality of handwork, but it makes possible elaborately colored designs at low cost.

Transfer printing involves more handwork, and so it is a somewhat more expensive method of decorating ware. The design is carefully engraved on a copper plate as jewelry is engraved. The engraved design is then filled with the desired color and transferred to a strong piece of tissue paper. The tissue paper that now has the imprint of the design is carefully applied to the dish and rubbed until the entire design has been transferred. The tissue is then removed, and the design fired onto the dish. Only one color may be put on at a time by this method. If other colors are desired, they are usually applied by hand. The design is then called a *hand-filled print*. Transfer printing may be recognized by the amount of detail and the fineness of the pattern. On fine-quality ware, lacy gold borders are applied by this method with a thick-quality gold known as *coin* gold, which has a rich, dull luster.

Stamping is an inexpensive imitation of the transfer print design. A pattern is cut into a rubber stamp. The stamp is then dipped into the desired color and pressed against the dish. This method is used especially for lacy border designs or one-color patterns on inexpensive dishes. When gold decoration is applied by this inexpensive stamping method, the gold used is called *liquid bright gold*. In place of the rich, dull luster of the coin gold, this bright gold has a shiny finish that needs no polishing. Since this gold is very thin, it wears away gradually when rubbed in washing or when dishes scratch against each other in being stacked.

HOW CERAMIC WARES ARE GRADED

In addition to the manufacture and application of decoration on dishes, the manufacturer's standards of perfection affect the price of the products being sold. A few manufacturers have built up fine reputations for quality merchandise. They have inspectors who examine every finished piece, and if it does not meet with the firm's standard of quality, the dish or ornament is broken to insure its not being sold. This practice, of course, raises the price of the dishes sold. Such rigid inspection results in dishes known as *selects.* These are found only in the fine quality brands.

Other manufacturers, however, in order to supply the demand for inexpensive dishes, adopt a less critical standard. Some place designs over the dark spots or dents on the dishes, and then these imperfections are hard to detect. Manufacturers use the following methods of grading.

Run of the kiln includes ware without any defects or with very minor defects not readily noticeable.

Second grade includes ware with noticeable minor defects that will not impair the wearing quality or the usefulness of the article.

Culls or lumps includes ware with defects that may hamper the article's usefulness and wearing qualities. These are dishes that are cracked, badly warped, chipped, or with noticeable errors in the design.

HOW PLASTIC DISHES ARE DECORATED

Plastic dishes may be white or colored due to the addition of special colors before the dishes are shaped. Some dishes are made with white inside and colored outside layers by fusing two layers of plastic during the forming of the dish. The addition of the colored layer increases the cost of manufacturing the dishes.

In 1955 the first decorative patterns became available in plastic dishes. These are applied by means of a *foil,* a sheet of melamine with the design imprinted upon it. This foil is placed in the mold, and the entire dish is fused in one operation. Thus the decoration is a permanent part of the product itself. It can never wash off or be rubbed away. Even gold colors are imbedded in the plastic itself and are permanent.

PUTTING THIS MERCHANDISE KNOWLEDGE TO USE

❭ DO YOU KNOW YOUR MERCHANDISE?

1. Define in the glaze, underglaze, overglaze.
2. Explain how a salesperson could illustrate the difference between underglaze and overglaze design to a customer.
3. Define hand painting, decalcomania, transfer printing, stamping.
4. What is the difference between coin gold and liquid bright gold in appearance? Which is more costly? Why cannot gold be applied underglaze?
5. Why is decoration on plastic dishes permanent?
6. Name and explain the three usual grades of ceramics. What is meant by the term *selects?* How can imperfections be camouflaged?

❭ INTERESTING THINGS TO DO

1. Prepare a 2-minute sales demonstration with another member of the class. If possible, bring a dish from home to illustrate your selling points.

2. Prepare a one-page manual for extra salespeople being hired to sell dishes at Christmastime.
3. Gather some broken or chipped dishes from your home and from friends' homes. List the colors used in the decorations. Which appeared to be underglaze? which overglaze? What method of design application do you think was used on each?

UNIT 84 CLASSIFICATIONS OF DISHES

BASIC SHAPES OF PLATES

While there may be many fancy flutings, borders, and contours, there are only two basic shapes for plates and other flat dishes: *coupe* and *rim.*

A *coupe* dish has no lip or flat edge by which it may be held while serving. This means the entire area of the plate or dish may be used to hold food and fewer dishes are consequently needed in serving a meal. Although one of the oldest shapes made by man, many people associate this shape with modern dishes. Almost half of the dishes sold today are in this coupe shape.

A *rim* dish has a convenient edge which may be held while serving. The edge also provides an attractive place for decoration that will not be hidden by food. The rim, however, reduces the overall space that may be used for food service on a plate. Many people think the rimmed dish looks more appropriate for traditional or period furnishings. These dishes, however, are also used with modern furnishings.

SIZES OF DISHES

Often the salesperson must play an important role in helping the customer who rushes into the department explaining that last night she accidentally broke one of Mrs. X's best dishes and she must have another just like it right away! Since many of the plates and bowls vary only slightly in size from one another, this may be a difficult task. The salesperson may determine what the customer wants by an actual measurement the customer has taken, or by the use to which the dish was put. There are two methods of measuring *flatware,* meaning plates, platters, and saucers: *overall* and *well-to-edge.*

Overall is the easiest, most convenient measurement to take. A ruler is used to measure the diameter of the dish from one edge to the other edge. Manufacturers of coupe shape dishes use this method of measurement. This

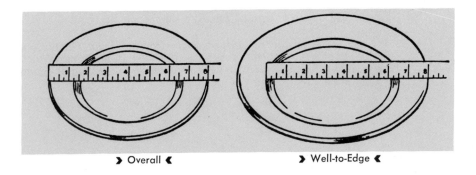

> Overall ◄   > Well-to-Edge ◄

is the type of measurement a person should use in reordering dishes to match a set.

Well-to-edge is the method adopted from English manufacturers. It is known as the *trade measurement*. Price lists of most older firms usually carry this type of measurement. A ruler is used to measure the dish from the inside ridge at the center across to the outside of the rim.

TYPES OF DISHES

Some types of dishes the salesperson in a chinaware department should be familiar with are:

Plates	Soup Dishes	Miscellaneous
4″ Bread and butter	Bouillons—cup with two side handles	Casserole — covered vegetable dish
5″ Dessert	Cream soups ⎡larger than	Demitasse cups—small cup used for after-dinner coffee
6″ Tea or salad	Onion soups ⎪bouillons, may	
7″ Luncheon	Puree soups ⎪or may not	Eggcups—double-purpose cup shaped like an hourglass with small section to fit eggshell on one end and large cup-shaped section for soft boiled eggs on the other end
8″ Dinner	Eared soups ⎣have handles	
9″ Service	Coupe soup—large bowl with no rim	
	Rimmed soup—large bowl with rim	Fruit dishes — small individual bowls for serving fruits or vegetables at the side of the dinner plate or for puddings or fruits for dessert
		Platters or trays—various sized oblong plates for serving meats and other foods
		Tureen—large serving bowl with cover; used for serving soup, beans, stew
		Vegetable dishes—round dishes are called nappies; oval ones, bakers

If you walk around a dinnerware department and notice the displays and signs, you will notice that dishes can be purchased in different combinations: sets, open stock, and place settings.

Sets

Most people today make their original purchase of dishes in sets. This is particularly desirable when the set has a quantity purchase price that means a saving of several dollars. Sets may vary in size according to the number of persons to be served and the number of dishes desired for each serving. Sets for four, six, eight, and twelve persons are usual. For example, sets may be:

20-Piece Service for 4	or	53-Piece Service for 8
including: 4 luncheon plates		8 luncheon or dinner plates
4 cups		8 cups
4 saucers		8 saucers
4 fruits		8 fruits
4 salad plates		8 salad plates
20		8 soups
		1 creamer
		1 sugar bowl
		1 sugar-bowl lid
		1 platter
		1 vegetable dish
		53

In counting the number of pieces in a set, each separate part is counted. A sugar bowl with a lid counts as two pieces. A salt-and-pepper set counts as two pieces. The usual sizes of sets are:

16 piece service for 4
20 piece service for 4
32 piece service for 6
53 piece service for 8
62 piece service for 8
93 piece service for 12
105 piece service for 12

Open Stock

If dishes are in *open stock,* it is possible to purchase additional pieces to match your set. When people purchase their sets they should make sure, if the set is expensive or if they intend to use it for a number of years, that individual dishes may be purchased to match in case of breakage or need to enlarge the set. A dish is in open stock only so long as the manufacturer continues to make the pattern. Some manufacturers of expensive lines guarantee that as long as they are in business they will keep the pattern in open stock.

Place Setting

The usual way to purchase expensive chinaware is by the *place setting.* This is particularly advisable for the person on a budget who is desirous of purchasing expensive ware a little at a time. Each place setting is a complete service for one person consisting of five pieces:

> 1 dinner plate
> 1 tea or salad plate
> 1 bread-and-butter plate
> 1 cup
> 1 saucer

Some place settings have six pieces and include a soup dish. Serving dishes and additional pieces are selected from open stock as needed.

CARE OF CERAMIC AND PLASTIC DISHES

Both kinds must be cared for; however, ceramic dishes require more careful handling than plastic dishes.

Ceramic

Since dishes that are cracked or chipped are not attractive, it is advisable to handle dishes carefully when washing or stacking them. Mild soapsuds and a soft dishcloth should be used, for steel wool and gritty cleaners will scratch the glazed surface. If dishes are rinsed shortly after being used, it will be unnecessary to scrub them later to remove hardened food particles. Foods containing vinegar when left in dishes may eat off overglaze decalcomania decoration.

Avoid drastic temperature changes that may crack the ware. Dishes placed in the refrigerator or in very hot water should be precooled or preheated in running water. Unless they are labeled *ovenware,* dishes should not be used in the oven for heating or baking.

Rings of rubber, cardboard, or cork placed over spouts on teapots or coffeepots will protect them from breaking while not in use.

Overglaze coloring on handles of cups will rub off if cups are stacked one inside the other. It is advisable to hang cups by handles on hooks, or provide ample space for each cup to stand separately.

Ease of care is one of the important selling points for plastic dishes. They are resistant to breakage, but they may crack or chip if they fall repeatedly on a hard floor. Very sharp knives used for cutting steaks can also scratch the surface.

Melamine plastic dishes resist extremes of temperature and can be used in the refrigerator and subjected to boiling hot water without harm. High heat from an oven and direct flame, such as crushing a lighted cigarette on a plate, can, however, damage the plastic.

Coffee and tea may stain cups. These stains may be removed by using a little baking soda in water and soaking the stains loose or by using regular commercial cleaners sold for this purpose. Gritty cleaners should never be used on plastics as they may scratch the surface.

Since melamine is about 60 per cent lighter in weight than other dishes, it is easy to stack and handle. The design being part of the dish itself cannot be worn away in use.

PUTTING THIS MERCHANDISE KNOWLEDGE TO USE ❯ ❯ ❯ ❯ ❯ ❯ ❯ ❯ ❯ ❯

❯ DO YOU KNOW YOUR MERCHANDISE?

1. Why is it important to know how to care for ceramic dishes? for plastic dishes?
2. Explain the following terms: coupe shape, rim shape, overall measurement, well-to-edge measurement, trade measurement.
3. If a customer did not know the size of a plate she wanted to match, how would you advise her to measure it?
4. How many pieces would each of the following represent in counting the dishes in a set: cup and saucer, sugar bowl with lid, casserole, eggcup, tureen?
5. Explain the following terms: sets, open-stock, place settings.
6. How should a customer be advised to care for coffee stains on plastic cups?
7. Why should abrasive cleaners not be used on dishes?

❯ INTERESTING THINGS TO DO

1. If you have a chipped or broken dish, clean a portion with a gritty cleaner. Press the sharp edge of a steak knife against the surface as if you were cutting steak. Record the results as an experiment.
2. From newspapers, record the sizes of dinner sets advertised. Which size sets were advertised most frequently? Why do you think they are the most common?
3. Visit a chinaware department in a store. Analyze the department. What proportion was devoted to the display of earthenware? of chinaware? of plastics? Were dishes shown in sets, as open stock, or as place settings? Write a report of your visit.

ADDITIONAL MERCHANDISE TERMS ❯❯❯❯❯❯❯❯❯❯❯❯❯❯❯❯❯❯❯❯

Belleek is a china originally made in Ireland. It has a cream-colored, extremely thin body with translucent quality resembling an *eggshell*. It appears fragile but is in reality very durable.

Coin gold is gold mixed with 10 per cent of some other metal such as copper and made into a thick paste by adding oil to the powder. The gold is applied overglaze, fired in the decorating kiln, then buffed or polished to make it shine. The thickness of the coating of gold determines its durability and price. This is also called *burnish gold*.

Delft is pottery first made in Holland, later in England, with colored clay body with an opaque white glaze. It was used in great quantity before the commercial development of European chinaware.

Dinnerware is china, earthenware, or glassware used for serving food.

Faience is peasant-type pottery originally made in Italy.

Flatware refers to flat articles of dinnerware such as plates, trays, saucers.

Holloware refers to hollow articles of dinnerware such as bowls, cups, vegetable dishes, or pitchers.

Jasperware is Wedgwood unglazed ware with bas-relief, cameolike figures in white, molded against a colored background.

Lenox is a famous American-made chinaware. This china has been the official White House china since 1917.

Limoges is a town in France where factories produce chinaware.

Liquid bright gold is a liquid with just a little gold present. It is called "liquid bright" because after being applied and fired it does not need to be polished as does coin gold.

Majolica is Italian peasant pottery with opaque glaze.

Melmac is a trade name used by some manufacturers for melamine dinnerware.

Noritake is a trade name for a famous chinaware made in Japan.

Queensware is Wedgwood white-bodied earthenware. It was originated by Josiah Wedgwood for the Queen of England.

Quimper is French peasant pottery.

Short lines are ceramic ornaments, vases, candelabra—articles usually carried in gift departments.

Shoulder is the inside raised edge which forms the rim of a plate or saucer or other flatware.

Spode, Josiah was the originator of famous bone china which bears his name. He was the first English potter who was successful in producing bone china in commercial quantities. The firm also makes a fine quality earthenware.

Staffordshire is the section of England which embraces many small towns famous for their ceramic products.

Stone china is an earthenware product that should not be represented as being true chinaware. It is also referred to as *ironstone*.

Stoneware is highly fired, vitrified, heat-resistant ware, usually rather heavy in appearance. Used often for jugs and sometimes for informal tablewares.

Wedgwood, Josiah was a well-known English potter, who contributed much to the development of ceramic ware in decorative quality, beauty of form, and in new mixtures and processes for making clay.

Glass— The Transparent Material

CHAPTER 28

UNIT 85 GLASS AND ITS USES

Only in legends are we told tales of the first discovery of glassware. We know from relics of excavations that, long before any history was recorded, people were using glass. At first it was used by the Egyptians as a coating for pottery dishes, figures, or beads. About 3000 B.C. they discovered that glass could be used by itself for ornaments, vases, and dishes. It was so beautiful that glass beads were considered as valuable as gold and semiprecious stones.

Although transparent, the walls of glassware hide many secrets mysteriously. The hard, transparent material which is so useful to us is made from common earthy substances, as is ceramic ware. Instead of clay, however, the basic ingredient is sand. Silica, the main ingredient in sand, is the most common mineral on our planet.

The sand and other chemicals are melted in a furnace. The molten "metal," as the glassmakers call it, is then shaped and cooled. After cooling is completed, the opaque sand has miraculously become transparent glass. Glass, then, is a molten substance shaped and cooled until it is a hard, nonporous, usually transparent object. All glass articles are nonporous or vitrified and are therefore sanitary.

IMPORTANT USES OF GLASSWARE

Many glass items are not sold in the glassware department, but in other parts of the store. They have added so much to man's progress that most everyone enjoys knowing some of the outstanding uses of glass.

Glass beads were found in the earliest tombs of the Egyptians who lived 4000 to 3000 B.C. Today there are few young ladies who do not possess a piece of costume jewelry set with glass stones in imitation of real stones. Rhinestones made of glass have long been an important jewelry item.

Window Glass

It is difficult for us to imagine homes or stores with little or no outside light permeating the dark interiors. Window glass has progressed very slowly, however, from the time when the Romans first used an almost opaque glass for small enclosures. The magnificent stained-glass windows used in famous old churches were created more for decoration than to let in rays of light. In the seventeenth century, the English imposed such prohibitive taxes on windows that only the smallest panes of glass could be used by the majority of the populace. This tax was not repealed until 1851. In contrast to the homes of a hundred years ago, the tendency today is to panel the entire sides of walls almost solidly with windows. Glass bricks, which are shells of heavy glass with a vacuum inside to act as an insulator, have become popular for use in homes, offices and manufacturing plants.

Interior Lighting

Man was particularly slow in adapting glass to interior lighting. To keep candle flames from being blown out, opaque metal covers were used. Into the metal covers were cut tiny holes from which the light was emitted. Quite accidentally, in the latter part of the eighteenth century, it was discovered that glass used as a chimney protected the candle flame and allowed the light to shine through. How thankful we are today for that discovery!

Edison's invention of the electric-light bulb in 1879 would have been impossible without the special properties of glass. The first bulbs were individually blown by glassworkers. This, of course, made the bulb expensive. By 1915 a method of blowing bulbs by machine had been perfected. The consequent lowered price made possible the universal adoption and use of electric lights. Today such light bulbs are machine blown by completely automated machinery that makes 1,000 bulbs a minute every minute of the day and night!

Miscellaneous Uses

Glass for optical use became important after printing was developed. All optical glasses require the purest, best-quality lead glass.

The ability of glass to magnify tiny objects has been of the greatest scientific importance. Without it, progress in medicine would have been hampered considerably. The ability of glass in a *telescope* to bring a distant article closer has been of invaluable aid to science in the study of the heavenly bodies surrounding the earth.

Glass for Christmas tree ornaments combines sparkling and colorful beauty with safety, for it creates no fire hazard. Today, tree balls are blown by machine in a similar manner to the blowing of light bulbs. Glass snow to be sprinkled on the Christmas tree is made by blowing bubbles of glass so thin they burst and crumble into fine flakes.

Glass fiber was first used as a dress fabric in 1893. Today glass fibers are used mainly for curtain and drapery materials. They have great tensile strength, are fireproof, and do not stretch or shrink. Glass fiber is also important when made into short fibers known as *glass wool* for use as insulation and for air filters. Glass wool has proved of great value to the refrigeration field as insulation. Glass fibers are also combined with plastics to make strong bodies for furniture, boat hulls, and bodies for experimental automobiles and some sport cars.

Pyroceram introduced in 1958 is the trade name for the newest type of heat-resistant glass. This is a material developed for the nose cone of outer-space projectiles that withstands extreme temperatures without being harmed. White in color, it resembles china and is used in the home as cook-and-serve ware. *Centura* is the trade name for Pyroceram dishes. (See page 582)

Glass has many other important uses, and as time progresses undoubtedly many new uses will be developed.

BASIC KINDS OF GLASS

Generally glassware is divided into three main groups: *lime, lead,* and *heat resistant.*

Lime

Because it is the least expensive, yet durable and serviceable, the great majority of glass today is *lime glass.* The milk bottles, soda bottles, window panes, mirrors, inexpensive drinking glasses, glass jars, and glass dishes we use are known as lime glass. The first glassmakers who lived 5,000 years ago developed the formula for this glass. It is a very durable, hard glass. If you examine a windowpane, you will find that although it is constantly subjected to wind, rain, snow, and other weather conditions, its surface is smooth and clear. Hold a bottle or an inexpensive glass by the base and tap it with a pencil. Notice that the glass has a rather dull tinkling sound when struck. Examine the luster or shine of the glass. This luster is not brilliant, therefore we refer to lime glass as having a *soft* luster.

Because its surface is hard and brittle, lime glass does not adapt itself to "cut" decorations. Designs may, however, be pressed into the glass when it is formed. For example, ordinary milk bottles often have the dairy firm's name pressed into the sides of the bottle.

Since 1950 some American manufacturers have improved the sparkle and cutting qualities of lime glass. Today some lime glasses are available that have machine-cut designs and a quite attractive sparkle.

Lead

The second type of glass, known as *lead glass,* was not developed until the latter part of the seventeenth century in England. The discovery of this glass led to some very interesting new artistic endeavors, for lead glass has a softer surface than lime glass, and can be cut readily, reflecting light with brilliance. Good quality rhinestones are made from lead glass because of this sparkle.

If you hold a lead glass to the light, you will notice the brilliance of its luster. Tap the edge with a pencil and listen to the bell-like tone. It sounds almost as if a gong had been struck! Because the surface of lead glass is softer than that of lime glass, it is more easily scratched. The ingredients used are more costly than those used in lime glass, therefore lead glass is used only in more expensive articles. It is used mainly for fine table glass, optical lenses, and imitation jewelry stones.

Heat Resistant

The third type of glass, heat resistant, is familiarly known by four of its trade names: *Pyrex, Glassbake, Fire King,* and *Pyroceram.* The first three are borosilicate, which formula was created in 1910 in response to a demand for glass that would not expand and contract so greatly when exposed to heat or cold. The chemists found that boric oxide would lower the coefficient of expansion of glass. Ordinary glass will break if subjected to extremes of temperature. Heat-resistant glass may be used in oven or refrigerator with little danger of breakage. This glass has many uses in chemical laboratories, but in the home it is mainly used for cooking. Some heat-resistant glass, known as *flameware,* can actually be used for cooking over the gas flame or electric plate. Most of this type of glass, however, is thicker and heavier *ovenware,* and it is used for baking. It has the advantages of holding the heat longer than metal containers, of enabling one to watch foods cook, and of being easy to clean, all of which make it very desirable for kitchen use.

This glass has little luster, and a rather dull sound when struck. It usually has a slightly cloudy transparency rather than a clear, colorless appearance. However, its qualities of durability and heat resistance are far more important than its lack of beauty, clarity, and tone. *Pyroceram,* developed in 1958, is made from a different formula and is opaque white in appearance.

PUTTING THIS MERCHANDISE KNOWLEDGE TO USE ❯ ❯ ❯ ❯ ❯ ❯ ❯ ❯ ❯ ❯

❯ DO YOU KNOW YOUR MERCHANDISE?

1. What is glass? Explain the differences between glassware and chinaware.
2. Name the three basic types of glassware. Explain the characteristics of each.
3. How did glass come to be used as the housing for electric lights?
4. How long have glass fibers been in use? What are some important uses today?
5. Why were people slow to adopt large windows for homes to permit light to enter?
6. What glass product initially developed for outer-space objects is used in homes today?

1. Make a list of all products in your home made from or containing glass.
2. Make a study of the uses of beads in the purchase of Manhattan Island. Write a short theme on this subject.
3. Analyze the buildings in your city or town. Are the uses of glass for windows different in the new buildings from the uses in the old buildings? Explain your findings in a short theme.

UNIT 86 MATERIALS AND MANUFACTURE OF GLASS

INGREDIENTS USED FOR GLASSMAKING

Strange, indeed, is the fact that an article whose main beauty and usefulness depends on its clear transparency has as one of its chief ingredients opaque sand. Only the finest, purest sand is used for good-quality glassware. The best sand in the United States is found in West Virginia. Other sand of good quality is found in Massachusetts, Pennsylvania, and Illinois.

To the sand, which is about 50 to 75 per cent of the formula, is added an alkali (soda or potash) which will aid the sand to melt. The third ingredient, lead, lime, or boric oxide, adds the qualities of brilliance or luster, hardness or softness of surface, tone, or resistance to temperature changes. Basic formulas for the three types of glassware might be specified as follows:

Lime	Lead	Heat-Resistant
Sand	Sand	Sand
Soda	Potash	Soda
Lime	Lead	Boric oxide

Many other chemicals may be used to get further variations of color, clearness, and hardness. Only the experienced chemist, however, would be able to analyze the chemicals used. The customer and salesperson are only interested in whether the glass is ordinary lime glass, lead glass, or ovenware or flameware. For coloring glass, mineral substances are added, such as chromium for green, cobalt for blue, copper or gold for ruby, and sulfur for yellow.

STEPS IN GLASSMAKING

There are two main steps in glassmaking: the preparing and firing of the ingredients and the shaping of the glass.

Preparing and Firing the Ingredients

After being carefully cleansed of all impurities and sieved, the raw ingredients including the coloring substances are mixed together. This mixture is known as *the batch*. To the batch is added broken glass scrap known as *cullet*. The cullet aids in the melting of the batch.

The batch and cullet are put into a specially made fire-clay pot or into a fire-clay tank furnace; fire performs the miracle of transforming the mixture into a molten, transparent liquid. The heat of the furnace necessary to melt the chemicals is about 2,700° F. This is a higher heat than any metals can withstand. The stove in your home has a maximum temperature of less than 700° F!

After one day of boiling and bubbling, the mixture, called the *metal,* is cooled slightly until it is a bright yellow-red, thick liquid about the consistency of hot taffy. The glass is then ready to be shaped into an article of usefulness and oftentimes of beauty.

Forming the Glass

Blown Glass. Originally strips of glass were wound around clay cores and after the glass had cooled, the clay centers were dug out. About 250 B.C. a glassmaker discovered quite accidentally that glass could be shaped by *blowing* much as one blows a soap bubble. This highly skilled method of shaping glass, still in use today, has changed little since its early beginning.

Into the red-hot thick liquid, the blower plunges the blow iron, a hollow steel tube from 4 to 6 feet in length. He gathers on its end some molten glass, places the other end of the blow iron to his mouth, and blows a bubble of air. This air bubble forms the inside of the article he is shaping.

By carefully rolling the blow iron, the blower can shape the glass in any desired way. He may also use tools or a dip mold to press against the outside of the glass bubble to make a variety of forms. Any marks so impressed against the glass remain throughout the additional shaping processes. As the glass cools, it hardens, so it is necessary to soften it again by placing it back in a small furnace known as a *glory hole.* As soon as the glass is softened, the blower can go on shaping it, adding stem, foot, and handles as required. In its semiliquid or viscous state, one mass of glass, such as a handle, can be joined permanently to the body of the article. The top of the glass bowl adhering to the blow iron may then be cut off and the rim shaped and smoothed by reheating in the glory hole, or by subsequent grinding and polishing.

Glassware blown in this method is expensive and is therefore rarely used except in good quality ware.

Molded Glass. A less expensive method of shaping glass, and one more widely used, is known as *molding.* In this process the glass is gathered on the blow iron, and a bubble of air is blown into the viscous glass; this bubble of

Steps in the Formation of Stemware. Top row, left: Molded stem is attached to goblet bowl. **Right:** Hand-fashioned foot is applied to stem. **Bottom row, left:** Smoothing the rim of the goblet. **Right:** Hand-molded piece in the mold. *(Courtesy Fostoria Glass Co.)*

glass is then inserted in a mold made of cast iron. Blowing through the blow iron forces the glass to expand and fill the sections of the mold. As the hot glass touches the mold, it is chilled and the outer form is shaped. The air shapes the inside of the glass.

The bottle is the best example of this type of craftsmanship. Originally all bottles were blown separately into molds. In the 1800's, when bottles became desirable for preserving and canning, a great demand for the article developed. This demand later led to the development of the first crude bottle-making machine by Michael J. Owens, an American inventor. Today the modern version of the bottle-making machine he invented turns out several bottles a minute after having performed every operation unaided by human touch. Each bottle is a marvel of perfection and accuracy, a thing undreamed of when each was laboriously handmade.

For products such as light bulbs that are used by the millions in America, automatic shaping machines that never stop are used to blow, mold, and eject the glass bulbs all ready for fitting with fine wire filaments.

Steps in Making Hand-Molded Giftware.

◀ Blowing a vase. Hand-forming the lip of a bowl. ▶ **Bottom row, left:** Hand-shaping a goblet foot. **Right:** Flaring a plate to shape. *(Courtesy Fostoria Glass Co.)*

The iron molds in which the glass is shaped may have designs cut into them. This in turn makes a raised design or indentation in the outside of the bottle or article being molded. Such decorative molds may fashion wares that resemble cut glass. Lime glass adapts itself particularly for molding.

Pressed Glass. The third method of shaping glass is known as *pressing*. Well known to all of us is the important role that glass beads played in acquiring America from the Indians. To have an adequate supply of these "baubles" on hand it was necessary to establish glass factories in America. The method of pressing glass into molds with a plunger instead of blowing the glass to shape the inside was first developed at the Sandwich factory in Sandwich, Massachusetts. Much of today's colonial type glassware is copied from early Sandwich pressed glass.

Hot glass will not flow readily into all the crevices of the mold. If not blown in, it must be forced into the crevices and corners by a metal plunger. At the same time this plunger shapes and makes the inner surface smooth. The outside of the glass may have an ornamental design imprinted on its surface. Pressed glass has blunt, rounded edges, and the designs on it are often symmetrical. Heat-resistant and lime glass are commonly made in this manner. Plates, fruit dishes, and other large rather flat articles are shaped by pressing. Stems of glassware may also be pressed and then attached to the base of the blown or molded glass.

Even round bowls may be made by pressing. First they are pressed into shape as flat plates, then while still plastic and hot, they are formed into bowl shapes as they revolve on a lathe.

Sheet Glass.   For flat surfaces, sheet glass, such as that used for windows and some mirrors, is shaped in still another manner. Ordinary window glass was originally blown, the bubble of glass cut open and flattened out while still in the molten state, making many swirls and lines in the glass. While not ordinarily used, glass of this type is made occasionally for fine furniture that reproduces the glass-front furniture of bygone days. Such glass panes are referred to as *crown glass.*

Since 1924, smooth window glass has been made by drawing the molten glass up through a machine that is so tall it goes through several floors in the building. As the glass is drawn upward, it is flattened and smoothed, and, when cool, passed between rows of rollers. The glass continues to cool slowly as it travels through the machine. On the floor at the top of the machine, the cooled flat glass is cut, examined, measured, and packed. This glass is also known as *window glass,* or *shock glass.*

Plate Glass.   The making of plate glass was developed by the French during the reign of Louis XIV. They discovered that the hot glass could be rolled on an iron table with iron cylinders that pressed out all the bubbles and wavy lines. After rolling, the rough surface of the glass is polished on both sides with abrasive substances until the glass is clear and smooth. Because the smooth, even surface of plate glass allows perfect vision, store windows and glass counters, safety glass for automobile windshields, and good quality mirrors are made from this glass.

The next time you look at yourself in a mirror, notice how far from the mirror you can stand and still get a true vision. When ordinary window glass is used for mirrors, your reflection is distorted at a short distance. With plate-glass mirrors, the vision is true even across a large room.

The thickness of the glass used in mirrors can be tested by holding a pencil point at an angle against the mirror. The distance between the pencil point and its reflection, which comes from the silver at the back of the mirror, shows the thickness of the glass. For large mirrors, the thicker the glass, the better the quality of the mirror.

Safety Glass. The accidental development of safety glass has proved a great boon to mankind. We are told that a chemist was working with Celluloid which he was heating in a glass tube. He dropped the tube, and expected the glass fragments to fly, as broken glass normally does. To his surprise, the glass broke; but the fragments adhered to the plastic substance inside the tube. He applied this principle and made a glass sandwich—two layers of glass with a clear, colorless layer of vinyl plastic in between. Thus safety glass was invented. Although it will break, the glass adheres to the plastic, and a person riding in a car is protected from being cut by flying glass fragments. Vinyl plastic is used as the transparent filler in today's safety glass.

MAKING GLASS DURABLE

A discussion of the two methods of making glass durable follows.

Heat Treatment

Some glasses are advertised as having rims that are very resistant to breakage, or the glasses themselves are described as break-resistant. Although glass is melted at very high temperatures, glass that is given additional heat treatment becomes far more durable. Thus, using 3,000° F temperatures to melt a smooth rim on the glass resulted in a bead of glass around the edge that was much tougher and more resistant to breakage than the rest of the glass. *Safedge* is a trade name for such an edge. Placing the entire glass in a tunnel oven with hot flames licking at the sides also imparts this added durability to the glass. Fine glassware, however, does not receive this extra heat treatment.

Annealing Glass

You have seen the cracked surface of dried mud. The surface of glass not properly cooled will crack in much the same way. Glass does not conduct heat well. Even though the glass is thin, the surface areas cool much more quickly than the center sections. This uneven surface cooling causes pressure which results in the cracking of the glass.

By putting the glass on a runway that carries it through an *annealing* oven where the heat is slowly diminished, the outer and inner layers of the glass are cooled simultaneously. Thus the glass emerges from this oven a useful, durable article. The length of time required for the slow cooling or annealing of the glass depends on the thickness of the article.

It is this same factor of internal pressure that makes it important that glass used in the home should not be subjected to a quick change from boiling water to freezing temperatures. Such extremes of temperature crack ordinary glass.

Testing Glassware. To be sure that glassware will give durable service, it is tested before leaving the factory. Each glass is examined under a strong light for imperfections that will mar its beauty or affect its wearing qualities. A special testing device known as a *polariscope* shows whether any stresses or strains are present that might later cause the glass to break.

Glass is also given a thermal test. It is plunged alternately into hot and cold water. If it withstands this test, the consumer can depend on the glassware to give her good service.

PUTTING THIS MERCHANDISE KNOWLEDGE TO USE ❯❯❯❯❯❯❯❯❯❯

❯ DO YOU KNOW YOUR MERCHANDISE?

1. What ingredients are used in the making of glassware? Explain how the use of different ingredients affects the finished glass.
2. Define batch, cullet, blow iron, glory hole.
3. Explain how the ingredients are transformed into glass.
4. What is meant by blown glass, molded glass, pressed glass, sheet glass, plate glass? Explain briefly how each is formed, and name a few articles made in each way.
5. What process is used to make glass durable? What is meant by annealing? Safedge? heat treatment?
6. Why is a polariscope used in testing glassware?

❯ INTERESTING THINGS TO DO

1. Make a list of three glassware items in your home that are made in one of the following ways: blown glass, molded glass, pressed glass.
2. Gather information in the library on the history of glass and write a short theme on this subject.
3. Analyze newspaper advertisements. How many mentioned the type of glass used (lead, lime, heat resistant)? How many told how the glassware was shaped? Explain why you believe that information was or was not given in the advertisements.

UNIT 87 DECORATING AND SELLING GLASSWARE

One glassware manufacturer asked in an advertisement addressed to salespeople, "Why do thousands of women pay $1.50 for a goblet when a 5-cent tumbler will hold water as well?"

"Because," the advertisement continued, "they have been educated to know beauty, they want it, and they will pay for it."

SURFACE DESIGNS WITH NO COLOR

The customer interested in purchasing glassware wants to know how different decorative effects are achieved. She takes pride in owning glassware that has handmade designs. The salesperson needs to know the answers to the customers' questions about the types of designs and the way they are applied. Understanding these makes it easier to explain the reasons for the price differences in glasses that appear to be somewhat similar.

Embossing

While glass is still taffylike, designs may be pressed with molds onto the surface. Such designs may resemble cut patterns, or they may simply have a cameolike look. This is an inexpensive method of decorating glass.

Cutting

One of the most beautiful and costly methods of decorating glassware, *cutting,* became possible after the invention of lead glass. Of course, the quality and amount of cutting can vary considerably. Small sandstone wheels are used for cutting. The glass with the design sketched on it is pressed against the revolving wheel by the artisan. Being an artist, he knows just the amount of pressure necessary to cut the design into the glass. Different sized and shaped wheels are used for the varying patterns in the design. The abrasive wheel leaves a grayed surface on the glass as it cuts the design. Inexpensive lime glass may be cut by machine.

Some designs for decorative contrast are left "in the gray." However, if the design is to be clear and to sparkle, the glass must be polished after it is cut.

Polishing may be accomplished by buffing with felt wheels or by dipping in acid. The buffing method is slow and costly, but it imparts a rich gleam to the glass. Glassware so polished is sold as "hand polished." The acid method is speedy and less expensive but does not make the glass quite so brilliant.

Copper-Wheel Engraving

On very select objets d'art the designs or monograms may be engraved on the glass. Delicate-looking, intricate forms are made by holding the glass against small copper discs that revolve on a lathe. The sections of the design that are hollowed out vary in depth. This creates interesting illusions from the right side of the glass. The design is left "in the gray" for contrast with the transparency of the rest of the glass. The bowl which former President Truman presented to Queen Elizabeth of England when she was married was copper-wheel engraved.

A popular method of applying designs to glass is by means of hydrofluoric acid. Glass is not affected by any acid except this one, which decomposes the glass wherever it touches the surface, leaving an indented, grayed surface. Entire sides of glass may have a *frosted* appearance by being dipped in the acid for a few moments, or designs may be achieved by exposing only parts of the glass. Wax, which is resistant to the acid, is applied to the glass. Any spaces uncovered by the wax will be attacked by the acid. The glass is submerged in the acid for the requisite amount of time, and then wax and acid are thoroughly washed off. The glass emerges with a grayed, grooved-out design wherever the acid was allowed to touch. The depth of the design depends on the strength of the acid and the length of time the article was left in the etching bath.

This method of etching can be fairly inexpensive if the glass is completely covered with wax and the design scratched through the wax by needles that are worked in unison by a machine. This makes a symmetrical line design, known as *needle etching*. If, however, the design is an intricate one which must be placed on as transfer-print designs are applied to ceramic ware, etching becomes an expensive and creative type of decoration. This latter method is known as *plate etching* and is used only on fairly costly glassware.

Sandblasting

Sand, blown forcibly against glass by means of compressed air, will pit the surface of the glass and leave a frosted appearance. If a design or monogram

Left: Hand cutting the design into the bowl. **Right:** Hand painting the metallic trim. *(Courtesy Fostoria Glass Co.)*

◀ 1. The design, etched on a metal plate, is covered with an inky wax, resistant to acid. The 2. A specially prepared tissue paper is next rubbed carefully over the plate so that every detail of the design is transferred. ❯

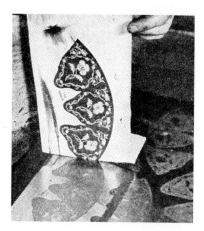

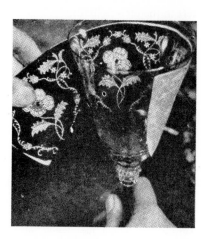

◀ 3. The paper containing the design transfer is removed from the plate and trimmed.
4. It is placed carefully against the sides of the goblet. The print is rubbed tightly onto the glass to be sure every bit of wax adheres to the surface. ❯

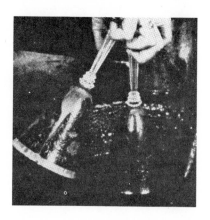

◀ 5. The paper is stripped off leaving the print on the glass.
6. Wax is then sprayed on the inside of the goblet to protect it from being attacked by the acid which will eat into all unprotected spots on the glass. ❯

❯ ❯ *Eight Steps in the Formation of a Plate-Etched Design on a Glass Goblet* ◀ ◀

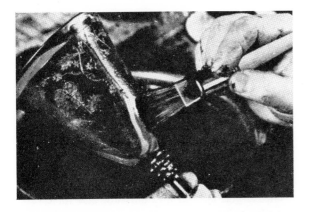

Left: 7. The operator now covers the entire piece with wax except where the pattern openings appear. **Right: 8.** The glass is placed in a hydrofluoric acid bath. The acid penetrates into those places that are left exposed. The acid and the wax are washed off and the finished goblet is wiped with sawdust. *(Courtesy Fostoria Glass Co.)*

is desired, a metal or rubber stencil which protects the glass from the sandblast except for the cut-out sections is used. Sandblasting leaves a rougher surface than etching does. When the design is deeply cut by sandblasting, the glass is known as *carved*.

COLORING GLASSWARE

If you have visited a glassware department recently, you probably noticed that most of the glass was colorless or "crystal color" named for the Greek word meaning "icelike." The colorless glass which we take for granted was considered a marvelous advancement by the Venetian craftsmen who first developed it in the sixteenth century. It was called *Cristallo* glass and was the envy of glassmakers throughout Europe until the secret was discovered. Cloudy or "off-color" glassware is the result of impurities of iron that are present in the sand.

Today even the least expensive glassware may be crystal clear in color. Chemists have learned how to neutralize the green tints caused by the iron impurities. In judging the quality of colorless glass today, the standard is "no color." Slight green or pink tints indicate inferior ingredients or improper mixing.

If colored glass is desired, various minerals are added to the ingredients. Since the color is an integral part of the glass, it never wears off. Popular colors are ruby red, cobalt blue, bottle green, and milky white.

For artistic cut effects, one layer of colored glass may be superimposed over a layer of crystal glass. Cutting through the colored layer reveals the crystal below. This is called *cased* glass, a fine quality decorative glassware made by some of the foremost European manufacturers.

An imitation of this method is achieved by merely applying a metallic coating over a stencil. This is known as *flashed* glass. This glass has an iridescent gleam and lacks the rich, deep colors found in cased glass.

COLORED DESIGNS

Mineral colors in the form of enamel, gold, silver, and platinum may be applied to the surface of the glass. Enameled colors may be stenciled or hand painted on the glass. After applying the color, the design is fired on for permanency. Any hand painting done in America makes the glassware costly. Stenciling is one of the most popular methods of decoration used by American manufacturers. It is used on cheese glasses and fine barware and tableware.

Platinum and gold lines may be painted on as they are in ceramic ware, then fired and polished for permanence and brilliancy. Applying gold over an etched surface is known as *encrusting;* the gold then being fired and polished. The price of this method of decoration varies depending on the quality of the gold used and the thickness of the layer applied. An inexpensive method of applying gold-colored decorations is known as the *cold gilt process.* Gilt paint covers a pressed-out design, which is then covered with a water-resistant lacquer. Being inexpensive and quick, this method may be used for decorative effects on less expensive types of glassware.

Silver is applied to glassware by a very unusual process called *electroplating.* Glass so decorated is known as *silver depositware.* To make silver adhere to glass, it is first necessary to paint or stencil the desired design on the glass with a metallic solution. After this solution has been fired onto the glass, it becomes white in color. If you look on the wrong side of a silver depositware item, you will see this white substance. The glass is then suspended in the electroplating bath, and the silver is deposited on the metal

In the process shown at the left, special ceramic colors are filtered through a screen onto the glass. The ware is then put through a lehr that actually fuses the decoration into the glass. *(Courtesy Libby Glass Company)*

design. Silver so deposited does not have to be fired. It will not rub off or wear off easily. To make it nontarnishable, the silver may be coated with another metal such as *rhodium,* which is costly and therefore used in very thin applications which eventually wear away.

CLASSIFICATIONS OF GLASSWARE

Glassware departments usually divide glass into sections: stemware, tumblers, barware sets, and accessories.

As in ceramic wares, plates, saucers, and flat serving dishes are called *flatware. Holloware* includes bowls, fruit dishes, and other hollow serving pieces. *Stemware* is the term used for drinking glasses that have a bowl, stem, and foot. These are used for formal and semiformal dining occasions. Water goblets, wine glasses, cocktail glasses, and sherbet glasses are included in this group. *Tumblers* are drinking glasses for less formal and informal service. These have no foot or stem. *Footed tumblers* have a foot but no stem. These come in various sizes ranging from fruit-juice glasses to iced-tea glasses. Miscellaneous glassware items include candleholders, vases, cigarette boxes, coupettes (for seafood cocktails), and ornaments.

HOW IS GLASSWARE SOLD?

Glassware is sold in sets and in open stock. Sets of glassware refer to special occasion groupings, such as water sets, iced-tea sets, salad sets, punch sets, fruit sets. Some firms make complete glassware lines in matching patterns. Such lines can usually be purchased in small quantities and filled in from time to time from open stock. Few people purchase entire matching sets of glass at once. It is wise, however, to point out to a customer the advantage of being able to fill in the glassware at a later date with other matching items. Some glassware for table use is made to match famous silverware and chinaware patterns.

Manufacturers have found a ready market for prepackaged glassware. Tumblers in water-glass and juice-glass size and some in highball size have been attractively packaged in sets of 4, 6, and 8 ready for the consumer. This saves packing time and eliminates extra handling of the glasses which might result in breakage. The cartons are attractive enough for gift wrapping also.

To aid the customer in understanding and appreciating the quality of the glassware, you should ask the customer to feel the smooth edge, a sign of good workmanship. Hold the glass to the light and point out the brilliant luster of the lead glass, or the softer glow of the lime glass. If it is lead glass you are selling, tap the edge of the glass carefully with your thumbnail or a pencil and ask the customer to listen to the tone. For contrast tap a lime glass and let her hear the difference. If she is purchasing crystal glassware, point out the fact that the lack of color or of cloudy or green tints means that the purest ingredients and finest mixing have been used in that glass. If the glassware is colored, mention the richness, the brilliance of the color. If only the design is colored, explain the method used and show the customer how it increases the beauty of the glass.

If the glass is hand cut, hold it up so the light is reflected by the cutting. Point out the beauty, gracefulness, proportion, and brilliance. If it is plate etched, stress the beauty and handwork necessary. Explain to the customer how difficult it is to make glassware "perfect." Make her feel proud of the glassware she is to own. If the manufacturer's name is on the glass, stress the quality standards his trademark represents. All these factors the customer will look for and the salesperson must be ready to point out.

CARE OF GLASSWARE

In addition to calling attention to the beauty and durability of an article, the glassware salesperson should advise the customer on the best methods of caring for her glassware. This, of course, is made easier if the department itself reflects the gleaming brightness of well-cared-for glassware. It is very difficult to sell the idea of beauty with a finger-smeared glass held before a fastidious customer.

Much of the inherent beauty of glassware depends on its sparkle. The plainest glass thoroughly cleansed and polished will reflect light attractively. Mild soapsuds or commercial detergents remove grease and other dirt. For cut glass, a small brush is necessary to cleanse all the grooves thoroughly. The glasses should then be rinsed in warm water and protected when placed on the drainboard by the use of a pad or folded towel. A good-quality linen towel that does not shed lint will give the requisite sparkle to the glass. Rubbing the glass with tissue paper will impart added sparkle.

The way the glass is handled while it is being dried is important. A lady had just received a gift of some exquisite glasses. When her sister offered to dry the dishes for her after dinner one evening, she warned her, "Be specially careful of these glasses. They are my pride and joy." The next day she noticed that every glass that had been used the night before had a bad scratch on the inside. Her sister had been careful in drying the glasses, but she had neglected to remove her diamond ring, and it had scratched the glasses wherever it touched them.

Glasses should never be stacked one inside the other, for there is danger of breakage. Glasses should stand upright on the shelves.

Avoid extremes of temperature in using glassware. Even heat-resistant glass should be heated or cooled with running water before being placed in the oven or the refrigerator. If glass cups are used for serving tea or coffee, pouring the hot liquid against a silver spoon placed in the cup lessens the danger of breakage.

The customer appreciates the interest you take in her purchase when you advise her about the proper care of her new glassware.

PUTTING THIS MERCHANDISE KNOWLEDGE TO USE ❯❯❯❯❯❯❯❯❯❯

❯ DO YOU KNOW YOUR MERCHANDISE?

1. Explain the following methods of decorating glassware: hand cutting, hand polishing, copper-wheel engraving, needle etching, plate etching, sandblasting.
2. What is a crystal glass? What is the best color for a crystal glass?
3. Define cased glass, flashed glass, cold gilt process, silver depositware.
4. What is the difference between stemware and tumblers? between tumblers and footed tumblers? If a customer wanted glassware for a formal occasion, what would you suggest? What is appropriate for semiformal service? for informal service?
5. What are the advantages of prepackaging glassware?
6. What advice should a customer be given about cleansing glassware? about wiping glassware? about stacking glassware? about extremes of temperature for glassware?

❯ INTERESTING THINGS TO DO

1. Prepare a sales talk on glassware. Bring samples of different kinds of glass to class for your demonstration.
2. Read advertisements in newspapers and magazines on glass. Copy selling points or technical terms from these advertisements. Be prepared to explain these terms.
3. Look up information in the library on one of the following topics and write a short theme about the company or product you studied: Venetian glass, Sandwich glass, Steuben glass.

ADDITIONAL MERCHANDISE TERMS ❯❯❯❯❯❯❯❯❯❯❯❯❯❯❯❯❯❯❯❯

Beveled mirror is a plate-glass mirror with the edges cut at an angle. This gives a finished look to the mirror and, of course, adds to its cost. Since this beveled edge is seldom put on mirrors other than those of good quality, people have come to associate beveled edges with quality mirrors.

Bubble glass is made by pricking a layer of glass and then superimposing another glass layer which traps the air in the depressions forming artistic bubbles.

Bulletproof glass is safety glass with three, five, or seven layers of glass, with plastic substances between each layer.

Carved glass is designed by being deeply sandblasted. Glass is not actually carved.

Champagne glass is a glass with a rather shallow wide bowl and a long hollow stem that permits the bubbles of the champagne to rise to the surface of the glass.

Coaster is a small flat saucer just large enough to hold the base of a glass. Used to keep contents of a glass from spilling on furniture.

Crackle glass is glass with hundreds of fine lines on the surface caused by plunging hot glass into cold water. The outer surface of the glass contracts and gives an attractive crackled effect.

Decanter is an attractively shaped bottle used to hold liqueurs.

Flint glass is a term synonymous with *lead* glass. It was originally used in England where lead glass was developed.

Glass bricks are building blocks made of two sections of cast glass fused together, developed in 1931. The partial vacuum created on the inside of the block forms an insulation that aids in keeping the room temperature comfortable. The diffused light that enters through the blocks is pleasant to work by because it eliminates possibilities of glare.

Hobnail glass is Early American style of glass made in molds that leave bumpy raised ball-like effects on the surface of the glass.

One-way vision glass has a very thin film of silver coated on one side of the glass. Looking from a dark room into a lighted room through such glass, one can see objects clearly. It appears like ordinary glass with a blue cast. However, looking from a lighted room to a dark one, one sees only reflections, for the thin silver coating acts as a mirror.

Optic glass is glassware blown into a mold that has lines along the sides. After removing the glass from the mold, the blower may continue to enlarge the size of the glass by blowing again. The lines become rather indistinct, but they add a sparkle to the glass. Sometimes the glass may be swirled so the lines curve around the glass. This is known as *swirled optic*. It also gives added sparkle to the glass.

Parfait glasses usually are V-shaped, deep, slender bowls with short stem and foot, used for fancy frozen desserts.

Pricking is a process of pushing the bottom of the glass in with a blunt instrument after the glass has been formed. The sides of this depression form a base on which the glass stands.

Rock crystal is a semiprecious stone—transparent, colorless quartz which is mined from the earth. It is used for such things as "crystal balls" for crystal gazers, and for jewelry and small art objects. The term *rock crystal* should never be used in referring to glass, regardless of quality.

Saucer champagne is a glass with a rather shallow, wide bowl and a long stem which is not hollow. This glass is used for serving champagne and also as a sherbet glass for the serving of various desserts.

Sham bottom is a heavy glass bottom used on tumblers. These camouflage the amount of liquid held by the glass and aid in keeping the glass from tipping over.

Water goblet is a deep-bowled glass with short or long stem, used for the serving of water. Long-stemmed goblets are used for formal occasions.

Wine glass is a small glass with rather short stem for serving wines.

Wire glass is ordinary window glass with a wire net placed in the glass while it is still in the viscous state. This glass is used as ordinary translucent window glass. The wire net helps to prevent breakage of the glass. It is also called armored glass.

Silver and Other Metals for Tablewares

CHAPTER 29

UNIT 88 THE METALS AND ALLOYS USED

The white or silvery color of silver has appealed to people for many centuries as the attractive complement on the table to dishes and glassware. Occasionally, gold or gold-colored metals become fashionable. Today's retail store carries sterling silver, silver plate, and stainless steel in the white-colored metals and gold plate and a copper-aluminum alloy for gold-look tableware.

SILVER

Silver has many qualities that make it desirable for ornaments, serving dishes, and eating utensils. Examine a silver teaspoon or a silver bowl. The first thing you notice is the color of the article, which is so lustrous and lovely that metals and other substances having a similar appearance are called "silvery" in honor of it.

Look at the finish on the pieces of silver—some may have a mirrorlike shine. Others are duller and have a softer sheen. Both finishes are attractive, yet they give variety to the silverware we use.

Notice the difference in the shapes of dishes, or knives, forks, and spoons made of silver. Because silver is soft, it can be worked easily—it can be pounded into thin sheets or it can be drawn into a fine wire. Designs can be stamped, hammered, or engraved into it. It bends without breaking because it is not brittle.

Next time you eat with a silver spoon, notice that the taste of the food is not affected by the metal. Many other metals used in this way seem to affect the taste of the food.

Most of the world's supply of silver comes from Mexico and the United

States. Canada, Peru, and Australia are the other important silver-producing countries. The people of the United States manufacture more silver articles and use more silverware than the people in any other country. Because it is readily available, its cost is only a fraction of the price of gold and platinum. Silver ranges around $1 an ounce while gold is $35 an ounce and platinum is about $80 an ounce.

The price of silverware items, however, may be quite costly or inexpensive depending on how much silver is used and how detailed and intricate the workmanship on the ware is.

Silver is used in the United States in three forms: as *sterling,* as *coin* silver, or as *plating.* Because of its softness, silver must be mixed with copper to form it into a useful *alloy* or it may be used to coat (plate) over base metals.

Sterling Silver

In order to make *solid* silver articles hard and firm so that they will be strong, will not dent very easily, and will really be useful, it is necessary to combine the silver with another metal. This combining of two or more metals is known as *alloying.* The metals are melted and mixed together the way ingredients for a cake are mixed. The ingredients must be carefully measured to insure the desired results. Copper is the metal added to silver which makes it firm and durable, without affecting its beauty and workability. *Sterling silver* is an alloy containing 925 parts of silver and 75 parts of copper. It is usually referred to as being 92½ per cent silver and 7½ per cent copper.

The name *sterling* comes, so history tells us, from the English in the twelfth century who referred to the Germanic traders who came to their ports from the East as *easterlings.* The coins these *easterlings* brought to England were of unusually fine quality, and they were known as *easterling coins.* Later this word, through usage, was shortened to *sterling* and came to signify a standard for quality in silver.

In 1906 the United States passed a law stating that articles stamped *sterling* must be 925 parts pure silver and 75 parts copper. Great Britain and Canada have the same standard. Sterling silver is also known as *solid* silver.

Although mixing silver with copper makes it considerably harder than pure silver, sterling silver articles must be quite thick if they are to hold up in use. One woman purchased a sterling salt-and-pepper set inexpensively. Two weeks later she noticed the set was dented in several places. Articles made of sterling silver can vary greatly in quality as well as in price—not because of any variation in the sterling itself, but because of thickness or thinness of the article. Since silver is so *malleable,* meaning that it can be rolled to paper thinness, manufacturers make inexpensive sterling articles very thin. Although these articles are attractive, they will dent or break rather easily. The durability of sterling, then, depends on the thickness of the article—the thicker the sterling, the more durable the article.

Sterling in varying thicknesses is used in making knives, forks, spoons, decorative items for the home, serving dishes, and jewelry.

Coin silver such as we use for dimes, quarters, and half dollars is an alloy containing 90 per cent silver and 10 per cent copper. Although this alloy is somewhat harder than sterling, it is not quite so workable or beautiful and, therefore, it is not used by manufacturers of tableware in the United States.

Sheffield Plate. In 1743, an Englishman accidentally discovered that with the aid of heat, silver could be rolled or coated (plated) on top of copper much as icing is spread on a cake. This was a revolutionary discovery because it meant that inexpensive base metals could be used to give a firm, heavy body, and the more expensive precious metal, silver, could be used as a coating only. Since this ware was made in Sheffield, England, it came to be known as *Sheffield plate*. Today all true Sheffield plate is classed as antique because this method of plating has not been in use since approximately 1840. Imitations of old Sheffield are sometimes advertised as "Sheffield designs," or "Sheffield reproductions."

Electroplating. In about the year 1840, a new process of coating base metals was developed known as *electroplating*. It was so far superior from the standpoint of speed, cost, and evenness of coating to the old method known as *Sheffield plate* that the latter was abandoned. Today all commercial silver-plated ware is made by the electroplating process.

Articles of the base metal to be silver coated are cleaned thoroughly by a succession of hot water, soap, chemical, and steam baths. The articles are then electroplated by being placed on a rack in a solution of silver cyanide, a salt of silver. Bars of pure silver in the tanks are decomposed by the electrical current which is run through the solution, and the pure silver particles are evenly deposited on the base-metal knives, forks, spoons, ornaments, or bowls.

The Electroplating Process. The current carries the metal from the anode (in this case the bar of pure silver) and deposits it in a uniform coating on the cathode (the spoons to be plated).

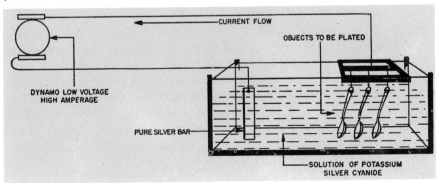

BASE METALS OR ALLOYS USED FOR SILVER-PLATING. *Nickel silver,* an alloy containing no silver, made by mixing nickel, copper, and zinc together in varying proportions, is considered the best base to use under silver-plating. It is the whitest, hardest base used. If the silver wears away, the alloy underneath is similar in color. The mark "EPNS" seen on the back of some silver-plated products means "electroplated on a nickel silver base."

White or Britannia metal, also silvery colored, is made by mixing tin, antimony, and copper together. This alloy is softer than nickel silver, dents and bends easily, and melts at a low temperature; it is therefore not nearly so durable. It is much too soft for flatware use. It is used for complicated shapes of holloware articles, such as spouts, knobs, and handles, and for decorative edges and borders on such articles as trays and coffeepots. Articles shaped of this metal may be stamped "EPWM" which means "electroplated over white metal."

Copper was the first metal used as a base for plating, and for that reason some people prefer silver-plated holloware with a copper base. Silver adheres to copper very well, but when the silver wears off, the reddish color of the copper shows through. Copper, being soft, dents considerably more easily than nickel silver does. It is therefore not used for flatware items. Holloware articles made with a copper base may be stamped "EPC," meaning "electroplated over copper."

Brass, an alloy of copper and zinc, may be used as the base of inexpensive silver-plated holloware. Brass shows yellow-colored metal when the silver begins to wear away, and the brass so exposed may turn green and be unusable.

Steel, made from refined iron and carbon, may be used for the poorest quality silver-plated products. Since silver is porous, the steel may rust through the silver coating. Silver does not plate smoothly and evenly over this poor quality base.

STAINLESS STEEL

First developed in 1915, stainless steel was then used only for kitchen utensils and cutlery in the home. Chemists discovered that the addition of a minimum of 11½ per cent chromium made the steel resistant to staining and rusting. Addition of more chromium improved its resistance and made it more attractive. Then they discovered that the addition of nickel further improved the whiteness and appearance as well as the durability of the stainless-steel product.

Today, qualities in stainless steel range from those having a minimum of 11½ per cent chromium to those having as much as 18 per cent. Some also have from 4 per cent to 8 per cent nickel content. The finest stainless steel used in knives, forks, and spoons is known as "18–8." This contains 18 per cent chromium, 8 per cent nickel and 74 per cent steel. This quality stainless steel most closely resembles silver in color.

It is fairly easy to determine whether or not a stainless steel contains nickel. In general, steel with nickel content will not be attracted by a magnet, while stainless steel made with just the addition of chromium will be attracted by a magnet.

Because stainless steel is so hard that it does not scratch or dent easily, and because it does not tarnish, rust, or stain, customers have begun to use it in the home in place of inexpensive silver-plated products. Designers of stainless steel have worked with the metal to develop attractive, eye-appealing shapes, and this has further increased the sales of this product for home use. Stainless steel ranges in price from very inexpensive to equally as costly as the finest silver plate.

GOLD-COLORED WARES

While pure gold may be plated over base metals or over sterling silver for tablewares, and gold alloys may also be used, few stores in the country carry such costly products. For customers who want gold-colored tableware, an aluminum, copper, nickel alloy trade-named "Dirilyte"[1] is available. This is a durable, attractive product that does not tarnish or scratch easily.

PUTTING THIS MERCHANDISE KNOWLEDGE TO USE ❯ ❯ ❯ ❯ ❯ ❯ ❯ ❯ ❯

❯ DO YOU KNOW YOUR MERCHANDISE?

1. Where does our main supply of silver come from? What is the cost of silver in comparison to the cost of gold and platinum?
2. What are the two basic factors that determine the price of a silverware article?
3. Differentiate between silver plate and sterling silver.
4. What determines the quality of sterling silver? Why do some sterling articles dent?
5. What are the qualities that have made silver famous for tablewares?
6. Explain Sheffield plate, Sheffield design, electroplate.
7. What base metals are used for silver-plated articles? Which is the best? Why?
8. What is nickel silver? Why do you think it is called by that name?
9. Why do customers like a copper base for silver-plated products?
10. What is stainless steel? How can you determine if stainless steel contains nickel? Why do customers like stainless steel?

❯ INTERESTING THINGS TO DO

1. Use a magnet on the stainless-steel articles in your home. Record the results. Do you think any of the stainless contained nickel? Why?
2. Visit a local store and look at their silverware department. Make a list of the kinds of products you see (sterling silver, silver plate, stainless steel, and so forth). Did you notice any difference in the appearance of these products? Which would you like for your home for everyday use? for company occasions?

[1] A product of the American Art Alloy Company.

UNIT 89 FLATWARE

Metal products for the table may be used as flatware or as holloware. *Flatware* refers to knives, forks, and spoons; *holloware,* to such items as bowls, plates, platters, pitchers, and vases.

HOW FLATWARE IS MADE

All flatware, whether sterling, silver-plated, stainless steel, or gold-colored alloy, follows somewhat similar basic processes. Originally, laborious hand-shaped methods were used. Today handcrafted flatware is rare. Mass production of these products using large, powerful machines is most common.

Before a piece can be made, the manufacturer must decide on the shape into which it will be formed and what design, if any, will be placed on it. Since the appearance of the flatware will affect the retail customer's desire to buy, the manufacturer selects the shapes and designs to be used very carefully. Often, polls are taken among young girls to see what patterns they might like when they begin to select their silver.

The outlines of the flatware shapes and any designs to be impressed on the handles must first be cut into very hard steel dies. These dies are then forced against the metal being shaped with such pressure that they cut it to the desired shape. Other dies impress the designs in a similar fashion.

Inexpensive forks and spoons are stamped into final shape from rather thin sheets of metal. The tip of the handle, the arch near the bowl, called the *shank,* and the bowl itself are all the same thickness. These forks and spoons bend easily under pressure and give poor service in use.

Better quality forks and spoons are first cut into chunky T-shaped *blanks* by huge steel dies, much as cookies are stamped with a cookie cutter. These T-shaped blanks are then thinned toward the end of the handle and across the bowl by rolling under pressure. The now *graded* (thick in some sections and thin in others) blank is cut into final form, stamped with dies that impart designs (except for plain patterns), arched for needed shaping, and trimmed so it is the correct size, shape, and thickness for durability and ease of handling. The prongs (tines) of forks are cut to shape and, in good quality flatware, are carefully finished later to make the edges smooth and round.

Knives may have hollow handles or flat handles. Flat-handled knives are usually inexpensive. Hollow handles are most costly to make. They may be stamped in two sections, the design stamped on each section, and then joined together by soldering with hot metal. Some hollow-handled knives are made without this soldered seam by repeatedly drawing the metal into a tubelike form. This makes a watertight handle. Knife blades usually made from stainless steel are then soldered into the hollow handle. These blades may be sharpened for a better cutting edge.

Die Making. The skilled die maker must cut each delicate detail of the design by hand out of the finest tool steel. It is slow, painstaking labor where one false move will ruin the work of days. *(Courtesy Oneida Ltd.)* ❯

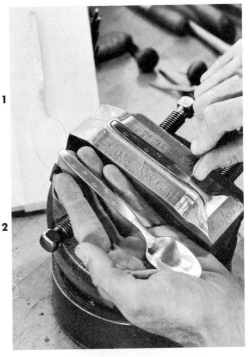

 ❮1

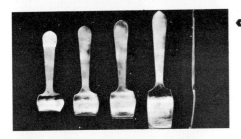 ❮2

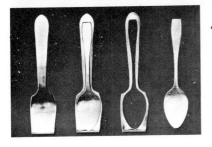 ❮3

 4❯

5❯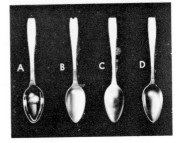

1. Powerful presses cut the "blanks" from a sheet of strong metal.

2. The "blanks" are then repeatedly rolled to give the proper length, width, and "contour," thinner at the bowl and end of the handle, thicker in the middle of the handle to resist bending.

3. The rolled blanks are then "cut to outline."

4. The pattern, or design, is applied by steel dies held in drop hammers which exert many tons pressure. Pieces are then "trimmed," "polished" and "buffed."

5. In the case of silverplate, the polished nickel silver spoon (A) is carefully cleaned with powerful chemicals and plated overall (B). Next it is overlaid (C), given an extra plate of solid silver on the area of wear to provide a balanced plate that gives years of extra service. Finally the spoon is finished (D), given a rigid inspection, wrapped in soft tissue and boxed. The polishing operations for stainless tableware are very similar except that it is, of course, not plated. *(Courtesy Oneida Ltd.)*

Careful workmanship in flatware items may be determined by the varied thicknesses of the metal, called *grading,* by the smooth edges of the spoons, the polished surfaces between the tines of the forks, and the smooth, hard-to-detect joining of the two halves of knife handles or by seamless handles. Knife blades used on quality products are carefully shaped by *forging,* pounding into desired thickness. These have thicker sections near the handle, called the *bolster,* and thinner blade sections for cutting.

Sterling Flatware

Sterling flatware is selected for the beauty of the article and for the weight of each piece. Different manufacturers use varying thicknesses of sterling to shape the original blanks. The heavier weights are more expensive but last much longer. Since sterling is easily worked, elegant and elaborate designs may be used. If they require much care in hand finishing and polishing, the price will be increased.

Silver-Plated Flatware

For silver-plated flatware, nickel silver is used for the blanks that are shaped into the finished forks, spoons, or knife handles. The nickel silver is then cleaned and polished because any speck of oil or dust will cause subsequent silver-plating to be imperfect. The articles are then attached to a rack and placed in a silver-plating bath where they remain until the requisite amount of silver has adhered to the base metal. They are then removed, polished, inspected, and wrapped ready for the consumer.

The quality of this plated flatware will depend on the type of workmanship and the amount of silver used to cover the base metal. Also, the thickness of the base metal itself will add to the durability of the flatware.

The amount of silver used on flatware determines whether it is *single plate, double plate, triple plate,* or *quadruple plate.* This refers to the thickness of the plate, not the number of times it was coated with silver. Thus, quadruple plate means the silver coating is four times as thick as single plate. The following chart shows the amount of silver applied to a gross of teaspoons. Forks, tablespoons, and other larger items have more silver applied based on this ratio:

	Grade	Silver Applied per Gross of Teaspoons
Al	single plate or standard	2 ounces
AA	double A	3 ounces
XX	double plate	4 ounces
XXX	triple plate	6 ounces
XXXX	quadruple plate	8 ounces

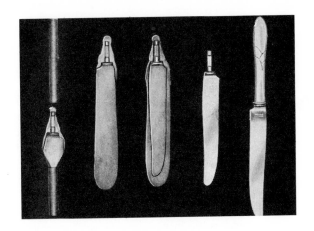

Forming the Knife Blade. A bar of stainless steel is heated red hot, and under powerful machines the bolster is *forged*. Then the blade is again heated and rolled out to the proper thickness. The finished blade is polished and soldered into the hollow handle. *(Courtesy Oneida Ltd.)*

Inexpensive, unmarked flatware is known as ¼ *standard* (one-quarter the amount of silver is used to coat a gross of teaspoons that is used for single plate) or ½ *standard* (one ounce of silver per gross of teaspoons). These are not only sparsely plated over a thin base, but they also lack fine workmanship in their manufacture. Tines of forks, for example, are not polished, and the base metal is not graded in thickness for utmost beauty and serviceability. They usually sell for 10 to 20 cents apiece.

Since customers are usually sold by trade name rather than by the grade of the product, only careful examination of the product and questioning of the salesperson will help to determine the quality.

Reinforcements. Examine the backs of several different teaspoons. Some better quality silver-plated flatware has a reinforcement of silver at the points of greatest wear on the most used pieces: teaspoons, dinner forks, soup spoons, and salad forks. The reinforced parts are at the bottom of the bowl and the tip of the handle where the article touches when it rests on the table.

This reinforcement may be an inlay or an overlay. The *inlay* is made by scooping a bit of metal out of the nickel-silver blank at these points and filling the space with sterling silver. The overall plating covers this reinforcement. Only Holmes & Edwards now uses the inlay method of reinforcement.

Most manufacturers use the *overlay* method. This is done after the plating by giving an extra coat of plating to the two points of wear on the flatware. The inlay does not show on the surface of the spoon, but the overlay leaves a slight ring at those two points. Since both of these methods add considerably to the durability of the silverware, they are desirable features to point out to the customer.

Some manufacturers use a plus sign (+) to indicate that the silver has an overlay. Thus, A1+ means single-plated ware with an overlay on the most used pieces.

Stainless-Steel and Gold-colored Alloy Flatware

Like sterling silver, stainless steel and the gold-colored alloy used for flatware require no plating. They differ, however, from sterling because they are so hard that it is difficult to impress any designs on the surface of the wares. Most manufacturers rely on interesting forms for these products rather than embossing fancy patterns on their surfaces.

Quality in these products is determined by thickness, grading, and fineness of finish along the edges of spoons and tines of forks.

HOW FLATWARE IS SOLD

Inexpensive flatware is popularly sold in sets and open stock. Sets of silverware come in various sizes and accommodate various numbers of people. Sets for 6, 8, and 12 are popular. All sets contain dinner (or dessert-size) knives and forks, and teaspoons in addition to other pieces.

Many people purchase a set of flatware and then wish later on to add pieces such as serving spoons, pie servers, tomato servers. These are purchased from open stock. Most silver-plated patterns are available from open stock for a number of years to permit the customer to fill in and replenish lost pieces.

Expensive flatware is popularly sold in open stock, place settings, and sets.

When a young couple first starts housekeeping, they may be unable to afford an entire set of sterling flatware or fine stainless; so they may purchase their flatware in place settings. These consist of six pieces: a dessert-size knife and fork, teaspoon, cream-soup spoon (or two teaspoons), salad fork, and butter spreader. Each additional setting allows them to set a complete place for another person. Serving pieces may then be added from open stock. Sets of sterling silver are also available as they are in plated ware.

Occasionally a retailer will advertise a five-piece place setting. He then prices the butter spreader separately.

ITEMS IN FLATWARE

A customer ordered a fork to match her sterling pattern. "Did you wish the dessert fork or the dinner fork?" the salesgirl asked.

"Oh, my—the *dinner* fork, of course," the customer replied.

When she opened the package at home and compared the fork she had just purchased, she found it was quite a bit larger than the forks in her set. She had not realized until then that she owned a set of so-called "dessert" forks. Since they resemble the dinner fork in every respect except for a slight difference in the length of the tines of the fork and the length of the handle, it is easy to confuse the two. The dessert fork is used by many people who prefer its daintier size to that of the main dinner fork.

It is important that the salesperson know the names and uses of all the various knives, forks, spoons, and serving pieces. Customers often want to know how certain pieces of flatware should be used and what their proper names are. A list of the more popular items is given below.

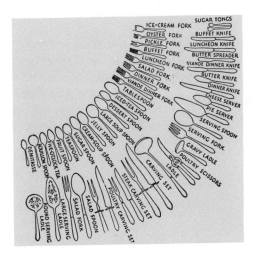

Types of Flatware. *(Courtesy Manchester Silver Co.)*

Knives

1. *Dinner Knife*. This is a regular-sized knife with knife blade that may be sharpened. This is used by the individual for cutting meat and vegetables.

2. *Viande Knife* (*grille*). This knife is the same length as the dinner knife, but with a short blade and a very long handle. It permits the forefinger to rest on the knife handle instead of the blade. It is used for cutting such things as steaks.

3. *Dessert or Luncheon Knife*. This is a slightly smaller knife than the dinner knife. It is used for luncheon service and is also used in some cases in place of the dinner knife.

4. *Fruit Knife*. This is a small knife with a sharp blade suitable for cutting and peeling fruit.

5. *Butter Knife*. This is a medium-sized knife used for cutting and serving butter.

6. *Butter Spreader*. This is a small individual knife with a blunt blade used by the individual for spreading butter on bread or rolls.

Forks

1. *Dinner Fork*. This large fork is used for dinner service with the dinner knife.

2. *Viande Fork* (*grille*). The short tines and long handle on this fork match the short blade and long handle of the viande knife.

3. *Dessert or Luncheon Fork*. This smaller-sized fork is used for luncheon or dinner service.

4. *Salad Fork or Pastry Fork*. This is a short fork with short tines. Used for salads and also popularly used for cake and pies.

5. *Ice-Cream Fork*. This fork is a cross between a fork and a spoon. It has a small bowl with short blunt tines on the end useful for eating ice cream.

6. *Cocktail or Oyster Fork*. This is a fork with a short, thin handle and three short tines. It is used for eating shrimp, clam, and oyster cocktails.

Spoons

1. *Teaspoon.* This is the regulation oval-shaped spoon.
2. *After-Dinner Coffee Spoon.* This small spoon is shaped like the teaspoon. It is appropriate for use with demitasse cups.
3. *Oval Bowl or Dessert Spoon.* This spoon is shaped like the teaspoon, but much larger. It is used mainly for eating soup and cereal in this country.
4. *Tablespoon.* This spoon is shaped like an oval-bowl spoon but considerably larger. It is used for eating spaghetti and for serving vegetables.
5. *Bouillon Spoon.* This spoon is about the size of a teaspoon, but with a round bowl. It is used to eat soup served in bouillon cups.
6. *Cream-Soup Spoon.* This larger spoon with a round-shaped bowl is used with cream, onion, and puree soup dishes.
7. *Round Bowl Soup Spoon.* This large spoon is shaped like the cream-soup spoon and is used with coupe soup or rim soup dishes.
8. *Iced-Tea Spoon.* This is like a teaspoon but has a long handle. It is used for stirring drinks served in tall glasses.
9. *Orange or Fruit Spoon.* This spoon is shaped like a teaspoon with a sharp pointed end useful in eating fruit served in the rind.
10. *Salt Spoon.* This tiny spoon is used for serving salt from an open salt dish.

Serving Pieces

1. *Jelly Server.* The flat edge on the side of the bowl of this server is used to cut and serve jelly.
2. *Pie Server.* The long, blunt, triangular-shaped blade is used to cut and serve pie and cake.
3. *Tomato Server.* The round, flat bowl is pierced to allow juice to drip through before serving sliced tomatoes and other sliced foods.
4. *Lemon Fork.* This is a short fork with two or three long narrow tines that are useful in serving sliced lemon.
5. *Cold-meat Fork.* This large serving fork is used for meats and salads.
6. *Berry Spoon.* This large serving spoon with rounded bowl is used for serving vegetables, fruits, and salads.
7. *Bonbon Spoon.* This small spoon with flattened pierced bowl is used for serving nuts and candies.
8. *Gravy Ladle.* This has a deep round bowl and a bent handle for use in serving gravy from sauceboat.
9. *Sugar Tongs.* These are like small pincers which are used for serving lump sugar.

HOW TO SHOW FLATWARE IN USE

Since display of these wares in a store helps to sell them and also illustrates their proper use in a home, every salesperson needs to know the general rules for placing flatware items on the table.

Rule 1. Knives and spoons go to the right of the plate and forks are placed on the left. The oyster fork, however, when not served on the plate is placed at the extreme right of the knives and spoons.

Rule 2. All knives, forks, and spoons are placed with the handles even one inch from the edge of the table. The cutting edge of the knife should be placed toward the plate.

Rule 3. All flatware items are placed in the order in which they will be used from the outside going toward the plate. Thus, if soup is to be served first, the soup spoon will be at the extreme right.

Rule 4. It is preferable not to place more than three pieces of silver on either side of a plate. If more pieces are needed, as for dessert, they may be brought in at the time dessert is served.

Rule 5. Butter spreaders when used are usually placed on or near the butter dish, which is at the upper left above the dinner plate.

Rule 6. Serving pieces may be placed on or near the dishes with which they will be used.

PUTTING THIS MERCHANDISE KNOWLEDGE TO USE ❯❯❯❯❯❯❯❯❯❯

❯ DO YOU KNOW YOUR MERCHANDISE?

1. Define flatware, holloware.
2. Explain briefly how flatware articles are made.
3. What is meant by single plate? triple plate? ½ standard plate?
4. Explain how flatware is sold. What is meant by place setting? open stock?
5. Explain the uses of the following: dessert knife, viande knife, butter knife, salad fork, ice-cream fork, dessert spoon, orange spoon, pie server, berry spoon.
6. In setting a table, on what side of the plate do the following pieces go: dinner knife? soup spoon? salad fork? oyster fork?
7. What is the maximum number of flatware items that should be placed at each place at the start of the meal?
8. Explain what makes some flatware items more costly than others.

❯ INTERESTING THINGS TO DO

1. Prepare a 2-minute sales talk for a flatware pattern. If possible, bring a piece of flatware to class to use as demonstration.
2. Bring knives, forks, and spoons from home and give the class a demonstration of incorrect and correct table settings.
3. Visit a store that sells flatware. Write a short theme telling how they displayed the flatware, what color backgrounds were used, how many table settings were on display, and how many flatware patterns were shown in boxes as complete sets. Explain which display method you liked best and tell why.

UNIT 90 HOLLOWARE

Bowls, trays, plates, and other holloware items may be made entirely by hand; or mass-production manufacturing methods may be used. Since holloware items do not have to be used as often as flatware, and since they do not need to be as strong as flatware items, the machinery to make them is less costly. Consequently, many more factories are able to make holloware items.

HOW HOLLOWARE IS MADE

In the handcraft classes in your school, some students may be shaping metal objects. Holloware is made by hand in a similar fashion. Of course, such methods are costly and are only used in a few factories in the United States today.

Most holloware is made by mass production by *stamping, spinning,* or *casting.* Some metals may be formed in one way, some in another.

Stamping shapes the metal to be used (sterling, stainless steel, base metal to be plated, and so forth) by squeezing the metal between shaped pieces of steel that keep pounding against it until the form has been completed. This is the most common method used for shaping holloware.

Spinning is used for small numbers of items where dies would be too costly to construct; however, only pliable, rather soft metals can be shaped by spinning. Thus, sterling silver and copper, the latter to be silver-plated, are the metals usually formed by spinning. To shape the metal, a flat sheet is placed against a wooden mold that is turning in a lathe. The workman forces a smooth steel rod against the sheet of metal as it turns, and it slowly molds to the form underneath. This is a hand-guided operation and thus is fairly costly.

Casting is used for complicated shapes, such as trophies, fancy borders, and handles. To cast, the metal must first be melted and then poured into a mold. While it is possible to melt and cast sterling, this process is usually limited to low-melting metals, such as white metal that will later be silver-plated.

After the article has been shaped, edges rounded, turned under, or reinforced with a simple or ornate border, and the handles joined, the metal is cleaned and polished.

Sterling Silver Holloware

Barbara Moore was asked by the floor superintendent to relieve in the silverware department during the noon hour because two of the regular salespeople were away. The first customer whom Barbara approached asked, "Why is this sugar and creamer so much more expensive than this other set?

Spinning. This is a method of shaping pieces of silver holloware by revolving a flat disc of silver over a mold made in the shape the silver is to assume. By means of a tool, the silver is spread over the form. *(Courtesy Wallace Silversmiths)*

They are both sterling!" Barbara tried to figure out an answer. She examined them both. Both sets were the same size, and when she lifted them, they appeared to weigh the same. Barbara looked very puzzled. "Well," exclaimed the customer who was obviously annoyed, "It's plain to see you don't know anything about the merchandise!" and she walked off in a huff.

When Barbara asked one of the regular salesgirls why the prices were so different, she was told that one set was a heavy or thick gauge of silver, and thus needed no weighting. The other set contained hollow bottoms that were filled with cement thus making them appear to be as good as the better sugar and creamer.

As Barbara learned, lightweight sterling holloware items may have a *weighted base.* This is formed by making the bottom of the item in a hollow shell-like form, then filling it with cement or pitch. This makes the article feel much heavier, and also gives it a sturdy base. Weighted articles must always be stamped *weighted* or *reinforced.* Heavy-gauge sterling articles do not need to be weighted.

The price of sterling holloware depends on the *thickness* of the sterling used, the size of the article, the workmanship and type of ornamentation.

Silver-Plated Holloware

Nickel silver, copper, white metal, and brass for better quality wares and steel for inexpensive wares are the metals and alloys used for the bases of silver-plated holloware. Since these metals are all relatively inexpensive, they may be made heavy enough to balance well and to feel sturdy. Thus no weighting is ever used in silver-plated items.

After the base materials have been shaped by stamping, spinning, or casting, and after the various parts have been soldered together, the metal is cleaned and polished and prepared for plating. The objects are then suspended in the silver-plating bath and the required amount of pure silver deposited thereon. There are no standards of single, double, or triple plate in holloware. The more costly the piece for its size, usually the thicker the silver plating.

Stainless-Steel Holloware

Customers have been reluctant to use stainless steel in place of sterling or silver plate for holloware until recently. As stainless steel has become more silvery in appearance and as the manufacturers have made more attractive bowls, plates, and trays, demand for these items has increased. Since this metal is much more difficult to work with than sterling or the base metals used for silver plate, fewer fancy designs and elaborate motifs have been made. The majority of stainless-steel holloware is made by stamping into rather plain shapes. Of course, no weighting is ever used in these products.

HOW HOLLOWARE IS SOLD

Holloware is usually purchased by the piece, although it may also be available in sets. Matching pieces to be sold as open stock are also made by the manufacturers. There are many popular holloware items.

Candelabra. These are candlesticks with two or more branches.

Candlesticks. These range in height up to 10 or 15 inches.

Centerpieces. These are large bowls with a deep center and a wide curved rim. They are used with a rack for flowers, or without a rack as fruit bowls.

Coffee and Tea Services. These include a coffeepot, teapot, sugar and creamer, and sometimes a *waste bowl* and waiter; they are popular in silver for serving at formal afternoon teas.

Compotes. These are short-stemmed and long-stemmed candy and nut bowls.

Console Sticks. These short candlesticks are sold in pairs. Used with a centerpiece or bowl, they form a *console set.*

Creamers and Sugars. These are sold as a set with or without a matching tray. Most sugar bowls have lids.

Gravy Boats. These are short, elongated lipped servers that may have a separate matching tray or that may be attached to a tray.

Guernsey Jugs. Small hot-water jugs for use with teapots are available in silver.

Plates. In various sizes these are used as service plates, salad or dessert plates, bread-and-butter plates, and for cake and cookie service.

Platters. Small and large, oblong, round, and square platters, which are useful in serving meats, salads and as trays are available in silver.

Salt-and-Pepper Shakers. Matching salt-and-pepper shakers for individual service or for use in the center of the table are available. Since silver is adversely affected by salt, open salt cellars with glass liners and tiny spoons for serving the salt are also available. These have regular pepper shakers to match.

Sherbet Dishes. These individual stemmed servers are available with or without glass liners. They are used for serving ice cream, sherbet, fruit, or seafood cocktails.

Vegetable Dishes. These are one of the most popular items in silverware. The covered vegetable dish that has a removable cover that may be turned upside down and also used as a vegetable dish is especially popular. Some vegetable dishes have a removable insert dividing the dish into two or three sections, so that it can be used for serving more than one vegetable.

Waiters and Trays. Large oblong, round, and square trays are known as *waiters.* These are used for serving such things as *hors d'oeuvres,* iced drinks, or for tea and coffee services. Smaller trays are used for bread, sandwiches, pickles, and so on.

Water Pitchers. Tall pitchers to hold water, milk, or iced drinks are available. Some have a special rim across the pouring spout called an *ice lip.* This is useful in pouring the liquid while keeping the ice in the pitcher.

PUTTING THIS MERCHANDISE KNOWLEDGE TO USE ❯❯❯❯❯❯❯❯❯❯

❯ DO YOU KNOW YOUR MERCHANDISE?

1. Explain the difference between flatware and holloware.
2. Explain the following terms: stamping, spinning, casting.
3. What is a weighted base in sterling holloware? Why are silverplate and stainless steel not weighted? When does a sterling holloware piece have weighting? How would the customer know a piece of holloware was weighted?
4. Do you think stainless-steel holloware will grow in popularity in years to come? Give reasons for your answer.
5. Explain the uses of the following: compotes, guernsey jugs, waiters.
6. What are the differences among the following: candelabra, candlesticks, console sticks, console set?
7. Why are glass liners used in some salt dishes?

❯ INTERESTING THINGS TO DO

1. A customer is looking for a wedding present and is willing to spend around $25. Prepare a sales talk for a sterling bowl that sells for $20 plus tax.
2. Repeat project 1 using a coffee service in silver plate for $25.

UNIT 91 DESIGNS, FINISHES, AND CARE OF FLATWARE AND HOLLOWARE

IMPORTANCE OF DESIGN ON FLATWARE AND HOLLOWARE

"Which pattern do you like?" the young bride asked her husband as they stood at the silverware counter.

"I don't know anything about those things—you decide."

The bride looked perplexed and examined the articles again. She just could not decide which she preferred.

Each flatware manufacturer makes several different patterns in the same quality flatware. Some may have as many as ten or twenty patterns from which to choose. When this number is multiplied by 20 or 30 manufacturers, it is no wonder the customer has a difficult time deciding among the vast number of designs she sees. Some patterns are available in matching hollo-ware lines. Occasionally, the pattern is used for chinaware and glassware too.

Since silver scratches rather easily, most manufacturers like to put some design on the silver, because this prevents the scratches from showing so noticeably. When people do purchase perfectly plain silverware, they often have a monogram engraved on the silver to give it a decorative surface and to prevent small scratches from showing too plainly.

Stainless steel and gold-colored alloys are so hard they are very resistant to scratches. This hardness also makes it difficult to put designs on the surface of these products.

HOW DESIGNS ARE APPLIED

Since the method of applying the design noticeably affects the price of the ware, it is important that the salesperson be acquainted with the methods used. Designs applied by hand require skilled workers and many man-hours of tedious, exacting artistic work. Even machine-made designs if well and attractively done require skill and much handwork in setting up the dies pre-paratory to stamping the design on the ware.

Some familiar methods of applying designs on metal products are described below.

Chasing

Beautiful designs are worked on the sterling silver or the copper base of plated wares by an artisan who taps sharp-pointed instruments against the surface of the silver and indents lines which outline the design. The metal is not removed; it is merely "pushed in" to form the design. This method of decoration is reproduced by machine by stamping the design in with steel dies.

Repoussé

This is the most expensive method of decorating silver by hand. Only ster-ling silver articles are usually decorated in this manner.

The artisan works the design from the *inside* of the dish giving a bas-relief or raised design on the surface of the silver. Tiny hammers are used to pound the silver and form the raised design. Often this is combined with chasing the outline of the design from the front. It is then known as *repoussé chasing.* Expensive coffee and tea sets, bowls, plates, and ornaments may have this

Left: Engraving. This is a process of hand decoration in which the surface of the metal is cut with engraving tools. The photograph shows a decorative scroll being engraved on the back of a mirror. **Right:** Engine Turning. This is a process of decorating by means of a machine-operated cutting tool controlled by a craftsman following a design that is cut into the metal from a master pattern or stencil. *(Courtesy Wallace Silversmiths)*

type of design applied. A machine-made replica of this is made by embossing the design on either sterling or plated ware by means of huge steel dies.

Engraving

Skilled workmen may cut a design into the metal's surface by means of sharp-pointed tools which gouge out the metal. Engraved designs may be applied at the factory, or the customer may have initials, coat of arms, or other insignia engraved on the item. Very thinly plated silverware or paper-thin sterling silver should not be engraved, for the sharp tools may scrape right through the silver.

Initials are popular on flatware and holloware. Popular styles are known as *script* which resembles handwriting, *block* which is plain and appropriate for modern designs, and *old English* which is rather ornate and suitable for period types of silver and more elaborate pieces.

Machine-controlled engraving known as *engine turning* puts geometric patterns on metal products.

Piercing

This is popular for both sterling silver and plated ware. It may be done by hand or machine on sterling and by machine only on plated ware.

Workmen using tiny saws and files may cut out designs or cutting dies may stamp holes in the ware. Edges of bowls and plates and the bowls of flatware pieces such as tomato and bonbon servers may have pierced designs.

Etching

Silver may be coated with wax which resists acid. A design is cut through the wax, and the article immersed in nitric acid. Where the silver is unprotected, it is attacked by the acid which etches or grooves out the design. The acid is then washed off and the wax removed. This method of decorating silver is infrequently used today.

Hammering

Tiny marks which give an attractive finish may be hammered onto the surface of the metal by hand or machine.

Embossing or Stamping

The design is first carefully engraved on steel plates or dies. These are placed in huge machines where tremendous pressure forces the pattern onto the object. Any metal may be given a design in this manner, but the softer metals take deeper, more attractive impressions. This is the process by which most flatware designs are applied.

HOW FINISHES ARE APPLIED

Not only is the beauty of form and design important to the customer, but the dull or shiny finish also affects her choice of metal products. A mirror-like finish known as *bright* is achieved by polishing the metal with brushes and buffing wheels. In silver, the main disadvantage of this highly polished surface is that tiny scratches will subsequently make it dull. Stainless steel and other hard alloys, however, maintain their bright finishes indefinitely.

Since silver does scratch rather easily, many people developed an appreciation for a duller finish which did not show fine scratches. This is called a *butler* or *gray* finish. The old silver that was polished repeatedly by butlers achieved this soft luster. In the factory this finish is applied by means of revolving brushes that scratch the surface. Since a dull finish on stainless steel makes it resemble old silver, dull finishes have become popular on that metal too.

Some silver holloware items may have the interior of bowls lined with a *gold wash,* a thin plating of pure gold that is applied by electroplating over the silver. This does not tarnish, but it will wear off in time.

FINISHES PREVENTING TARNISH

To prevent silver from tarnishing, European manufacturers developed a clear enamel finish that was baked on holloware items. This permitted them to be used for display, or for food service without discoloring. Scratches, however, would expose the silver and permit tarnishing. In time, the finish would wear away. Colored enamel finishes are baked inside some holloware.

In 1960 a new silicone finish (made from sand and oil) for silver holloware

This unretouched photo shows two silver pieces that were half treated with silicone finish over five years ago, and the treated side has not tarnished yet! (*Courtesy The Bron-Shoe Co.*)

articles was introduced. The silicone is applied as a very thin coating (1/10,000th of an inch thick). It cannot be seen, does not alter the appearance of the silver, is long lasting unless it is scratched, and it keeps the silver shiny and untarnished until it wears away. Even hot coffee can be served in silicone treated silver. The finish is used both on sterling and silver-plated holloware. "Siloxi" is a trade name for this finish.

CARE OF FLATWARE AND HOLLOWARE

Nearly every customer interested in purchasing silver says, "I love silver when it's new and shiny, but it *tarnishes* so badly!"

Fruit juices, ordinary acids, or foods do not discolor silver. It is, however, subject to discoloration by sulfur which may be present in the air, in eggs, and in rubber and some other materials. Leave a silver spoon in a soft-boiled egg for a few minutes. When you remove it, you notice that the spoon has become discolored. This is known as *tarnish* and is considered the only real objection to silver. Tarnish, while it does detract from the appearance of the silver until it is removed, has not really harmed the silver article. A chemical reaction takes place between the silver and the sulfur causing the formation of silver sulfide, a brown discoloration that leaves a stained appearance.

Removing Tarnish

Tarnish is easily rubbed off with any good silver polish and a soft cloth. Ornate designs may be cleaned by first dipping a soft brush in the polish and using it on the grooved portions of the design, then cleaning the entire article with a soft cloth. The silver is then washed and dried thoroughly.

Tarnish may also be removed by placing the silver to be cleaned in an aluminum pan containing a teaspoon each of baking soda and common salt. The silver is then covered with water and boiled for a few minutes until a chemical change occurs which removes the brown deposit. This is a quick, easy method of cleaning inexpensive items, but it leaves a dull surface and removes any oxidized coloring on the silver.

Proper care of silverware may keep tarnish at a minimum. Silver in constant use, which is being washed daily in hot soapy water and dried thoroughly, is not apt to tarnish nearly so readily as silver that is just on display. Such silverware, when it is not to be used to hold food, may be lacquered. This colorless lacquer coating does not mar the beauty of the silver, but it does keep it from being attacked by chemicals in the air. However, the lacquer may peel off and then the silver will tarnish until relacquered.

Silver that is not being used except for special occasions should be packed away in felt bags or tarnish-resistant chests. Since silver scratches easily, pieces should not be allowed to knock against each other in drawers.

Common household salt will corrode silver if left in it for a long period of time; however, the salt will not harm the silver container if it is removed shortly after using.

The beauty and value of attractive silver articles is worth the little trouble it takes to keep them bright and shiny.

Stainless steel owes much of its acceptance to the ease with which it maintains its attractive appearance with nothing other than occasional soap and water baths. Since it does not tarnish, stain, or rust, and since there is no plating to wear away, the only care it needs is to remove food particles or soil. For housewives who dislike household drudgery, this is indeed an important selling point.

Like stainless steel, the gold-colored alloys require little care. They may get a slight dulling film in use that needs on occasion to be polished, but they require little more than washing and wiping after use.

PUTTING THIS MERCHANDISE KNOWLEDGE TO USE ❯ ❯ ❯ ❯ ❯ ❯ ❯ ❯ ❯ ❯

❯ DO YOU KNOW YOUR MERCHANDISE?

1. Explain what is meant by a bright finish; a butler finish; a gold wash.
2. Explain how decorations are applied by chasing, repoussé, engraving, piercing, embossing, engine turning.
3. What is tarnish? How can tarnish be removed from silver?
4. How would you advise a customer to care for silver in use? not in use?
5. How may tarnish on silver be prevented?
6. What special care does stainless steel require?

1. Leave a stainless-steel spoon and a silver-plated spoon in a soft-boiled egg for 10 minutes. Examine the spoons. Write a short report describing this experiment and its results.

2. Ask your mother and two or three of her housewife friends what they like and what they dislike about silver. Write a short report describing their answers.

3. Prepare a short discussion to be held with new salespeople about the care of silver products.

ADDITIONAL MERCHANDISE TERMS ❯❯❯❯❯❯❯❯❯❯❯❯❯❯❯❯❯❯❯❯❯❯

Active patterns are flatware patterns that are available in open stock and sets for immediate delivery.

Antique silver is sterling or plated silverware manufactured over 100 years ago.

Buffing is a process of shining silver by polishing the surface with wheels coated with rouge or pumice stone.

Elderly silver is silver that was manufactured many years ago, but which is not old enough to be classed as antique.

Engine turning is an engraving on silver which is applied by following a master pattern or stencil. It does not require such intricate handwork as does regular engraving.

Flash plate is very inexpensive plated silverware which has a thin coating of silver. Manufacturers do not use their identifying trademarks on this poor quality ware.

German silver is a white metal alloy of nickel, copper, and zinc. It contains no silver. It is similar to nickel silver.

Inactive patterns are flatware designs which were previously available in open stock from the manufacturers but which are no longer selling in volume. The manufacturer, however, keeps the dies, permits the stores to take special orders, and periodically (depending on demand) makes sufficient items to cover the orders. Often the customer must wait almost a year to obtain these items.

Oxidizing is the process of darkening the outline of a design in silver by use of a chemical.

Pewter is a soft alloy containing tin, antimony, and copper, which is used for ornaments and holloware items. Since it does not tarnish and takes and holds a lovely soft, lustrous finish, it is an attractive alternate for silver.

Rouge used in silver factories is an iron oxide which serves to polish silver.

Vermeil is a gold finish on silver plate or sterling. It is available through Tiffany's in New York.

Furniture for the Home

CHAPTER 30

UNIT 92 KINDS OF FURNITURE

Although from earliest periods in history furniture has been an important factor in the lives of individuals, yet little is known by the average person about the materials and construction of the furniture he uses constantly. The salesperson, therefore, has to be particularly well informed. People selecting furniture for several years of use want to be sure of the value of the articles they are purchasing. The new *Trade Practice Rules for the Household Furniture Industry,* issued by the Federal Trade Commission on December 18, 1963, to become effective on March 18, 1964, will aid both the customer and the salesperson in buying and selling furniture intelligently. A digest of these rules appears on page 653.

FURNITURE CLASSIFICATIONS

Furniture departments are usually divided into occasional furniture, case goods, upholstered furniture, and bedding. In addition to these major groupings, there are also other kinds of furniture, such as infants' (cribs, high chairs, carriages); unpainted furniture; cedar chests; summer furniture; dinette furniture; and kitchen furniture. Since these minor classifications are made in general from the same materials as the four major groupings, the salesman who knows about the main furniture products can easily adapt his knowledge to the minor furniture types.

When a salesperson is first placed in the furniture department, he is usually assigned to sell *occasional furniture,* which includes small furniture items, such as coffee tables, magazine racks, lamp tables, radio and television tables, whatnots, and small desks and chairs. These are considered furniture accessory items, as they add comfort and charm to a home.

The salesman who has developed skill in selling these small items may next be transferred to *case goods*. Technically *case* refers to cabinets. Desks, china closets, chests, and bookcases come under this grouping. Since sets of furniture include some of these items and are often bought as a unit, case goods refers to bedroom furniture, dining-room furniture, and the tables, breakfronts, and large desks used in living rooms.

Probably one of the most difficult assignments is the *upholstered furniture* section. This includes furniture made with filling materials, such as couches, settees, club chairs, wing chairs, barrel chairs, love seats, and sofas. Since most of the values of upholstered furniture are hidden from view, the salesman must know his merchandise thoroughly in order to explain its qualities to the customer who can see only the surface covering. One of the new developments in upholstered furniture has been the increased use of sectional pieces. In place of one large sofa, two or three smaller sofas without arms or with arms just on the end pieces may be placed together. This facilitates rearrangement of the furniture as needed and adds flexibility to room settings.

Bedding is the name for mattresses and springs as well as furniture that serves as seating pieces during the day and as beds at night. Sofa beds, chair beds, day beds, and ottoman beds are all included in the bedding classification.

PERIOD CLASSIFICATIONS

Within each of the major classifications listed above, furniture will again be divided by period or style. The major style groupings are modern, traditional, colonial, and provincial. These were discussed in detail in Unit 19.

Modern refers to furniture made with broad flat or slightly curved lines with a minimum of ornamentation. The furniture is built to serve today's way of living in compact space with the need for considerable storage space and areas that can be kept clean with a minimum of work. Natural finishes, comfort, usability, ease of care are all selling features of modern furniture.

Traditional furniture refers to those styles originally made in Europe in the 17th and 18th centuries. Included in this grouping is furniture made from exotic woods. such as mahogany and walnut usually stained in dark, rich colors and featuring designs made famous by Chippendale, Hepplewhite, Sheraton, and other masters of furniture styles from that age. This furniture varied from massive to delicate and was often richly ornamented.

Colonial, or *Early American,* furniture refers to those items used by the early settlers in America. In general, it was sturdy, functional furniture made from woods available in the inhabited sections of the country—maple, birch, cherry, and pine.

Provincial furniture was first made in the French provinces during the 16th to 18th centuries. Since the provinces were located far from the center of court life, the furniture reflected the simple life and tastes of the people. Gentle curves, and sturdy yet attractive appearance characterized this popular style.

＞ DO YOU KNOW YOUR MERCHANDISE?

1. Why is it important for the furniture salesman to be informed about the products he sells?
2. What are the major classifications of furniture? Explain what furniture items are included in each classification.
3. How would you classify the following items (a) chest of drawers, (b) lamp table, (c) cocktail table, (d) dining-room table, (e) sectional sofa, (f) dresser, (g) sofa bed, (h) breakfront, (i) mattress?
4. What are the distinguishing features of modern furniture?
5. What are the distinguishing features of traditional furniture?
6. What are the distinguishing features of colonial furniture?
7. Why is French Provincial furniture less ornate than other French period furniture?

＞ INTERESTING THINGS TO DO

1. Visit a local museum and make sketches of furniture characteristic of the periods mentioned in this text.
2. Analyze three furniture advertisements appearing in newspapers or magazines. Did the ads mention the style of the furniture? If so, what styles were mentioned? If not, could you recognize the styles? How would you classify them?
3. Prepare a 3-minute talk for the class on one of the styles of furniture. Obtain your information from books on interior decoration or magazine articles that discuss furniture styles.

UNIT 93 VENEERS AND SOLID WOODS

Wood has always been the most used material for furniture. Even with the recent progress in the use of metals, glass, and synthetic substances, wood for certain parts of furniture still has many advantages. It is easily worked, has beauty of grain pattern, is pleasant to feel, is relatively noise-free, and takes and holds attractive finishes. If damaged, it is quite easy to repair.

When the early settlers came to America, they had to clear forest areas to make room for their homes and farmlands. The trees they chopped down were used to build their homes and to make the interiors comfortable with benches, tables, beds, and chests. All over the world, throughout all history, furniture has been obtainable in the same way. Since trees grow almost every place where man can live, he has always had his raw material readily available.

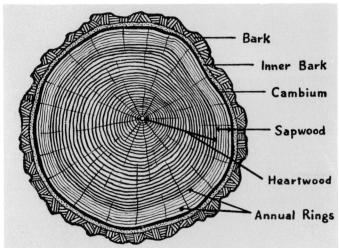

Cross Section of Tree Trunk.

Bark

Inner Bark

Cambium

Sapwood

Heartwood

Annual Rings

HOW DO TREES GROW?

Trees grow taller by means of new shoots that push from the trunk of the tree. If you mark your height by placing a nail in the tree, years later you will find the nail the same distance from the ground. However, it may be embedded in the tree trunk as it grows outward. Trees grow thicker by cells that multiply under the bark and form new woods and new bark. See above. for a cross section of a tree. Here are several layers which tell much about this tree:

1. The Bark. The outer layer is the skin of the tree that protects the inner fibers, tells what kind of tree it is, and also may be useful for its by-products such as tannin, quinine, eucalyptus, or cascara.

2. Cambium Layer. The layer just under the bark is composed of living cells that are constantly dividing and forming new bark and new wood. Since these newly formed cells vary in size from large loosely formed ones in the spring to small, compactly formed ones in the late summer, they form a line that is known as the *annual ring*. These rings add to the beauty of the grain pattern of the wood. By counting these lines or rings, the age of the tree may be determined. In tropical grown woods, where the seasons are not marked by weather changes, these rings are not so noticeable.

3. Sapwood. The new wood formed by the cambium layer is known as the *sapwood*. This is the living wood of the tree which is lighter in color than the center wood of the tree, contains more moisture, and is less compactly formed.

4. Heartwood. The darker center portion of the tree which was once sapwood but has now become inactive wood is known as *heartwood*. This portion of the tree is more durable than sapwood and is more desirable for furniture use. The fibers are more compact, making a denser, sturdier wood.

SUBSTANCES IN WOOD

Cellulose, the basis of all plant life, which forms a large portion of the wood, is the material that makes up the cell wall. The cells which are long and narrow are called *fibers*. These fibers in general run vertically in the tree's trunk and branches; it is because of this vertical arrangement that a log splits up and down with comparative ease. The fibers are sometimes compared to the warp in cloth. They form the vertical *grain structure of the wood*. Other cells known as *medullary rays* run crosswise (like the filling threads in cloth) and bind the warp cells together. They add strength to the grain cells and beauty to the wood when it is cut. They are particularly noticeable in oak.

Other materials contained in wood are mineral matter, resin or pitch, lignin (a complicated substance resembling cellulose), and moisture. The percentages of all these materials vary in every tree.

The tree is nourished by the roots, which draw minerals and water from the soil, and by the foliage, which absorbs carbon from the air. This food combines in the tree to make a substance known as the *sap*.

After the trees are cut and shipped to the lumber mill, they are prepared for manufacture into furniture. The cutting of the tree is very important, because the beauty of the finished piece of furniture depends on the angle at which the logs are cut.

Freshly cut logs contain as much as 50–60 per cent moisture. The excess moisture must be removed, or the wood swells and shrinks after it is made into furniture. This warping causes dresser drawers to stick in damp weather and to rattle in dry seasons. The removal of this excess moisture, which is known as *seasoning,* is accomplished by carefully stacking cut wood in the yard and allowing the moisture to evaporate slowly over a period of many

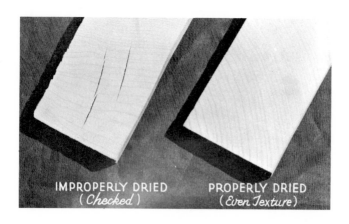

IMPROPERLY DRIED
(*Checked*)

PROPERLY DRIED
(*Even Texture*)

A board improperly dried looks like that on the left. The one on the right is kiln-dried evenly, inside and out, and reduced to the desired moisture content. *(Courtesy Kindel Furniture Company)*

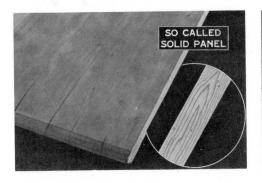

Left: Furniture made of solid lumber may look all right when new but may eventually develop checks and cracks. **Right:** Plywood panels for table tops and other flat surfaces. The United States Department of Commerce advises that a properly built plywood panel is approximately 80 per cent stronger than a solid piece of wood of equal thickness. *(Courtesy Kindel Furniture Co.)*

months. This *air seasoning* reduces the moisture content to about 15 per cent. For good-quality furniture, further moisture is removed by *kiln drying,* which reduces moisture content to approximately 4 to 8 per cent by controlled drying in heated and air-conditioned chambers. Wood that has been well kiln-dried seldom warps in use. Wood may be dried totally in kilns, but this is a costly process.

SOLID WOOD AND VENEERED WOOD

Before the wood is cut, it is necessary to know whether it is to be used to make solid-wood furniture or veneered furniture. For *solid-wood* furniture, thick boards of wood are used. These are cut to the correct size and shape, planed, sanded, and then joined together and finished. These thick boards are known as *lumber.*

Veneered-wood furniture is made of thin layers of wood which may be only $\frac{1}{20}$ to $\frac{1}{28}$ of an inch in thickness. These thin layers of wood are glued together so that the grains of the individual layers run at right angles to each other. They may have a center core of thicker lumber.

Some people believe that solid-wood furniture is better than veneered furniture. Actually, the salesperson needs to know the advantages and disadvantages of both in order to advise the customer in her selection. Generally speaking, the term *solid wood* denotes quality to customers. They feel that anything that is solid must be durable. Yet some of the oldest known pieces of furniture—built in the days of the Egyptians—have been unearthed in good condition and found to be of veneered construction. The most expensive piece of furniture ever constructed, a desk Louis XV ordered for Madame Pompadour, reputed to be worth about $100,000, is veneered.

It is easy to distinguish solid-wood furniture from veneered furniture. Solid-wood pieces never have very fancy grain pattern designs. An open drawer or door if solid may be rounded at the top or have a "worn-edge" design and it will show just the one large section of wood. Veneered woods, on the contrary, occasionally show elaborately matched patterns in the form of "V's" or diamonds in the front and top panels of the furniture. The edges of the doors or drawers show several layers of very thin pieces of wood glued together. Another term for veneered furniture is *plywood*.

Most furniture today is made from a combination of plywoods and solid-wood sections. For example, a desk may have the large flat panels forming the top, front sections and sides of plywood. The legs and posts would be made from solid wood. This piece would be labeled "veneered wood and solid wood."

Facts about Solid-Wood Furniture

Solid-wood furniture may be exquisitely carved, turned or grooved as chair legs are; it can be planed down if it becomes scratched or chipped, and it may be refinished after years of use. Very old, much-used solid-wood furniture may have the edges rounded from wear, but since it is the same piece of wood throughout, the appearance of the wood does not change. If properly constructed, solid-wood furniture is particularly desirable for very moist areas like Florida and the Gulf States.

Disadvantages. The greatest disadvantage of solid-wood furniture is its tendency to warp and crack. If the sections of the furniture are held tightly by other pieces of wood (as the side of a desk which is held by the bottom and top panels and the front and back posts), there is little chance of warping. Solid-wood school-desk tops, however, which are not held securely on the edges, often warp and crack. To reduce this tendency to warp, manufacturers of solid-wood furniture today cut the wood into strips 2½ to 4 inches wide and reverse every other strip and then glue them together. This reduces to a minimum the amount any given strip may warp.

Another disadvantage of solid-wood construction is that the cost of rare or

The Veneer Slicing Machine. Strips of veneer $\frac{1}{28}$ of an inch in thickness are being sliced by this automatic slicer. Notice that sheets adjacent to one another have similar grain patterns, making various matchings possible. *(Courtesy Mahogany Association, Inc.)*

  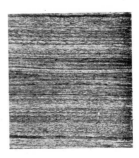

Veneer Slicing of American Walnut. Left: Rotary Cut. **Center:** Flat Cut. **Right:** Quarter-Sliced. *(Courtesy Veneer Association)*

expensive woods is high, and the beautiful wood pattern instead of gracing many furniture pieces, as it could do if thin veneers were used, can only make one or two pieces of solid furniture.

Facts about Veneered Furniture

In order to understand what veneered furniture is and what its advantages and disadvantages are, we should first see how it is obtained.

Steps in Production. The log with the bark removed is first soaked or steamed so that the wood fibers are pliable and soft. The log is then rolled against huge razor-sharp knives that slice off thin strips of wood in a continuous strip much as you might unroll a bolt of cloth or unwrap a roll of adhesive tape. These veneer strips may be as much as $\frac{3}{16}$ or as little as $\frac{1}{28}$ of an inch in thickness; however, $\frac{1}{28}$th-inch veneers are the most frequently used for furniture surfaces. Veneers so cut are known as *rotary sliced* and are used for the hidden parts of furniture, door panels, wall panels, and the surfaces of mass-produced furniture such as school chairs. *Flat-cut* veneers, sliced after first cutting the log in half, show more attractive grain patterns combining cone-shaped patterns and straight-line designs. *Quarter-cut* veneers are sliced from logs that have been quartered first. This is a fairly costly method of cutting as it wastes more wood. It yields ribbon-stripe patterns that are attractive for use on the surfaces of furniture.

After the veneer strips are sliced into sizes easy to handle, they are carefully dried and stacked so that matching sections come together. They are now ready for use in furniture.

The next important step in veneering comes when the thin veneer layer is attached to the other layers of wood to form what is known as *plywood*. Most plywood has 3, 5, 7 or more layers. In three-ply, two layers of veneer are bonded with another layer of veneer called a *crossband* or with a core of lumber in the center.

The reason veneered construction does not warp readily is because the grain of the top and back veneer runs at right angles to the grain of the cross-band or core wood. This means that the grains pull against each other and equalize tension, reducing the possibility of warping and cracking of the wood. This is one of the salesman's strongest selling points for veneered construction. Five-plywood has one face veneer, one crossband veneer with grain running at right angles, one core with grain running parallel to that of the face veneer, another crossband, and a back veneer. This construction is stronger than the three-ply; likewise, seven-ply is stronger than five-ply, and so on. Five-ply veneer is the most common for furniture use.

Gluing the Wood. Plywood is only as strong as the glue used to hold the various plies of wood together. It is like the chain that is only as strong as its weakest link. If a poor quality glue has been used, the veneer may come loose, crack, chip, or break and then, of course, the furniture needs refinishing, a costly and involved process on veneered furniture. The difficulty of repairing surface damages of veneered furniture represents one of its greatest disadvantages.

Vegetable glue, made from the root of a type of tapioca plant, is inexpensive, easy to handle, but not waterproof. It is little used today. *Animal glues,* obtained from waste products from slaughterhouses and tanneries, make good quality glues. They must, however, be heated when applied; and they are not waterproof although considerably better than vegetable glue. *Casein glue,* made from a milk base, is practically waterproof, more costly to use, and available on good quality furniture. *Plastic resin* glues are the most costly of all to use. They are not only waterproof but also will last indefinitely. Only large manufacturers use this glue, since it requires costly machinery to set the glue with heat and pressure.

Veneer Patterns. Veneer patterns on the fronts and tops of attractive furniture may be matched to give striking designs. Grain patterns are meticulously put together to make this attractive effect. Two apparently ordinary-looking veneers when rearranged often make striking symmetrical designs.

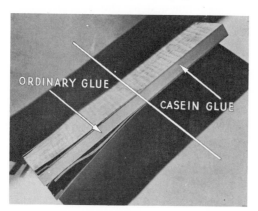

ORDINARY GLUE

CASEIN GLUE

The use of waterproof glue is important when furniture is submerged in water or subjected to humid conditions. This five-ply panel was soaked in water to observe the action of the waterproof glue. *(Courtesy Kindel Furniture Co.)*

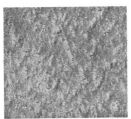
Bird's eye maple.

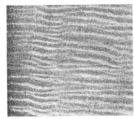
Curly maple.

Maple stumpwood.

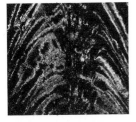
Crotch mahogany.

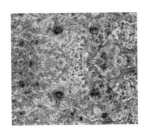
Carpathian elm burl, 2-piece book matched.

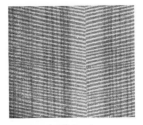
Peroba fiddleback, 2-piece book matched.

❮ Book-matched mahogany.

Diamond-matched mahogany with satinwood border. ❯

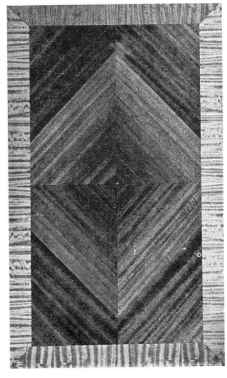

❯ ❯ Types of Veneer Patterns ❮ ❮

❮ Broken-stripe mahogany.

(Courtesy Mahogany Assoc. and Veneer Assoc.)

Matchings are called *book matching, slip matching, end matching* and *four-way matching.*

Various sections of a tree yield more beautiful patterns than others. Some of the better-known veneer patterns are:

Butt—Swirled pattern caused by the unusual grain structure formed by the joining of the root and the trunk of the tree. This is especially famous in walnut veneers. It is also called *stumpwood.*

Burl—Unusual growths on a tree cause these small oval and round markings. These are famous in walnut, redwood, and some unusual woods. (See page 631.)

Bird's-eye—This unusual tiny marking peculiar to maple has never been satisfactorily explained, but it is thought to be caused by buds unable to break through the bark of the maple tree. (See page 631.)

Crotch—Branches extending from the tree cause this beautiful "V"-shaped or featherlike pattern effect. (See page 631.)

Fiddleback—Fine, wavy lines run crosswise at right angles to the regular grain markings. This unusual design is found in some mahogany and maple woods and some fancy woods. (See page 631.)

Mottle—A blurred figure is made by the grain running in various directions.

Stripe—Some woods such as walnut, mahogany, satinwood produce straight band effects in shadings of dark and light. (See page 631.)

These figures properly matched add great beauty to the furniture. Because matching causes waste of wood and requires much skill, the price of furniture with these lovely patterns is often somewhat costly.

To match a whole set of furniture with similar pattern and color is practically impossible. Remember that the tree is one of nature's products, and mother nature does not grow two trees with the same grain pattern, nor are two sections of the same tree identical, any more than two sides of a person's face. The resultant variations in appearance add interest to furniture groupings.

PUTTING THIS MERCHANDISE KNOWLEDGE TO USE ❯❯❯❯❯❯❯❯❯❯

❯ DO YOU KNOW YOUR MERCHANDISE?

1. Which substance is most used for furniture construction? Why?
2. Explain the following parts of the tree: bark, cambium layer, sapwood, heartwood. Which part is used for furniture?
3. How is wood prepared for use?
4. What are the selling points of solid-wood furniture?
5. What are the selling points of veneered furniture?
6. Which glue is best for furniture? Why do not all furniture manufacturers use the best quality glue?
7. Why are matched panels of veneer on furniture costly to make?
8. Explain why a customer should not expect all pieces of furniture in a set to match perfectly in appearance of the wood.

1. Examine the furniture in your own home. Are the pieces veneered or solid or a combination? Which pieces have veneered surfaces? Do you have any matched grain veneers? How do you think they were matched?
2. Analyze five newspaper advertisements for furniture. How many told the customer whether the wood was solid or veneered? Copy the statements made about the woods if any such statements were used.
3. Prepare a 2-minute sales talk on a piece of veneered furniture.

UNIT 94 — HARDWOODS AND SOFTWOODS USED IN FURNITURE

Ask almost any person what kind of floors he has in his house or what kind of wooden furniture, and if he does not know the name of the wood, he usually says "hardwood." Ask these same people what they mean by "hardwood" and the only answer they can give is that "The wood is hard—it does not dent easily." Few people actually know what is meant by *hardwood* or *softwood*. The furniture salesman, however, must be prepared to explain the difference to customers. Actually, the *hardness* of the tree is not the reason for the term; it is the kind of tree that determines this designation. When we speak of *hardwoods,* we mean trees with broad, flat leaves; trees that lose their leaves in the fall. The technical term for these trees is *deciduous.* In contrast to these trees are the evergreen or coniferous trees known as the *softwoods.* These trees have pinelike needles. Both deciduous and coniferous trees are used in furniture, but the hardwoods generally have a more attractive grain pattern and a structure that permits them to hold glue or nails and screws more securely. Hardwoods also take a better polish, and they do not burn so rapidly as softwoods.

HARDWOODS

Most of the hardwoods used for our furniture are grown in the United States, only a very small percentage being imported. Some well-known hardwoods are birch, gumwood, oak, mahogany, maple, and walnut. Dozens of other woods are used, but if the person selling furniture can identify and know the advantages of the most-used woods, he can learn the characteristics of the less-used woods more easily.

The best way to study woods is to examine them. If possible, visit museums where trees are on display, examine furniture at home, in advertisements, in store windows, and when you go shopping in furniture departments. The following descriptions will aid you to recognize these woods and to know why they are so popular for furniture.

Walnut

One of the best-known cabinet woods is walnut. A large percentage of dining-room and bedroom furniture boasts of having walnut veneers or being made of solid walnut. Not only does this wood have a beautiful grain, but it often has some of the most attractive and unusual patterns suitable for veneered surfaces. It also is adapted to furniture construction because it warps very little, carves beautifully, keeps its rich color without fading, becomes more beautiful with age and use, and is very strong. Because it holds its shape so well, it has been the ideal wood for gunstocks. Delicate gun fittings are never pulled askew by its warping. True walnut is from the Juglans family.

The walnut tree grows in America as well as in European countries. It is known here as the *black walnut* in contrast to the butternut tree, which is known as the *white walnut*. The butternut tree produces a softer, lighter wood than the black walnut, and its lacks the beauty of the unusual patterns. Walnut has rich brown shades, a smooth grain, and the pattern of the wood is enhanced by darker markings throughout the design.

Mahogany

There are probably very few homes that do not boast of some mahogany furniture. Real mahogany does not grow in the United States (except for a few trees in Florida). It is obtainable in Cuba, Santo Domingo, Mexico, Honduras, and South America. A related species of fine quality from the Gold Coast of Africa must be labeled "African mahogany." The wood labeled "Philippine mahogany" is not so good a wood but has a similar color.

Mahogany is a light-brown wood with a slightly reddish cast which is usually darkened by staining to resemble the appearance of woods which have aged for centuries. It has a rich-looking smooth surface, which is often marked by beautiful patterns. Many attractive veneered panels are achieved by matching crotch figures, ribbon stripes, and mottles.

Historians tell us that mahogany was first made into furniture when Queen Elizabeth saw and admired some mahogany planks used to repair the boat in which Sir Walter Raleigh had made a trip to the West Indies. He had the planks removed and made into furniture for Her Majesty.

Not only does mahogany possess rare beauty of grain and color, but it is also desirable for furniture use because of its resistance to warping, its durability, and the ease with which it can be worked.

Oak

Oak is a pale colored, coarse-grained wood. Because it is a rugged, sturdy-looking wood, it is adaptable to heavy, masculine-looking types of furniture. It is very durable and strong, but splinters easily causing snagging of hosiery. Oak wood may be carved, and the attractive grain of the wood is revealed by quarter sawing the veneered sections.

Birch

This is a moderately priced wood used extensively for the structural (unexposed) parts of furniture, for furniture with walnut, mahogany, or maple finish, and for bleached or medium-toned furniture.

Birch is one of the strongest, hardest woods. It polishes well, takes an attractive finish and has a lustrous sheen. It has a smooth, close-grained appearance, often showing rather decided dark streaks of color. Because it resists dents and marks, it makes a sturdy wood for furniture meant to endure hard service.

Maple

This is the wood people think of when they select furniture for a colonial type home. It was the wood our New England forefathers used to build their homes and their furniture. There are two general types of maple, the best of which is called *hard, rock, northern,* or *sugar* maple. It grows largely in Vermont, New York, and Michigan and yields the famous maple sugar. This wood is the best for furniture. The other maple, known as soft or silver maple, grows in the southern states, and does not have the strength or heaviness desirable for furniture uses.

Maple wood is light in color and usually has a straight grain pattern. A few unusual patterns occur in maple. One, known as the famous *bird's-eye,* is used for veneers. There are also some *wavy* and *curly* patterns available for veneer. (See page 631.)

Maple is desirable because of its attractive smooth, close-grained appearance, its light color which adapts itself to bleaching or staining in various shades, its resistance to shock, and its hardness which prevents its denting too easily.

Gumwood

Red gum and sweet gum, as the woods are called, are southern hardwoods used for the unexposed parts of furniture and also in inexpensive furniture for the exposed parts to imitate walnut and mahogany. Some copy writers refer to this wood as *ambarwood* because the tree has an amber-colored juice that exudes from it; however, since customers do not know this term, it is misleading and should not be used.

Until kiln-drying methods were perfected, this wood was little used because it warped and twisted during seasoning. Now, however, it is one of the most-used woods in furniture construction. It has a rosy hue, and a smooth, uniform grain structure that dents rather easily even when a fingernail is pressed against it. Although it splits easily and is somewhat brittle, it is strong, and when kiln-dried it holds its shape well.

Gumwood is commonly used for the legs, posts, and other solid-wood portions of moderate-priced or inexpensive furniture having broad surface areas of walnut or mahogany veneer. Thus, you often see furniture advertised as "Mahogany veneer and gumwood," or "Walnut veneer and walnut-finished gumwood."

Other Native Hardwoods

Chestnut, black gumwood, tupelo, basswood, and yellow poplar are commonly used hardwoods for structural and hidden parts of furniture. Ash, which is famous for baseball bats, is used for kitchen furniture. Cherry, apple, pear, and other fruit woods are noted for their beauty and coloring. Because they are rather scarce today, they are used mainly as trimming woods or veneers.

Other Imported Hardwoods

The well-known imported hardwoods used in furniture in addition to mahogany are *ebony,* which is striped dark brown to yellow and not plain black at all; *rosewood,* which gets its name from the rose odor of the newly cut wood; *satinwood,* a golden-colored wood having a beautiful striped pattern and a golden shimmer which makes it desirable for use as trimming in combination with mahogany; and *zebrawood,* which has black stripes against a yellow background.

SOFTWOODS

While coniferous trees or softwoods do not have the structural advantages that deciduous or hardwoods have, there are a few used for furniture construction: red cedar, Douglas fir, white pine, and spruce are typical.

Red Cedar

Perhaps the most familiar of the softwoods is the cedar known as eastern, Tennessee, or aromatic red cedar. This is the wood used for pencils. It has an oil that vaporizes and destroys moth larvae, the clothing moths in the worm stage, that eat hair and woolen fibers. They cannot live if they whiff strong enough odors of the cedar oil. Since the knots in the wood contain more of the oily substance, a cedar chest or cedar closets lined with knotty cedar will be more effective than one lined with plain wood. Unless the wood is at least ¾ of an inch thick and the doors or drawers kept tightly closed, the aroma will not be strong enough to kill the moth larvae. A light sanding once a year will release additional cedar oil.

Pine

White pine, sugar pine, and Pacific Coast soft pine are used in making inexpensive unpainted furniture, as the base or core of veneered furniture, or for rustic types of furniture. They are particularly adaptable to light-colored or painted furniture. Because they carve well, they are also used for decorative mounts. Some knotty pine is used as veneers on colonial furniture.

PUTTING THIS MERCHANDISE KNOWLEDGE TO USE ›››››››››

› DO YOU KNOW YOUR MERCHANDISE?

1. Define hardwood, softwood, deciduous, coniferous.
2. Why are hardwoods more extensively used than softwoods for furniture?
3. Name three important woods that are hardwoods. Name three well-known woods that are softwoods.
4. What are the advantages of hardwoods in furniture construction?
5. What does the average customer think hardwood means? Give an example of a hardwood that is soft enough to dent when pressed with the fingernail.
6. Name two important softwoods. What unique advantages do they possess?

› INTERESTING THINGS TO DO

1. If possible, obtain a piece of softwood and a piece of hardwood from a local lumberyard. Examine the woods and write a short report on the differences you note.
2. Analyze five furniture advertisements. Was the word "hardwood" used? Why would the advertiser not use the word "softwood"?
3. Prepare a 2-minute sales talk for the class on the advantages of hardwood furniture.

UNIT 95 JOINING, DECORATING, AND FINISHING FURNITURE

JOINING

After the plywood or lumber sections have been cut into the desired size and shape, they are ready to be joined together to make a piece of furniture. Even though the best wood has been used, unless the furniture is carefully and securely put together, the customer may have trouble with it in use. One of the important selling points about furniture is the manner in which the various sections of wood have been connected. Since many of these joints cannot be seen, they become one of the hidden values to be explained to the interested customer.

Furniture is joined by using nails, screws, and/or glue. Nails are used primarily for inexpensive furniture, but even some medium-priced furniture may have nails in the back. Screws, because of their threads, will hold pieces of wood together more securely than nails, and where necessary will give good support. Backs and under parts of quality furniture usually contain screws.

Almost all joints are held together by glue. Well-glued joints that are hidden should have the glue oozing out around the joint. Skimping on glue is a fault of many production plants.

COMMONLY USED JOINTS

Furniture may be joined by plain butt, dado, tongue-and-groove, dowel, mortise-and-tenon, and dovetail joints.

The *plain butt* is the simplest. One piece of wood is simply glued, nailed, or screwed to another piece of wood. It is the poorest type of joint because it does not have sufficient reinforcement.

The *dado joint* has a groove into which another piece of wood is fitted. It is particularly adapted for joining shelves to sides of furniture, for securing drawer bottoms to sides of drawers, and may be used to hold sides of furniture to front and back panels.

The *tongue-and-groove* joint has a projection that fits into a groove. This is often used for fitting sides of desk or bureau drawers together.

Dowel joints are one of the finest types but demand precision and accuracy of workmanship. The dowel is a tiny piece of kiln-dried hardwood about the size of a piece of chalk, carved out of a block of wood. It usually has spiral grooves cut around it which let air escape. Holes are drilled in the two blocks of wood to be joined, glue inserted in the holes, the dowels are fitted into the holes and a secure joint is obtained. *Double doweling,* the use of two dowels spaced a short distance from each other, is superior to the single dowel. The dowel joints are used especially on various parts of chairs and sofas, both plain and upholstered, and for joining legs to the body of tables and desks.

Another excellent joint is known as the *mortise-and-tenon*. This works on

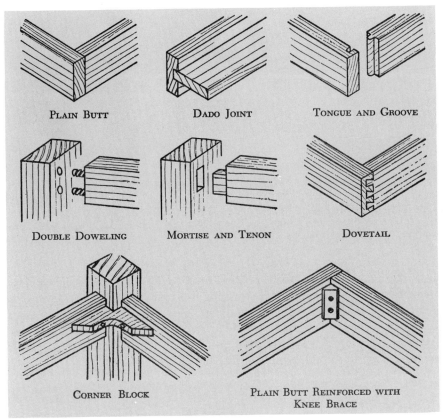

PLAIN BUTT	DADO JOINT	TONGUE AND GROOVE
DOUBLE DOWELING	MORTISE AND TENON	DOVETAIL
CORNER BLOCK		PLAIN BUTT REINFORCED WITH KNEE BRACE

❯ ❯ Types of Joints ❮ ❮

the same principle as the dowel except that the projection (known as the tenon) is formed by cutting away the wood from one section and a hole is grooved out of the other section for an exact fit. This joint, which is usually square or rectangular in shape, is also used for the joining of sections of chairs, couches, beds, and desks.

For secure drawer joinings, the best construction is the *dovetail*. When accurately and neatly done, it creates a strong, durable joint that cannot warp out of shape or come apart at the corners.

In addition to the various types of joints, good furniture is also usually reinforced. Look for these "extra selling points" on the furniture you sell. Turn a chair upside down and see if there are extra blocks of wood at the corners where legs join the seat of the chair. These are known as *corner blocks* or *knee braces* and are underneath most tables, chairs, and other well-made pieces of furniture.

Even drawers have reinforcements in the form of tiny wood blocks glued at the corners and sides underneath the drawer to give added support. The *center guides* under the drawers in the inexpensive furniture keep the drawers

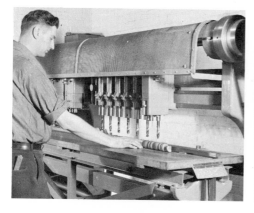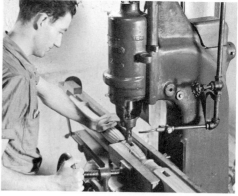

Hole Boring Methods. Left: This multiple spindle-boring machine bores as many as 22 dowel holes simultaneously. **Right:** This is a square-hole mortiser that always bores holes perfectly and quickly. *(Courtesy Kindel Furniture Co.)*

from warping out of shape too badly. In good furniture they help to resist pressure when one handle of a two-handle drawer is pulled. *Dustproof sections,* which can be seen when drawers are removed, are made from plywood in better furniture and from wood fibers or reinforced cardboard in less expensive furniture. When securely dadoed into the frame, these add extra reinforcement to the entire piece of furniture.

DECORATING FURNITURE

Through the ages, as man developed new products, he soon began to ornament them. The outline of the furniture may provide sufficient design appeal, or the elaborate wood used may supply enough decorative design. There are, however, many other ways of decorating furniture.

One of the oldest and most beautiful methods is *carving*. A solid piece of wood may be chiseled by hand, an expensive and difficult procedure; or it may be carved by a machine known as a *spindle. Multiple spindle* carving means that several spindles are attached to the main one, and as a man guides one spindle over a piece of wood, the others simultaneously make the same carvings on the pieces of wood to which they are attached. An inexpensive imitation of carving may be obtained by *molding* a synthetic substance or plaster and pasting it on the furniture. This of course does not have the beauty or the durability of carved wood. It is known as *applied ornament.*

Legs of furniture and posts often are *turned.* The wood piece is placed on a lathe where it revolves against a revolving knife blade or a series of knife blades that groove out symmetrical sections, shaping and rounding the leg or post.

Another type of decoration is done by *hand painting.* An inexpensive imi-

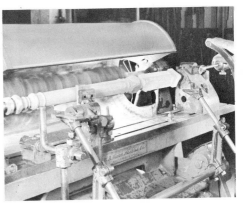

Left: Rope-Twist Cutter. This automatic twist cutter puts the design on easily, quickly, and with geometrical accuracy. **Right:** Turning. In these lathes the wood is slowly turned against rapidly revolving cutting blades. *(Courtesy Kindel Furniture Co.)*

tation of hand painting is a transfer pattern known as *decalcomania*. The design painted on cellophane is glued onto the wood and when the furniture is varnished, the "decal" is permanently affixed.

Two of the most beautiful decorations, and usually very costly ones, are known as *inlay* and *marquetry*. For *inlay* a small groove is cut in the wood and another strip of a different type of wood or material is fitted in and glued. In *marquetry,* rather elaborate designs are formed by fitting together pieces of wood, metal, or shells, like the pieces of a jig-saw puzzle, and then this veneer surface is glued to the furniture.

Elaborate gold-colored metal trimmings on furniture are known as *ormolu*. These trimmings, usually made of polished brass, were popular on French period furniture.

Hand Carving. This highly skilled operation requires 190 different chisels to achieve desired effects. The experienced craftsman shows the young apprentice how to use the tools. *(Courtesy Kindel Furniture Co.)*

Left: Spindle carving is really a hand-carving operation. Instead of pushing a chisel against the wood, the operator, with technical skill, guides and presses the wood against one of a variety of cutters, revolving at ten thousand revolutions a minute. **Right:** Multiple Spindle Carving. This machine reproduces on several pieces simultaneously the design on the hand-carved model which is traced by the operator's right hand. *(Courtesy Kindel Furniture Co.)*

FINISHING FURNITURE

The last thing a boy does when he makes a model airplane is to paint it. Furniture, too, must be painted or finished. This process is, however, a much more complicated one than it would seem.

The finish accomplishes a number of things. It may make less expensive woods look like better quality woods. Gumwood posts and legs on a desk or chest may be made to look like the mahogany veneers used on the tops, sides, and drawer fronts. When wood is finished to look like another wood, the term "finish" is used in describing it. Thus "mahogany veneer and mahogany-finished gumwood" would be an accurate description of the furniture described above.

In addition to making the furniture more attractive by changing the color or toning the colors to match, finishes also keep the moisture out of wood thus aiding in preventing warping; they help to keep the furniture clean by giving it a smooth somewhat nonporous surface; and they protect the furniture against minor scratches and scars.

A finish may merely change the color but still reveal the grain of the wood. This is known as a *transparent* finish. *Opaque* finishes change the color and hide the grain of the wood. These are usually used on less attractive woods or scarred woods.

Various kinds of plastics are being used on furniture both as ornaments and as surface finishes. Some bedroom sets have tops entirely made from a plastic layer that is waterproof. Living-room table tops with wood-grained plastic surfaces are alcohol- and water-resistant. Some are even impervious to cigarette burns.

Steps in Finishing

After a piece of furniture has been finished, it is difficult to tell what materials were used in it. Yet the quality and price of these materials varies considerably. There are many steps in finishing furniture. A typical piece might be finished as follows:

First a coloring matter is applied known as *staining*. Since this generally raises the grain, *sanding* follows. Then for coarse-grained woods (oak and ash) and medium-grained woods (walnut and mahogany) a paste made of a form of fine sand known as a *filler* is rubbed into the pores of the wood. This filler may be used to cover defects, or if colored, to accent the pores. This filler is *sealed* with a coat of shellac or lacquer, and *sanded*. Then the finish coat of shellac, varnish, or lacquer is applied. Final waxing imparts a rich sheen to the wood.

Special treatments such as alcohol-resistant finishes and fire-resistant finishes may also be given to the furniture at an added cost.

A good-quality finish appears *even* and does not have thick blobs of paint in spots. The color matches throughout if the furniture is well stained and finished.

Antiquing Furniture. Newly constructed furniture that is made to resemble elderly or antique furniture has special finishes applied that are known as *antiqued* or *distressed*. These are applied after the steps outlined above. The

Left: A workman bores holes in a desk drawer preparatory to placing drawer pulls in position. **Right:** An assembly line of chairs is carried to the finishing department. Notice the corner blocks, visible at the joint of legs and chair bottom. *(Courtesy Drexel Furniture Co.)*

antique appearance may be achieved by darkening the edges of the furniture, by painting small marks over its surface that resemble small scratches and dents, by actually denting and scratching the furniture with the use of chains that are struck against its surface, by boring small holes that resemble worm holes, or by a combination of these methods. When artistically done, such finishes make a new furniture item look worn and old, and they may add considerably to the cost of the piece.

CARE OF CASE GOODS

When the furniture first arrives at the customer's home, she will be occupied with the arrangement and rearrangement of the room. After the preliminary enjoyment of the new furniture, she will need to start to care for it. It will need to be dusted, polished, and cleaned. The salesperson who advises her on the correct methods for care will aid her in keeping the furniture beautiful.

Well-kept furniture should be dusted every day with a soft cloth that does not shed lint. Fingermarks and greasy spots may be removed from wooden, metal, or plastic furniture by using a soft cloth dipped in a mild suds of soap and lukewarm water. After rubbing over the area, wipe with a clean damp cloth and then rub dry. Any moisture left on the furniture will cause watermarks. Water spots on wood furniture may be removed by rubbing with a little furniture wax or polish.

Polishing furniture requires first that all dirt be removed by washing carefully and drying thoroughly. Most furniture experts recommend a good wax polish that is rubbed with the grain of the wood until no marks are noticeable. This gives the furniture its beautiful *patina*—that rich luster which is highly prized on expensive furniture.

PUTTING THIS MERCHANDISE KNOWLEDGE TO USE ❯ ❯ ❯ ❯ ❯ ❯ ❯ ❯ ❯ ❯

❯ DO YOU KNOW YOUR MERCHANDISE?

1. How are nails and screws used in furniture construction? Which is better? Why?
2. Explain the following methods of joining furniture: plain butt, dado, tongue-and-groove. Give an example of the use of each joint.
3. How do the mortise-and-tenon and double dowel joints differ? What sections of furniture use these joints?
4. Explain how the dovetail joint is used. What is the advantage of this joint?
5. Why is furniture finished?
6. Explain the differences between transparent and opaque finishes.
7. What is meant by an antique or distressed finish? How is it accomplished? What are its advantages?
8. What are the ways of carving wood today?
9. Explain the following terms: decalcomania; turned leg; inlaid; ormolu.

1. Examine a desk, table, or chest of drawers in your home. Make a list of the methods of reinforcing the furniture. Is the furniture solid or wobbly when in use? Do drawers slide open easily in all weather? Is the surface of the wood smooth and free from checks and cracks? How has the furniture been joined? Have corner blocks been used for reinforcement? Are drawers dustproof?

2. Plan a furniture sales talk to be given before the class. Use some article of furniture available in the classroom as your merchandise. Point out all the qualities of the wood, finish, and construction. Include information on the proper care of the furniture.

3. Analyze furniture advertisements that you read in newspapers and magazines. Copy on a sheet of paper all the technical phrases that you have studied in your furniture class. Be prepared to explain these to the class.

UNIT 96 UPHOLSTERED FURNITURE

For soft, loungy comfort the customer seeks upholstered furniture. She may see two upholstered chairs that appear to be similar yet are priced quite differently. Since virtually all the quality of upholstered furniture, except the surface cover, is hidden from view, the customer relies upon the informed salesman to tell her what the differences are.

DESIRABLE QUALITIES

Quality upholstered furniture will give durable, comfortable service for many years, while poorly constructed furniture, which may look quite good when new, may sag and lump and become uncomfortable in a few short months.

What are the qualities that customers look for and salesclerks must know about upholstered furniture? The customer looks first at the color, texture, and pattern of the fabric covering, then at the style and type of chair or couch sized to specifications to fit the room she is furnishing. Then she sits in the chair to see if it is comfortable, if it is the right depth and height from the floor for utmost enjoyment and utility.

Many stores feature upholstered furniture to be sold "in muslin." The customer then selects any covering material she wishes and eliminates the problem of the color, texture, and pattern in selecting the chair. The furniture is not actually in the muslin, but has a sample cover on it. The price quoted on such furniture includes the chair (or sofa) and the labor for covering. The price also may or may not include the cost of the fabric to cover the chair. The customer may wish to purchase the covering material separately. In some stores, different prices are quoted for the same chair depending on the quality of the covering material selected.

In general, it is far more difficult to construct a soft, luxurious item that holds its shape than it is to make a firm, rigid upholstered item. The former is, therefore, usually costly, while the latter may be considerably less expensive.

Construction of Upholstered Furniture

Certain desirable qualities should be checked in each construction part of upholstered furniture.

Frame. A look behind the scenes at a furniture factory is the best way of knowing what to look for and what to stress in upholstered furniture. The workmen first assemble the wooden frame. The best frame will be made of good-quality hardwood, such as ash, oak, birch, or maple; and the exposed parts of the frame that will be seen after the furniture is finished should be of walnut, mahogany, maple, or other desired wood. Sections of the frame should, of course, be doweled or have mortise-and-tenon joints, and should be reinforced for sturdiness. Less expensive frames will be made from gumwood or yellow poplar and the least desirable from pine or fir.

Webbing. The space between the frame across the seat of the furniture, the back, and along the sides of the arms may have a number of different constructions. Heavy webbing material that is about 2½ to 3 inches wide may be interlaced in a checkerboard effect and securely nailed to the frame. If the webbing is closely interlaced and securely nailed, and preferably if it is double, this is an excellent construction. Other good constructions consist of heavy cotton material stretched across the chair bottom, back or sides and held in place with tiny springs that work like clothespins in holding the material taut. Sometimes steel or wooden slats are used instead of webbing or cloth. While these are very strong, they do not always have the requisite amount of elasticity for utmost comfort.

Springs. To the webbing or the slats are secured double-cone steel springs. These are firmly tied to each other with a heavy cord, so that all the springs work in unison and do not cause unsightly or uncomfortable bumps in the finished furniture. The way the springs are tied and the number of knots used determines the quality and comfort to be had from the use of the furniture. Some furniture has only four knots to each spring. Better furniture has eight knots.

The size and number of springs used varies with the section and size of the furniture. Inexpensive furniture, of course, will have fewer springs than will better furniture. Tiny springs are used in the arms and larger ones in the seat and back sections. In poor quality furniture as few as six springs may be used to a seat section; nine are used in medium quality and as many as twelve in quality furniture.

The types of springs just described are used in traditional sofas and chairs. In place of double-cone springs for lightweight but sturdy modern furniture, zigzag springs that require no tieing and no interlaced webbing may be used. The frame, however, needs to be strong if zigzag springs are used.

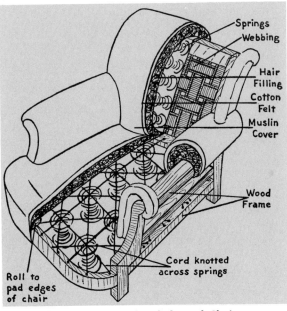

> > Construction of Upholstered Chair < <

Filling. Over the springs is placed a heavy burlap covering which supports the filling materials. Individual states' bedding laws governing cleanliness, sanitation, and newness of material and labeling of ingredients apply to

Lightweight but sturdy spring construction is accomplished by these zigzag springs that require no base of webbing and eliminate hand-tying operations. Small helical springs join the sections and hold them firm. (*Courtesy No Sag Spring Co.*)

this part of the furniture. The important thing for the salesman is the ability to read these labels and explain them to the customers.

Horsehair is the best stuffing material because each long, wiry hair after receiving a "permanent wave" by being tightly twisted, steamed, and dried, forms a tiny spring. Thousands of these horsehair springs add to the resiliency of the furniture. Horsetail, being longer, is superior to horse mane for this purpose. Hog hair, moss, palm fiber, and kapok are considered fairly good stuffing materials. In poor quality furniture, coconut fiber, tow (short flax fibers), excelsior (shredded, curled sections of wood), and even paper may be used. These filling materials, to prevent shifting during use, must be sewed or quilted into position.

New types of filling materials eliminate the need for quilting. These are thick layers of rubberized hair for better furniture and rubberized sisal (a straw) for less expensive furniture. The hair or sisal is impregnated with rubber and then formed into layers one or more inches in thickness. These are placed either directly over the springs with a backing material or over the burlap that covers the springs. The rubberizing process prevents the hair covering from being attacked by moths and thus serves a double purpose.

In good-quality furniture, a muslin inner lining is placed over the filling materials to hold them securely in position. This is eliminated in less expensive constructions. A layer of cotton felt which resembles absorbent hospital cotton is laid directly over the filling materials or in better furniture, over the muslin lining to form a smooth foundation for the outer cover. It also helps to prevent filling materials from working through the outer cover.

One-eighth to one-inch-thick sheets of foam rubber or urethane (a plastic foam) may be laid over the filling materials for added buoyancy.

Cushions. When furniture is made with filling materials only, but with no separate cushions, it is known as "tight seat" construction. Most furniture, however, has separate cushions.

The cushions may be *spring filled,* then covered with a layer of cotton felt to make them soft and comfortable. For very soft cushions, down and feathers may be used. *Down* is the fine covering next to the skin of the duck. It gives buoyancy and resiliency to cushions. Some feathers are mixed with the down to give body to the cushion. An excellent combination is 75 per cent down and 25 per cent feathers.

Foam-rubber cushions provide the comfort of down and feathers with the resiliency of springs. They cost about the same as down-filled cushions, and since they keep their shape better, they have proved to be an important selling point for upholstered furniture.

Moderate-priced furniture may contain pieced foam rubber which uses large leftover sections and glues them together to make moderately comfortable cushions. Shredded foam rubber is made from tiny scraps that have been macerated and joined to give a fairly firm cushioning material for inexpensive furniture. This must be accurately labeled as "pieced" or "shredded" respectively.

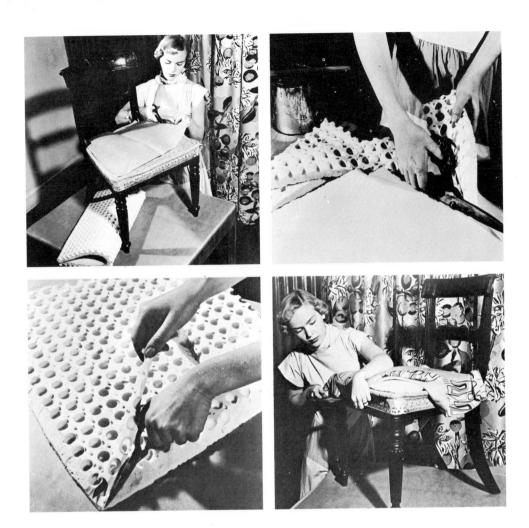

Reupholstering a Chair at Home. Top row, left: The first step in renovating a sagging chair seat is to strip off the old covering and worn cushioning materials. Next cut a paper pattern to fit the chair seat, allowing an extra quarter inch all around. **Right:** Latex foam may be used to form a new cushion. Mark the pattern on the sheet of latex foam and cut it out with a pair of household shears. Experts say you'll do a better job if you dip the shears in water occasionally as you cut. **Bottom row, left:** You will have a neater finish if you cut tapered edges on the underside of the foam padding. **Right:** Final step is to put padding in place and tack on the covering material. To guard against slipping, dot the chair seat lightly with rubber cement, and press padding firmly in place. If a loose-weave or slippery upholstery fabric is used, cover the latex foam cushion with muslin before putting the upholstery fabric in place. *(Courtesy Natural Rubber Bureau)*

Urethane foam, which is about one-half the price of foam rubber, is also used where economies must be effected. This is a resilient plastic foam that is slightly less buoyant than foam rubber, but it is durable, holds its shape, and is noticeably lighter in weight. It must be accurately labeled as "urethane foam." (See p. 312.)

Some modern upholstered chairs and sofas with wooden arms and exposed legs eliminate the costly filling, webbing, and springing process described above. Slats of wood or rubber slats are used for the back and bottom of the chair. A foam-rubber or urethane cushion completes the construction. These chairs are quite comfortable. If the cushion covers have zippers, the problem of cleaning upholstered furniture is easily solved.

Tufting. Diamond tufting which is very deep and rather firm has been used for many generations on upholstered furniture, and it is still available on traditional pieces. It takes great skill and is costly when used on furniture.

For modern furniture, a type of loose, block-shaped tufting known as "biscuit" tufting is used. In both diamond and biscuit tufting, buttons are used to hold the tufts or folds of material in shape. These buttons should be securely anchored to the background webbing so they do not become loosened in use.

Covering Materials. Virtually any fabric may be used to cover upholstered furniture. The tighter the weave and the stronger the yarn, the better the wear the fabric will give. In addition, customers are concerned with the care the fabric will need. If it is washable, the cost of cleaning will be kept at a minimum.

In addition to fabrics, genuine leathers, which are costly, and vinyl plastics, which resemble leather or fabric, are used. Both of these materials are strong and will give many years of service if properly cared for. Leather needs to be waxed from time to time, while vinyl plastic needs merely to be wiped with a damp cloth to remove surface soil. This is a particularly important selling point for the plastic covers. Coverings must be labeled accurately.

CARE OF UPHOLSTERED FURNITURE

The special attachments on vacuum cleaners may be used to clean many pieces of upholstered furniture. These attachments should not be used on down-filled cushions, however, as the light fluffy down might be pulled through the covering fabric by the suction force. Occasional brushing keeps surface dirt from becoming imbedded in the fabric covering on such cushions.

When the fabric covering is soiled, special solutions for washing upholstered furniture may be used. Advise the customer to follow directions carefully or to have an expert do the work. To test colorfastness of the fabric before cleaning, a small section at the back of the furniture should first be washed. Plastic covers usually wash without any difficulty.

PUTTING THIS MERCHANDISE KNOWLEDGE TO USE ❯❯❯❯❯❯❯❯❯❯

❯ DO YOU KNOW YOUR MERCHANDISE?

1. Explain what is meant by hidden values in upholstered furniture.
2. How is the customer assured of knowing what filling materials have been used in upholstered furniture?
3. Explain the differences between the traditional and the modern constructions in upholstered furniture.
4. What are the advantages of rubberized hair fillings?
5. What are the differences between foam-rubber and urethane cushions?
6. Name three qualities of foam rubber for cushions. Which is better? Why?
7. What steps are eliminated by the use of zigzag springs?
8. What types of button tufts are used on furniture? What are the differences in these types?
9. What care would you advise a customer to take with upholstered furniture?

❯ INTERESTING THINGS TO DO

1. Analyze upholstered furniture advertisements. What construction features did they mention? What covering materials were mentioned? what cushioning materials?
2. Look for the bedding tag on furniture you have at home. Is the tag still on the furniture? What filling materials and cushioning materials did it list?

ADDITIONAL MERCHANDISE TERMS ❯❯❯❯❯❯❯❯❯❯❯❯❯❯❯❯❯❯❯❯❯

Barrel chair is a type of upholstered chair in which the rounded back is stitched to resemble staves of a barrel.

Bleaching is a finishing process which makes wood paler by oxidizing the color with a strong chemical such as oxalic acid.

Chaise longue is a chair with seat extended so that a person may recline. The chair is generally used in the bedroom.

Chestnut is a little-known wood because it is often infested by worms which eat holes into it. For this reason it is rarely used for the exposed parts of furniture, but it is still desirable for the unexposed parts—the backs of furniture and core stock for veneers. It warps and twists very little, is easy to work, but it is rather weak and brittle.

Chip core is composed of sawdust or small chips of wood glued together and compressed into sheets about ¾ inch thick. These are used in place of lumber as core stock.

Circassian walnut is a fine quality of highly figured walnut from Europe.

Club chair is a massive, mannish-looking upholstered chair which is low and comfortable. These chairs are often upholstered in leather and are popularly used in dens and men's club rooms.

Coconut fibers are shredded fibers from the husk of the coconut, twisted for more resiliency. They are used as filling in inexpensive upholstered furniture.

Coffee table is a small, low table for use in the living room for decorative ornaments, or to hold coffee or tea service, bonbon dishes, etc.

Contemporary refers to furniture made for today's living. It is not synonymous with *modern,* although it may refer to modern furniture. Traditional styles of furniture made to scale and size for today's homes may be referred to as being contemporary.

Excelsior is made of shredded curled strips of wood and is used as filling in poor-quality upholstered furniture.

Floating construction is a method of allowing solid wood furniture to expand without buckling by placing screws that hold the tops and sides of furniture together in slotted screw holes. This permits the sides and top to expand or contract without damage.

Highboy is a tall chest of drawers.

Hog hair is hair from pigs and hogs which makes a filling suitable for medium-priced furniture. This does not have the resiliency of horsehair.

Kapok is a silklike fiber from the fruit of a tropical tree. It cannot be woven, but is resilient and light when used as filling in furniture and bedding. Since it is buoyant in water, it is used in life belts.

Lamp table is a small table suitable for use as a base for small lamps.

Lawson chair and couch are upholstered pieces having square-shaped seat cushions and a short, square back rest.

Lowboy is a low chest of drawers.

Moss is a vegetable hairlike growth from the southern section of the United States, which makes a desirable filling for medium-priced upholstered furniture.

Occasional table is a small table for use in the living room, den or foyer. May be used to hold ornaments, or as a coffee table.

Palm fiber is made of palm leaves shredded and twisted to give them a curled effect and added resiliency. They are then used as filling in medium-quality upholstered furniture.

Side chair is a chair with no arms such as those used in dining rooms, at desks, and as occasional chairs.

Splat is the center rail running vertically between the top rail on the back of a side or armchair and the seat.

Stretchers are rails which reinforce the legs of chairs, tables, and desks. These rails join the furniture legs by running between the two back legs, two side legs, or from the front legs to the back legs.

Top slat is the top rail running horizontally across the back of a side or armchair.

Tow is made of short ends and waste material from the flax plant. It is used as stuffing in inexpensive upholstered furniture.

Transitional is a term that refers to furniture which is neither completely modern nor is it traditional but combines some features of both.

Wing chair is a large, upholstered chair with high back that has winglike sides. It was originally designed to keep drafts off the person sitting in the chair.

DIGEST OF TRADE PRACTICE RULES
FOR THE HOUSEHOLD FURNITURE INDUSTRY

On December 18, 1963, "Trade Practice Rules for the Household Furniture Industry" were issued by the Federal Trade Commission, to become effective March 18, 1964, for industry use. To protect members of the furniture industry, the retail trade, and the public, these rules require both manufacturers and retailers to be truthful in any claims or statements made about their furniture products. In most cases, labeling is not required; but if any statements are made, they must be accurate and not mislead or deceive those who read them. These rules cover information about woods, wood names, imitations of wood, leather and its imitations, other outer coverings, filling materials, origin of styles, and used materials. The rules also include information about deceptive retailing practices in pricing, advertising, and so forth.

As you read this chapter, you will have seen how these rules apply to the merchandise covered in this text. The rules include the following:

Woods used for exposed parts of furniture must be described accurately. Thus, birch, for example, cannot be labeled "maple" although it resembles maple and has similar properties.

Thin layers of wood, called *veneers*, which are glued over other woods cannot be labeled "solid wood" nor can just the accepted name of the face wood, such as mahogany, be used. Instead the piece must be described as "mahogany veneer."

Nonlumber materials cannot be labeled "wood." Hardboard, for example, which is made from wood fibers, must be called "hardboard" or "fiberboard."

When a surface has an imitation grain, it must be correctly labeled as, for example, "mahogany veneer with imitation crotch figures."

Products made with plastic, metal, hardboard, or other surface with a woodlike finish should accurately state this as, for example, "walnut-grained plastic surface."

Fillings used in upholstered or padded furniture to make it comfortable must be accurately labeled. If other than new materials are used, this fact must be disclosed as, for example, "cushions made from reused shredded foam rubber."

Geographic origins of furniture also must be accurate. Furniture manufactured in the United States, for example, may not be described as "Danish" or "Swedish modern." Such furniture may be labeled or advertised as "Danish style" or "Swedish modern style." Similarly, trade names must not mislead as to the origin of the furniture. For example, "Grand Rapids Furniture" would mean that the products were made in Grand Rapids, Michigan. Foreign-made furniture should be identified by the country of origin; however, terms such as "French Provincial" or "Chinese Chippendale," because of long usage and general understanding by the public, are considered to be descriptive of the respective style rather than of the country of origin and, therefore, do not violate the rule stated above. Such rules as these make it even more important for the furniture retailer to "know his merchandise."

Index

Onyx, 477, 483
Opal, 470, 471, 472, 477, 480–481
Opaque paints, 338–339
Opaque stones, 472
Open stock
  dishes, 575–576
  flatware, 608
  glassware, 595
  holloware, 614
  stationery, 353
Open-handled furs, 432
Open-shank sandal, 396, 400
Opera pump, 396
Opera slippers, 397, 400
Opossum, 456–457
Optical glass, 580, 598
Ore, 557
Organdy, 21, 42, 61, 64, 85, 88, 154, 192, 215, 425; *illus.,* 153
  embroidered, 71, 73
  silk, 191
Organic solvents, 312, 318
Oriental cat's-eye, 471, 492
Oriental emerald, 493
Oriental pearls, 481
Oriental rugs, 279, 280; *illus.,* 291
  American, 282, 287
  cleaning of, 294
  selling points of, 291
Oriental topaz, 493
Orlon, 32–33, 37 (*see also* Acrylic fibers)
Ormolu, 641
Ostrich leather, 361, 378, 419; *illus.,* 377
Ottoman (fabric), 188, 204
Outseam, glove, 405–406; *illus.*
Overalls
  children's, 160, 161, 240
  infants', 152, 154, 155
  men's and boys', 240
Overglaze, 569–570
Overlay method, flatware, 607
Overnight case, 428
Overseam, glove, 406; *illus.,* 405
Oxford chinaware, 559
Oxford shirting, 66, 223
Oxford shoe, 396–397
Oxidation, 343, 467

Pacs, 397, 400
Paint stains, removal of, 110
Paintbrushes, 341–342
Painting on fabrics, 103
Paints
  aerosol, 342
  materials used in, 338–339
  types of, 339–340
Pajamas
  children's, 161
  men's and boys', 230–231; *illus.*
  women's and girls', 168; *illus.,* 169

Palladium, 464, 465, 490
Palm fibers, 648, 652
Palm oil, 500, 522
Panama hats, 211
Panties, 161, 170
Paper, 25–26, 344–354, 358
  differences in, 345
  finishes on, 348–350
  history of, 345–346
  kinds of, 358
  manufacture of, 346–348
    chemical method, 347
    materials used in, 346–347
    mechanical method, 346–347
  stationery, 351–353
  uses for, 344–345, 358
Papier-mâché, 344, 358
Papyrus, 345
Para dyes, 517
Para rubber, 325
Parasols, 425
Parchment, 345, 358, 374, 379
  vegetable, 350, 358
Parchment finish, 358
Parfait glasses, 598
Parkas, 33, 237; *illus.,* 159
Paste setting, 468
Paste stones, 493
Pasteurization, 532–533
Patchwork quilts, 263
Patent leather, 359, 369–370, 412
  care of, 370
Pattina, 389
Peanut oil, 500, 522
Pearls, 471, 472, 477, 481–482
Peau de soie, 188
Pebble crepe, 189
Pedal pushers, 160, 196
Peeler cotton, 21
Pegging of shoes, 394
Peltry, 431, 441; *illus.,* 438
Pencils, 354–355
Pens, 355–356
Perbunan rubber (Buna-N), 323
Percale, 43, 46, 61, 64, 154, 198, 255, 256; *illus.,* 153
Perfumes, 507–508
  care of, 509
Period styles
  American, 145–148, 623
    Colonial, 146, 623
    contemporary, 147–148
    Early, 145–146, 623
    Federal, 146–147
    modern, 147, 623
  English, 140–143, 623
    Adam, 141–142; *illus.,* 143
    Chippendale, 141
    Georgian, 141–142
    Jacobean, 140
    Queen Anne, 141
    Regency, 142
    Victorian, 142–143
    William and Mary, 141
  fabrics suitable for
    drapery, 269–271
    upholstery, 274–275
  French, 143–145

Period styles (*Continued*)
  Directoire, 144–145
  Empire, 145
  Louis XIV, 143–144
  Louis XV, 144
  Louis XVI, 144
  Provincial, 145, 623
Periodot, 493
Permanent finishes, 88, 95–97, 106, 154–155
Permanent-wave kits, 518
Persian lamb, 430, 436, 440, 444–445, 455
Persian paw, 441, 455
Personalized stationery, 353
Perspiration stains, removal of, 110, 112
Perspiration-resistant finishes, 92–93
Petrolatum, 522
Petroleum, 322, 333–334
Petticoats, 161, 167–168
Pewter, 621
Phenol, 302, 318
Phenol-formaldehyde plastics, 298, 299, 302, 314
  trade names of, 314, 315
Philippine mahogany, 634
Phosphorescent paints, 339
Phosphorus, 539
Photographic printing, 104, 129
Pick glass, 60–61, 62; *illus.*
Picking, 62
Piece dyeing, 42, 101, 102, 105, 129
Piercing of flatware and holloware, 617
Pigment dyeing, 102, 379
Pigment yarns, 53
Pigmented lacquers, 341
Pigmented paints, 338–339
Pigskin, 376, 402, 419
Pile weave, 68–71, 86–87, 155, 242; *illus.,* 65
  cotton fabrics in, 186
Pillbox hats, 214; *illus.,* 213
Pilling, 58, 152, 208
Pillow lace, 80
Pillowcases
  selection of, factors in, 255–259
Pillows, 254–255
Pima cotton, 21, 223
Pin-lever watches, 489
Pin seal, 368, 376; *illus.,* 369
Pine, 636, 637, 646
Pinking, 164
Pins (jewelry), 487
Piqué, 73, 155, 192, 196; *illus.,* 153
Piqué seam, glove, 406; *illus.,* 405
Place settings
  dishes, 576
  flatware, 608

Repoussé, 616–617
Residual shrinkage, 94–95
Resilient construction, 220
Resin finish, 84, 94, 155, 156, 164, 221, 267
Resins, 318, 341
Resist printing, 105, 163
Retanned cowhide, 379
Retanning, 367
Retreating colors, 139
Retting, 24
Reused wool, 262
Rhea, 25
Rhinestones, 493, 579
Rhodium, 464, 493
Rib knitting, 75
Rice, 524
Rings, types of, 487–488
Roasting pans, 549
Rock crystal, 477, 483, 598
Rock maple, 635
Rodent family, 446–449
Rolled gold, 464, 466–467
Romaine crepe, 189
Rose cut, 493
Rose point lace, 80
Rosewood, 636
Rotary-sliced veneers, 629; *illus.*
Rouge, 514
  for silver, 621
Round-thread linen, 250
Royalene, 34
Rubber
  articles made from, 31, 328–329 (*see also* Tires)
  care of, 329
  cold, 343
  importance of, 319
  kinds of, 324–325
  manufacture of, 325–326
  origin and history of, 320–321
  production of, 321–322
  reclaimed, 326, 330–331
  in shoes, 387, 388, 394, 397
  synthetic, 31, 321, 322–324, 339, 343
    trade names of, 37
  vulcanization of, 31, 38, 321, 326, 331, 394
Rubber balls, 329
Rubber cement, 329
Rubber yarns, *table,* 54–55
  selling points of, 127
Rubberized hair, 648
Rubbers, 397, 400
Ruby, 469–471, 478
  synthetic, 478
Rugs and carpets
  bath, 246
  care of, 291–295
  cleaning of, 285, 293–294
  cotton fibers in, 246, 282
  cushions for, 291
  distinction between, 280–281
  handmade, 290–295
  hand-tied, 279, 290; *illus.,* 291
  knitted, 285

Rugs and carpets (*Continued*)
  machine-made, 280–281, 286
  man-made fibers in, 282–283, 284
  moth prevention for, 294-295
  Oriental, 279, 280; *illus.,* 291
    American, 282, 287, 290
  selling points of, 283, 288, 290–291
  tufted, 284–285
  wool used in, 281–282
  worsted and woolen yarns in, 281–282
  woven, 285–288
    hand-, 290
Run-resist hosiery, 174–175
Rush, 26
Rush rugs, 288
Rust stains, removal of, 110, 112
Ruthenium, 465
Rutile, 470

Sable, 440, 443, 449
Sacques, infants', 151, 152, 156
Saddle leather, 372
Saddle oxfords, 397
Safedge, 588
Safety glass, 310, 588; *illus.*
Safety paper, 358
Sailcloth, 216, 240, 263, 266, 277, 278
Sailor hats, 210, 214; *illus.,* 213
Salesman's case, 428
Salt-and-pepper shakers, 614
Saltwater pearls, 481
Sandals, 389, 391, 396
Sandblasting, 591, 593
Sanforized process, 95, 120, 240
Sapphire, 469–471, 478
  synthetic, 478
Sapwood, 625
Saran, 33–34, 275, 311
  care of, 118
  characteristics of, 37
  trade names of, 37
Sardonyx, 477, 483
Sash curtains, 265–266
Sateen, 21, 67, 171, 207, 262
Sateen weave, 67
Satin, 47, 171, 204, 215, 216, 270, 271, 277
Satin crepe, 67, 191, 207
Satin weave, 66–67; *illus.,* 65
  selling points of, 67
Satinwood, 636
Saucepans and saucepots, 548
Saucer champagne glass, 598
Scarfs
  fabric, 215, 218
  fur, 453, 461
Schiffli embroidery, 73, 181
Scorch stains, removal of, 110, 114
Scotch grain, 372
Scotch topaz, 493
Screen printing, 104, 129; *illus.*

Scuffs, 397, 400
Sculptured rug or carpet, 286
Scutching, 24
Sea Island cotton, 21
Seal
  fur, 431, 457
  hair, 460
  Hudson, 447
Sealskin, 376, 419
Seam slippage, 90
Seamless hosiery, 76–77, 174
Seams, 164, 172, 244
  on gloves, 405–406, 428
  skin-on-skin, 439
Searosole, 387
Seasoning
  of cast-iron utensils, 541
  of leather, 368
  of wood, 626–627
Secondary colors, 130
Seersucker, 86, 154–155, 190, 196, 198, 206; *illus.,* 87
Self-opening umbrellas, 424, 426
Self-sealing envelopes, 329
Self-winding watches, 490
Selling points, 3–6
  acetate, 123–124
  acrylics, 124–125, 156, 208, 283
  attractiveness as, 4–5
  bedspreads, 263
  blended yarns, 127, 156
  blouses, 195–196
  carded and combed yarns, 45–46
  care required as, 6
  children's wear, 164–165
  comfort as, 5
  cotton fabrics, 46, 120–121
  curtains and draperies, 269–271
  durability as, 4
  electrical appliances, 556
  fashion as, 4
  finishing processes as, 85–86
  foundation garments, 181–182
  fur garments, 458
  glass fibers, 126–127
  glassware, 595–596
  handbags, 415
  handkerchiefs, 216
  health and safety as, 5–6
  hosiery, 77, 177–178
  jewelry, 491
  knitted fabrics, 77, 208
  leather, 361
  leno weave, 71
  linen, 121, 247–250
  luggage, 418–421
  metallic fibers, 126
  modacrylics, 125, 283
  neckties, 219–220
  nylon, 124, 283
  plain weave, 67
  plastics, 317
  polyesters, 125–126
  price as, 5
  pride of ownership as, 5
  rayon, 123–124, 283
  rubber yarns, 127
  rugs and carpets, 283, 288, 290–291
  satin weave, 67